Lecture Notes in Computer Science 16053

Founding Editors

Gerhard Goos
Juris Hartmanis

Editorial Board Members

Elisa Bertino, *Purdue University, West Lafayette, IN, USA*
Wen Gao, *Peking University, Beijing, China*
Bernhard Steffen ⓘ, *TU Dortmund University, Dortmund, Germany*
Moti Yung ⓘ, *Columbia University, New York, NY, USA*

The series Lecture Notes in Computer Science (LNCS), including its subseries Lecture Notes in Artificial Intelligence (LNAI) and Lecture Notes in Bioinformatics (LNBI), has established itself as a medium for the publication of new developments in computer science and information technology research, teaching, and education.

LNCS enjoys close cooperation with the computer science R & D community, the series counts many renowned academics among its volume editors and paper authors, and collaborates with prestigious societies. Its mission is to serve this international community by providing an invaluable service, mainly focused on the publication of conference and workshop proceedings and postproceedings. LNCS commenced publication in 1973.

Vincent Nicomette · Abdelmalek Benzekri ·
Nora Boulahia-Cuppens · Jaideep Vaidya
Editors

Computer Security – ESORICS 2025

30th European Symposium
on Research in Computer Security
Toulouse, France, September 22–24, 2025
Proceedings, Part I

 Springer

Editors
Vincent Nicomette
INSA Toulouse
Toulouse, France

Abdelmalek Benzekri
Université Toulouse- Paul Sabatier
Toulouse, France

Nora Boulahia-Cuppens
Polytechnique Montreal
Montreal, QC, Canada

Jaideep Vaidya
Rutgers University
Newark, NJ, USA

ISSN 0302-9743 ISSN 1611-3349 (electronic)
Lecture Notes in Computer Science
ISBN 978-3-032-07883-4 ISBN 978-3-032-07884-1 (eBook)
https://doi.org/10.1007/978-3-032-07884-1

© The Editor(s) (if applicable) and The Author(s), under exclusive license
to Springer Nature Switzerland AG 2026

This work is subject to copyright. All rights are solely and exclusively licensed by the Publisher, whether the whole or part of the material is concerned, specifically the rights of translation, reprinting, reuse of illustrations, recitation, broadcasting, reproduction on microfilms or in any other physical way, and transmission or information storage and retrieval, electronic adaptation, computer software, or by similar or dissimilar methodology now known or hereafter developed.
The use of general descriptive names, registered names, trademarks, service marks, etc. in this publication does not imply, even in the absence of a specific statement, that such names are exempt from the relevant protective laws and regulations and therefore free for general use.
The publisher, the authors and the editors are safe to assume that the advice and information in this book are believed to be true and accurate at the date of publication. Neither the publisher nor the authors or the editors give a warranty, expressed or implied, with respect to the material contained herein or for any errors or omissions that may have been made. The publisher remains neutral with regard to jurisdictional claims in published maps and institutional affiliations.

This Springer imprint is published by the registered company Springer Nature Switzerland AG
The registered company address is: Gewerbestrasse 11, 6330 Cham, Switzerland

If disposing of this product, please recycle the paper.

Preface

It is our great pleasure to welcome you to the thirtieth edition of the European Symposium on Research in Computer Security (ESORICS 2025). This symposium was founded to further the progress of research in computer, information and cyber security and in privacy, by establishing a European forum for bringing together researchers in this area, by promoting the exchange of ideas with system developers and by encouraging links with researchers in related areas.

Since its inception in 1990, ESORICS has been hosted in a series of European countries and has established itself as the premiere European research event in computer security. Starting biannually in 1990 in Toulouse, the symposium has been held annually since 2002. We are delighted to welcome you to the 30th edition of the symposium in Toulouse, where it was first held.

As one of the longest-running reputable conferences focused on security research, ESORICS 2025 attracted numerous high-quality submissions from all over the world, with authors affiliated with diverse academic, non-profit, governmental, and industrial entities. After two rounds of submissions, each followed by an extensive reviewing period, we wound up with an excellent program, covering a broad range of timely and interesting topics. A total of 605 unique submissions were received: 150 in the first round and 475 in the second (of which 20 were invited resubmissions). Three to four reviewers per submission in a single-blind review driven by selfless and dedicated PC members (and external reviewers) collectively did an amazing job providing thorough and insightful reviews. Some PC members even "went the extra mile" by reviewing more than their share. The end result was 100 accepted submissions: 10 and 90, in the first and second rounds, respectively – giving an overall acceptance rate of 16.52%.

The ESORICS 2025 technical program was organized into 27 tracks held in 3 parallel sessions as well as 3 impressive keynote talks by internationally prominent and active researchers across academia and industry: Carlos Aguilar, Pierangela Samarati, and V. S. Subrahmanian. The program testifies to the level of excellence and stature of ESORICS.

Putting together ESORICS 2025 was a team effort. We would like to express our sincere gratitude to:

- Authors and contributors: without high-quality submissions from the authors, the success of the conference would not have been possible.
- PC members and additional reviewers: for the effort they put into the evaluation and high-quality in-depth reviews.
- Organization Chairs: Denise Gross from ICO, Justine Praneuf from LAAS-CNRS, Charlotte Sébastien from Université de Toulouse, and Tifanny Vest from Université de Toulouse for all of their efforts in organizing the conference and managing all of the logistics.
- Publicity Chairs: Paria Shirani from the University of Ottawa, Canada, Wenjuan Li from Hong Kong Polytechnic University, China, and Sebastien Bardin from Software

Safety and Security Lab, CEA, France, for their efforts in spreading the word about ESORICS 2025.
- Web Chairs: Charlotte Sébastien from Université de Toulouse and Tifanny Vest from Université de Toulouse for their efforts and continuous and quick updates of the website.
- Workshops Chair Romain Laborde from IRIT, Université de Toulouse for handling the workshops organization and being involved in other organizational aspects.
- Sponsor Chair Giorgia Macilotti from Airbus Protect for helping to arrange sponsorship for the symposium.
- The ESORICS Steering Committee and in particular, the Steering Committee Chair Joaquin Garcia-Alfaro for providing advice with numerous organizational issues.
- Easychair for providing an excellent conference management system.

In closing, we believe that ESORICS 2025 was an overall success and we hope that all attendees enjoyed the symposium and their stay in Toulouse, France.

July 2025

Vincent Nicomette
Abdelmalek Benzekri
Nora Boulahia-Cuppens
Jaideep Vaidya

Organization

General Chairs

Vincent Nicomette — LAAS-CNRS, INSA de Toulouse, France
Abdelmalek Benzekri — IRIT, Université de Toulouse, France

Program Chairs

Nora Boulahia-Cuppens — Polytechnique Montréal, Canada
Jaideep Vaidya — Rutgers University, USA

Publicity Chairs

Paria Shirani — University of Ottawa, Canada
Wenjuan Li — Education University of Hong Kong, China
Sebastien Bardin — CEA, France

Organization Chairs

Denise Gross — ICO, France
Justine Praneuf — LAAS-CNRS, France
Charlotte Sébastien — Université de Toulouse, France
Tifanny Vest — Université de Toulouse, France

Workshops Chair

Romain Laborde — IRIT, Université de Toulouse, France

Sponsor Chair

Giorgia Macilotti — Airbus Protect, France

Web Chairs

Charlotte Sébastien — Université de Toulouse, France
Tifanny Vest — Université de Toulouse, France

Steering Committee

Joachim Biskup — University of Dortmund, Germany
Frédéric Cuppens — Polytechnique Montréal, Canada
Sabrina De Capitani di Vimercati — Università degli Studi di Milano, Italy
Joaquin Garcia-Alfaro (Chair) — Institut Polytechnique de Paris, France
Dieter Gollmann — Hamburg University of Technology, Germany
Sushil Jajodia — George Mason University, USA
Sokratis Katsikas — Norwegian University of Science and Technology, Norway

Mirek Kutyłowski — Wrocław University of Technology, Poland
Javier Lopez — Universidad de Málaga, Spain
Jean-Jacques Quisquater — Université catholique de Louvain, Belgium
Peter Y. A. Ryan — University of Luxembourg, Luxembourg
Pierangela Samarati — Università degli Studi di Milano, Italy
Einar Snekkenes — Norwegian University of Science and Technology, Norway

Michael Waidner — Technische Universität Darmstadt, Germany
Edgar Weippl — University of Vienna & SBA Research, Austria

Program Committee

Andrea Agiollo (Round 2) — TU Delft, The Netherlands
Massimiliano Albanese — George Mason University, USA
Cristina Alcaraz — University of Málaga, Spain
Abdelrahaman Aly — Technology Innovation Institute, United Arab Emirates

Shengwei An (Round 2) — Virginia Tech, USA
Hafiz Asif (Round 2) — Hofstra University, Rutgers University, USA
Mikael Asplund — Linköping University, Sweden
Vijay Atluri — Rutgers University, USA
Daniel Augot (Round 1) — Inria Saclay, France
Samiha Ayed (Round 2) — Université de technologie de Troyes, France
Sebastien Bardin — CEA LIST, France
Alessandro Barenghi — Politecnico di Milano, Italy

Ken Barker (Round 1)	University of Calgary, Canada
Giampaolo Bella (Round 2)	University of Catania, Italy
Abdelmalek Benzekri	Université de Toulouse, France
Elisa Bertino	Purdue University, USA
Clara Bertolissi (Round 2)	Aix-Marseille University, France
Bruhadeshwar Bezawada (Round 2)	Southern Arkansas University, USA
Smriti Bhatt (Round 2)	Purdue University, USA
Giuseppe Bianchi (Round 2)	University of Rome "Tor Vergata", Italy
Alex Biryukov	University of Luxembourg, Luxembourg
Jorge Blasco (Round 1)	Universidad Politécnica de Madrid, Spain
Carlo Blundo	Università degli Studi di Salerno, Italy
Tamara Bonaci (Round 2)	Northeastern University, USA
Rainer Böhme (Round 2)	University of Innsbruck, Austria
Pino Caballero-Gil	University of La Laguna, Spain
Maurantonio Caprolu (Round 2)	King Abdullah University of Science and Technology, Saudi Arabia
Xavier Carpent	University of Nottingham, UK
Aldar C.-F. Chan (Round 2)	University of Hong Kong, China
Bo Chen (Round 2)	Michigan Technological University, USA
Rongmao Chen (Round 2)	National University of Defense Technology, China
Xiaofeng Chen (Round 2)	Xidian University, China
Yuan Cheng (Round 2)	University of Nottingham Ningbo China, China
Sherman S. M. Chow (Round 2)	Chinese University of Hong Kong, China
Pietro Colombo (Round 2)	Università dell'Insubria, Italy
Michal Choras (Round 1)	Bydgoszcz University of Science and Technology, Poland
Mauro Conti	University of Padua, Italy
Bruno Crispo (Round 2)	University of Trento, Italy
Michel Cukier (Round 2)	University of Maryland, USA
Frédéric Cuppens	Polytechnique Montréal, Canada
Tooska Dargahi	Manchester Metropolitan University, UK
Saptarshi Das (Round 2)	Pennsylvania State University, USA
Sabrina De Capitani di Vimercati	Universita' degli Studi di Milano, Italy
Hervé Debar	Télécom SudParis, France
Jose Maria De Fuentes (Round 1)	Universidad Carlos III de Madrid, Spain
Soumyadeep Dey (Round 2)	IIT Kharagpur, India
Roberto Di Pietro (Round 2)	King Abdullah University of Science and Technology, Saudi Arabia
Tassos Dimitriou (Round 2)	Kuwait University, Kuwait
Xuhua Ding (Round 1)	Singapore Management University, Singapore

Josep Domingo-Ferrer — Universitat Rovira i Virgili, Spain
Andreas Ekelhart (Round 1) — Secure Business Austria, Austria
Santiago Escobar (Round 2) — Universitat Politècnica de València, Spain
David Espes (Round 2) — Université de Bretagne Ouest, France
Shuya Feng (Round 2) — University of Connecticut, USA
Anna Lisa Ferrara — Università degli studi del Molise, Italy
Josep Lluís Ferrer Gomila (Round 2) — Universitat de les Illes Balears, Spain
Philip W. L. Fong (Round 2) — University of Calgary, Canada
Olga Gadyatskaya — University of Leiden, The Netherlands
Debin Gao — Singapore Management University, Singapore
Joaquin Garcia-Alfaro — Institut Polytechnique de Paris, France
Essam Ghadafi — Newcastle University, UK
Giorgio Giacinto — University of Cagliari, Italy
Alberto Giaretta (Round 1) — Örebro Universitet, Sweden
Dieter Gollmann — Hamburg University of Technology, Germany
Lorena González Manzano — Universidad Carlos III de Madrid, Spain
Dimitris Gritzalis (Round 1) — Athens University of Economics & Business, Greece
Stefanos Gritzalis (Round 2) — University of Piraeus, Greece
Maanak Gupta (Round 2) — Tennessee Tech University, USA
M. Emre Gursoy (Round 2) — Koç University, Turkey
Gregory Gutin (Round 2) — Royal Holloway, University of London, UK
Hannes Hartenstein (Round 2) — Karlsruhe Institute of Technology, Germany
Hongxin Hu (Round 2) — University at Buffalo, SUNY, USA
Xinyi Huang (Round 2) — Fujian Normal University, China
Hugo Jonker — Open University of the Netherlands, The Netherlands
Sokratis Katsikas — Norwegian University of Science and Technology, Norway
Stefan Katzenbeisser — University of Passau, Germany
Jörg Keller — FernUniversität in Hagen, Germany
Latifur Khan (Round 2) — University of Texas at Dallas, USA
Hiroaki Kikuchi — Meiji University, Japan
Hyoungshick Kim (Round 2) — Sungkyunkwan University, South Korea
Ram Krishnan (Round 2) — University of Texas at San Antonio, USA
Marina Krotofil — Maersk, Switzerland
Christopher Kruegel (Round 2) — University of California Santa Barbara, USA
Alptekin Küpçü — Koç University, Turkey
Romain Laborde — Université de Toulouse, France
Peeter Laud — Cybernetica AS, Estonia
Maryline Laurent — Télécom SudParis, France

Zeyu Lei (Round 2)	Purdue University, USA
Shujun Li (Round 2)	University of Kent, UK
Wenting Li (Round 2)	Peking University, China
Jun Li (Round 2)	University of Oregon, USA
Kaitai Liang	Delft University of Technology, The Netherlands
Hoon Wei Lim (Round 2)	NCS Group, Singapore
Dan Lin (Round 2)	Vanderbilt University, USA
Peng Liu (Round 2)	Pennsylvania State University, USA
Giovanni Livraga	University of Milan, Italy
Valeria Loscri	Inria, France
Wenjing Lou (Round 2)	Virginia Tech, USA
Rongxing Lu (Round 2)	Queen's University, Canada
Haibing Lu (Round 2)	Santa Clara University, USA
Xiapu Luo (Round 2)	Hong Kong Polytechnic University, China
Eduard Marin	Telefónica Research, Spain
Jean-Yves Marion	Université de Lorraine, France
Fabio Martinelli (Round 2)	IIT-CNR, Italy
Amir Masoumzadeh (Round 2)	University at Albany - SUNY, USA
Barbara Masucci	University of Salerno, Italy
Wojciech Mazurczyk	Warsaw University of Technology, Poland
David Megías	Universitat Oberta de Catalunya, Spain
Weizhi Meng	Lancaster University, UK
Donika Mirdita (Round 2)	Fraunhofer Secure Information Technology, Germany
Chris Mitchell (Round 2)	Royal Holloway, University of London, UK
Barsha Mitra (Round 2)	BITS Pilani Hyderabad Campus, India
Sudip Mittal (Round 2)	Mississippi State University, USA
Meisam Mohammady (Round 2)	Iowa State University, USA
Haralambos Mouratidis (Round 2)	University of Essex, UK
Guillermo Navarro-Arribas	Autonomous University of Barcelona, Spain
Jianting Ning (Round 2)	Singapore Management University, Singapore
Antonino Nocera	University of Pavia, Italy
Gabriele Oligeri	Hamad Bin Khalifa University, Qatar
Melek Önen (Round 2)	EURECOM, France
Philippe Owezarski	LAAS-CNRS, France
Balaji Palanisamy (Round 2)	University of Pittsburgh, USA
Stefano Paraboschi (Round 2)	Università di Bergamo, Italy
Sikhar Patranabis (Round 2)	IBM Research India, India
Günther Pernul (Round 2)	Universität Regensburg, Germany
Josef Pieprzyk	CSIRO/Data61, Australia
Joachim Posegga	University of Passau, Germany
Mir Mehedi Pritom (Round 2)	Tennessee Tech University, USA

Megha Quamara (Round 2)	King's College London, UK
Silvio Ranise (Round 2)	University of Trento, Italy
Kai Rannenberg (Round 2)	Goethe University Frankfurt, Germany
Siddharth Prakash Rao (Round 2)	Nokia Bell Labs, Finland
Danda B. Rawat (Round 2)	Howard University, USA
Indrakshi Ray (Round 1)	Colorado State University, USA
Indrajit Ray (Round 2)	Colorado State University, USA
Peter Rønne	University of Luxembourg, Luxembourg
Carlos Rubio Medrano (Round 2)	Texas A&M University, USA
Peter Y. A. Ryan	University of Luxembourg, Luxembourg
Reihaneh Safavi-Naini	University of Calgary, Canada
Pierangela Samarati	Università degli Studi di Milano, Italy
Neetesh Saxena	Cardiff University, UK
Neta Rozen-Schiff (Round 2)	Hebrew University of Jerusalem, Israel
Dominique Schröder	Universität Erlangen-Nürnberg, Germany
Jörg Schwenk	Ruhr-Universität Bochum, Germany
Savio Sciancalepore	Eindhoven University of Technology, The Netherlands
R. Sekar (Round 2)	Stony Brook University, USA
Basit Shafiq (Round 2)	Lahore University of Management Sciences, Pakistan
Ankit Shah (Round 2)	Indiana University, USA
Siamak Shahandashti	University of York, UK
Alessandro Sorniotti (Round 1)	IBM Research Europe, Switzerland
Shantanu Sharma (Round 2)	New Jersey Institute of Technology, USA
Wenbo Shen (Round 2)	Zhejiang University, China
Weidong Shi (Round 2)	University of Houston, USA
Arunesh Sinha (Round 2)	Rutgers University, USA
Jayesh Soni (Round 2)	Florida International University, USA
Angelo Spognardi	Sapienza Università di Roma, Italy
Riccardo Spolaor	Shandong University, China
Natalia Stakhanova (Round 2)	University of Saskatchewan, Canada
Thorsten Strufe (Round 2)	Karlsruhe Institute of Technology, Germany
Wenhai Sun (Round 2)	Purdue University, USA
Shamik Sural (Round 2)	Indian Institute of Technology Kharagpur, India
Luis Suárez (Round 2)	Ericsson, Canada
Qiang Tang (Round 2)	University of Sydney, Australia
Nadia Tawbi	Laval University, Canada
Vicenc Torra	Umeå University, Sweden
Jacob Torrey (Round 2)	Thinkst Applied Research, USA
Ari Trachtenberg (Round 2)	Boston University, USA
Stacey Truex (Round 2)	Denison University, USA

Jalaj Upadhyay (Round 2)	Johns Hopkins University, USA
Tobias Urban (Round 2)	Westphalian University of Applied Sciences, Germany
Daniele Venturi	Sapienza University of Rome, Italy
Rakesh Verma (Round 2)	University of Houston, USA
Tran Viet Xuan Phuong (Round 2)	University of Arkansas at Little Rock, USA
Joao P. Vilela (Round 2)	University of Porto, Portugal
Di Wang (Round 2)	State University of New York at Buffalo, USA
Haining Wang (Round 2)	Virginia Tech, USA
Cong Wang (Round 2)	City University of Hong Kong, China
Xinyue Wang (Round 2)	Renmin University of China, China
Lingyu Wang (Round 2)	Concordia University, Canada
Han Wang (Round 2)	University of Kansas, USA
Wenqi Wei (Round 2)	Fordham University, USA
Edgar Weippl	University of Vienna, Austria
Avishai Wool (Round 1)	Tel Aviv University, Israel
Christos Xenakis (Round 2)	University of Piraeus, Greece
Yang Xiang (Round 2)	Swinburne University of Technology, Australia
Yue Xiao (Round 2)	IBM Research, USA
Shouhuai Xu (Round 2)	University of Colorado Colorado Springs, USA
Runhua Xu (Round 2)	Beihang University, China
Peng Xu (Round 2)	Huazhong University of Science and Technology, China
Guomin Yang (Round 2)	Singapore Management University, Singapore
Zhihao Yao (Round 2)	New Jersey Institute of Technology, USA
Roland Yap (Round 2)	National University of Singapore, Singapore
Miuyin Yong Wong (Round 2)	Georgia Institute of Technology, USA
Chuan Yue (Round 2)	Colorado School of Mines, USA
Stefano Zanero (Round 1)	Politecnico di Milano, Italy
Yuan Zhang (Round 2)	Fudan University, China
Zhikun Zhang (Round 2)	Zhejiang University, China
Kehuan Zhang (Round 2)	Chinese University of Hong Kong, China
Liang Zhao (Round 2)	Emory University, USA
Ziming Zhao (Round 2)	Northeastern University, USA
Yunlei Zhao (Round 2)	Fudan University, China
Jianying Zhou (Round 2)	Singapore University of Technology and Design, Singapore
Sencun Zhu (Round 2)	Pennsylvania State University, USA
Rui Zhu (Round 2)	Indiana University, USA

Additional Reviewers

Abbadini, Marco
Abdelgawad, Mahmoud
Abdullahi, Ahmed
Abu Jabal, Amani
Afzal, Zeeshan
Aghayarzadeh, Hamed
Agrawal, Anand
Ahmed, Basharat
Ahmed, Faisal
Akbar, Khandakar Ashrafi
Akbarzadeh, Aida
Al Kadri, Mhd Omar
Al Mahmud, Tamim
Alborch Escobar, Ferran
Alhaidari, Abdulrahman
Allami, Ali
Almani, Dimah
Almasan, Paul
Almutaitri, Abeer
Amaral Simões, Sancho
Arazzi, Marco
Armanuzzaman, Md
Arriaga, Afonso
Arrus, Aurora
Aryal, Kshitiz
Aung, Yan Lin
Avizheh, Sepideh
Azizli, Elmaddin
Bacho, Renas
Baecker, Ruben
Bashir, Shadaab Kawnain
Belguith, Sana
Benaloh, Josh
Beneš, Martin
Beretta, Michele
Berlato, Stefano
Bertrand, Léo
Bertrand, Simon
Bezawada, Bruhadeshwar
Bianchi, Federica
Binosi, Lorenzo
Binte Haq, Hina
Birashk, Amin

Biswas, Chinmoy
Bisways, Chinmoy
Boyapally, Harishma
Carlson, Trevor E.
Carminati, Michele
Carvalho, Tânia
Casagrande, Marco
Castiglione, Arcangelo
Castiglione, Gianpietro
Catuogno, Luigi
Cecconello, Stefano
Charlès, Alex
Chaturvedi, Bhuvnesh
Chawla, Abhimanyu
Chekole, Eyasu Getahun
Chen, Depeng
Chen, Juntao
Chen, Yumin
Chen, Zeyu
Chong, Chun Jie
Chouchoulis, Ioannis
Chu, Hien Thi Thu
Cihangiroglu, Mert
Cimato, Stelvio
Collu, Matteo Gioele
Cui, Hui
Cunha, Mariana
Dai, Jiongyu
Dai, Xushu
Daneshmand, Arash
Dang, Hai-Van
Das, Debayan
Das, Prajit Kumar
Das Chowdhury, Partha
Daudén-Esmel, Cristòfol
Deidda, Nicola
Demetrio, Luca
Demir, Nurullah
Demirkiran, Ferhat
Dey, Kunal
Di Gennaro, Marco
Di Paolo, Edoardo
Ding, Weikang

Dipta, Debopriya Roy
Dolati, Mahdi
Donadel, Denis
Droll, Jan
Du, Linkang
Du, Minxin
Duck, Gregory
Dunbar, Arthur
Eichhammer, Philipp
Erinola, Nurullah
Esposito, Sergio
Facchinetti, Dario
Fadavi, Mojtaba
Falanji, Reyhane
Falebita, Oluwatosin
Faraj, Omair
Farasat, Talaya
Feng, Hanwen
Ferrari, Stefano
Ferré-Queralt, Joan
Flamini, Andrea
Fotiadis, Georgios
Fouotsa, Tako Boris
Galeazzi, Alessandro
Gao, Yang
Garbelini, Matheus
García Díaz, Jorge Francisco
García Fernández, Pablo
George, Aleena Elsa
Ghorbel, Bassem
Ghosh, Soumyadyuti
Giannakopoulos, Thrasyvoulos
Giapantzis, Konstantinos
Gimenez, Pierre-François
Glas, Magdalena
Golinelli, Matteo
Gomes, Catarina
Gowdanakatte, Shwetha
Grill, Johannes
Grisafi, Michele
Groszschaedl, Johann
Grundmann, Matthias
Guiot, Miquel
Guo, Jinduo
Gupta, Deepti

Haefner, Kyle
Haffar, Rami
Haffey, Preston
Hamm, Peter
Hamm And Lieberknecht, Two Subreviewers Peter And Ann-Kristin
Han, Qiang
Han, Yanni
Haque, Md Shahedul
Hassanpour, Seyedeh Bahereh
Herranz, Javier
Hopkins, Jacob
Hore, Soumyadeep
Hosseini, Henry
Hou, Chenxi
Howard, Samuel
Hu, Chengcong
Huang, Mengdie
Huang, Qiqing
Huang, Zhicheng
Huso, Ingrid
Ibarrondo, Alberto
In, Junbeom
Ioannidis, Thodoris
Irfan, Muhammad
Jacob, Florian
Jacqmin, Quentin
Jiang, Shan
Jiang, Yuning
Jin, Heng
Jorba, Josep
Kaaniche, Nesrine
Kammueller, Florian
Kanpak, Halil Ibrahim
Karim Imtiaz
Katsis Charalampos
Kei, Andes Y. L.
Kembu, Vignesh Kumar
Kermabon-Bobinnec, Hugo
Kern, Sascha
Khan, Younas
Kimm, Hanke
Koffas, Stefanos
Koohpayeh Araghi, Tanya
Korichi, Youcef

Kouko, Gildas
Kumar, Gulshan
Kumari, Komal
Kunwar, Pradip
Lalande, Jean-Francois
Lara, Carlos
Laura Madison, Axel Durbet
Le Mouel, Florian
Leinweber, Marc
Lerch-Hostalot, Daniel
Li, Adrian Shuai
Li, Fagen
Li, Xiang
Li, Xiaoguo
Li, Yamin
Li Calsi, Davide
Liang, Yu
Ligier, Damien
Lin, Chao
Litzinger, Sebastian
Liu, Gaoxiang
Liu, Jiahao
Liu, Jianghua
Loh, Jia-Chng
Lombard-Platet, Marius
Longo, Riccardo
Lopez Morales, Efren
Lotto, Alessandro
Luchini, Chiara
Luo, Nanqing
Lybarger, Kevin
Löbner, Sascha
Ma, Jack P. K.
Ma, Jinhua
Ma, Wanlun
Ma, Zheyuan
Maehren, Marcel
Maffei, Ivo
Maitra, Sudip
Makropodis, Ioannis
Maldonado, Mark
Manzanares-Salor, Benet
Martins, Óscar
Marty, Pierre
Massidda, Emmanuele

McCarthy, Andrew
Meadows, Catherine
Meng, Qiaoran
Mercer, Rebekah
Merzdovnik, Georg
Michaud, Quentin
Mishra, Nimish
Mishra, Sagar
Mitra, Shaswata
Mohammadi, Sareh
Mondragon, Jennifer
Mostafiz, Mir Imtiaz
Mura, Raffaele
Müller, Mathis
Nagasubramaniam, Piyush
Nath, Souradip
Nelson, Jonathan
Neudert, Raphael
Nguyen, Hieu
Nicolazzo, Serena
Niknia, Ahad
Niow, Choon Hock
Noble, Daniel
P., Vinod
Palihawadana, Chamath
Pan, Ying-Yu
Panebianco, Francesco
Panja, Somnath
Patel, Raj
Paudel, Diwas
Persiano, Giuseppe
Pimpinella, Giovanni
Podder, Rakesh
Praharaj, Lopamudra
Preatoni, Riccardo
Psychogyiou, Aikaterini
Pucher, Michael
Puchta, Alexander
Pérez-Ramos, Edgar
Qiu, Tian Qu, Jiashu
Quadrio, Giacomo
Quinci, Arianna
Qureshi, Amna
Raciti, Mario
Rasul, Md Fazle

Regano, Leonardo
Reijsbergen, Daniel
Rizzi, Matteo
Rosenblattl, Jakob
Rossi, Matthew
Roy, Shovan
Russo, Luigi
Saadi Dadmarzi, Hamidreza
Sacchetta, Juri
Saha, Rahul
Samdaliri, Mahya
Sanna, Alessandro
Saqlain, Sabbir Ahmed
Sato, Shingo
Sauger, Gabriel
Senn, Judith
Serra-Ruiz, Jordi
Sha, Kailun
Shafir, Lior
Shahriar, Md Hasan
Sharif, Amir
Shen, Zilin
Shepherd, Carlton
Shi, Shanghao
Siemer, Jan Niklas
Singh, Animesh
Singh, Gurjot
Sinha, Sayani
Skandylas, Charilaos
Skrobot, Marjan
Song, Yongcheng
Song, Zirui
Soria-Comas, Jordi
Spadafora, Chiara
Spiesberger, Patrick
Srivastava, Gautam
Stifter, Nicholas
Streicher, Klaus
Stylianou, Ioannis
Sun, Shihua
Sözen Esen, Derya
Thomas, Julian
Thomas, Tony
Tian, Guohua
Tian, Jianwen

Tippe, Pascal
Todd, James
Torabi, Sadegh
Tripathi, Himanshu
Trombetta, Alberto
Tsado, Yakubu
Tuck, Bryan
Tureček, Philip
Udovenko, Aleksei
Valeriani, Lorenzo
Vasilopoulos, Dimitrios
Wan, Guoan
Wang, Cheng-Long
Wang, Hongxiao
Wang, Jingzhe
Wang, Lulu
Wang, Shuo
Wang, Wenli
Wang, Xinhai
Wang, Yuyu
Wazan, Ahmad Samer
Wen, Tian
Wong, Harry W. H.
Wu, Jiaojiao
Wu, Pengfei
Xie, Xinhong
Xu, Chenming
Xu, Difei
Xu, Peng
Xu, Shengmin
Xue, Haiyang
Yan, Yingfei
Yang, Fan
Yang, Yang
Yang, Zeyu
Yin, Zihao
Younas, Affan
Yu, Chia-Mu
Yu, Hexuan
Yu, Tianchi
Yuan, Quan
Yuan, Wei
Yuan, Yijun
Zari, Oualid
Zhang, Bokang

Zhang, Chaoyu
Zhang, Ke
Zhang, Zicheng
Zhao, Rui

Zhou, Ming
Zhu, Rui
Zhu, Xiaogang
Özfatura, Kerem

Contents – Part I

Time-Distributed Backdoor Attacks on Federated Spiking Learning 1
   Gorka Abad, Stjepan Picek, and Aitor Urbieta

TATA: Benchmark NIDS Test Sets Assessment and Targeted Augmentation . . . 21
   Omar Anser, Jérôme François, Isabelle Chrisment, and Daishi Kondo

Abuse-Resistant Evaluation of AI-as-a-Service via Function-Hiding
Homomorphic Signatures 42
   Nuttapong Attrapadung, Goichiro Hanaoka, Ryo Hiromasa,
   Yoshihiro Koseki, Takahiro Matsuda, Yutaro Nishida, Yusuke Sakai,
   Jacob C. N. Schuldt, and Satoshi Yasuda

PriSM: A Privacy-Friendly Support Vector Machine 62
   Michele Barbato, Alberto Ceselli, Sabrina De Capitani di Vimercati,
   Sara Foresti, and Pierangela Samarati

Towards Context-Aware Log Anomaly Detection Using Fine-Tuned Large
Language Models 83
   Hugo Breniaux and Djedjiga Mouheb

PROTEAN: Federated Intrusion Detection in Non-IID Environments
Through Prototype-Based Knowledge Sharing 103
   Sara Chennoufi, Yufei Han, Gregory Blanc, Emiliano De Cristofaro,
   and Christophe Kiennert

KeTS: Kernel-Based Trust Segmentation Against Model Poisoning Attacks 126
   Ankit Gangwal, Mauro Conti, and Tommaso Pauselli

Machine Learning Vulnerabilities in 6G: Adversarial Attacks
and Their Impact on Channel Gain Prediction and Resource Allocation
in UC-CFmMIMO 147
   Mahmoud Ghorbel, Selina Cheggour, Valeria Loscri, Youcef Imine,
   Hamza Ouarnoughi, and Smail Niar

FuncVul: An Effective Function Level Vulnerability Detection Model
Using LLM and Code Chunk 166
   Sajal Halder, Muhammad Ejaz Ahmed, and Seyit Camtepe

LUMIA: Linear Probing for Unimodal and MultiModal Membership
Inference Attacks Leveraging Internal LLM States 186
  *Luis Ibanez-Lissen, Lorena Gonzalez-Manzano,
  Jose Maria de Fuentes, Nicolas Anciaux, and Joaquin Garcia-Alfaro*

Membership Privacy Evaluation in Deep Spiking Neural Networks 207
  Jiaxin Li, Gorka Abad, Stjepan Picek, and Mauro Conti

DUMB and DUMBer: Is Adversarial Training Worth It in the Real World? 228
  Francesco Marchiori, Marco Alecci, Luca Pajola, and Mauro Conti

Countering Jailbreak Attacks with Two-Axis Pre-detection and Conditional
Warning Wrappers 249
  Hyunsik Na, Hajun Kim, Dooshik Yoon, and Daeseon Choi

How Dataset Diversity Affects Generalization in ML-Based NIDS 269
  Benoit Nougnanke, Gregory Blanc, and Thomas Robert

Llama-Based Source Code Vulnerability Detection: Prompt Engineering
vs Fine Tuning 289
  Dyna Soumhane Ouchebara and Stéphane Dupont

DBBA: Diffusion-Based Backdoor Attacks on Open-Set Face Recognition
Models 309
  *Fuqi Qi, Haichang Gao, Boling Li, Guangyu He, Yuhong Zhang,
  and Jiacheng Luo*

Evaluation of Autonomous Intrusion Response Agents in Adversarial
and Normal Scenarios 328
  Matthew Reaney, Kieran McLaughlin, and Sandra Scott-Hayward

Trigger-Based Fragile Model Watermarking for Image Transformation
Networks 346
  *Preston K. Robinette, Thuy Dung Nguyen, Samuel Sasaki,
  and Taylor T. Johnson*

Let the Noise Speak: Harnessing Noise for a Unified Defense Against
Adversarial and Backdoor Attacks 366
  *Md Hasan Shahriar, Ning Wang, Naren Ramakrishnan,
  Y. Thomas Hou, and Wenjing Lou*

On the Adversarial Robustness of Graph Neural Networks with Graph
Reduction 388
  Kerui Wu, Ka-Ho Chow, Wenqi Wei, and Lei Yu

SecureT2I: No More Unauthorized Manipulation on AI Generated Images from Prompts 410
Xiaodong Wu, Xiangman Li, Qi Li, Jianbing Ni, and Rongxing Lu

GANSec: Enhancing Supervised Wireless Anomaly Detection Robustness Through Tailored Conditional GAN Augmentation 430
Jiali Xu, Shuo Wang, Valeria Loscri, Alessandro Brighente, Mauro Conti, and Romain Rouvoy

Fine-Grained Data Poisoning Attack to Local Differential Privacy Protocols for Key-Value Data 450
Terumi Yaguchi and Hiroaki Kikuchi

The DCR Delusion: Measuring the Privacy Risk of Synthetic Data 469
Zexi Yao, Nataša Krčo, Georgi Ganev, and Yves-Alexandre de Montjoye

StructTransform: A Scalable Attack Surface for Safety-Aligned Large Language Models 488
Shehel Yoosuf, Temoor Ali, Ahmed Lekssays, Mashael AlSabah, and Issa Khalil

Author Index 509

Time-Distributed Backdoor Attacks on Federated Spiking Learning

Gorka Abad[1,2,3(✉)], Stjepan Picek[1,4], and Aitor Urbieta[2]

[1] Radboud University, Nijmegen, The Netherlands
{abad.gorka,stjepan.picek}@ru.nl
[2] Ikerlan Technology Research Centre, Arrasate-Mondragón, Spain
aurbieta@ikerlan.es
[3] University of Bergen, Bergen, Norway
[4] University of Zagreb, Zagreb, Croatia

Abstract. This paper investigates the vulnerability of federated learning (FL) with spiking neural networks (SNNs) to backdoor attacks using neuromorphic data. Despite the efficiency of SNNs and the privacy advantages of FL, particularly in low-powered devices, we demonstrate that these systems are susceptible to such attacks. We first assess the viability of using FL with SNNs using neuromorphic data, showing its potential usage. Then, we evaluate the transferability of known FL attack methods to SNNs, finding that these lead to sub-optimal attack performance. Consequently, we explore backdoor attacks involving single and multiple attackers to improve the attack performance. Our main contribution is developing a novel attack strategy tailored to SNNs and FL, which distributes the backdoor trigger temporally and across malicious clients, enhancing the attack's effectiveness and stealthiness. In the best case, we achieve a 100% attack success rate, 0.13 MSE, and 98.9 SSIM. Moreover, we adapt and evaluate existing defenses against backdoor attacks, revealing their inadequacy in protecting SNNs. Our code is publicly available. (https://github.com/GorkaAbad/Time-Bandits).

Keywords: Backdoor · Spiking Neural Network · Federated Learning

1 Introduction

Deep neural networks (DNNs) achieve outstanding performance across tasks like computer vision and natural language processing (NLP) by learning from large datasets, but require significant energy and computation [11]. In contrast, spiking neural networks (SNNs) enable energy-efficient computing through neuromorphic data, which is time-encoded and highly compressed [13]. SNNs perform comparably to traditional models while drastically reducing energy consumption. Real-world applications highlight the practicality of SNNs. Intel's Loihi chip recognizes hazardous chemicals in real-time [24], and CarSNN [52] enables low-latency autonomous driving. Industry solutions, such as SynSense[1] for real-time vision and audio processing and Prophesee[2] for event-based object tracking, further demonstrate their utility.

Privacy-preserving machine learning (ML), such as federated learning (FL), decentralizes training across devices without sharing data, which benefits edge-computing environments [36]. FL has been tested with SNNs on non-neuromorphic data [51,53], but its evaluation with neuromorphic data remains unexplored. Neuromorphic inputs require time-sensitive processing, are highly sparse and event-driven, and differ fundamentally from conventional image datasets. This makes standard FL frameworks suboptimal unless adapted to the unique characteristic of SNNs. While recent work has shown the vulnerability of SNNs to backdoors in centralized settings [2], no prior work has studied the persistence, stealthiness, or federated-specific defenses in neuromorphic FL, which we address in this paper. Merging FL with SNNs offers opportunities for energy-efficient, high-accuracy training but introduces new security challenges. Security concerns in ML include adversarial, model inversion, and backdoor attacks [23]. While SNNs are vulnerable to adversarial [42] and backdoor attacks [2], unique threats arise when combining FL with neuromorphic data.

Backdoor attacks in FL have shown practicality in real-world settings [44], with methods like model scaling [8] and multi-attacker coordination [55] improving attack persistence. Attacks such as Perdoor [4] and Neurotoxin [57] ensure backdoor persistence across training rounds by targeting stable model parameters. Backdoor attacks in FL span various tasks, including images and text [19]. Time-encoded neuromorphic data allows attackers to distribute backdoor triggers across time frames, making detection harder than pixel-based triggers. Spiking neuron mechanisms, which process event-based inputs, are perfectly suited for time-based perturbations, enabling novel attack strategies. In this work, we evaluate backdoor attacks in FL using neuromorphic data and propose a novel attack, *Time Bandits*, where triggers are split across time and multiple attackers. Our contributions include i) pioneering backdoor attacks in FL with neuromorphic data, where we design the *Time Bandits* attack, which leverages time-split triggers; ii) evaluating single and multiple attacker scenarios and the stealthiness of time-based triggers; and iii) assessing the applicability of standard FL defenses under neuromorphic data.

While our attacks are not designed for physical deployment, they have real-world implications. i) In FL settings using SNNs, a malicious client can inject backdoors into the global model, requiring specialized defenses. ii) Coordinated attackers can exploit the time dimension to enhance stealth, complicating detection. Recent advancements in neuromorphic computing are reflected in emerging hardware like Loihi [10], TrueNorth [3], Spinal Flow [35], and H2Learn [30], with applications where neuromorphic systems outperform traditional computing: i) **Power grids:** Neuromorphic computing enables faster, energy-efficient anomaly detection for expanding electrical grids, critical for sustainability goals [40]. ii)

---

[1] https://www.synsense.ai.
[2] https://www.prophesee.ai.

Drones: On-the-fly image processing supports applications like disaster victim searches, plant inspection, and logistics [39]. iii) **Research:** Systems like the Large Hadron Collider and European Low-Frequency Array generate vast data volumes (>100 PB/year). Neuromorphic hardware achieves up to $1\,000\times$ lower energy use and $10\times$ faster computation [27].

2 Background

SNNs and Neuromorphic Data. Neuromorphic data is inspired by biological neural systems, encoding information through temporal dynamics in an event-driven, asynchronous manner. It has significant applications in visual processing, particularly using dynamic vision sensors (DVSs) cameras and SNNs. DVSs cameras capture luminance changes over time as streams of events, enabling real-time, efficient visual representations. SNNs process these events through spiking neurons, leveraging neuromorphic data for energy-efficient computation.

Formally, let $I(\omega)$ represent the neuromorphic input at time ω. The behavior of a spiking neuron j is defined by the leaky integrate-and-fire (LIF) model:

$$h_j(\omega) = \begin{cases} 1, & \text{if } V_j(\omega) \geq \nu_j, \\ 0, & \text{otherwise,} \end{cases} \qquad (1)$$

where $V_j(\omega)$ is the membrane potential, and ν_j is the firing threshold. After emitting a spike, the membrane potential resets. Since Eq. (1) is non-differentiable, standard backpropagation cannot be applied. Specialized training methods like spike timing-dependent plasticity (STDP) or surrogate gradients approximate the derivatives to enable backpropagation. We use Adam, which achieves better performance [28], over alternatives like stochastic gradient descent (SGD).

Federated Learning. FL [34] is a decentralized ML technique enabling collaborative model training across clients while keeping data private, unlike centralized approaches that require raw data sharing. Federated Averaging (FedAvg) [34] is a common FL aggregation method, where client updates are averaged. Let $\mathcal{D}_1, \mathcal{D}_2, \ldots, \mathcal{D}_n$ be the local datasets of n clients, where each client trains a local model parameterized by θ_i. FL aims to learn a global model Θ by aggregating updates from a subset of clients $\mathcal{B}_t$ selected at iteration t. This ensures the global model benefits from distributed knowledge while preserving data privacy.

Backdoor Attacks. Backdoor attacks manipulate model behavior during training, causing misclassification of inputs containing a trigger while performing correctly on clean inputs [20]. In data poisoning backdoors, malicious samples with a trigger are added to the training set. Formally, an algorithm $f_\theta(\cdot)$ is trained on a dataset mixing clean and backdoor data, where the mixing ratio is $\epsilon = \frac{m}{n}$ ($m \ll n$). The backdoor dataset $\mathcal{D}_{bk}$ contains samples $\{(\hat{\mathbf{x}}, \hat{y})\}$, where $\hat{\mathbf{x}}$ includes the trigger, and $\hat{y}$ is the target label. In FL, malicious clients inject poisoned samples into local training [8]. With many clients, the backdoor effect may vanish during aggregation. To amplify their impact, attackers scale their local model by $\gamma = \frac{n}{\hat{n}}$, where $\hat{n}$ is the number of malicious clients [8].

3 Threat Model

Federated SNNs have been explored in various studies [47,51], including privacy-preserving approaches [22]. Still, these works focus on regular data, leaving practical applications with neuromorphic data unexplored. Neuromorphic data enhances SNNs's efficiency, enabling real-time pattern recognition and sensory data interpretation. This approach leverages the biological plausibility of SNNs while addressing critical challenges in energy efficiency, making it ideal for IoT, robotics, and edge computing [37]. FL complements this by offering decentralized training, preserving data privacy, and reducing bandwidth usage [26]. This is particularly important for neuromorphic datasets, which often include sensitive or high-volume sensory data. While SNNs excels with neuromorphic inputs, their ability to handle regular data further expands their versatility in sensory information processing.

We adopt a standard threat model for backdoor attacks in FL [8,19,55]. Clients collaboratively train a shared model on a specific task using FL to preserve data privacy. The central server initializes the model, aggregates client updates, and repeats this process until convergence. We assume one or more coordinated attackers among benign clients. In practical FL, factors like communication delays, asynchronous updates, and variable client participation can impact attack success. We simulate scenarios where attackers are intermittently involved by varying client participation rates.

The attacker can access private data and modify the local training process, but cannot interfere with benign clients or model aggregation. Coordinated attackers can freely collaborate but still operate on their private data. The attacker aims to inject a backdoor into the global model via dirty-label poisoning [8,20,49], crafting poisoned samples for local training. Dirty-label refers to a backdoor injection technique, where the label of the modified sample are swapped to an attacker-selected target label. In contrast to clean-label attacks, where the label is not altered. Attackers may scale their models to increase influence during aggregation. We focus on digital backdoor attacks in the image domain rather than physical attacks [7]. Our study considers horizontal FL [56], where clients have distinct data samples but share the same features (e.g., a smart keyboard collects similar text input data across devices and shares model updates).

4 Methodology

Single Attacker. In a single-attacker scenario, the attacker injects a backdoor into the global model using its private data and model (Fig. 1a). We adapt the *vanilla* backdoor attack [8] to neuromorphic data. The attacker selects a trigger size, location, and polarity based on prior work [2], using a 30% trigger size placed in the top-left corner with polarity 1 (light blue). We consider different trigger sizes in Sect. 5.1. This configuration achieves high attack success rate (ASR) without degrading the global model's benign performance. For neuromorphic data, larger triggers may be needed to overcome its complex and noisy nature, ensuring consistent model manipulation. While a 30% trigger may seem visually obvious, its placement and polarity can remain undetectable [2].

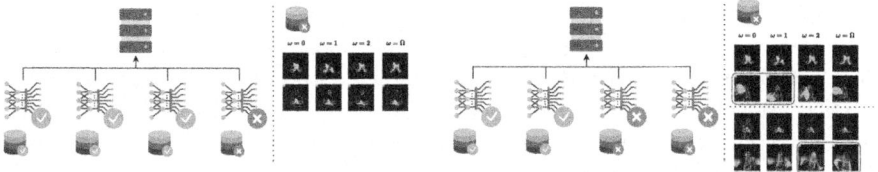

(a) Overview of the single-attacker backdoor attack.

(b) Time Bandits attack with two attackers splitting the trigger in time.

Fig. 1. Comparative visualization of the single-attacker and multiple-attacker (Time Bandits) backdoor attacks.

The attacker adds poisoned samples (controlled by ϵ) to the local dataset, placing the trigger consistently across all frames Ω with constant polarity.[3] After local training, the attacker scales the malicious model $\hat{\theta}$ and sends it to the server for aggregation. The attacker's participation depends on client selection probability, which impacts attack performance (see Sect. 5.1).

Multiple Attackers - Time Bandits. In a multiple-attacker scenario, malicious clients collaborate to inject a backdoor into the global model (see Fig. 1b). Inspired by Xie et al. [55], where triggers are spatially split, we propose the novel *Time Bandits* attack, leveraging neuromorphic data's temporal properties by splitting triggers across time frames. Instead of placing the trigger spatially, each malicious client injects it into a subset of frames. For instance, with two attackers and $\Omega = 16$ frames, one attacker poisons the first 8 frames, while the other poisons the last 8. This strategy generalizes to any number of attackers. At test time, the trigger, present in all frames, activates the backdoor. A shorter trigger (a subset of frames) is also considered; see Sect. 5.1.

Formally, let N be the total clients and M the malicious ones. Each data sample $\mathbf{x}$ contains Ω frames: $\mathbf{x} = \{\mathbf{x}_1, \mathbf{x}_2, \ldots, \mathbf{x}_\Omega\}$. The binary function $B_i(\omega)$ determines trigger injection for client i as follows:

$$B_i(\omega) = \begin{cases} 1, & \text{if } i \leq M \text{ and } s_i \leq \omega \leq e_i, \\ 0, & \text{otherwise,} \end{cases} \quad s_i = \left\lfloor \frac{(i-1)\Omega}{M} \right\rfloor + 1, \; e_i = \left\lfloor \frac{i\Omega}{M} \right\rfloor,$$

where $B_i(\omega) = 1$ injects the trigger, and each attacker has a distinct dataset $\mathcal{D}_{A_1} \neq \mathcal{D}_{A_2}$.

---

[3] Injecting the trigger in all frames means that the trigger is applied consistently across all time steps of the sample, making the backdoor temporally persistent. In Time-Bandits, this is distributed across clients to maximize stealthiness.

In SNNs, input patterns are encoded as spike trains over time, and models are trained to recognize complex spatio-temporal signatures. Let $x(t)$ denote an input spike train over discrete time steps $t \in [1, T]$, and let f_θ be the SNN with parameters θ. A standard backdoor attack introduces a consistent trigger pattern $\tau(t)$ into $x(t)$ such that $f_\theta(x(t) + \tau(t)) \to y_{\text{target}}$. In our case, the trigger $\tau(t)$ is *distributed* across time steps and across malicious clients, such that no single client introduces the full pattern. Due to the temporal integration properties of SNNs, this fragmented injection can still result in the learning of a stable temporal association with the target label. From a FL perspective, this strategy benefits from two key properties:

1. **Cumulative Effect Over Rounds:** While each attacker contributes a small part of the trigger, the global model aggregates updates over multiple rounds. This allows the backdoor to be slowly and subtly embedded into the model without raising the norm of any individual update significantly.
2. **Distributed Injection Reduces Outlier Detection:** In contrast to centralized attacks, where the backdoor signal is easily detectable, distributing the trigger over clients and time results in sparse, low-magnitude updates that are directionally aligned with benign updates. This allows the attack to evade defenses based on update magnitude (e.g., norm clipping) or direction (e.g., cosine similarity), see Sect. 6.

5 Experiments

Datasets. We use three datasets: N-MNIST [38], CIFAR10-DVS [29] (N-CIFAR10), and DVS128-Gesture [5] (Gesture). The non-neuromorphic counterparts of N-MNIST and N-CIFAR10 are used for benchmarking security and privacy in ML.

Models. We use three network architectures based on prior work [15].[4] The N-MNIST model has one convolutional and one fully connected layer, trained for 10 rounds and a single local epoch. Gesture and N-CIFAR10 use two convolutional layers with batch normalization, max pooling, dropout, and a voting layer, trained for 64 and 30 rounds, respectively, with two local epochs. Baseline single-client accuracies are 99.27% (N-MNIST), 94.09% (Gesture), and 67.60% (N-CIFAR10). In federated settings, accuracy drops with more clients or lower participation. For example, N-MNIST drops to 93.71% (50 clients, 50% sampled), N-CIFAR10 to 30.4%, and Gesture to 44.4%, with the latter most affected due to limited data per client. We measure the ASR at the final round.

Warm-up and Data Augmentation. Warm-up training improves performance in FL when datasets are small or imbalanced (non-IID) [6]. While common in FL [54,58], warm-up has not been explored for SNNs. We propose a warm-up phase for 10% of federated rounds to enhance training convergence. Gesture

---
[4] SEW-ResNet [14] and spiking VGG-16 yielded similar results on N-CIFAR10 and are omitted.

ensuring consistent model manipulation. While a 30% trigger may seem visually obvious, its placement and polarity can remain undetectable [2].

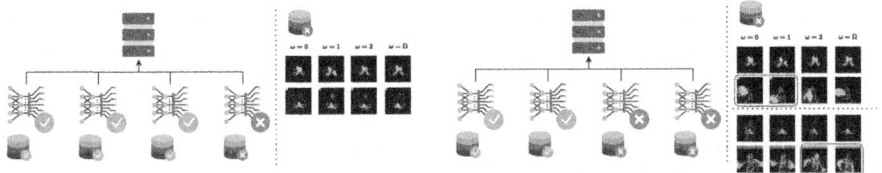

(a) Overview of the single-attacker backdoor attack.

(b) Time Bandits attack with two attackers splitting the trigger in time.

Fig. 1. Comparative visualization of the single-attacker and multiple-attacker (Time Bandits) backdoor attacks.

The attacker adds poisoned samples (controlled by ϵ) to the local dataset, placing the trigger consistently across all frames Ω with constant polarity.[3] After local training, the attacker scales the malicious model $\hat{\theta}$ and sends it to the server for aggregation. The attacker's participation depends on client selection probability, which impacts attack performance (see Sect. 5.1).

Multiple Attackers - Time Bandits. In a multiple-attacker scenario, malicious clients collaborate to inject a backdoor into the global model (see Fig. 1b). Inspired by Xie et al. [55], where triggers are spatially split, we propose the novel *Time Bandits* attack, leveraging neuromorphic data's temporal properties by splitting triggers across time frames. Instead of placing the trigger spatially, each malicious client injects it into a subset of frames. For instance, with two attackers and $\Omega = 16$ frames, one attacker poisons the first 8 frames, while the other poisons the last 8. This strategy generalizes to any number of attackers. At test time, the trigger, present in all frames, activates the backdoor. A shorter trigger (a subset of frames) is also considered; see Sect. 5.1.

Formally, let N be the total clients and M the malicious ones. Each data sample $\mathbf{x}$ contains Ω frames: $\mathbf{x} = \{\mathbf{x}_1, \mathbf{x}_2, \ldots, \mathbf{x}_\Omega\}$. The binary function $B_i(\omega)$ determines trigger injection for client i as follows:

$$B_i(\omega) = \begin{cases} 1, & \text{if } i \leq M \text{ and } s_i \leq \omega \leq e_i, \\ 0, & \text{otherwise,} \end{cases} \quad s_i = \left\lfloor \frac{(i-1)\Omega}{M} \right\rfloor + 1, \; e_i = \left\lfloor \frac{i\Omega}{M} \right\rfloor,$$

where $B_i(\omega) = 1$ injects the trigger, and each attacker has a distinct dataset $\mathcal{D}_{A_1} \neq \mathcal{D}_{A_2}$.

---

[3] Injecting the trigger in all frames means that the trigger is applied consistently across all time steps of the sample, making the backdoor temporally persistent. In Time-Bandits, this is distributed across clients to maximize stealthiness.

In SNNs, input patterns are encoded as spike trains over time, and models are trained to recognize complex spatio-temporal signatures. Let $x(t)$ denote an input spike train over discrete time steps $t \in [1, T]$, and let f_θ be the SNN with parameters θ. A standard backdoor attack introduces a consistent trigger pattern $\tau(t)$ into $x(t)$ such that $f_\theta(x(t) + \tau(t)) \to y_{\text{target}}$. In our case, the trigger $\tau(t)$ is *distributed* across time steps and across malicious clients, such that no single client introduces the full pattern. Due to the temporal integration properties of SNNs, this fragmented injection can still result in the learning of a stable temporal association with the target label. From a FL perspective, this strategy benefits from two key properties:

1. **Cumulative Effect Over Rounds:** While each attacker contributes a small part of the trigger, the global model aggregates updates over multiple rounds. This allows the backdoor to be slowly and subtly embedded into the model without raising the norm of any individual update significantly.
2. **Distributed Injection Reduces Outlier Detection:** In contrast to centralized attacks, where the backdoor signal is easily detectable, distributing the trigger over clients and time results in sparse, low-magnitude updates that are directionally aligned with benign updates. This allows the attack to evade defenses based on update magnitude (e.g., norm clipping) or direction (e.g., cosine similarity), see Sect. 6.

5 Experiments

Datasets. We use three datasets: N-MNIST [38], CIFAR10-DVS [29] (N-CIFAR10), and DVS128-Gesture [5] (Gesture). The non-neuromorphic counterparts of N-MNIST and N-CIFAR10 are used for benchmarking security and privacy in ML.

Models. We use three network architectures based on prior work [15].[4] The N-MNIST model has one convolutional and one fully connected layer, trained for 10 rounds and a single local epoch. Gesture and N-CIFAR10 use two convolutional layers with batch normalization, max pooling, dropout, and a voting layer, trained for 64 and 30 rounds, respectively, with two local epochs. Baseline single-client accuracies are 99.27% (N-MNIST), 94.09% (Gesture), and 67.60% (N-CIFAR10). In federated settings, accuracy drops with more clients or lower participation. For example, N-MNIST drops to 93.71% (50 clients, 50% sampled), N-CIFAR10 to 30.4%, and Gesture to 44.4%, with the latter most affected due to limited data per client. We measure the ASR at the final round.

Warm-up and Data Augmentation. Warm-up training improves performance in FL when datasets are small or imbalanced (non-IID) [6]. While common in FL [54,58], warm-up has not been explored for SNNs. We propose a warm-up phase for 10% of federated rounds to enhance training convergence. Gesture

---

[4] SEW-ResNet [14] and spiking VGG-16 yielded similar results on N-CIFAR10 and are omitted.

accuracy increases from 44.44% to 80.90% (50 clients), and N-CIFAR10 improves from 30.4% to 57.90%. Data augmentation [46] further boosts performance by expanding datasets through transformations. We apply random rotations and padding to the Gesture dataset, increasing it to 2 800 samples. Combining warm-up and augmentation improves model accuracy by up to 20%.

Excluding Gesture Results for 25/50 Clients. We omit Gesture results for 25 and 50 clients due to limited data per client (e.g., 40 samples in IID settings). Smaller datasets lead to unstable training, high variance, and poor performance, particularly in non-IID settings. SNNs are sensitive to weight initialization [13, 41, 48], worsening instability when data is sparse. Therefore, we focus on settings that allow robust and reliable training outcomes.

5.1 Results

Single Attacker. In the single attacker scenario, the attacker crafts poisoned data and includes them in the local dataset, so the backdoor is injected into the model through local training. We consider a case where all the clients in the networks are selected in every round, i.e., $|\mathcal{B}_t|/n = 1$, and when only half of the clients are randomly selected, i.e., $|\mathcal{B}_t|/n = 0.5$. We observe that without scaling, the attack results are ineffective; see Table 1a and Table 1b. The attack achieves a 39.59% ASR with ten clients and a 9.74% with 50 clients for N-MNIST. As expected, the more benign the clients, the worse the attack performance. The same effect is also noticeable for the other datasets. We also evaluate the backdoor performance under model scaling. The attacker scales the model by a scalar based on the number of total clients on the network. The attack performance increases in all the settings (see Table 1b). In most cases, the performance is not as good as the state-of-the-art [8]. Since attacking neuromorphic data is more complex [2], requiring (in general) specific methods for attacking federated SNNs.

Table 1. ASR (%) of a single attacker backdoor attack under different settings with and without scaling (n = number of total clients). $\epsilon = 0.1$.

	(a) Without Scaling						(b) With Scaling					
n	10		25		50		10		25		50	
$|\mathcal{B}_t|/n$	0.5	1	0.5	1	0.5	1	0.5	1	0.5	1	0.5	1
N-MNIST	38.39	30.38	10.09	10.66	9.48	9.74	100	100	100	100	100	100
N-CIFAR10	44.97	29.60	11.20	10.83	10.67	9.27	97.63	99.60	94.93	97.83	25.70	48.53
Gesture	7.06	7.75	-	-	-	-	85.06	82.29	-	-	-	-

Attacking FL with SNNs is generally more complex than attacking its non-neuromorphic counterpart due to the lower performance of SNNs and data complexity. However, the attack achieves top backdoor performance, i.e., 100% ASR, on less complex datasets such as N-MNIST, where the samples are simple and have less noise. For N-CIFAR10, the attack performance also improves with scaling, achieving an ASR of up to 97.63% with ten clients. However, it drops to 48.53% with 50 clients, indicating the difficulty of maintaining high attack success with larger numbers of clients. The Gesture dataset also shows a notable improvement, with ASR reaching up to 85.06% with ten clients when scaling is applied. It is important to note the importance of the rounds at which the attacker is selected. If the attacker is only selected in an early round, the backdoor effect will not be retained and will vanish. This will also be important in later experiments. Furthermore, the results highlight a critical aspect of backdoor attacks in federated learning: the necessity of a careful attacker strategy. The effectiveness of the backdoor attack is significantly influenced by the attacker's ability to manipulate the model scaling process and the timing of their participation in the training rounds. We underscore this by considering a multiple-attacker scenario (Sect. 5.1), where the attackers have more chances of being selected.

Multiple Attackers - Time Bandits. Under a multiple-attacker setup, we use our novel Time Bandits attack. We consider various scenarios where clients are collaborating to achieve the same goal. Precisely, we begin considering two malicious clients, where, in a coordinated manner, they split the trigger through time and include it in their respective dataset (more malicious clients are considered in Sect. 5.1). Note that two malicious clients comprise 20%, 8%, and 4% of the total federated network for 10, 25, and 50 clients. Compared with the single attacker scenario, we observe a significant increase in the performance of the attack (see Table 2), regardless of the dataset. Recall that in a multiple attacker setup, the trigger is split into multiple parts, and the malicious samples are different per client, i.e., attacker 1 contains different samples than attacker 2, only sharing the trigger at different time steps. Thus, the model learns a more complex trigger-target-task relation than in the single-client setup.

By analyzing the results, we observe a noticeable improvement in the attack performance, mostly with complex datasets such as Gesture and N-CIFAR10. This is mainly because of three implications. i) There is an additional attacker. Thus, more samples are compromised; ii) the impact on the aggregated model is larger; and iii) there are more chances of an attacker being selected than with a single attacker. The best performance of Time Bandits is exhibited when the network comprises many clients, i.e., 50. For instance, the performance on N-CIFAR10 improves from 25.70% to 98.47%, an improvement of 72.77%. In that case, using the single attacker setup does not succeed in achieving a successful backdoor, and therefore, the improvement with Time Bandits is substantial.

The stealthiness of the backdoor samples in the multiple attackers scenario is also improved compared to the single attacker scenario since fewer time steps are modified. In the single attacker scenario, the attacker poisons a few data samples. Those contain the trigger for all the timesteps. However, using Time Bandits with two attackers will poison half of the timesteps, which results in a more stealthy attack (more details in Sect. 6.2).

Table 2. ASR (%) of the Time Bandits attack under different settings (n = number of total clients). $\epsilon = 0.1$.

n	10		25		50	
$|\mathcal{B}_t|/n$	0.5	1	0.5	1	0.5	1
N-MNIST	100	100	100	100	100	100
N-CIFAR10	99.70	100	100	98.80	98.47	98.64
Gesture	100	96.18	-	-	-	-

Overall, using Time Bandits compared to a single attacker setup (even when using a scaling factor) generally improves the attack performance and stealthiness. Similarly, the Time Bandits attack gives the attacker more flexibility and control over the trigger, which could be adapted to bypass known defenses.

Effect of the Number of Attackers. We consider the effect of different numbers of malicious clients for the Time Bandits attack. Precisely, we split the trigger among 2, 4, 6, 8, 10, and 12 malicious clients. We set the maximum value to 12, comprising half of the total number of 25 clients. Tables 3a and 3b show ASR of different attack setups with 25 and 50 total clients, respectively.

Table 3. ASR (%) of the Time Bandits attack under different settings ($n = 25$ and $n = 50$ number of total clients). $\epsilon = 0.1$.

	(a) $n = 25$ Clients												(b) $n = 50$ Clients											
$|\mathcal{B}_t|/n$	0.5						1						0.5						1					
# Attackers	2	4	6	8	10	12	2	4	6	8	10	12	2	4	6	8	10	12	2	4	6	8	10	12
N-MNIST	100	100	100	100	100	100	100	100	100	100	100	100	100	100	100	100	100	100	100	100	100	100	100	100
N-CIFAR10	100	99.95	98.80	99.90	87.90	91.20	98.80	100	99.20	99.40	99.30	99.80	98.47	40.70	100	76.80	60.30	65.90	98.64	100	99.01	100	92.40	82.70

Starting with 25 total clients in the network, we observe that Time Bandits achieves 100% ASR when attacking the N-MNIST dataset, regardless of the number of attackers, and without degrading the clean performance. Indeed, the clean accuracy drops to less than 1%. This shows that Time Bandits finds an excellent trade-off between attack and clean performance, mainly boosted by the scaling factor, which adapts depending on the number of attackers.

On a more complex dataset such as N-CIFAR10, the attack performance is still high, with a minimum of 87.90% ASR with ten attackers. The performance can be lower when a few clients (50% of the total clients in this case) are selected because the rounds in which the attacker is selected directly correlate with the attacker's performance. The clean accuracy, in this case, drops to a minimum of 57.5% (from 59.20%) with 25 clients and down to 56.1% (from 57.50%) with 50 clients, with 12 attackers. The downgrade is less than 3% when compared to the baseline. Overall, Time Bandits exhibit success in a wide range of settings, granting the attacker flexibility for attacking FL.

A similar trend is observed with 50 total clients; see Table 3b. Attacking N-MNIST achieves 100% ASR in every setting without noticeable degradation in the clean accuracy. Moving to N-CIFAR10, The Time Bandits attack still achieves great performance in most cases. However, there are some cases where ASR is not as good as with 25 total clients. Precisely, the degradation in the attack performance is influenced by the randomness of the attackers being selected. Note that with four attackers, when half of the clients are selected in each round, ASR is 40.70%. When all the clients are selected in every round, the performance improves to 100% ASR. As observed in earlier experiments, the round in which the attacker is selected heavily influences the attack's success.

Overall, the more attackers in the network, the higher the chances of being selected, improving the attack performance. Moreover, the stealthiness is boosted. That is, the more attackers, the more the trigger is split; therefore, the subtler the perturbation in the samples. More about stealthiness in Sect. 6.2.

Effect of the IID-ness. In addition to the number of clients in the network, other properties, such as the data distribution, also affect the performance of the FL network. This section evaluates how SNNs and the attack perform as the data distribution becomes non-IID. We systematically create the non-IID data using the Dirichlet distribution, a standard method in FL [60]. We set the non-IID degree to 50%[5]. We also consider training solely on clean data to compare its performance with the IID version. Based on the results (see Table 4), we observe a slight degradation in the accuracy. However, the degradation is not severe and also happens in regular non-spiking networks when non-IID data is used [51].

Table 4. Clean accuracy (%) baseline for different FL setups under non-IID settings (n = number of total clients).

n	10		25		50	
$|\mathcal{B}_t|/n$	0.5	1	0.5	1	0.5	1
N-MNIST	98.31	98.17	97.31	97.14	95.94	96.11
N-CIFAR10	56.90	61.40	56.5	26.70	20.35	18.30
Gesture	84.37	87.84	-	-	-	-

Considering ten clients in the network, we achieve 100% ASR with N-MNIST and N-CIFAR10, regardless of the number of clients selected in each federated round. With Gesture, when half of the clients are selected per round, ASR equals 88.19%, and with all the clients selected, it equals 97.56%. With ten clients, the performance of Time Bandits is high, regardless of IID or non-IID settings. Additionally, we consider 25 and 50 clients in the network, with varying numbers of attackers: 2, 4, 6, 8, 10, and 12, see Tables 5a and 5b.

---

[5] We also considered different degrees of IID-ness. We observed that Time Bandits is required to achieve a successful attack. We excluded the results due to page limitations.

Table 5. ASR (%) of the Time Bandits attack under different settings ($n = 25$ and $n = 50$ number of total clients). $\epsilon = 0.1$.

	(a) $n = 25$ Clients											(b) $n = 50$ Clients										
$|\mathcal{B}_t|/n$	0.5						1					0.5					1					
# Attackers	2	4	6	8	10	12	2	4	6	8	10	12	2	4	6	8	10	12	2	4	6	8	10	12
N-MNIST	100	100	100	100	100	100	100	100	100	100	100	100	100	100	100	100	100	100	100	100	100	100	100	100
N-CIFAR10	93.20	100	91.80	100	100	100	100	100	100	100	100	100	77.90	94.0	82.10	99.80	93.10	100	100	100	61.10	100	97.20	77.90

We observe a similar behavior as in the IID case; N-MNIST achieves 100% ASR regardless of the number of attackers and the number of clients selected per round. Moving to N-CIFAR10, ASR also remains high; however, the performance lowers in specific settings, e.g., six attackers out of 50 total clients with ASR equal to 61.10%. The degradation is subject to random initialization of both the weights and the samples selected for the trigger injection. Overall, the attack was successful regardless of the data distribution.

Effect of the Trigger Length. An attacker injects the backdoor by placing the trigger in every time step of the input data or splitting it into shorter ones when using Time Bandits. At test time, the full-length trigger is given to launch the backdoor. However, *is the full-length trigger necessary to execute the backdoor?*

That is, can an attacker use a shorter trigger, which is only present in some frames at test time? To answer this question, we attacked different models with the Time Bandits attack (2 attackers and ten total clients with IID distribution), and then we evaluated ASR by varying the length of the trigger at test time. We chose this setup to isolate the trigger length effect from others that are attack-related, allowing a better understanding of the result. Precisely, we vary the trigger length from 2 frames to a total of 16, i.e., where every frame is poisoned. The starting frame is randomly selected, and the consequent frames are poisoned up to the trigger length. For example, if a length of 4 frames is selected, the initial trigger time step is randomly selected, e.g., frame 2. Then, frames 2, 3, 4, and 5 will contain the trigger while the rest remain unaltered.

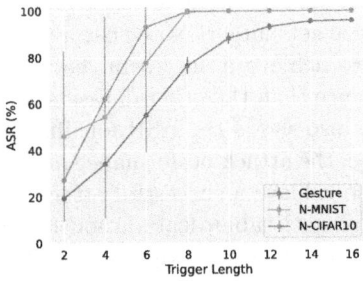

Fig. 2. The effect of the trigger length on ASR.

We present the results in Fig. 2. For every tested model, there is a direct correlation between the length of the trigger and ASR. For N-MNIST, ASR reaches top performance with just 25% of the total length. For the Gesture dataset, with 50% of the total trigger length, the attack achieves around 80% ASR and then keeps increasing slightly. Similarly, N-CIFAR10 achieves excellent ASR with 6 out of 16 total frames, and then ASR keeps increasing up to 100%. Overall, the attacker could use a shorter trigger at test time, around half of the total sample length, to achieve excellent ASR while improving the stealthiness, as shown in Sect. 6.2.

Effect of the Trigger Size. Based on prior literature [1,2], we selected the trigger size to be 30% of the input size. Even the goal of this paper is not to find the optimal trigger size an attacker can use but rather to exploit the time dimension of the triggers; we investigate different trigger sizes, i.e., 0.01, 0.05, 0.1, 0.2, and 0.3. We consider a federated network with ten clients and two attackers to highlight the influence of the trigger size. We consider Gesture, N-MNIST, and N-CIFAR10 datasets.

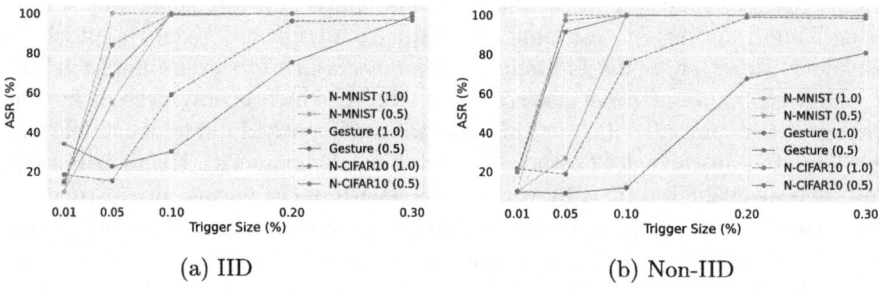

Fig. 3. Analysis of attack performance with different trigger sizes. (1.0) represents all clients participating in every federated round; (0.5) represents half.

Figure 3a shows the ASR for different trigger sizes, fractions of clients per federated round, and N-MNIST and Gesture datasets using IID data. The ASR increases as the trigger size gets larger. Note that a small trigger as 0.05% of the input image is enough to achieve a successful backdoor. The gesture dataset gets overall less performance than the other datasets, mainly because it contains fewer samples. Figure 3b also shows the ASR for different trigger sizes but with non-IID data. In this case, the attack performance also increases with the trigger size. An attacker can also achieve a successful attack with a 0.05% trigger size. We have not noticed any noticeable degradation of clean accuracy in the N-MNIST case for any of the settings. In the Gesture and N-CIFAR10 case, the drop in the clean accuracy is neither large. However, the degradation is larger as the trigger size increases.

5.2 On Vertical FL

We have discussed how to attack horizontal FL, which considers that the clients share the same features but for distinct data records. In vertical FL, however, the clients may overlap on the data records, but they differ on the features. We hypothesize that Time Bandits would still be effective. Different clients ($\mathcal{C}$) share the same data IDs (same images); however, they differ in their features ($\mathcal{F}$). The attacker coordinates and injects the trigger in their feature region and in the intended time frames (ω).

6 Defense Evaluation

FedAvg is known to be vulnerable to Byzantine behaviors and model poisoning attacks [9]. Several robust alternatives exist, including Krum [16], Trimmed Mean [9], and norm-clipping [8] defenses. While these have not yet been adapted for neuromorphic settings, their evaluation is important for understanding the transferability of defenses. Several defenses have been proposed against backdoor attacks in the image domain [17], categorized into data analysis [18,50], secure aggregation [9], and post-training methods [32,59]. For neuromorphic data, prior work [2] has only explored data analysis and post-training defenses with limited success. Post-training methods are largely ineffective due to the distinct mechanisms of SNNs, and secure aggregation remains unexplored. We focus on the data analysis method strong intentional perturbation (STRIP) [2] and the post-training method channel Lipschitzness-based pruning (CLP), which we adapt for SNNs and share in our repository. On the robust aggregation side, we consider clipping and cosine similarity-based rejection. The adaptation of secure aggregation mechanisms for neuromorphic data remains an open challenge.

STRIP. We consider STRIP [18] as a local defense for benign clients, detecting triggers by measuring sample entropy. At inference, STRIP rejects inputs

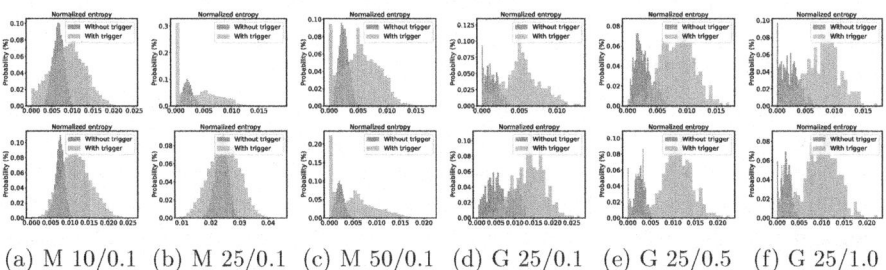

(a) M 10/0.1 (b) M 25/0.1 (c) M 50/0.1 (d) G 25/0.1 (e) G 25/0.5 (f) G 25/1.0

Fig. 4. STRIP defense results for the Time Bandits attack. N: N-MNIST, G: Gesture. Number clients/fractions per epoch. The first row in each set is non-IID, and the second row is IID. Blue represents samples without triggers. Orange samples with triggers. (Color figure online)

with anomalous entropy based on a detection boundary derived by superimposing clean samples and measuring Shannon entropy. Methods like artificial brain stimulation (ABS) [32] are ineffective for SNNs with neuromorphic data [2], so we exclude them. We tested the Time Bandits attack on N-MNIST and Gesture datasets under varying client numbers and sampling fractions. We also considered N-CIFAR10, which showed similar results. We omit it due to length constraints. Results (Fig. 4) show that clean and malicious samples exhibit similar entropy distributions, making boundary detection challenging. For IID and non-IID data, malicious samples overlap clean data entropy, making differentiation infeasible. Gesture further complicates detection due to noisy, non-normal distributions, making STRIP ineffective at filtering malicious samples.

Channel Lipschitzness-based Pruning. CLP [59] detects and repairs backdoored models by pruning neurons with high Lipschitz constants, as backdoor-related channels exhibit higher sensitivity. The threshold τ for pruning is calculated as $\tau_l = \mu_l + u \cdot \sigma_l$, where μ_l and σ_l are the mean and standard deviation of the Channel Lipschitz constant (UCLC), and u controls the sensitivity budget. We adapt CLP for neuromorphic data and SNNs, testing u values from 0.1 to 0.9. Results show limited effectiveness: the best performance occurs at

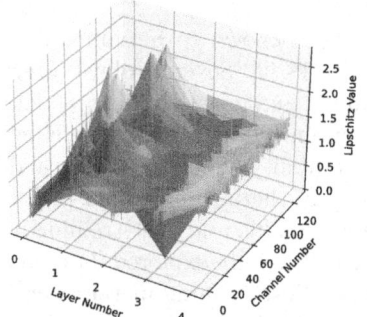

Fig. 5. Lipschitz values for clean (green) and malicious (red) models at $u = 0.3$. (Color figure online)

$u = 0.1$ for the N-MNIST dataset, reducing ASR while maintaining accuracy. However, clean and malicious models share similar Lipschitz constants (Fig. 5), particularly in deeper layers, making neuron separation challenging. Neuromorphic triggers, which rely on temporal sparsity rather than spatial pixel coherence, further complicate detection. Given this, CLP struggles to identify backdoors in temporally distributed attacks. Effective defenses for neuromorphic data may require temporal coherence checks or anomaly detection that monitors input spike patterns over time.

Clipping. Scaling the model lead to stronger attacks, however, the norm of the model will substantially increase. Thus, a defender, could easily discard or clip such updates in before averaging, mitigating the backdoor [45]. Nevertheless, an adaptive attacker that knows that such technique is applied, could limit the scaling factor in order to prevent being rejected by the aggregator [8]. Precisely, the attacker locally trains the backdoor model using the standard procedure, and instead of directly scaling the model by an arbitrary scalar, the attacker carefully chooses the scale so the norm remain below the clipping threshold. A defender sets the clipping threshold $\mathcal{C}$, so $||\theta||_2 \leq \mathcal{C}$. Thus, an attacker aware of $\mathcal{C}$, should constraint the norm of the update such as: $||\alpha \cdot \Delta||_2 \leq \mathcal{C}$, where $\Delta = \theta_{\text{global}} - \hat{\theta}$, thus the scaling factor is obtained from $\alpha = \frac{\mathcal{C}}{||\Delta||_2}$. We observed that the attacker norm is larger than the benign clients, which norm is around 100. Thus, we set the $\mathcal{C} = 100$. The attacker sets the scaling factor accordingly to be below the threshold remaining unnoticed.

Cosine Similarity. Another defense targets the *direction* of client updates, using *cosine similarity* to distinguish benign from malicious behavior. Benign clients, optimizing toward a common goal, tend to produce directionally similar updates (cosine similarity ≈ 1), while backdoored updates deviate. Let $\Delta_i = \theta_i - \theta_{\text{global}}$ be the update from client i, with similarity defined as $\cos\_\text{sim}(\Delta_i, \Delta_j) = \frac{\Delta_i \cdot \Delta_j}{\|\Delta_i\|\|\Delta_j\|}$. An aggregator can discard updates that are less similar to others. We observe that under our attack, both the benign model and the attacked model are similar to the global model. However, in case we want to enforce the attacker to evade detection, an attacker can align its update with the global model by optimizing: $\mathcal{L} = \mathcal{L}_{\text{clean}} + \mathcal{L}_{\text{backdoor}} + \lambda \left(1 - \cos(\theta_{\text{global}}, \hat{\theta})\right)$, where λ acts as a regularizer.

6.1 Towards Secure SNNs

Next, we discuss potential defenses against backdoor attacks in SNNs using neuromorphic data, focusing on mechanisms that leverage SNN-specific properties. We first consider input encoding types, such as rate, temporal, and delta modulation encoding [13]. Rate encoding uses spike frequency to represent input features, temporal encoding relies on spike timing, and delta modulation converts temporal changes into spikes. These methods differ in robustness to noise and perturbations; for example, alternative encodings have shown improved robustness against adversarial examples [43]. Another promising direction is certified defenses. For adversarial robustness, S-IBP and S-CROWN [31] adapt existing techniques to handle the non-linear behavior of spiking neurons, providing robustness guarantees. Additional approaches include robust hyperparameter tuning [12] and input filtering [33], which, while designed for adversarial examples, warrant exploration for backdoor resilience.

6.2 Stealthiness

Although there is no precise method for measuring the stealthiness of a trigger in backdoor attacks or the perturbation in adversarial examples, mean squared error (MSE) and structural similarity index (SSIM) are commonly used [21,25]. Following recent work [2], we also utilize these metrics for evaluating the stealthiness of the neuromorphic triggers. Note that these metrics measure the stealthiness of the triggers for constructing the malicious samples, i.e., visual imperceptibility [4]. This is mostly relevant at test time once the model is deployed. Detecting malicious samples can prevent the models from processing those inputs and, therefore, not executing the malicious behaviors. Similarly, when collecting samples from untrusted sources, less stealthy samples can be discarded and, therefore, not used for training. MSE compares the pixel-wise difference between the clean and the backdoored sample. MSE does not consider the context, e.g., the neighboring pixels, making its measurement local. SSIM overcomes this limitation by considering the context of the image. The SSIM and MSE metrics used in our evaluation are adapted for neuromorphic data by averaging across time frames. Precisely, for a batch of clean $b = \{\mathbf{x}_1, \mathbf{x}_2, \cdots, \mathbf{x}_n\}$ and malicious samples $\hat{b} = \{\hat{\mathbf{x}}_1, \hat{\mathbf{x}}_2, \cdots, \hat{\mathbf{x}}_n\}$, where n is the size of the batch. We compare SSIM or MSE per sample and per time-step ω.

Table 6 shows the average stealthiness of the proposed triggers. We use the same attacking setup as presented in Sect. 5 to be consistent with the experimental setup. We observe that the triggers' stealthiness is high regardless of the number of attackers. Nevertheless, we notice that the more malicious clients in the network, the higher the stealthiness because fewer frames include the trigger. This empirical result is interesting because in the extreme case where the number of attackers is equal to the number of frames, the poisoned image is left (almost) unchanged except for a single frame, boosting its stealthiness.

Table 6. Average stealthiness of single attacker and the Time Bandits attacks with a trigger size of 30% of the source image.

# of Attackers	MSE ↓			SSIM ↑		
	1	2	3	1	2	3
N-MNIST	8.57	2.14	**0.84**	87.72	88.77	**90.01**
Gesture	10.11	2.05	**0.98**	91.67	92.31	**92.97**
N-CIFAR10	1.28	0.56	**0.13**	98.17	97.52	**98.88**

7 Conclusions and Future Work

Using neuromorphic data in IID and non-IID settings, we demonstrated the feasibility of FL with SNNs. Existing backdoor methods like BadNets show suboptimal performance as the number of clients increases, highlighting the complexity of compromising SNNs compared to DNNs. We improved attack performance by scaling the malicious model's importance during aggregation. Further, we introduced a novel backdoor attack, *Time Bandits*, where multiple attackers split the trigger over time and collaboratively inject it. This increases stealthiness by making the link between the trigger and the backdoor task more complex, reducing detectability. We evaluated four defenses: STRIP, CLP, clipping, and cosine similarity-based rejection. STRIP struggles to differentiate clean and malicious samples due to similar entropy levels. CLP, which prunes neurons based on their Lipschitz values, fails as clean and attacked SNNs exhibit similar Lipschitz behavior. Similarly, we show that our attack can bypass both clipping and cosine similarity-based defenses. Additionally, we propose promising directions towards securing SNNs. Splitting triggers in time and among attackers introduces novel opportunities, such as triggers with changing shape, position, or polarity, which we plan to explore in future work.

References

1. Abad, G., Ersoy, O., Picek, S., Ramírez-Durán, V.J., Urbieta, A.: Poster: backdoor attacks on spiking NNS and neuromorphic datasets. In: Proceedings of the 2022 ACM SIGSAC Conference on Computer and Communications Security, pp. 3315–3317 (2022)
2. Abad, G., Ersoy, O., Picek, S., Urbieta, A.: Sneaky spikes: uncovering stealthy backdoor attacks in spiking neural networks with neuromorphic data. In: NDSS (2024)
3. Akopyan, F., et al.: TrueNorth: design and tool flow of a 65 mw 1 million neuron programmable neurosynaptic chip. IEEE Trans. Comput. Aided Des. Integr. Circuits Syst. **34**(10), 1537–1557 (2015). https://doi.org/10.1109/TCAD.2015.2474396
4. Alam, M., Sarkar, E., Maniatakos, M.: PERDOOR: Persistent non-uniform backdoors in federated learning using adversarial perturbations. arXiv preprint arXiv:2205.13523 (2022)
5. Amir, A., et al.: A low power, fully event-based gesture recognition system. In: Proceedings of the IEEE Conference on Computer Vision and Pattern Recognition, pp. 7243–7252 (2017)
6. Arafeh, M., Ould-Slimane, H., Otrok, H., Mourad, A., Talhi, C., Damiani, E.: Data independent warmup scheme for Non-IID federated learning. Inf. Sci. **623**, 342–360 (2023)
7. Bagdasaryan, E., Shmatikov, V.: Blind backdoors in deep learning models. In: Usenix Security (2021)
8. Bagdasaryan, E., Veit, A., Hua, Y., Estrin, D., Shmatikov, V.: How to backdoor federated learning. In: International Conference on Artificial Intelligence and Statistics, pp. 2938–2948. PMLR (2020)
9. Blanchard, P., El Mhamdi, E.M., Guerraoui, R., Stainer, J.: Machine learning with adversaries: Byzantine tolerant gradient descent. In: Advances in Neural Information Processing Systems, vol. 30 (2017)
10. Davies, M., et al.: LOIHI: a neuromorphic manycore processor with on-chip learning. IEEE Micro **38**(1), 82–99 (2018)
11. Dhar, P.: The carbon impact of artificial intelligence. Nat. Mach. Intell. **2**(8), 423–425 (2020)
12. El-Allami, R., Marchisio, A., Shafique, M., Alouani, I.: Securing deep spiking neural networks against adversarial attacks through inherent structural parameters. In: 2021 Design, Automation & Test in Europe Conference & Exhibition (DATE), pp. 774–779. IEEE (2021)
13. Eshraghian, J.K., et al.: Training spiking neural networks using lessons from deep learning. In: Proceedings of the IEEE (2023)
14. Fang, W., Yu, Z., Chen, Y., Huang, T., Masquelier, T., Tian, Y.: Deep residual learning in spiking neural networks. Adv. Neural. Inf. Process. Syst. **34**, 21056–21069 (2021)
15. Fang, W., Yu, Z., Chen, Y., Masquelier, T., Huang, T., Tian, Y.: Incorporating learnable membrane time constant to enhance learning of spiking neural networks. In: Proceedings of the IEEE/CVF International Conference on Computer Vision, pp. 2661–2671 (2021)
16. Fung, C., Yoon, C.J., Beschastnikh, I.: Mitigating sybils in federated learning poisoning. arXiv preprint arXiv:1808.04866 (2018)

17. Gao, Y., et al.: Backdoor attacks and countermeasures on deep learning: a comprehensive review. arXiv preprint arXiv:2007.10760 (2020)
18. Gao, Y., Xu, C., Wang, D., Chen, S., Ranasinghe, D.C., Nepal, S.: Strip: A defence against trojan attacks on deep neural networks. In: Proceedings of the 35th Annual Computer Security Applications Conference, pp. 113–125 (2019)
19. Gong, X., Chen, Y., Wang, Q., Kong, W.: Backdoor attacks and defenses in federated learning: state-of-the-art, taxonomy, and future directions. IEEE Wirel. Commun. **30**(2), 114–121 (2022)
20. Gu, T., Liu, K., Dolan-Gavitt, B., Garg, S.: BadNets: evaluating backdooring attacks on deep neural networks. IEEE Access **7**, 47230–47244 (2019)
21. Hameed, M.Z., Gyorgy, A.: Perceptually constrained adversarial attacks. arXiv preprint arXiv:2102.07140 (2021)
22. Han, B., Fu, Q., Zhang, X.: Towards privacy-preserving federated neuromorphic learning via spiking neuron models. Electronics **12**(18), 3984 (2023)
23. He, Y., Meng, G., Chen, K., Hu, X., He, J.: Towards security threats of deep learning systems: a survey. IEEE Trans. Softw. Eng. **48**(5), 1743–1770 (2020)
24. Imam, N., Cleland, T.A.: Rapid online learning and robust recall in a neuromorphic olfactory circuit. Nat. Mach. Intell. **2**(3), 181–191 (2020)
25. Jordan, M., Manoj, N., Goel, S., Dimakis, A.G.: Quantifying perceptual distortion of adversarial examples. arXiv preprint arXiv:1902.08265 (2019)
26. Konečný, J., McMahan, H.B., Yu, F.X., Richtárik, P., Suresh, A.T., Bacon, D.: Federated learning: strategies for improving communication efficiency. arXiv preprint arXiv:1610.05492 (2016)
27. Kösters, D.J., et al.: Benchmarking energy consumption and latency for neuromorphic computing in condensed matter and particle physics. APL Mach. Learn. **1**(1), 016101 (2023)
28. Lee, J.H., Delbruck, T., Pfeiffer, M.: Training deep spiking neural networks using backpropagation. Front. Neurosci. **10**, 508 (2016)
29. Li, H., Liu, H., Ji, X., Li, G., Shi, L.: Cifar10-DVS: an event-stream dataset for object classification. Front. Neurosci. **11**, 309 (2017)
30. Liang, L., et al.: H2Learn: high-efficiency learning accelerator for high-accuracy spiking neural networks. IEEE Trans. Comput. Aided Des. Integr. Circuits Syst. **41**(11), 4782–4796 (2021)
31. Liang, L., Xu, K., Hu, X., Deng, L., Xie, Y.: Toward robust spiking neural network against adversarial perturbation. Adv. Neural. Inf. Process. Syst. **35**, 10244–10256 (2022)
32. Liu, Y., Lee, W.C., Tao, G., Ma, S., Aafer, Y., Zhang, X.: ABS: scanning neural networks for back-doors by artificial brain stimulation. In: Proceedings of the 2019 ACM SIGSAC Conference on Computer and Communications Security, pp. 1265–1282 (2019)
33. Marchisio, A., Pira, G., Martina, M., Masera, G., Shafique, M.: DVS-attacks: adversarial attacks on dynamic vision sensors for spiking neural networks. In: 2021 International Joint Conference on Neural Networks (IJCNN), pp. 1–9. IEEE (2021)
34. McMahan, B., Moore, E., Ramage, D., Hampson, S., y Arcas, B.A.: Communication-efficient learning of deep networks from decentralized data. In: Artificial intelligence and statistics, pp. 1273–1282. PMLR (2017)
35. Narayanan, S., Taht, K., Balasubramonian, R., Giacomin, E., Gaillardon, P.E.: SpinalFlow: an architecture and dataflow tailored for spiking neural networks. In: 2020 ACM/IEEE 47th Annual International Symposium on Computer Architecture (ISCA), pp. 349–362. IEEE (2020)

36. Nguyen, D.C., Ding, M., Pathirana, P.N., Seneviratne, A., Li, J., Poor, H.V.: Federated learning for internet of things: a comprehensive survey. IEEE Commun. Surv. Tutorials **23**(3), 1622–1658 (2021)
37. Nunes, J.D., Carvalho, M., Carneiro, D., Cardoso, J.S.: Spiking neural networks: a survey. IEEE Access **10**, 60738–60764 (2022)
38. Orchard, G., Jayawant, A., Cohen, G.K., Thakor, N.: Converting static image datasets to spiking neuromorphic datasets using saccades. Front. Neurosci. **9**, 437 (2015)
39. Paredes-Vallés, F., Hagenaars, J.J., Dupeyroux, J., Stroobants, S., Xu, Y., de Croon, G.: Fully neuromorphic vision and control for autonomous drone flight. Sci. Robot. **9**(90), eadi0591 (2024)
40. Park, S., Pandey, A.: Anomaly detection in power grids via context-agnostic learning. arXiv preprint arXiv:2404.07898 (2024)
41. Rossbroich, J., Gygax, J., Zenke, F.: Fluctuation-driven initialization for spiking neural network training. Neuromorphic Comput. Eng. **2**(4), 044016 (2022)
42. Sharmin, S., Panda, P., Sarwar, S.S., Lee, C., Ponghiran, W., Roy, K.: A comprehensive analysis on adversarial robustness of spiking neural networks. In: 2019 International Joint Conference on Neural Networks (IJCNN), pp. 1–8. IEEE (2019)
43. Sharmin, S., Rathi, N., Panda, P., Roy, K.: Inherent adversarial robustness of deep spiking neural networks: effects of discrete input encoding and non-linear activations. In: Vedaldi, A., Bischof, H., Brox, T., Frahm, J.-M. (eds.) ECCV 2020. LNCS, vol. 12374, pp. 399–414. Springer, Cham (2020). https://doi.org/10.1007/978-3-030-58526-6_24
44. Shejwalkar, V., Houmansadr, A., Kairouz, P., Ramage, D.: Back to the drawing board: a critical evaluation of poisoning attacks on production federated learning. In: 2022 IEEE Symposium on Security and Privacy (SP), pp. 1354–1371. IEEE (2022)
45. Shen, S., Tople, S., Saxena, P.: AUROR: defending against poisoning attacks in collaborative deep learning systems. In: Proceedings of the 32nd Annual Conference on Computer Security Applications, pp. 508–519 (2016)
46. Shorten, C., Khoshgoftaar, T.M.: A survey on image data augmentation for deep learning. J. Big Data **6**(1), 1–48 (2019)
47. Skatchkovsky, N., Jang, H., Simeone, O.: Federated neuromorphic learning of spiking neural networks for low-power edge intelligence. In: ICASSP 2020-2020 IEEE International Conference on Acoustics, Speech and Signal Processing (ICASSP), pp. 8524–8528. IEEE (2020)
48. Tavanaei, A., Ghodrati, M., Kheradpisheh, S.R., Masquelier, T., Maida, A.: Deep learning in spiking neural networks. Neural Netw. **111**, 47–63 (2019). https://doi.org/10.1016/j.neunet.2018.12.002
49. Tolpegin, V., Truex, S., Gursoy, M.E., Liu, L.: Data poisoning attacks against federated learning systems. In: Chen, L., Li, N., Liang, K., Schneider, S. (eds.) ESORICS 2020. LNCS, vol. 12308, pp. 480–501. Springer, Cham (2020). https://doi.org/10.1007/978-3-030-58951-6_24
50. Tran, B., Li, J., Madry, A.: Spectral signatures in backdoor attacks. Tech. rep. (2018). https://doi.org/10.48550/arXiv.1811.00636, arXiv:1811.00636
51. Venkatesha, Y., Kim, Y., Tassiulas, L., Panda, P.: Federated learning with spiking neural networks. IEEE Trans. Signal Process. **69**, 6183–6194 (2021)
52. Viale, A., Marchisio, A., Martina, M., Masera, G., Shafique, M.: CARSNN: an efficient spiking neural network for event-based autonomous cars on the loihi neuromorphic research processor. In: 2021 International Joint Conference on Neural Networks (IJCNN), pp. 1–10. IEEE (2021)

53. Wang, Y., Duan, S., Chen, F.: Efficient asynchronous federated neuromorphic learning of spiking neural networks. Neurocomputing **557**, 126686 (2023)
54. Wazzeh, M., Ould-Slimane, H., Talhi, C., Mourad, A., Guizani, M.: Privacy-preserving continuous authentication for mobile and IoT systems using warmup-based federated learning. IEEE Netw. **37**, 224–230 (2022)
55. Xie, C., Huang, K., Chen, P.Y., Li, B.: DBA: distributed backdoor attacks against federated learning. In: International Conference on Learning Representations (2020)
56. Yang, Q., Liu, Y., Chen, T., Tong, Y.: Federated machine learning: concept and applications. ACM Trans. Intell. Syst. Technol. (TIST) **10**(2), 1–19 (2019)
57. Zhang, Z., et al.: Neurotoxin: durable backdoors in federated learning. In: International Conference on Machine Learning, pp. 26429–26446. PMLR (2022)
58. Zhao, Y., Li, M., Lai, L., Suda, N., Civin, D., Chandra, V.: Federated learning with Non-IID data. arXiv preprint arXiv:1806.00582 (2018)
59. Zheng, R., Tang, R., Li, J., Liu, L.: Data-free backdoor removal based on channel lipschitzness. In: Avidan, S., Brostow, G., Cissé, M., Farinella, G.M., Hassner, T. (eds.) European Conference on Computer Vision, pp. 175–191. Springer (2022). https://doi.org/10.1007/978-3-031-20065-6_11
60. Zhu, H., Xu, J., Liu, S., Jin, Y.: Federated learning on Non-IID data: a survey. Neurocomputing **465**, 371–390 (2021)

TATA: Benchmark NIDS Test Sets Assessment and Targeted Augmentation

Omar Anser[1(✉)], Jérôme François[1,2], Isabelle Chrisment[1], and Daishi Kondo[3]

[1] Inria, Université de Lorraine, CNRS, LORIA, Nancy, France
{omar.anser,jerome.francois,isabelle.chrisment}@inria.fr
[2] SnT - University of Luxembourg, Esch-sur-Alzette, Luxembourg
jerome.francois@uni.lu
[3] Information Technology Center, The University of Tokyo, Bunkyo, Japan
daishi.kondo@nc.u-tokyo.ac.jp

Abstract. Research works on Network Intrusion Detection Systems (NIDSs) using Machine Learning (ML) usually reports very high detection rate, often well above 90%. However, these results typically originate from overly simplistic NIDS datasets, where the test set, often just a subset of the overall dataset, mirrors the training set distribution, failing to rigorously assess the NIDS's robustness under more varied conditions. To address this shortcoming, we propose a method for **T**est sets **A**ssessment and **T**argeted **A**ugmentation (TATA). TATA is a model-agnostic approach that assesses and augments the quality of benchmark ML–based NIDS test sets. First, TATA encodes both training and test sets in a structured latent space via a contrastive autoencoder, defining three quality metrics (diversity, proximity, and scarcity) to identify test set gaps where the ML-based classification is harder. Next, TATA employs a reinforcement learning (RL) approach guided by these metrics, configuring a testbed that produces realistic data specifically targeting these gaps, creating a more robust test set. Using CIC-IDS2017 and CSE-CIC-IDS2018, we observe a positive correlation between higher metric values and increased detection difficulty, confirming their utility as meaningful indicators of test set robustness. With the same datasets, TATA's RL-based augmentation significantly raises detection difficulty for multiple NIDS models, revealing previously overlooked weaknesses.

Keywords: NIDS · ML · Data quality · Data augmentation

1 Introduction

In Network Intrusion Detection System (NIDS) research, Machine Learning (ML) and Deep Learning (DL) have become foundational tools (throughout this paper, NIDS refers exclusively to systems that use ML or DL). Benchmark NIDS datasets play a crucial role in the design and comparative evaluation of these systems. For instance, LUCID [3] (a state-of-the-art DDoS detector) used ISCXIDS2012 [34], CIC-IDS2017 [33] (IDS2017), and CSE-CIC-IDS2018 [33]

(IDS2018); both ADA [35] (an adaptive NIDS with minimal data requirements) and FlowTransformer [25] (a transformer-based model capturing intricate traffic patterns) utilized UNSW-NB15 [26]. FlowTransformer additionally relied on NSL-KDD and IDS2018. Although these datasets are widely adopted, they can contain errors and biases in data collection, labeling, post-processing, and even after publication [4,20,21].

Besides, one of the key issues with NIDS datasets is their simplicity [1,6,7], often illustrated by minimal heterogeneity among traffic that shares the same label identifying the different types of attacks or benign flows. Flood *et al.* [7] use Principal Component Analysis (PCA) to analyze the DoS Hulk labeled flows in IDS2017, showing that its training and test subsets exhibit near-complete overlap in feature-value distributions. They attribute this phenomenon to both IDS2017 and IDS2018 being generated using automated tools with limited attack exploration. Consequently, concerns arise about the relevance of these largely used datasets—particularly their test sets, often just subsets of the same data—for evaluating an NIDS, since their limited heterogeneity may lead to an overestimation of detection performance and fail to meaningfully reflect the system's robustness under operational conditions [36].

Existing metrics can analyze intrinsic dataset characteristics to quantify its overall quality [6,7], while ignoring the downstream NIDS-classification task. For instance, they highlight issues such as mislabeled flows, dubious labeling assumptions, and near-duplicate attacks. Others evaluate a dataset from a classification perspective, assessing how challenging it is for a NIDS to separate the training labeled traffic to build its decision boundaries [4,21,22] without examining the later testing stage which relies on a test set and its quality to challenge the system. Prior studies in non-NIDS domains propose methods for assessing test set quality [14,17,30], then extend these efforts with augmentation strategies [31,32] to better challenge the models. Yet most of these approaches rely on model-dependent indicators (e.g., neuron activation), which can be impractical when the NIDS model is unknown or closed-source. Moreover, this model-centric focus does not provide a comprehensible view of how much the distribution of a test set is aligned relative to the training set. To the best of our knowledge, only two studies address the problem of test set augmentation in the NIDS domain [6,7], but their solutions are manual and thus not generalizable across NIDS datasets.

Given these challenges, we aim at answering two research questions:
RQ1. How can we **assess** the quality of test sets in challenging NIDS models, ensuring a robust evaluation of their detection capabilities?
RQ2. How to **augment** these test sets to better evaluate the robustness and real-world applicability of NIDS models?

To address these questions, we introduce a method for **T**est sets **A**ssessment and **T**argeted **A**ugmentation, **TATA**. TATA tackles RQ1 by defining comprehensive quality metrics to evaluate a test set relative to a training set, without relying on model internals. TATA trains a contrastive autoencoder [11,16] to increase both inner and intra-label separability of the training set in the latent space, thus approximating the decision boundaries. Once trained, the autoencoder additionally projects the test data points, enabling the measuring of **diversity** (captures the range of test data points, reflecting whether the test set broadly spans the feature space or remains redundant), **proximity** (how test data points lie close to differently labeled training data points, indicating how borderline they are for classification), and **scarcity** (how uniformly test data points are spread across the decision boundaries, ensuring multiple boundary regions are tested). Higher values imply a more challenging test for the NIDS.

Addressing RQ2, TATA uses Reinforcement Learning (RL) [37]. The RL agent iteratively generates configurations, such as network conditions (e.g., bandwidth constraints or latency) or traffic patterns (e.g., bursty or steady flows). Using these on a testbed, real traffic is generated, unlike model-based data augmentation techniques (e.g., Generative Adversarial Networks, or GANs), which remains synthetic. To improve the quality of the test set, this generation is guided by the predefined quality metrics. Once trained, the agent can be applied to multiple NIDS test sets without retraining, a practical transferability that could pave the path to an easier generalization.

We evaluate TATA on the IDS2017 and IDS2018 datasets, showing that diversity, proximity, and scarcity effectively quantify a test set's challenging aspects. For example, we examine how changes in proximity correlate with detection performance for the three NIDS models used in this paper (Random Forest (RF), Support Vector Machine (SVM), and a Deep Neural Network (DNN)). We use these metrics to guide TATA's RL-based test set augmentation on IDS2018, applying the learned strategy to IDS2017. TATA increases the original metrics (diversity, proximity, scarcity) by approximately 437%, 190%, and 136% respectively by generating benign traffic only, which in turn reduces each model's macro-averaged F1-score (macro-F1) by nearly 30 points, exposing previously overlooked NIDS weaknesses hidden by the original test split. Beyond IDS2017 and IDS2018, we conducted a broader temporal and comparative analysis across multiple network-intrusion datasets showing that the test set quality is far from being satisfactory for research on NIDS.

2 Related Work

Research on test set quality assessment (RQ1) and augmentation (RQ2) has been prominent in DL, software engineering, and software testing fields. Table 1 categorizes the main studies, as identified in the literature, into **Neuron Coverage**, **Surprise Coverage**, and **Mutation Testing**, linking them to RQ1 and/or RQ2 while highlighting limitations. Notably, only one study, under mutation testing, addresses both RQ1 and RQ2, while others focus solely on RQ1. Additionally, two uncategorized methods [6,7] address only RQ2. All categorized methods share a common limitation: requiring model access, a critical issue in the NIDS domain where access is often restricted, for example assuming commercial products.

Neuron coverage methods interpret higher neuron activations as broader model exploration, with [30] introducing neuron coverage (NC) as a metric that measures the proportion of neurons activated by a test set. However, these approaches offer limited insight into how training and test sets align, require

Table 1. Methods & limitations for test set assessment (RQ1) & augmentation (RQ2)

Method category	Studies	RQ1	RQ2	Limitations	
Neuron coverage	[23, 24, 30]	✓	✗	– Need for model access – Ignores training–test alignment	– High sensitivity to hyperparameters – Not adapted to non NN models
Surprise coverage	[17, 18, 40]	✓	✗	– Need for model access – Not adapted to non NN models	– Only proximity-based analysis
Mutation testing	[13, 14, 38]	✓	✗	– Need for model access – Lack of adaptability to model changes	– Ignores training–test alignment
Mutation testing	[31]	✓	✓	– Same limitations as [13,14,38] – Needs a new training run per dataset	– Use of a data generator that may produce unrealistic data points
N/A	[6, 7]	✗	✓	– Focus solely on increasing proximity	– Manual and unguided test set augmentation

delicate hyperparameter tuning [12], and are limited to neural networks, excluding widely used NIDS models (e.g., RF). Other methods [5,10,41] employ similar coverage criteria for RQ2 but remain primarily fuzzing-based, focusing on stress-testing with diverse or adversarial inputs that lack semantic or real-world coherence, contrasting with our emphasis on realistic test set augmentation.

Surprise coverage methods assess how unexpected a test data point is by comparing its activation pattern (i.e., hidden-layer outputs of a neural network) with those of the training set. Various implementations (e.g., distance-based or likelihood-based) share the core idea that test data points whose activations deviate substantially from the training set are considered surprising [17]. This category mainly focuses on proximity in activation space and thus overlook other test set problems unlike our method that also incorporates scarcity and diversity considerations, leading to a more comprehensive evaluation.

Mutation testing introduces modifications to the model and its training set, producing **mutants** whose detection rate (the mutation score) indicates test set quality. A higher mutation score means a more robust test set. These solutions relies on mutation operators specific to each model, requiring new operators whenever the model changes. They also evaluate test sets in isolation, without relating them to the training set. Riccio et al. [31] extend prior mutation testing work [14] with test set augmentation but, in addition to mutation-testing limits, these approaches depend on human-interpretable, image-based generators [32], which are unsuited to the complex, non-visual nature of network traffic. Their approach requires re-training on each new dataset, further limiting its reusability.

Two NIDS-oriented works [6,7] are not categorized in Table 1, yet each includes a subsection discussing test set augmentation (RQ2). Flood et al. [6] propose a complexity metric capturing spatial and temporal diversity, while Flood et al. [7] use heuristics to quantify dataset quality, both focusing on overall dataset aspects (rather than explicit test–train alignment as excepted in RQ1). They augment IDS2017 by replaying DoS-Hulk traffic on a testbed [2], randomly sampling page sizes and attacker bandwidths. Capturing traffic on a live testbed preserves protocol semantics, a strategy we also adopt, unlike fully synthetic GAN outputs (e.g., NetShare [42]), diffusion models (e.g., NetDiffusion [15]), or simple feature-jittering [39], which can break flow coherence. However, their procedure remains manual, unguided, and purely random, as the configuration values are chosen without reference to any quality metric; consequently, the added data points may leave key coverage gaps unaddressed in the latent space.

TATA addresses the identified gaps: it evaluates test data points in relation to the training set through diversity, proximity, and scarcity, then augments the test set via RL with realistic network traffic data points to better assess the NIDS robustness. It is model-independent, requires no model access, and, in principle, the trained RL agent can be applied to new NIDS datasets without retraining.

3 Test Sets Assessment and Targeted Augmentation

3.1 TATA Overview

TATA operates on a labeled NIDS training set ($\mathcal{D}_{\text{train}}$) and test set ($\mathcal{D}_{\text{test}}$), each containing network traffic data points $(\mathbf{x}, l_k)$, where $\mathbf{x}$ is a high-dimensional feature vector including information about traffic flow (e.g., the number of bytes exchanged), and $l_k \in \mathcal{L} = \{l_1, \ldots, l_n\}$ is the label (e.g., benign or a type of attack). Figure 1 outlines TATA using an illustrative example with $\mathcal{L} = \{\text{Benign}, \text{Attack-1}, \text{Attack-2}\}$. TATA proceeds in three steps: (i) a preliminary phase that constructs a structured latent space from $\mathcal{D}_{\text{train}}$, (ii) phase

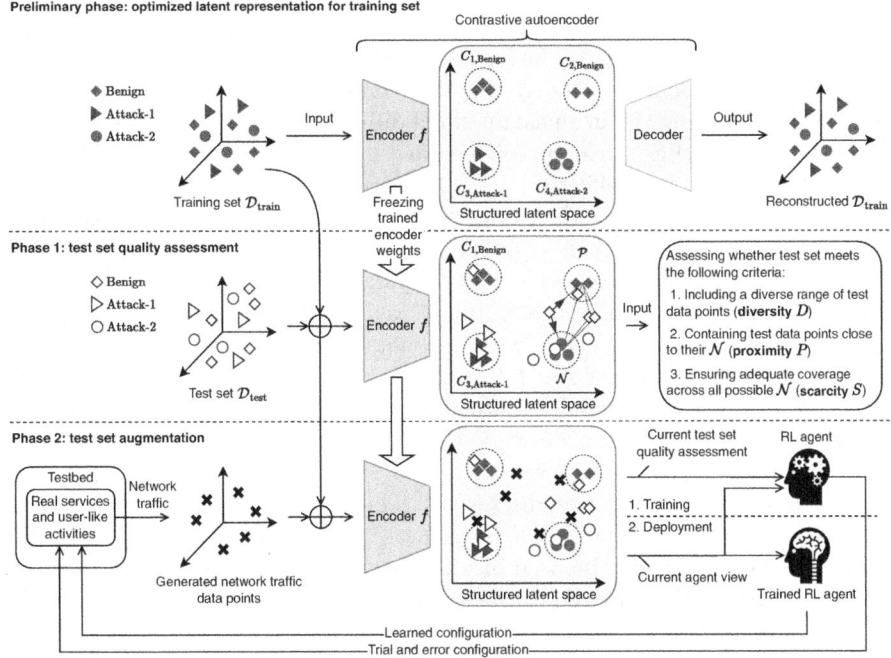

Fig. 1. TATA, a method to assess and augment the quality of a test set

1 that assesses $\mathcal{D}_{\text{test}}$'s quality, and *(iii)* phase 2 that augments $\mathcal{D}_{\text{test}}$. $\mathcal{L}$ is the set of labels that the NIDS must classify.

The preliminary phase provides the latent space foundation by training a **contrastive autoencoder** with encoder f, parameterized by $\boldsymbol{\theta}$, on $\mathcal{D}_{\text{train}}$. During training, the contrastive objective [11,16] shapes the latent space into well-separated clusters, each containing encoded training data points with similar labels and closely aligned input feature values, while preserving reconstruction accuracy. This process yields a trained f that encodes each $\mathbf{x} \in \mathcal{D}_{\text{train}}$ into a latent representation $\mathbf{z} = f(\mathbf{x}; \boldsymbol{\theta})$, forming $\mathcal{Z}_{\text{train}} = \{\mathbf{z} \mid \mathbf{z} = f(\mathbf{x}; \boldsymbol{\theta}),\ \mathbf{x} \in \mathcal{D}_{\text{train}}\}$. We determine the number of clusters in $\mathcal{Z}_{\text{train}}$ using the silhouette score, then apply k-means to assign each $\mathbf{z} \in \mathcal{Z}_{\text{train}}$ to a cluster C_{i,l_k} (where i is the cluster index and l_k is the majority label among its members). All clusters form the set $\mathcal{C}$ knowing that a single label may correspond to multiple clusters (e.g., $C_{1,\text{Benign}}$ and $C_{2,\text{Benign}}$ in Fig. 1), which reflects intra-class variability in $\mathcal{D}_{\text{train}}$. By reducing the data's dimensionality, the contrastive autoencoder not only speeds up subsequent computations but also approximates the decision boundaries inherent in $\mathcal{D}_{\text{train}}$, all without being tied to a specific NIDS model.

In phase 1, we use the trained f to encode $\mathcal{D}_{\text{test}}$ into the same structured latent space as $\mathcal{D}_{\text{train}}$. We obtain $\mathcal{Z}_{\text{test}} = \{\mathbf{z} \mid \mathbf{z} = f(\mathbf{x}; \boldsymbol{\theta}),\ \mathbf{x} \in \mathcal{D}_{\text{test}}\}$, which positions each test data point relative to $\mathcal{D}_{\text{train}}$'s distribution. For each $\mathbf{z} \in \mathcal{Z}_{\text{test}}$ with input label l_k, we compute its Euclidean distance $\|\mathbf{z} - \boldsymbol{\mu}_{C_{i,l_j}}\|$ to every cluster centroid $\boldsymbol{\mu}_{C_{i,l_j}}$ in $\mathcal{C}$. Among these distances, the cluster C_{i,l_j} whose label l_j matches l_k and minimizes $\|\mathbf{z} - \boldsymbol{\mu}_{C_{i,l_j}}\|$ is termed as its positive cluster $\mathcal{P}(\mathbf{z})$. Conversely, the cluster C_{i,l_j} whose label differs ($l_j \neq l_k$) and minimizes that distance is its negative cluster $\mathcal{N}(\mathbf{z})$. Figure 1 illustrates this pairing by arrows linking a Benign encoded test data point to its positive and negative clusters, representing the intrinsic maximal difficulty to make the right decision. Accordingly, we define three complementary metrics (diversity, proximity, and scarcity) to assess how effectively $\mathcal{D}_{\text{test}}$ challenges the NIDS in its detection task. They are computed in the structured latent space on a **per-cluster basis** (details in Sect. 3.2). We then aggregate each metric's results across all clusters $C_{i,l_k} \in \mathcal{C}$ to measure how effectively $\mathcal{D}_{\text{test}}$ challenges each subgroup of $\mathcal{D}_{\text{train}}$.

In phase 2 (detailed in Sect. 3.3), the RL agent is trained by iteratively interacting, through trial and error, with a configurable testbed that it directs to generate network traffic (see Fig. 1). At each iteration, the agent first consults its current view of the structured latent space and then selects a traffic-generation configuration. The resulting network traffic is merged into the evolving $\mathcal{D}_{\text{test}}$ and, after encoding, is re-assessed with TATA's predefined metrics, yielding a quality measure that serves as the reward. This reward guides the agent's configuration choices, which are refined over multiple iterations. Once training, the agent's learned policy can be used on the same or other NIDS datasets without requiring further retraining (i.e., without additional reward signals).

3.2 Test Set Quality Assessment

Because TATA's metrics are computed on a per-cluster basis, we begin by defining the subset of encoded test data points tied to each cluster C_{i,l_k}. Specifically, for each C_{i,l_k}, we focus on $\mathcal{Z}_{\text{test}}^{(C_{i,l_k})} = \{\mathbf{z} \in \mathcal{Z}_{\text{test}} \mid \mathcal{P}(\mathbf{z}) = C_{i,l_k}\}$, the $\mathcal{Z}_{\text{test}}$ subset of **encoded test data points whose positive cluster is** C_{i,l_k}. To support metrics computation, we also introduce the function $\text{PairNeg}(\mathcal{Z}_{\text{test}}, C_{i,l_k}) = \{(\mathbf{z}, \mathcal{N}(\mathbf{z})) \mid \mathbf{z} \in \mathcal{Z}_{\text{test}}^{(C_{i,l_k})}\}$ that pairs every $\mathbf{z} \in \mathcal{Z}_{\text{test}}^{(C_{i,l_k})}$ with its negative cluster $\mathcal{N}(\mathbf{z})$. Each pair $(\mathbf{z}, \mathcal{N}(\mathbf{z}))$ indicates the nearest differently labeled cluster that could challenge the classification of $\mathbf{z}$ away from its positive cluster C_{i,l_k} (*i.e.* leading to a classification error so).

Diversity. A common testing requirement is to cover a wide range of test cases. Diversity (D) captures the variability among the data points in $\mathcal{Z}_{\text{test}}^{(C_{i,l_k})}$. A higher D reflects a $\mathcal{D}_{\text{test}}$ in which individual data points exhibit minimal redundancy and more fully cover the available feature space.

D is calculated using the Vendi Score [8] (denoted as V_{i,l_k}), which quantifies how evenly the data points span the feature space by computing the von Neumann entropy of their normalized similarity matrix. Since V_{i,l_k} ranges from 1 (minimal diversity) to the size of $\mathcal{Z}_{\text{test}}^{(C_{i,l_k})}$ (maximal diversity), we min–max normalize it to $[0,1]$. Finally, we average these normalized scores across all clusters to obtain:

$$D = \frac{1}{|\mathcal{C}|} \sum_{C_{i,l_k} \in \mathcal{C}} V_{i,l_k} \qquad (1)$$

Proximity. Because diverse data points lying far from decision boundaries are typically simpler to classify, proximity (P) measures how close data points in $\mathcal{Z}_{\text{test}}^{(C_{i,l_k})}$ are to their negative clusters. A higher P suggests that $\mathcal{D}_{\text{test}}$ includes data points near differently labeled training data point, which are more likely to challenge the NIDS.

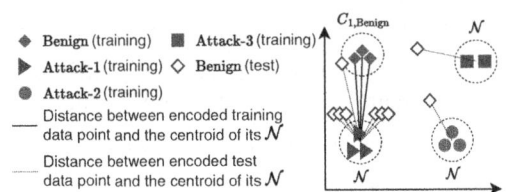

Fig. 2. Training vs. Test Distances for $C_{1,\text{Benign}}$

Formally, for each cluster C_{i,l_k}, we define:

$$d_{\text{test}_i} = \left\{\|\mathbf{z} - \boldsymbol{\mu}_{\mathcal{N}(\mathbf{z})}\| \mid (\mathbf{z}, \mathcal{N}(\mathbf{z})) \in \text{PairNeg}(\mathcal{Z}_{\text{test}}, C_{i,l_k})\right\} \qquad (2)$$

as the set of Euclidean distances from each $\mathbf{z} \in \mathcal{Z}_{\text{test}}^{(C_{i,l_k})}$ to the centroid of its negative cluster. To determine whether these encoded test data points lie farther from C_{i,l_k} than their training counterparts $\mathbf{z} \in \mathcal{Z}_{\text{train}}$ assigned to C_{i,l_k} (and thus pose a greater challenge to the NIDS), we analogously define d_{train_i}. Figure 2 illustrates d_{test} (dashed) and d_{train} (solid) derived for the set $\mathcal{Z}_{\text{test}}^{(C_{1,\text{Benign}})}$. Using the empirical cumulative distribution functions F_{test_i} and F_{train_i} of d_{test_i} and d_{train_i}, we derive the maximum positive difference using the one-sided Kolmogorov–Smirnov statistic $\mathrm{KS}_{C_{i,l_k}} \in [0,1]$. A high value means that the distances in d_{test_i} are significantly smaller than those in d_{train_i}, so the encoded test data points are very close to their negative clusters. To capture the worst-case, we define P as the maximum KS value computed across all $\mathcal{Z}_{\mathrm{test}}^{(C_{i,l_k})}$ (for $C_{i,l_k} \in \mathcal{C}$):

$$P = \max_{C_{i,l_k} \in \mathcal{C}} \left(\mathrm{KS}_{C_{i,l_k}} \right). \tag{3}$$

Scarcity. Beyond diversity and proximity, a robust test approach must ensure that test data points appear across multiple decision boundaries where misclassifications may arise. Scarcity (S) evaluates how uniformly data points in $\mathcal{Z}_{\mathrm{test}}^{(C_{i,l_k})}$ are spread across **all possible negative clusters**. Fig. 3 depicts an optimal scenario where each of the three possible negative clusters of $C_{1,\mathrm{Benign}}$ is assigned an equal number of encoded test data points (three points each). In contrast, Fig. 4 shows a non-optimal scenario and reflects thus a poor scarcity.

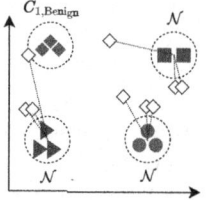

Fig. 3. Optimal scarcity scenario

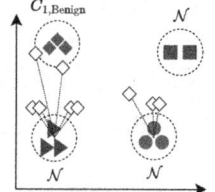

Fig. 4. Non-optimal scarcity scenario

Formally, we define the set of all possible negative clusters of C_{i,l_k} as:

$$\mathcal{N}_{\mathrm{all}}(C_{i,l_k}) = \{ C_{j,l_p} \in \mathcal{C} \mid j \neq i,\ l_p \neq l_k \} \tag{4}$$

For each $C_{j,l_p} \in \mathcal{N}_{\mathrm{all}}(C_{i,l_k})$, we define the number of associated data points as:

$$\mathrm{PointCount}(C_{j,l_p}) = \left| \{ \mathbf{z} \mid (\mathbf{z}, \mathcal{N}(\mathbf{z})) \in \mathrm{PairNeg}(\mathcal{Z}_{\mathrm{test}}, C_{i,l_k}) \wedge \mathcal{N}(\mathbf{z}) = C_{j,l_p} \} \right| \tag{5}$$

Normalizing $\mathrm{PointCount}(C_{j,l_p})$ by $|\mathrm{PairNeg}(\mathcal{Z}_{\mathrm{test}}, C_{i,l_k})|$ yields the distribution R_{i,l_k}. The complement of the Gini Coefficient measures its uniformity:

$$R_{i,l_k} = \left\{ \frac{\mathrm{PointCount}(C_{j,l_p})}{|\mathrm{PairNeg}(\mathcal{Z}_{\mathrm{test}},\ C_{i,l_k})|}, \forall\, C_{j,l_p} \in \mathcal{N}_{\mathrm{all}}(C_{i,l_k}) \right\}, G_{i,l_k} = 1 - \mathrm{Gini}(R_{i,l_k}) \tag{6}$$

Values of G_{i,l_k} range from 0 to 1, where higher values indicate a more even distribution among negative clusters. S is the average of G_{i,l_k} for all $C_{i,l_k} \in \mathcal{C}$:

$$S = \frac{1}{|\mathcal{C}|} \sum_{C_{i,l_k} \in \mathcal{C}} G_{i,l_k}. \tag{7}$$

3.3 Test Set Targeted Augmentation

We formulate the augmentation of $\mathcal{D}_{\mathrm{test}}$ as a Partially Observable Markov Decision Process (POMDP) and train a RL agent whose policy π—a learnable rule that maps the current view of the latent space (the observation), to the next testbed configuration (the action)—interacts with this POMDP to maximise the three test set quality objectives: diversity, proximity, and scarcity. The main components of this POMDP are:

- **Observations** Ω. Each observation $o \in \Omega$ is a compressed summary of the structured latent space, comprising the cluster centroids $\boldsymbol{\mu}_{C_{i,l_k}}$ (for all $C_{i,l_k} \in \mathcal{C}$) and basic statistics (mean, min, max, variance, std) computed over $\mathcal{Z}_{\text{test}}$.
- **Actions** $\mathcal{A}$. Each action $a \in \mathcal{A}$ specifies a traffic-generation configuration (e.g., bandwidth throttling, latency injection, or packet corruption) that the testbed uses to generate one new network traffic data point.
- **Reward** R. After each action, the agent receives a scalar reward r quantifying the improvement in test set quality in terms of diversity D, proximity P, and scarcity S. Formally, $R = \frac{1}{\frac{w_D}{D} + \frac{w_P}{P} + \frac{w_S}{S}}$, where w_D, w_P, and w_S are tunable hyperparameters.

During training, the agent first observes the cluster centroids and the summary of the initial $\mathcal{Z}_{\text{test}}$, denoted by o_0, while its policy π is randomly initialized. We implement this policy using Deep Reinforcement Learning (DRL), where a neural network approximates π. At each step t, the agent selects a traffic-generation configuration a_t (i.e., how the testbed should create one network traffic data point). In response, the configured testbed instantiates real network traffic under those conditions, yielding a new data point. It is then encoded, $f(\mathbf{x})$, and appended to $\mathcal{Z}_{\text{test}}$. The updated $\mathcal{Z}_{\text{test}}$ is summarized to yield, with the cluster centroids, the new partial observation o_{t+1}, and the test set is evaluated using the three quality metrics to compute the reward r_t. Upon receiving the transition tuple (o_t, a_t, r_t, o_{t+1}), the agent updates π with the aim of increasing future rewards. This process repeats for multiple steps, with each step adding one new encoded data point to $\mathcal{Z}_{\text{test}}$. If a target test set quality is reached or a maximum step budget is met, the current episode terminates and the environment resets to the original test set (or a fresh copy), after which a new episode begins. Over multiple episodes, π converges to a better policy π^*, learning a strategy for configuring the testbed to generate network traffic flows that progressively enhance the diversity, proximity, and scarcity of the test set.

Once the training phase is complete, π^* can be reused during testing to augment either the same $\mathcal{D}_{\text{test}}$ or another NIDS dataset. In the latter case, the preliminary phase and phase 1 must first be carried out to establish a compatible structured latent space for that new NIDS dataset; the pre-trained agent can then directly apply π^* to guide the generation of additional network traffic.

4 Experiments and Results

4.1 Experimental Setup

Experiments were conducted on a server running Ubuntu 22.04.3 LTS with an Intel(R) Xeon(R) Gold 6258R CPU @ 2.70 GHz processor, 500 GB of RAM, and an NVIDIA RTX A6000. Our implementation is provided.[1]

---

[1] https://gitlab.inria.fr/oanser/tata.

Datasets. We used refined versions of the IDS2017 and IDS2018 datasets [21], recognized benchmarks for NIDS [7] yet noted for their relatively low input complexity [6] and classification complexity [22]. Both are flow-based using CICFlowMeter [21] to create bidirectional flows enriched with statistical features. While both cover the same number of attacks, they differ in scale: about 926k benign and 253k attack flows for IDS2017 and about 59.8M benign and 4.1M attack flows for IDS2018. Benign traffic is mostly DNS, HTTP, and HTTPS flows with other minority protocols (e.g., SSH, FTP, SMTP). The attack types range from infiltration and port scanning to DoS, DDoS, and web exploits. Due to the very low occurrence (10 to 20 flows) of certain attack types in IDS2017, a pattern not observed in IDS2018, we removed these attack types.

NIDS Models. We show TATA's model-agnostic nature using three multi-class ML models: RF, SVM, and a DNN which features three fully connected ReLU layers (128 neurons each) and a softmax output. These models are widely used in NIDS research, showing strong results on IDS2017 and IDS2018 [28]. Each dataset is stratified 60/20/20 into training ($\mathcal{D}_{\text{train}}$), validation ($\mathcal{D}_{\text{val}}$), and test ($\mathcal{D}_{\text{test}}$) splits; $\mathcal{D}_{\text{val}}$ is used to select model hyper-parameters via random search.

Contrastive Autoencoder. The contrastive autoencoder is a multilayer perceptron selected after a grid search over candidate architectures and training hyper-parameters. The best configuration, ranked according to the Silhouette-guided k-means accuracy, uses three fully connected layers with 64, 32, and 16 neurons, and ReLU activations. It is trained for 250 epochs with a batch size of 128 and a learning rate of 0.001. The contrastive loss employs a margin of 10 and a regularisation factor of $\lambda = 0.1$, while the latent space is three-dimensional.

4.2 Preliminary Phase: Evaluating the Contrastive Autoencoder

We evaluate the output from the contrastive autoencoder (the cluster set $\mathcal{C}$, derived from $\mathcal{Z}_{\text{train}}$) comparing it to a vanilla autoencoder (which omits the contrastive loss). Both autoencoders are trained on ten distinct 60%-$\mathcal{D}_{\text{train}}$ splits of IDS2017 and IDS2018, each generated with a different random seed, and assessed via silhouette score (a measure of cluster separability) and K-Means (KM) accuracy (alignment of clusters with true labels).

The contrastive autoencoder achieves significantly higher silhouette scores ($0.96_{\pm 0.00}$ vs. $0.73_{\pm 0.05}$ on IDS2017 and $0.98_{\pm 0.00}$ vs. $0.76_{\pm 0.02}$ on IDS2018), indicating that the clusters in $\mathcal{Z}_{\text{train}}$ are both well-grouped and clearly divided. These strong internal structures yield near-perfect KM Accuracy (over 99% on both datasets), indicating that each cluster is almost entirely composed of encoded data points from the same input label. In contrast, the vanilla autoencoder's lower KM Accuracy (around 60%) reveals considerable label mixing.

Takeaway: The contrastive autoencoder yields a highly discriminative and well-structured latent space, outperforming a vanilla autoencoder.

4.3 Phase 1: Test Set Assessment Metrics in Practice

Having introduced each metric's rationale, we now address RQ1 by examining whether their values vary in alignment with the performance of the implemented NIDSs. We use a single 60/20 $\mathcal{D}_{\text{train}}$–$\mathcal{D}_{\text{test}}$ stratified split on the IDS2017 dataset (IDS2018 yields similar observations). Because this split alone gives each metric a single value, we selectively manipulate $\mathcal{D}_{\text{test}}$ to produce varying test set qualities, as detailed in the subsections below. We measure correlation using Pearson's r for linear relationships and Spearman's ρ for rank-based (monotonic) trends, so both absolute differences and relative orderings are captured.

Diversity. We investigate whether including additional traffic types (labels) in the NIDS evaluation (an inherently more challenging scenario) correlates with higher diversity. To do this, we generate all sub-test sets from IDS2017's $\mathcal{D}_{\text{test}}$ corresponding to each label combination of size k (k ranges from 1 to 9 since IDS2017 includes 9 types of traffic).

We then compute and plot the resulting diversity values in Fig. 5, observing a perfect correlation (Pearson's $r = 1$, Spearman's $\rho = 1$) between the number of labels and mean diversity. As k grows from 1 to 9, diversity rises monotonically from near-minimal to a maximum of 0.1209.

Takeaway: The diversity metric captures the increased evaluation challenge that results from adding more label types, which increases the range of traffic types the NIDS must handle.

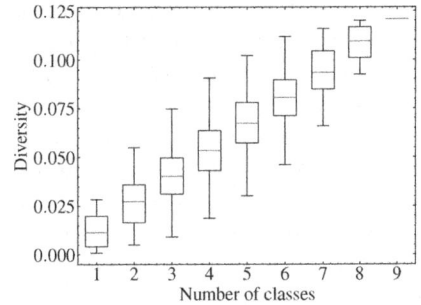

Fig. 5. Box plots of the diversity metric for sub-test sets of size $k = 1, \ldots, 9$

Proximity. To assess proximity, we compute each encoded test data point's distance to its negative cluster. We rank these distances from largest to smallest and split the ordered list into 100 cumulative sub-test sets: the first contains the top 1 %, the second the top 2 % (including the first), and so on. As we move from sets with the largest distances to those with smaller ones, the average distance decreases, thereby increasing the proximity metric. Using each sub-test set, we evaluate whether higher proximity levels challenge the NIDS, as indicated by increased error.

In Fig. 6, each circular marker represents a sub-test set, with its average proximity (x-axis)

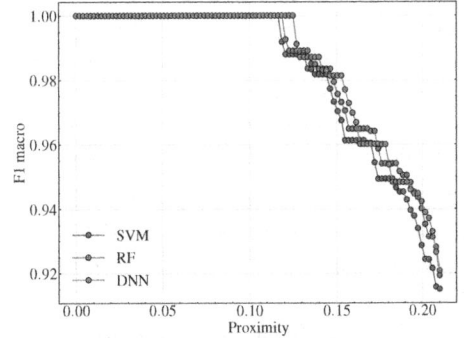

Fig. 6. Effect of Proximity on NIDS Performance

plotted against the macro-F1 of the three NIDS (RF, DNN, SVM). All three NIDS maintain macro-F1=1.0 across more than half the sub-test sets (proximity ≤ 0.11–0.14), but macro-F1 gradually declines (to about 0.92 for RF/DNN and 0.91 for SVM) as more borderline data points appear. We observe a strong negative Spearman correlation ($\rho = -0.90 \pm 0.01$) and a similarly negative Pearson correlation ($r = -0.86 \pm 0.01$), both averaged across the three NIDS, confirming that higher proximity corresponds to lower macro-F1. Their nearly identical trajectories (pairwise correlations Pearson > 0.98, Spearman > 0.97) indicate that proximity is agnostic to the ML model.

Takeaway: Proximity captures the escalating difficulty posed by borderline test data points, as higher proximity values coincide with lower NIDS performance.

Scarcity. As with proximity, we investigate whether scarcity correlates with $\mathcal{D}_{\text{test}}$'s difficulty and thus affects NIDS performance. Defined in Sect. 3.2, scarcity measures how uniformly encoded test data points distribute across all possible negative clusters. To produce sub-test sets with different scarcity levels, we run each NIDS on $\mathcal{D}_{\text{test}}$, record misclassified data points, and map them to their latent representations. We then systematically redistribute these misclassified instances among the available negative clusters in 10 steps, transitioning from a less-uniform (clustered) to a more-uniform (dispersed) arrangement. As with proximity, we therefore create sub-test sets with an increasing scarcity and evaluate how this impacts the NIDS performance.

Because our objective is to create a wide range of types of misclassification errors (*i.e.* mixing different labels), macro-F1 is also considered, correcting imbalance effect of a particular label. In overall, a strong negative Spearman correlation ($\rho = -1 \pm 0$, averaged across models) and a strong negative Pearson correlation ($r = -0.8885 \pm 0.0055$) clearly indicate that higher scarcity corresponds to a lower macro-F1. In details, Fig. 7 shows that, after the first redistribution step, macro-F1 shows a sharp decline. Performance then continues to decrease more gradually and monotonically; for instance, the macro-F1 of the RF-based NIDS falls below 0.78 when the scarcity level reaches 0.53.

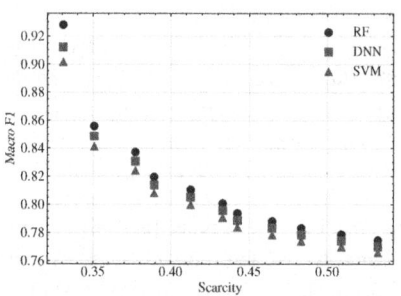

Fig. 7. Effect of Scarcity on NIDS Performance

Takeaway: A more uniform spread of misdetection data points across decision boundaries increases scarcity and decreases the macro-averaged F1-score, confirming scarcity's relevance as a difficulty indicator.

4.4 Phase 2: Test Set Augmentation Evaluation

In this second phase, TATA focuses on augmenting $\mathcal{D}_{\text{test}}$ with Benign flows only, as a proof of concept. The RL agent relies on a two-host testbed (client and server) exchanging Benign SSH traffic (a protocol present in IDS2017 and IDS2018). While RL ideally operates at millisecond timescales, allowing the collection of numerous transition tuples (o_t, a_t, r_t, o_{t+1}) for effective learning, our full pipeline (traffic generation, flow conversion, encoding with f and metrics computation) requires seconds, making a conventional online loop infeasible. Thus, we employ offline RL, training on a static dataset of transitions (o_t, a_t, r_t, o_{t+1}) derived from IDS2018 while reserving IDS2017 for final testing. We omit the reverse scenario because IDS2018's larger cluster set $\mathcal{C}$ exceeds what an agent trained on IDS2017 can handle as observation input.

To construct these transition tuples, we first split IDS2018 into $\mathcal{D}_{\text{train}}$ and an initial $\mathcal{D}_{\text{test}}$ and augment the latter iteratively with a random traffic-generation configuration (action) on the SSH traffic, drawn from uniform parameter ranges (forming the action set a_t): loss [5%, 10%], jitter [4 ms, 10 ms], delay [10 ms, 40 ms], duplication [0.1%, 5%], corruption [0.1%, 10%], reordering [0.1%, 50%], and correlation [50%, 100%]. The action is applied with the Linux tc command on the client side while running a predefined SSH scenario creating large random files, performing frequent file operations, executing complex commands, modifying file permissions, and cleaning up. Next, we convert the resulting network traffic into flow(s) using CICFlowMeter, after which we apply our pipeline (metric computation and reward calculation with weights $w_P = w_S = w_D = 1$). If 5,000 steps have elapsed or the reward exceeds 0.9, we reset the initial $\mathcal{D}_{\text{test}}$ to begin a new episode. Across these episodes, we collect roughly 500,000 transitions without any filtering, deliberately retaining failed episodes to ensure the offline RL algorithms (CQL [19] and TD3+BC [9], chosen for continuous-action support and for penalizing out-of-dataset actions to remain within known transitions, and tuned via grid search) encounter a diverse range of outcomes.

After training, we evaluate each RL agent for 20 episodes on IDS2017, using different random seeds to define an 60–20 train–test split each time. During these evaluations, the agent manipulates traffic configurations on the same SSH testbed, but no further policy updates or reward signals occur. Newly generated flows are labeled benign and added to the IDS2017 test set. Finally, we measure how this augmentation affects (i) our test-set quality metrics and (ii) NIDS detection performance (macro-averaged precision and recall). We report mean and standard deviation over the 20 episodes. Three baselines are considered:

– **Random Agent:** The agent selects traffic-shaping parameters (loss, jitter, delay, etc.) at random, using no learned strategy.
– **GAN-Based Method (Netshare [42]):** Netshare employs a GAN to synthesize network traffic. Although it attempts to mimic real-world distributions, its generated flows may not fully capture the complexity of realistic network behavior.
– **Augmentation guided with NC [30]:** This variant uses the TATA's offline RL pipeline but replaces the default reward with a neuron-coverage metric from the DNN-based NIDS. During training, after each newly generated traffic flow, we measure the fraction of activated neurons (e.g., 70% activation yields a reward of 0.7).

We compare only methods with publicly available, working code that can be adapted to NIDS; others, such as [31], focus on image-based augmentation and are therefore omitted.

Figure 8 summarizes our results, plotting each augmentation method alongside the test set (no augmentation) on the x-axis.

Our TATA approach focuses on CQL-based findings, as TD3+BC produces similar outcomes that do not change our conclusions. The y-axis shows both quality metrics (diversity, proximity, and scarcity) and NIDS performance metrics (macro-averaged precision and recall), all normalized to [0,1].

Both the Random agent and Netshare dramatically reduce diversity, driving it close to zero. However, the impact on proximity is negligible (the Random agent lowers it slightly, while Netshare raises it slightly) whereas scarcity declines for both. Together, these changes have nearly no effect on NIDS performance. In contrast, TATA increases proximity by about 190%, scarcity by roughly 136%, and diversity by around 437%, whereas the augmentation guided with NC focuses on proximity, increasing it by approximately 129%. This limitation arises because neuron coverage targets data points near negative clusters, those most stressful to the NIDS, while overlooking diversity and scarcity. These differences also influence precision and recall. For example, for the RF-based NIDS,

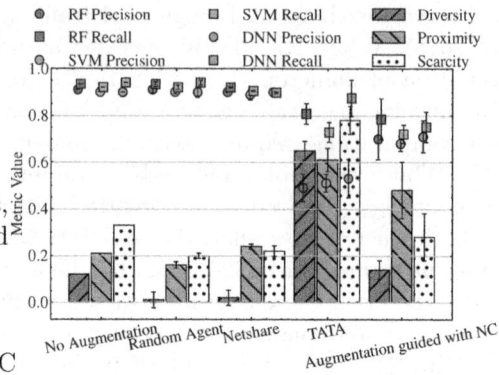

Fig. 8. Impact of TATA and Baselines on Test-Set Quality Metrics and Detection Performance

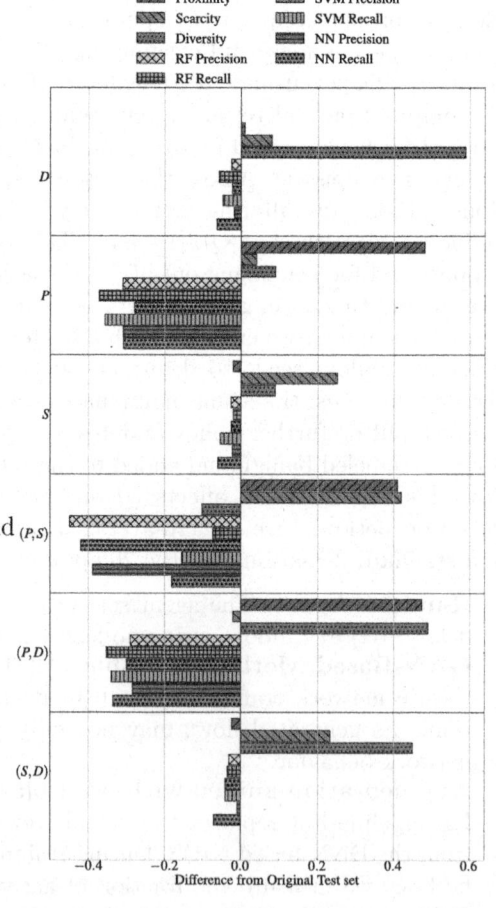

Fig. 9. Impact of Partial Metric Combinations on Test-Set Quality and NIDS Performance

TATA lowers precision by roughly 46%, compared with about 23% for NC, while recall drops by around 13% with TATA versus 16% with NC. We see that scarcity, by distributing misclassified points more widely, strongly affects precision (tied to false positives).

Takeaway: TATA comprehensively stresses the NIDS through diversity, proximity, and scarcity, creating a more challenging test set (thus lower precision/recall) than augmentation guided with NC, which focuses solely on proximity.

To have a higher understanding of the importance of the quality metrics, the reward is now calculated from a single metrics or any combination of two of them resulting in 6 different cases reported in Fig. 9 where D, P, and S stands for diversity, proximity, and scarcity respectively. Horizontal bars, centered at zero, illustrate how much each configuration improves or degrades performance relative to the original set. Combinations that include proximity $(P), (P, S), (P, D)$ offer the greatest challenge to the NIDSs, while the others have minimal impact. This is because proximity targets the decision boundary of negative clusters, where the NIDS struggles most with detection. For example, with the RF-based NIDS, in the (P, S) combination, recall declines by about 8% (from 0.934 to 0.862) and precision by about 49% (0.910 to 0.460), whereas in (S, D), they fall by roughly 4% (0.934 to 0.900) and 3% (0.910 to 0.880), respectively.

Takeaway: Proximity emerges as the critical factor in stressing the NIDSs, whereas scarcity and diversity offer complementary effects by covering all possible decision boundaries and avoiding redundant test cases, together expanding test coverage.

4.5 Datasets Analysis

We applied TATA's metrics to various networking-related datasets, including intrusion detection and other traffic-classification benchmarks, to assess their test sets over time.

Table 2 highlights studied benchmarks, from early, small-scale examples like NSL-KDD (2009) to more recent, encrypted-oriented sets (ISCX Tor, VPN-NonVPN) and IoT-focused ones (Bot-IoT, ToN-IoT). They have evolved toward more realistic testbeds, extensive logging, and multi-vector attacks.

Using ten 60/20 training–test splits, Fig. 10 plots our metrics. As shown, proximity

Table 2. Datasets Summary

Dataset	Key Highlights	#Attacks	#Feat
NSL-KDD (2009)	DARPA'98 refinement; ~148k records	22	41
CTU-13 (2011)	13 botnet scenarios; >15M flows	13	15
ISCX IDS 2012	24-host lab; ~2.5M flows	4	14
UNSW-NB15 (2015)	Cyber-Range lab; 2.54 M flows	9	49
CIC-UNSW (2015)	Augmented UNSW-NB15; ~450 k flows	9	~80
ISCX Tor (2016)	5-user Tor traffic; 2 scenarios	2	28
VPN-NonVPN (2016)	Multi-app data; VPN vs non-VPN	14	84
CIC-IDS 2017	18-host testbed; 3.12M flows	7	83
CSE-CIC-IDS 2018	Enterprise-scale net; 16.23 M flows	7	~80
Bot-IoT (2018)	Simulated IoT; >72 M records	4	46
CIC-DDoS 2019	Lab network; multi-vector DDoS	13	80
ToN-IoT (2020)	IoT/IIoT testbed; ~0.48 M flows	9	42

remains fairly stable (mostly 0.2–0.3), though early versions of IDS2017 and IDS2018 (with labeling errors) reach around 0.5. Diversity shows a broader range, from near zero to about 0.5, without a clear monotonic trend. Scarcity largely tracks proximity until CIC-IDS2017 (errors present), then aligns more with diversity and fluctuates more. Across all ten splits, each metric exhibits minimal, often negligible, standard deviation.

These findings suggest that, despite increasingly complex testbed designs over time (including more attacks, applications, and intricate topologies), the core quality of these datasets' test sets remains consistent, and their inherent difficulty has not substantially increased. In contrast, widely used image classification benchmarks, MNIST and CIFAR-10, exhibit higher complexity. Notably, we adapted our contrastive autoencoder with convolutional layers for image data.

Takeaway: Even with recent advances in dataset design, reference datasets differ widely in difficulty across application domains, and our metrics reveal that most NIDS test sets still pose only a moderate challenge, highlighting the network-security community's ongoing shortage of truly demanding, well-suited datasets.

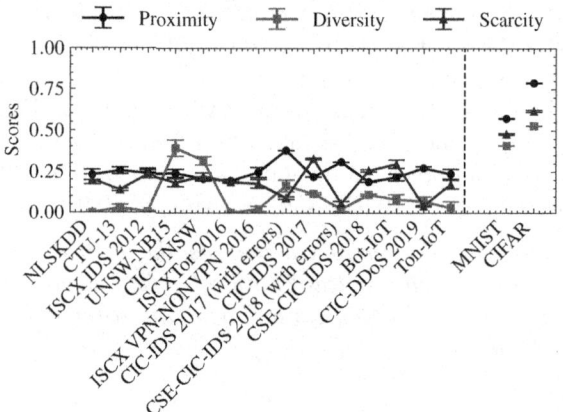

Fig. 10. Test Sets Assessment of NIDS Datasets

5 Conclusion

In this paper, we presented TATA, a model-agnostic method to assess and augment the quality of benchmark NIDS test sets. TATA uses a contrastive autoencoder to build a structured latent space from a training set, derives three comprehensive metrics (diversity, proximity, scarcity) from the test set, and combines them with RL to guide realistic traffic augmentation. Our evaluation shows that the contrastive autoencoder effectively organizes the latent space, these dataset-centric metrics capture test set difficulty, and the RL-based agent increases the challenge for various ML-based NIDS models.

TATA's pipeline still exhibits some limitations. *(i) Computational overhead.* Assessing a new test set currently entails retraining the contrastive autoencoder and running an exhaustive hyperparameter search, which dominates the total runtime. We aim to reduce this cost by starting the preliminary phase from a pre-trained autoencoder and fine-tuning only lightweight adapters. *(ii) Limited traffic diversity.* So far, the augmentation phase produces only benign SSH flows. We plan to enrich the testbed with additional benign protocols and with attack traffic by adopting a multi-agent design in which each agent generates a specific traffic type. *(iii) Fixed-cluster assumption.* The present RL agent is built for a fixed number of clusters, preventing its use on datasets that contain more clusters than expected. *(iv) Unverified RL generalization.* Evaluation has been restricted to the IDS2017 benchmark. The agent's ability to generalize to datasets with markedly different feature distributions (such as UNSW-NB15 and Bot-IoT) remains untested. Assessing performance across a broader suite of NIDS benchmarks is therefore a central goal of future work.

Acknowledgement. The authors acknowledge partial support from the French National Research Agency through the France 2030 initiative (project *Superviz*, ANR-22-PECY-0008) and additional funding in part from the Luxembourg National Research Fund (FNR, grant C23/IS/18088425/COCTEL). The opinions expressed are solely those of the authors and do not necessarily reflect the views of the French government.

A Computational Complexity of Test Set Assessment

To assess a given test set $\mathcal{D}_{\text{test}}$, TATA follows a workflow that begins with contrastive autoencoder training and concludes with computing the cluster–wise metrics D, P, and S.

(i) Preliminary phase (contrastive autoencoder training). The contrastive autoencoder is trained on the corresponding training set $\mathcal{D}_{\text{train}}$. A hyperparameter tuning examine H candidate configurations; for each one, the autoencoder is trained for E complete epochs over $\mathcal{D}_{\text{train}}$. A single forward–backward pass scales with the number of parameters in the model, and the worst case is obtained with the largest candidate network, whose size is $|\theta_{\max}|$. Hence, the overall cost of the preliminary phase is: $\boxed{O(H\,E\,|\mathcal{D}_{\text{train}}|\,|\theta_{\max}|)}$.

(ii) Phase 1-a (cluster identification). On the embeddings from the best run, silhouette-guided k-means performs I refinement rounds, yielding a cost of: $\boxed{O(I\,|\mathcal{D}_{\text{train}}|\,|\mathcal{C}|)}$.

(iii) Phase 1-b (centroid assignment). Every embedding $\mathbf{z} \in \mathcal{Z}_{\text{train}} \cup \mathcal{Z}_{\text{test}}$ is then compared with the $|\mathcal{C}|$ centroids to locate its $\mathcal{P}(\mathbf{z})$ and $\mathcal{N}(\mathbf{z})$ clusters, for a total of $\boxed{O((|\mathcal{D}_{\text{train}}| + |\mathcal{D}_{\text{test}}|)\,|\mathcal{C}|)}$ distance evaluations.

(iv) Phase 1-c (metric computation). A single linear pass over $\mathcal{Z}_{\text{test}}$ updates the per-cluster counters needed for D, P, and S, costing: $\boxed{O(|\mathcal{D}_{\text{test}}| + |\mathcal{C}|)}$.

Combining the four steps, the overall time complexity becomes:

$$\boxed{O\bigl(H\,E\,|\mathcal{D}_{\text{train}}|\,|\theta_{\max}| + I\,|\mathcal{D}_{\text{train}}|\,|\mathcal{C}| + (|\mathcal{D}_{\text{train}}| + |\mathcal{D}_{\text{test}}|)|\mathcal{C}|\bigr)}$$

Pre-training the encoder once on an heterogeneous set of network traffic and then fine-tuning a small adapter on $m \ll |\mathcal{D}_{\text{train}}|$ data points for $\tilde{E} \ll E$ epochs cuts the training component from $H\,E\,|\mathcal{D}_{\text{train}}|\,|\theta_{\max}|$ to $\tilde{E}\,m\,|\theta_\star|$, yielding an overall per-dataset complexity of:

$$O(\tilde{E}\,m\,|\theta_\star| + I\,|\mathcal{D}_{\text{train}}|\,|\mathcal{C}| + (|\mathcal{D}_{\text{train}}| + |\mathcal{D}_{\text{test}}|)\,|\mathcal{C}|), \quad \text{where } |\theta_\star| \ll |\theta_{\max}|$$

B Offline RL Hyperparameter Tuning

We adopt the Split-Select-Retrain pipeline proposed by Nie *et al.* [27]. Concretely, we create $K = 20$ independent 50/50 train/validation splits of the offline dataset. For each algorithm–hyperparameter configuration (CQL or TD3+BC variants), we train a candidate policy on every training split. We then estimate each policy's expected return on the corresponding validation split using Fitted Q Evaluation (FQE), a simple method that learns a reward-predicting value function from the logged data and reuses it to score a policy without any new environment interaction, originally introduced by Paine *et al.* [29]. Averaging the K FQE estimates yields a robust performance metric for each configuration; we choose the configuration with the highest mean score and retrain the agent on the full offline dataset before deployment.

References

1. Catillo, M., Pecchia, A., Villano, U.: Machine learning on public intrusion datasets: academic hype or concrete advances in NIDS? In: 2023 53rd Annual IEEE/IFIP International Conference on Dependable Systems and Networks - Supplemental Volume (DSN-S) (2023)
2. Clausen, H., Flood, R., Aspinall, D.: Traffic generation using containerization for machine learning. In: Proceedings of the 2019 Workshop on DYnamic and Novel Advances in Machine Learning and Intelligent Cyber Security (2022)
3. Doriguzzi-Corin, R., Millar, S., Scott-Hayward, S., Martínez-del Rincón, J., Siracusa, D.: LUCID: a practical, lightweight deep learning solution for DDoS attack detection. IEEE Trans. Netw. Serv. Manage. **17**, 876–889 (2020)
4. Engelen, G., Rimmer, V., Joosen, W.: Troubleshooting an intrusion detection dataset: the cicids2017 case study. In: 2021 IEEE Security and Privacy Workshops (SPW) (2021)
5. Feng, Y., Shi, Q., Gao, X., Wan, J., Fang, C., Chen, Z.: DeepGini: prioritizing massive tests to enhance the robustness of deep neural networks. In: Proceedings of the 29th ACM SIGSOFT International Symposium on Software Testing and Analysis. ISSTA 2020 (2020)
6. Flood, R., Aspinall, D.: Measuring the complexity of benchmark NIDS datasets via spectral analysis. In: 2024 IEEE European Symposium on Security and Privacy Workshops (EuroS&PW) (2024)
7. Flood, R., Engelen, G., Aspinall, D., Desmet, L.: Bad design smells in benchmark NIDS datasets. In: 2024 IEEE 9th European Symposium on Security and Privacy (EuroS&P) (2024)
8. Friedman, D., Dieng, A.B.: The vendi score: A diversity evaluation metric for machine learning (2023)

9. Fujimoto, S., Gu, S.S.: A minimalist approach to offline reinforcement learning. In: Advances in Neural Information Processing Systems (2021)
10. Guo, J., Jiang, Y., Zhao, Y., Chen, Q., Sun, J.: DLFUZZ: differential fuzzing testing of deep learning systems. In: Proceedings of the 2018 ACM Joint Meeting on European Software Engineering Conference and Symposium on the Foundations of Software Engineering (2018)
11. Hadsell, R., Chopra, S., LeCun, Y.: Dimensionality reduction by learning an invariant mapping. In: 2006 IEEE Computer Society Conference on Computer Vision and Pattern Recognition (CVPR 2006) (2006)
12. Harel-Canada, F., Wang, L., Gulzar, M.A., Gu, Q., Kim, M.: Is neuron coverage a meaningful measure for testing deep neural networks? In: Proceedings of the 28th ACM Joint Meeting on European Software Engineering Conference and Symposium on the Foundations of Software Engineering. ESEC/FSE 2020 (2020)
13. Hu, Q., Ma, L., Xie, X., Yu, B., Liu, Y., Zhao, J.: Deepmutation++: a mutation testing framework for deep learning systems. In: 2019 34th IEEE/ACM International Conference on Automated Software Engineering (ASE) (2019)
14. Humbatova, N., Jahangirova, G., Tonella, P.: DeepCrime: mutation testing of deep learning systems based on real faults. In: Proceedings of the 30th ACM SIGSOFT International Symposium on Software Testing and Analysis. ISSTA 2021 (2021)
15. Jiang, X., et al.: NetDiffusion: network data augmentation through protocol-constrained traffic generation. Proc. ACM Meas. Anal. Comput. Syst. **8**, 1–32 (2024)
16. Khosla, P., et al.: Supervised contrastive learning. In: Advances in Neural Information Processing Systems
17. Kim, J., Feldt, R., Yoo, S.: Guiding deep learning system testing using surprise adequacy. In: Proceedings of the 41st International Conference on Software Engineering. ICSE 2019 (2019)
18. Kim, J., Feldt, R., Yoo, S.: Evaluating surprise adequacy for deep learning system testing. ACM Trans. Softw. Eng. Methodol. **32**, 1–29 (2023)
19. Kumar, A., Zhou, A., Tucker, G., Levine, S.: Conservative q-learning for offline reinforcement learning. In: Advances in Neural Information Processing Systems (2020)
20. Lanvin, M., Gimenez, P.F., Han, Y., Majorczyk, F., Mé, L., Totel, E.: Errors in the CICIDS2017 dataset and the significant differences in detection performances it makes. In: Risks and Security of Internet and Systems: 17th International Conference, CRiSIS 2022, Sousse, Tunisia, 7-9 December 2022, Revised Selected Papers (2023)
21. Liu, L., Engelen, G., Lynar, T.M., Essam, D.L., Joosen, W.: Error prevalence in NIDS datasets: a case study on CIC-IDS-2017 and CSE-CIC-IDS-2018. 2022 IEEE Conference on Communications and Network Security (CNS) (2022)
22. Lorena, A.C., Garcia, L.P.F., Lehmann, J., Souto, M.C.P., Ho, T.K.: How complex is your classification problem? a survey on measuring classification complexity. ACM Comput. Surv. **52**, 1–34 (2019)
23. Ma, L., et al.: DeepCT: tomographic combinatorial testing for deep learning systems. In: 2019 IEEE 26th International Conference on Software Analysis, Evolution and Reengineering (SANER) (2019)
24. Ma, L., et al.: DeepGauge: multi-granularity testing criteria for deep learning systems. In: Proceedings of the 33rd ACM/IEEE International Conference on Automated Software Engineering. ASE 2018 (2018)

25. Manocchio, L.D., Layeghy, S., Lo, W.W., Kulatilleke, G.K., Sarhan, M., Portmann, M.: FlowTransformer: a transformer framework for flow-based network intrusion detection systems. Expert Syst. Appl. **241**, 122564 (2024)
26. Moustafa, N., Slay, J.: UNSW-NB15: a comprehensive data set for network intrusion detection systems (UNSW-NB15 network data set). In: 2015 Military Communications and Information Systems Conference (MilCIS)
27. Nie, A., Flet-Berliac, Y., Jordan, D.R., Steenbergen, W., Brunskill, E.: Data-efficient pipeline for offline reinforcement learning with limited data. In: NeurIPS (2022)
28. Owezarski, P.: Investigating adversarial attacks against random forest-based network attack detection systems. In: NOMS 2023-2023 IEEE/IFIP Network Operations and Management Symposium (2023)
29. Paine, T.L., et al.: Hyperparameter selection for offline reinforcement learning. arXiv preprint (2020)
30. Pei, K., Cao, Y., Yang, J., Jana, S.: DeepXplore: Automated Whitebox testing of deep learning systems. In: Proceedings of the 26th Symposium on Operating Systems Principles, pp. 1–18. ACM (2017)
31. Riccio, V., Humbatova, N., Jahangirova, G., Tonella, P.: DeepMetis: augmenting a deep learning test set to increase its mutation score. In: Proceedings of the 36th IEEE/ACM International Conference on Automated Software Engineering. ASE 2021 (2022)
32. Riccio, V., Tonella, P.: When and why test generators for deep learning produce invalid inputs: an empirical study. 2023 IEEE/ACM 45th International Conference on Software Engineering (ICSE) (2022)
33. Sharafaldin, I., Lashkari, A.H., Ghorbani, A.A.: Toward generating a new intrusion detection dataset and intrusion traffic characterization. In: Proceedings of the 4th International Conference on Information Systems Security and Privacy, (ICISSP) (2018)
34. Shiravi, A., Shiravi, H., Tavallaee, M., Ghorbani, A.A.: Toward developing a systematic approach to generate benchmark datasets for intrusion detection. Comput. Secur. **31**, 357–374 (2012)
35. Singla, A., Bertino, E., Verma, D.: Preparing network intrusion detection deep learning models with minimal data using adversarial domain adaptation. In: Proceedings of the 15th ACM Asia Conference on Computer and Communications Security. ASIA CCS 2020 (2020)
36. Sudyana, D., et al.: Quality analysis in ids dataset: impact on model generalization. In: 2024 IEEE Conference on Communications and Network Security (CNS) (2024)
37. Sutton, R.S., Barto, A.G.: Reinforcement Learning: An Introduction (2018)
38. Tufano, M., et al.: DeepMutation: a neural mutation tool. In: 2020 IEEE/ACM 42nd International Conference on Software Engineering: Companion Proceedings (ICSE-Companion) (2020)
39. Wang, C., Finamore, A., Michiardi, P., Gallo, M., Rossi, D.: Data augmentation for traffic classification. In: Richter, P., Bajpai, V., Carisimo, E. (eds.) Passive and Active Measurement (2024)
40. Weiss, M., Chakraborty, R., Tonella, P.: A review and refinement of surprise adequacy. In: 2021 IEEE/ACM Third International Workshop on Deep Learning for Testing and Testing for Deep Learning (DeepTest) (2021)
41. Xie, X., et al.: DeepHunter: a coverage-guided fuzz testing framework for deep neural networks. In: Proceedings of the 28th ACM SIGSOFT International Symposium on Software Testing and Analysis (2019)

42. Yin, Y., Lin, Z., Jin, M., Fanti, G., Sekar, V.: Practical GAN-based synthetic IP header trace generation using NetShare. In: Proceedings of the ACM SIGCOMM 2022 Conference. SIGCOMM 2022 (2022)

Abuse-Resistant Evaluation of AI-as-a-Service via Function-Hiding Homomorphic Signatures

Nuttapong Attrapadung[1], Goichiro Hanaoka[1], Ryo Hiromasa[2], Yoshihiro Koseki[2], Takahiro Matsuda[1], Yutaro Nishida[2], Yusuke Sakai[1(✉)], Jacob C. N. Schuldt[1], and Satoshi Yasuda[2]

[1] National Institute of Advanced Industrial Science and Technology (AIST), Tokyo, Japan
{n.attrapadung,hanaoka-goichiro,t-matsuda,yusuke.sakai, jacob.schuldt}@aist.go.jp
[2] Mitsubishi Electric Corporation, Kamakura, Japan
Hiromasa.Ryo@aj.MitsubishiElectric.co.jp,
Koseki.Yoshihiro@ak.MitsubishiElectric.co.jp,
Nishida.Yutaro@da.MitsubishiElectric.co.jp,
Yasuda.Satoshi@ea.MitsubishiElectric.co.jp

Abstract. Artificial intelligence (AI) has emerged as an incredibly useful tool with wide-ranging applications. This has given rise to numerous companies specializing in the development and training of AI models. Access to these models is often provided via cloud services—an approach referred to as "AI as a service" (AIaaS). An AIaaS provider typically offers limited free access to the service to entice users to buy full access, e.g., a bounded number of queries per month. Such free trial access is useful for users who want to determine whether the functionality and performance of the AI are sufficient for their use case. However, free trial access may also be abused by malicious users who might try to circumvent the trial restrictions e.g., by posing as many different users, in an attempt to gain full access to the AIaaS or potentially to try to mount a model extraction attack. As a first attempt to address this issue, we construct a cryptographic mechanism that enables users to test the performance of an AI while simultaneously preventing abuse caused by granting users full model access. Specifically, using our mechanism, users will be restricted to a pre-specified category of inputs or modifications thereof which prevents users from freely specifying the input while still ensuring input diversity. From a technical perspective, we achieve this by formalizing a new cryptographic primitive, function-hiding homomorphic signatures, and instantiating this via a construction based on non-interactive zero-knowledge proofs.

1 Introduction

1.1 Background

AI Models as High-Value Intellectual Property. Artificial intelligence (AI) is widely believed to be a transformative technology and has already been shown to be incredibly useful in many practical applications. In particular two prominent architectures, convolutional neural networks (CNNs) and large language models (LLMs), have emerged as excellent tools for classification tasks and natural language processing, respectively.

However, constructing an AI model is a resource-intensive process. Firstly, finding the optimal model structure can be challenging and may require significant research and development. Secondly, training an AI model requires a substantial amount of data, which will have to be gathered and potentially preprocessed before any training can be done. The preprocessing step in itself might be a non-trivial and time-consuming task. To further complicate matters, the required training data may in some cases only be available to a very limited group of entities who might not grant access to this without compensation. As a result, creating an AI model is often a significant investment.

The high cost of constructing an AI model naturally makes those who constructed the model reluctant to publicly release this without a way to recover their investment. AI as a service (AIaaS) is a suitable business model for this. In this approach, the service provider does not publicize the AI model. Instead, users access the AI model through an Internet service by sending their input to the AIaaS provider and receiving the output of the AI model. For a user to obtain access, the user is required to pay a fee to the service provider. This allows the service provider to recover the model construction costs while maintaining control over the model's use and distribution.

Testing the Quality of a Private AI Model. The AIaaS paradigm raises a fundamental question: *Without direct access to an AI model and the underlying training data, how can users be assured of the quality of the AI model?* As highlighted above, users need to enter a service agreement with the AIaaS provider to be allowed to submit queries to the AI. However, reasonably, users want to confirm the quality of the AI model before doing so. Users do not want to find the AI model to be of low quality and insufficient for their use case after committing to an agreement with the AIaaS provider.

The issue becomes more acute if the AI output is intended to be used and relied upon by a third party e.g. a use case highlighted in related works [4] is that of a user obtaining a medical diagnose via AI classification and then presenting this to an insurance company. In this case, the third party (the insurance company) would like to be assured of the quality of the used AI model, but would not be able to access the model without entering into a service agreement with the AIaaS provider. If different users make use of different AIaaS providers, the third party would potentially have to enter into service agreements with all of these, which is likely undesirable for the third party.

To balance the needs of service providers and users, demonstrating the quality of the AI model via black-box testing seems like the only reasonable option. Specifically, a user (or a third party) could be convinced about the quality of the AI model by observing a sufficient number of diverse input queries to the AI and the resulting outputs. This would be in line with the interest of the AIaaS provider to keep the AI model private, and if the black-box testing can be done without requiring users to enter a service agreement with the AIaaS provider, the interest of users can likewise be met. However, this approach is not straightforward to realize as testing done by the AIaaS provider by itself would not be trustworthy to users while the AIaaS provider might want to limit a tester's access to the AI model for reasons discussed in the following.

Can We Allow Testers to Choose Inputs? When approaching AI model quality assurance via black-box testing, a natural question to ask is: Can we allow the tester to choose test inputs arbitrarily? Below we observe that there are multiple concerns when we allow a tester to do so.

Free-Riders. The first concern is that black-box testing potentially allows free-riders. Specifically, a service provider may offer a free trial to users to allow them to test the model. However, if this free trial is accessible to the public without any restriction (e.g., on the number of trial queries), users could simply use the free trial to obtain access to the AI without entering into a service agreement with the provider.

The current solution to this free-rider issue is to restrict the number of trial queries per hour/day/month, which is not a perfect solution. Firstly, the service provider needs to keep track of the number of queries for each user. Furthermore, a mechanism for ensuring that the same user does not create multiple trial accounts is needed. Secondly, this approach still allows free-riders if the user only requires a smaller number of queries.

Model Extraction Attacks. The second concern is model extraction attacks. A model extraction attack attempts to recover the model parameters of an AI model by using black-box access to the AI [15]. To keep the AI model parameters private, the service provider must take steps to prevent model extraction attacks. In particular, if it is possible to mount a model extraction attack using a trial service (i.e. within the restriction on the number of queries per hour/day/month), the AI model parameter becomes available to malicious users, and the service provider potentially loses the investment done to develop the AI model.

Notably, the current solution (restricting the number of queries per time period) is not very effective for avoiding model extraction attacks. This is because model extraction attacks can be optimized by carefully crafting the inputs to the model as opposed to observing many random queries and corresponding outputs.[1] At the very least, even if a model extraction attack requires sending many queries to the victim AIaaS service, who may restrict the number of trial queries per time period, the attacker can mount the attack by waiting a sufficiently long time.

---

[1] There is an upper bound on the number of queries to mount a model extraction attacks against some type of neural networks [23].

1.2 Our Contribution

In this paper, we provide the first attempt at enabling abuse-resistant evaluation of AI models, allowing limited, verifiable testing without granting full access to the model.

Conceptually, our proposed solution is simple; we provide a new cryptographic mechanism that enables restricting the input to an AI model to some pre-specified evaluation category. At a high level, our mechanism works as follows. After an initial system setup, an evaluation authority generates public information describing the pre-specified evaluation category. Then, when a user sends an input to the AIaaS provider, the mechanism enables the user to attach a certificate certifying that the input belongs to the pre-specified evaluation category. The AIaaS service provider can then verify the certificate without maintaining state. In this way, the service provider is guaranteed that the input belongs to the pre-specified category of allowed test inputs.

However, for this approach to be effective, the pre-specified evaluation category needs to satisfy two conflicting requirements. Firstly, the category should have sufficient diversity to allow a proper evaluation of the AI model i.e. a malicious service provider should not be able to train an AI model that provide good performance on the pre-specified inputs but has poor general performance. Secondly, the category should be sufficiently restricted to prevent free-riders and extraction attacks. The challenge is to design a mechanism which is sufficiently flexible to support this.

Furthermore, in some use cases, it would be highly desirable to let the evaluation authority dynamically and regularly update the set of authorized inputs in the evaluation category. This will further discourage a malicious service provider from attempting to construct a malicious AI model that performs well for a specific test set but is not guaranteed to perform well for general inputs. This dynamic update is difficult to achieve if we simply apply existing mechanisms. For example, PhotoProof [25] provides a solution for certifying image editing, however, it only supports a weaker proof-of-knowledge guarantee which prohibits adaptively chosen inputs. Similar mechanisms in other works [7,8,17,21] does not meet a sufficient secrecy condition. This hinders the mechanisms from being applied to our context.

We formalize our mechanism as a new cryptographic primitive named *function-hiding homomorphic signatures*. As opposed to standard homomorphic signatures, function-hiding homomorphic signatures hide the function with which the homomorphic evaluation was performed. This is a crucial security property in our application of testing the quality of an AI model. Looking ahead, the function in a homomorphic evaluation will be chosen randomly, and this randomness will make the test input unpredictable from the service provider's viewpoint. This unpredictability ensures a sufficient variety of the pre-specified inputs and the corresponding signature will function as a certificate. Here, the evaluation category will then correspond to transformations of a set of inputs provided by the evaluation authority. We discuss these aspects in more detail in the technical overview in Sect. 2.

Note that employing function-hiding homomorphic signatures as briefly outlined above (and discussed in detail in Sect. 6), we can effectively address the AIaaS security concerns raised above regarding user-selected test input. Specifically, the free-rider issue is addressed by limiting users evaluating the AI model to inputs from the pre-specified evaluation category which can be verified by the AIaaS provider via the attached certificates i.e. the users will be prevented from freely specifying the input. Note that a potentially malicious user will not gain an advantage by creating multiple accounts or posing as multiple users, as he will still be restricted to submitting input belonging to the evaluation category. Finally, the issue of model extraction is also mitigated by the restriction to authorized test inputs. Concretely, our solution prevents efficient model extraction attacks relying on input specifically crafted to optimize extraction. We note, however, that any input-output pair of an AI model will theoretically leak some information about the model, but this leakage is unavoidable if users are allowed to observe/verify any input/output at all.

Lastly, we provide a generic construction of function-hiding homomorphic signatures based on a non-interactive zero-knowledge proof system and a signature scheme. We provide a carefully chosen instantiation and measure the performance of this. The details regarding this are discussed in the construction overview in Sect. 2.

To summarize, the contribution of this paper is a follows.

- As the first attempt to resolve the problem of testing the quality of (a possibly malicious) AIaaS, we propose a cryptographic mechanism (i.e. function-hiding homomorphic signatures) that enables the restriction of inputs to an AI model to a flexible pre-specified category.
- We provide a generic construction of a function-hiding homomorphic signature scheme from a non-interactive zero-knowledge proof system and a signature scheme.
- We carefully chose a pairing-based instantiation of our generic construction, implemented a proof of concept, and conducted experiments to measure the efficiency of the construction.

1.3 Related Work

To the best of our knowledge, we are the first to provide a cryptographic solution to the evaluation problem for AIaaS. While we are not aware of any other works that consider a similar setting in connection with AIaaS, there are several prior works focused on proving authenticity of an edited image ([7,8,17,21,25]). Specifically, these works aim to show in zero-knowledge that a given image was obtained by an allowable transformation of a (hidden) original image which has been authenticated via a signature (e.g. a trusted module inside a camera might sign all images taken). PhotoProof [25] used proof-carrying data [6] to achieve this goal and supports repeatedly applying transformations to already transformed images with corresponding proofs. However, the PhotoProof construction comes with the inherent limitation of a weak proof-of-knowledge guarantee that prevents adaptively chosen inputs (see [25] Section IV-C). This makes the scheme unsuitable for our application in which images can be authenticated after system setup. ZK-IMG [17] used a different approach based on succinct zero-knowledge non-interactive arguments of knowledge (zk-SNARKs) and commitments to the original and intermediate images. This was improved by Datta, Chen, and Boneh [7] by using lattice-based hash functions to reduce the cost of proving knowledge of a preimage of a hash function, which in turn is needed to prove knowledge of a signature on a hidden original image. Li et al. [21] improved efficiency for local transformations (e.g. hiding a person's face in an image) by dividing the original image into tiles, while Monica et al. ([8]) expanded Li et al.'s idea to global transformations. However, ZK-IMG and all of the follow-up works do not hide the transformation being applied to the image. This is a crucial difference to our work in which the transformation is required to remain hidden to obscure the relation to the (public) original images.

Our main technical contribution, function-hiding homomorphic signatures, is related to the existing works on homomorphic signatures. This line of research was initiated by Johnson et al. [16], and while many of the early works only supported a very restricted class of evaluations, Gorbunov, Vaikuntanathan, and Wichs [11] proposed the first *fully* homomorphic signature scheme from standard lattice assumptions. Note that in a standard homomorphic signature scheme, a message/signature pair is verified with respect to a function, and successful verification guarantees that the message was obtained by evaluating the function on an unknown signed message. In contrast, our new notion of function-hiding homomorphic signatures additionally hides the evaluation function but guarantees that the function is drawn from a restricted class of functions.

Lastly, our approach is related to computation on authenticated data [3,5]. This is likewise based on restricted homomorphic signatures, and guarantees that the output is obtained by combining authenticated input data via evaluation of a restricted functionality. However, employing the approach of [3,5] in our setting would require employing a tag for each original image, which in turn would reveal the original image being transformed.

2 Technical Overview

In this section, we provide a technical overview of our construction.

Technical Difficulties. To illustrate the difficulties in constructing a suitable solution, we first discuss a naive construction, which is neither secure nor efficient. However, this will serve as an easy-to-understand stepping stone toward our generic construction. In the naive construction, the evaluation authority signs each possible input in the pre-specified evaluation category. This set of input-signature pairs constitutes the information that the evaluation authority makes public. A tester chooses one of the inputs and the corresponding signature and sends this pair to the service provider. The service provider verifies the signature and thereby convinces itself that the input belongs to the pre-specified category.

This naive construction does not meet our stated goal. Specifically, because the service provider can learn all possible test inputs, it is trivial for the provider to maliciously construct a model that has a good performance on the pre-specified inputs but might perform poorly in general.

To prevent this, one might attempt to make the pre-specified evaluation category consist of so many diverse inputs that a good performance on these test inputs would imply a good general performance. While this would make the construction inefficient as each input would have to be signed and made public, it is furthermore not fully addressing the problem as long as it is feasible for the malicious service provider to process all possible test inputs.

Input Diversity via Transformations. To improve efficiency, we let the evaluation authority sign a small number of inputs and let a tester transform one of the inputs signed by the evaluation authority. In this way, the number of the possible inputs that the service provider may receive is large, i.e., the number of the signed inputs times the number of the possible transformations.

Still, a tester should not be allowed to transform the inputs arbitrarily. Firstly, the signed inputs should be chosen to represent a diverse selection from the input space. Then the set of allowed transformations should be chosen such that the "meaning" of the original input remains the same. In this way, the possible inputs after transformations are restricted to variants of the original inputs, which prevent a malicious tester from injecting his own input (i.e. being a free-rider) and mounting a model extraction attack (due to the restricted set of inputs). Simultaneously, there are many different inputs (i.e. variants) that will be used for testing. However, it is crucial that the expressiveness of the transformations should make it hard for a malicious service provider to train an AI model that only guarantees good performance on the pre-specified inputs while not guaranteeing a good performance in general. We note that the appropriate selection of inputs and possible transformations is application specific and striking the right balance between diversity and the potential for model extraction attacks is a non-trivial research topic. In this paper, our main focus is on the cryptographic mechanism that will enable this kind of AI model testing.

To make our approach concrete, we consider the example of image inputs and transformations corresponding to affine image transformations. This type of transformations includes parallel transformations, rotations, distortions, etc. and captures many possible variations. However, at the same time, the image subject is not changed, which will prevent model extraction techniques such as combining images of different inputs.

Another example of inputs and transformations could be prompts in generative AI based on LLMs (e.g. like ChatGPT [26]). Here, users input a prompt (sentences) to an AI model and obtains a reply. Our approach to AI model testing could likewise be employed for these systems. Namely, an evaluation authority could provide a set of prompts which demonstrates the performance of the AI model as well as a set of transformations that provides semantic diversity of the prompts while still not allowing a user to freely specify the input. We envision that transformations of this type can be implemented by techniques of natural language processing but defer to future work investigating the possibility of realizing inputs and transformations for generative AI (see Sect. 7.2).

(Function-Hiding) Homomorphic Signatures. Our core contribution is a cryptographic mechanism that allows the above described authentication of a set of inputs and their transformations. Specifically, this is a type of homomorphic signatures. In the following, we quickly review homomorphic signatures.

In homomorphic signatures, a signer can sign a message x. Later, an evaluator can modify the signature on x to a signature on $y = f(x)$. A verifier can verify the modified signature with respect to the message y and the function f i.e. verify that the signature is obtained from a signature on some unknown x and known f.

In our context, x is an original input which the evaluation authority signs and f is a transformation which a tester applies to x. With this, the verifier (the service provider) can convince itself that the input $y = f(x)$ comes from one of the inputs signed by the evaluation authority with an allowed transformation f applied to x.

A subtle difference in the security requirements of standard homomorphic signatures and of our setting is that we need to hide f from the verifier (the service provider). If the service provider knows f, the service provider can invert f and learn the original input before the transformation. Since the number of the original inputs is small, a malicious service provider might construct a model that only works reliably for these, and when an input is received, simply invert the transformation and use the maliciously trained AI model to classify the input. Thereby the malicious service provider mislead the tester into believing that the service provider has an AI model that correctly classifies all variants of the inputs even though this might not be the case.

Formalization and Construction. We formalize our variant of homomorphic signatures as *function-hiding homomorphic signatures*. While the syntax is almost the same as that of homomorphic signatures, there are three security requirements: Signature unforgeability, proof unforgeability, and privacy.[2] Signature unforgeability is simply the unforgeability of signatures before evaluations and proof unforgeability is the unforgeability of signatures after evaluations. Privacy requires that the original message x and the function f are not leaked from a signature after an evaluation.

While signature unforgeability and privacy are relatively straightforward, proof unforgeability is tricky to define. In a straightforward candidate definition, the winning condition of the security game is *not efficiently checkable*, which we elaborate on below. As in the standard unforgeability game, in the candidate definition, an adversary is allowed to issue signing queries and obtain many message-signature pairs. Then the adversary outputs a forged after-evaluation signature τ^* on y^*. The issue is that, since our primitive hides the function f^* from which an after-evaluation signature is obtained, the verification of τ^* is with

---

[2] We use the name "proof unforgeability" due to our main use case of this primitive where the signer is the evaluation authority and the evaluator is the tester who sends a "proof" of a correct transformation to the verifier, i.e., the service provider.

respect to only y^* but not with respect to y^* and a function f^*. If verification were with respect to y^* and f^*, the winning condition would be that

for all queried x, it holds that $y^* \neq f^*(x)$,

to forbid a trivial forgery of querying the signing oracle with some x, transforming the before-evaluation signature with f^*, and obtaining an after-evaluation signature on $y^* = f^*(x)$. However, since verification is with respect to y^*, the winning condition is that

for all queries x and for all possible f, it holds that $y^* \neq f(x)$,

to forbid the same strategy above of making a trivial forgery. Because the number of the possible f's is large and exponential in general, the experiment cannot check $y^* \neq f(x)$ for all the f.

To avoid this inefficient winning condition, we define proof unforgeability to require an efficient *extractor* which extracts an original message x^*, a signature σ^* on it, and a function f^* from an adversary's forgery (y^*, τ^*). With this extractor, the winning condition is that one of the followings holds:

- The extracted x^* is not queried;
- the extracted f^* is not an allowable transformation;
- it does not hold that $y^* = f^*(x^*)$; or,
- the message-signature pair (x^*, σ^*) is not valid.

If all the conditions do not hold, we can say that the extractor succeeded in tracking the origin of the forgery, which means that the adversary's output is a trivial forgery. If some of the conditions hold, we can say the extractor fails to track the origin, which we define as winning of the adversary.

Finally, we briefly explain our construction. In our generic construction, a before-evaluation signature is a standard digital signature σ on a message x. To evaluate this signature σ, an evaluator generates a non-interactive zero-knowledge proof proving knowledge of a message-signature-function triple (x, σ, f) satisfying that $y = f(x)$ and that σ is a valid digital signature on x. If the non-interactive proof is extractable, we can extract the origin of the transformed signature and then can achieve the extractability-based definition of proof unforgeability.

Instantiation and Proof of Concept Implementation. We provide a construction of function-hiding homomorphic signatures using a non-interactive zero-knowledge proof system and a signature scheme. As highlighted in the works by Datta, Chen, and Boneh [7], a typical bottleneck in proving knowledge of a signature on an image is having to deal with a hash function in the signature verification in the zero-knowledge proof system. While the above works reduced this cost by using a lattice-based hash function, we choose to use structure-preserving cryptography [1]. Structure-preserving cryptography allows us to prove knowledge of a signature on a message efficiently without dealing with a hash function. This way we eliminate the need to deal with a hash function in our construction.

More concretely, we first prove the security of our construction in a generic manner, assuming the building blocks are secure. Then, to instantiate our scheme, we made a careful choice of building blocks, i.e., a non-interactive zero-knowledge proof system and a signature scheme. Specifically, to avoid the above discussed potentially large cost of proving signature-related statements in zero-knowledge, we use the Groth-Sahai proof system [14] and a structure-preserving signature scheme [1]. This choice reduces the complexity of our instantiation.

We furthermore implemented our proposed instantiation as a proof of concept. The purpose of our implementation is to clarify whether our construction can, with reasonable efficiency, generate and verify a proof. As our construction involves complex statements to be proven, this might not be immediately clear. Conducting experiments, we found that, while there is room for improvement, our construction can generate and verify a proof within a reasonable amount of time. More concretely, our implementation can authorize a 28×28 image in 13.62 s with a corresponding verification time of 47.58 s. For a 32×32 image, authorization takes 18.22 s and verification takes 63.48 s. However, we stress that our implementation is merely an unoptimized proof of concept.

3 Preliminaries

A non-interactive proof system for an NP relation R consists of the following algorithms.

- ZK.Setup(1^k) → crs. The setup algorithm takes as input a security parameter 1^k and outputs a CRS crs.
- ZK.Prove(crs, x, w) → π. The proving algorithm takes as input a CRS crs, a statement x, and a witness w and outputs a proof π.
- ZK.Verify(crs, x, π) → 0 or 1. The verification algorithm takes as input a CRS crs, a statement x, and a proof π and outputs a bit 0 or 1.
- ZK.ExtSetup(1^k) → (crs, xk). The extractable setup algorithm takes as input a security parameter 1^k and outputs a CRS crs and an extraction trapdoor xk.
- ZK.Extract(crs, xk, x, π) → w. The extraction algorithm takes as input a CRS crs, an extraction trapdoor xk, a statement x, and a proof π and outputs a witness w.
- ZK.SimSetup(1^k) → (crs, zk). The simulatable setup algorithm takes as input a security parameter 1^k and outputs a CRS crs and a simulation trapdoor zk.
- ZK.Simulate(crs, zk, x) → π. The simulation algorithm takes as input a CRS crs, a simulation trapdoor zk, and a statement x, and outputs a proof π.

We say that (ZK.Setup, ZK.Prove, ZK.Verify, ZK.ExtSetup, ZK.Extract, ZK.SimSetup, ZK.Simulate) is a non-interactive proof system for relation R, if for all $k \in \mathbb{N}$, all crs ← ZK.Setup(1^k), all $(x, w) \in R$, and all π ← ZK.Prove(crs, x, w), it holds that ZK.Verify(crs, x, π) = 1.

We require a non-interactive proof system to be zero-knowledge and extractable. The definitions are found in [13].

4 Function-Hiding Homomorphic Signatures

In this section, we define the cryptographic primitive of function-hiding homomorphic signatures.

As mentioned in the introduction, function-hiding homomorphic signatures hide the function used to homomorphically derive a new signature. This property is formalized as privacy (Definition 3). This definition requires the existence of a simulator that simulates a homomorphically derived signature without knowing the original message x, a signature σ on it, and the function f but with using the after-evaluation message $f(x)$. The secrecy of the function is formalized by not providing f to the simulator, which ensures that the evaluated signature does not include the knowledge of the function f.

In contrast to this, the context-hiding notion for (standard) homomorphic signatures is not intended to hide the function f. In this context-hiding notion, the simulator takes as input a (description of) function f. This means that a homomorphically derived signature may include knowledge of the function f.

4.1 Syntax

We define the syntax and security definitions of function-hiding homomorphic signatures. A function-hiding homomorphic signature scheme for the function class $\mathcal{F}$ with domain $\mathcal{X}$ and range $\mathcal{Y}$ consists of the following algorithms.

- HS.Setup(1^k) $\to$ pp. The setup algorithm takes as input a security parameter 1^k and outputs a public parameter pp.
- HS.Kg(pp) $\to$ (vk, sk). The key generation algorithm takes as input a public parameter pp and outputs a pair (vk, sk) of a verification key and a signing key.
- HS.Sign(pp, vk, sk, x) $\to \sigma$. The signing algorithm takes as input a public parameter pp, a verification key vk, a signing key sk, and a message $x \in \mathcal{X}$ and outputs a signature σ.
- HS.VerifyS(pp, vk, x, σ) $\to$ 0 or 1. The signature verification algorithm takes as input a public parameter pp, a verification key vk, a message x, and a signature σ and outputs a bit 0 or 1.
- HS.Evaluate(pp, vk, x, σ, f) $\to (y, \tau)$. The evaluation algorithm takes as input a public parameter pp, a verification key vk, a message x, a signature σ, and a transformation $f \in \mathcal{F}$ and outputs a transformed message y and a proof τ.
- HS.VerifyP(pp, vk, y, τ) $\to$ 0 or 1. The proof verification algorithm takes as input a public parameter pp, a verification key vk, a transformed message $y \in \mathcal{Y}$, and a proof τ and outputs a bit 0 or 1.

We say that (HS.Setup, HS.Kg, HS.Sign, HS.VerifyS, HS.Evaluate, HS.VerifyP) is a function-hiding homomorphic signature scheme, if for all $k \in \mathbb{N}$, all pp $\leftarrow$ HS.Setup(1^k), all (vk, sk) $\leftarrow$ HS.Kg(pp), all $x \in \mathcal{X}$, all $\sigma \leftarrow$ HS.Sign(pp, vk, sk, x), all $f \in \mathcal{F}$, and all $(y, \tau) \leftarrow$ HS.Evaluate(pp, vk, x, σ, f), it holds that HS.VerifyS(pp, vk, x, σ) = 1 and HS.VerifyP(pp, vk, y, τ) = 1.

4.2 Security Notions

We require a function-hiding homomorphic signature scheme to be signature unforgeable, proof unforgeable, and private.

Definition 1. *We say that a function-hiding homomorphic signature scheme* (HS.Setup, HS.Kg, HS.Sign, HS.VerifyS, HS.Evaluate, HS.VerifyP) *is signature unforgeable if for all probabilistic polynomial-time adversaries* $\mathcal{A}$,

$$\Pr\begin{bmatrix} \mathsf{pp} \leftarrow \mathsf{HS.Setup}(1^k); (\mathsf{vk}, \mathsf{sk}) \leftarrow \mathsf{HS.Kg}(\mathsf{pp}); \\ (x^*, \sigma^*) \leftarrow \mathcal{A}^{\mathsf{HS.Sign}(\mathsf{pp},\mathsf{vk},\mathsf{sk},\cdot)}(\mathsf{pp}, \mathsf{vk}) \\ : \mathsf{HS.VerifyS}(\mathsf{pp}, \mathsf{vk}, x^*, \sigma^*) = 1 \wedge x^* \notin Q \end{bmatrix}$$

is negligible in k *where* Q *is the set of the queries that* $\mathcal{A}$ *issued during the execution.*

Definition 2. *We say that a function-hiding homomorphic signature scheme* (HS.Setup, HS.Kg, HS.Sign, HS.VerifyS, HS.Evaluate, HS.VerifyP) *is proof unforgeable if (1) there exists probabilistic polynomial-time algorithm* HS.ExtSetup *satisfying that for all probabilistic polynomial-time adversaries* $\mathcal{A}$

$$\left| \Pr\begin{bmatrix} b \leftarrow \{0,1\}; \mathsf{pp}_0 \leftarrow \mathsf{HS.Setup}(1^k); \\ (\mathsf{vk}_0, \mathsf{sk}_0) \leftarrow \mathsf{HS.Kg}(\mathsf{pp}_0); (\mathsf{pp}_1, \mathsf{vk}_1, \mathsf{sk}_1, \mathsf{xk}) \leftarrow \mathsf{HS.ExtSetup}(1^k); \\ b' \leftarrow \mathcal{A}(\mathsf{pp}_b, \mathsf{vk}_b, \mathsf{sk}_b) : b = b' \end{bmatrix} - \frac{1}{2} \right|$$

is negligible in k *and (2) for all probabilistic polynomial-time adversaries* $\mathcal{A}$, *there exists probabilistic polynomial-time algorithm* HS.Extract *satisfying that*

$$\Pr\begin{bmatrix} (\mathsf{pp}, \mathsf{vk}, \mathsf{sk}, \mathsf{xk}) \leftarrow \mathsf{HS.ExtSetup}(1^k); \\ \mathsf{rand} \leftarrow \{0,1\}^{\mathrm{poly}(k)}; \\ (y^*, \tau^*) \leftarrow \mathcal{A}^{\mathsf{HS.Sign}(\mathsf{pp},\mathsf{vk},\mathsf{sk},\cdot)}(\mathsf{pp}, \mathsf{vk}; \mathsf{rand}); \\ (x^*, \sigma^*, f^*) \leftarrow \mathsf{HS.Extract}(\mathsf{pp}, \mathsf{vk}, \mathsf{sk}, \mathsf{xk}, \mathsf{rand}, y^*, \tau^*) \\ : \mathsf{HS.VerifyP}(\mathsf{pp}, \mathsf{vk}, y^*, \tau^*) = 1 \\ \wedge (x^* \notin Q \vee f^* \notin \mathcal{F} \vee y^* \neq f^*(x^*) \vee \mathsf{HS.VerifyS}(\mathsf{pp}, \mathsf{vk}, x^*, \sigma^*) \neq 1) \end{bmatrix}$$

is negligible in k *where* Q *is the set of the queries that* $\mathcal{A}$ *issued during the execution.*

Definition 3. *We say that a function-hiding homomorphic signature scheme* (HS.Setup, HS.Kg, HS.Sign, HS.VerifyS, HS.Evaluate, HS.VerifyP) *is private if there exist probabilistic polynomial-time algorithms* HS.SimSetup *and* HS.Simulate *satisfying that for all probabilistic polynomial-time adversaries* $\mathcal{A}$,

$$\left| \Pr\begin{bmatrix} b \leftarrow \{0,1\}; \mathsf{pp}_0 \leftarrow \mathsf{HS.Setup}(1^k); \\ (\mathsf{pp}_1, \mathsf{zk}) \leftarrow \mathsf{HS.SimSetup}(1^k); (\mathsf{vk}, \mathsf{sk}) \leftarrow \mathsf{HS.Kg}(\mathsf{pp}_b); \\ b' \leftarrow \mathcal{A}^{\mathcal{O}}(\mathsf{pp}_b, \mathsf{vk}, \mathsf{sk}) \\ : b = b' \end{bmatrix} - \frac{1}{2} \right|$$

is negligible in k *where* $\mathcal{O}$ *takes as a query* (x, σ, f) *and returns* $\perp$ *if* $\mathsf{HS.VerifyS}(\mathsf{pp}_b, \mathsf{vk}, x, \sigma) = 0$, $x \notin \mathcal{X}$, *or* $f \notin \mathcal{F}$, *returns* $\tau_0 \leftarrow \mathsf{HS.Evaluate}(\mathsf{pp}_0, \mathsf{vk}, x, \sigma, f)$ *if the three checks pass and* $b = 0$, *and returns* $\tau_1 \leftarrow \mathsf{HS.Simulate}(\mathsf{pp}_1, \mathsf{zk}, \mathsf{vk}, f(x))$ *if the three checks pass and* $b = 1$.

5 Construction from Non-Interactive Zero-Knowledge

In this section, we present a construction of function-hiding homomorphic signatures from a non-interactive zero-knowledge proof system (ZK.Setup, ZK.Prove, ZK.Verify, ZK.ExtSetup, ZK.Extract, ZK.SimSetup, ZK.Simulate) and a signature scheme (Sig.Kg, Sig.Sign, Sig.Verify) (whose definition is found in [10]). We use a non-interactive zero-knowledge proof system for the following NP relation R:

$$(\langle \mathsf{vk}, y \rangle, \langle x, \sigma, f \rangle) \in R$$
$$\iff x \in \mathcal{X} \land f \in \mathcal{F} \land y = f(x) \land \mathsf{Sig.Verify}(\mathsf{vk}, x, \sigma) = 1 \quad (1)$$

The construction is as follows.

- HS.Setup(1^k). Choose crs $\leftarrow$ ZK.Setup(1^k) and sets pp $\leftarrow$ crs. Output pp.
- HS.Kg(pp). Choose (vk, sk) $\leftarrow$ Sig.Kg(1^k) and output (vk, sk).
- HS.Sign(pp, vk, sk, x). Generate $\sigma \leftarrow$ Sig.Sign(vk, sk, x) and output σ.
- HS.VerifyS(pp, vk, x, σ). Output Sig.Verify(vk, x, σ).
- HS.Evaluate(pp, vk, x, σ, f). Compute $y = f(x)$ and set $x = \langle \mathsf{vk}, y \rangle$ and $w = \langle x, \sigma, f \rangle$. Compute $\pi \leftarrow$ ZK.Prove(crs, x, w). Output (y, π).
- HS.VerifyP(pp, vk, y, τ). Set $x = \langle \mathsf{vk}, y \rangle$ and output ZK.Verify(crs, x, τ).

We can prove the security of this construction. The full proofs are deferred to the full version, due to the page limitation.

Theorem 1. *The construction is signature unforgeable if the underlying signature scheme is unforgeable.*

Theorem 2. *The construction is proof unforgeable if the underlying signature scheme is unforgeable and the underlying non-interactive proof system is extractable.*

Theorem 3. *The construction is private if the underlying non-interactive proof system is zero-knowledge.*

The signature unforgeability follows from the unforgeability of the signature scheme. To see the proof unforgeability, we use the extractor of the proof system to extract a witness $\langle x^*, \sigma^*, f^* \rangle$, which should satisfy Eq. (1). Thus, the winning condition $x^* \notin Q \lor f^* \notin \mathcal{F} \lor y^* \neq f^*(x^*) \lor \mathsf{HS.VerifyS}(\mathsf{pp}, \mathsf{vk}, x^*, \sigma^*) \neq 1$ implies that $x^* \notin Q$, which means that (x^*, σ^*) is a forgery against the signature scheme. The privacy follows from the zero-knowledge property of the proof system.

6 Evaluating AIaaS Using Function-Hiding Homomorphic Signatures

In this section, we outline how our function-hiding homomorphic signatures can be used to test an AI model held by an AIaaS provider.

6.1 Functionality

Setup. To set up the system, a trusted entity runs the setup algorithm HS.Setup to obtain public parameters pp and the key generation algorithm HS.Kg to obtain a verification-signing key pair (vk, sk). The trusted entity then makes (pp, vk) public and delivers the signing key to an evaluation authority responsible for authorizing test inputs (the trusted entity could potentially also play the role of the evaluation authority in which case he will just keep the signing key secret). The evaluation authority then specifies a test category by deciding the original inputs $(x_1, \ldots x_n)$ which will be transformed into test inputs. To authorize these original inputs, for each input x_i, the evaluation authority generates a signature $\sigma_i \leftarrow$ HS.Sign(pp, vk, sk, x_i). Finally, the evaluation authority makes the $\{(x_i, \sigma_i)\}_{i=1,\ldots,n}$ values public.

Test Input Generation. To test an AI model, a tester randomly transforms one of the inputs authorized by the evaluation authority. To do this, the tester randomly chooses one of the original inputs (x_i, σ_i) and one of the allowed transformations $f \in \mathcal{F}$, and transforms the input to obtain $(y, \tau) \leftarrow$ HS.Evaluate(pp, vk, x_i, σ_i, f), where τ is a signature on the transformed input $y = f(x)$. Finally, the tester sends (y, τ) to the AIaaS service provider.

Test Input Verification. Upon receiving (y, τ), the service provider confirms that the input y is a transformation of one of the authorized inputs by the evaluation authority. To do this, the service provider simply verifies the signature by running HS.VerifyP(pp, vk, y, τ). By verifying the signature, the service provider can confirm that the input sent by the tester is a transformation of one of the authorized inputs. Once confirmed, the service provider runs the AI model on the input sent by the tester and sends back the output of the AI model.

Output Evaluation. When receiving the output of the AI model, the tester confirms the output of the AI model corresponds to the expected output. In the image classification case, the transformation might be chosen such that they do not change the output of the AI model, in which case the tester simply confirms that the output is identical to the classification of the original image. More generally, we can assume that a tester, given an original input and a transformation, can determine whether the output of the AI model is acceptable. This allows the tester to confirm that the AI model behaves as expected and thereby confirm the quality of the AI model.

6.2 Security Considerations

It should be clear from the above description that the privacy of the function-hiding homomorphic signature will guarantee that the AIaaS provider learns no information about the test input beyond that this belongs to the set of authorized test input. Furthermore, the unforgeability and proof unforgeability of the function-hiding homomorphic signature scheme imply that a potentially malicious tester will not be able to convince an honest AIaaS service provider to provide the AI model output for an input not authorized by the evaluation authority.

However, as highlighted in the introduction, the basic premise of this approach to AIaaS evaluation is that the transformed input are sufficiently diverse to guarantee that a good performance on these will imply a high quality AI model and that constructing an AI model for the transformed inputs is essentially as hard as constructing a good general model. To determine an appropriate set of inputs and allowed transformations requires an in-depth analysis of the concrete AI model in question, and while this is an important aspect to recognize, we consider this slightly out of scope for this paper, which is focused on the cryptographic aspect of the problem.

We note that it is possible to cryptographically hide the transformed input from the service provider by using an appropriate multiparty computation (MPC) protocol for the classification (e.g. [24]). This can somewhat mitigate a weaker set of transformations that could potentially allow a malicious service provider to exploit the relation between the original and transformed input. It should be noted though that our proposed setup will reveal the test input space, as the set of original inputs and possible transformations will be known to the service provider. However, by choosing a sufficiently diverse input space, the cost of building a high quality AI for this should ideally approach the cost of building a full-fledged model, in which case a service provider will arguably lose the incentive to maliciously construct his AI model.

Another approach to mitigating a weaker set of inputs and transformations can be letting the evaluation authority issue new authorized inputs dynamically and regularly. This can dissuade a service provider from constructing an AI model for a specific test set (possibly "overfitting" an AI model to this set) because such an overfitted model will not perform well on newer inputs. We note that this requires adaptively authorizing inputs after the public parameters are set up.

Finally, in the above scenario, we assume the service provider responds to a user's queries by applying a (possibly inadequate) AI model in his possession. We note that it is possible to cryptographically ensure that the service provider consistently applies the same model by requiring the service provider to provide a commitment to the AI model and a proof that the classification was obtained by using the AI model that was committed to [4,9,20,22,27].

6.3 Towards Practical Deployments

Integration into Existing AIaaS Services. Our mechanism can be integrated into an existing AIaaS system by relatively simple modifications. That is, our mechanism simply requires trial users to submit proofs of correct test input generation and the AIaaS provider to respond only to queries with a valid proof. An alternative to the AIaaS provider checking the (in)validity of the proofs by himself, would be to introduce a security gateway between trial users and the AIaaS service provider which performs this task. Note though that unlike standard AIaaS, we do require a third-party authority to provide the initial set of pre-specified test input.

Role of Evaluation Authority. We envision that the evaluation authority could be implemented in various ways. For example, the role of this authority can be played by a standardization body, or a consortium among AIaaS companies.

Collusion Between the Evaluation Authority and Users. While the evaluation authority can potentially collude with users (to publicize inputs that correlate with the users' interests), the fact that the test inputs will be made public discourages the authority from doing this. Specifically, once the test inputs are made public, anyone can examine the input, and potentially detect suspicious choices indicating collusion. Furthermore, if multiple entities play the role of the evaluation authority, agreement upon the chosen input will make it more difficult for a malicious actor to inject maliciously chosen test inputs.

Table 1. Evaluation Result

Input Size	Signing Time (s)	Verification Time (s)	Signature Size (KB)
2×2	0.089	0.335	3.23
4×4	0.297	1.09	4.54
8×8	1.12	3.98	7.17
16×16	4.41	15.67	12.4
32×32	18.22	63.48	22.9
64×64	70.51	248.1	43.9
128×128	284.6	986.2	85.9
256×256	1140.6	4051.1	169.9
512×512	5063.0	17491.4	337.9

7 Implementation and Evaluation

To evaluate the performance of our function-hiding homomorphic signature scheme, we implemented it in Rust.

7.1 Implementation Details and Results

Our scheme is constructed by using a non-interactive zero-knowledge proof system and a signature scheme described in Sect. 5. In our implementation, we used the following specific schemes. First, we used the Groth-Sahai proof system as a non-interactive zero-knowledge proof system [14] and its Rust library.[3] Second, as a signature scheme, we used a structure-preserving signature scheme in bilinear groups [2]. Both schemes were implemented on the BLS12-381 curve.

---

[3] https://github.com/jdwhite48/groth-sahai-rs.

We chose these instantiations in order to make the cost of signature verification in a zero-knowledge proof smaller. Proving the validity of a signature in a zero-knowledge proof is a potential bottleneck. In particular, to prove knowledge of a preimage of a hash function incurs a large computational cost. To avoid this, we employed structure-preserving signatures [1] and the Groth-Sahai proof system [14]. This enables us to prove signature-related statements (like knowledge of a valid signature on some message) without dealing with hash functions in the zero-knowledge proof system. This choice significantly reduced the complexity of our implementation.

Next, we describe the class of functions used in the implementation. Our research aims to verify the performance of AI services, such as image recognition services. Therefore, in this implementation, we used a two-dimensional matrix as a message, such as images, and a linear transformation as a transformation f. We used the following equations to generate a proof of such a transformation. Let an input image be a $(2^w \times 2^h)$-pixel image and the color of each pixel be $p[x, y]$ and let an output image be a $(2^W \times 2^H)$-pixel image and the color of each pixel be $P[X, Y]$. For each $(X, Y) \in \{0, \ldots, 2^W - 1\} \times \{0, \ldots, 2^H - 1\}$,

$$\begin{pmatrix} x[X,Y] \\ y[X,Y] \end{pmatrix} = \begin{pmatrix} T_{1.1} & T_{1.2} \\ T_{2.1} & T_{2.2} \end{pmatrix} \begin{pmatrix} X \\ Y \end{pmatrix} + \begin{pmatrix} c_1 \\ c_2 \end{pmatrix},$$
$$P[X, Y] = p[x[X, Y], y[X, Y]].$$

This relationship indicates that the point $(x[X, Y], y[X, Y])$ is moved to (X, Y) and that the colors of the source and destination points are the same.

Table 1 shows the performance of our implementation, and these experiments were performed on Windows 11, 12th Gen Intel Core i3-12100 3.30 GHz, 32GB RAM. In the experiment, for each size of an image, we chose a single image and ran our algorithm on this image. We expect that the running times of the algorithms do not vary depending on the image content, but only depend on the size of the image. For this reason, we did not change the image content for each size. For the image size 32×32, which is the same as the images in CIFAR-10 [18], signature generation took 18.22 s and signature verification took 63.48 s. For the image size 28×28, which is the same as the image of MNIST [19], signature generation took 13.62 s and signature generation took 47.58 s.

Multiple homomorphic signature schemes and image authentication schemes have been proposed in the literature (see Sect. 1.3). However, as these do not fulfill our security requirement of hiding the transformation function or only achieve a weaker level of unforgeability (proof-of-knowledge property), an efficiency comparison with these is arguably less interesting, and we do not provide one here.

7.2 Discussions of Our Implementation

On the Efficiency of Our Implementation. We note that our implementation might not be sufficiently efficient for some practical applications. However, we emphasize that our implementation is an unoptimized proof of concept and that better performance is likely to be achieved by an optimized implementation. Furthermore, while we leave this as an open problem, we envision that efficiency gains can be achieved via structural improvements in terms of the used signature and NIZK and how these are combined to prove the applied transformation is valid. In particular, we note that making different instantiation choices will provide trade-offs between different efficiency metrics. For example, we could use a zk-SNARK (e.g., Groth's zk-SNARKs [12]) instead of the Groth-Sahai proof system. A zk-SNARK has very efficient verification, which would yield efficient verification of a transformed signature in our scheme and would furthermore provide compact proofs. However, a drawback of using a zk-SNARK is the need for dealing with the computation required for signature verification, which must be converted into appropriate arithmetic circuits, and prover time is furthermore likely to increase.

On Implementing a Full AIaaS System. For an efficiency comparison, it is sufficient to implement the cryptographic algorithms that will be required for testing an AI model. Our proposal entails letting the evaluation authority, service provider, and tester run the appropriate algorithms from our function-hiding homomorphic signature scheme, i.e., the HS.Setup, HS.Sign, HS.Evaluate, and HS.VerifyP algorithms. The classification of the AIaaS is orthogonal to this and, from an efficiency standpoint, will not be affected by our scheme. For this reason, we did not implement a full AIaaS system.

On the Types of Images. To evaluate the efficiency of our scheme, it is sufficient to conduct an experiment for a single image i.e. it is not needed to conduct experiments for various image dataset. This is because the type of image (e.g. images of physical objects, handwritten digits, etc.) does not affect the running time of the proof generation and verification. Specifically, in our instantiation, the proof captures general geometric transformations and only the image size will affect the running time. Hence, we simply conducted experiments for images of varying sizes.

Beyond Image Transformations. While in our experiment, we only considered image transformations, we can extend our approach to support other types of inputs and transformations. For example, we could consider text transformations, which transform a set of texts into semantically close ones. Such semantic transformations can be implemented by exploiting semantic embeddings which capture the semantic meaning of an input as a vector. Combining these with function-hiding homomorphic signatures that ensure closeness of vectors, and thereby semantic meaning, would then allow a user to transform a given text. Note that this requires users to be able to compute the semantic embeddings corresponding to a chosen text. Concretely, these transformations can be implemented as above using the Groth-Sahai proof system to show the closeness of two vectors.

Acknowledgments. The authors would like to thank the anonymous referees for their valuable comments and helpful suggestions. This work was partially supported by JST CREST Grant Number JPMJCR22M1.

References

1. Abe, M., Fuchsbauer, G., Groth, J., Haralambiev, K., Ohkubo, M.: Structure-preserving signatures and commitments to group elements. J. Cryptol. **29**(2), 363–421 (2015). https://doi.org/10.1007/s00145-014-9196-7
2. Abe, M., Groth, J., Haralambiev, K., Ohkubo, M.: Optimal structure-preserving signatures in asymmetric bilinear groups. In: Rogaway, P. (ed.) CRYPTO 2011. LNCS, vol. 6841, pp. 649–666. Springer, Heidelberg (2011). https://doi.org/10.1007/978-3-642-22792-9_37
3. Ahn, J.H., Boneh, D., Camenisch, J., Hohenberger, S., Shelat, A., Waters, B.: Computing on authenticated data. In: Cramer, R. (ed.) TCC 2012. LNCS, vol. 7194, pp. 1–20. Springer, Heidelberg (2012). https://doi.org/10.1007/978-3-642-28914-9_1
4. Attrapadung, N., et al.: Privacy-preserving verifiable CNNs. In: Pöpper, C., Batina, L. (eds.) ACNS 2024, Part II. LNCS, vol. 14584, pp. 373–402. Springer, Cham (2024). https://doi.org/10.1007/978-3-031-54773-7_15
5. Attrapadung, N., Libert, B., Peters, T.: Computing on authenticated data: New privacy definitions and constructions. In: Wang, X., Sako, K. (eds.) ASIACRYPT 2012. LNCS, vol. 7658, pp. 367–385. Springer, Heidelberg (2012). https://doi.org/10.1007/978-3-642-34961-4_23
6. Chiesa, A., Tromer, E.: Proof-carrying data and hearsay arguments from signature cards. In: Yao, A.C.C. (ed.) ICS 2010, pp. 310–331. Tsinghua University Press (2010)
7. Datta, T., Chen, B., Boneh, D.: VerITAS: verifying image transformations at scale. In: 2025 IEEE Symposium on Security and Privacy (SP), pp. 97–97. IEEE Computer Society, Los Alamitos, CA, USA (2025). https://doi.org/10.1109/SP61157.2025.00097
8. Della Monica, P., Visconti, I., Vitaletti, A., Zecchini, M.: Trust nobody: privacy-preserving proofs for edited photos with your laptop. In: 2025 IEEE Symposium on Security and Privacy (SP), pp. 14–14. IEEE Computer Society, Los Alamitos, CA, USA (2025). https://doi.org/10.1109/SP61157.2025.00014
9. Feng, B., Qin, L., Zhang, Z., Ding, Y., Chu, S.: ZEN: An optimizing compiler for verifiable, zero-knowledge neural network inferences. Cryptology ePrint Archive, Report 2021/087 (2021). https://eprint.iacr.org/2021/087
10. Goldwasser, S., Micali, S., Rivest, R.L.: A digital signature scheme secure against adaptive chosen-message attacks. SIAM J. Comput. **17**(2), 281–308 (1988)
11. Gorbunov, S., Vaikuntanathan, V., Wichs, D.: Leveled fully homomorphic signatures from standard lattices. In: Servedio, R.A., Rubinfeld, R. (eds.) 47th ACM STOC, pp. 469–477. ACM Press (2015). https://doi.org/10.1145/2746539.2746576
12. Groth, J.: On the size of pairing-based non-interactive arguments. In: Fischlin, M., Coron, J.S. (eds.) EUROCRYPT 2016, Part II. LNCS, vol. 9666, pp. 305–326. Springer, Heidelberg (2016). https://doi.org/10.1007/978-3-662-49896-5_11
13. Groth, J., Ostrovsky, R., Sahai, A.: New techniques for noninteractive zero-knowledge. J. ACM **59**(3), 1–35 (2012)
14. Groth, J., Sahai, A.: Efficient noninteractive proof systems for bilinear groups. SIAM J. Comput. **41**(5), 1193–1232 (2012)
15. He, Z., Zhang, T., Lee, R.B.: Model inversion attacks against collaborative inference. In: Balenson, D. (ed.) ACM ACSAC 19, pp. 148–162. ACM Press (2022). https://doi.org/10.1145/3548606.3559393

16. Johnson, R., Molnar, D., Song, D.X., Wagner, D.: Homomorphic signature schemes. In: Preneel, B. (ed.) CT-RSA 2002. LNCS, vol. 2271, pp. 244–262. Springer, Berlin, Heidelberg (2002). https://doi.org/10.1007/3-540-45760-7_17
17. Kang, D., Hashimoto, T., Stoica, I., Sun, Y.: ZK-IMG: attested images via zero-knowledge proofs to fight disinformation. arXiv:2211.04775 (Nov 2022)
18. Krizhevsky, A.: The CIFAR-10 dataset. https://www.cs.toronto.edu/~kriz/cifar.html
19. LeCun, Y., Cortes, C., Burges, C.J.C.: The MNIST database of handwritten digits. http://yann.lecun.com/exdb/mnist/
20. Lee, S., Ko, H., Kim, J., Oh, H.: VCNN: verifiable convolutional neural network based on ZK-Snarks. IEEE Trans. Dependable Secure Comput. **21**(4), 4254–4270 (2024)
21. Li, K.H., Hsu, C.F., Chang, M.C., Liu, F.H., Chien, S.Y., Chen, W.C.: Region-aware photo assurance system for image authentication. In: MIPR 2023, pp. 1–6. IEEE Computer Society Press (2023). https://doi.org/10.1109/MIPR59079.2023.00037
22. Liu, T., Xie, X., Zhang, Y.: zkCNN: zero knowledge proofs for convolutional neural network predictions and accuracy. In: Vigna, G., Shi, E. (eds.) ACM CCS 2021, pp. 2968–2985. ACM Press (2021). https://doi.org/10.1145/3460120.3485379
23. Milli, S., Schmidt, L., Dragan, A.D., Hardt, M.: Model reconstruction from model explanations. In: Proceedings of the Conference on Fairness, Accountability, and Transparency, pp. 1–9. Association for Computing Machinery, New York, NY, USA (2019)
24. Mohassel, P., Zhang, Y.: SecureML: a system for scalable privacy-preserving machine learning. In: 2017 IEEE Symposium on Security and Privacy, pp. 19–38. IEEE Computer Society Press (2017). https://doi.org/10.1109/SP.2017.12
25. Naveh, A., Tromer, E.: PhotoProof: cryptographic image authentication for any set of permissible transformations. In: 2016 IEEE Symposium on Security and Privacy, pp. 255–271. IEEE Computer Society Press (2016). https://doi.org/10.1109/SP.2016.23
26. OpenAI: ChatGPT (2024). https://openai.com/chatgpt/
27. Weng, J., Weng, J., Tang, G., Yang, A., Li, M., Liu, J.N.: PVCNN: privacy-preserving and verifiable convolutional neural network testing. IEEE Trans. Inf. Forensics Secur. **18**, 2218–2233 (2023)

PriSM: A Privacy-Friendly Support Vector Machine

Michele Barbato, Alberto Ceselli, Sabrina De Capitani di Vimercati, Sara Foresti, and Pierangela Samarati

Università degli Studi di Milano, 20133 Milano, Italy
{michele.barbato,alberto.ceselli,sabrina.decapitani,sara.foresti,
pierangela.samarati}@unimi.it

Abstract. Today's society is witnessing not only an evergrowing dependency on data, but also an increasingly pervasiveness of related analytics and machine learning applications. From business to leisure, the availability of services providing answers to questions brings great benefits in diverse domains. On the other side of the coin, the need to provide input data that the services need to compute a response. However, some data may be considered sensitive or confidential and users would legitimately be reluctant to release them to third parties.

Considering classification tasks in machine learning applications, we introduce our PriSM (Privacy-friendly Support vector Machine) approach for computing a privacy-friendly model. PriSM anticipates the training phase of the classifier with a phase for discovering correlations among attributes that can indirectly expose sensitive information. It then trains the classifier excluding from consideration not only sensitive attributes but also other sets of attributes that have been learned as correlated to them. The result is a privacy-friendly classifier that does not require any of such information as input from the users. Our experimental evaluation on both synthetic and real-world datasets confirms the effectiveness of PriSM in protecting privacy while maintaining classification accuracy.

Keywords: PriSM · privacy-friendly classifier · sensitive attribute · sensitive correlation

1 Introduction

In machine learning, data classification is a method where a model tries to predict the correct label of a given input data. The model learns to predict labels during a *training* phase, where a statistical relationship between attribute values and labels is identified by analyzing a large number of samples with known attributes and labels. After training the model (classifier) for *prediction*, with the attribute values of a user as input the model generates a corresponding label as output. Clearly, the more the data available the more accurate the classification, and a data-hungry approach would try to employ all available attributes for classification, which in turn will require users of the classifier application to provide input for all such attributes.

In this paper, we consider the problem of building, from a training dataset, a classifier that can be made available to third parties and that end users can use for classifying their data. In this context, some attributes may be considered sensitive (or company-confidential for business application scenarios) and users of the application would not be willing to disclose them, hence a privacy-friendly classifier should not assume their availability and therefore sensitive attributes should also not be used in the training phase so that classification does not depend on them. As a motivating example, consider a medical center that has information about patients and aims at releasing a classifier that people can use at home to have suggestions on suitable physical activities to improve their fitness. The classifier is not run by the medical center but offered through an external provider. The set of attributes in the medical dataset includes various information about the patients. While some of the attributes are not considered sensitive (e.g., age), others are to be considered sensitive (e.g., a disease) and their values should remain confidential to the provider (i.e., the classifier should not require them). If the classification model does not depend on an attribute (e.g., either because it is irrelevant or because it has been artificially excluded), the corresponding value is not required for performing the prediction on the label. Note that, excluding sensitive information from the training process not only enables producing a classifier that does not require it for prediction but also ensures that the model released to the external provider does not leak sensitive information from the training data. A naive approach to enforce such protection would be to simply discard sensitive attributes from the dataset before training and hence ignore them all throughout. However, such an approach would still be exposed to improper sensitive information leakage through data dependencies and correlations. As a matter of fact, values of the sensitive attributes may be indirectly leaked by other attributes that - individually or in combination - can convey information on sensitive attributes. For instance, a disease (sensitive attribute) may be indirectly exposed by the values of medicine prescriptions (the cure) or by a combination of values of some physical parameters. While some data dependencies, such as the ones just mentioned, may be known, others may be hidden in the data and a truly privacy-friendly approach should ensure protection even with respect to them (in fact, the external provider servicing the application to the user can employ a classification process at their side as well).

Our approach, called PriSM (for Privacy-friendly Support vector Machine), addresses this problem by excluding from the training process sensitive attributes as well as attributes that may leak information on them. More precisely, PriSM first learns correlations of other attributes in the dataset with sensitive attributes. It then restricts the training process forcing the classifier to exclude from consideration not only the sensitive attributes but also sets of attributes that can leak them. It does so while, at the same time, minimizing the effect of such protection on the correctness of the classification. Even more, PriSM accounts for the fact that what can be considered sensitive are, in some cases,

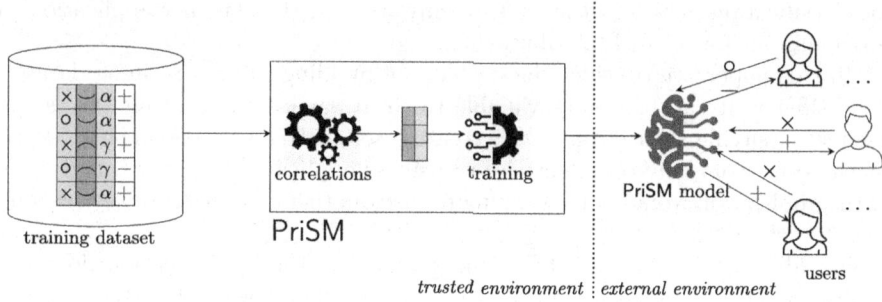

Fig. 1. Reference scenario

only specific values. For instance, while a disease like flu may be considered non problematic, values of other rarer or discriminatory diseases need strong protection. In learning correlations for attributes for which only some values are critical, we specifically address correlations with respect to such critical values so to find those correlations that are problematic (in contrast to any correlation). This notwithstanding the fact that the sensitive attribute is to be excluded in its entirety in training the classifier.

Figure 1 illustrates the overall scenario of our approach. The training phase is performed within the trusted environment under the data owner control, and hence with visibility of the whole dataset. The result is a classifier to be released to an external environment and made available to users. Users can input their data and receive a response as predicted by the classifier.

The remainder of the paper is organized as follows. Section 2 presents the main concepts and the formulation of the problem introducing our PriSM approach to compute a privacy-friendly classifier. Sections 3 and 4 describe the two phases of PriSM, discovering correlations among attributes in the dataset and then training the classifier to exclude from consideration sensitive attributes as well as other sets of attributes that have been learned as correlated to them. Section 5 presents our experimental evaluation confirming the effectiveness of PriSM in protecting privacy while minimizing the impact on the quality of the classification. Section 6 discusses related works. Finally, Sect. 7 presents our conclusions. Appendix A reports theorems proving the correctness of PriSM.

2 PriSM

For concreteness, we assume a support vector machine as a classifier. We note, however, that our approach can be extended to more general classification problems and to other data analytics tasks (e.g., regression tasks). Also, we assume a single sensitive attribute (which can be sensitive in its entirety or for which only some values may be defined as critical), and a binary classification problem, that is, the classification (*label*) attribute has domain in $\{+1, -1\}$.

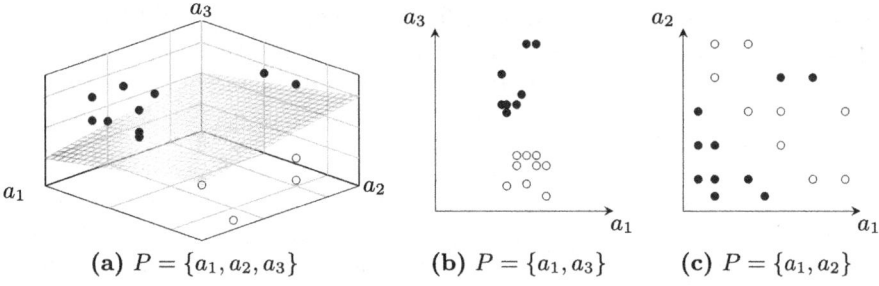

Fig. 2. An example of linear classifier in a 3-dimensional space (a) and of the projection of points in the 3D space over two bi-dimensional spaces (b)-(c)

The training dataset is modeled as a relational table r defined over schema $R(A, s, l)$, where $A = \{a_1, \ldots, a_n\}$ is a set of attributes other than the sensitive attribute s and the label attribute l. Training a classifier on r for predicting l means learning from the tuples in r how the value of l can be predicted based on the values of the other attributes in a tuple (i.e., learning the relationships between the values of the attributes in $R \setminus \{l\}$ and known labels in a training dataset). Assuming to represent the projection of tuples in r over $R \setminus \{l\}$ as points in a $|R \setminus \{l\}|$-dimensional space, the training phase of a support vector machine classifier finds a hyperplane that well separates the points with positive ($+1$) from the points with negative (-1) label, corresponding to the two classes. The predicted label will depend on the side of the hyperplane where the point representing the user's data falls in the multi-dimensional space. For instance, Fig. 2(a) illustrates a hyperplane in a 3-dimensional space that well separates positive (filled circles) from negative (empty circles) points.

Our goal is to ensure the classifier to be *privacy-friendly*, and perform predictions based only on a subset P of attributes in $R\setminus\{l\}$ that does not include the sensitive attribute nor other attributes that can leak its values (or those values specified as critical for it).

PriSM works in two phases: the first phase identifies sensitive correlations of other attributes with the sensitive attribute; the second phase trains the classifier in a controlled way to restrict the choice of predictor attributes so that privacy is respected, while minimizing the impact on the quality of the classifier. More precisely, the first phase of PriSM learns from the training dataset the correlations among the other attributes A and the sensitive attribute s, meaning the sets of attributes that can well predict the sensitive attribute (we will elaborate more on this in Sect. 3). We note that if a set X of attributes is correlated with s, denoted $X \leadsto s$, so it is clearly any set $Y \supset X$. Also, blocking an inference channel from X to s, forbidding the classifier to use all the attributes in X as predictor attributes, trivially blocks the inference channel from any $Y \supset X$ to s. We are therefore interested in the identification of a set of minimal sensitive correlations for r, as formally captured by the following definition.

Definition 1 (Set of minimal sensitive correlations). *Let $R(A, s, l)$ be a relation schema, with s the sensitive attribute and l the label attribute. The set of minimal sensitive correlations for s is a set $\mathcal{X}$ of subsets of A such that: 1) $\forall X \in \mathcal{X} : X \rightsquigarrow s$; 2) $\forall X_i \rightsquigarrow s : \exists X_j \in \mathcal{X}$ s.t. $X_j \subseteq X_i$; 3) $\forall X_i, X_j \in \mathcal{X}, i \neq j$: $X_i \not\subseteq X_j$ and $X_j \not\subseteq X_i$.*

In the definition, the first two conditions ensure that $\mathcal{X}$ includes only existing correlations (Condition 1) and that all correlations are captured (Condition 2). Condition 3 ensures that only minimal correlations are explicitly represented. Besides correlations learned from the training dataset, $\mathcal{X}$ can also include additional (minimal) correlations specified by the data owner [8]. Given a set of minimal sensitive correlations for a relation R, a classifier is said to be privacy-friendly if the set of attributes used for classification does not include the sensitive attribute s nor (in its entirety) any set X of attributes correlated to it. This concept is formally captured by the following definition of privacy-friendly classifier.

Definition 2 (Privacy-friendly classifier). *Let $R(A, s, l)$ be a relation schema, with s the sensitive attribute and l the label attribute. A classifier C for l using as predictor attributes a set $P \subseteq R \setminus \{l\}$ of attributes is* privacy-friendly *iff: $s \notin P$ and $\forall X \subseteq P, X \not\rightsquigarrow s$.*

In other words, a classifier is privacy-friendly if the set P of attributes that it uses as predictor attributes does not include any set in $\mathcal{X}$ (formally, $\forall X \in \mathcal{X}$: $X \not\subseteq P$). Note that for a set X of attributes not to be included in P it is sufficient to exclude one (any) of its attributes. In fact, while on one hand excluding more attributes can clearly increase privacy (the less the data, the less the potential inference on the sensitive attribute) on the other hand removing more attributes than needed (e.g., at the extreme, all the attributes involved in a correlation) can affect severely the ability of the classifier to predict the value of the label attribute, destroying any utility of the classifier. Since the set of correlations is minimal, such an aggressive exclusion is not needed, as ensuring exclusion of one attribute for each of the correlations would have the same effect. Additionally, the same attribute can solve more than one correlation.

Clearly, there can be different choices for a set of predictors that satisfy Definition 2, each with a different impact on the quality of the classifier, with the usual dichotomy between privacy and utility. The challenge is to find a set P of attributes that ensures privacy while minimizing the effect on the prediction quality of the classifier. As an example, consider Fig. 2(a), where $X=\{a_1,a_2,a_3\}$ is a sensitive correlation. If the set of selected predictor attributes is $P=\{a_1,a_3\}$ (Fig. 2(b)), it is possible to find a linear classifier that well separates the positive (filled circles) from the negative (empty circles) points. By contrast, using $P=\{a_1,a_2\}$ (Fig. 2(c)) would imply a higher misclassification since the positive and negative points are not linearly separable.

Capturing the impact on the quality of a classifier C in terms of misclassification [16], denoted $\epsilon(C)$, our problem is formalized as follows.

Problem 1 *Given a training dataset r defined over relation schema $R(A, s, l)$, with s the sensitive attribute and l the label attribute, find a classifier C that is privacy-friendly (Definition 2) and that minimizes misclassification. That is, there is no classifier C' satisfying Definition 2 such that $\epsilon(C') \leq \epsilon(C)$.*

PriSM solves the problem in two phases, first learning from the training dataset the set of minimal correlations representing inference channels to the sensitive attribute (Sect. 3), and then performing training of the classifier controlling and restricting the choice of the set of predictor attributes (Sect. 4).

3 Sensitive Correlations Discovery

The first phase of our approach aims at learning sensitive correlations from the training dataset, that is, correlations that may leak (critical) values of the sensitive attribute. More formally, the first phase aims to find the set $\mathcal{X} = \{X_1, \ldots, X_n\}$ of all minimal sensitive correlations $X_i \leadsto s$, $i = 1, \ldots, n$. In the following, we first discuss how to determine whether, for a given set $X \subseteq A$ of attributes, $X \leadsto s$ holds (Sect. 3.1), and then how to identify the set of candidates X against which a correlation needs to be evaluated (Sect. 3.2).

3.1 Assessing Correlations

A set X of attributes is correlated with s if X is a good predictor for the values of s. Intuitively, correlation between X and s can be evaluated running a classifier (i.e., treating s as the label) and comparing some metrics on the classifier result with a threshold value τ (reflecting the accuracy of the prediction). Correlation exists whenever the metrics evaluates above the threshold.

As already mentioned, our approach for discovering such correlations also accounts for situations in which only specific values of the sensitive attribute are considered critical. Notwithstanding the fact that the sensitive attribute is to be discarded in its entirety in training (and prediction), considering those values that are critical (if not all are) for s in discovering correlations enables to be more precise in spotting those correlations that lead to a critical value, and not just any value of the sensitive attribute. The identification of correlations for the case where not all values of the sensitive attribute are critical deserves some considerations. In particular, a question to solve is whether correlations should be identified considering the set of critical values as a whole (single encoding) or considering each critical value individually (multiple encoding). Intuitively, considering the critical values of the sensitive attribute as a whole equates to consider a binary label λ for s, with $\lambda = +1$ for all tuples t such that $t[s]$ is critical; $\lambda = -1$, otherwise. This enables to detect the set of attributes that are correlated to the whole set of critical values. By contrast, considering the different sensitive values separately implies considering a binary label λ_v for each critical value v with $\lambda_v = +1$ for all tuples t such that $t[s] = v$; $\lambda_v = -1$, otherwise. We note that neither of the two approaches subsumes the other since each of them

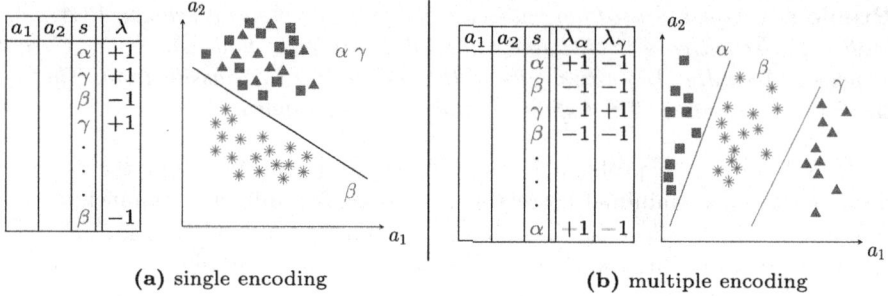

Fig. 3. An example of two datasets with single (a) or multiple encoding (b) together with their multidimensional representation

can discover sensitive correlations that would go undetected from the other. To illustrate, consider two datasets where $A=\{a_1,a_2\}$ and, among the values of the sensitive attribute, only α and γ are critical. Figure 3 illustrates the tuples in these two datasets as points in a bi-dimensional space where the dimensions correspond to a_1 and a_2. In the bi-dimensional space, α and γ are denoted with a red square (for α) and a red triangle (for γ) while a green star denotes any other value. Suppose that we aim at discovering whether there is a correlation between $X=\{a_1,a_2\}$ and the sensitive attribute s. For the first dataset, the critical values taken all together are linearly separable from the non-critical ones, while each critical value singularly taken is not linearly separable from all the other values (critical or not critical). Therefore, single encoding finds the correlation between values in X and s while multiple encoding would not. On the contrary, for the second dataset, the critical values taken all together are not linearly separable from the non-critical ones, while each critical value singularly taken is linearly separable from all the other values (critical or not critical). Therefore, multiple encoding finds the correlation between values in X and s while single encoding would not.

We further note that, while in principle correlations can be learned by running a classifier (e.g., training an SVM having non-zero value only for the coefficients of the hyperplane of the attributes in the set X to be evaluated), this would be quite computationally intensive. We use instead correlation coefficients [16] as a proxy for such evaluation. The specific correlation coefficient, or combination of them, that can perform better may depend on the specific dataset. In preliminary experiments we compared many options, finding Pearson's correlation coefficient and Cramer's V test of statistical independence to be a good choice in general.

3.2 Finding Potential Candidates

To identify the candidate sets of attributes against which correlations need to be evaluated, we leverage the natural monotonicity of sensitive correlations similarly to Apriori strategy for frequent itemset mining [1], that is, if $X \leadsto s$, then $X' \leadsto s$ $\forall X' \subset R$ such that $X' \supset X$. We do so by performing different iterations over

INPUT   dataset r on $R(A,s,l)$
           sensitive attribute s (and critical values)
           maximum cardinality of the set of predictor attributes $pmax$
           threshold correlation τ
OUTPUT set $\mathcal{X}$ of minimal sensitive correlations for s

MAIN
1: $\mathcal{X} := \emptyset$
2: $c := 0$
3: **repeat**
4:    $c := c + 1$
5:    **if** $c = 1$
6:    **then** let $\mathcal{Y}_1$ be the set of all sets $\{a\}$ s.t. $a \in A$
7:    **else** let $\mathcal{Y}_c$ be the set of all sets Y with $|Y| = c$
       s.t. $Y = \bigcup_i X_i \in Q$, with $Q \subseteq \mathcal{Y}_{c-1}$, $|Q| = c$
8:    **for each** $Y \in \mathcal{Y}_c$ **do**
9:      **if** correlation(Y,s)$\geq \tau$ /* correlation with single and/or multiple encoding */
10:      **then** $\mathcal{Y}_c := \mathcal{Y}_c \setminus \{Y\}$
11:         $\mathcal{X} := \mathcal{X} \cup \{Y\}$
12: **until** $c = pmax$ OR $|\mathcal{Y}_c| \leq c$

Fig. 4. Procedure computing sensitive correlations

variable c corresponding to the cardinality of X (e.g., $c = 1$ for evaluating individual attributes at the first iteration), with each iteration determining the set $\mathcal{Y}_c$ of candidates of cardinality c. Differently from Apriori, which generates candidates for iteration c by joining pairs of sets from iteration $c - 1$ that have the first $c - 2$ attributes in common, our algorithm considers as candidates for iteration c only those sets produced by the union of c sets from iteration $c - 1$. For instance, assume at the end of iteration 2, $\mathcal{Y}_2$ to include $\{a_i, a_j\}$ and $\{a_i, a_z\}$, but not $\{a_j, a_z\}$, joining the two sets would produce as candidate to consider $\{a_i, a_j, a_z\}$. However, such a set cannot belong to $\mathcal{X}$, since one of its subsets already does and $\mathcal{X}$ is a minimal set (Definition 1). In fact, $\{a_j, a_z\} \notin \mathcal{Y}_2$ implies that at least one between $\{a_j\} \in \mathcal{X}$ and $\{a_z\} \in \mathcal{X}$ holds. Our construction avoids producing such candidates that would then be discarded for minimality, ensuring to produce all and only candidates that are not a superset of sets already included in $\mathcal{X}$ in a previous iteration (see Theorem 2 in the Appendix). The algorithm assumes also a limit $pmax$ on the number of attributes in candidate sensitive correlations, corresponding to the maximum number of predictor attributes used by PriSM (see Sect. 4). The reason for such a limit is both efficiency, to limit the iterations, as well as supporting a principle of *parsimony* for the number of attributes to be used as predictors and hence requested as input to the users of the application (clearly $pmax = |A|$ implies no limitation).

Figure 4 illustrates the procedure for computing the set of sensitive correlations. Starting from the set $\mathcal{Y}_1$ of candidate correlations including one attribute only (line 6), for each Y in $\mathcal{Y}_1$, the algorithm verifies if $Y \leadsto s$ holds and, if this is the case, it removes Y from $\mathcal{Y}_1$ inserting Y into $\mathcal{X}$ (lines 9–11). After evaluating all the singleton sets, $\mathcal{Y}_1$ will include only those attributes a such that $\{a\} \not\leadsto s$. The algorithm then checks all the pairs in $\mathcal{Y}_2$ composed of attributes in $\mathcal{Y}_1$, because for any other pair X of attributes there exists an attribute $a \in X$ that has been removed from $\mathcal{Y}_1$ (and included in $\mathcal{X}$), therefore X does not need to be inserted into $\mathcal{X}$. The algorithm evaluates candidate sets Y of increasing size c. For each value of c, the check is limited to the candidate correlations Y including c attributes, obtained as the union of c sets in $\mathcal{Y}_{c-1}$ (line 7). This restricts $\mathcal{Y}_c$ to the sets Y such that all the subsets of Y of cardinality $c-1$ belong to $\mathcal{Y}_{c-1}$. Indeed, if at least a subset X of Y does not appear in $\mathcal{Y}_{c-1}$, it means that a correlation $X \leadsto s$ dominating $Y \leadsto s$ has already been learned by the algorithm. The algorithm stops when c reaches $pmax$ attributes (larger correlations would for sure not be exposed by a classifier using at most $pmax$ predictors), or when the candidate set of correlations including c attributes has less than $c+1$ subsets of attributes (any set of $c+1$ attributes would not have all its subsets of c attributes in $\mathcal{Y}_c$, hence $\mathcal{Y}_{c+1}$ would be empty).

The output of the first phase is then the set $\mathcal{X}$ of minimal correlations among attributes A in the dataset and the sensitive attribute. Note that this phase does not enforce any choice (or removal) of attributes from the classifier. It is for the second phase (next section) to determine the optimal set of attributes that does not include in its entirety any set in $\mathcal{X}$ and optimizes label prediction.

4 Classifier Training

The second phase of our approach consists in simultaneously selecting the set of attributes and training a classifier, thus solving Problem 1. While the problem applies to a general classification task, and the first phase (Sect. 3) is agnostic with respect to the classifier, the execution of this second phase depends on the classifier to be considered. As already noted in the previous sections, we consider classification with a Support Vector Machine (SVM).

We then design a variant of SVM that controls and restricts predictor attributes selection. In the following, we use boldface for denoting vectors. Similarly to classical SVMs, each tuple t in the training dataset r is modeled as a point in a multi-dimensional space, having a dimension for each attribute in $R \setminus \{l\}$. The classification model is geometrically represented as a hyperplane $\mathcal{H}$ in the multidimensional space. Training a SVM then corresponds to learn the coefficients $\mathbf{w} \in \mathbb{R}^{|R|-1}$ and $b \in \mathbb{R}$ of a hyperplane $\mathcal{H} = \{\mathbf{t} \in \mathbb{R}^{|R|-1} : \mathbf{w} \cdot \mathbf{t} = b\}$, with $\mathbf{t}$ being the vector of values of tuple $t[R \setminus \{l\}] \in r$. The hyperplane must separate well (i.e., place on different sides) points with positive ($t[l] = +1$) and negative ($t[l] = -1$) label in the training dataset. Each coefficient $\mathbf{w}[a]$, with $a \in R \setminus \{l\}$, used in the definition of $\mathcal{H}$ represents the slope of the hyperplane in the dimension that corresponds to attribute a. Since finding a hyperplane that separates positive from negative points might not always be possible (e.g., when the positive and negative classes are not linearly separable), our training phase relies on soft margin [6]. Intuitively, it considers a misclassification penalty when maximizing the distance between the positive and negative classes.

Differently from standard SVMs, our problem has a combinatorial nature. A straightforward adaptation would require to enumerate all possible subsets of predictors, testing each of them for sensitive correlations, and solve a SVM training problem for the remaining attributes. Such an approach, having a time complexity exponential in the number of predictors, would be computationally infeasible. We solve Problem 1 by extending the classical formulation of the SVM training problem as an optimization problem, formulated as a Mixed Integer Program [27] imposing *privacy-friendliness* (the predictors cannot include the sensitive attribute nor any set correlated to it) and *parsimony* (use at most *pmax* attributes as predictors) as model constraints. Figure 5 illustrates the formalization of the optimization problem, where the parameters and variables are as follows.

$$\min \frac{1}{2}||\mathbf{w}||_2^2 + \pi \sum_{i=1}^{|r|} \mathbf{z}[t_i] \quad (1)$$

$$t_i[l](\mathbf{w} \cdot \mathbf{t}_i - b) \geq 1 - \mathbf{z}[t_i] \qquad i = 1, \ldots, |r| \quad (2)$$

$$\mathbf{z}[t_i] \geq 0 \qquad i = 1, \ldots, |r| \quad (3)$$

$$\mathbf{w}[a] \in \mathbb{R}, b \in \mathbb{R} \qquad \forall a \in R \setminus \{l\} \quad (4)$$

$$\mathbf{p}[a]\mathbf{w}^\mathbf{L}[a] \leq \mathbf{w}[a] \leq \mathbf{p}[a]\mathbf{w}^\mathbf{U}[a] \qquad \forall a \in R \setminus \{l\} \quad (5)$$

$$\sum_{a \in R \setminus \{l\}} \mathbf{p}[a] \leq pmax \quad (6)$$

$$\mathbf{p}[s] = 0 \quad (7)$$

$$\sum_{a \in X} \mathbf{p}[a] \leq |X| - 1 \qquad \forall X \in \mathcal{X} \quad (8)$$

$$\mathbf{p}[a] \in \{0, 1\} \qquad \forall a \in R \setminus \{l\} \quad (9)$$

Fig. 5. Mixed Integer Programming formulation of the PriSM training problem

- $pmax \in [1, |R|)$: input parameter representing the maximum number of predictors that can be used by the classifier.
- $\pi \in \mathbb{R}$: input parameter representing the relative penalty for misclassification errors (higher values correspond to a smaller probability of misclassification, at the price of smaller separation between positive and negative classes).
- $\mathbf{w^U} \in \mathbb{R}^{|R|-1}, \mathbf{w^L} \in \mathbb{R}^{|R|-1}$: input parameters representing the upper and lower bounds on the values of $\mathbf{w}$ for each attribute in $R \setminus \{l\}$ (which represent the maximum and minimum slope of the hyperplane allowed in the

corresponding direction). They forbid the degenerate choice of vertical hyperplanes, and improve the numerical stability of our optimization procedure (narrow bounds speed up convergence, looser ones reduce the risk of cutting off solutions that are potentially optimal [2]).

- $t_i \in \mathbb{R}^{|R|-1}, t_i[l] \in \{-1, +1\}$: input vector of values for attributes in $R \setminus \{l\}$ and label, respectively, for each tuple $t_i \in r$ in the training dataset.
- $\mathbf{p} \in \{0,1\}^{|R|-1}$: resulting binary variables modeling the selection (value 1) or exclusion (value 0) of each attribute $a \in R \setminus \{l\}$ from the set of predictors.
- $\mathbf{w} \in \mathbb{R}^{|R|-1}, b \in \mathbb{R}$: resulting coefficients of the hyperplane.
- $\mathbf{z} \in \mathbb{R}^{|r|}$: resulting misclassification error for each tuple $t \in r$.

Equation 1 is the classical soft-margin optimization function used in training SVM classifiers, and Eqs. 2–4 correspond to classical constraints of the definition of the SVM, when formulated as a Quadratic Program. The additional constraints (Eqs. 5–9), enforce instead restrictions which are specific for our PriSM problem. The semantics of the constraints is as follows.

(2) models the possible error $\mathbf{z}$ in classification using the trained classifier. More precisely, $(\mathbf{w} \cdot \mathbf{t}_i - b)$ has a positive value if the predicted label for t_i is $+1$; it has a negative value if the predicted label is -1. The product between $(\mathbf{w} \cdot \mathbf{t}_i - b)$ and the correct label $t_i[l]$ is positive if the predicted class is correct; it is negative otherwise. Therefore, $\mathbf{z}[t_i]$ is 0 if the prediction is correct (it cannot be a negative number, see (3)); it has a positive value measuring the misclassification error (i.e., the distance from the hyperplane), otherwise.
(3) limits the values of $\mathbf{z}$ to be non-negative numbers. This ensures to properly consider the penalty of misclassification in the objective function (i.e., to prevent positive and negative misclassifications that compensate each other).
(4) specifies the domain of coefficients $\mathbf{w}$ and b to be $\mathbb{R}$.
(5) constrains the values of the slope coefficient $\mathbf{w}[a]$ to be in the range $[\mathbf{w}^\mathbf{L}[a], \mathbf{w}^\mathbf{U}[a]]$ for each attribute $a \in R \setminus \{l\}$ selected as predictor (i.e., $\mathbf{p}[a]=1$); at the same time it forces $\mathbf{w}[a]=0$ when the attribute is not selected (i.e., $\mathbf{p}[a]=0$).
(5) limits the number of predictors to be at most $pmax$ by setting the sum for binary variables $\mathbf{p}[a]$, with $a \in R \setminus \{l\}$, to be lower than or equal to $pmax$.
(6) excludes the sensitive attribute from the set of predictors by setting $\mathbf{p}[s]$ to 0. Note that this also implies constraining $\mathbf{w}[s]$ to be equal to 0 (see (5)).
(7) imposes the number of attributes included in the set of predictors from each set $X \in \mathcal{X}$ to be smaller than the cardinality of X. This ensures that, for each X, at least one attribute is excluded from the set of predictors. The constraint forces the solution to have at least one of the binary variables $\mathbf{p}[a]$, with $a \in X$, set to 0 thus making their sum lower than the cardinality of X. Like for s, $\mathbf{p}[a] = 0$ implies $\mathbf{w}[a] = 0$, meaning the attribute is excluded from consideration.
(8) restricts the domain of $\mathbf{p}$ to be $\{0,1\}$ (0 being exclusion, and 1 inclusion).

Intuitively, the objective function (Eq. 1) aims at balancing two needs: *i)* maximize separation between the positive and the negative class, and *ii)* minimize misclassifications. To maximize separation between classes, the SVM maximizes the distance from the hyperplane of the nearest positive point and the nearest negative point in the training dataset. This is guaranteed by the first term in the objective function. The second term instead represents the misclassification penalty, obtained by multiplying the overall misclassification error of tuples in the training set by coefficient π. PriSM then offers a global optimality guarantee to choose a given number of predictors containing no sensitive correlations, minimizing misclassification error (see Theorem 2 in the Appendix). We note that, in general, finding effective formulations of hard problems as ours is far from trivial [2]. Our model, however, enjoys two properties that permit to keep training times under control: *i)* the number of binary variables is linear in the number of predictors, independently from the number of tuples in the dataset; *ii)* when integrality conditions on these (few) binary variables are relaxed, we obtain a convex quadratic model, which allows for effective resolution algorithms. This is confirmed by our experimental results, where training times were always of few seconds with about one minute at most on datasets with 16 attributes and more than 40,000 tuples.

5 Experimental Results

We performed a series of experiments to assess the effectiveness of PriSM in training a classifier that provides high accuracy in the prediction of the label attribute, without revealing critical values of the sensitive attribute.

5.1 Experimental Setting and Datasets

We implemented PriSM in `python3`, using the `python` API of `Gurobi 10.1` to solve the Mixed Integer Programming formulation of PriSM in Fig. 5 with a branch-and-cut algorithm [27]. We assumed correlations of at most 5 attributes each, and used as correlation coefficient the Cramer's V test with p-value 0.05 and threshold τ to either 0.02 or 0.2 (depending on the dataset). These thresholds ensure that no subset of predictors can be selected, unless it is independent from the sensitive attribute with very high probability or its association strength is statistically very low. Based on preliminary testing, we set $\mathbf{w}^U[a] = 1000$ and $\mathbf{w}^L[a] = -1000$ for all attributes in $R\setminus\{l\}$. These values are large enough for not affecting optimality while enhancing computational performance [2]. The results reported in the following have been obtained using a PC equipped with an Intel Core i5-1135G7 at 2.40 GHz and 32 GB of memory.

For assessing the effectiveness of PriSM, we considered a synthetic dataset and a real-world dataset. We generated the synthetic dataset as a stress-test of PriSM to enable us to control all the features that might affect our approach.[1] It contains 40,000 tuples and is defined over a relational schema with 15 attributes, including 13 candidate predictors defined over a ternary domain,

---

[1] https://doi.org/10.13130/RD_UNIMI/Y4LVV5.

a binary sensitive attribute, and a binary label attribute. The frequency distributions of the two values of the sensitive attribute and of the two values of the label attribute are balanced (52% and 50% occurrences of positive values, respectively) and all the attributes have an impact on the classification task. We selected, as real-world dataset, the binarized version of *Bank Marketing* dataset[2] that well represents the heterogeneity of real-world data. The dataset collects information about a marketing campaign of a Portuguese bank. It includes 45,211 tuples and is defined over a relational schema including 16 attributes (4 binary, 6 categorical, 6 numerical). The binarized version has been obtained performing a one-hot encoding on all the attributes, after proper binning of numerical attributes. We consider attribute `default`, defined over a binary domain and representing whether the customer has credits in default, as sensitive. The label is attribute `class` defined over a binary domain and indicating whether the customer subscribed a bank term deposit. The frequency distributions of the two values of the sensitive attribute and of the two values of the label are highly unbalanced (more than 98% of occurrences of the non-critical value for attribute `default`, and 88% of 0 for attribute `class`).

5.2 Results

To assess the effectiveness of our PriSM approach, we evaluated: *i)* the quality of classification results when introducing constraints to protect critical values of the sensitive attribute, and *ii)* the ability to reconstruct critical values of the sensitive attribute starting from the predictor attribute used by the classifier. To this purpose, we compared the results obtained using three classifiers:

- SVM: a classical SVM classifier (considering Constraints 2-4 in Fig. 5 and setting $\mathbf{w}[s]=0$ to exclude the sensitive attribute), which represents our baseline, to assess the impact of protecting against (direct or indirect) release of sensitive information on classification results;
- Parsimony: a parsimonious SVM classifier that limits the number of predictor attributes used by the classifier to at most *pmax* (considering Constraints 2-7 and 9 in Fig. 5), to assess the impact of the parsimony requirement on classification results;
- PriSM: our privacy-friendly classifier (considering all the constraints in Fig. 5).

Accuracy. Limiting the number of predictors and constraining the choice of the same to prevent disclosure of sensitive attributes (and of correlations that might reveal them) is expected to reduce the ability of the classifier to predict the label of data items. Figure 6 compares the accuracy of PriSM and of Parsimony with the baseline accuracy obtained using a traditional SVM (black horizontal line), varying the maximum number *pmax* of predictor attributes used by PriSM and Parsimony from 3 to 12. We did not consider values higher than 12

---

[2] https://archive.ics.uci.edu/dataset/222/bank+marketing Binarized version available at https://gitlab.tudelft.nl/jgmvanderlinde/dpf [17].

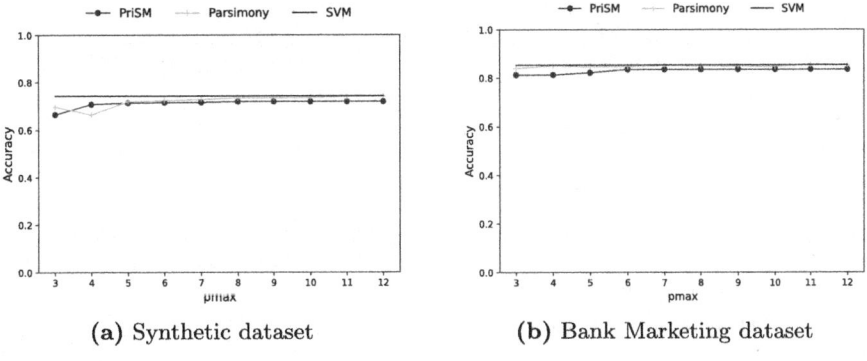

Fig. 6. Accuracy of the classifier varying $pmax$

since for higher values Parsimony produces the same solutions as SVM (parsimony requirement was not binding anymore). Also, Constraint 8 (preventing the classifier from using a set of predictors including sensitive correlations) in PriSM formulation does not permit to select more than 9 predictor attributes. In other words, setting $pmax > 9$ produces the same solution as $pmax = 9$. (Note that such a theoretical limit can be discovered computing a hitting set on the set of minimal sensitive correlations, avoiding unnecessary runs of the training phase.) As expected, the accuracy of PriSM grows with the maximum number of predictors that the classifier can use. As visible from the figure, protecting the sensitive attribute with PriSM has a limited impact on accuracy, both compared with the results of the SVM baseline and with the ones obtained by Parsimony. Indeed, allowing the classifier to use $pmax \geq 8$ predictors, PriSM loses only 2% accuracy with respect to SVM baseline (Parsimony reaches the same gap with 5 predictors) for both the synthetic and Bank Marketing datasets.

Protection. While noting that PriSM guarantees that no set of attributes with a correlation higher than τ with the sensitive attribute is used by the trained classifier, we empirically analyze the ability of an adversary to predict s based on the predictor attributes used by the classifier produced by PriSM. We then consider a worst case scenario and assume that the adversary trains a classification model for predicting the sensitive attribute values using a dataset having exactly the same distribution of values as the one used by PriSM. In our experiments, this translates in using the same training set for both PriSM and for the adversary model. For simulating the adversary predicting the sensitive attribute, we use ν-SVC (which is a reliable classification model [22]) trained with a nested cross validation, performing hyperparameters tuning in an inner loop.

Figure 7(a) compares the accuracy of PriSM, Parsimony, and SVM in predicting the sensitive attribute values of the synthetic dataset, varying $pmax$ from 3 to 12. As visible from the figure, PriSM is much more effective than SVM and Parsimony in protecting the sensitive attribute values. In fact, the accuracy of the adversary classifier remains below 58% with PriSM, while it is about 72% with the SVM. Also with Parsimony the sensitive attribute is gradually more

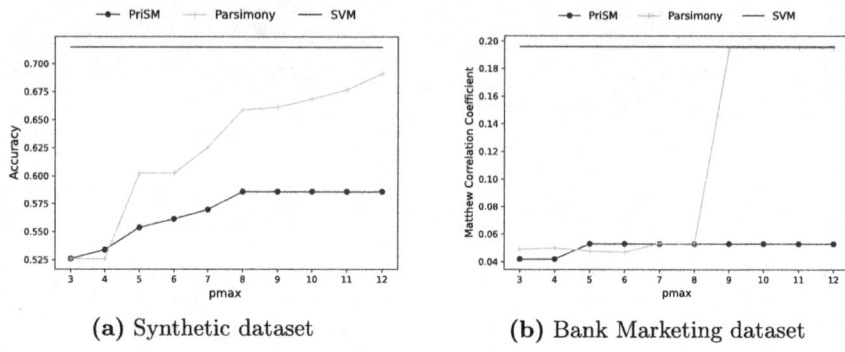

Fig. 7. Correlation with the sensitive attribute values varying $pmax$

exposed as $pmax$ increases, eventually reaching a risk similar to that of SVM. It is interesting to note that, with PriSM, the accuracy of the adversary remains close to the theoretical accuracy lower bound given by the class frequency (52% in our dataset).

Figure 7(b) compares the Matthew's Correlation Coefficient (MCC) of PriSM, Parsimony, and SVM in predicting the sensitive attribute values of the Bank Marketing dataset, varying $pmax$ from 3 to 12. We decided to use the MCC for the Bank Marketing dataset since the critical value is very unfrequent (only 2% of the tuples). Similarly to what observed on the synthetic dataset, PriSM protects well the sensitive attribute: the MCC score is stable and as low as 0.05 (against 0.20 for SVM). The behavior of Parsimony is instead peculiar: the MCC remains around 0.05 (similar to PriSM) until $pmax=8$, and suddenly worsens at $pmax=9$ reaching the MCC of the SVM. From a more in depth analysis of results, we noticed that this change is due to a strong reduction in the number of false positives, which increases the precision of the adversary model in guessing a positive data item from about 1 case over 50 (which, in practice, approaches a random guess), to about 1 case over 10. This is due to the use by Parsimony of an additional predictor that, combined with the ones already taken, implies the set of predictors to contain a sensitive correlation. Note that in our experiments this happens with $pmax = 9$, but with other training rounds and other cross validation splittings it could happen for lower values of $pmax$.

The experimental results confirm that PriSM maintains high classification accuracy, while protecting the sensitive attribute and its critical values from indirect disclosure through sensitive correlations.

6 Related Work

Several works have addressed the problem of protecting privacy of data in machine learning scenarios (e.g., [20,21,28]). Indeed, sensitive data in the training datasets can be exposed to various inference attacks that could violate data privacy (e.g., [7,11,13,15,23,29]). To block such attacks, different privacy-preserving machine learning algorithms have been proposed. Each of these solutions operates at a specific step of the machine learning process (i.e., data acquisition, training, and prediction), with the goal of guaranteeing individuals' privacy and preventing data leakage (e.g., [12]).

Privacy-preserving machine learning approaches follow two main strategies: *i)* protect the dataset (e.g., using anonymization approaches [9]) before using it for training the machine learning model; and *ii)* train the machine learning model using a privacy-preserving approach (e.g., a differentially private training [10,14]). The adoption of anonymization techniques for protecting the training set, while effective in protecting the privacy of the dataset, clearly reduces the accuracy of the machine learning model trained over it. Therefore, recent proposals have focused on the analysis of such an impact on accuracy and of the provided privacy guarantees (e.g., [4,24]). Other proposals instead addressed the problem of developing utility-aware anonymization techniques that protect data and, at the same time, preserve as much as possible utility for the data analytics working downstream (e.g., [3]). An alternative to anonymization for protecting training datasets is represented by homomorphic encryption that, together with secure multi-party computation, can be used to protect the training dataset while used to train a machine learning model (e.g., [5]). Cryptographic-based approaches, however, typically imply higher computational overhead and loss of precision [12]. The problem of protecting training datasets including confidential information requires particular attention when different parties contribute with their data to the training phase. Indeed, while aiming at collaboration, each data owner also needs to keep their dataset confidential to the other owners (e.g., [19,26]). PriSM differs from all these proposals since it does not use privacy-preserving techniques neither on the training dataset nor on the machine learning model. The focus is on protecting user's privacy during the prediction phase, ensuring that the machine learning model does not ask (directly or indirectly) any sensitive information as input to provide an accurate prediction.

Related lines of work addressed the problems of overlearning and of fair learning. Overlearning happens when a machine learning model unintentionally learns sensitive attributes (which are not even correlated with the target label) at inference time [25]. Fair learning instead is concerned with producing accurate machine learning models without learning bias like, for instance, in case of unbalance among classes (e.g., [18]). While related, these lines of work are orthogonal to the problem addressed in this paper.

7 Conclusions

We proposed an approach, PriSM, for generating a privacy-friendly classifier that requires neither sensitive information nor information correlated with it for classifying user's data. This goal is reached by first identifying sets of attributes that could (indirectly) reveal the sensitive attribute, and then training the classifier excluding the sensitive attribute as well as other sets of attributes that have been learned as correlated to it. The formulation of the problem as a Mixed Integer Programming problem guarantees protection of the sensitive attribute and misclassification minimization, keeping training times under control. The experiments, performed over both a synthetic and a real-world datasets, confirm that PriSM protects sensitive information also against inference channels due to correlated information, minimizing impact on classification accuracy. The paper leaves space for future works, including the consideration of different families of classifiers (e.g., non linear classifiers) as well as other data analytics tasks.

Acknowledgements. This work was supported in part by the EC under projects GLACIATION (101070141) and EdgeAI (101097300), by the Italian MUR under PRIN project POLAR (2022LA8XBH), and by project SERICS (PE00000014) under the MUR NRRP funded by the EU - NGEU. Project EdgeAI is supported by the Chips Joint Undertaking and its members including top-up funding by Austria, Belgium, France, Greece, Italy, Latvia, Netherlands, and Norway under grant agreement No. 101097300. Views and opinions expressed are however those of the authors only and do not necessarily reflect those of the European Union, the Chips Joint Undertaking, or the Italian MUR. Neither the European Union, nor the granting authority, nor Italian MUR can be held responsible for them.

A Minimization of the Misclassification Error

Theorem 1 (Correctness of data correlation discovery). *Given a training dataset r defined over relation schema $R(A, s, l)$, with s a sensitive attribute, a set V_S of sensitive values in the domain of s, the maximum number pmax of predictors used by the classifier, and a correlation threshold τ, the procedure in Fig. 4 finds the minimal set $\mathcal{X}$ of correlations for s.*

Proof. To prove that the procedure in Fig. 4 computes the set $\mathcal{X}$ of minimal correlations for s, we separately prove the three conditions in Definition 1. Note that we consider a monotone correlation function, that is, the correlation between Y and s is higher than or equal to the correlation between X and s, $\forall X \subseteq Y$.
Condition 1. We first prove that each set Y in $\mathcal{X}$ is a sensitive correlation. Since a set Y is inserted into $\mathcal{X}$ only if the correlation between Y and s is above the given threshold τ (lines 9–11), all the sets Y in $\mathcal{X}$ are such that $Y \rightsquigarrow s$.
Condition 2. We prove that $\mathcal{X}$ captures all the sensitive correlations, either directly or through a dominating correlation. To this purpose, we prove by induction that, at the end of the **repeat-until** loop: *i)* $\mathcal{Y}_c$ contains all the subsets of A of cardinality c that do not represent a sensitive correlation, and *ii)* $\mathcal{X}$ includes all the sensitive correlations with at most c attributes.

For $c = 1$ (base case of the induction), $\mathcal{Y}_1$ contains all the singleton sets of attributes in A that do not represent a sensitive correlation for s. Similarly, $\mathcal{X}$ contains all the singleton sets of attributes in A that represent a sensitive correlation for s. Indeed, $\mathcal{Y}_1$ is initialized to the set of all singleton sets $\{a\}$ with $a \in A$ (line 6). The procedure then checks each set Y in $\mathcal{Y}_1$ and removes it from $\mathcal{Y}_1$ (line 10) inserting it into $\mathcal{X}$ (line 11) if the correlation between Y and s is above threshold τ (line 9).

Let us now assume that the hypothesis holds for $c-1$ with $c>1$, that is: *i)* $\mathcal{Y}_{c-1}$ contains all subsets of A of cardinality $c-1$ that do not represent a sensitive correlation, and *ii)* $\mathcal{X}$ includes all the sensitive correlations with at most $c-1$ attributes. It is immediate to see that the procedure inserts into $\mathcal{X}$ only sensitive correlations including c attributes. In fact, the sets of attributes in $\mathcal{Y}_c$ include c attributes by construction (line 7) and Y is inserted into $\mathcal{X}$ only if the correlation between Y and s is above threshold τ (line 9). Similarly, at the end of the **repeat-until** loop $\mathcal{Y}_c$ contains only subsets of c attributes that do not represent a sensitive correlation for s, because each set Y in $\mathcal{Y}_c$ representing a sensitive correlation for s is removed from $\mathcal{Y}_c$ (line 10). To prove that $\mathcal{Y}_c$ contains all the subsets of interest (i.e., those subsets of A of cardinality c that do not represent a sensitive correlation), suppose, by contradiction, that there exists a set $Y \subseteq A$ of cardinality c such that all its subsets do not represent sensitive correlations, which does not belong to $\mathcal{Y}_c$ when generated at line 7. That would imply that, at the beginning of the **repeat-until** loop, it has not been possible to find c subsets of Y including $c-1$ attributes in $\mathcal{Y}_{c-1}$ (i.e., at least one of the subsets of Y of cardinality $c-1$ does not belong to $\mathcal{Y}_{c-1}$). Since, by the induction hypothesis, $\mathcal{Y}_{c-1}$ contains all the subsets of attributes of cardinality $c-1$ that do not represent sensitive correlations, the missing subset of Y would be a sensitive correlation, therefore also Y would represent a sensitive correlation, thus leading to contradiction. Similarly, to prove that $\mathcal{X}$ includes all the sensitive correlations with at most c attributes, we start from the observation that $\mathcal{X}$ includes all the sensitive correlations with at most $c-1$ attributes at the beginning of the **repeat-until** loop by hypothesis. Let us assume, by contradiction, the existence of a set Y of cardinality c that represents a sensitive correlation, which is not included in $\mathcal{X}$ at the end of the **repeat-until** loop. This means that Y either has not been inserted into $\mathcal{Y}_c$ at line 7, or it has not been removed from $\mathcal{Y}_c$ at line 10. Since Y represents a sensitive correlation, it cannot be maintained in $\mathcal{Y}_c$ since the condition at line 9 would be satisfied by Y. If Y is not inserted into $\mathcal{Y}_c$ at line 7, it means that it does not have c subsets of $c-1$ attributes each in $\mathcal{Y}_{c-1}$, that is, that do no represent a sensitive correlation. Since a set of c attributes has exactly c subsets of $c-1$ attributes, if not all these subsets belong to $\mathcal{Y}_{c-1}$, there is at least a subset of Y representing a sensitive correlation that, by induction hypothesis, already belongs to $\mathcal{X}$. Therefore, Y is already represented in $\mathcal{X}$.

Since the invariant holds for each value of c, it holds also for $c = pmax$ (and, in the worst case, for $c = |A|$), thus proving that $\mathcal{X}$ captures all the sensitive correlations.

Condition 3. We prove that $\mathcal{X}$ does not include any sensitive correlation that is a superset of another sensitive correlation in $\mathcal{X}$. The satisfaction of this condition follows by construction of sets $\mathcal{Y}_c$. As illustrated above, for Y to be included in $\mathcal{X}$, it must be generated as a candidate sensitive correlation as the union of c sets of attributes of cardinality $c-1$ that do not represent sensitive correlations (line 7). Therefore, the condition holds. □

Theorem 2. (Correctness of PriSM). *Given a training dataset r defined over relation schema $R(A, s, l)$, with s the sensitive attribute and l the label attribute,* and the minimal set $\mathcal{X}$ of sensitive correlations for s, PriSM *computes a privacy-friendly classifier that minimizes misclassification (i.e., solves Problem 1).*

Proof. Since any classifier computed as a solution to the Quadratic Programing formulation of PriSM training problem satisfies all the constraints in Fig. 5, the classifier is privacy-friendly (Definition 2). Indeed, Constraint 7 excludes the sensitive attribute s from the set of predictors, and Constraint 8 excludes from the set of predictors at least one attribute for each sensitive correlation $X \in \mathcal{X}$. In fact, Constraint 7 is satisfied only if $\mathbf{p}[s]$ is 0, and Constraint 8 is satisfied only if $\mathbf{p}[a]$ is 0 for at least one attribute a in X, for each $X \in \mathcal{X}$. Thanks to Constraint 5, if $\mathbf{p}[a]=0$ then $\mathbf{w}[a]=0$. Therefore, any solution to the Quadratic Programing problem in Fig. 5 is privacy-friendly (Definition 2).

Since the Mixed Integer Programming formulation of PriSM in Fig. 5 defines a binary variable $\mathbf{p}[a]$ for each candidate predictor attribute in $R \setminus \{l\}$, it implicitly encodes all the (combinatorially many) possible choices of subsets of $R \setminus \{l\}$ as predictors. Constraint 6 limits to at most *pmax* the number of attributes for which $\mathbf{p}[s]=1$, and then the number of predictors. Solving the problem in Fig. 5 is then equivalent to (implicitly) explore all the possible choices of predictors as subsets of $R \setminus \{l\}$ of cardinality at most *pmax*.

Relaxing integrality conditions on $\mathbf{p}$ variables, we obtain a continuous optimization problem. Such a residual optimization problem has a quadratic convex objective function (it is the sum of a linear function and a squared norm-2 term) and linear constraints. It is therefore a convex optimization problem, which can be solved to proven global optimality by means of many effective algorithms. Branch-and-bound, branch-and-cut [27] or even more effective algorithms can therefore be used to solve the problem in Fig. 5 to proven global optimality, in terms of both choice of predictors and final hyperplane. Since the objective function of the formulation of PriSM in Fig. 5 is the classical objective function of the Mixed Integer Programming formulation of the SVM problem, the solutions to the problem in Fig. 5 minimize misclassification. □

References

1. Agrawal, R., Srikant, R.: Fast algorithms for mining association rules. In: Proceedings of VLDB. Santiago, Chile (1994)
2. Barbato, M., Ceselli, A.: Mathematical programming for simultaneous feature selection and outlier detection under l1 norm. Eur. J. Oper. Res. **316**(3), 1070–1084 (2024)
3. Barezzani, S., De Capitani di Vimercati, S., Foresti, S., Ghirimoldi, V., Samarati, P.: TA_DA: Target-aware data anonymization. IEEE TP **2**, 15–26 (2025)
4. Caruccio, L., Desiato, D., Polese, G., Tortora, G., Zannone, N.: A decision-support framework for data anonymization with application to machine learning processes. Inf. Sci. **613**, 1–32 (2022)
5. Chen, C., Wei, L., Xie, J., Shi, Y.: Privacy-preserving machine learning based on cryptography: a survey. ACM TKDD **19**(4), 1–33 (2025)
6. Cortes, C., Vapnik, V.: Support-vector networks. Mach. Learn. **20**, 273–297 (1995)

7. Coscia, P., Ferrari, S., Piuri, V., Salman, A.: Synthetic and (Un)secure: evaluating generalized membership inference attacks on image data. In: Proceedings of SECRYPT. Bilbao, Spain (2025)
8. De Capitani di Vimercati, S., Foresti, S., Jajodia, S., Livraga, G., Paraboschi, S., Samarati, P.: Fragmentation in presence of data dependencies. IEEE TDSC **11**(6), 510–523 (2014)
9. De Capitani di Vimercati, S., Foresti, S., Livraga, G., Samarati, P.: k-Anonymity: from theory to applications. Trans. Data Priv. **16**(1), 25–49 (2023)
10. Demelius, L., Kern, R., Trügler, A.: Recent advances of differential privacy in centralized deep learning: a systematic survey. ACM CSUR **57**(6), 1–28 (2025)
11. Dick, T., Dwork, C., Kearns, M., Liuc, T., Roth, A., Vietri, G., Wu, Z.: Confidence-ranked reconstruction of census microdata from published statistics. PNAS **120**(8), e2218605120 (2023)
12. El Mestari, S., Lenzini, G., Demirci, H.: Preserving data privacy in machine learning systems. COSE **137**, 103605 (2024)
13. Fredrikson, M., Lantz, E., Jha, S., Lin, S., Page, D., Ristenpart, T.: Privacy in pharmacogenetics: an end-to-end case study of personalized warfarin dosing. In: Proceedings of USENIX. San Diego, CA, USA (2014)
14. Jayaraman, B., Evans, D.: Evaluating differentially private machine learning in practice. In: Proceedings of USENIX. Santa Clara, CA, USA (2019)
15. Jia, J., Gong, N.Z.: AttriGuard: a practical defense against attribute inference attacks via adversarial machine learning. In: Proceedings of the USENIX. Baltimore, MD, USA (2018)
16. Larose, D.T.: Data Mining and Predictive Analytics. Wiley (2015)
17. van der Linden, J., de Weerdt, M., Demirović, E.: Fair and optimal decision trees: a dynamic programming approach. Adv. Neural. Inf. Process. Syst. **35**, 38899–38911 (2022)
18. Mehrabi, N., Morstatter, F., Saxena, N., Lerman, K., Galstyan, A.: A survey on bias and fairness in machine learning. ACM CSUR **54**(6), 1–35 (2022)
19. Mohassel, P., Zhang, Y.: SecureML: a system for scalable privacy-preserving machine learning. In: Proceedings of IEEE S&P. San Jose, CA, USA (2017)
20. Rao, B., Zhang, J., Wu, D., Zhu, C., Sun, X., Chen, B.: Privacy inference attack and defense in centralized and federated learning: a comprehensive survey. IEEE TAI **6**(2), 333–353 (2025)
21. Rigaki, M., Garcia, S.: A survey of privacy attacks in machine learning. ACM CSUR **56**(4), 1–34 (2023)
22. Scholkopf, B., Smola, A., Williamson, R., Bartlett, P.: New support vector algorithms. Neural Comput. **12**(5), 1207–1245 (2000)
23. Shokri, R., Stronati, M., Song, C., Shmatikov, V.: Membership inference attacks against machine learning models. In: Proc. of IEEE S&P. San Jose, CA, USA (2017)
24. Slijepčević, D., Henz, M., Klausner, L., Dam, T., Kieseberg, P., Zeppelzauer, M.: k-anonymity in practice: how generalisation and suppression affect machine learning classifiers. COSE **111**, 102488 (2021)
25. Song, C., Shmatikov, V.: Overlearning reveals sensitive attributes. In: Proceedings of ICLR. virtual (2020)
26. Vaidya, J., Yu, H., Jiang, X.: Privacy-preserving SVM classification. Knowl. Inf. Syst. **14**, 161–178 (2008)

27. Wolsey, L.: Integer Programming. Wiley, Ltd (2020)
28. Xue, M., Yuan, C., Wu, H., Zhang, Y., Liu, W.: Machine learning security: threats, countermeasures, and evaluations. IEEE Access **8**, 74720–74742 (2020)
29. Zhu, L., Liu, Z., Han, S.: Deep leakage from gradients. In: Proceedings of NIPS. Vancouver, Canada (2019)

Towards Context-Aware Log Anomaly Detection Using Fine-Tuned Large Language Models

Hugo Breniaux[✉] and Djedjiga Mouheb

Department of Computer Science and Software Engineering, Université Laval,
Québec, QC, Canada
{hugo.breniaux.1,djedjiga.mouheb.1}@ulaval.ca

Abstract. With the expansion of complex IT systems, the volume of generated log data continues to escalate, intensifying the challenges of monitoring and securing these systems. Recent advances in log-based anomaly detection demonstrate effectiveness in leveraging deep learning techniques to answer these challenges. However, most approaches remain limited in their ability to extract complex relationships and understand contextual patterns from log data. In this work, we present a log-based anomaly detection approach based on fine-tuned large language models (LLMs), designed to improve context-aware and intelligent detection methods without using degrading parsing techniques or log templates. The model learns normal behaviors through self-supervised fine-tuning on normal system and network log data, aiming to complete a next log prediction task from a sequence of raw logs. The predicted log is then compared to the ground truth using cosine similarity to assess the deviation from expected behavior and identify anomalies. The experiments showcase notable results on system logs, exceeding state-of-the-art F1 scores with 0.945 on BGL, 0.926 on Thunderbird, and 0.920 on Spirit datasets. Furthermore, despite using a language model, our approach unveils promising results over network logs, mainly composed of numerical values, with an F1 score of 0.957 on NLS-KDD.

Keywords: Cybersecurity · Anomaly Detection · Log · Large Language Model · Deep Learning

1 Introduction

Defensive tools are more critical than ever as cyber threats continue to become increasingly prevalent. A substantial adoption of digital technologies has been noticed amidst recent years, increasing the exposition of data and services across the internet. According to The Strategic Counsel *Canada's Internet Factbook 2022* [7], among Canadian citizens working from home in 2022, only 37% reported that they worked remotely at least some of the time prior to the COVID-19 pandemic. This resulted in a growing volume of logging information that, combined with the lack of a common standard for both the content and the format of logs, makes anomaly detection a notably challenging task. Along with the growing reliance on digital technologies, the sophistication of malicious actors' techniques and tools is getting progressively faster over time, coercing defenders to speed up as well [22]. These enhancements lead to amplified attacks as well as subtler AI-assisted cyberattacks from threat actors relying on LLMs as assistant [14] for script generation, social engineering, and bridging knowledge gaps[1]. Based on Unit 42 *2024 and 2025 Incident Response Report* [1], these AI-assisted cyberattacks are harder to detect due to a lack of indicators and their refined efficacy and speed, resulting in a median time between compromise and exfiltration of solely one day in 2024 compared to nine days in 2022.

As the flow of complex logs multiplies and accelerates, it becomes strenuous and time-consuming to manually analyze log data in search of anomalies. These limitations led to the development of automatic analysis mechanisms, now predominantly powered by artificial intelligence algorithms. Tools comparable to LogFiT [2] leverage Pre-trained Language Models (PLMs) to effectively extract and compute features from text-based logs. These models offer notably superior feature extraction and representation methods, increasing the context understanding in the logs and overcoming limited traditional log-based anomaly detection models. This led downstream tasks to perform more efficiently, supplanting lacking methods such as log parsing [26,42]. Language models are frequently defined by their size; for example, Large Language Models (LLMs) like GPT-4 [31] are trained on more extensive resources and datasets, resulting in much larger models compared to Small Language Models (SLMs) such as BERT [9]. Thanks to their scale, LLMs unveil unprecedented and upgraded natural language processing (NLP) capabilities [46]. These models also support larger maximum sequence lengths, surpassing BERT's 512-token limit, allowing the extraction of more information in the logs. However, as most state-of-the-art anomaly detection tools use BERT to process logs, the use of LLMs in this domain is still underexplored. Only a few approaches study either LLMs in specific stages [37,45] or as the full log anomaly detection pipeline [13,33,35]. These researches explore limitations on the methods used, the prompt sensitivity, and the hallucinations of the models without deeply exploring fine-tuned LLMs in a local environment, improving security and privacy toward log anomaly detection.

In this research, we develop a log-based anomaly detection tool based on a fine-tuned LLM. The aim is to explore how LLMs can enhance the detection of anomalies, specifically in system and network logs likely to contain malicious actions compromising system security. Furthermore, the integration of LLMs is carried out without running them on distant cloud services. We first leverage an LLM by fine-tuning it on curated logs data. Later the model is integrated into our pipeline, where we can evaluate the overall performance. To the best of our knowledge, this is the first approach that uses fine-tuned local LLMs for anomaly detection. The contributions of this paper can be summarized as follows:

- We introduce an approach to detect anomalies in system and network logs, exploiting the generative capacity of a fine-tuned LLM over log data. Employing a next-log prediction task on raw logs, the pipeline avoids relying on parsing or template techniques that impact pipeline performance.

---

[1] https://www.crowdstrike.com/en-us/global-threat-report/.

– We demonstrate the potential of LLMs to effectively capture log data patterns and assist in detecting anomalies. This research leverages LLMs' reasoning, predictive, and context-aware capabilities for better understanding log data patterns in a bigger context and for finer predictions.
 – We propose a local and private pipeline using large language models to replace reliance on cloud-based inference, avoid associated operational costs, and eliminate the exchange of sensitive information to external servers.

In summary, this approach processes raw logs directly without relying on parsing or template-based methods, using a fine-tuned LLM on a next-log prediction task for enhanced context-aware analysis. Furthermore, the data and the model are handled locally, assuring better privacy and control over them. Through this approach, the results unveil strong efficacy in extracting insights from textual data with limited context while displaying narrow capabilities on numerical data from network logs. The pretrained models and datasets are available on Hugging Face[2]. Though documentation is in progress, early access is provided to support reproducibility. The data set preparation and fine-tuning code will also be released after cleanup and verification on GitHub[3].

The paper is organized as follows: we first explore existing works and their limitations in Sect. 2. Then, we define in Sect. 3 the methodology of our approach for anomaly detection using large language models. In Sect. 4, we evaluate our results and experimentation, followed by a discussion on the limitations and challenges of our approach in Sect. 5. Finally, we conclude our paper and outline potential future directions in Sect. 6.

2 Related Work

Over the years, a variety of tools have been developed to address log-based anomaly detection and improve existing capabilities. Focuses vary between obstacles like maximizing feature extraction from logs, strengthening detection models, or interpreting the results while keeping a fast and accurate process. Previous anomaly detection tools rely on traditional machine learning algorithms; however, they share limitations in terms of efficiency, adaptability, and robustness [34]. In comparison, deep learning [27] approaches have been shown to outperform conventional machine learning algorithms and their limitations [21].

Recent research [23,42] has demonstrated that traditional deep learning methods do not perform as well as the newest deep learning tools, such as Transformers [40] and their attention mechanisms. Transformers allow solving problems of computational efficiency for processing long sequences and gradient vanishing, which are the weak points of convolutional neural networks and recurrent neural networks, two traditional deep learning architectures. Furthermore, Transformers makes it possible to capture complex and ambiguous contextual

---

[2] https://huggingface.co/collections/LogAD-laval/towards-context-aware-log-anomaly-detection-esorics-2025-685da9e57e4a3810db6d1452.
[3] https://github.com/hubaval/LogAD.

relationships and is used in [12,16,20]. The emergence of such architecture has also enabled the democratization of extremely high-performance language models. Lee et al. [28] and Almodovar et al. [2] address different uses in anomaly detection of BERT, an SLM, removing the need for a parser or tackling variability issues. While BERT showcases impressive performances, it cannot be considered an LLM due to the difference in scalability and capacities of the models [46]. LLMs are pre-trained models that excel in NLP contexts, unlike SLMs, which are much more limited. A case in point demonstrating LLMs' advantages is ChatGPT[4], a chatbot previously based on GPT-4 [31] large language model that has made a big splash in recent years with its conversational and comprehension capabilities. Qi et al. [35] and Egersdoerfer et al. [13] introduce uses of ChatGPT for anomaly detection with prompt engineering methods to analyze log data, highlighting several limitations on prompt sensitivity, model hallucinations, and inference time. Song et al. [37] also use a chatbot in a multi-agent approach by breaking down the overall process. A key limitation in these approaches is the reliance on an external API used for ChatGPT. This implies that the model is run in an external facility, raising privacy and security concerns, and it can quickly get costly with numerous API calls.

Rather than using isolated LLMs, it is possible to integrate them with external tools. Pan et al. [33] focus on implementing a retrieved augmented generation (RAG) approach to overcome the LLM's constraints like token capacity, memory, and hallucinations. Importantly, all presented LLM approaches rely on could-based OpenAI's GPT models raising concerns about data control, privacy, and security. This is troubling given the sensitivity of the information involved.

3 Methodology

Through this section, we present our proposed approach to tackle the previously discussed challenges related to keeping control of data privacy and security, avoiding the use of weakening methods for data parsing, and enabling the extraction of context-aware insights from log data. We justify the motivations behind every step of our methodology and describe the architecture harnessed.

This tool utilizes a pre-trained large language model (LLM), namely Llama 3.1 [11], which has been fine-tuned using a self-supervised one-class learning approach, specifically for the next-log prediction task. By relying on normal log data for the one-class learning approach, the model is able to learn the properties and patterns that characterize normal behavior in log data. When given a context representing a sequence of normal logs, the model aims to predict the next typical log entry used to determine if the actual log entry is an anomaly. This simplicity is a deliberate design choice aimed at avoiding additional architectural complexity that could further increase resource overhead beyond that of the fine-tuned LLM. As shown in Fig. 1, the workflow comprises: (1) log data pre-processing for prompt crafting; (2) LLM fine-tuning on normal logs for domain-specific adaptation and the next log prediction task; and, (3)

---
[4] https://openai.com/chatgpt.

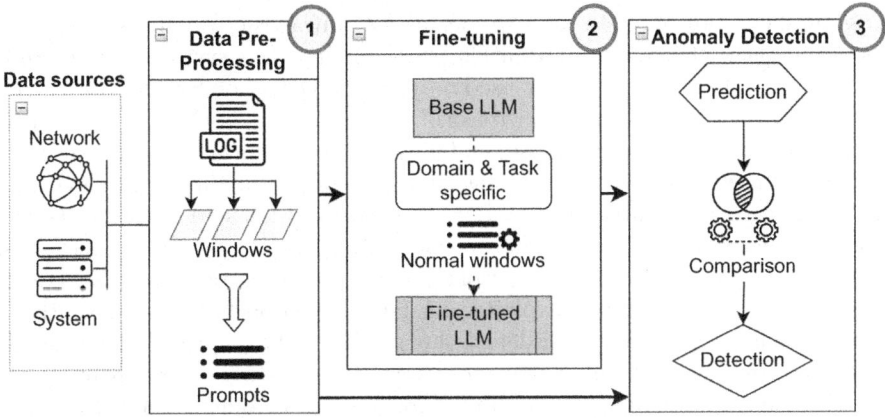

Fig. 1. Workflow of our proposed log anomaly detection approach

log anomaly detection through a comparison of predicted logs and actual log entries.

3.1 Data Pre-processing

The way data logs are handled has a great influence over the behavior and performance of our model. The overall data process is presented in Fig. 2 with the construction of prompts from log data. We first select systems and network logs as a grounding base because of the diverse information they transmit.

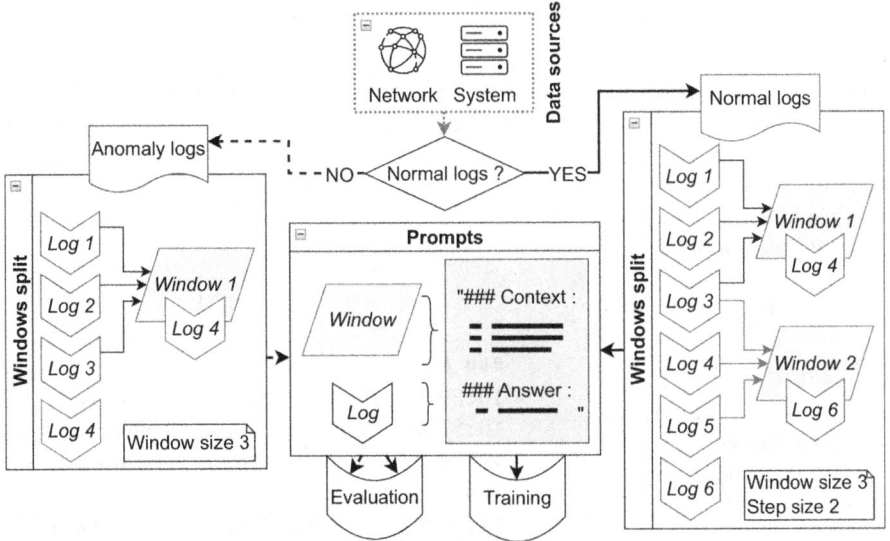

Fig. 2. Data pipeline

Log Sources. In order to improve defenses of infrastructure and systems, we choose to gather thorough information by examining their systems and network logs. Network logs are commonly used in Intrusion Detection Systems (IDS) [41] or, more precisely, in Network Intrusion Detection Systems (NIDS). These logs contain the source, the destination, and miscellaneous information on each interaction in the network, making it easier to trace potential threats and cyberattacks. Another log source used in IDS, specifically in Hosted Intrusion Detection Systems (HIDS), is system logs representing records of system activities, including running services, applications, and system events. In anomaly detection, system logs are mainly exploited for fault detection but less frequently to improve defense capacities and detect threats. Nevertheless, they offer valuable insights, providing a comprehensive overview of the system environment.

The one-class learning approach used for fine-tuning our model will leverage normal logs from both network and system logs, giving the model the possibility to learn benign features in our data. This approach is justified by how difficult finding labeled anomalous log data is, thus privileging normal logs, and by the potential to detect both known and unknown threats.

Partitioning. During training and anomaly detection, working with all the logs at once in the context is practically impossible due to resource constraints, so it is recommended to split them into a more practical and compact form [23,25]. By splitting the log data into overlapping sliding windows, we can train and run the model on smaller contexts, reducing the resources needed and computational costs. Sliding windows, like fixed windows, are built with Δ, a duration or a finite number of logs. These methods differ in the choice of distance between the windows to allow overlapping. Sliding windows partitioning proposes smaller contexts to learn and work on while allowing the capture of more nuances and patterns that might not be visible with non-overlapping windows.

Prompts. The produced contexts are then transformed into prompts to be used in the next-log prediction task, allowing the model to easily recognize and process the inputs. The idea is to work with logs as raw as possible, preventing the need for parsing tools known to reduce workflow performances [2,18], or convert logs using templates [10,15]. We defined a prompt template leveraging raw logs to guide the model during fine-tuning and inference:

Prompt template	Example
### Context : {CONTEXT SEQUENCE} ### Answer : {NEXT LOG}	### Context : 10:32:00.25 INFO User A connected 10:37:07.57 INFO User B connected 12:04:46.25 INFO User A disconnected ### Answer : 12:30:54.12 INFO User B disconnected

The extraction of insights is done between the context sequence given to the prompt after the "Context" tag, and the next log represented after the "Answer" tag. The prompt represent our task and helps define a structure the model can follow for training and generation. Once ingested by the LLM, the prompt is converted into a vector representation, allowing the model to leverage learned features to produce coherent and context-aware responses.

3.2 Fine-Tuning Strategy

Pre-trained LLMs like Llama 3.1 generally perform better on textual data compared to numerical data, as evidenced by their mathematical reasoning and understanding. However, we believe that LLMs can also handle numerical values effectively, using the same method as when working on textual data. Furthermore, in their pre-trained state, LLMs exhibit good overall results and generalizations across a wide range of tasks. To fully harness their potential, it is essential to adapt the model for specific tasks or domains. This fine-tuning requires fewer resources and less time than training a model "from scratch".

Fine-Tuning Process. To maximize the potential of our base LLM and enhance its performance, we choose to break down the fine-tuning process into two distinct steps, as shown in Fig. 3. The first step is to fine-tune the model on domain-specific knowledge, improving its understanding of logs. The second step is a task-specific fine-tuning for next-log prediction to adapt the model behavior.

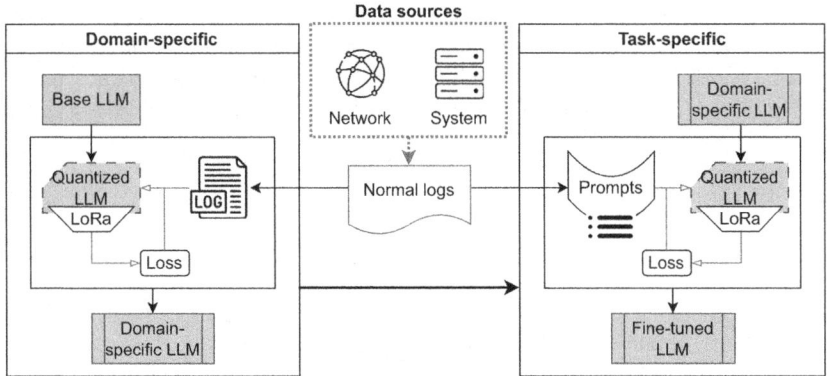

Fig. 3. Fine-tuning steps

The way in which a model is updated has a major impact on its capabilities. In our case, the domain-specific fine-tuning process focuses primarily on self-supervised learning, allowing the base LLM to learn from unlabeled textual patterns and build a comprehensive understanding of the log data. The self-supervised approach is popular for anomaly detection, as it enables models to autonomously learn patterns from data. Such approach often utilizes next-sequence prediction to detect deviations from the norm. This domain-specific LLM then serves as the foundation for the subsequent task-specific fine-tuning. For task-specific fine-tuning, we aim to enhance the model's abilities to generate normal logs. It implies fine-tuning our model on normal logs using a one-class approach and self-supervised learning, enabling it to learn the normal distribution. By combining the strengths of both supervised and unsupervised learning, the semi-supervised learning approach "one-class classification" (or "novelty detection") relies solely on "normal" data. This makes training more convenient when anomalous data is insufficient, and allows the model to understand the expected flow of log data, making it able of generating logs that are coherent with the learned distribution. To do so, we define the task as predicting the next log of a sequence, using contexts built from normal log data. The fine-tuning is done using created prompts, employing separate log types to produce type-specific models, allowing for deeper evaluations of the performance reached.

Given the resource-intensive nature of LLM training, optimization plays a key role in improving training speed and reducing computation costs. To achieve this, we use a combination of LoRa [19] and 4-bit quantization [8].

The final fine-tuned LLM is highly specialized in understanding normal log patterns and generating logs following these patterns. This makes it a robust groundwork for further analysis and anomaly detection systems, where deviations in real logs can be identified by comparing them to the generated logs.

3.3 Anomaly Detection

The inference part is composed of the anomaly detection pipeline depicted in Fig. 4. The model predicts the next log based on a given normal context (sequence of logs); if the actual next log is too different from this predicted normal log, then it is flagged as an anomaly. This approach is widely used in existing research

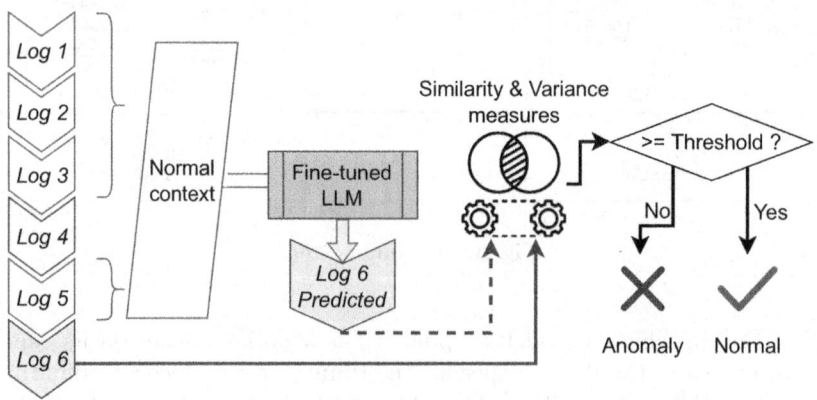

Fig. 4. Inference pipeline

[4,15] and allows one to define if an actual log is too far away from a normal distribution represented by the predicted log.

Our approach only considers normal logs as valid inputs to build a normal context used for the model generation. This means that each detected anomaly log is excluded from the context, ensuring the model relies solely on normal logs. One important parameter influencing the prediction of our model is the temperature. The temperature acts on the creativity of a model, modifying the probability distribution of the next token, taking a risky or safe choice.

Feature Extraction. To better analyze the predictions from the fine-tuned LLM, we parse them into separate timestamps and textual information. Doing so, it is easier to process each part differently because the timestamp is a numerical value and the textual information is a string. Textual similarity focuses on quantifying the resemblance between logs using similarity measures, which implies comparing the textual content of the generated logs and actual logs to determine how closely they match. The similarity score computed then helps in figuring out the nature of analyzed logs.

4 Evaluation

In this section, we describe the motivations behind the dataset choices. We then focus on fine-tuning our model with the various selected datasets of different types to better evaluate the performances and limits of our approach.

Experiment Setup. The research was carried out with computing resources provided by the Digital Research Alliance of Canada[5]. We trained our model using 64 GB of total GPU memory (4 V100SXM2 with 16 GB of memory each) and an 8-core CPU. Python, torch, bitsandbytes, as well as the transformers, datasets, accelerate, trl, and peft libraries from Hugging Face[6] are the main components involved in the fine-tuning process. The model evaluation and inference were performed with only one V100SXM2 and an 8-core CPU.

4.1 Data Selection

The selection of data logs is principally influenced by their source and what anomalies they contain, which justifies their quality and relevance for analysis. Furthermore, to efficiently assess the performances of our proposed approach against previous research, we decided to follow leading benchmarks. Several systems datasets exist, as shown by Zhu et al. [47] on GitHub[7] listing various types of log datasets from different systems. We consider these datasets to be a good representation of the diverse log types that can be found. As such, it can be

---

[5] https://alliancecan.ca/en.
[6] https://huggingface.co/.
[7] https://github.com/logpai/loghub.

used to initiate our model with basic domain knowledge over many logs. By aggregating two thousand row samples for the 16 different log types, the domain fine-tuning dataset sums up to 32k log lines.

To fine-tune the model on a specific task, we first use BGL, Thunderbird, and Spirit [30], three different system datasets providing an ample amount of normal categorized logs on which the model can efficiently learn the distribution. The choice of different datasets is aimed at prioritizing the generalization capabilities of the model and furthering the study of its behaviors across different environments. Also, it is pertinent to use a widely used benchmark dataset to determine our approach's pertinence against other anomaly detection models.

– **Blue Gene/L (BGL)** is a convenient dataset due to its use across several studies [2,15,44] and its role as an anomaly detection benchmark. BGL logs come from the Blue Gene/L supercomputer system at Lawrence Livermore National Laboratory, California. The dataset is composed of 4,747,963 log messages, with 348,460 (7.34%) manually labeled as anomalous.
– **Thunderbird** is a large log dataset containing 211,212,192 log messages, with 3,248,239 manually flagged anomalies. Collected on real-world supercomputer systems at Sandia National Laboratory in Albuquerque, New Mexico, Thunderbird is also widely used across studies [2,15,44].
– **Spirit** dataset was collected at Sandia National Laboratory in New Mexico, from a Linux production cluster. It contains 272,298,696 log messages, of which 172,816,564 are anomalies, and was used in a few studies [35,44].

To further extend the evaluation of our LLM capacities over different data sources, we selected three network datasets widely used [24]: CIC-IDS2017 [36], CSE-CIC-IDS2018 [36], and NSL-KDD [39]. These datasets contain network data with various types of threats and are used to train different models and assess their performance over threat detection rather than fault detection.

– **CIC-IDS2017** is an intrusion detection evaluation dataset from the Canadian Institute for Cybersecurity and the University of New Brunswick used in numerous studies [5,41,43]. The dataset contains benign traffic and common attacks, which resemble the true real-world data. The total number of records is 2,830,743, with 471,453 (16,66%) attack records.
– **CSE-CIC-IDS2018**[8] is also a dataset from the Canadian Institute for Cybersecurity and the Communications Security Establishment. It is a benchmark for intrusion detection, totaling 16,232,963 events and behaviors seen on the network over ten days, including benign traffic and seven different attack scenarios representing roughly 17% of the dataset. As the successor of the CIC-IDS2017 dataset, many research studies use this dataset [17,41].
– **NSL-KDD** dataset is a benchmark for evaluating intrusion detection system performance. It is an improved version of the original KDD Cup 1999 dataset[9], containing 158,514 records with 77,052 being benign and 71,462 (45,08%) being attacks. NSL-KDD is explored in a few studies [3,32].

---

[8] https://registry.opendata.aws/cse-cic-ids2018/.
[9] https://kdd.ics.uci.edu/databases/kddcup99/kddcup99.html.

4.2 Training and Inference

For evaluation purposes, we fine-tune the model distinctly on three source types during the task-specific adaptation. This approach allows us to ensure that the model not only performs well on the specific task at hand but also shows its capabilities to adapt with different and unseen data logs. Furthermore, we explore how the pipeline and flagging performances vary when applying different similarity metrics and flagging methods on the textual information from the logs.

Model Fine-Tuning. We selected Llama 3.1, a pre-trained model from the META Llama family, totaling 8 billion parameters [11]. The advantage of such models is their openly available model weights, hardly obtainable without using colossal resources, architecture, and training configurations for research and development purposes, allowing anyone to fine-tune or evaluate the model on specific domains and tasks. This foundation model with a context of up to 128k tokens uses dense transformers and Grouped-Query Attention (GQA) for improved inference scalability. Llama 3.1 has been trained on over 15 trillion tokens from multiple publicly available sources, bringing better understanding of contexts and, at the same occasion, better generation capabilities than SLMs.

Using both domain-specific and task-specific approaches, we fine-tune the model on different datasets to improve generalization across various contexts. By tackling a diverse set of training data, we enhance the model's ability to adapt to a wide range of anomalies and system behaviors. Fine-tuning contexts are defined with a window size of 10 logs and a step size of 7 so that each context shares logs with other contexts by overlapping. We develop three different models: the first, STB, specialized on system logs; the second, NETNOSTAMP, on network logs with timestamps; and the third, NETSTAMP, on network logs without timestamps. By doing so, we can evaluate the capacities and reactions of the model over different sources and data types. The models are fine-tuned using datasets corresponding to their assigned data type.

The training process, exploiting libraries developed by Hugging Face, is defined with an effective batch size of 4 using gradient accumulation every two steps and a batch size of 2. We also utilize a context length of 1024 and 2048 tokens with packing to optimize memory usage. For parameter-efficient fine-tuning (PEFT) and the learning rate, we select specific values tailored to the task, which are tuned based on preliminary experiments. The total training time took approximately 20 h for the domain-specific fine-tuning and around 18 h for the task-specific fine-tuning on each type of source.

Inference Pipeline. To determine what similarity measures are adapted in differentiating the logs, we examine various textual comparison methods, namely the Jacquard Index, Levenshtein Distance, Exact Matching, and Cosine Similarity using the logs' embeddings.

As shown in Table 1, we compare the metrics for different similarity measures. We found that cosine similarity performs better on the BGL dataset for anomaly

Table 1. Performance metrics for different similarity measures on BGL anomaly detection

Label	F1 Score	Recall	Precision	Specificity	Threshold
Jacquard Index	0.959	0.980	0.938	0.936	0.350
Levenshtein Distance	0.961	0.983	0.940	0.937	0.482
Exact Match	0.947	0.955	0.940	0.939	0.676
Cosine Similarity	**0.980**	**0.991**	**0.969**	**0.968**	**0.882**

detection. This measure is also used in other research, like Nour et al. [29] for graph similarity, and is highlighted due to its robustness and capacity to handle multidimensional data. The cosine similarity score represents the cosine of the angle between two non-zero vectors; in our case, it allows us to check the degree of similarity between the predicted and actual logs. To compute the similarity score, we manipulate the embedding vectors recovered from the textual information. We use **A**, the predicted log textual embedding, and **B**, the actual log textual embedding, as vectors for the cosine similarity measure defined in Eq. (1).

$$\text{Cosine Similarity} = \frac{\mathbf{A} \cdot \mathbf{B}}{\|\mathbf{A}\|\|\mathbf{B}\|} \quad (1)$$

Log Flagging. Textual similarity's optimal threshold is generated using AUC metrics to maximize the efficiency of anomaly detection, balancing the true positive (TP) rate and false positive (FP) rate represented in Fig. 5a. Then, leveraging the optimal threshold and using computed similarity values, we determine the nature of the given results as being an anomaly or not. If the score exceeds the threshold, it indicates that logs are similar enough, flagging the result as normal. Whereas, if the score falls under the threshold, logs are too divergent, flagging the result as an anomaly. Figure 5b depicts the number of anomalies detected based on the similarity score from the cosine similarity between sets of three thousand normal and abnormal logs from the STB dataset. The optimized threshold highlights a high true anomaly detection while keeping the false detection rate around 16%.

4.3 Experimental Results

To experiment on our developed approach, we use unseen logs with a consistent context size of 10 and set the LLM predictions temperature at 0.2 to control the diversity of the generations. Evaluation took around 10 h per model, from log generation to similarity computing. Following the inference pipeline, we then compare the predicted log to the real log in our test dataset to extract metrics.

Benchmark Assessment. In an anomaly detection task, several methods and metrics exist, but not all are suitable, such as accuracy (not suitable if the

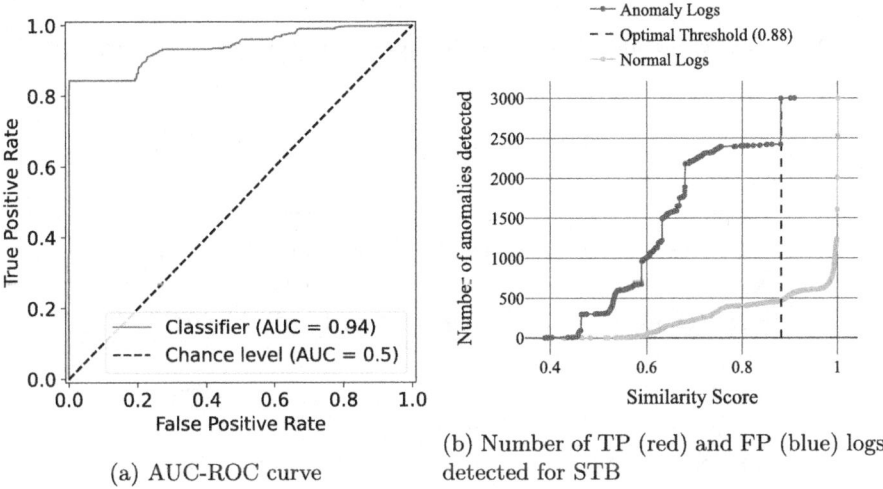

Fig. 5. Threshold on STB evaluation

(a) AUC-ROC curve

(b) Number of TP (red) and FP (blue) logs detected for STB

dataset is not balanced) [38]. Other metrics such as precision, F1-score or recall are used in various state-of-the-art tools and can thus be considered as a means of benchmark evaluation on anomaly detection [2,12].

We compare our STB fine-tuned model on systems logs against three different other approaches in Table 2: DeepLog by Du et al. [10], LogGPT by Qi et al. [35] and LogFit by Almodovar et al. [2]. For network logs evaluation on NETSTAMP and NETNOSTAMP, we compare them to Cai et al. [5], Han et al. [17], Bamber et al. [3] in Table 3. The results for STB highlight the robustness of the model, maintaining high performance across three different datasets with minimal misclassifications. Specifically, our model performs the best overall, with F1-score equal to or higher than that of the other models in all tested scenarios, along with very high precision, recall, and specificity. We attribute the improvements to the model's fine-tuning, which enhances consistency, and to simplified prompts that help focus on relevant information, as compared to LogGPT more complex prompt engineering approach. In comparison to DeepLog reliance on static templates and fixed sequences, STB adapts better to dynamic log formats, likely due to its language modeling capabilities and learned semantic patterns.

For network logs, NETNOSTAMP shows impressive performance on the NSL-KDD dataset with high precision, recall, and specificity. However, the performance drops on CIC-IDS2017 and CSE-CIC-IDS2018 (with NETSTAMP), where it struggles to detect anomalies effectively. A key distinction lies in modeling: traditional methods like CDDA-MD, ECNet rely on structured features and temporal cues, while LLMs like NETNOSTAMP infer patterns from raw inputs. This offers flexibility but struggles with logs that are mainly numerical or subtle timing-based anomalies. NETNOSTAMP was also tested on the NETSTAMP dataset to assess its generalization across network data. It surpass STB results on

Table 2. Performance comparison by datasets and models on system logs

BGL				
Model	F1-score	Recall	Precision	Specificity
LogFit	0.899	0.944	0.858	0.989
DeepLog	0.793	0.707	0.902	0.983
NETNOSTAMP (Ours)	0.670	0.647	0.695	0.873
NETSTAMP (Ours)	0.608	0.492	0.795	0.873
STB (Ours)	0.945	0.976	0.916	0.910
Thunderbird				
LogFit	0.939	0.986	0.897	0.977
DeepLog	0.736	0.994	0.651	0.893
NETNOSTAMP (Ours)	0.909	0.975	0.852	0.830
NETSTAMP (Ours)	0.865	0.914	0.821	0.800
STB (Ours)	0.926	1.000	0.863	0.841
Spirit				
LogGPT	0.601	0.985	0.432	0.333
DeepLog	0.521	1.00	0.352	0.053
NETNOSTAMP (Ours)	0.895	0.965	0.835	0.809
NETSTAMP (Ours)	0.651	0.535	0.832	0.892
STB (Ours)	0.920	0.930	0.910	0.908

Table 3. Performance comparison by datasets and models on network logs

NSL-KDD				
Model	F1-score	Recall	Precision	Specificity
CNN-LSTM	0.910	0.860	0.960	...
NETNOSTAMP (Ours)	0.957	0.947	0.968	0.969
STB (Ours)	0.688	0.765	0.625	0.542
CIC-IDS2017				
CDDA-MD	0.986	0.994	0.651	0.893
NETNOSTAMP (Ours)	0.791	0.825	0.759	0.738
STB (Ours)	0.639	0.639	0.639	0.639
CSE-CIC-IDS2018				
ECNet	0.934	0.951	0.918	...
NETSTAMP (Ours)	0.660	0.720	0.610	0.540
NETNOSTAMP (Ours)	0.542	0.503	0.588	0.648
STB (Ours)	0.502	0.482	0.525	0.564

timestamped data, highlighting its strength in pattern recognition. To evaluate broader generalization, we tested network-tuned models on system logs and STB on network logs. Network models showcase encouraging results over systems logs evaluation, particularly on Thunderbird and Spirit datasets with F1-scores close to the state-of-the-art. However, STB model results over network logs remain low even on timestamped data. This suggesting that the STB model struggles with temporal cues and relies more log content instead.

These shortcomings likely arise from the variability of network logs across datasets and their predominantly numerical nature, which LLMs handle less effectively than textual data, potentially limiting model performance.

Context Size. We evaluated inference on context sizes of 5, 10, and 20 to understand our models' behaviors in Figs. 6a, 6b, and 6c. Overall, the model shows consistent performance over different context sizes even though it has been trained exclusively on windows of size 10. The NETSTAMP (no stamp) model contains logs without temporal information (timestamps), conversely to NETSTAMP,

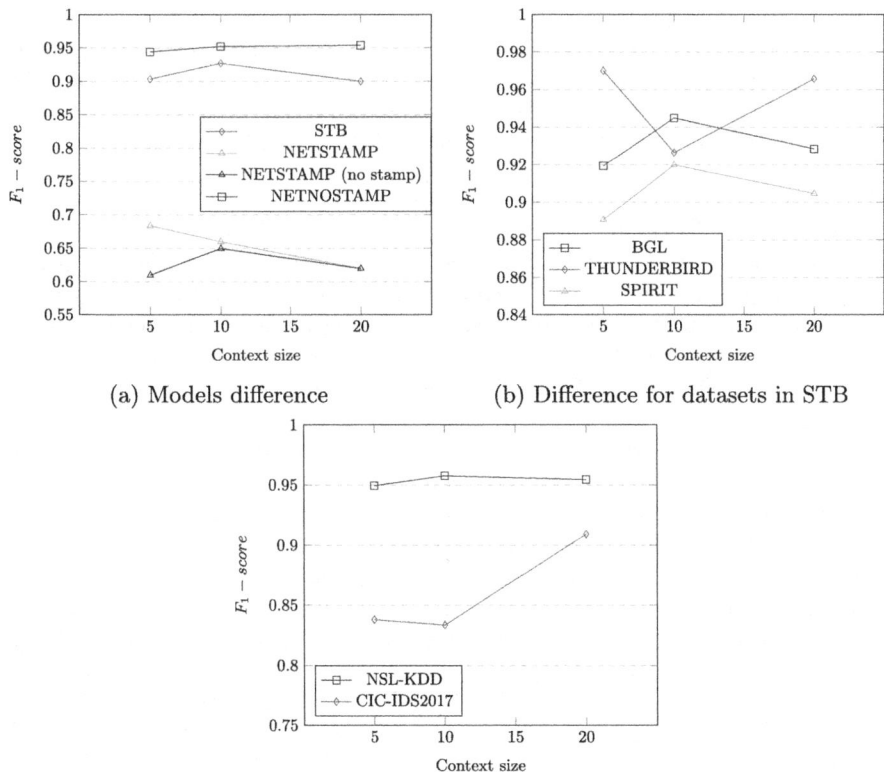

(a) Models difference

(b) Difference for datasets in STB

(c) Difference for network datasets in NETNOSTAMP

Fig. 6. Context size performance

where the full log is kept during evaluation. Except for the NETSTAMP model, this implies that the models are able to leverage different context sizes without greatly impacting the performances.

Inference Speed Evaluation. We evaluate the inference performance on 1000 samples, comparing the baseline (unquantized) models to their BitsAndBytes (bnb) quantized counterparts. The STB model achieves the highest throughput with 0.505 samples/s in the unquantized setting and 0.288 with bnb quantization. In contrast, NETSTAMP and NETNOSTAMP perform lower, with NETSTAMP reaching 0.132 (base) and 0.084 (bnb), and NETNOSTAMP achieving 0.334 (base) and 0.201 (bnb). Lower throughput is mainly due to longer inputs sequences (up to 300 tokens versus 128 for STB) and the abundance of numerical values, which likely increase decoding complexity. These results highlight how input characteristics and quantization impact real-time performance, especially in resource-limited settings using quantization methods like bnb.

5 Discussion and Limitations

Efficient models for anomaly detection tend to use a deep learning approach overcoming the limitations of ML models [21,27] but are slower to train due to their complexity [6]. LLMs also brings multiple restrictions on real world deployment, in anomaly detection LLMs' limitations tend to negatively impact the workflow, unveiling challenges to be addressed:

- **Computing Capacity**: LLMs require significant resources and can be too slow for real-time anomaly detection, especially in security contexts where quick responses are necessary. Current inference time during evaluation is way too important to be considered a viable option at the moment
- **Labeled Data**: The lack of anomalous data makes it difficult to train LLMs in a supervised manner. Without a sufficient quantity of anomalies, it is harder to train the model efficiently.
- **Context Range**: While LLMs handle long dependencies, they may falter with noisy data. Careful data selection and preprocessing are essential.
- **Interpretation**: Model interpretation represents a major challenge when using LLMs, as they act as black boxes. Providing explanations for the model's choices is essential for validation and trust in the model.
- **Data Shift**: As data evolve over time, the model needs to adapt to new patterns. Following the data shift is a crucial step over time, as the model can adapt to new distributions.

6 Conclusion and Future Work

In conclusion, leveraging large language models (LLMs) for anomaly detection offers a promising approach to identifying unusual logs. Using their capabilities to process and analyze raw data depending on context, LLMs can partake in the detection of anomalies that traditional methods may overlook. This ability to handle complex data is a significant advantage where data patterns are intricate and variable. Findings from our research show that LLMs can enhance detection accuracy in systems environments, particularly with textual logs, independently of the context size used. However, network logs present challenges due to their numerical nature negatively impacting performance. The complexity in network data with its heavy reliance on numerical values may not make the most of the strengths of LLMs and necessitate further adjustment. While our method is relatively simple, we show that it performs competitively.

Future work should focus on fine-tuning LLMs to optimize their efficiency and adaptability, particularly across network logs. Enhancing memory and resource use are key to effective, cost-conscious real word anomaly detection. Current efforts aim to develop risk-aware, proactive detection to improve early identification and decision-making. Additionally, ensuring consistency in model outputs and integrating safeguards will help address ethical and security concerns. As LLMs evolve, they promise faster, scalable detection but must overcome challenges in reliability and resource demands.

References

1. Unit 42: 2025 Unit 42 global incident response report (2025)
2. Almodovar, C., Sabrina, F., Karimi, S., Azad, S.: LogFit: log anomaly detection using fine-tuned language models. IEEE Trans. Netw. Serv. Manage. **21**(2), 1715–1723 (2024). https://doi.org/10.1109/TNSM.2024.3358730
3. Bamber, S.S., Katkuri, A.V.R., Sharma, S., Angurala, M.: A hybrid CNN-LSTM approach for intelligent cyber intrusion detection system. Comput. Secur. **148**, 104146 (2025). https://doi.org/10.1016/j.cose.2024.104146
4. Boffa, M., et al.: Logprécis: unleashing language models for automated malicious log analysis. Comput. Secur. **141**, 103805 (2024). https://doi.org/10.1016/j.cose.2024.103805
5. Cai, S., Tang, H., Chen, J., Hu, Y., Guo, W.: CDDA-MD: an efficient malicious traffic detection method based on concept drift detection and adaptation technique. Comput. Secur. **148**, 104121 (2025). https://doi.org/10.1016/j.cose.2024.104121
6. Chen, Z., Liu, J., Gu, W., Su, Y., Lyu, M.R.: Experience report: deep learning-based system log analysis for anomaly detection (2022). arXiv:2107.05908
7. Counsel, T.S.: Canada's internet Factbook 2022 (2023)
8. Dettmers, T., Pagnoni, A., Holtzman, A., Zettlemoyer, L.: QLoRA: efficient fine-tuning of quantized LLMs. In: Oh, A., Naumann, T., Globerson, A., Saenko, K., Hardt, M., Levine, S. (eds.) Advances in Neural Information Processing Systems, vol. 36, pp. 10088–10115. Curran Associates, Inc. (2023)
9. Devlin, J., Chang, M.W., Lee, K., Toutanova, K.: BERT: Pre-training of deep bidirectional transformers for language understanding (2019). arXiv:1810.04805
10. Du, M., Li, F., Zheng, G., Srikumar, V.: DeepLog: anomaly detection and diagnosis from system logs through deep learning. In: Proceedings of the 2017 ACM SIGSAC Conference on Computer and Communications Security, pp. 1285–1298. ACM, Dallas Texas USA (2017). https://doi.org/10.1145/3133956.3134015

11. Dubey, A., Jauhri, A., Pandey, A., Kadian, A., Al-Dahle, A., et al.: The Llama 3 herd of models (2024). arXiv:2407.21783
12. Ede, T.V., et al.: DEEPCASE: semi-supervised contextual analysis of security events. In: 2022 IEEE Symposium on Security and Privacy (SP), pp. 522–539. IEEE, San Francisco, CA, USA (2022). https://doi.org/10.1109/SP46214.2022.9833671
13. Egersdoerfer, C., Zhang, D., Dai, D.: Early exploration of using ChatGPT for log-based anomaly detection on parallel file systems logs. In: Proceedings of the 32nd International Symposium on High-Performance Parallel and Distributed Computing, pp. 315–316. ACM, Orlando FL USA (2023). https://doi.org/10.1145/3588195.3595943
14. European union agency for cybersecurity.: ENISA threat landscape 2024: July 2023 to June 2024. Publications Office, LU (2024)
15. Guo, H., Yuan, S., Wu, X.: LogBERT: log anomaly detection via BERT. In: 2021 International Joint Conference on Neural Networks (IJCNN), pp. 1–8. IEEE, Shenzhen, China (2021). https://doi.org/10.1109/IJCNN52387.2021.9534113
16. Guo, H., et al.: LogFormer: a pre-train and tuning pipeline for log anomaly detection. In: Proceedings of the AAAI Conference on Artificial Intelligence, vol. 38, no. 1, pp. 135–143 (2024). https://doi.org/10.1609/aaai.v38i1.27764
17. Han, X., Liu, S., Liu, J., Jiang, B., Lu, Z., Liu, B.: ECNET: robust malicious network traffic detection with multi-view feature and confidence mechanism. IEEE Trans. Inf. Forensics Secur. **19**, 6871–6885 (2024). https://doi.org/10.1109/TIFS.2024.3426304
18. He, S., He, P., Chen, Z., Yang, T., Su, Y., Lyu, M.R.: A survey on automated log analysis for reliability engineering. ACM Comput. Surv. **54**(6), 1–37 (2022). https://doi.org/10.1145/3460345
19. Hu, E.J., et al.: LoRA: low-rank adaptation of large language models (2021). arXiv:2106.09685
20. Huang, S., Liu, Y., Fung, C., Wang, H., Yang, H., Luan, Z.: Improving log-based anomaly detection by pre-training hierarchical transformers. IEEE Trans. Comput. **72**(9), 2656–2667 (2023). https://doi.org/10.1109/TC.2023.3257518
21. Jordan, M.I., Mitchell, T.M.: Machine learning: trends, perspectives, and prospects. Science **349**(6245), 255–260 (2015). https://doi.org/10.1126/science.aaa8415
22. Labs, F.: Fortinet 2025 global threat landscape report (2025)
23. Landauer, M., Onder, S., Skopik, F., Wurzenberger, M.: Deep learning for anomaly detection in log data: a survey. Mach. Learn. Appl. **12**, 100470 (2023). https://doi.org/10.1016/j.mlwa.2023.100470
24. Landauer, M., Skopik, F., Frank, M., Hotwagner, W., Wurzenberger, M., Rauber, A.: Maintainable log datasets for evaluation of intrusion detection systems. IEEE Trans. Dependable Secure Comput. **20**(4), 3466–3482 (2023). https://doi.org/10.1109/TDSC.2022.3201582, arXiv:2203.08580
25. Landauer, M., Skopik, F., Wurzenberger, M., Rauber, A.: System log clustering approaches for cyber security applications: a survey. Comput. Secur. **92**, 101739 (2020). https://doi.org/10.1016/j.cose.2020.101739
26. Le, V.H., Zhang, H.: Log-based anomaly detection without log parsing. In: 2021 36th IEEE/ACM International Conference on Automated Software Engineering (ASE), pp. 492–504. IEEE, Melbourne, Australia (2021). https://doi.org/10.1109/ASE51524.2021.9678773
27. LeCun, Y., Bengio, Y., Hinton, G.: Deep learning. Nature **521**(7553), 436–444 (2015). https://doi.org/10.1038/nature14539

28. Lee, Y., Kim, J., Kang, P.: LanoBert: system log anomaly detection based on BERT masked language model. Appl. Soft Comput. **146**, 110689 (2023). https://doi.org/10.1016/j.asoc.2023.110689
29. Nour, B., Pourzandi, M., Qureshi, R.K., Debbabi, M.: AUTOMA: automated generation of attack hypotheses and their variants for threat hunting using knowledge discovery. IEEE Trans. Netw. Serv. Manag., 1 (2024). https://doi.org/10.1109/TNSM.2024.3378972
30. Oliner, A., Stearley, J.: What supercomputers say: a study of five system logs. In: 37th Annual IEEE/IFIP International Conference on Dependable Systems and Networks (DSN 2007), pp. 575–584. IEEE, Edinburgh, UK (2007). https://doi.org/10.1109/DSN.2007.103
31. OpenAI, Achiam, J., Adler, S., Agarwal, S., Ahmad, L., et al.: GPT-4 technical report (2024). https://doi.org/10.48550/arXiv.2303.08774, arXiv:2303.08774
32. Pai, H.T., Kang, Y.H., Chung, W.C.: An interpretable generalization mechanism for accurately detecting anomaly and identifying networking intrusion techniques. IEEE Trans. Inf. Forensics Secur. **19**, 10302–10313 (2024). https://doi.org/10.1109/TIFS.2024.3488967
33. Pan, J., Liang, W.S., Yidi, Y.: RAGLog: log anomaly detection using retrieval augmented generation. In: 2024 IEEE World Forum on Public Safety Technology (WFPST), pp. 169–174. IEEE, Herndon, VA, USA (2024). https://doi.org/10.1109/WFPST58552.2024.00034
34. Pang, G., Shen, C., Cao, L., Hengel, A.V.D.: Deep learning for anomaly detection: a review. ACM Comput. Surv. **54**(2), 1–38 (2022). https://doi.org/10.1145/3439950
35. Qi, J., Huang, S., Luan, Z., Yang, S., Fung, C., et al.: LogGPT: exploring ChatGPT for log-based anomaly detection. In: 2023 IEEE International Conference on High Performance Computing & Communications, Data Science & Systems, Smart City & Dependability in Sensor, Cloud & Big Data Systems & Application (HPCC/DSS/SmartCity/DependSys), pp. 273–280. IEEE, Melbourne, Australia (2023). https://doi.org/10.1109/HPCC-DSS-SmartCity-DependSys60770.2023.00045
36. Sharafaldin, I., Habibi Lashkari, A., Ghorbani, A.A.: Toward generating a new intrusion detection dataset and intrusion traffic characterization: In: Proceedings of the 4th International Conference on Information Systems Security and Privacy, pp. 108–116. SCITEPRESS - Science and Technology Publications, Funchal, Madeira, Portugal (2018). https://doi.org/10.5220/0006639801080116
37. Song, C., Ma, L., Zheng, J., Liao, J., Kuang, H., Yang, L.: Audit-LLM: multi-agent collaboration for log-based insider threat detection (2024). arXiv:2408.08902
38. Su, J., et al.: Large language models for forecasting and anomaly detection: a systematic literature review (2024). arXiv:2402.10350
39. Tavallaee, M., Bagheri, E., Lu, W., Ghorbani, A.A.: A detailed analysis of the KDD CUP 99 data set. In: 2009 IEEE Symposium on Computational Intelligence for Security and Defense Applications, pp. 1–6. IEEE, Ottawa, ON, Canada (2009). https://doi.org/10.1109/CISDA.2009.5356528
40. Vaswani, A., et al.: Attention is all you need (2023). arXiv:1706.03762
41. Wang, M., Yang, N., Forcade-Perkins, N.J., Weng, N.: PROGEN: projection-based adversarial attack generation against network intrusion detection. IEEE Trans. Inf. Forensics Secur. **19**, 5476–5491 (2024). https://doi.org/10.1109/TIFS.2024.3402155
42. Wu, X., Li, H., Khomh, F.: On the effectiveness of log representation for log-based anomaly detection. Empir. Softw. Eng. **28**(6), 137 (2023). https://doi.org/10.1007/s10664-023-10364-1

43. Yi, T., Chen, X., Li, Q., Zhu, Y.: An anomaly behavior characterization method of network traffic based on spatial pyramid pool (SPP). Comput. Secur. **141**, 103809 (2024). https://doi.org/10.1016/j.cose.2024.103809
44. Yin, Z., Kong, X., Yin, C.: Semi-supervised log anomaly detection based on bidirectional temporal convolution network. Comput. Secur. **140**, 103808 (2024). https://doi.org/10.1016/j.cose.2024.103808
45. Zhong, A., et al.: LogParser-LLM: advancing efficient log parsing with large language models. In: Proceedings of the 30th ACM SIGKDD Conference on Knowledge Discovery and Data Mining, pp. 4559–4570. ACM, Barcelona Spain (2024). https://doi.org/10.1145/3637528.3671810
46. Zhou, K., et al.: A survey of large language models (2023). https://doi.org/10.48550/ARXIV.2303.18223
47. Zhu, J., He, S., He, P., Liu, J., Lyu, M.R.: LogHub: a large collection of system log datasets for AI-driven log analytics. In: 2023 IEEE 34th International Symposium on Software Reliability Engineering (ISSRE). pp. 355–366. IEEE, Florence, Italy (2023). https://doi.org/10.1109/ISSRE59848.2023.00071

PROTEAN: Federated Intrusion Detection in Non-IID Environments Through Prototype-Based Knowledge Sharing

Sara Chennoufi[1(✉)], Yufei Han[2], Gregory Blanc[1], Emiliano De Cristofaro[3], and Christophe Kiennert[1]

[1] SAMOVAR, Télécom SudParis, Institut Polytechnique de Paris, Palaiseau, France
sara.chennoufi@telecom-sudparis.eu
[2] PIRAT, INRIA Rennes, Rennes, France
[3] University of California, Riverside, USA

Abstract. In distributed networks, participants often face diverse and fast-evolving cyberattacks. This makes techniques based on Federated Learning (FL) a promising mitigation strategy. By only exchanging model updates, FL participants can collaboratively build detection models without revealing sensitive information, e.g., network structures or security postures. However, the effectiveness of FL solutions is often hindered by significant data heterogeneity, as attack patterns often differ drastically across organizations due to varying security policies. To address these challenges, we introduce PROTEAN, a Prototype Learning-based framework geared to facilitate collaborative and privacy-preserving intrusion detection. PROTEAN enables accurate detection in environments with highly non-IID attack distributions and promotes direct knowledge sharing by exchanging class prototypes of different attack types among participants. This allows organizations to better understand attack techniques not present in their data collections. We instantiate PROTEAN on two cyber intrusion datasets collected from IIoT and 5G-connected participants and evaluate its performance in terms of utility and privacy, demonstrating its effectiveness in addressing data heterogeneity while improving cyber attack understanding in federated intrusion detection systems (IDSs).

1 Introduction

Cyber intrusions vary widely, challenging detection efforts. Signature-based methods lack adaptability, while Machine Learning (ML)-based IDSs trained on local data struggle with unseen threats. This highlights the need for collaborative intelligence [9], though data sharing raises serious privacy concerns. FL has emerged as a privacy-friendly alternative for distributed ML-based IDS without disclosing local training data [18]. Each participating organization trains the model locally and shares only model updates to jointly aggregate a global model.

In the practice of distributed IDS, FL faces the notable non-IID challenge raised by heterogeneous data distributions of different end-point devices. In distributed IDS applications, certain types of cyber intrusions may be specific to a subset of participants while being rare or completely absent in others, resulting in highly imbalanced distributions of attack data across participants. For example, while DDoS attacks are common across various types of organizations, entities that primarily host database servers are more frequently targeted by SQL injection or brute-force attacks aimed at gaining unauthorized database access. Conversely, botnet attacks, such as those involving Mirai, are more likely to affect organizations with IoT infrastructure. Although prior research has proposed aggregation techniques to mitigate the effects of non-IID data in FL (e.g., [8,12,13,25]), these methods primarily address heterogeneous training data distribution caused by varying class proportions across participants and are less effective when the class imbalance arises from the absence or rarity of certain classes in local datasets. Specifically, they enhance the overall performance of the globally aggregated model [8,13,25], or adapt the global model to heterogeneous local data distributions, i.e. personalization of the global model [12]. Nevertheless, they overlook the class-specific accuracy for rarely appearing classes that can be only seen by a few participants.

Moreover, FL shares only global model parameters, which does not provide a comprehensive understanding of the threat across participants. This is particularly evident in non-IID scenarios. When shared back with local participants, the globally aggregated model fails to reveal characteristics of attacks that are not locally observed by the client. Understanding the attack class distribution is crucial to grasping the broader threat landscape beyond merely achieving accurate detection and is needed to make ML based detection more explainable.

As a result, we set out to achieve two main objectives. **First**, jointly trained detection models of a distributed IDS should reach high accuracy in the presence of highly skewed distributions of different cyber attack types. Specifically, we consider a cross-silo scenario where attacks are distributed in a highly imbalanced manner, aiming to improve detection performance over rarely appearing attack types. **Second**, beyond reaching accurate detection results, cyber attack knowledge sharing should also boost the explainability of the detection model, helping reach a comprehensive understanding of the distribution of cyber attack types.

To do so, our work introduces PROTEAN, a collaborative intrusion detection mechanism. Unlike standard FL, PROTEAN draws from prototype learning [22,24]. It operates by sharing model parameters for aggregation alongside class-specific prototypes of attack behaviors encountered by local participants during federated training. PROTEAN enforces a two-fold alignment process: 1. **(Model parameter)** Detection model parameters trained locally by different participants should converge to a unified global model. 2. **(Class prototype)** PROTEAN requires class prototypes of the same attack type generated by different participants to be as similar as possible. This improves training convergence by minimizing discrepancies between locally trained models, thereby enhancing detection capabilities in environments where attacks are heterogeneously distributed across participants. Additionally, sharing class-specific prototypes enables participants to generalize their understanding of various cyber attack types. For example, a participant with limited exposure to a rare attack type can learn to identify and classify it by receiving the corresponding prototype during training. This not only accelerates convergence in heterogeneous and imbalanced attack class distributions but also promotes the transfer of attack knowledge among participants.

Overall, our work aims to answer the following research questions:

1. Can PROTEAN improve the FL-based IDS detection performance under heterogeneous attack data distributions with highly imbalanced cyber attack types?
2. Can attack knowledge sharing via sharing class-specific prototypes help detect rare or unique cyber attacks on local participants?
3. Can sharing attack class prototypes and model updates allow attackers to perform reconstruction attacks [23,29] to recover training data, triggering privacy risk of the FL IDS?

We theoretically prove the convergence of PROTEAN and provide complexity analysis to demonstrate the applicability of PROTEAN for distributed IDS training. We also show the superior performance of PROTEAN compared to prior FL-based IDS methods in heterogeneous environments on two IoT and 5G intrusion detection datasets: *5G-NIDD* [21] and *X-IIoTID* [2]. In extremely imbalanced data distributions, PROTEAN improves on the state-of-the-art (SOTA) FL-based IDS method [18] with F1 scores 23% higher on the X-IIoTID dataset and 5% on the 5G-NIDD dataset. Finally, we audit the privacy leakage risks using a reconstruction attack with an adversary observing the shared prototypes either on a compromised local participant or via a semi-honest global server. This follows previous insights from Zhu et al. [23,29], which has proved effective in reconstructing training data in FL. We experimentally show that the attack fails to recover meaningful feature values of the original data from the local participants. We also evaluate the impact of differential privacy (DP) on utility and privacy preservation.

2 Related Work

FL with Non-IID Data. A few aggregation techniques have been proposed to address non-IIDness and heterogeneous data distributions in FL. Some use optimization techniques to avoid model divergence: e.g., FedProx [13] incorporates a proximal term to keep the local model close to the global one; FedOpt [3] adapts classic optimizers like Adam and SGD-Momentum, while FedNova [26] normalizes contributions from participants, and SCAFFOLD [8] adds control variables to account for the data drift over local participants. These robust aggregation methods focus on smoothing the federated optimization process facing the heterogeneous local data distributions, improving the convergence speed of FL methods.

The other line of non-IID FL methods relies on personalizing techniques. For instance, FedAlt /FedSim [20] aggregate parts of the model while keeping other parts private. Ditto [12] simultaneously tunes the locally adapted models and the global aggregated model, forcing the consistency between the local and global models. By transferring the knowledge from other participants while keeping parts frozen, transfer learning helps adapt the model even when data distributions are different. Additionally, Model-Contrastive Federated Learning (Moon) [11], and Model-Agnostic Meta-Learning (MAML) [5] have been used in the context of FL heterogeneity. The personalized FL algorithms are dedicated to adapting the global model to the local data distributions of different participants. However, previous efforts to improve non-IID federated training often prioritize evaluating the overall performance of the aggregated

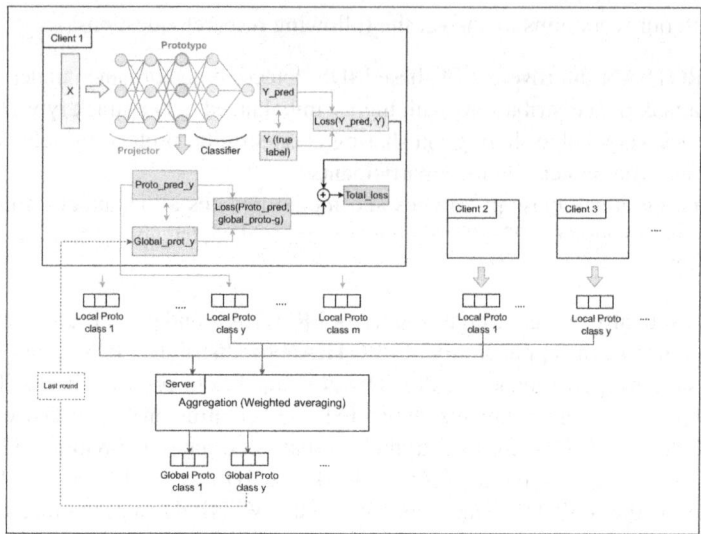

Fig. 1. PROTEAN training process. Each participant trains a local model and extracts prototypes that summarize observed attacks. These prototypes and models are sent to the server, which aggregates them and sends the aggregated results to the participants to refine their knowledge using both local and global insights.

global model. Nevertheless, they overlook the specific detection performance for classes that appear rarely, existing only in the training data of a few participants. Consequently, commonly used global metrics, heavily influenced by majority classes, can mask poor performance on these minority classes, leading to an inaccurate assessment of accuracy for underrepresented classes.

FL-Based IDSs. Similar FL techniques have also been applied to IDSs with heterogeneous data [1,6]. The evaluation only focuses on eliminating specific attacks for some participants while maintaining an IID distribution for other classes. Federated clustering [4] is also applied for non-IID cases. But it largely ignores the class-specific detection performance and does not show how well participants benefit from knowledge sharing on new classes.

Knowledge Sharing in FL. A major challenge of vanilla FL is the degradation of model performance due to the aggregation of local models trained on highly skewed class distributions of local training datasets. This results in a global model that struggles to generalize effectively. Local models often overfit to their specific data distributions, limiting the effectiveness of global knowledge sharing. Pei et al. [19] propose integrating transfer learning into the FL framework to enhance knowledge sharing. However, their approach primarily addresses the semi-supervised learning scenario and does not fully tackle the non-IID bottleneck. On the contrary, Federated Prototype Learning (FPL) [15,24] offers a more effective approach to knowledge sharing, particularly under non-IID data conditions. Nevertheless, as unveiled in our study, the two vanilla FPL algorithms [15,24] fail to reach accurate detection in the extreme heterogeneous environments, where some cyber attack types mostly appear on a few participants' local training data, while barely exist in the others' datasets. The core reason is that the imbalanced distribution of the attack types across local participants leads to a significant distribution drift between the embedding space spanned by locally trained ML models, which makes the aggregation of local class prototypes in FPL diverge in the training process.

3 Methodology

3.1 Notations

Let M denote the number of participants and K the total number of cyber attack classes. Each participant i owns data D_i; $d_i \subseteq D_i$ is a batch. For any class j, $N_{i,j}$ designates the number of samples of that class on participant i, and $N_i = \sum_{j=1}^{K} N_{i,j}$ the total number of samples on that participant. Let $f_\omega(x) \to y$ be the locally trained detection model with ω the parameters of f. We denote x and y as the features of a cyber attack and the corresponding predicted attack type, respectively. To clarify, we further decompose the detection model as $y = f_\omega(x) = c(\phi(x))$, where c and ϕ are the classification head and embedding layers of the detection model, respectively. For instance, for a ten-layered convolutional neural network (CNN), we use the first eight layers as the embedding function and the remaining two layers as the classification head. An input x is first fed into the embedding function then the classification head c is applied to the generated embedding $\phi(x)$ to produce the attack type prediction. At round t, the model parameters trained by participant i are denoted as ω_i^t. The logit output on x_i from the locally trained detection model with respect to class j is denoted as $p_{i,j} = f(\omega_i^t; x_i)$. Each participant also builds a local prototype $C_{i,j}^t$ for every class j by averaging the embeddings of its class j samples; the server aggregates those local prototypes into the global prototype $\bar{C}_j^t$. The dimensionality of a prototype denoted as d, and the number of model parameters as m. Let L_S denote the cross-entropy loss, L_R the prototype alignment loss. λ and μ are hyper-parameter scalars to balance the loss terms in the optimization objective.

3.2 Description of PROTEAN

The workflow of PROTEAN is outlined in Algorithm 1 and illustrated in Fig. 1. Its training process is established based on the FL protocol. Each participant trains the parameters ω of the detection model locally using privately owned training samples. Simultaneously, each participant i also generates the class prototype vector $C_{i,j}$, as given in Eq. 1:

$$C_{i,j} = \frac{1}{N_{i,j}} \sum_{x_{i,j} \in \text{class } j} \phi(x_{i,j}) \tag{1}$$

These locally computed class prototypes encapsulate the essential characteristics of each attack type observed by the participant, with one prototype vector per attack type. At each federated training round, each participant transmits the locally generated class

Algorithm 1: PROTEAN

1: **Input:** $D_i, \omega_i, i = 1, \ldots, M$
2: Initialize the global prototypes $\{\bar{C}_j^0\}, j = 1, \ldots, K$ for all K classes
3: **Server executes:**
4: **for** each round $t = 1, 2, \ldots$ **do**
5:     **for** each participant i in parallel **do**
6:         $\{C_{i,j}^t\}, \omega_i^t \leftarrow$ LocalUpdate$(i, \bar{C}_j^{t-1}, \omega^{t-1})$
7:     **end for**
8:     Aggregate the local model parameters ω^t on the central server (Eq. 2)
9:     Update the global prototypes by aggregating the local prototypes $\{C_{i,j}^t\}$ (Eq. 2)
10:    Share back the global prototypes $\{\bar{C}_j^t\}$ and the global model parameters ω^t to local clients
11: **end for**

12: **Function LocalUpdate**$(i, \bar{C}_i^{t-1}, \omega^{t-1})$
13: **for** each local epoch **do**
14:     **for** each batch $(x_i, y_i) \in d_i$ **do**
15:         Compute local prototypes using the embedding layers of the detection model
16:         Optimize the learning objective in Eq. 3 to update local model parameters ω_i^t
17:     **end for**
18: **end for**
19: **return** $\{C_{i,j}^t\}, \omega_i^t$

prototypes $\{C_{i,j}\}$, as well as the parameters ω of the local detection model to a central server.

As given in Eq. 2, the server then aggregates these local class prototypes. Each $\bar{C}_j$ represents the shared knowledge of the attack class j observed by different participants. The global prototypes, and the aggregated detection model parameters, are then redistributed to the participants, allowing each one to retrain its local detection model using both its local data and the globally shared prototypes. This iterative process enables each participant to align both the detection model parameters and the class prototypes, ensuring that the shared knowledge remains representative of the data distribution across all participants. During inference, the global detection model and prototypes are used by each local participant to detect attack classes on its device.

The global class prototypes and model parameters are computed on the central server as:

$$\omega^t = \frac{1}{M} \sum_{i=1}^{M} \omega_i^t, \quad \bar{C}_j^t = \frac{1}{M} \sum_{i=1}^{M} C_{i,j}^t \qquad (2)$$

The objective of local training, as shown in Eq. 3, is to optimize each participant's local classification performance and align the local prototypes with the global prototypes. This learning objective incorporates three items. First, it minimizes the cross-entropy loss $\mathcal{L}_S$, encouraging accurate classification of cyber intrusions. Second, minimizing the prototype alignment loss $\mathcal{L}_R$ ensures that the local prototypes $C_{i,j}$ generated by participant i for each class j are closely aligned with the corresponding global prototypes $\bar{C}_j$. We denote $\|C_{i,j}^t - \bar{C}_j^{t-1}\|$ the L^2 distance between the two prototypes, with a lower distance indicating that the local prototype $C_{i,j}$ is better aligned to the global prototype $\bar{C}_j$. Enforcing the alignment between the local and global class prototypes in the embedding space acts as a regularization requiring locally trained models to provide similar class prototypes. This prototype alignment term hence encourages the convergence of the federated model training across different participants. Furthermore, the third term enforces model parameter alignment between different participants. It penalizes the locally trained parameters ω_i^t of the detection model if they deviate significantly from the global model parameters derived in the last round ω^{t-1}. Intuitively, with the model parameter alignment, locally tuned model parameters should stay close to the globally aggregated model parameters. It suppresses the bias from the distribution drift of local training datasets hosted by different participants. Jointly applying the prototype alignment (the second term) and model alignment (the third term) thereby boosts the convergence of the training process in the extreme heterogeneous training data distribution [13]:

$$\omega_i^{*t} = \arg\min_{\omega_i^t} \sum_{(x_i,y_i) \sim d_i} \mathcal{L}_S(f(\omega_i^t; x_i), y_i) + \lambda \sum_{j=1}^{K} \mathcal{L}_R(\bar{C}_j^{t-1}, C_{i,j}^t) + \frac{\mu}{2} \|\omega_i^t - \omega^{t-1}\|^2 \text{ s.t.}$$

$$\mathcal{L}_S(f(\omega_i^t; x_i), y_i) = -\frac{1}{N_i} \sum_{(x_i,y_i) \sim d_i} \sum_{j=1}^{K} y_{i,j} \log(p_{i,j}), \quad \mathcal{L}_R(\bar{C}_j^{t-1}, C_{i,j}^t) = \|C_{i,j}^t - \bar{C}_j^{t-1}\|^2$$

(3)

where x_i and y_i are the features and attack class labels of the training sample hosted by the participant i. $\bar{C}_j^{t-1}$ is the global prototype of the attack class j obtained in the $t-1$-th round and shared back to the local participants at the beginning of the t-th federated training round. During inference, the global model classifies new instances by assigning the label of the global prototype with the smallest L^2 distance to the instance's embedding. To guarantee the applicability of PROTEAN, we perform the theoretical reasoning of the asymptotic convergence of PROTEAN. Due to the space limit, we provide the convergence proof in Appendix A.

3.3 Direct Knowledge Sharing to Detect Rare Cyber Attacks

Introducing the prototypes does not only aim to improve federated model training with non-IID training data but also facilitates direct knowledge sharing about cyber attacks between the participating organizations. In the context of PROTEAN, a global attack class prototype $\bar{C}_j$ serves as a representation of typical features associated with a specific attack type j. Note that one attack has multiple local prototypes $C_{i,j}$. These class prototypes reflect the diverse modes of data distribution for this attack type. This multi-prototype approach enables direct knowledge sharing by allowing various local participants – each equipped with excessively non-IID cyber attack data – to exchange these refined representations of different attack types.

Consider, for instance, an FL network deployed with various organizations as the local participants. Each organization monitors its own network traffic to raise alerts to malicious activity. Rather than exchanging raw network data, which may include confidential information, the organizations can access the global cyber attack class prototypes generated by the PROTEAN framework to estimate the distribution of various types of cyber attacks. These attack class-specific prototypes are high-level summaries that encapsulate the collective insights and characteristics of the respective attacks as observed across all participants. These participants collaborate by sending their local class prototypes to a central server. For example, if one participant generates a prototype $C_{i,DDoS}$ that captures specific traffic patterns indicative of this attack, this can be aggregated with prototypes from other participants. The result is a *global prototype* $\bar{C}_{DDoS}$ that reflects a comprehensive view of how such attacks manifest across diverse networks. By continuously updating their local prototypes in response to insights gained from the global prototype, the participants collectively strengthen the overall detection capabilities.

Once the global prototype is established, each participant receives it, enabling them to enhance their local models. If a participant has only limited or even no training samples for specific attack, e.g., DDoS Attack, the global prototype of this attack aggregated on the central server can be used as a valuable reference for the participant. It can help him to learn the representative profiles of this rarely appearing or previously unseen attack within the embedding space of the globally learned detection model. In other words, local participants can rely on this global prototype to identify potential DDoS attacks in future traffic flows. By aggregating and sharing these global prototypes of attacks across all participants, local participants gain the ability to perform few-shot or zero-shot [27] learning on rare or previously unseen attack types, enhancing IDS capabilities even in the presence of heterogeneous data distributions.

3.4 Comparison with FPL in Extreme Heterogeneous Environments

For a local participant, the detection model trained with FPL [24] struggles when tested on the rarely or unseen attack classes due to the lack of optimization for these classes during training. If a participant's embedding model has never been tuned with training samples from such classes, the local training process will introduce a statistical bias into the detection model, which prevents the model from learning meaningful representations of these classes. Consequently, during inference, the embedding layer of this locally trained model generates noisy local prototypes for these unseen or rarely appearing classes. It results in poor alignment with the corresponding global prototypes formed by the other participants who have encountered these classes. This misalignment results in diverged prototype representations between different participants, which in turn causes incorrect detection output.

PROTEAN addresses this issue by simultaneously aggregating both local prototypes and model parameters. This design reduces the discrepancies between the embedding spaces of locally trained models, ensuring that the embeddings of locally generated prototypes align more closely with the global prototype representations of the same class. This alignment enhances the convergence of prototype generation and improves consistency across locally trained models. In addition, PROTEAN introduces a regularization term (the final term in Eq. 3) in the loss function, dragging the parameters of local models close to those of the globally aggregated model. Benefitting from the design, we show that PROTEAN can reach 35% higher classification accuracy than the SOTA FPL algorithm in extreme heterogeneous data distributions.

3.5 Computational and Communication Complexity of PROTEAN

Prototype dimensionality d, is much smaller than the number of model parameters m. Thus, communication and computational cost caused by prototype transfer is negligible.

The per-round **communication** cost for classic FL (e.g., FedAvg) is $2Mm$ as each participant transmits its model parameters to the server, which then sends the aggregated model back to the participants. In contrast, PROTEAN incurs a per-round communication cost of $2M(m + dK)$, where the additional term dK accounts for the transmission of prototype data, consisting of one d-dimensional vector per class across K classes.

The additional **computational** cost introduced by PROTEAN compared to classical FL primarily stems from three operations: (i) aggregating participant prototypes by class on the server side, (ii) aggregating prototypes over all batches on the participant side, and (iii) computing the prototype loss on the participant side too. Since these operations involve only small vectors, their cost is minimal relative to the full model parameter updates.

On the server side, aggregating model parameters requires $O(mM)$ operations for classic FL. PROTEAN also aggregates participant prototypes, adding a computational cost of $O(MKd)$. However, since $Kd \ll m$, the overall server-side computational complexity remains $O(mM)$. On the participant side, let e denote the number of epochs, s the total number of training instances, and b the batch size. For each batch, the forward pass requires $O(bm)$ operations, and the loss computation requires $O(b(K + d) + m)$ operations for PROTEAN (due to prototype-related computations). The backward pass requires approximately $O(bm)$ operations. As a result, the per-batch complexity remains dominated by $O(bm)$, leading to an overall per-participant complexity of $O(esm)$ for all approaches. Although PROTEAN introduces an additional term $O\left(\frac{K d s}{b}\right)$ for prototype processing, this term is negligible relative to $O(esm)$ because $Kd \ll m$.

4 Evaluating the Knowledge Sharing in PROTEAN

In this section, we present an experimental evaluation of PROTEAN to assess its feasibility in terms of utility and knowledge sharing for rare attacks.

4.1 Experimental Setup

Datasets. We use benchmark datasets, namely X-IIoTID [2] and 5G-NIDD [21]. Both datasets capture real-world network attack data from distributed end-point devices, such as IoT devices and 5G end-devices. X-IIoTID is often used in the context of intrusion detection in Industrial Internet of Things (IIoT), a key use case in 5G studies. It includes both general and specific attack classes. The general classes are: Normal, Weaponization, Ransom Denial of Service (RDOS), Reconnaissance, Lateral Movement, Exfiltration, Exploitation, Tampering, Command and Control (C&C), and Crypto-ransomware. We remove Crypto-ransomware as it contains very few instances with valid values.

The 5G-NIDD dataset was collected from the 5G Test Network Finland (5GTN) at Oulu University, with additional testbed elements like Nokia Pico Base Stations, attacker nodes, and benign traffic-generating participants. It consists of live traffic using protocols like HTTP, HTTPS, SSH, and SFTP. The dataset covers various types of DoS attacks, such as ICMP Flood, UDP Flood, SYN Flood, HTTP Flood, and Slowrate DoS. It also incorporates various port scanning techniques, including SYN Scan, TCP Connect Scan, and UDP Scan.

Non-IID Attack Data Distributions. We adopt the Dirichlet distribution model to simulate various non-IID levels of data across local participants [10,17]. By changing the α hyperparameter of the Dirichlet distribution, we control the degree of heterogeneity across different local participants, with smaller values of α corresponding to less uniform distributions (non-IID-like behavior). We conduct our experiments using different α values, i.e., $\{0.75, 0.5, 0.25\}$. By focusing on lower α values and thus more heterogeneous distributions of attack data, we study how well knowledge sharing in PROTEAN can help detect unseen attacks in heterogeneous environments.

Baselines. We involve the Four SOTA FL methods applied in collaborative training of attack detection models, including Cerberus [18], MOON [11], FedProx [13] and FedProto [24]. Cerberus applies the standard FedAvg aggregation. MOON and FedProx are non-IID FL methods, enforcing the consistency constraint over locally trained models to bridge the distribution gap between local participants. FedProto is the vanilla federated prototype learning method, which only aggregates local prototypes. In contrast, PROTEAN performs the aggregation of the locally trained class prototypes and detection model parameters, reaching the alignment of class prototypes and models. In the empirical study, these baselines are noted as *Cerberus*, *MOON-IDS*, *FedProx-IDS* and *FPL-IDS*. In addition, we include a variant of PROTEAN, which aggregates the parameters of the embedding layers $\phi(*)$ of the detection model instead of all the parameters. We name this baseline as *PROTEAN-embedding*. We compare PROTEAN and PROTEAN-embedding to verify the model aggregation strategy adopted in PROTEAN.

Detection Model. We use a CNN implemented in Pytorch consisting of two convolutional layers (64 and 128 filters) with ReLU activations, each followed by max pooling and dropout (0.2 and 0.5). The flattened output is passed through a dense layer with 128 units, followed by the final classification layer. The architecture outputs both a class prediction via log-softmax and the global class prototype vectors. For the proximal term in Eq. 3, we use $\mu = 0.1$.

Evaluation Settings and Metrics. PROTEAN targets cross-silo FL scenarios involving a limited number of participants [14], e.g. companies and ISPs. With this setting, we assume 10 participants in the following experiments. For each dataset, we split the samples into 80% for training and 20% for testing, and distribute the former to the participants in a non-IID manner according to the Dirichlet distribution. We train PROTEAN with 10 rounds of federated training and three epochs of local training on each participant. To evaluate the performance of the detection model over multiple classes, we use *Macro accuracy, Accuracy, F1 score*, and *Precision*. Experiments were done on a Linux Ubuntu 22.04.4 with 11th Gen Intel® Core™ i7-11800H processor (16 threads, 4.6 GHz max) and 31 GiB of RAM.

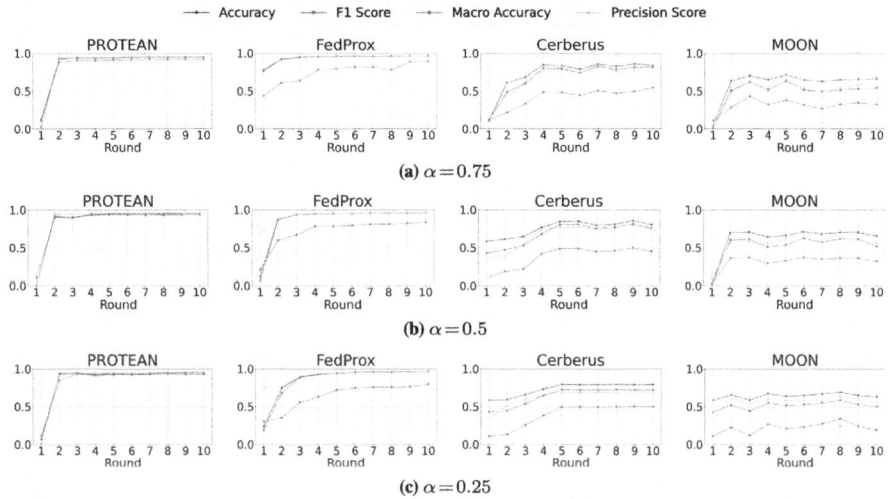

Fig. 2. Per-round accuracy, F1 score, macro accuracy, and precision of PROTEAN, FedProx-IDS, Cerberus, and MOON-IDS with $\alpha = 0.75, 0.5$, and 0.25 on the X-IIoTID dataset.

4.2 Utility of PROTEAN in Heterogeneous Environments

We start by evaluating the accuracy scores on each local participant and report the average over all 10 participants as the PROTEAN's global utility metrics in detecting different attacks. The empirical results can be found in Table 1. These results demonstrate that PROTEAN outperforms Cerberus, MOON, FedProx-IDS, and FPL-IDS across all α values and on both datasets. For instance, in a very heterogeneous environment with $\alpha = 0.25$, on the X-IIoTID dataset, PROTEAN achieves 40%, 66.45%, 6.33% and 36.3% higher utility than the baselines.

PROTEAN outperformed the original FPL. Specifically, in the X-IIoTID dataset, where each participant has a skewed class distribution with $\alpha = 0.5$, 5 out of 10 participants lack 2 to 4 classes in their training sets. When evaluated across all classes—including those unseen during training—FPL-IDS achieves a macro-averaged classification accuracy of 68.06% vs. 92.24% for PROTEAN. Under an even more severely skewed distribution with $\alpha = 0.25$, where 8 out of 10 participants miss between 1 and 5 classes, FPL-IDS's macro-averaged accuracy drops to 63.92% vs. 93.64% for PROTEAN. Similarly, for the 5G-NIDD dataset at $\alpha = 0.75$, 7 out of 10 users are missing 1 to 3 classes, with one user missing 5 classes. Under these conditions, FPL-IDS achieves a macro accuracy of 60.14%, compared to 88.07% for PROTEAN. At $\alpha = 0.5$, with 8 out of 10 users missing between 1 and 5 classes, FPL-IDS's macro accuracy further decreases to 51.63% while PROTEAN's is 83.84%. Finally, for $\alpha = 0.25$, FPL-IDS records a macro accuracy of 48.88% while PROTEAN achieves 85.88%. This demonstrates PROTEAN's effectiveness in leveraging prototype-based knowledge, enabling robust detection of unseen or rare classes, even in highly heterogeneous environments.

PROTEAN increasingly improves over the baselines with lower α values. This is due to the divergence of prototypes and model parameters locally tuned by par-

Table 1. Mean and standard deviation of the macro accuracy with varying α values on X-IIoTID and 5G-NIDD datasets. Results for each α are averaged over three runs with different random seeds.

Algorithm	X-IIoTID			5G-NIDD		
	$\alpha = 0.75$	$\alpha = 0.50$	$\alpha = 0.25$	$\alpha = 0.75$	$\alpha = 0.50$	$\alpha = 0.25$
Cerberus	52.23 (5.19)	56.52 (16.64)	53.57 (4.81)	66.05 (5.4)	54.45 (2.22)	47.40 (11.19)
Moon-IDS	41.1 (1.81)	35.58 (3.59)	27.17 (5.34)	39.06 (2.46)	31.55 (4.32)	25.03 (7.5)
FedProx-IDS	89.72 (0.87)	89.15 (3.75)	87.29 (5.41)	82.27(0.21)	77.98 (6.71)	71.67 (5.96)
FPL-IDS	64.57 (2.48)	65.46 (3.06)	57.32 (4.92)	56.06 (2.89)	51.08 (0.47)	44.93 (8.04)
PROTEAN-embedding	90.88 (1.36)	91.31 (1.37)	92.2 (0.47)	78.78(2.58)	77.42 (0.13)	81.52 (0.24)
PROTEAN (Ours)	**92.67 (0.32)**	**93.62 (0.29)**	**93.43 (0.16)**	**85.83 (3.14)**	**82.50 (0.95)**	79.97 (5.72)

ticipants during training Cerberus, FedProx-IDS, and FPL-IDS. It impedes effective aggregation and hinders the ability to generalize in highly heterogeneous distributions. FedProx-IDS achieves higher macro accuracy than Cerberus by mitigating model divergence across different participants but still underperforms compared to PROTEAN due to its introduction of prototypes and model parameter alignment into the training process. Both alignment-driven learning objectives shrink the gap between locally tuned class prototypes. These prototypes, in turn, enhance accuracies over rarely appearing attack classes of each participant, thereby increasing the overall utility.

Furthermore, PROTEAN achieves higher macro-accuracy compared to PROTEAN-embedding. This result highlights the importance of aggregating all parameters to improve classification performance, especially for infrequently occurring attack classes. Theoretically, this full-parameter aggregation promotes greater consistency within the embedding space formed by the locally trained models. Such a design enhances knowledge sharing by aggregating the local class prototypes, which in turn improves the accuracy for low-prevalence attack classes.

Convergence. We also evaluate the convergence speed of PROTEAN in heterogeneous environments, via the evolution of accuracy, F1 score, macro accuracy, and precision scores for increasing FL rounds. We report the results in Figs. 2 and 7, respectively, for the X-IIoTID and the 5G-NIDD datasets, with α valued as 0.75, 0.5 and 0.25. Due to the space limit, we leave all Figures on the 5G-NIDD dataset in the appendix. We omit FPL-IDS as its performance is significantly lower than the other detection models over all the rounds.

For both datasets, PROTEAN outperforms Cerberus across all metrics; once again, this is primarily due to FedAvg's tendency to diverge in non-IID settings. PROTEAN also achieves higher macro accuracy than FedProx-IDS and exhibits faster convergence. This stems from sharing prototypes by class, enhancing detection accuracy for each class. In other words, by improving the accuracy of each class, PROTEAN effectively boosts the overall macro accuracy. We also tested with higher number of participants (20) and found out that PROTEAN maintained essentially the same effectiveness. For example, for $\alpha = 0.25$ it attained 95.4% accuracy 95.4% F_1, 91.7% macro-accuracy and

95.5% precision on X-IIoTID, and 97.1% accuracy, 97.5% F_1, 83.7% macro-accuracy and 98.0% precision on 5G-NIDD.

Moreover, PROTEAN converges faster for both datasets in the second round, while FedProx-IDS converges in the fourth round for X-IIoTID and the fifth for 5G-NIDD, and Cerberus converges in the fifth round for both datasets. This reduces the number of communication rounds required to reach good performance, which is beneficial in FL settings where communication costs may be significant.

4.3 Knowledge Sharing for Detecting Rare Attacks

For each local participant, we choose the 2 attack types with the least training samples as the *rare* attack classes collected on the corresponding local participant. By setting $\alpha = 0.25, 0.5$ and 0.75, the 2 rare attack classes amount for, on average, less than 0.39%, 0.59% and 0.12% for X-IIoTID and 0.32%, 0.59%, 1.46% for 5G-NIDD of training samples hosted by the other attack types across different local participants.

On each data set, we average the accuracy score of the 2 rare attack classes for each local participant with PROTEAN and Cerberus, noted as $\mathcal{A}_{\text{PROTEAN}}$ and $\mathcal{A}_{\text{Cerberus}}$. We then compare the averaged accuracy scores of PROTEAN and Cerberus in Figs. 3 and 8. In the analysis of the X-IIoTID dataset, PROTEAN consistently outperforms Cerberus in detecting both rare attacks across all participants. Specifically, for α values of 0.5 and 0.25, Cerberus failed to detect rare attacks on participants 6 and 7, and participants 4 and 5, respectively, resulting in an accuracy close to 0%. In contrast, PROTEAN significantly improves detection accuracies to over 80% for rare attacks on these participants. Similarly, on 5G-NIDD, all rare attacks are being better detected for some participants for $\alpha = 0.5$ but the difference between $\mathcal{A}_{\text{PROTEAN}}$ and $\mathcal{A}_{\text{Cerberus}}$ for these values is less than 6%. On the other hand, other participants make an improvement with PROTEAN of more than 55% and, for participants 0, 1 and 5, the attacks were not detected with Cerberus but detected with PROTEAN. For other α values, we observe that $\mathcal{A}_{\text{PROTEAN}}$ is higher than $\mathcal{A}_{\text{Cerberus}}$ for all the cases and improvement achieved was higher than 80% for participant 9 when $\alpha = 0.25$. Furthermore, we perform the Mann-Whitney U hypothesis test [16] over $\mathcal{A}_{\text{PROTEAN}}$ and $\mathcal{A}_{\text{Cerberus}}$ of all the participants on X-IIoTID and 5G-NIDD datasets. The hypothesis test shows that $\mathcal{A}_{\text{PROTEAN}}$ is significantly larger than $\mathcal{A}_{\text{Cerberus}}$ with a p-value less than $2e-4$ for the X-IIoTID dataset. For the 5G-NIDD dataset, the p-value is less than $5e-2$ with $\alpha = 0.75$ and 0.25, indicating a significantly larger value of $\mathcal{A}_{\text{PROTEAN}}$ than $\mathcal{A}_{\text{Cerberus}}$. The only exception is at $\alpha = 0.5$ on 5G-NIDD, the p-value is larger than $1e-2$. The possible reason is that the two attack classes selected to measure $\mathcal{A}_{\text{PROTEAN}}$ and $\mathcal{A}_{\text{Cerberus}}$ on some of the participants have relatively more samples inside the 5G-NIDD dataset compared to the situation on the X-IIoTID dataset. Therefore, the accuracy gap between PROTEAN and Cerberus shrinks on these participants. We also compute the average of $\mathcal{A}_{\text{PROTEAN}}$ and $\mathcal{A}_{\text{Cerberus}}$ scores derived on all the participants, which gives 91.32% and 58.08% respectively. We observe that globally PROTEAN can reach 33.24% higher detection accuracy than Cerberus on the rarely appearing attack types across all the local participants.

These empirical observations convey a two-fold message. First, via sharing the global attack class prototypes in PROTEAN, the local participants with the rare attacks can use the distribution of these attack data in the embedding space to enhance the training of their local models, thus mitigating the training data bias induced by the local imbalanced data. This is achieved by integrating the prototype regularization into the learning objective of PROTEAN in updating local detection models in each round, according to Eq. 3 in Sect. 3. Second, compared to Cerberus, we find that PROTEAN can effectively boost the detection performances over the rarely appearing attack classes. Though sharing model parameters in Cerberus facilitates driving the federated training to converge to a global detection model, local model training in Cerberus is prone to the statistical bias caused by the class imbalance between the rare attack types and other attack classes. As a result, the globally aggregated model is impacted by the bias of class imbalance of local ones, which deteriorates the detection performance over rare classes.

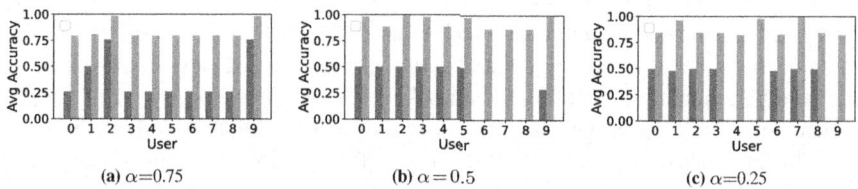

Fig. 3. Comparison of the averaged accuracy on two rare classes of each participant on the X-IIoTID dataset with different α values. Blue and orange bars represent Cerberus and PROTEAN, respectively. (Color figure online)

Zero-Shot Learning of Unseen Cyber Intrusions via Knowledge Sharing. For each participant, we further examine the detection accuracy of PROTEAN across attack classes for which the participant has no training samples (zero-shot learning [27]). After training the IDS model using PROTEAN, we compare the accuracy score for each attack class between models trained with PROTEAN and those trained only locally (i.e., *without FL*) in Figs. 4 and 9 (in the appendix) for α values of 0.75, 0.5 and 0.25, for X-IIoTID and 5G-NIDD datasets, respectively. For the setting without FL, the detection model is locally trained with the training samples of cyber intrusions hosted by the participant. In this case, this local participant can only detect the attack types present in his own training data. Using the locally trained detection model, there are some participants limited to detecting just one or two types of cyber intrusions. By comparison, after applying PROTEAN, local participants using the shared model and prototypes were able to detect all types of attacks. For example, for X-IIoTID dataset and for α = 0.75, participant 5 does not have any instances of classes RDOS, Reconnaissance, Tampering and Weaponization. With the locally trained detection model, the accuracy scores of these classes are all 0%. With PROTEAN, the accuracy of these classes are increased to 99.61%, 77.18%, 100% and 99.98% respectively. For the same dataset with α = 0.5, participant 6 does not have any training instances of the same classes. With the locally trained detection model, the accuracy scores are null for these classes on that participant. With PROTEAN, the accuracy is raised to 99.80%, 76.91%, 99.61%, and

99.62% on these classes respectively. For the 5G-NIDD dataset and $\alpha = 0.75$, participant 5 does not have any instances of all classes except benign. With only the locally trained model, the accuracy of these classes is null. With PROTEAN, their accuracies are increased to 76.19%, 91.78%, 98.45%, 99.59%, 77.03%, 99.10%, and 99.88%. This indicates that local participants can share their knowledge about cyber intrusions and detect unseen attacks in their own local datasets. The empirical results demonstrate the effectiveness of PROTEAN in knowledge sharing and effectively detecting attacks not present in the local training data.

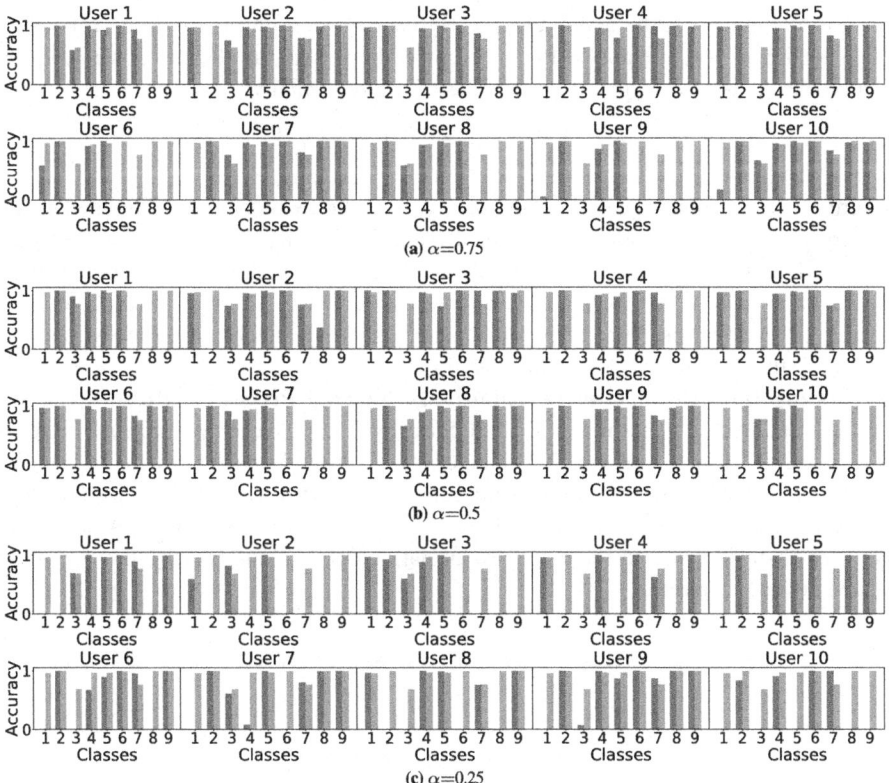

Fig. 4. Per-class accuracy for all users using PROTEAN on the X-IIoTID dataset with different α values. Blue and orange bars represent the accuracy without FL and with PROTEAN, respectively. (Color figure online)

5 Audit of Privacy Risks in PROTEAN

Privacy Risk. We start by investigating potential privacy violations in PROTEAN, more precisely, from sharing the prototypes of the attack classes and the detection model's parameters. To do so, we use data reconstruction attacks geared to recover the feature values of the raw network traffic flow data. We assume that the attacker controls a semi-honest central server. The attacker has full access to the parameters of the local detection models and local class-specific prototype vectors submitted by a local participant. The attacker's goal is to infer sensitive data (e.g., input samples) hosted by the local participant, from the shared information – the parameters of the local detection model and local prototypes. In other words, we wish to assess the feasibility of reconstructing original data points from the shared elements or learning any information about them. The data reconstruction attack is formulated as a minimization of squared error (MSE) problem. For a given participant i, the attacker attempts to recover a representative raw feature profile $\hat{x}_{i,j}$ of the attack class j. By passing through the embedding layer of the detection model, the goal is to get an embedding vector as close as possible to the shared local class prototype $C_{i,j}$ of the class j. More formally:

$$\hat{x}_{*i,j} = \arg\min_{\hat{x}_{i,j}} \|\phi_i(\hat{x}_{i,j}) - C_{i,j}\|^2 \qquad (4)$$

where $\phi_i(\hat{x}_{i,j})$ denotes the embedding vector produced by passing the estimated attack feature profile of the class j to the local model owned by the participant i, respectively. After estimating $\hat{x}_{*i,j}$, we compute the MSE between it with the average feature vector of all data in the class j hosted by the participant i. The larger (resp., smaller) the L_2 distance is, the less (resp., more) successful the attacker is in recovering the representative feature profiles in the class j.

Evaluating Data Privacy in the Knowledge Sharing Process of PROTEAN. We perform data reconstruction attacks as defined by Eq. 4 for each participant. Figure 5 reports the MSE value averaged over all the classes hosted by each participant, noted as *Reconstructed MSE*. Besides, we introduce the average MSE value derived by a random guess of the averaged feature values of each class, noted as *Random MSE*. A larger gap between them indicates a more successful data reconstruction attack, thus the more severe privacy leak risk.

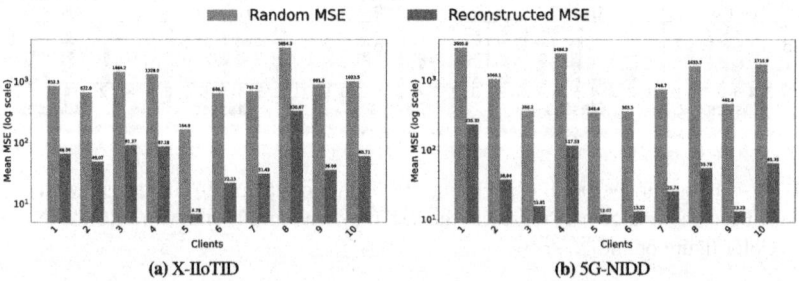

Fig. 5. Comparison between Random and Reconstructed MSEs per client (with $\alpha = 0.75$). Larger/smaller gap between the two MSE values indicates more/less accurate data reconstruction.

This attack can only reconstruct class representatives for each participant but not the data itself. The leakage is restricted to a high-level summary rather than a complete reconstruction of the data. To further enhance privacy, we applied DP by adding Gaussian noise to the local prototypes, making it more difficult to reconstruct representatives: $C_{i,j} = C_{i,j} + \mathcal{N}(0, \sigma^2)$.

We evaluate the impact of using DP to make the reconstruction attack more challenging. We analyze the impact on utility (F1-score) and privacy loss (reconstructed MSE and Peak Signal-to-Noise Ratio (PSNR) values) by varying the noise level. The PSNR is a widely used metric to quantify reconstruction quality [28]. In our evaluation, PSNR is computed per feature based on the per feature MSE and the feature range of the original training samples. It is defined as: $\text{PSNR} = 10 \log_{10}\left(\frac{(\text{Range})^2}{\text{MSE}}\right)$. The final PSNR value is obtained by averaging the per-feature PSNRs. Higher PSNR values indicate better reconstruction. Results are shown in Figs. 6 and 10 for X-IIoTID and 5G-NIDD datasets, respectively. Higher noise variance improves privacy (higher MSE). With the addition of DP noise, we observe larger MSE values and lower PSNR values, indicating that the noise perturbation effectively reduces the success of reconstructing the averaged feature profile for each class. The F1-score remains largely unaffected by the noise, suggesting that the utility is preserved. The average of the random guess baseline MSE are 1112.75, 1380.42, and PSNR are 11.82, 14.13 for X-IIoTID and for 5G-NIDD. For the reconstructed profiles without DP, the average MSE are 74.10, 66.89 and PSNR are 31.78, 33.19 for X-IIoTID and for 5G-NIDD. However, compared to the MSE and PSNR values of the random guess baseline, the MSE and PSNR values after adding the DP noise are still high. It implies that on one hand, adding DP alleviates, yet does not completely mitigate the privacy risk in the proposed system, appealing for more effective privacy protection strategies. On the other hand, the reconstruction attack can estimate no more than the averaged feature profile of one given class of network attacks. Compared to the data reconstruction attack scenarios described in previous privacy attack research [7], the reconstructed result can not be used to uncover accurate privacy-related information in the training data.

6 Conclusion

In this work, we present PROTEAN, an FPL-IDS designed for environments with distributed sensors and participants. The core contribution of PROTEAN is its knowledge-sharing process, where class-specific prototypes are shared across participants to enhance the detection of rare attacks in non-IID distributions. We also address key challenges such as privacy risks. Our findings show that PROTEAN maintains data privacy, as sharing prototypes does not reveal sensitive training data features. Our future work will focus on integrating secure computing techniques, such as Multi-Party Computing (MPC), to further strengthen privacy. We also aim to study PROTEAN's resilience to poisoning attacks and how to detect malicious participants.

Acknowledgements. This work was carried out in the context of Beyond5G, a project funded by the French government as part of the economic recovery plan, namely "France Relance" and the investments for the future program. This work has been partially supported by the French National Research Agency under the France 2030 label, SuperviZ (ANR-22-PECY-0008) and HiSec (ANR-22-PEFT-0009) projects, as well as the GRIFIN project (ANR-20-CE39-0011)

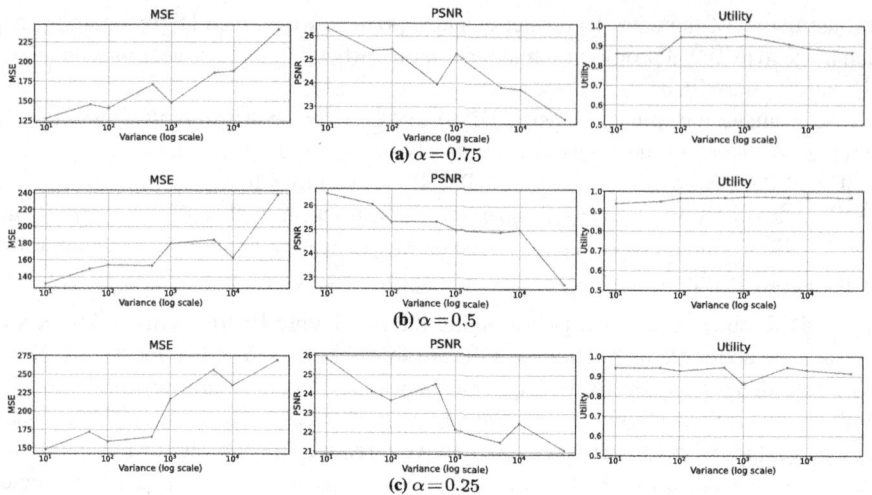

Fig. 6. Reconstructed MSE, PSNR and Utility for $\alpha = 0.75$, 0.5 and 0.25 on the X-IIoTID dataset.

and a grant from CISCO research gift on "Privacy-Friendly Collaborative Threat Mitigation." The views reflected herein do not necessarily reflect the opinion of the funders.

A Convergence Analysis of PROTEAN

We first provide the Lipschitz continuity and smoothness assumptions posed to the model trained in PROTEAN. Note that Lipschitz continuity and smoothness hold for most deep neural network models, as the learning objective function and non-linear transform encoded by deep neural networks inherently limit the rate of change and ensure smooth behavior.

Assumption 1 *Lipchitz Smoothness. For each participant, the learning objective $\mathcal{L}$ of PROTEAN, as given in Eq. 3 is L_1-Lipschitz smooth, which means,*

$$\|\nabla_\omega \mathcal{L} - \nabla_{\omega'} \mathcal{L}\|_2 \leq L_1 \|\omega - \omega'\|_2 \ s.t. \ \forall \omega, \omega' \in \Omega \tag{5}$$

where ω and ω' denote two parameter values of the detection model in the parameter value space Ω. $\|\ \|_2$ denotes the Euclidean distance. With L_1-Lipschitz smoothness, we can derive the quadratic bound of $\mathcal{L}(\omega')$ as:

$$\mathcal{L}(\omega') \leq \mathcal{L}(\omega) + \langle \nabla_\omega \mathcal{L}, (\omega' - \omega) \rangle + \frac{L_1}{2} \|\omega' - \omega\|_2^2 \tag{6}$$

Assumption 2 *Lipschitz Continuity of the embedding function. The embedding vectors produced by the embedding function ϕ has the L_ϕ-Lipschitz continuity. For any input x, we give*

$$\|\phi'(x) - \phi(x)\|_2 \leq L_\phi \|\omega_\phi - \omega'_\phi\|_2 \tag{7}$$

where ω_ϕ and ω'_ϕ are the parameters of two embedding functions ϕ and ϕ'.

Assumption 3 *Lipschitz Continuity of the objective function with respect to the embedding.* For each participant, the learning objective $\mathcal{L}$ of PROTEAN is L_2-Lipschitz continuous with respect to the embeddings. It gives for any training sample (x,y):

$$|\mathcal{L}(\phi') - \mathcal{L}(\phi)| \leq L_2 \|\omega'_\phi - \omega_\phi\|_2 \tag{8}$$

where ω_ϕ and ω'_ϕ are the parameters of the two different embedding functions ϕ' and ϕ.

Theorem 1. *The upper bound of the learning objective descent at one federated training round.* For each participant i, we use $\mathcal{L}^i_{t+1}$ and $\mathcal{L}^i_t$ to denote the learning objective values of a participant of PROTEAN, which are derived at the successive federated training rounds $t+1$ and t. We assume the local learning rate as η and locally the model is trained with T steps of stochastic gradient descent. Given that Assumptions 1, 2, and 3 hold, we can bound the expectation of the learning objective at the communication round $t+1$, $\mathcal{L}^i_{t+1}$, as given in Eq. 9.

$$\mathbb{E}[\mathcal{L}^i_{t+1}] \leq \mathcal{L}^i_t - (\eta - \frac{L_1 \eta^2}{2}) \sum_{k=1}^{T} \|\nabla_{\omega^t_{i,k}} \mathcal{L}^i\|_2^2 + \frac{L_1 T \eta^2}{2} \sigma^2 + (L_2 + 2\lambda L_\phi)\eta L_2 T \tag{9}$$

where σ is the upper bound of the variance of the stochastic gradient in the local training of the participant. Between the federated training rounds t and $t+1$, each participant conducts local training of the detection model. $\omega^t_{i,k}$ are the locally tuned detection model parameters of the participant i derived at the local training step k. $\nabla_{\omega^t_{i,k}} \mathcal{L}^i$ is the gradient of the learning objective of the local training process of participant i with respect to the model parameters $\omega^t_{i,k}$.

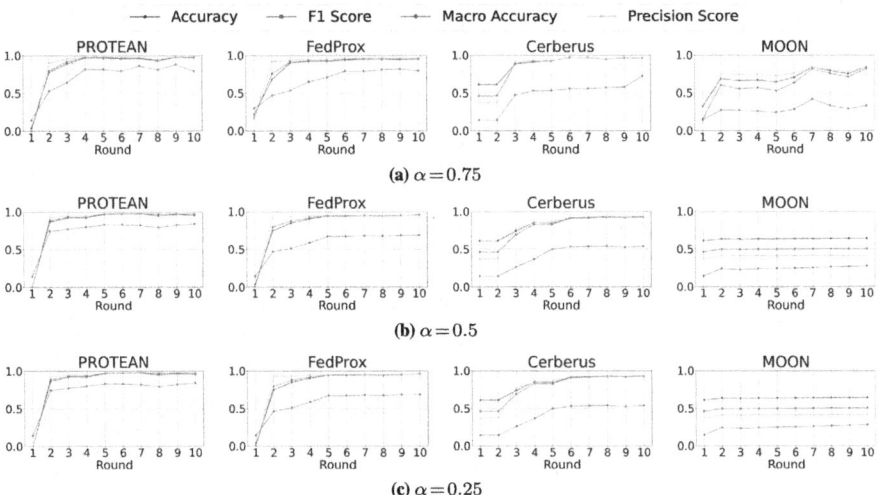

Fig. 7. Per-round accuracy, F1 score, macro accuracy, and precision of PROTEAN, FedProx-IDS, Cerberus, and MOON-IDS with $\alpha = 0.75, 0.5,$ and 0.25 on the 5G-NIDD dataset.

(a) α=0.75 (b) α=0.5 (c) α=0.25

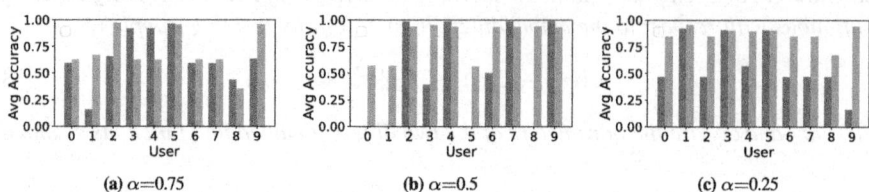

Fig. 8. Comparison of the averaged accuracy on two rare classes of each participant on the on 5G-NIDD dataset with different α values. Blue and orange bars represent Cerberus and PROTEAN, respectively. (Color figure online)

(a) α=0.75

(b) α=0.5

(c) α=0.25

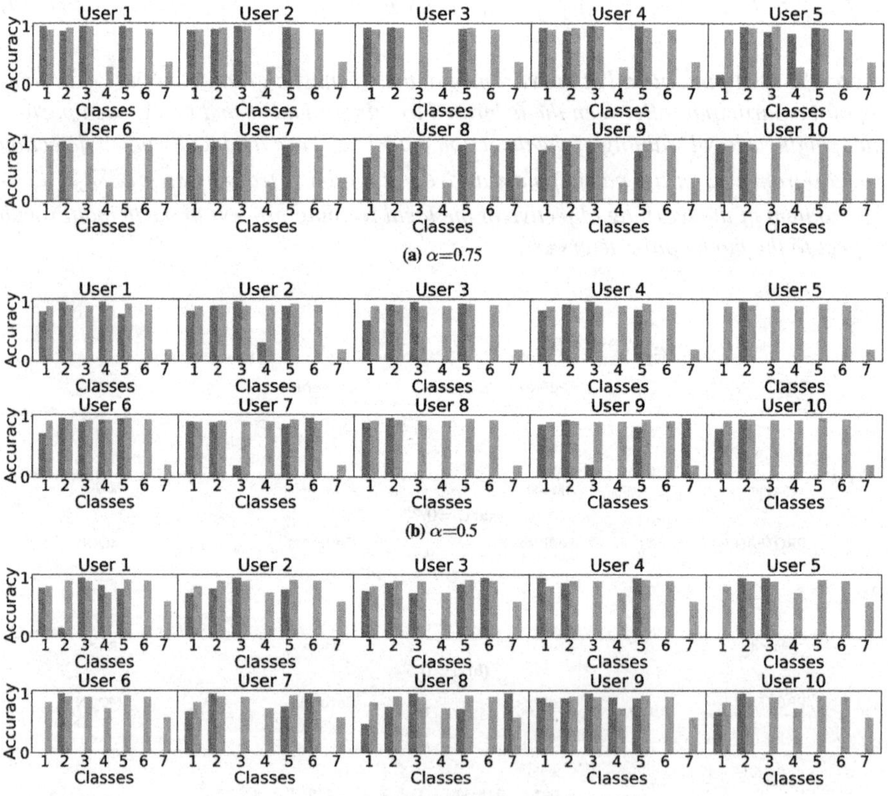

Fig. 9. Per-class accuracy for all users using PROTEAN on the 5G-NIDD dataset with different α values. Blue and orange bars represent the accuracy without FL and with PROTEAN, respectively. (Color figure online)

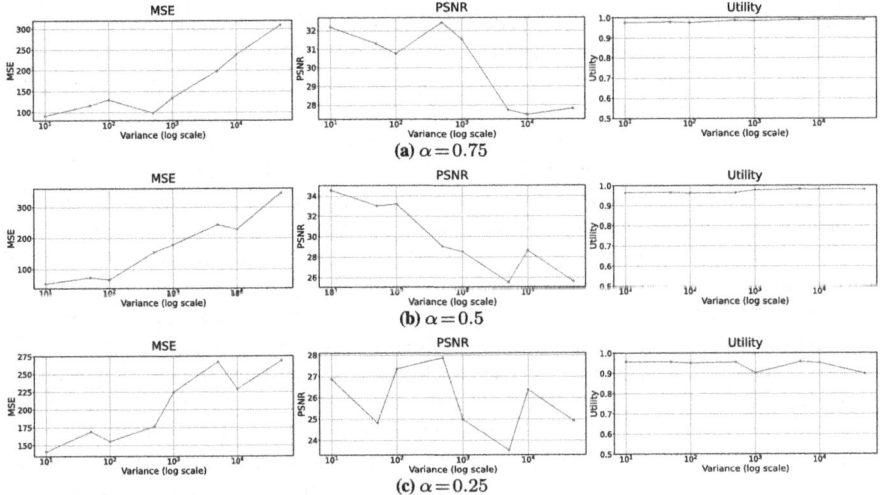

Fig. 10. Reconstructed MSE, PSNR and Utility for $\alpha = 0.75$, 0.5 and 0.25 on the 5G-NIDD dataset.

Theorem 2. *Convergence of PROTEAN. With η in Eq. 10 set as:*

$$\eta \leq \frac{\kappa - \tau}{\psi + \kappa L_1/2}, \quad \kappa = \sum_{i=1}^{T} \|\nabla_{\omega_i} \mathcal{L}_k\|_2^2, \quad \tau = (L_2 + 2\lambda L_\phi)L_2 T, \quad \psi = \frac{L_1 T \sigma^2}{2} \tag{10}$$

The convergence of the training process of PROTEAN holds.

B Evaluation on the 5G-NIDD Dataset

We report the classification performances in Figs. 7 and 8 on the 5G-NIDD datasets. After training the IDS model using PROTEAN, we compare the accuracy score for each attack class between models trained with PROTEAN and those trained only locally (i.e., *without FL*) in Figs. 9. In Fig. 10, we report the privacy attack results on the 5G-NIDD dataset.

References

1. Abosata, N., Al-Rubaye, S., Inalhan, G.: Customised intrusion detection for an industrial IoT heterogeneous network based on machine learning algorithms called FTL-CID. Sensors **23**(1) (2023)
2. Al-Hawawreh, M., Sitnikova, E., Aboutorab, N.: X-IIoTID: a connectivity- and device-agnostic intrusion dataset for industrial internet of things **9**(5), 3962–3977. https://doi.org/10.21227/mpb6-py55 (2021)
3. Asad, M., Moustafa, A., Ito, T.: FedOpt: towards communication efficiency and privacy preservation in federated learning. Appl. Sci. **10**(8) (2020)

4. Briggs, C., Fan, Z., Andras, P.: Federated learning with hierarchical clustering of local updates to improve training on non-IID data. In: IJCNN (2020)
5. Fallah, A., Mokhtari, A., Ozdaglar, A.: Personalized federated learning: a meta-learning approach. arXiv preprint 2002.07948 (2020)
6. Fan, Y., Li, Y., Zhan, M., Cui, H., Zhang, Y.: IoTDefender: a federated transfer learning intrusion detection framework for 5G IoT. In: IEEE BigDataSE (2020)
7. Geiping, J., Bauermeister, H., Dröge, H., Moeller, M.: Inverting gradients-how easy is it to break privacy in federated learning? Adv. Neural. Inf. Process. Syst. **33**, 16937–16947 (2020)
8. Karimireddy, S.P., Kale, S., Mohri, M., Reddi, S., Stich, S., Suresh, A.T.: SCAFFOLD: stochastic controlled averaging for federated learning. In: ICML (2020)
9. Lavaur, L., Pahl, M.O., Busnel, Y., Autrel, F.: The evolution of federated learning-based intrusion detection and mitigation: a survey. IEEE Trans. Netw. Serv. Manag. **19**(3) (2022)
10. Li, Q., Diao, Y., Chen, Q., He, B.: Federated learning on non-IID data silos: an experimental study. In: 2022 IEEE 38th International Conference on Data Engineering (ICDE) (2022)
11. Li, Q., He, B., Song, D.: Model-contrastive federated learning. In: IEEE CVPR (2021)
12. Li, T., Hu, S., Beirami, A., Smith, V.: DITTO: fair and robust federated learning through personalization. In: Meila, M., Zhang, T. (eds.) Proceedings of the 38th International Conference on Machine Learning. Proceedings of Machine Learning Research, vol. 139, pp. 6357–6368. PMLR (2021). https://proceedings.mlr.press/v139/li21h.html
13. Li, T., Sahu, A.K., Zaheer, M., Sanjabi, M., Talwalkar, A., Smith, V.: Federated optimization in heterogeneous networks. In: MLSys (2020)
14. Liu, K., Hu, S., Wu, S.Z., Smith, V.: On privacy and personalization in cross-silo federated learning. Adv. Neural Info. Process. Syst. **35** (2022)
15. Long, G., Ma, J., Jiang, J., Liu, L., Zhou, T., Tan, Y.: FedPCL: learning to blend representations for federated prototype learning. In: AAAI (2022)
16. Mann, H.B., Whitney, D.R.: On a test of whether one of two random variables is stochastically larger than the other. Ann. Math. Stat. **18**(1), 50–60 (1947)
17. Marfoq, O., Neglia, G., Bellet, A., Kameni, L., Vidal, R.: Federated multi-task learning under a mixture of distributions. In: NeurIPS (2021)
18. Naseri, M., Han, Y., Mariconti, E., Shen, Y., Stringhini, G., De Cristofaro, E.: Cerberus: exploring federated prediction of security events. In: Proceedings of the 2022 ACM SIGSAC Conference on Computer and Communications Security, pp. 2337–2351. CCS '22, Association for Computing Machinery (2022)
19. Pei, X., Deng, X., Tian, S., Zhang, L., Xue, K.: A knowledge transfer-based semi-supervised federated learning for IoT malware detection. IEEE Trans. Depend. Sec. Comput. **20**(3) (2022)
20. Pillutla, K., Malik, K., Mohamed, A.R., Rabbat, M., Sanjabi, M., Xiao, L.: Federated learning with partial model personalization. In: ICML (2022)
21. Samarakoon, S., et al.: 5G-NIDD: a comprehensive network intrusion detection dataset generated over 5G wireless Network. arXiv preprint 2212.01298 (2022)
22. Snell, J., Swersky, K., Zemel, R.: Prototypical networks for few-shot learning. In: Proceedings of the 31st International Conference on Neural Information Processing Systems, pp. 4080–4090. NIPS'17, Curran Associates Inc. (2017)
23. Tan, Q., Li, Q., Zhao, Y., Liu, Z., Guo, X., Xu, K.: Defending against data reconstruction attacks in federated learning: an information theory approach. In: 33rd USENIX Security Symposium (USENIX Security 24), pp. 325–342 (2024)
24. Tan, Y., Long, G., Liu, L., Zhou, T., Lu, Q., Jiang, J., Zhang, C.: FedProto: federated prototype learning across heterogeneous clients. In: AAAI (2022)
25. Wang, H., Yurochkin, M., Sun, Y., Papailiopoulos, D., Khazaeni, Y.: Federated learning with matched averaging. arXiv preprint 2002.06440 (2020)

26. Wang, J., Liu, Q., Liang, H., Joshi, G., Poor, H.V.: A novel framework for the analysis and design of heterogeneous federated learning. IEEE Trans. Signal Process. **69** (2021)
27. Xian, Y., Lampert, C.H., Schiele, B., Akata, Z.: Zero-shot learning–a comprehensive evaluation of the good, the bad and the ugly. IEEE Trans. Pattern Anal. Mach. Intell. **41**(09), 2251–2265 (2019)
28. Xiao, D., Li, J., Li, M.: Privacy-preserving federated compressed learning against data reconstruction attacks based on secure data. In: International Conference on Neural Information Processing, pp. 325–339. Springer (2023)
29. Zhu, L., Liu, Z., Han, S.: Deep leakage from gradients. In: NeurIPS (2019)

KeTS: Kernel-Based Trust Segmentation Against Model Poisoning Attacks

Ankit Gangwal[1], Mauro Conti[2], and Tommaso Pauselli[3](✉)

[1] IIIT Hyderabad, Hyderabad, India
gangwal@iiit.ac.in
[2] University of Padua, Padua, Italy
mauro.conti@unipd.it
[3] Politecnico di Milano, Milan, Italy
tommaso.pauselli@mail.polimi.it

Abstract. Federated Learning (FL) enables multiple users to collaboratively train a global model in a distributed manner without revealing their personal data. However, FL remains vulnerable to model poisoning attacks, where malicious actors inject crafted updates to compromise the global model's accuracy. We propose a novel defense mechanism, Kernel-based Trust Segmentation (*KeTS*), to counter model poisoning attacks. Unlike existing approaches, *KeTS* analyzes the evolution of each client's updates and effectively segments malicious clients using Kernel Density Estimation (KDE), even in the presence of benign outliers. We thoroughly evaluate *KeTS*'s performance against the six most effective model poisoning attacks (i.e., *Trim-Attack*, *Krum-Attack*, *Min-Max* attack, *Min-Sum* attack, and their variants) on four different datasets (i.e., MNIST, Fashion-MNIST, CIFAR-10, and KDD-CUP-1999) and compare its performance with three classical robust schemes (i.e., *Krum*, *Trim-Mean*, and *Median*) and a state-of-the-art defense (i.e., *FLTrust*). Our results show that *KeTS* outperforms the existing defenses in every attack setting; beating the best-performing defense by an overall average of > 24% (on MNIST), > 14% (on Fashion-MNIST), > 9% (on CIFAR-10), > 11% (on KDD-CUP-1999). A series of further experiments (varying poisoning approaches, attacker population, etc.) reveal the consistent and superior performance of *KeTS* under diverse conditions. *KeTS* is a practical solution as it satisfies all three defense objectives (i.e., fidelity, robustness, and efficiency) without imposing additional overhead on the clients. Finally, we also discuss a simple, yet effective extension to KeTS to handle consistent-untargeted (e.g., *sign-flipping*) attacks as well as targeted attacks (e.g., *label-flipping*).

Keywords: Federated Learning · Model Poisoning · Outlier Detection

1 Introduction

Federated Learning (FL) is a crucial paradigm for machine learning on resource-constrained devices (such as mobile, edge, and IoT devices) [1,17,18]. Big tech companies such as Google have already adopted it (e.g., for the next-word prediction in Android's Gboard [16]). FL also has profound applications in healthcare for handling sensitive data [26]. Given its potential to safeguard private and proprietary client data, FL holds significant promise, especially in light of emerging privacy regulations, e.g., GDPR. In FL, multiple devices with privacy-sensitive data collaborate to optimize a machine learning model under the guidance of a central server, while keeping the data decentralized and private.

The process of FL typically consists of three main steps that are repeated iteratively. First, the service provider's server distributes the current global model to the clients or a selected subset of them. Second, each client then adapts the global model using its own local training data to create a local model and sends the updates back to the server. Third, the server aggregates the local model updates according to a specified rule to generate a global model update, which is used to update the global model. A widely used FL method for aggregation in non-adversarial settings is *FedAvg* [17], which was developed by Google. This method computes the average of local model updates, weighted by the sizes of the local training datasets, to produce the global model update.

Given the decentralized nature of FL, it is vulnerable to adversarial attacks from malicious clients. These clients may either be artificially introduced by attackers or are legitimate clients that have been compromised. As a result, FL faces the risk of various model poisoning attacks [3,10], where attackers submit malicious updates that can undermine the global model. An attacker can compromise the global model either by poisoning the local dataset (*data poisoning attacks* [4,19]) or by directly manipulating the model updates (*local model poisoning attacks* [1,3,8,19]). When the attacker's goal is to indiscriminately degrade the global model's predictions across a wide range of test samples, it is called an untargeted attack [8]. Conversely, when the objective is to cause misclassification for a specific class label, it is called a targeted attack [1,3]. Several robust aggregation rules have been proposed to address model poisoning attacks, e.g., *Krum* [5], *Trim-Mean* [28], and *Median* [28], which rely on statistical analyses. To the best of our knowledge, *FLTrust* [6], *RECESS* [27], *DnC* [24] are the state-of-the-art solutions against model poisoning attacks in FL. Due to the unavailability of code, we do not consider *DnC* and *RECESS* in our evaluation.

Motivation: Existing classical defense schemes [5,28] that rely on statistical analyses are vulnerable to optimization-based model poisoning attacks [8,24], resulting in a decline in global model accuracy. The primary issue with these techniques is the non-Independent and non-Identically Distributed (non-IID) nature of datasets across clients. The state-of-the-art defense, *FLTrust*, is also vulnerable in highly non-IID environments because its root dataset diverges significantly from clients' local data distributions. As a result, benign client updates are frequently misclassified as statistical outliers. Therefore, a solution is missing in the literature that can distinguish malicious clients from benign clients in highly non-IID environments and in the presence of benign outliers.

Contributions: The major contributions of our work are as follows:

1. We propose Kernel-based Trust Segmentation (*KeTS*), a novel defense mechanism against model poisoning attacks. *KeTS* analyzes each client's updates to compute an individual trust score that takes into account their historical contributions. *KeTS* segments the trust scores via Kernel Density Estimation (KDE) [20] to distinguish between benign and malicious clients effectively, even in the presence of benign outliers.

2. We empirically evaluate *KeTS* against six untargeted model poisoning attacks in a white-box scenario, which is the most difficult combination to defend against. We perform our evaluations using both image and tabular datasets (i.e., MNIST [12], Fashion-MNIST [25], CIFAR-10 [11], and KDD-CUP-1999 [21]). Our results show that *KeTS* not only outperforms the existing defenses, but it also achieves all three defense objectives (i.e., fidelity, robustness, and efficiency).

3. In a series of further experiments, we (i) analyze the behavior of different clients with KeTS; assess the impact of (ii) changing the degree of non-IID partitions, (iii) attacker population, (iv) poisoning approaches, (v) number of local epochs; and finally, (vi) we propose a simple extension to KeTS to handle consistent-untargeted as well as targeted attacks.

Organization: This paper is organized as follows. Section 2 reports the background and key concepts in FL. Section 3 presents our threat model. Section 4 elucidates our proposed approach. Section 5 presents our evaluation results. Finally, Sect. 6 concludes the paper.

2 Related Works

2.1 Background

Common FL Framework: *FedAvg* [17] has established itself as the de facto standard for FL, which works as follows. At the beginning of each round, the server sends the global model to a randomly chosen subset of clients. These clients train the model on their local datasets over multiple local epochs. Next, the clients upload their trained models back to the server. The server then aggregates these updates by calculating a weighted average of each client's gradient. Here, the weight is proportional to the size of the client's training dataset. In contrast to traditional distributed stochastic gradient descent (which typically uses a single epoch), *FedAvg*'s use of multiple epochs significantly reduces the number of communication rounds; which makes it far more communication-efficient.

Non-IIDness in FL: Non-IID data in FL is characterized by substantial differences in distribution and features across the data contributed by different client participants. In real-world scenarios, such variability stems from various interconnected factors (including user behaviors, and data collection methods) [15]. Non-IID scenarios are typically emulated using: (1) *label distribution skew*, where the label distributions $P(y_i)$ vary across parties; or (2) *feature distribution skew*, where the feature distributions $P(x_i)$ vary across parties. Nonetheless, the conditional probability $P(y_i \mid x_i)$ remains the same [14]. We adopt the former strategy using a distribution-based label imbalance to simulate our non-IID settings. Specifically, each party is allocated a proportion of samples for each label according to a *Dirichlet* distribution.

2.2 Poisoning Attacks in FL

An attacker can compromise the global FL model by either modifying the local dataset (*data poisoning attacks* [4,19]) or manipulating the model updates themselves (*local model poisoning attacks* [1,3,8,19]). An untargeted attack [8] aims to degrade the global model's performance across a range of test samples, while a targeted attack [1,3] seeks to cause misclassification for a specific class.

Krum-Attack and Trim-Attack: Fang et al. [8] introduced a general framework for local model poisoning attacks that can be tailored to any aggregation rule. Their approach formulates the attack as an optimization problem. Here, the goal is to maximize the deviation of the global model update from the original update direction, achieved by crafting poisoned gradients from malicious clients. Depending on the aggregation rule, the optimization problem takes on different forms. Specifically, they designed attacks for *Krum* (termed as *Krum-Attack*), as well as for *Trim-Mean* and *Median* (termed as *Trim-Attack*).

Aggregation Attacks: The optimization problem can be refined by incorporating perturbation vectors and scaling factors [24]. By embedding the product of the perturbation vector and the scaling factor into the optimization objective, the scaling factor can be iteratively adjusted to maximize the attack's effectiveness. The authors [24] propose three specific attacks: AGR-tailored, AGR-agnostic *Min-Max*, and AGR-agnostic *Min-Sum*. In the AGR-tailored attack, the attacker utilizes knowledge of the server's aggregation rules to design an objective function that maximizes the scaling factor while adhering to those rules. Conversely, when the aggregation rules are unknown, the AGR-agnostic attacks focus on crafting poisoned gradients that deviate significantly from the majority of benign updates while evading detection by defense mechanisms. In the *Min-Max* attack, the malicious gradient is crafted so that its maximum distance from any other gradient is bounded by the maximum distance between any two benign gradients. Conversely, in the *Min-Sum* attack, the malicious gradient is designed to ensure that the sum of its squared distances from all benign gradients is bounded by the sum of squared distances between any benign gradient and the rest of the benign gradients. The perturbation vector represents any direction within the upload space that, when multiplied by the scaling factor, is utilized to perturb the mean of the benign gradients. We considered two different types of perturbation gradients: (1) inverse unit vector (denoted as Unit-Vector), which is a unit vector pointing in the opposite direction of the mean of the benign gradients; and (2) inverse standard deviation (denoted Std.-Vector), which is the negative component-wise standard deviation of the benign uploads.

2.3 Existing Byzantine Robust Aggregation Rules

A summary of the existing key defenses against poisoning attacks is as follows:

Krum [5]: It is a majority-based method. Given c malicious and n total clients, *Krum* identifies the gradient that minimizes the sum of squared distances to the $n - c - 2$ closest neighbors and selects it as the final aggregation result.

Trimmed-Mean (Trim-Mean) [28]: It is a robust aggregation method that considers each coordinate of the upload separately, making it a coordinate-wise aggregation technique. For each model parameter, the server collects and sorts its value from all clients' updates. Using a trim parameter k (where $k < \frac{n}{2}$ over n total clients), the server discards the k smallest and k largest values, then calculates the mean of the remaining $n - 2k$ values. To ensure robustness, k should be at least as large as the number of attackers; i.e., the *Trim-Mean* approach is effective only when the proportion of malicious clients is below 50%.

Median [28]: It is another coordinate-wise aggregation method. For each model parameter, it sorts the values across all local model updates. Rather than using the mean value after trimming, the *Median* method selects the median value of each parameter as its corresponding value in the global model update.

FLTrust [6]: The server in *FLTrust* utilizes a small dataset to participate in each iteration and generate a gradient benchmark. As outlined by the authors [6], we sample the root dataset uniformly at random from the union of the clients' clean training datasets while maintaining a homogeneous distribution of samples across classes, ensuring each class contains an equal number of samples. Each local model update is normalized to have the same magnitude as the server's model update. Clients whose cosine similarity between the updates and the server's update is negative are not considered for aggregation. The remaining normalized updates are aggregated via a weighted average based on their cosine similarity.

DnC [24]: It leverages singular value decomposition based spectral methods for outliers detection and removal. DnC provides strong theoretical robustness guarantees for removing malicious updates when benign updates are *iid* but, it struggles in *non-iid*, white-box scenarios.

RECESS [27]: This proactive defense constructs test gradients to analyze client responses. Benign clients optimize toward their local data distribution, while malicious ones introduce erratic changes to maximize poisoning. It detects gradient abnormalities via directional and magnitude shifts. A key limitation of RECESS is its reliance on querying clients with constructed gradients, which can introduce significant overheads and hinder scalability in large FL systems.

3 Threat Model

Attacker: Our attacker aims to degrade the global model's accuracy without being detected. We adopt the attack settings from previous works [6,27]. Specifically, the server remains uncompromised while an attacker controls malicious clients. These malicious clients may either be fake clients injected by the attacker or genuine clients compromised by the attacker. The malicious clients can send crafted local model updates to the server in each iteration of the FL training process. We primarily focus on untargeted attacks against established aggregation schemes, as they result in greater losses in the final accuracy of the global model. Typically, the attacker has partial knowledge of the FL system, including the local training data, local model updates from the malicious clients, the loss function, and the learning rate. We consider the white-box scenario, in which the attacker can access benign clients' updates and compute an attack based on this knowledge. Such a strong adversary represents the most impactful threat model.

Defender: The defense is assumed to be implemented on the server side, which is unaware of the number of attackers and does not have access to the client datasets. However, the server has complete access to the global model and the local model updates from all clients during each iteration. Additionally, it gathers updates from all the clients across previous iterations.

Defense Goal: The goal is to develop an FL technique that accomplishes Byzantine resilience against harmful clients without compromising accuracy. An effective defense mechanism must achieve all the following three defense objectives [6]:

1. **Fidelity:** When there are no adversarial attacks, the defense technique should guarantee that the classification performance of the global model is unaffected. In particular, the technique should be able to generate a global model with a classification accuracy similar to *FedAvg*, assuming no attacks.

2. **Robustness:** In the presence of malevolent clients carrying out severe poisoning attacks, the method should maintain the classification accuracy of the global model. The aim is to design a method that can train a global model amid an attack while maintaining performance comparable to a global model trained by *FedAvg* in a non-adversarial situation.

3. **Efficiency:** The approach shouldn't result in additional communication and computation costs, particularly for the clients. The clients in FL are often devices with limited resources. Thus, the goal is to create a technique that does not add to the client's workload.

4 Kernel-Based Trust Segmentation (*KeTS*)

We propose *KeTS*, a novel defense against model poisoning attacks in FL. *KeTS* derives its name from its reliance on Kernel-Based methods to estimate the probability density function of clients' trust scores. *KeTS* aims to detect malicious gradient without labeling honest clients as false positives even in largely non-IID environments. The intuition behind *KeTS* is that benign and malicious clients behave differently, i.e., benign clients aim to minimize a loss function related to their data while malicious clients aim to maximize the poisoning of the global model without being detected solving an optimization problem. In essence, benign gradients tend to point to their local distribution and remain consistent during the epochs. On the other hand, malicious gradients - solved on the basis of the optimization problems - change inconsistently. The same is demonstrated in Sect. 5.3, where the cosine similarity and Euclidean distance exhibit an inconsistent pattern for malicious clients. The existing defense schemes (*FLTrust* [6], *Krum* [5], *Trim-Mean* [28], *Median* [28]) rely on statistical analyses of the uploaded values or on utilizing similarities/differences among various uploads/previous global update. In contrast, we focus on analyzing each client individually and their history by calculating trust scores. Each client's trust score is based solely on its submitted uploads, which enables *KeTS* to function effectively in heterogeneous scenarios; where updates may vary significantly due to a non-IID distribution of class labels across clients. Figure 1 presents an overview of *KeTS*.

We now present the following related to our scheme: general setting in Sect. 4.1, reputation score and penalty in Sect. 4.2, trust score in Sect. 4.3, segmentation in Sect. 4.4, and then aggregation in Sect. 4.5.

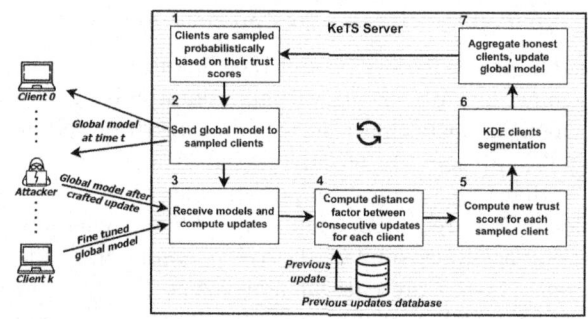

Fig. 1. An overview of *KeTS*.

4.1 General Setting

The server sends a global model to the sampled clients at each global epoch. The sampling method is based on trust scores, in fact the higher the trust score, the higher the probability of being sampled. At the outset, all trust scores are initialized to 1. Therefore, in the first global round, we sample all the clients to quickly observe variations in the trust scores, allowing us to start detecting potential attackers and avoid aggregating malicious updates. Each client will fine-tune its local model on its local dataset for a certain number of local epochs and send the resulting model updated to the server. To prevent any additional calculations on the client side, the server computes the resulting update u for each client i at a given epoch t, as defined by:

$$u_i^t = Local\_model_i^t - Global\_model_i^{t-1}, \qquad (1)$$

where each client i fine-tunes its local model at each local training iteration k according to:

$$LocalModel_i^{k+1} = LocalModel_i^k - \eta \cdot \nabla \mathcal{L}_i, \qquad (2)$$

where η is the fixed learning rate for all the clients and $\nabla \mathcal{L}$ is local Loss function. Once the sampled clients send their updates, the server collects and stores them.

4.2 Reputation Score and Penalty

We define the updates as $u = \{u_0, u_1, u_2, \ldots, u_n\}$, where each update corresponds to a client's local update. After computing the updates for each client, the server calculates a reputation score by analyzing two measures of abnormality: *direction* and *magnitude*.

The attacker can control the direction of malicious updates in order to deviate from the original direction of the global gradient. As noted in Sect. 5.3, the upload direction of benign clients points to its distribution of the local dataset since it minimizes its local loss function and is consistent with the upload of the previous global epoch. We use *cosine similarity* (S_i) as a metric to detect the angular change in direction between the upload of client i at time t (denoted as $\mathbf{u}_i^t$.) and the update at time $t-1$ (denoted as $\mathbf{u}_i^{t-1}$).

$$S_i\left(u_i^t, u_i^{t-1}\right) = \frac{u_i^t \cdot u_i^{t-1}}{\|u_i^t\|_2 \cdot \|u_i^{t-1}\|_2}. \tag{3}$$

An attacker can also manipulate the magnitude of the poisoned gradients, particularly when larger than the benign gradients. Hence, we decide to leverage l_2 distance to measure the magnitude difference between two consecutive updates. Formally:

$$\|\mathbf{u}_i^t - \mathbf{u}_i^{t-1}\|_2 = \sqrt{\sum_j \left(u_i^{t,(j)} - u_i^{t-1,(j)}\right)^2}. \tag{4}$$

Now, we introduce penalty. The penalty serves as a measure of dissimilarity between two consecutive updates, focusing exclusively on the updates of an individual client, without considering their distance from other clients' updates (as in *Krum* [5], *Trim-Mean* [28], *Median* [28]) or the server's update (as in *FLTrust* [6]).

Theorem 1 (Penalty). *In our FL setting, the penalty Py for the update uploaded by the i-th client can be defined as:*

$$Py = \begin{cases} (1 - S_i\left(u_i^t, u_i^{t-1}\right)) + \|u_i^t - u_i^{t-1}\|_2, & \text{if } S_i\left(u_i^t, u_i^{t-1}\right) \geq 0, \\ \frac{TScore_i^{t-1}}{\beta} & \text{otherwise} \end{cases} \tag{5}$$

where β is a fixed-parameter that influences speed of the score shift, and $TScore^{t-1}$ is the trust score of i-th client at the end of the previous global round.

Cosine similarity is initially used to discriminate malicious updates. Clients, whose update direction deviates from the previous one and have a cosine similarity lower than 0 are promptly discarded; and their trust score is set to 0. It is achieved by assigning a penalty, which, when multiplied by β, results in the previous trust score, leading it to be set to 0 (cf. Equation 6). The trust score update process is described in Sect. 4.3. Penalty is negatively correlated to the Cosine Similarity S_i and positively correlated to the Euclidean Distance l_2. Using the sum between the variables, rather than the product, ensures that the penalty remains responsive to changes in both S_i and l_2 independently.

4.3 Trust Score

The clients' trust scores are based on the history of each client's updates, enabling the tracking of long-term performance rather than focusing solely on the current iteration. By using trust scores, we can analyze the long-term behavior of clients; as their value is not determined by the current epoch alone, but is the cumulative result of the entire training process. Initially at $t = 0$, we assign the same trust score $=1$ to each client. Then at each iteration, we update it in the following way:

$$\text{Trust}^t = \max\left(0, \text{Trust}^{t-1} - \beta \times Py\right). \tag{6}$$

The rule above prevents the trust scores to be lower than 0. In fact, when a client reaches 0, it means that it will no longer be sampled and is eliminated from the clients pool.

4.4 Segmentation

Once we have our trust scores for the sampled clients, we want to segment them in order to detect the malicious clients. They can be easily divided into two distinct groups. To this end, we use Kernel Density Estimation (KDE) [20]. We chose KDE for its statistical robustness in one-dimensional clustering (in our case, clustering of trust scores). One-dimensional data is inherently more structured and sortable, making KDE a statistically sound and well-suited; because it efficiently detects local minima in the density distribution - unlike multidimensional techniques that are unnecessary and less effective in such settings.

Theorem 2 (Kernel Density Estimation). *Let $X_1, X_2, \ldots, X_n \in \mathbb{R}^d$ be an independent and identically distributed (IID) random sample drawn from an unknown distribution P with density function p. The KDE of the probability density function p at any point x can be expressed as:*

$$\hat{p}_n(x) = \frac{1}{nh^d} \sum_{i=1}^{n} K\left(\frac{x - X_i}{h}\right), \tag{7}$$

*where $K : \mathbb{R}^d \to \mathbb{R}$ is a smooth function called the kernel function, and $h > 0$ is the bandwidth parameter that controls the degree of smoothing. A common kernel function is the **Gaussian Kernel**, defined as:*

$$K(x) = \frac{\exp\left(-\frac{x^2}{2}\right)}{v_{1,d}}, \tag{8}$$

where $v_{1,d}$ is given by the integral:

$$v_{1,d} = \int_{\mathbb{R}^d} \exp\left(-\frac{x^2}{2}\right) dx. \tag{9}$$

KDE smooths each data point into a continuous bump, with the shape of the bump determined by the particular kernel function K(x). Individual bumps are summed to obtain a density estimate. In regions with a high concentration of observations, the density will be higher because many bumps contribute to the estimate. Inversely, in regions with fewer observations, the density will be lower as only a small number of bumps influence the density estimate. Then we consider the local minima of the resulting density function as the boundaries for our clusters. The bandwidth h at every iteration is estimated using *estimate_bandwidth* function from *scikit-learn*; this function chooses the bandwidth by calculating the maximum distance between a point and its nearest neighbors for each sample in the dataset. It then averages these distances to determine the bandwidth. We note that KDE is used solely to segment a 1D vector of n trust scores. Given m evaluation points (1000 in our setting), KDE has a complexity of $O(nm)$ (without optimization), while *bandwidth* selection requires $O(n^2)$. Since n is bounded by the number of clients, the complexity overhead is negligible. Algorithm A.1 in Appendix A presents *KeTS'* segmentation process.

4.5 Aggregation

Let the Kernel Density Estimator be $\hat{p}_n(x)$, where trust scores $x \in [0,1]$. We denote the local minima of $\hat{p}_n(x)$ as $m_1, m_2, \ldots, m_k$, such that $m_1 < m_2 < \cdots < m_k$, and m_k is the last local minimum before $x = 1$. The set of trust scores higher than m_k can be written as:

$$S = \{x \mid x > m_k,\ x \in [0,1]\}, \tag{10}$$

where m_k is given by:

$$m_k = \max\{x_i \mid \hat{p}_n'(x_i) = 0,\ \hat{p}_n''(x_i) > 0,\ x_i \in [0,1]\}. \tag{11}$$

Here, $\hat{p}_n'(x_i)$ and $\hat{p}_n''(x_i)$ denote the first and second order derivative of $\hat{p}_n(x_i)$, respectively. We consider the uploads of the selected clients as honest and aggregate them using an algorithmic equivalent of *FedAvg* [17], i.e., first computing a weighted average of the selected uploads and then adding the resulting update to the previous global model [17]. Prior works (such as RECESS [27] and *FLTrust* [6]) use a weighted aggregation mechanism based on trust scores. Their approach sacrifices the weight each client has based on its dataset cardinality, at the risk of more false positives. Moreover, selecting the clients to be aggregated allows us more flexibility in the final aggregation scheme.

KeTS focuses on detecting untargeted model poisoning attacks by identifying inconsistencies in client update histories. Although data poisoning attacks (e.g., label flipping [4,9]) lead to consistent updates from corrupted datasets, they shall appear benign to our method. By combining *KeTS* with traditional Byzantine-robust aggregation schemes (such as *Median* and *Trim-Mean*), we can first detect model poisoning attacks and then address data poisoning through traditional defenses. Algorithm A.2 in Appendix A presents *KeTS'* aggregation process.

5 Evaluation

5.1 Settings

We evaluate *KeTS* against untargeted model poisoning attacks in FL. Our focus is primarily on non-IID settings as these scenarios pose significant challenges to traditional robust aggregation schemes due to the high number of benign client outliers. To simulate non-IID scenarios among clients, we use the *Dirichlet Partitioner* (originally from *Flower* [2]) as in the work [29]. We sequentially divide the data over each label. A fraction of the data for each label is drawn for each client from *Dirichlet* distribution and adjusted for balancing.

Datasets: All our experiments are written in Python 3.10.10 environment. We use MNIST [12], Fashion-MNIST [25], KDD-CUP-1999 [21], CIFAR-10 [11] datasets in our experiments. We set *Dirichlet* concentration parameter = **0.5** for the first three datasets and **2.0** for CIFAR-10 to simulate non-IID client partitions. For MNIST, we use a simple fully connected network ($712 \times 512 \times 10$). For Fashion-MNIST, we employ a CNN with two convolutional layers (32 and 64 filters of size 3×3), followed by ReLU activations and 2×2 max-pooling. The output is then flattened and passed through two fully connected layers (600 and 120 units) with a 25% dropout. For KDD-CUP-1999 we used a fully connected network (41×128 x 23). We used a VGG [23] for CIFAR-10.

Configurations: All attacks are conducted in a white-box scenario, where the attacker has access to all clients' updates, making it the **most difficult** to defend against. We consider a fixed number of global and local epochs. We use mini-batch gradient descent; we used in CIFAR-10 a momentum of 0.9. The initial trust scores are set to 1, and the baseline β is set to 0.1. The number of clients is fixed, with attackers accounting for 20%. Table 1 shows our experiment settings.

Table 1. Dataset details.

Dataset	Classes	Size	Dimension	# of clients	# of selected clients	# of local epochs	# of global epochs	Batch size	Learning rate	% of attackers
MNIST 0.5 [12]	10	60,000	$28 \times 28 \times 1$	100	80	5	50	200	0.001	20
Fashion-MNIST 0.5 [25]	10	60,000	$28 \times 28 \times 1$	100	80	5	50	128	0.001	20
CIFAR-10 2.0 [11]	10	50,000	$32 \times 32 \times 3$	50	50	4	50	200	0.01	20
KDD-CUP-1999 0.5 [21]	23	800,000	41	100	80	1	30	128	0.001	20

Attacks and Defenses: We consider six different poisoning attacks, viz., *Trim-Attack* [8], *Krum-Attack* [8], *Min-Max* (Unit-Vector) [24], *Min-Max* (Std.-Vector) [24], *Min-Sum* (Unit-Vector) [24], and *Min-Sum* (Std.-Vector) [24]. As for the defenses, we consider three classical robust schemes (i.e., *Krum* [5], *Trim-Mean* [28], and *Median* [28]) and one state-of-the-art defense (i.e., *FLTrust* [6]). We do not consider *DnC* defense [24] due to the unavailability of its code. The parameters for these defense mechanisms are configured to their default specified values. For *Trim-Mean*, the parameter k is configured to correspond to the number of attackers. We use accuracy as the metric to evaluate the performance of trained models (both with and without poisoning). The decrease in accuracy indicates the severity of an attack, and a higher accuracy signifies a stronger defense. All the reported results are averaged over 10 runs.

5.2 Performance Results Against Poisoning Attacks

Due to our *Dirichlet*-based splitting method (cf. Sect. 5.1), all the datasets exhibit a high level of non-IID in the class distribution across clients. Furthermore, once a client is considered an attacker by KeTS, its dataset is no longer available for the training process. Due to the high heterogeneity in class distribution among clients, an excluded dataset may contain the majority of samples for a particular class. In our evaluation, the excluded datasets are always the same, i.e., the attackers are consistently the same clients while evaluating different defenses. Figures 2(a)-(d) show the average FL accuracy on the server test set for MNIST, Fashion-MNIST, KDD-cup-1999, and CIFAR-10, respectively.

As shown in Fig. 2, *KeTS* outperforms the existing defenses in effectively defending against all the untargeted poisoning attacks considered. Furthermore, *KeTS* fulfills all the three defense objectives outlined in Sect. 3 as follows:

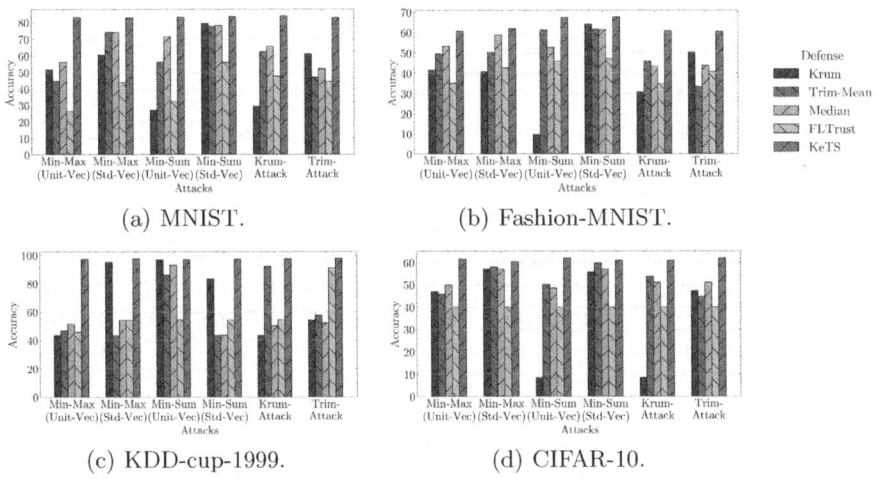

Fig. 2. The average FL accuracy with different defense mechanisms against different poisoning attacks over all the four datasets in a white-box scenario.

- **Fidelity:** We now evaluate the accuracy achieved by KeTS in the absence of attacks and compare it with the accuracy obtained by FedAvg under the same conditions. Our results demonstrate that KeTS achieves comparable performance, thereby satisfying the fidelity objective. In particular, without attacks, KeTS reaches an accuracy of 83.67% on MNIST compared to 83.77% with FedAvg; 71.23% on Fashion-MNIST compared to 71.37% with FedAvg; 97.13% on KDD-Cup-1999 compared to 97.20% with FedAvg; and 62.17% on

CIFAR-10 compared to 63.29% with FedAvg. Our results confirm that KeTS does not significantly impact model performance in benign settings.

- **Robustness:** Unlike other defenses, *KeTS* is robust because its average accuracy under any attack (i.e., > 82% on MNIST, > 60% on Fashion-MNIST, > 97% on KDD-cup-1999, and > 60% on CIFAR-10) clearly beating the existing defenses in every case (cf. Fig. 2).

- **Efficiency:** In *KeTS*, clients incur no computational overhead while the server performs relevant basic operations (e.g., storing each client's previous update, calculating cosine similarity and Euclidean distance, and executing segmentation using *KDE*). Therefore, *KeTS* is efficient and has negligible computational complexity (cf. Sect. 4.4).

Discussion: We find that the existing techniques could not defend as effectively as *KeTS*, because one or both are true for the existing defenses: (1) Benign outliers are misclassified as false positives due to the heterogeneity of client dataset partitions, which prevents their aggregation by the server. (2) Aggregation-agnostic attacks (i.e., *Min-Max*, *Min-Sum*; both variants) are designed to bypass classical aggregation rules. On the other hand, aggregation-tailored attacks (i.e., *Trim-Attack* and *Krum-Attack*) are transferable to other aggregation schemes [8], which allows malicious updates to be aggregated by the server.

5.3 Analysis of Client Behavior

We now evaluate the behavior of malicious clients in the context of four optimization and aggregation-tailored attacks, i.e., *Min-Max* (cf. Fig. 3(a)), *Min-Sum* (cf. Fig. 3(b)), *Krum-Attack* (cf. Fig. 3(c)), and *Trim-Attack* (cf. Fig. 3(d)). These scenarios are essential for: (1) showcasing how attackers behave in a distinct and diverse manner compared to honest clients, and (2) demonstrate the effectiveness of *KeTS* for detection and mitigation.

For each attack, we analyze the evolution of trust scores for both benign and malicious clients. Additionally, we examine the changes in cosine similarity and Euclidean distance. Cosine similarity (cf. Eq. 3) ranges from -1 to 1, where 1 signifies vectors pointing in the same direction and -1 indicates vectors pointing in opposite directions. Euclidean distance (cf. Eq. 4) accounts for the l_2 norm between consecutive updates, which helps in detecting modifications in the magnitude of the update that can amplify the poisoning effect. Each curve in Fig. 3 represents the mean values for the metrics while shaded regions indicate standard deviations across clients sampled in a given round. Please note that malicious clients are excluded from sampling once their trust scores reach zero, which is marked by the disappearance of the red curves. Moreover, we note that the trust scores can increase between rounds, even though the formula should not allow this. This occurs because different clients may be sampled in different rounds, leading to variations in the mean value of the trust scores.

As illustrated in Fig. 3, it is clear that malicious clients exhibit distinct behavior compared to benign clients. The trust scores for malicious clients in all four attacks sharply declines. Malicious clients experience drastic changes in update directions, as indicated by cosine similarity dropping below zero or its erratic

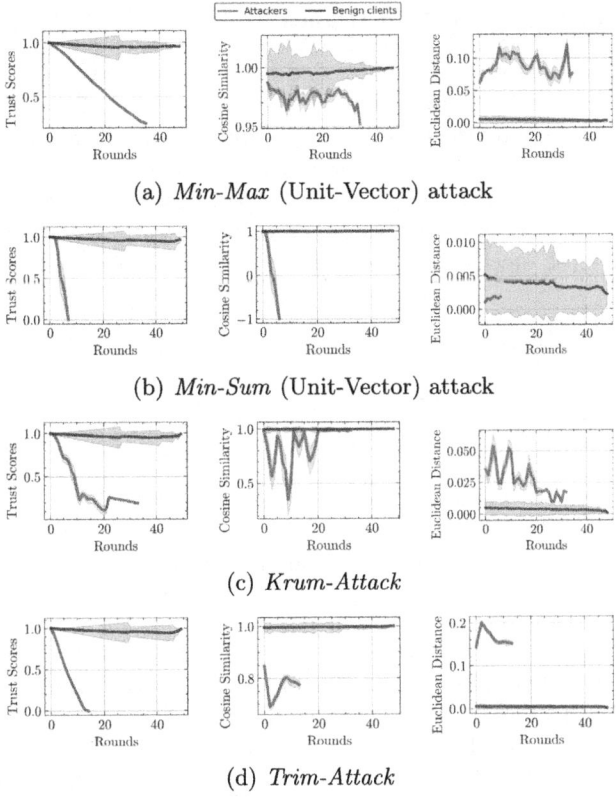

Fig. 3. Performance of *KeTS* under different attacks.

fluctuation. The Euclidean distance for malicious clients also tends to drift away from zero (in the case of the *Min-Sum* attack, *KeTS* quickly penalizes attackers based on the other two metrics). On the contrary, benign clients exhibit consistent behavior under all four attacks. In particular, benign clients maintain a stable trust score, cosine similarity near 1, and the Euclidean distance near zero. To summarize, *KeTS* is capable of identifying attackers in both optimization and aggregation-tailored attacks due to their distinct behavior.

For our further investigations (i.e., Sect. 5.4 onwards), we present results for the MNIST dataset only; mainly due to the page limit, and the results for other datasets are congruent. We chose *Min-Max* (Unit-Vector) attack in these experiments because the trust score for malicious clients declines gradually (cf. Fig. 3) as compared to other attacks. Thus, it much more difficult to defend against. All other settings remain the same as described in Sect. 5.1, unless specified otherwise.

5.4 Effect of Degree of Non-IIDnes

Next, we aim to analyze how *KeTS* and classical defenses respond to modifications in the *Dirichlet* factor, which influences the level of non-IIDness in the class distribution among the clients. Specifically, a lower value indicates a higher degree of non-IIDness in the class distributions. A higher degree of non-IIDness enables adversaries to craft more malicious gradients without detection, thereby amplifying the impact of their attacks. Figure 4 presents the detection accuracy of different defense mechanisms concerning the degree of non-IIDness.

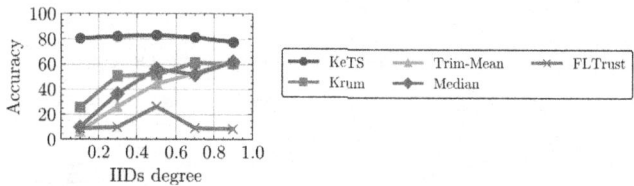

Fig. 4. Detection accuracy with respect to the degree of non-IIDness.

It is evident from Fig. 4 that the majority of defense schemes perform better when the class distribution among clients becomes more balanced (i.e., with a higher *Dirichlet* factor). It is because the more the class samples are distributed in an IID manner, the fewer benign outliers there will be. *FLTrust* demonstrates consistent yet suboptimal performance. This happens primarily due to the root dataset being too small to effectively represent the entire dataset; particularly in extreme non-IID environments, where it significantly deviates from the client's local data distributions. The accuracy in *Krum*, *Trim-Mean*, and *Median* is directly proportional to the degree of IID-ness. Those defense techniques typically rely on statistical analyses of the update population, where the aggregation is computed based on the comparative information derived from multiple updates. However, such an approach is susceptible to failure in non-IID settings, where client data distributions exhibit significant disparities. In such scenarios, the presence of outliers can distort the aggregation results, even when robust measures such as the *Median* or *Trim-Mean* are applied. In contrast, *KeTS* mitigates this issue by focusing on the individual update of each client. By evaluating updates independently, KeTS eliminates aggregation dependencies and reduces the influence of outliers. Our approach not only outperforms other defense techniques but also ensures stable accuracy across varying levels of non-IIDness.

5.5 Impact of Percentage of Attackers

We also evaluate the impact of the attackers' population on detection accuracy. As shown in Fig. 5, existing defense methods experience a substantial decline in performance as the number of attackers increases. For the same reason discussed in Sect. 5.4, this decline occurs because these methods rely on statistical analyses of the update population, where the aggregation is based on comparative information from multiple updates. As the number of attackers increases, the distribution of updates becomes increasingly skewed by malicious updates, impairing the effectiveness of these defenses. In contrast, *KeTS* focuses on analyzing each client's update independently. Its performance remains consistent, with only minimal deterioration as the percentage of attackers increases.

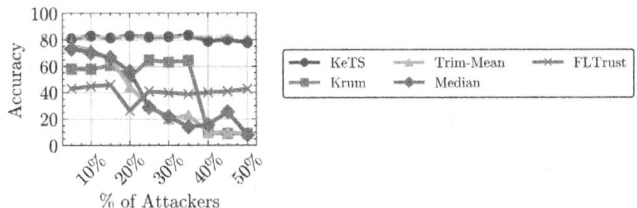

Fig. 5. Accuracy on the server test set with respect to the percentage of attackers.

5.6 Different Poisoning Approaches

In all the previous experiments, the attacker consistently sent malicious updates starting from the first epoch. We now consider two different poisoning strategies. In the first approach, the attacker begins to send malicious updates once the FL training has already started, i.e., during a global epoch > 0. *KeTS* promptly identifies such attacks, as the injected uploads are highly inconsistent with the previous legitimate updates. Specifically, these uploads exhibit a cosine similarity < 0, leading to an immediate assignment of a trust score of zero (cf. Fig. 6(a)).

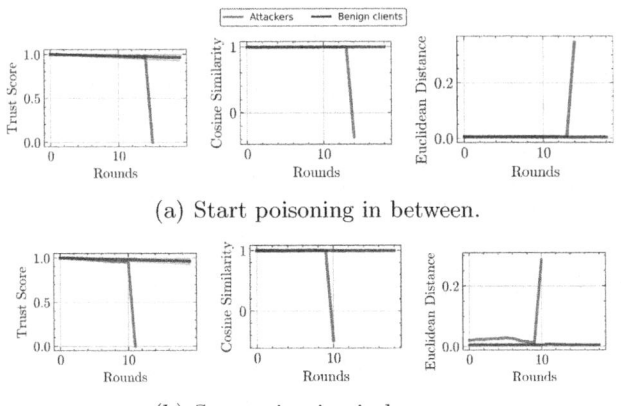

(a) Start poisoning in between.

(b) Stop poisoning in between.

Fig. 6. Performance of *KeTS* under different poisoning approaches.

In the second approach, we analyze the scenario where an attacker ceases to send malicious updates and instead submits legitimate ones after training on its dataset. In this case, *KeTS* detects the abrupt change in direction, identifies all the attackers, and sets their trust scores to 0 (cf. Fig. 6(b)).

5.7 Impact of Number of Local Epochs

We now investigate how changing the number of local epochs for each client influences the speed at which trust scores decrease for attackers. Figure 7 shows that increasing the number of local epochs causes the attackers' trust scores to decrease more rapidly, resulting in their exclusion from sampling in a shorter amount of time. We hypothesize that this happens because, with more local epochs, the updates become larger and more heterogeneous. It allows the attacker to have a bigger radius of search to find a malicious upload. As a result, the difference in direction and magnitude for the attacker becomes more pronounced.

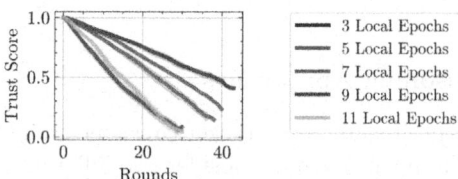

Fig. 7. Trust score decline for attackers in *KeTS* over different numbers of local epochs.

6 Conclusion

In this paper, we propose *KeTS* - a novel defense for FL against untargeted model poisoning attacks. We choose a direction based on the evaluation of each client individually. Our evaluations demonstrate that *KeTS* outperforms existing defenses and effectively handles the honest outlier problem. Moreover, *KeTS* is a scalable solution because it incurs minimal computation and storage overheads on the server and imposes no additional overhead on the clients.

Appendix A Algorithms

Algorithm A.1 KeTS-KDE-Segmentation

input : $TScores$ (list of trust scores), $SampledClients$ (list of sampled clients id), $EstimateBandwidth$ (function to estimate the bandwidth).
output: $HonestClients$ list of honest Clients

1 $bandwidth \leftarrow$ EstimateBandwidth$(TScores)$; // get the kernel bandwidth estimation
2 $density \leftarrow$ EstimateDensity$(TScores, bandwidth)$; // Generate the density estimation
3 $x_d \leftarrow$ Generate density values in range $(0, \max(TScores) + 1)$
4 $MinimaIndices \leftarrow$ FindLocalMinima$(density)$; // Indexes of local minima of density function
5 $ClusterBoundaries \leftarrow x_d[MinimaIndices]$; // Trust scores that mark the beginning of segments
6 $HonestSegment \leftarrow ClusterBoundaries[-1]$; // Index of the Trust Score marking the start of the segment
7 **for** $client\ c \in SampledClients$ **do**
8   **if** $TScores[c] >= HonestSegment$ **then**
9   Append c to $HonestClients$
10   **end**
11 **end**

Algorithm A.2 KeTS-Aggregation

input : $TScores$ (Trust scores), β (constant), Py (penalty), G (set of uploaded updates by sampled clients), $SampledClients$ (list of sampled clients id), $ClientsUpdates$ (list of previous updates for each client), w (no. of samples in each client dataset).
output: New aggregated update

1 **foreach** $client\ c \in SampledClients$ **do**
2     $sim \leftarrow$ CosineSimilarity$(client\_updates[c][-1], G[c])$
3     $eudist \leftarrow$ Euclidean distance$(ClientsUpdates[c][-1], G[c])$
4   **if** $sim < 0$ **then**
5         $TScores[c] \leftarrow 0$
6   **else**
7         $Py \leftarrow (1 - sim) + eudist$
8         $Tscores[c] \leftarrow \max(0, TScores[c] - \beta \cdot Py)$
9   **end**
10 **end**
11 $HonestClients \leftarrow$ KDESegmentation$(TScores, SampledClients)$
12 $TotalSamples \leftarrow \sum_{i \in \text{HonestClients}} w[i]$
13 $AggregatedUpdate \leftarrow \sum_{i \in \text{HonestClients}} \frac{w[i]}{TotalSamples} ClientUpdates[i]$; // Same aggregation as *FedAvg* but with updates rather then models. The resulting update will be added to the previous global model.

Appendix B Can *FLTrust* Match *KeTS*'s Performance?

We now analyze if *FLTrust*, a state-of-the-art defense, can achieve the same performance as *KeTS* under the same settings as those used in Fig. 2(a). By increasing the size of the root dataset, the performance of *FLTrust* improves (cf. Fig. 8). *FLTrust* requires over 2000 samples (which is over three times the size of a client's dataset in this setting; cf. Table 1) in the root dataset to match the performance with *KeTS*. This requirement poses significant challenges for the server and is practically infeasible[1] in FL.

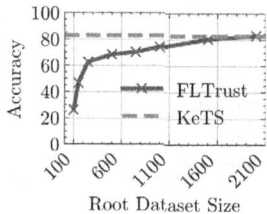

Fig. 8. Comparison with *FLTrust*.

Appendix C *KeTS'* Extension for Consistent-Untargeted and Targeted Attacks

We now demonstrate that KeTS can be easily extended to counter other attacks that exhibit a more natural sequence of updates (i.e., consistent-untargeted and targeted attacks). In particular, we examine the *sign-flipping* attack [7,13,22], where the attacker computes the update in a legitimate manner, after which the sign is flipped, resulting in consistent updates that point in an adversarial direction. Next, we consider the *label-flipping* attack [4,9], where labels are altered before the training process begins, causing the updates to follow a natural progression. We explore the following two solution avenues:

1. Use KeTS as a preliminary step/filter before any aggregation scheme. Here, KeTS detects untargeted, inconsistent attacks (as discussed throughout this paper), after which any standard aggregation method can be applied to the client updates. This approach enhances the effectiveness of the existing defenses.

2. A simple extension of KeTS, referred to as KeTSv2, handles attacks that misdirect updates to hinder convergence. Unlike crafted attacks that mimic benign behavior, these attacks rely on updates derived from legitimate training

---
[1] Due to strict privacy constraints, the server is prohibited from directly accessing client data, preventing it from sampling client data to estimate their distribution. As a result, the server must rely on externally sourced datasets. This limitation is further exacerbated in non-IID settings, where clients often hold only a subset of classes.

but oriented in a divergent direction. After filtering clients based on trust scores, KeTSv2 computes the cosine similarity between each client update and the previous global update, discarding those falling below a defined threshold. This method assumes that the number of attackers is less than half of the clients. The previous global update - used in the similarity check - is computed at each epoch using a momentum-based update rule: $\theta_t = (1 - \mu) \cdot \theta_{t-1} + \mu \cdot update_{new}$.

Table 2 shows our results on the final accuracy, based on the server test set, on Fashion-MNIST using $\mu = 0.1$, a Dirichlet distribution with concentration parameter 2.0, over 80 global rounds, 5 local training rounds per client, and 80 clients with full client participation at each round. These results showcase that KeTS is a complete solution against both targeted and untargeted attacks.

Table 2. KeTS (v1, as a pre-filter, v2) against *sign-flipping* and *label-flipping* attacks. In pre-filter setting, we test KeTS + Median as Median is the best among existing defenses.

Attacks	Existing defenses				KeTS (v1)	KeTS as a pre-filter to another defense	KeTS (v2)
	Median	FLTrust	Trim-Mean	Krum		**KeTS+Median**	
Sign-flipping	59.54%	65.07%	59.17%	69.30%	30.00%	59.97%	73.16%
Label-flipping	69.18%	65.13%	69.09%	66.90%	60.47%	69.28%	72.20%

References

1. Bagdasaryan, E., Veit, A., Hua, Y., Estrin, D., Shmatikov, V.: How to backdoor federated learning. In: AISTATS, pp. 2938–2948 (2020)
2. Beutel, D.J., et al.: Flower: a friendly federated learning research framework. arxiv:2007.14390 (2020)
3. Bhagoji, A.N., Chakraborty, S., Mittal, P., Calo, S.: Analyzing federated learning through an adversarial lens. In: ICML, pp. 634–643 (2019)
4. Biggio, B., Nelson, B., Laskov, P.: Poisoning attacks against support vector machines. arxiv:1206.6389 (2012)
5. Blanchard, P., El, M., Guerraoui, R., Stainer, J.: Machine learning with adversaries: byzantine tolerant gradient descent. NeurIPS **30** (2017)
6. Cao, X., Fang, M., Liu, J., Gong, N.Z.: Fltrust: byzantine-robust federated learning via trust bootstrapping. arxiv:2012.13995 (2020)
7. Chelli, M., et al.: FedGuard: selective parameter aggregation for poisoning attack mitigation in federated learning. IEEE CLUSTER, pp. 72–81 (2023)
8. Fang, M., Cao, X., Jia, J., Gong, N.: Local model poisoning attacks to byzantine-robust federated learning. In: USENIX SEC, pp. 1–18 (2020)
9. Fung, C., Yoon, C.J., Beschastnikh, I.: The limitations of federated learning in sybil settings. In: RAID, pp. 301–316 (2020)
10. Guerraoui, R., Rouault, S., et al.: The hidden vulnerability of distributed learning in Byzantium. In: ICML, pp. 3521–3530 (2018)
11. Krizhevsky, A., Hinton, G., et al.: Learning Multiple Layers of Features from Tiny Images. University of Toronto (2009)

12. LeCun, Y.: The MNIST database of handwritten digits. http://yann.lecun.com/exdb/mnist/ (1998)
13. Li, L., Xu, W., Chen, T., Giannakis, G.B., Ling, Q.: RSA: byzantine-robust stochastic aggregation methods for distributed learning from heterogeneous datasets. In: AAAI Conf. on AI, vol. 33, pp. 1544–1551 (2019)
14. Li, Q., Diao, Y., Chen, Q., He, B.: Federated learning on non-IID data silos: an experimental study. In: IEEE ICDE, pp. 965–978 (2022)
15. Lu, Z., Pan, H., Dai, Y., Si, X., Zhang, Y.: Federated learning with non-IID data: a survey. IEEE IoT J. **99** (2024)
16. McMahan, B., Ramage, D.: Federated Learning: Collaborative Machine Learning without Centralized Training Data. Google Research Blog (2017)
17. McMahan, B., et al.: Communication-efficient learning of deep networks from decentralized data. In: AISTATS, pp. 1273–1282 (2017)
18. McMahan, H.B., et al.: Federated learning: strategies for improving communication efficiency. In: NIPS, pp. 1–6 (2016)
19. Nelson, B., et al.: Exploiting machine learning to subvert your spam filter. LEET **8**(16), 1–9 (2008)
20. Parzen, E.: On estimation of a probability density function and mode. Ann. Math. Stat. **33**(3), 1065–1076 (1962)
21. Salvatore, S., Wei, F., Wenke, L., Andreas, P., Philip, C.: KDD Cup 1999 Data. UCI Machine Learning Repository (1999). https://doi.org/10.24432/C51C7N
22. Sharma, A., Marchang, N.: Probabilistic sign flipping attack in federated learning. In: ICCCNT, pp. 1–6 (2024)
23. Simonyan, K., Zisserman, A.: very deep convolutional networks for large-scale image recognition. arXiv:1409.1556 (2014)
24. Virat, S., Amir, H.: Manipulating the byzantine: optimizing model poisoning attacks and defenses for federated learning. In: NDSS (2021)
25. Xiao, H., Rasul, K., Vollgraf, R.: Fashion-MNIST: a novel image dataset for benchmarking machine learning algorithms. arxiv:1708.07747 (2017)
26. Xu, J., et al.: Federated learning for healthcare informatics. J. Healthcare Info. Res. **5**, 1–19 (2021)
27. Yan, H., et al.: Recess vaccine for federated learning: proactive defense against model poisoning attacks. NeurIPS **36** (2024)
28. Yin, D., et al.: Byzantine-robust distributed learning: towards optimal statistical rates. In: ICML, pp. 5650–5659 (2018)
29. Yurochkin, M., et al.: Bayesian nonparametric federated learning of neural networks. In: ICML, pp. 7252–7261 (2019)

Machine Learning Vulnerabilities in 6G: Adversarial Attacks and Their Impact on Channel Gain Prediction and Resource Allocation in UC-CFmMIMO

Mahmoud Ghorbel[1]([✉]), Selina Cheggour[2], Valeria Loscri[2], Youcef Imine[1], Hamza Ouarnoughi[1], and Smail Niar[1]

[1] University of Polytechnique Hauts-de-France, CNRS, INSA, LAMIH-UMR CNRS 8201, 59313 Valenciennes, France
mahmoud.ghorbal@uphf.fr
[2] Université de Lille France and Inria Lille, Lille, France

Abstract. Machine learning (ML) models integrated into physical-layer functions in wireless systems are increasingly vulnerable to adversarial attacks. Although prior research has investigated such threats in conventional massive MIMO architectures, the security risks in future 6G topologies, particularly user-centric cell-free massive MIMO (UC-CFmMIMO) deployed in vehicular environments, remain largely unexplored. These architectures depend heavily on frequency-domain channel gain estimation, which opens new attack surfaces. In this work, we present a black-box adversarial framework tailored to UC-CFmMIMO networks operating in dynamic vehicular environments. The attacker passively collects RF data to train a surrogate model and crafts perturbations using the FGSM attack. A local anomaly detector is integrated to assess stealth prior to uplink injection via pilot contamination. Our method significantly disrupts channel gain estimation and subband allocation, while requiring no access to the target model's internals. These results underscore emerging vulnerabilities in ML-enabled wireless systems and highlight the need for robust, context-aware defenses.

Keywords: Adversarial Attacks · Dynamic Vehicular Environments · UC-CFmMIMO · Physical-Layer Security · Resource Allocation

1 Introduction

The rise of sixth-generation (6G) wireless networks is set to transform connectivity by enabling unprecedented capacity, reliability, latency, and intelligence. As applications like autonomous driving, industrial automation, and immersive communications push current architectures to their limits, the demand for adaptive, flexible, and densely deployed systems continues to grow [2]. A key enabler of this vision is the User-Centric Cell-Free Massive MIMO (UC-CFmMIMO) architecture, which eliminates cell boundaries and leverages a dense Access Point

© The Author(s), under exclusive license to Springer Nature Switzerland AG 2026
V. Nicomette et al. (Eds.): ESORICS 2025, LNCS 16053, pp. 147–165, 2026.
https://doi.org/10.1007/978-3-032-07884-1_8

(AP) deployment to ensure seamless user service across distributed antennas. This makes it especially suitable for high-mobility use cases such as vehicular communications, where persistent connectivity is essential [21]. However, deploying UC-CFmMIMO in practice raises major challenges in resource allocation, including AP clustering, beamforming, power control, scheduling, and spectrum management. The scale and dynamics of such systems render traditional optimization methods computationally expensive and difficult to achieve under real-time constraints [15,27,37].

To address this, native Artificial Intelligence (AI), including Machine Learning (ML) and Deep Learning (DL) techniques, is increasingly being considered as a cornerstone in 6G system design. By embedding AI algorithms directly into the network stack, systems can adapt to their environment and make autonomous decisions with reduced latency and overhead. Nevertheless, a common requirement across AI-based resource management strategies is access to accurate environmental knowledge, particularly in the form of channel state information (CSI) [13,20].

In high-mobility environments, such as vehicular networks operating in the 5.88–5.92 GHz band, the channel is characterized by rapid temporal and frequency variations, largely due to Doppler effects and multipath fading. These conditions make *frequency-dependent channel modeling and prediction* a key enabler for robust and intelligent communication system design [11]. Accurate prediction of frequency-selective fading can improve the performance of downstream modules such as beamforming, handover, and interference mitigation.

However, the increasing reliance on ML and DL models for physical-layer tasks introduces new vulnerabilities. These models can become targets of adversarial attacks, where carefully crafted perturbations are introduced to the input data in order to mislead or disrupt the model's behavior [8,12,32]. Adversarial attacks are typically categorized into white-box attacks, where the attacker has full knowledge of the model architecture and parameters, and black-box attacks, which are more challenging as the attacker only observes the model's input-output behavior without knowing its internal structure [28,41]. To counter such threats, recent research has explored the use of machine learning-based misbehavior detection systems (MDS) that monitor and identify anomalous patterns suggestive of adversarial manipulation [5,8,31]. These systems are designed to enhance the resilience of AI-driven components by detecting suspicious input behaviors, thereby helping to preserve the integrity and reliability of essential wireless functions. Nevertheless, MDS has drawbacks, such as difficulties in identifying internal assaults, decreased efficacy because of physical layer fluctuations, and scaling problems that might impair performance [6,7].

1.1 Related Work

Adversarial machine learning (AML) in wireless communications has become an increasingly active research domain, driven by the growing integration of machine learning across physical-layer operations such as modulation recognition, beamforming, power allocation, and channel estimation. This has created new attack surfaces for adversaries capable of crafting imperceptible perturbations to disrupt downstream decisions.

A first line of research has targeted ML-based classification systems in wireless signal processing. The work in [3] demonstrated that adversarial examples, crafted using white-box and black-box gradient-based methods, can drastically degrade the performance of autoencoder-based communication and modulation classification models. The authors introduced robustness and undetectability constraints, making their attack relevant beyond classification and into constrained optimization. In a related effort, [38] showed that adversaries using the Fast Gradient Sign Method (FGSM) could mislead protocol classifiers under various partial-knowledge scenarios, including mismatched models and datasets. These findings confirmed the susceptibility of RF learning systems across different ML architectures.

Other works have focused on resource allocation and beam prediction modules. In [25], FGSM-based perturbations were applied to ML-driven power allocation strategies in massive MIMO systems, revealing vulnerabilities in both white-box and black-box settings. Similarly, [26] showed how surrogate model-based attacks can disrupt regression-driven power control decisions, significantly affecting feasibility rates. In the beamforming context, [9, 22] demonstrated that DNNs for mmWave beam prediction are highly vulnerable to small perturbations, which can cause beam misalignment and performance loss, even in black-box scenarios. These methods primarily operated over static inputs and did not consider adaptive stealth mechanisms or attacker-side refinement.

On the detection front, [1] proposed a multi-scale Isolation Forest and SVM framework to detect FGSM-based adversarial attacks in real-time video analysis for autonomous vehicles. While developed in a computer vision context, their use of unsupervised anomaly detection offers conceptual parallels to attacker-side stealth evaluation, where patterns in input-output behavior are used to assess detectability.

Other domain-specific attacks have emerged more recently. The MAGMAW framework in [10] targets JSCC-based wireless systems and introduces multi-modal perturbations transferable across protocols, models, and RF conditions. It uses a surrogate model and gradient-based adversarial objectives to generate black-box perturbations with minimal information leakage. Similarly, [16] focuses on attacking GNN-based resource allocation mechanisms, using spectral graph manipulation to deteriorate

Surveys such as [23, 33] present detailed taxonomies of adversarial threats and defenses, categorizing attack methods by knowledge level, domain specificity, and defensive strategies. These works highlight the maturity of AML as a research field and emphasize its growing relevance across domains, particularly within communication systems. Their comprehensive treatment of black-box models, surrogate training, and adaptive defense underscores the timeliness of developing new strategies that extend these principles to sequence-based and frequency-aware wireless estimators under realistic mobility conditions.

Recent work by [24] expands on this by demonstrating the effectiveness of FGSM-based attacks specifically in deep learning-powered power allocation within massive MIMO (maMIMO) systems. Their findings show that even small perturbations introduced at the input layer, such as user position coordinates, can lead to highly infeasible power allocation outputs, with white-box FGSM attacks causing up to 86% infeasibility under certain conditions. These results emphasize the significant threat posed by adversarial perturbations to physical-layer regression tasks in large-scale antenna systems, and strongly support the motivation for studying such attacks in UC-CFmMIMO contexts.

Most prior work assumes attackers have access to static datasets or full knowledge of the target system. In contrast, realistic high-mobility settings demand limited observability and real-time adaptation. Our framework addresses this by enabling an adaptive, transfer-based attack using local environmental observations and a surrogate model, combined with a self-evaluation loop to minimize detection. This design supports scalable adversarial manipulation in emerging 6G environments, where dense deployments and sequence-driven estimation govern communication reliability. In addition, to the best of our knowledge, we are the first to address adversarial attacks in the context of user-centric cell-free massive MIMO for tasks such as gain prediction and resource allocation.

1.2 Contributions

Building upon recent advances in AML in wireless networks, this work investigates the vulnerability of UC-CFmMIMO systems to black-box adversarial attacks targeting CSI used for resource allocation. The attack, based on a frequency-domain channel predictor utilizing Long Short-Term Memory (LSTM) networks [18], manipulates predicted channel gains through imperceptible perturbations, evading ML-based anomaly detection. This approach is applicable to vehicular environments, considering frequency-selective fading and uplink pilot-based injection.

The main contributions of this paper are summarized as follows:

- We develop a simulation framework for UC-CFmMIMO networks in high-mobility vehicular scenarios, using QuaDRiGa to model 3D geometry-based, frequency-selective propagation with dynamic bandwidth sharing.
- We implement a black-box attack within the simulated network that targets the input space of channel gain estimators, using a surrogate model trained on passively collected RF data to approximate gradients and craft perturbations without internal model access.
- We employ the FGSM to generate perturbations that alter channel gain predictions. Despite its simplicity, the attack effectively transfers across multiple model architectures, including LSTM, XGBoost, and Random Forest.
- We evaluate the downstream effects of perturbed predictions on frequency resource allocation performance, showing that small input distortions can cascade into significant allocation mismatches, highlighting the system-level vulnerability of AI-driven wireless networks.

2 System Model Description

We consider a user-centric cell-free massive MIMO (UC-CFmMIMO) system operating in a 2 km × 2 km urban vehicular environment, reflecting the dynamic and latency-sensitive design goals of 6G networks. The network comprises $L = 100$ distributed access points (APs), each with $N = 4$ antennas, jointly serving $K = 40$ single-antenna user equipments (UEs). All APs are connected to a central processing unit (CPU) via low-latency fronthaul links to enable centralized scheduling, CSI aggregation, and misbehavior detection.

The system operates over the 5.88–5.92 GHz band, which is reserved for vehicular communications and characterized by strong frequency selectivity and Doppler effects. UEs and APs are placed according to realistic urban distributions inspired by the works [14, 17]. The total available bandwidth B is partitioned into S orthogonal subbands indexed by $s \in \{1, \ldots, S\}$. On each subband, the downlink channel between AP l and UE k is represented by the frequency-domain vector $\mathbf{h}_{k,l,s} \in \mathbb{C}^{1 \times N}$, generated via QuaDRiGa's geometry-based stochastic channel model (GSCM). The global channel vector is:

$$\mathbf{h}_{k,s} = [\mathbf{h}_{k,1,s}, \ldots, \mathbf{h}_{k,L,s}] \in \mathbb{C}^{1 \times NL}.$$

At the start of each coherence interval, estimated CSI, obtained via pilot signaling or machine-learned prediction, is used for spectrum allocation and beamforming. Resource allocation is managed by an AI-based scheduler at the CPU, which dynamically assigns UEs to subbands based on link quality and interference metrics. Several IA models can be used to perform this task [39]. This assignment is encoded in a binary matrix $\mathcal{A} \in \{0,1\}^{S \times K}$, where $\mathcal{A}_{s,k} = 1$ indicates that UE k is scheduled on subband s.

The signal transmitted from AP l on subband s is:

$$\mathbf{x}_{l,s} = \sum_{k \in \mathcal{A}_s} \mathbf{w}_{k,l,s} a_k,$$

where $a_k \in \mathbb{C}$ is the data symbol for UE k, and $\mathbf{w}_{k,l,s} \in \mathbb{C}^{N \times 1}$ is the Zero Forcing (ZF) precoding vector computed using CSI from co-scheduled users. The received signal at UE k is:

$$y_{k,s} = \mathbf{h}_{k,s} \sum_{i \in \mathcal{A}_s} \mathbf{w}_{i,s} a_i + n_{k,s},$$

where $\mathbf{w}_{i,s} \in \mathbb{C}^{NL \times 1}$ denotes the global precoder across APs and $n_{k,s} \sim \mathcal{CN}(0, \sigma^2)$ is AWGN.

UE performance is measured via SINR:

$$\text{SINR}_{k,s} = \frac{|\mathbf{h}_{k,s} \mathbf{w}_{k,s}|^2}{\sum_{i \in \mathcal{A}_s \setminus \{k\}} |\mathbf{h}_{k,s} \mathbf{w}_{i,s}|^2 + \sigma^2}.$$

The CPU hosts a sequence-aware LSTM model to predict future channel gains, which assists in proactive subband-user scheduling for high-mobility users.

To protect the integrity of CSI predictions, an ML-based anomaly detector monitors the spatiotemporal structure of predicted channels, flagging deviations that may signal adversarial behavior.

This system model serves as the foundation for evaluating black-box adversarial attacks on channel gain predictors in UC-CFmMIMO systems.

3 Threat Model

This section formally outlines the threat model, focusing on adversarial attacks targeting ML-based channel prediction systems in UC-CFmMIMO architectures. The CPU is assumed to use an unknown ML-based gain prediction model, inaccessible to the attacker. The attack is framed under realistic assumptions about adversary behavior, resource access, and system interaction, representing a black-box, physically feasible attack scenario in vehicular wireless environments.

3.1 Adversarial Model

The adversary launches a two-phase attack designed to deceive the frequency-domain channel gain predictor used by the CPU for subband allocation and beamforming decisions.

Phase 1: Passive Observation and Surrogate Model Approximation. The adversary initiates the attack by passively collecting wireless propagation data using a custom-built, portable channel sounder. This device operates in environments similar to those of legitimate users, capturing spatially and temporally correlated channel state information (CSI)-like measurements. Notably, the construction of such portable and cost-effective channel sounders is well-documented in the literature; for instance, [4] present a real-time ultra-wideband channel sounder designed for frequencies ranging from 3 to 18 GHz, demonstrating the practicality of deploying such equipment for field measurements. While the adversary's sounder may not occupy the exact physical location of an AP, positioning it within the same propagation environment allows for the collection of data that reflects similar multipath characteristics and channel dynamics. This is due to the spatial consistency properties of wireless channels, where measurements taken in close proximity can exhibit correlated fading patterns [34]. Consequently, the gathered data, which can be considered as proxy data, is sufficient to train a surrogate model that approximates the behavior of the legitimate channel gain estimation process, which may rely on various models including LSTM, XGBoost, or Random Forest. This surrogate model is used to estimate the gradient landscape necessary for crafting adversarial perturbations using the FGSM attack, in accordance with the assumptions in [30], where a surrogate model acts as an oracle for black-box attacks, enabling adversarial transferability (Fig. 1).

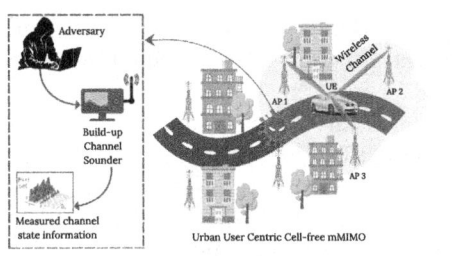 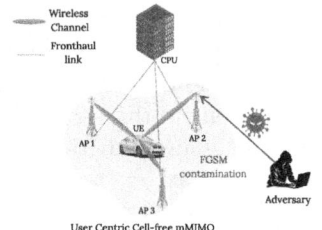

(a) Phase 1 of the threat model. (b) Phase 2 of the threat model.

Fig. 1. Overview of the two attack phases in the proposed threat model.

Phase 2: Adversarial Injection via Uplink Manipulation. Building upon the surrogate model developed in Phase 1, the adversary crafts adversarial perturbations using FGSM in a black-box setting. The attacker leverages a substitute LSTM model trained on proxy data to approximate the behavior of the target system. To simulate potential countermeasures that might be deployed by the operator, such as a misbehavior detection system, the adversary trains a classifier using both clean and adversarial proxy data. This classifier is then used as a constraint in the perturbation selection process to ensure that the crafted inputs remain under the anomaly detection threshold.

The crafted adversarial inputs are introduced into the system by actively transmitting manipulated CSI-related signals during the uplink phase. The attacker impersonates a legitimate User Equipment (UE) and transmits corrupted pilot sequences, misleading the Central Processing Unit's (CPU) channel estimation pipeline. This attack, known as pilot spoofing, relies on reusing pilot sequences to contaminate channel estimates, thereby degrading the accuracy of resource allocation decisions.

Massive MIMO systems are particularly susceptible to such spoofing mechanisms, which have been shown to compromise CSI integrity and impair downstream processes such as scheduling and beamforming [42]. These vulnerabilities are also present in next-generation network architectures, including 5G and beyond, particularly in Non-Orthogonal Multiple Access (NOMA) scenarios where pilot contamination significantly reduces CSI precision [29]. In this work, the attack is assessed across multiple target architectures, including LSTM, Random Forest, and XGBoost, demonstrating its transferability and robustness against different channel estimation techniques.

3.2 Adversary's Goal

The proposed attack targets the resource allocation process in a UC-CFmMIMO network under a black-box setting, where the adversary lacks access to the CPU' internal models. It exploits the strong dependency between transmission gain estimation and scheduling decisions. Prior studies have established that real-time gain predictions critically inform resource allocation in 5G and beyond

[35,36,40], and even non-predictive schemes like water-filling rely on accurate gain values [19]. This motivates the attacker to corrupt gain estimation in order to misguide downstream decisions.

To implement this strategy, the attacker trains a surrogate LSTM model that mimics the gain prediction module of the CPU. Using this model, adversarial perturbations are crafted via FGSM and fine-tuned to induce prediction errors. Although designed without access to the target model, these perturbations are evaluated for transferability and potential to degrade scheduling and beamforming.

The attacker's goal is twofold:

- **Stealth:** Ennsure perturbations remain subtle and undetectable by incorporating a local anomaly detector into the attack pipeline, despite being crafted without access to the target model.
- **Deception:** Induce corrupted channel gain estimates that, through transferability from a surrogate LSTM model trained to mimic the CPU's predictor, lead to degraded scheduling and beamforming decisions.

3.3 Adversary's Capability and Practical Limitations

The adversary is modeled as a physically present but externally uninvolved entity, operating under a black-box assumption with no direct access to the internal parameters or architecture of the system's channel estimation or detection modules. However, the adversary is assumed to possess the following realistic capabilities:

- Environmental Presence and Mobility: The adversary can deploy a custom channel sounder and physically move within or near the target service area, collecting CSI-like measurements in propagation environments that share spatial and temporal similarities with those experienced by legitimate UEs.
- Surrogate Model Training: Using collected RF data, the adversary is capable of training a surrogate model that approximates the behavior of the legitimate frequency-domain channel gain estimation module. This model is not used for prediction, but rather to enable adversarial gradient estimation required for crafting FGSM-based perturbations.
- Uplink Injection Capabilities: The adversary is equipped to transmit CSI-like feedback or pilot signals into the network, effectively impersonating a legitimate UE. This includes the ability to conduct pilot spoofing or CSI contamination attacks, as supported by existing studies in massive MIMO and 5G contexts [29,42].
- Black-Box Feedback Awareness: Although the adversary has no visibility into the internal workings of the system, it can observe the input-output behavior of its surrogate model and use that as a proxy to infer transferability. Additionally, the attacker leverages a local anomaly detection mechanism to evaluate the stealthiness of generated perturbations before injecting them, thereby refining attack parameters without requiring access to the system's monitoring components.

Practical Limitations: Despite these capabilities, the adversary faces several constraints that limit the effectiveness and scope of the attack. High mobility in vehicular environments imposes strict timing constraints, requiring perturbations to be computed and injected within short channel coherence intervals. The adversary is also limited by power and protocol-level constraints in uplink transmissions, making large or obvious deviations detectable. Lastly, the anomaly detection mechanism used by the adversary is only an approximation of any system-side detector and may not fully capture the true detection boundary, potentially leading to suboptimal stealth (Fig. 2).

4 Adversarial Attack Strategy

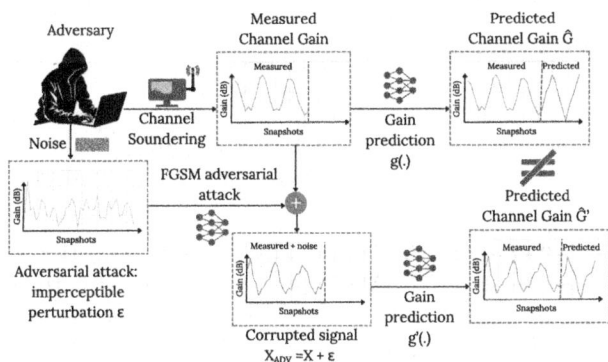

Fig. 2. Overview of the adversarial attack based on FGSM attack.

This section presents our adversarial attack strategy. The objective is to craft subtle perturbations that can degrade prediction accuracy and, consequently, the allocation of bandwidth, while remaining difficult to detect by defense mechanisms. To generate adversarial examples, we adopt the FGSM attack, a widely used technique in adversarial machine learning. FGSM perturbs input data by adding a small amount of noise in the direction that maximally increases the model's loss. This is done by computing the sign of the gradient of the loss with respect to the input and scaling it by a factor ϵ. The resulting adversarial input is expressed as:

$$X_{\text{adv}} = X + \epsilon \cdot \text{sign}(\nabla_X \mathcal{L}(X, y))$$

where $\mathcal{L}(X, y)$ denotes the loss function, typically Mean Squared Error (MSE) in regression tasks. Although FGSM is traditionally used in classification settings, we adapt it here to a regression context. Instead of aiming for class misclassification, our goal is to maximize prediction error. The procedure remains unchanged: we perturb the input slightly but purposefully, pushing the model's output away from the true value.

Algorithm 1. Adversarial Attack Construction and Evaluation Pipeline

Require: Proxy dataset X_{proxy}, perturbation range $\{\epsilon_i\}$, real dataset X_{real}
Ensure: Adversarial samples X_{adv}, classifier C
1: **Step I: Attack Preparation on Proxy Data**
2: **I. Train Substitute LSTM Model**
3: Train a substitute LSTM model $\hat{M}$ on the proxy dataset X_{proxy}
4: **II. Select Perturbation Level**
5: **for** each ϵ_i in a predefined range **do**
6:     Compute gradient: $\nabla_X \mathcal{L}(\hat{M}, X_{\text{proxy}})$
7:     Generate adversarial data: $X_{\text{adv}}^{\epsilon_i} = X_{\text{proxy}} + \epsilon_i \cdot \text{sign}(\nabla_X \mathcal{L})$
8:     Evaluate the impact of ϵ_i on model predictions to select candidate ϵ^*
9: **end for**
10: **III. Train Misbehavior Detection Classifier**
11: Use $X_{\text{adv}}^{\epsilon^*}$ and X_{proxy} to train classifier C_{ϵ^*}
12: **Step II: Evaluation on Real Data**
13: **IV. Transfer Attack to Real Data**
14: **for** each ϵ_j in a predefined range **do**
15:     Generate $X_{\text{adv}}^{\text{real}}[\epsilon_j]$ from X_{real} using $\hat{M}$ and ϵ_j
16:     Apply classifier C_{ϵ^*} to $X_{\text{adv}}^{\text{real}}[\epsilon_j]$
17:     Measure detection sensitivity and prediction impact
18: **end for**
19: **return** All $X_{\text{adv}}^{\epsilon_j}$ and classifier C_{ϵ^*}

Our attack pipeline, detailed in Algorithm 1, unfolds in two main steps: attack preparation on a proxy dataset and evaluation on real-world data.

Step I: Attack Preparation. We begin by training a substitute LSTM model on a proxy dataset (lines 1–2 in Algorithm 1). This model is then used to craft adversarial inputs using FGSM, where we vary the perturbation strength ϵ across a predefined range. For each value, we evaluate the impact of the resulting adversarial samples on the model's predictions (lines 5–9 in Algorithm 1). The candidate value ϵ^* is selected based on its ability to balance attack effectiveness while maintaining a small perturbation that is less likely to be detected, as we do not have prior knowledge of the target model's architecture or the perturbation thresholds that might be used by the CPU in a real scenario. Since this is a black-box attack, we only have access to an aproximation to find a suitable perturbation. Adversarial examples generated with ϵ^* are then combined with clean data to train a detection classifier (lines 11–12 in Algorithm 1).

Step II: Real-World Evaluation. We transfer the attack to real data by generating adversarial inputs using the same substitute model and several ϵ_j values. These perturbed samples are fed to the misbehavior detector trained during Step I. This allows us to observe how different levels of perturbation influence prediction accuracy while evaluating their detectability in a more realistic scenario (line 14–18 in Agorithme 1). Importantly, both the substitute LSTM model used to generate adversarial examples and the misbehavior detection classifier are trained exclusively on proxy data. This setup simulates a black-box scenario where the attacker has no access to the target model's architecture or training data.

5 Experiments

We take the following steps to evaluate how our attack affects the distribution of resources. We start by assessing how the attack impacts the prediction of channel gain. Next, we use the resource allocation model suggested in [11] to investigate how these prediction errors propagate into resource allocation decisions.

5.1 Evaluation Framework and Predictive Models

In this section, we evaluate machine learning-based channel gain predictors, which are crucial for subband scheduling and resource allocation, as described in Sect. 2. These predictors directly impact CPU decisions in UC-CFmMIMO systems, making them significant targets for adversarial attacks. By perturbing gain predictions, we can disrupt scheduling, degrade SINR, and cause misallocations.

For the purpose of our adversarial attack, we chose the LSTM model because the FGSM attack requires a differentiable model to compute the gradient. However, in black-box attack scenarios, the attacker has no knowledge of the deployed model. Thus, we will later evaluate the transferability of the attack to other predictive models. In this section, we focus on the performance of various models to provide an idea of their effectiveness and demonstrate that LSTM is a strong candidate for adversarial attacks.

We evaluate the following models on both clean data and proxy data:

- **LSTM (victim)**: A first LSTM model considered as the target of the attack
- **Random Forest (RF)**: An ensemble regressor with 20 trees and a maximum depth of 5.
- **Gradient Boosting (XGB)**: A boosting model with 20 trees and depth 8.
- **LSTM Substitute**: A secondary LSTM model trained on proxy data, used to simulate the black-box attacker scenario.

All models are trained on 80% of the data and validated on the remaining 20%. We use standard regression metrics, including MSE, MAE, RMSE, R^2, and Explained Variance, to establish a quantitative reference for clean performance and adversarial analysis.

As shown in Fig. 3, the LSTM model captures the temporal variations in channel gain effectively on a representative link, demonstrating strong predictive accuracy. This highlights its relevance as a target for adversarial attacks.

To quantify the predictive accuracy of each model, we report the evaluation results on the clean validation set in Table 1. These metrics include Mean Squared Error (MSE), Mean Absolute Error (MAE), Root Mean Squared Error (RMSE), the coefficient of determination (R^2), and the Explained Variance score.

The LSTM models slightly outperform both Random Forest and Gradient Boosting across all metrics. These results suggest that LSTM is a strong candidate for both clean predictions and adversarial targeting and highlight the effectiveness of FGSM as a strong surrogate in black-box attack scenarios. As we move forward, we will assess the transferability of adversarial attacks on LSTM to other predictive models, such as Random Forest and XGB, to understand the broader applicability of our attack strategy.

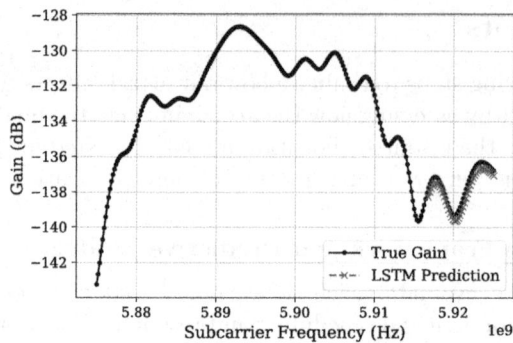

Fig. 3. Example prediction of channel gain using LSTM. The model captures the temporal pattern with relatively high accuracy.

Table 1. Performance of models on clean validation data

Model	MSE	MAE	RMSE	R^2	Var. Score
LSTM (clean)	0.097	0.198	0.311	0.948	0.948
Random Forest	0.123	0.232	0.351	0.936	0.936
Gradient Boosting	0.112	0.224	0.334	0.941	0.941
LSTM (Substitute)	0.095	0.196	0.308	0.949	0.949

5.2 Adversarial Robustness

Impact of Perturbation Strength and Corruption Level. To assess the susceptibility of learning-based channel predictors to adversarial manipulation, we evaluate the effect of test-time perturbations generated via the FGSM. In this scenario, an attacker seeks to alter the predicted gain values while keeping the perturbations imperceptible in magnitude. We simulate a black-box threat model, where the adversary trains a substitute LSTM model on a clean substitute (or proxy) dataset collected during the passive observation step as described in Sect. 3.1 and then fits attacks that transfer to the target model used by the CPU. For a complete evaluation, the attack was conducted using various epsilon values and different corruption levels, defined as the proportion of CPU-to-UE links deliberately targeted by the adversary. Figure 4 shows the degradation in R^2 of the LSTM victim predictor under adversarial conditions. Model performance drops sharply with increasing ϵ and corruption percentage, especially for $\epsilon \geq 1$ and 80–100% corruption.

The impact of the attack was also evaluated on the two alternative prediction models that could potentially be deployed by the CPU, namely Random Forest and XGB, in order to assess the transferability of the perturbations. As shown in the Fig. 4, despite not being involved in the attack's training phase, both models exhibit noticeable performance degradation, confirming that the crafted adversarial noise effectively transfers across model architectures. To illustrate the impact of the attack under low corruption conditions, Fig. 5 shows the LSTM-

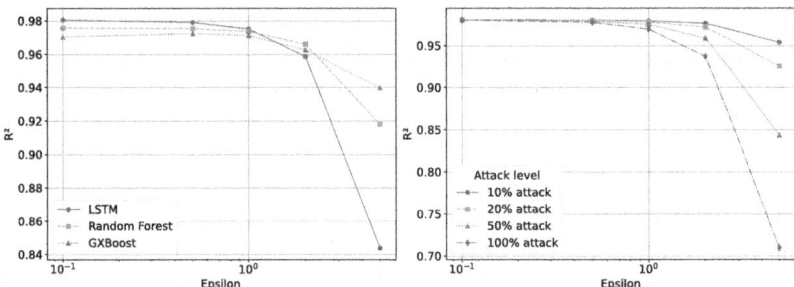

Fig. 4. Effect of perturbation strength and corruption percentage on R^2. The first figure shows the performance of LSTM, Random Forest, and GXBoost under 50% attack. The second figure displays the LSTM performance under different attack levels. Performance degrades significantly under strong or widespread attacks.

predicted channel gain for the same UE under clean and adversarial inputs, with a corruption level of 20% and a perturbation strength of $\epsilon = 0.5$. While the adversarial signal (MSE = **1.69 dB^2**) closely resembles the clean input (MSE = **0.50 dB^2**), we believe that small, structured perturbations are sufficient to mislead the resource allocation process (this will be confirmed by the results presented later). Such discrepancies, although visually subtle, can propagate through the pipeline and degrade SINR and fairness in a non-negligible manner.

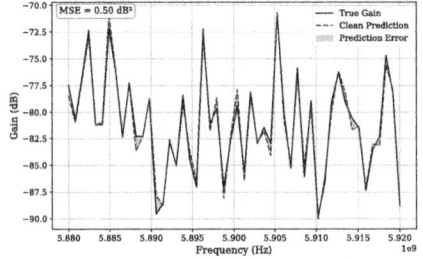
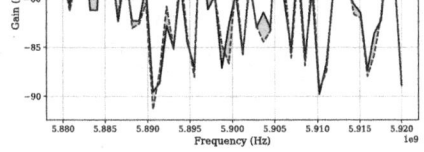

(a) Clean LSTM prediction.

(b) Adversarial LSTM prediction (FGSM, $\epsilon = 0.5$).

Fig. 5. Comparison of predicted frequency-domain gain under clean and adversarial conditions for the same user and antenna. The adversarial case shows greater deviation and a higher MSE, despite visually subtle differences.

The Constraint of Attack Detection. Until now, the evaluation we have carried out did not take into account the possible use of an attack detection system. In the following, we add this constraint by training classifiers that play the role of MDS. We used four classifiers usually implemented in the literature as MDS (Random Forest, KNN, Decision Tree, and SVM) [6]. Those classifiers were trained on the substitute dataset (50% clean and 50% FGSM corrupted data with (ϵ) = 1). The obtained results, as shown in Table 2, demonstrate that such classifiers can easly detects the attack under those conditions. Therefore, it is crucial to consider this constraint when developing the attack. A more thorough evaluation is required to determine the appropriate epsilon value and the level of corruption.

That is why we analyzed the sensitivity of the MDS to two key parameters: the perturbation magnitude (ϵ) and the proportion of corrupted samples in the validation set. Given that the classifiers were trained using the surrogate LSTM and proxy data, we can now proceed to the inference phase, where the attack is executed using real-world data. Figures 6a and 6b present detailed performance curves for the Random Tree-based detector, showcasing its accuracy across varying configurations. The other three classifiers gave similar trends with slight variations in performance. Figure 6a presents detection accuracy as a function of perturbation strength ϵ, across different corruption levels. Accuracy improves with stronger perturbations, particularly when a larger fraction of the data is adversarial. Near-perfect detection is achieved for $\epsilon \geq 2.5$ when at least 80% of inputs are perturbed.

Table 2. Detection accuracy of different classifiers on mixed (50% clean, 50% adversarial) test data. Attacks were generated using FGSM based on the LSTM substitute model.

Model	Detection Accuracy
Decision Tree	91.17%
Random Forest	94.19%
KNN	91.62%
SVM	89.71%

Figure 6b shows detection performance versus the proportion of corrupted samples, for fixed ϵ values. For small perturbations (e.g., $\epsilon \leq 0.25$), accuracy remains consistently low regardless of corruption level. In contrast, higher ϵ values lead to steadily improving detection with increasing attack prevalence. These results demonstrate that both the magnitude and coverage of adversarial perturbations significantly influence detectability. Sparse, low-intensity attacks remain difficult to identify, while stronger or more pervasive manipulations are reliably flagged.

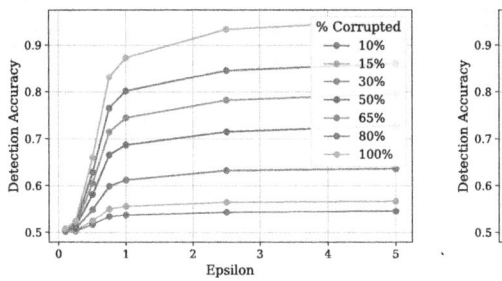 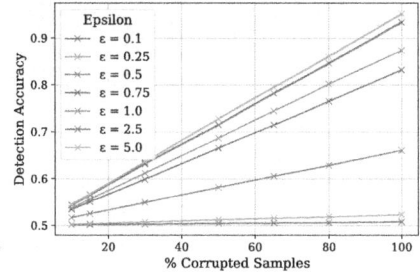

(a) Detection Performance vs. ϵ for Different Corruption Levels

(b) Corruption percentage impacts detection accuracy when ϵ is fixed.

Fig. 6. Detection accuracy behavior under varying perturbation parameters using Random Tree-based detector.

5.3 Impact on Resource Allocation Consistency

The choice of perturbation parameters in the following resource allocation analysis is guided by insights gained from the detection experiments. Specifically, we focus on configurations where detection becomes less reliable, typically at lower corruption rates or moderate perturbation strengths, since these represent realistic adversarial strategies aiming to remain covert while still exerting noticeable influence. This setup allows us to examine how attacks that fly under the radar of detection systems can still undermine downstream tasks such as scheduling and allocation.

To assess the downstream impact of adversarial perturbations on system functionality, we compare the subband-user assignments generated by algorithm proposed in the paper [11] under clean and adversarial CSI predictions. In this experiment, we inject FGSM-crafted perturbations with $\epsilon = 0.5$ into 10% of the CSI inputs and perform scheduling separately on both the clean and perturbed datasets. As proposed in [11], subband-user allocations are computed using a Simulated Annealing (SA) algorithm across 30 frequency subbands. This scheduling is driven by predicted channel gains, which become susceptible to adversarial manipulation. Allocation stability is assessed via Jaccard similarity. The Jaccard similarity measures the overlap between the subband-user allocations generated under clean and adversarial CSI predictions, with a value of 1 indicating no change, higher values indicating greater similarity, and lower values reflecting more significant discrepancies in the allocation process. While Fig. 7a shows noticeable allocation changes even under 10% corruption with $\epsilon = 0.5$, the impact becomes more pronounced in Fig. 7b, where $\epsilon = 2$ induces greater divergence despite the same corruption level. These results emphasize the SA algorithm's sensitivity to perturbations in predicted CSI, even when input distortions remain limited.

Even a slight adversarial perturbation in the predicted channel gains can severely affect the subsequent resource allocation process. Specifically, mises-

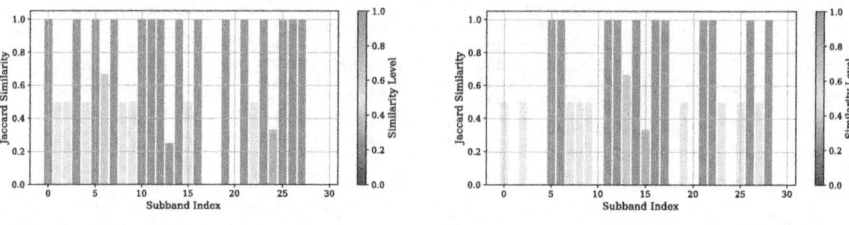

(a) FGSM, $\epsilon = 0.5$, 10% corruptions. (b) FGSM, $\epsilon = 2$, 10% corruption.

Fig. 7. Jaccard similarity between subband-user allocations under clean and adversarial CSI.

timated gains result in incorrect subband-to-user mappings during scheduling, undermining the optimality and fairness of the allocation strategy. This misalignment increases inter-user interference, reduces spectral efficiency, and can destabilize the system under high load conditions. These results highlight the critical need for adversarial resilience, not only at the model prediction level but also in the design of the end-to-end communication system.

6 Conclusion

In this study, we deploy a black-box attack on an LSTM-based frequency-domain predictor to subtly modify channel gains and subband-user allocations while avoiding anomaly detection. The findings reveal that even little adversarial perturbations can severely disturb channel gain predictions and scheduling consistency in UC-CFmMIMO systems. These perturbations result in significant increases in prediction error and decreased Jaccard similarity in subband-user assignments. The findings support the transferability of black-box assaults across model architectures while emphasizing the difficulty of identifying low-magnitude attacks. Future work will investigate adversarial attack strategies that integrate learnable epsilon values, which adapt to the constraints of detection systems and optimize their effectiveness against ML models. The current use of FGSM serves as an initial step in analyzing the attack surface, with plans to incorporate more sophisticated techniques in subsequent studies.

Acknowledgment. The authors gratefully acknowledge the support from the Regional STIMULE CORTESE project of the Hauts-de-France Region.

References

1. Abhulimhen-Iyoha, A., Ditzler, G., Krishnan, S.: Isolation forest and support vector machine for detecting adversarial examples in autonomous vehicles. IEEE Trans. Intell. Veh. **7**(1), 123–134 (2022). https://doi.org/10.1109/TIV.2021.3134567

2. Akbar, M.S., Hussain, Z., Ikram, M., Sheng, Q.Z., Mukhopadhyay, S.: On challenges of sixth-generation (6G) wireless networks: a comprehensive survey of requirements, applications, and security issues. J. Netw. Comput. Appl. 104040 (2024). https://doi.org/10.1016/j.jnca.2024.104040
3. Bahramali, A., Gagnon, F., Loranger, M., et al.: Adversarial attacks on deep learning-based modulation recognition. IEEE Trans. Cogn. Commun. Netw. **9**(1), 123–135 (2023). https://doi.org/10.1109/TCCN.2023.3245679
4. Bas, C.U., Kristem, V., Wang, R., Molisch, A.F.: Real-time ultra-wideband channel sounder design for 3-18 GHz. In: 2018 IEEE International Conference on Communications Workshops (ICC Workshops), pp. 1–6. IEEE (2018)
5. Boualouache, A., Engel, T.: A survey on machine learning-based misbehavior detection systems for 5G and beyond vehicular networks. IEEE Commun. Surv. Tutorials **25**(2), 1128–1172 (2023). https://doi.org/10.1109/COMST.2023.3242504
6. Boualouache, A., Engel, T.: A survey on machine learning-based misbehavior detection systems for 5G and beyond vehicular networks. IEEE Commun. Surv. Tutorials **25**(2), 1128–1172 (2023)
7. Bouchouia, M.L., et al.: A survey on misbehavior detection for connected and autonomous vehicles. Veh. Commun. **41**, 100586 (2023)
8. Catak, E., Catak, F.O., Moldsvor, A.: Adversarial machine learning security problems for 6G: mmWave beam prediction use-case. In: 2021 IEEE International Black Sea Conference on Communications and Networking (BlackSeaCom), pp. 1–6. IEEE (2021). https://doi.org/10.1109/BlackSeaCom52164.2021.9527860
9. Catak, F.O., Sagduyu, Y.E., Shi, Y.: Adversarial beamforming attack and defense for wireless networks. IEEE Trans. Wireless Commun. **22**(5), 3123–3135 (2023). https://doi.org/10.1109/TWC.2023.3245678
10. Chang, J., Sun, K., Heydaribeni, N., Hidano, S., Zhang, X., Koushanfar, F.: Magmaw: Modality-agnostic adversarial attacks on machine learning-based wireless communication systems. arXiv preprint arXiv:2311.00207 (2023). https://arxiv.org/abs/2311.00207
11. Cheggour, S., Loscri, V.: Frequency channel selectivity in vehicular CFmMIMO systems: a multi-objective optimization approach. In: VNC 2025-IEEE Vehicular Networking Conference (2025)
12. Chou, H.F., et al.: Edge AI empowered physical layer security for 6G NTN: Potential threats and future opportunities. arXiv preprint arXiv:2401.01005 (2023)
13. Cui, Q., et al.: Overview of AI and communication for 6G network: Fundamentals, challenges, and future research opportunities. arXiv preprint arXiv:2412.14538 (2024)
14. Felez, J., Maroto, J., Cabanellas, J.M., Mera, J.M.: A full-scale simulation model to reproduce urban traffic in real conditions in driving simulators. SIMULATION **89**(9), 1099–1114 (2013)
15. Fu, J., Zhu, P., Ai, B., Wang, J., You, X.: Resource allocation in cell-free MU-MIMO multicarrier system with finite blocklength. In: 2023 IEEE 98th Vehicular Technology Conference (VTC2023-Fall), pp. 1–5. IEEE (2023). https://doi.org/10.1109/VTC2023-Fall58003.2023.10305591
16. Ghasemi, P., Saad, W., Mandayam, N.B., et al.: Adversarial attacks on graph neural networks for wireless network resource allocation. In: Proceedings of IEEE Global Communications Conference (GLOBECOM), pp. 1–6 (2021). https://doi.org/10.1109/GLOBECOM46510.2021.9685357
17. Gonçalves, F., et al.: Urban traffic simulation using mobility patterns synthesized from real sensors. Electronics **12**(24), 4971 (2023)

18. Hochreiter, S., Schmidhuber, J.: LSTM can solve hard long time lag problems. Adv. Neural Inf. Process. Syst. **9** (1996)
19. Jang, J., Lee, K.B.: Transmit power adaptation for multiuser OFDM systems. IEEE J. Sel. Areas Commun. **21**(2), 171–178 (2003)
20. Karachalios, O.A., Zafeiropoulos, A., Kontovasilis, K., Papavassiliou, S.: Distributed machine learning and native AI enablers for end-to-end resources management in 6G. Electronics **12**(18), 3761 (2023). https://doi.org/10.3390/electronics12183761
21. Kassam, J., Castanheira, D., Silva, A., Dinis, R., Gameiro, A.: A review on cell-free massive MIMO systems. Electronics **12**(4), 1001 (2023). https://doi.org/10.3390/electronics12041001
22. Kim, B., Sagduyu, Y.E., Shi, Y., et al.: Beamattack: adversarial beamforming in wireless networks. In: Proceedings of IEEE Conference on Communications and Network Security (CNS), pp. 1–9 (2020). https://doi.org/10.1109/CNS49298.2020.9162263
23. Li, X., He, D., Zhang, Y., et al.: Cybersecurity in 5G: a comprehensive review and directions for secure deployment. IEEE Commun. Surv. Tutorials **24**(3), 1729–1762 (2022). https://doi.org/10.1109/COMST.2022.3150946
24. Manoj, B., Sadeghi, M., Larsson, E.G.: Adversarial attacks on deep learning based power allocation in a massive MIMO network. arXiv preprint arXiv:2101.12090 (2021). https://arxiv.org/abs/2101.12090
25. Manoj, M., Kalantari, N., Avestimehr, S., et al.: Adversarial attacks on deep learning-based power allocation in massive MIMO systems. In: Proceedings of IEEE International Conference on Communications (ICC), pp. 1–6 (2021). https://doi.org/10.1109/ICC42927.2021.9500473
26. Manoj, M., Kalantari, N., Avestimehr, S., et al.: Adversarial attacks on deep learning-based power allocation in massive MIMO systems. In: Proceedings of IEEE International Conference on Communications (ICC), pp. 1–6 (2021). https://doi.org/10.1109/ICC42927.2021.9500473
27. Mohammadi, M., Mobini, Z., Ngo, H.Q., Matthaiou, M.: Next-generation multiple access with cell-free massive MIMO. Proc. IEEE (2024). https://doi.org/10.1109/JPROC.2024.3363457
28. Moisejevs, I.: Adversarial attacks and defenses in malware classification: a survey. Int. J. Artif. Intell. Expert Syst. **8** (2019)
29. Nashat, D., Khairy, S.: Statistical-based detection of pilot contamination attack for NOMA in 5G networks. Sci. Rep. **15**(1), 3726 (2025)
30. Papernot, N., McDaniel, P., Goodfellow, I.: Transferability in machine learning: from phenomena to black-box attacks using adversarial samples. arXiv preprint arXiv:1605.07277 (2016)
31. Saeed, M.M., Saeed, R.A., Abdelhaq, M., Alsaqour, R., Hasan, M.K., Mokhtar, R.A.: Anomaly detection in 6G networks using machine learning methods. Electronics **12**(15), 3300 (2023). https://doi.org/10.3390/electronics12153300
32. Son, B.D., et al.: Adversarial attacks and defenses in 6g network-assisted IoT systems. IEEE Internet Things J. (2024). https://doi.org/10.1109/JIOT.2024.3364024
33. Wang, T., Zhang, Y., Wang, X., et al.: Adversarial machine learning in wireless communications: a survey on attacks and defenses. IEEE Commun. Surv. Tutorials **25**(1), 1–20 (2023). https://doi.org/10.1109/COMST.2023.1234567
34. Wu, C., Zhu, Y., Wang, W., Wang, C.X., Gao, X.: Improvement of the cluster-level spatial consistency of channel simulator with reference points transition method. In: IEEE Transactions on Vehicular Technology. vol. 69, pp. 11447–11459. IEEE (2020)

35. Xiong, J., Hu, H., Cheng, P., Yang, C., Shi, Z., Gui, L.: Wireless resource scheduling for high mobility scenarios: a combined traffic and channel quality prediction approach. IEEE Trans. Broadcast. **68**(3), 712–722 (2022)
36. Yan, M., Feng, G., Zhou, J., Sun, Y., Liang, Y.C.: Intelligent resource scheduling for 5G radio access network slicing. IEEE Trans. Veh. Technol. **68**(8), 7691–7703 (2019)
37. Zaeem, R.M., Duncan, J.C.M., Martins, W.A., Ha, V.N., Chatzinotas, S., Ottersten, B.: Resource allocation and user scheduling design for user-centric cell-free massive MIMO systems. In: 2023 IEEE 34th Annual International Symposium on Personal, Indoor and Mobile Radio Communications (PIMRC), pp. 1–6. IEEE (2023). https://doi.org/10.1109/PIMRC56786.2023.10287069
38. Zhang, W., Ditzler, G., Krunz, M.: Application of adversarial machine learning in protocol and modulation misclassification. IEEE Trans. Cogn. Commun. Netw. **9**(3), 789–801 (2023). https://doi.org/10.1109/TCCN.2023.3291223
39. Zhao, Y., Zhao, J., Zhai, W., Sun, S., Niyato, D., Lam, K.-Y.: A survey of 6G wireless communications: emerging technologies. In: Arai, K. (ed.) FICC 2021. AISC, vol. 1363, pp. 150–170. Springer, Cham (2021). https://doi.org/10.1007/978-3-030-73100-7_12
40. Zheng, J., Chen, R., Zhang, Y.: Dynamic resource allocation based on service time prediction for device-to-device communication underlaying cellular networks. IET Commun. **9**(3), 350–358 (2015)
41. Zheng, M., Yan, X., Zhu, Z., Chen, H., Wu, B.: BlackboxBench: A comprehensive benchmark of black-box adversarial attacks. arXiv preprint arXiv:2312.16979 (2023)
42. Zhou, X., Zhang, L., Song, L., Han, Z.: On pilot spoofing attack in massive MIMO systems: detection and countermeasures. IEEE Trans. Inf. Forensics Secur. **15**, 2630–2645 (2020)

FuncVul: An Effective Function Level Vulnerability Detection Model Using LLM and Code Chunk

Sajal Halder, Muhammad Ejaz Ahmed[(✉)], and Seyit Camtepe

Data61, CSIRO, Eveleigh, Australia
{sajal.halder,ejaz.ahmed,seyit.camtepe}@data61.csiro.au

Abstract. Software supply chain vulnerabilities arise when attackers exploit weaknesses by injecting vulnerable code into widely used packages or libraries within software repositories. While most existing approaches focus on identifying vulnerable packages or libraries, they often overlook the specific functions responsible for these vulnerabilities. Pinpointing vulnerable functions within packages or libraries is critical, as it can significantly reduce the risks associated with using open-source software. Identifying vulnerable patches is challenging because developers often submit code changes that are unrelated to vulnerability fixes. To address this issue, this paper introduces FuncVul, an innovative code chunk-based model for function-level vulnerability detection in C/C++ and Python, designed to identify multiple vulnerabilities within a function by focusing on smaller, critical code segments. To assess the model's effectiveness, we construct six code and generic code chunk based datasets using two approaches: (1) integrating patch information with large language models to label vulnerable samples and (2) leveraging large language models alone to detect vulnerabilities in function-level code. To design FuncVul vulnerability model, we utilise Graph-CodeBERT fine tune model that captures both the syntactic and semantic aspects of code. Experimental results show that FuncVul outperforms existing state-of-the-art models, achieving an average accuracy of 87–92% and an F1 score of 86–92% across all datasets. Furthermore, we have demonstrated that our code-chunk-based FuncVul model improves 53.9% accuracy and 42.0% F1-score than the full function-based vulnerability prediction. The model code and datasets are publicly available on GitHub (https://github.com/sajalhalder/FuncVul).

Keywords: Function code · Vulnerability Detection · Code Chunk · Software Supply Chain · Large Language Model

1 Introduction

With the rapid expansion of technology, cybersecurity has become a growing priority. By October 2024, the National Vulnerability Database (NVD) recorded over 240,000 reported Common Vulnerabilities and Exposures (CVEs) [3,21]. This number has steadily risen, with an average growth rate of 15–20% per year. Detecting vulnerabilities in C/C++ and Python code is a challenging process that demands thorough analysis of the codebase's structure, syntax, and semantics to reveal potential weaknesses

© The Author(s), under exclusive license to Springer Nature Switzerland AG 2026
V. Nicomette et al. (Eds.): ESORICS 2025, LNCS 16053, pp. 166–185, 2026.
https://doi.org/10.1007/978-3-032-07884-1_9

exploitable by attackers. Identifying vulnerable functions within the package is crucial because it allows developers to focus their efforts on resolving the specific issue rather than discarding the entire package. It enables organizations to prioritize fixes based on the severity and significance of the affected functions. Moreover, identifying vulnerable source enables the developer to resolve them quickly, minimizing the impact on customers and ensuring service continuity. Identifying vulnerable functions within the vast number of packages released daily is both time-consuming and requires specialized expertise in security. Thus, an automated model capable of effectively identifying vulnerable functions is essential.

Existing research has explored code similarity techniques to detect vulnerable code patterns using machine learning [22], deep learning [2,14,30], and graph-based models [27]. Yuan et al. [35] combined serialized features from Gated Recurrent Units (GRUs) and structural features from Abstract Syntax Trees (ASTs) via Gated Graph Recurrent Networks (GGRNs), addressing data scarcity and imbalance with a Random Forest model, achieving superior performance. Vo et al. [26] found that pre-trained deep models for vulnerability type identification (VTI) offered limited improvement over classical TF-IDF baselines and enhanced them by identifying key code tokens. Wang et al. [29] developed ReposVul, a repository-level dataset created using an automated framework with modules for untangling vulnerabilities, dependency extraction, and filtering outdated patches. Other works explored context-aware embeddings [31], RoBERTa models pre-trained on open-source C/C++ code [9], and Word2Vec-LSTM pipelines for Python code [30]. However, these approaches face two key limitations. First, while they can identify whether a function is vulnerable, they cannot determine the exact number of vulnerabilities within the function. Second, pinpointing the precise lines of code that contain vulnerabilities remains a challenge. As a result, security analysts are compelled to manually review functions, significantly increasing the time and effort required for vulnerability analysis. Addressing these limitations is vital for streamlining the vulnerability identification process and improving efficiency.

To address these limitations, we propose a code chunk-based model for function-level vulnerability detection that can identify multiple vulnerabilities within a single function. Real world vulnerabilities often reside in small, contiguous segments of code rather than spanning entire functions or files. Motivated by this, our proposed model focuses on these minimal yet informative regions referred to as code chunks to enhance the accuracy of vulnerability detection.

To sum up, in this paper we aim to answer the following research questions.

RQ1: What modeling strategies can be employed to accurately detect function level vulnerabilities?

RQ2: Does leveraging code chunks enhance model performance compared to analyzing full-function code?

RQ3: Does the FuncVul model leverage generalized code properties for vulnerability detection?

RQ4: How effective is our approach at detecting vulnerabilities in unseen projects?

RQ5: How does the performance of our approach vary with different numbers of source lines in a code chunk?

RQ6. Is our proposed model capable of detecting multiple vulnerabilities within a single function's code?

To evaluate the performance of our proposed FuncVul model, we compared it against several state-of-the-art models: CodeBERT [5], CustomVulBERTa [9], BERT [12] and VUDENC [30] across six datasets. The main contribution of this research work are as follows.

- We propose a novel code chunk-based **Func**tion **Vul**nerability (**FuncVul**) detection model capable of identifying multiple vulnerabilities within a function and, importantly, to identify the specific, smaller code segments responsible for those vulnerabilities.
- We collected and curated four datasets from diverse data sources, such as project source codes from GitHub and vulnerability advisory databases, i.e., OSV. Additionally, we developed novel methods to analyze, process, and curate source code using large language models (LLMs).
- We employ a fine-tuned GraphCodeBERT model for function-level vulnerability prediction, as it effectively captures both syntactic and semantic similarities within the code.
- Our experimental results demonstrate that the proposed FuncVul model outperforms state-of-the-art baselines, achieving an average accuracy of 89.39% and an F1 score of 88.94% across the six datasets.
- Additionally, we show that the FuncVul model is highly generic, capable of handling diverse code chunks and identifying new vulnerable patterns effectively.

The remaining part of the paper is organized as follows. We briefly describe the relevant existing works in Sect. 2. Then, we discuss the problem statement in Sect. 3. We introduce our proposed model in Sect. 4. After that, we present our experiments in Sect. 5. Finally, we conclude the paper with potential future research directions in Sect. 6.

2 Existing Works

Software vulnerability detection is a critical research area in both academia and industry. Existing work can be broadly categorized into the following areas:

Vulnerability Dataset Creation: Constructing reliable vulnerability datasets is foundational to enabling supervised learning approaches. Wang et al. [29] developed *ReposVul*, a repository-level dataset using an automated framework that untangles fixes, extracts multi-level dependencies, and filters outdated patches. Li et al. [15] introduced *VulPecker*, which identifies known vulnerabilities using patch-derived features and code similarity techniques. Lu et al. [18] presented a well-balanced C/C++ vulnerability dataset enriched with VCCs, filtered for noise, and refined using the ESC technique to ensure label reliability.

Traditional Deep Learning-Based Vulnerability Detection: Hanif et al. [9] introduced *VulBERTa*, a RoBERTa-based model pre-trained on real-world C/C++ code using a specialized tokenization pipeline. Warschinski et al. [30] proposed *VUDENC*, which combines Word2Vec embeddings with an LSTM network for detecting vulnerabilities in Python code. Wei et al. [31] utilized pre-trained ELMo embeddings and a Bi-LSTM layer to capture deep contextual representations. Yuan et al. [35] presented a hybrid model combining GRU-based serialized features with structural features from Gated Graph Recurrent Networks (GGRNs), using Random Forests to address data imbalance. Fu et al. [6] proposed *LineVul*, a Transformer-based model for line-level vulnerability detection in C/C++. Tran et al. [24] introduced *DetectVul*, a statement-level detection model for Python that employs self-attention to learn patterns directly from raw code. Li et al. [16] developed *VulDeePecker*, which uses code gadgets—semantically related but non-consecutive code lines—to form vector representations of programs.

Graph-Based Vulnerability Detection: Graph Neural Network (GNN)-based methods have shown significant promise by capturing structural dependencies in code. Hin et al. [10] proposed *LineVD*, combining GNNs and transformers for statement-level vulnerability detection. Zhou et al. [36] developed *Devign*, a graph-level classifier using semantic code representations. Wang et al. [28] applied GGNNs to capture data, control, and call dependencies with traditional classifier ensembles. Li et al. [13] introduced a feature-attentive GCN over program dependency graphs, while Wu et al. [33] proposed *VulCNN*, which transforms code into semantic-preserving images for CNN processing. Nguyen et al. [20] developed *ReGVD*, integrating token embeddings from pre-trained models with residual connections and pooling techniques. Wen et al. [32] improved performance by refining graph structures in *AMPLE*, capturing long-range dependencies. Islam et al. [11] introduced Poacher Flow edges to bridge static and dynamic analysis for richer vulnerability detection.

Pre-trained Language Models for Code Understanding: Pre-trained transformer models have transformed vulnerability detection by leveraging large-scale semantic knowledge. Liu et al. [17] presented *RoBERTa*, while Feng et al. [5] introduced *CodeBERT* for code and natural language pairs. Guo et al. [7] proposed *GraphCodeBERT*, which incorporates data flow graphs alongside code tokens to learn structural relationships. These models have significantly improved tasks such as automated program repair [34] and function-level vulnerability detection. However, most of these models either provide binary function-level predictions or miss granular vulnerability information such as exact line locations or number of vulnerable lines within a function.

Large Language Models for Vulnerability Detection: The recent surge of Large Language Models (LLMs) has extended to vulnerability detection due to their general-purpose reasoning and code understanding capabilities. Lu et al. [19] proposed *GRACE*, enhancing LLM-based detection by integrating graph structural information and in-context learning. Akuthota et al. [1] used LLMs to identify and monitor software vulnerabilities. Guo et al. [8] evaluated LLMs beyond traditional usage, investigating their effectiveness in security-critical tasks.

However, our proposed model is different than the prior traditional approaches that rely solely on code similarity existing models (e.g. [6,30]), where we use LLM to generate datasets and use code based fine tune model to detect vulnerability.

2.1 Differences with Previous Works

Our proposed function-level vulnerability detection model introduces several key advancements over state-of-the-art techniques. First, unlike existing approaches that analyse entire functions or line-based vulnerability detection, our model focuses on code chunk-based vulnerability detection in C/C++ and Python. This approach significantly reduces the time required by experts or developers to address vulnerabilities. Second, the code chunk-based method enables the detection of multiple vulnerabilities within a function, whereas existing models typically provide only a binary assessment of whether a function is vulnerable. Third, our model leverages a large language model that is capable of supporting code chunks from different programming languages, eliminating the need for language-specific preprocessing required by existing methods. Finally, we utilise the pre-trained GraphCodeBERT model to build a function-level vulnerability detection framework that effectively captures both syntactic and semantic features, surpassing traditional approaches that rely solely on code similarity.

3 Preliminaries and Problem Statement

In this section, we first present the key preliminary definitions and then describe the problem statement.

Definition 1 (Function Code Chunk): *A Function Code Chunk (FC) refers to a contiguous segment of lines extracted from a function's source code, typically centered around a code change or edit. It includes a few lines before and after the change to preserve local context for vulnerability analysis.*

Definition 2 (Generic Code Chunk): *Generic Code Chunk represents the segments of code where variable names, function names, and other identifiers have been replaced with generic placeholders (e.g., F_1, F_2,...,F_n for functions and V_1, V_2, ..., V_n for variables).*

This generic code chunk transformation standardizes the code, removing specific naming conventions or contextual biases, and ensures a consistent format that focuses on structural and syntactic patterns.

Definition 3 (3-Line Extended-Based Code Chunk): *3-Line Extended-Based Code Chunk refers to a segment of code centered on an edited line (or lines), augmented with three preceding and three succeeding lines from the edited lines in the function.*

This design captures the semantic context of code for vulnerability detection. Generally, the code edited lines is fewer than 10 lines. If the edited length is more than 10 lines, we consider edited lines only to make the code chunk. Thus, we can define the code chunk as follows.

$$\text{Code Chunk} = \begin{cases} \{L_i \mid i \in [\min(E) - 3, \max(E) + 3]\} & \text{if } |E| \leq 10 \\ E & \text{if } |E| > 10 \end{cases} \quad (1)$$

where L_i represents the ith line of the function code, $min(E)$ and $max(E)$ refer starting and ending edited lines, respectively. This code chunk approach provides a contextualized view of the code, enabling better understanding and analysis of the detected lines within their surrounding context.

Problem Definition: Given a C/C++ or Python based software patch information based modified function code chunk (fc_i). The main goal of this research work is to develop a vulnerable code detector $\mathcal{V}$ which can identify patch-modified codes as vulnerable or non-vulnerable. It can be defined as follows.

$$\mathcal{V}(fc_i) = \begin{cases} 1, & \text{if } fc_i \text{ is vulnerable,} \\ 0, & \text{non-vulnerable} \end{cases} \quad (2)$$

To solve the problem, we propose 3-line extended based code chunk to detect function label vulnerability using code-based fine-tune models in C/C++ or Python code.

4 Proposed Model

In this paper, we propose an effective function-level vulnerability detection framework that leverages large language models (LLMs) alongside specialized code vulnerability detection techniques. To generate ground truth data, we utilise two distinct types of LLM prompts and employ an additional prompt to transform code chunks into generic code chunks. Subsequently, we fine-tune the prediction models using advanced code vulnerability identification techniques. The next two subsections provide a detailed explanation of the data generation process and the proposed *FuncVul* models.

4.1 Data Generation

Labeling data is critical for training any prediction model, yet identifying vulnerable data often poses significant challenges. In this study, we construct two types of ground truth datasets: code chunks and generic code chunks, derived from function source code and corresponding patch information. Figure 1 illustrates the processes involved in generating these datasets. Detailed descriptions of the ground truth generation for both code chunks and generic code chunks are provided in the following subsections.

In this study, we focus on function code chunks rather than full function code for two key reasons. First, vulnerabilities often exist within just one or two lines of code inside a function, and models trained on entire functions may struggle to pinpoint these specific vulnerable lines that potentially leading to inaccurate predictions. Second, using code chunks reduces the search space and minimizes the number of tokens processed by the tokenizer, enabling the fine-tuned model to more effectively distinguish between vulnerable and non-vulnerable patterns.

In this work, we generate code chunks by leveraging function source code and patch information. Patch information highlights the modifications made to the code, marking added lines with a plus sign (+) and removed lines with a minus sign (-) at the beginning of each line. Additionally, it includes a chunk header that specifies the location and range of the changes, indicating where the modifications begin and the consequences of changes using line numbers.

The Algorithm 1 extracts relevant code chunk segments from a function based on patch information. It first parses the patch details to retrieve the chunk header, removed lines, and added lines in line 1. Next, it extracts the starting lines and corresponding modification ranges for both the removed and added lines in line 2. Context parameters are initialized to include three lines before and after the modified region (for three line strategy) in line 3. The algorithm then initialises indices of the removed lines within

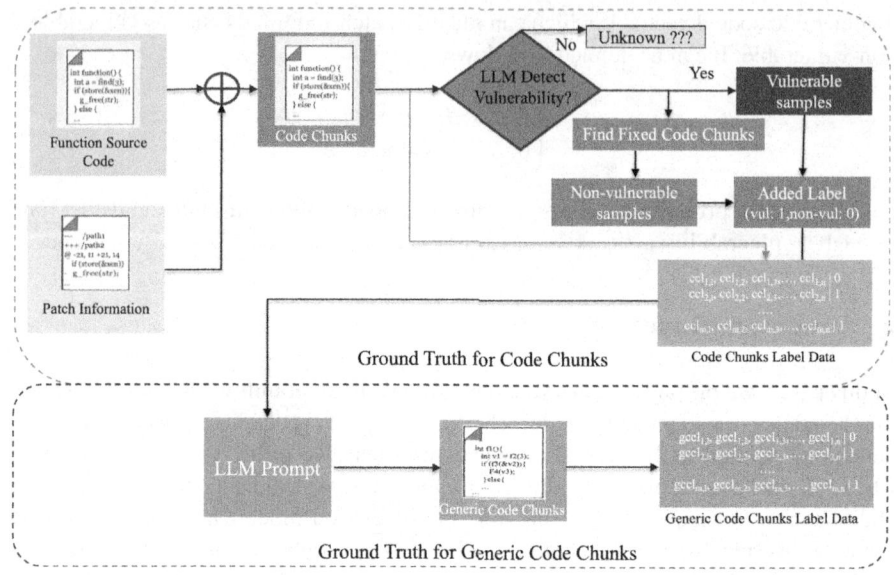

Fig. 1. Code Checks and Generic Code Chunks Label Data Generation.

the function, recording them in a list called modified_index in line 4. If no matches are found, it returns an empty result in line 9. For matched lines, the algorithm determines the bounds of the code chunk using a heuristic for small regions (≤ 10 lines) to include additional context, or directly uses the minimum and maximum indices for larger regions in lines 11–16. Finally, it extracts and returns the code chunk based on the calculated bounds in line 16 and line 17, respectively.

Generic Code Chunks: Generic code chunk converts code chunks to a generic format. In this work, we have transformed function code into a generic format by renaming functions as $F_1, F_2, ..., F_m$ and variables as $v_1, v_2, ..., v_n$. The key advantage lies in mitigating the variations introduced by different developers who often use diverse functions and variable names to achieve the same functionality. The LLM prompt designed to standardize code chunks by converting them into their generic format is presented in Appendix A.1.

In this work, we leverage the Gemini 1.5 Pro [23] LLM model to efficiently transform generic code chunks. A key advantage of utilizing this LLM model is its ability to seamlessly convert code across various programming languages, including C/C++, Java, and Python.

Vulnerable and Non-vulnerable Samples: Our primary objective is to detect vulnerabilities using function-level code, whether in its original form as code chunks or transformed into generic code chunks. To develop a robust vulnerability detection model, we require a ground truth dataset comprising both vulnerable and non-vulnerable samples. To construct this dataset, we adopt a dual-strategy approach that combines code-based heuristics with predictions from a LLM. This methodology enhances the ability to iden-

Algorithm 1: Find Function Code Chunk (F, P)

Data: F: Function source code; P: Patch information.
Result: FC: Extracted function code chunk.

1. chunk_header, removed_lines, added_lines ← P
2. removed_start_line, removed_line_range, added_start_line, added_line_range ← chunk_header
3. before_lines, after_lines = 3, 3
4. modified_index ← {}
5. **for** *index, line ∈ enumerate(F[removed_start_line : removed_start_line + removed_line_range])* **do**
6.   **if** *line ∈ removed_lines* **then**
7.   modified_index.append(removed_start_line + index)
8. **if** *modified_index == {}* **then**
9.   **return** {}
10. **if** *max(modified_index) - min(modified_index) ≤ 10* **then**
11.   start_index ← max(modified_index[0]) - before_lines, 0)
12.   end_index ← min(max(modified_index[-1]) + after_lines + 1, len(F))
13. **else**
14.   start_index ← min(modified_index)
15.   end_index ← max(modified_index)
16. Extract function code chunk FC = F[start_index:end_index]
17. **return** FC;

tify functions with a higher likelihood of containing vulnerabilities, ensuring greater confidence in the dataset's accuracy.

Property 1 *Code-Based Heuristic (Patch Modification Hypothesis):* *We hypothesize that functions containing only a single modification within a CVE patch are more likely to contain the vulnerability. This hypothesis stems from the assumption that smaller, localized patches often address specific vulnerabilities directly. This property does not guarantee that the code chunks will always be vulnerable, as developers may modify patches to enhance code quality.*

Our study consists of clean and localized vulnerability cases from OSV.dev, where our empirical study shows 80.04% (6515 out of 8139) of CVEs have a single Git commit patch. Therefore, we restricted our study to single-patch CVEs, aligning with VFCFinder [4]. Multiple modifications make it unclear which change corresponds to the vulnerability. For dataset reliability, we excluded multifile patch information. Each modified patch contains chunk headers with deleted and added lines between code versions. The before version shows the vulnerable state, while the after version shows the fixed code.

Property 2 *LLM-Based Heuristic (Vulnerable Line Detection):* *We utilise a LLM Gemini-1.5 Pro [23] to predict vulnerable lines within code chunks. This model is presented with either (i) the code chunk alone or (ii) the code chunk alongside its corresponding CVE description. This dual input strategy aims to leverage both code structure* *and vulnerability context for improved ground vulnerability predictions. Appendix A.2 shows the two different prompts that we use in this work to identify vulnerable samples.*

Vulnerable Ground Truth: A code chunk is classified as vulnerable (class label: 1) and included in the ground truth dataset if it satisfies the following criteria:

- **Property 1** must be fulfilled.
- According to **Property 2**, the LLM response for *vul_lines* is not *None*.
- There is at least one overlapping line between the *vul_lines* identified by the LLM and the deleted lines in the patch modification.

If any of the above criteria are not met, the code chunk is labeled as Unknown (see Fig. 1).

Non-vulnerable Ground Truth: After the labeling of vulnerable code chunks, we extract fixed code from the after version using patch modification details and construct non-vulnerable code chunk samples. Additionally, we include random 5 to 10 lines of code from fixed functions in the after version. These samples are classified as non-vulnerable (class label: 0).

Code Chunks and Generic Code Chunks Label Data: Figure 1 illustrates the process of generating labeled data for code chunks and generic code chunks. These chunks are constructed using two types of LLM prompts (detailed in Table 6). Therefore, based on two LLM prompts and code chunks and generic code chunks, we generate four label datasets (Dataset 1, Dataset 2, Dataset 3 and Dataset 4) that shown in dataset section (*c.f.* Sect. 5.1) in Table 1.

We further created two additional datasets, Dataset 5 and Dataset 6 (*c.f.* Sect. 5.1), by providing the full function code to a large language model (LLM) to identify vulnerable lines. If the LLM successfully detects at least one vulnerable line, we apply the N-line code chunking approach to generate positive samples. The same strategy used for generating negative samples in Datasets 14 is applied here for consistency.

4.2 Proposed FuncVul Model

Figure 2 provides an overview of the architecture for the proposed FuncVul model, designed to detect function-level vulnerabilities effectively. The process begins with the input data, which consists of either code chunks or generic code chunks. These inputs are preprocessed and split into two subsets: 80% for training and 20% for testing. The training data is then tokenized using the tokenizer from the pre-trained GraphCodeBERT model. This tokenization step transforms the raw code chunks into numerical representations that encode the syntactic and semantic features of the code. Subsequently, the tokenized training data is passed through the pre-trained GraphCodeBERT model, which has been fine-tuned to capture rich features specific to programming languages.

GraphCodeBERT [7] is a pre-trained model for programming languages that incorporates the semantic structure of code, focusing on data flow rather than abstract syntax

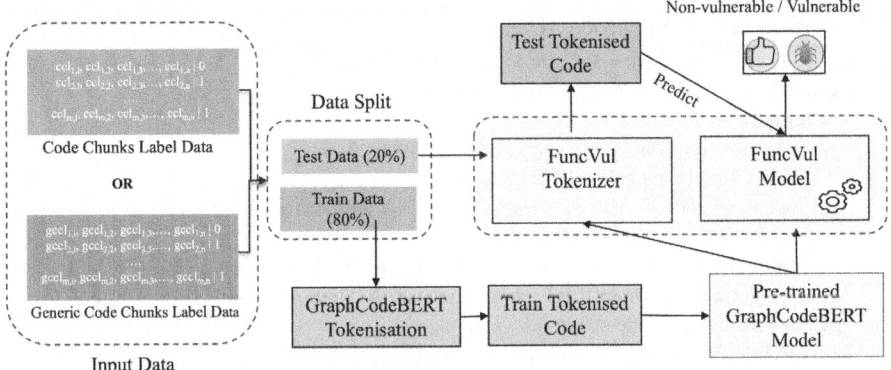

Fig. 2. Proposed code chunk based function vulnerability detection model (FuncVul) architecture.

trees (AST). Data flow represents variable relationships through a graph, simplifying complexity and enhancing efficiency. The model introduces two structure-aware pre-training tasks: data flow edge prediction to learn code structure representation and variable alignment to bridge source code and data flow representations. Built on a Transformer [25] architecture, GraphCodeBERT extends it with a graph-guided masked attention mechanism, enabling it to effectively integrate code structure and improves code representation learning.

In Fig. 2, we illustrate the fine-tuning process of the GraphCodeBERT model using our generated code chunk or generic code chunk data. After fine-tuning, the GraphCodeBERT model builds a new model and tokeniser, which we refer to as the FuncVul model and FuncVul tokeniser, respectively. To evaluate the model's performance on the test data, the test code is first tokenised using the FuncVul tokeniser. The tokenised code is then fed into the FuncVul model, which predicts whether the code chunk is vulnerable or non-vulnerable.

4.3 FuncVul Algorithm

The Algorithm 2 presents the training and testing process for the function-level vulnerability detection model, FuncVul. During the training phase, the data is split into training (80%) and testing (20%) sets (line 2). Next, the GraphCodeBERT tokenizer and model are loaded (line 3), and the training data is tokenized using the GraphCodeBERT tokenizer to create train_tokenised_code (line 4). Training parameters, such as epochs, batch size, and learning rate, are configured (line 5). Using the tokenized training data, the GraphCodeBERT model is fine-tuned to produce the FuncVul model $\mathcal{M}$ and tokenizer $\mathcal{T}$ (line 6). These are saved for future use (line 7).

In the testing phase, the test data is tokenized using the FuncVul tokenizer $\mathcal{T}$ (line 9). The FuncVul model $\mathcal{M}$ then predicts vulnerability labels for the tokenized test data (line 10). Model performance is evaluated by comparing the predicted labels with the ground

---
Algorithm 2: FuncVul Model (Data)

Data: Data: Code chunks or Generic code chunks data
Result: FuncVul model $\mathcal{M}$ and FuncVul tokeniser $\mathcal{T}$

1 **Training Phase:**
2 Split Data into train_data (80%) and test_data (20%)
3 $\mathcal{M}_\mathcal{G}, \mathcal{B}_\mathcal{G} \leftarrow$ Load GraphCodeBERT tokeniser and model
4 train_tokenised_code $\leftarrow$ Tokenize train_data using GraphCodeBERT tokenizer $\mathcal{T}_\mathcal{G}$(test_data).
5 Set training parameters (e.g., epochs, batch size, logging steps, learning rate).
6 $\mathcal{M}, \mathcal{B} \leftarrow$ Train GraphCodeBERT using train_data $\mathcal{M}_\mathcal{G}$(train_tokenised_code) and parameters and generate new model and tokeniser
7 Save the FuncVul model $\mathcal{M}$ and FuncVul tokenizer.
8 **Testing Phase:**
9 test_tokenised_code $\leftarrow$ Tokenize test_data using FuncVul tokeniser $\mathcal{T}$(test_data).
10 predict_label $\leftarrow$ Predict vulnerabilities (vulnerable or non-vulnerable) using FuncVul model $\mathcal{M}$ (test_tokenised_code).
11 Evaluate the model's performance on the test_data label and predict_label.
12 **return** $\mathcal{M}, \mathcal{T}$
---

truth labels from the test data (line 11). Finally, the algorithm returns the FuncVul model and tokenizer (line 12).

5 Experiments

5.1 Experimental Setup

All experiments in this paper were conducted using Python on a MacBook Pro with an Apple M3 processor and 24GB of RAM. For the FuncVul implementation, a batch size of 8 was used with a chunk code embedding vector length of 512. The model was trained for 3 epochs with 50 warmup steps, a weight decay of 0.05, and automatic reloading of the best model at the end.

Datasets: In this research work, we generate six datasets. The dataset generation process is discussed in detail in the corresponding section (*c.f.* Sect. 4.1). The first four datasets were created by combining patch information (removed lines) with lines detected by the LLM, ensuring that at least one common line is present between the two. In contrast, datasets 5 and 6 were generated solely using code chunks identified by the LLM, without incorporating any removed line information. For identifying vulnerable lines using LLMs, we employ two prompts: one that utilises only the code information and another that incorporates both the code and its description. Table 1 provides details of six datasets, including the code type, and the number of vulnerable and non-vulnerable samples.

Baselines: We compare our proposed FuncVul model with five baselines: **CodeBERT** [5], **CustomVulBERTa** [9], **BERT** [12], **VUDENC** [30] and **LineVul** [6]. These baselines' detailed descriptions are given in Appendix A.3.

Table 1. Details of various datasets.

Dataset	Prompt	Code Type	Vulnerable Defined By	Vulnerable	Non-vulnerable
1	Code + Description	Code Chunk	LLM + Patch Information	1810 (43.4%)	2357 (56.6%)
2	Code	Code Chunk	LLM + Patch Information	2120 (42.6%)	2851 (57.4%)
3	Code + Description	Generic Code Chunk	LLM + Patch Information	1810 (43.4%)	2357 (56.6%)
4	Code	Generic Code Chunk	LLM + Patch Information	2120 (42.6%)	2851 (57.4%)
5	Code + Description	Code Chunk	LLM	3169 (50%)	3169 (50%)
6	Code	Code Chunk	LLM	6041 (50%)	6041 (50%)

Evaluation Metrics: In the prediction models analyses, we applied various evaluation metrics indicating the model performances. Our main goal is to predict code vulnerability. Thus, we evaluate our results using Accuracy, Precision, Recall, F1-score and Matthews Correlation Coefficient (MCC). The details of these evaluation metrics are defined in Appendix A.4.

5.2 Results Analysis

To evaluate the proposed model FuncVul performance, we run a set of experiments to answer our six research questions.

FuncVul Model Performance (RQ1): We compare our proposed FuncVul model against five baseline methods across six benchmark datasets. As shown in Table 2, FuncVul consistently outperforms all other models, ranking first in most evaluation metrics—including F1-Score, Accuracy, Precision, and MCC—across all datasets. Specifically, it achieves the highest score in 25 out of 30 cases and ranks second in two additional cases. The LineVul model also demonstrates strong performance, obtaining the highest Recall in four cases and second-best results in three others. CodeBERT and CustomVulBERTa exhibit competitive results in certain settings, with CodeBERT achieving the second-highest score in 18 cases. CustomVulBERTa achieves seven second-best results and one best-case performance. All experiments are conducted using an 80/20 train-test split, and results are reported as the average of five-fold cross-validation. Our model, FuncVul, operates at the function level using extended 3-line code chunks. This design makes the model more selective in labeling functions as vulnerable, often requiring strong semantic or syntactic cues to trigger a positive prediction. As a result, vulnerabilities with subtle or distributed patterns may be overlooked, contributing to a relatively lower recall. However, this selectivity leads to a notable reduction in false positives, thereby significantly improving the F1 score, which reflects a better balance between precision and recall and is particularly important for reliable vulnerability prediction. Overall, Table 2 confirms that FuncVul delivers the most consistent and superior performance, effectively answering RQ1.

Table 2. Comparison of FuncVul and baselines across six datasets, with bold for best scores, underline for second-best, and bracketed numbers indicating F1-score rankings (1 = best, 6 = worst).

Dataset	Model	Accuracy	Precision	Recall	F1-Score	MCC
1	CodeBERT	0.8707 ± 0.00020	0.7928 ± 0.0216	0.9505 ± 0.0269	0.8641 ± 0.0095 (5)	0.7683 ± 0.0283
	CustomVulBERTa	0.8648 ± 0.0060	0.7974 ± 0.0224	<u>0.9816 ± 0.204</u>	0.8816 ± 0.0091 (3)	0.7898 ± 0.0102
	BERT	0.8812 ± 0.0103	<u>0.8067 ± 0.0168</u>	0.9548 ± 0.0443	0.8739 ± 0.0167 (4)	0.7742 ± 0.0282
	VUDENC	0.8598 ± 0.0111	0.8058 ± 0.0090	0.8560 ± 0.0380	0.8404 ± 0.0225 (6)	0.7166 ± 0.0241
	LineVul	<u>0.8874 ± 0.0074</u>	0.7937 ± 0.0174	0.9802 ± 0.0.0	<u>0.8849 ± 0.0708 (2)</u>	<u>0.7976 ± 0.0118</u>
	FuncVul	**0.8906 ± 0.0042**	**0.8108 ± 0.0136**	**0.9840 ± 0.0206**	**0.8888 ± 0.0055 (1)**	**0.9477 ± 0.0025**
2	CodeBERT	0.8950 ± 0.0117	<u>0.8151 ± 0.0315</u>	0.9777 ± 0.0322	<u>0.8882 ± 0.0111 (2)</u>	<u>0.8039 ± 0.0183</u>
	CustomVulBERTa	0.8908 ± 0.0130	0.7975 ± 0.0232	<u>0.9976 ± 0.0053</u>	0.8863 ± 0.0132 (3)	0.8022 ± 0.0200
	BERT	0.8902 ± 0.0119	0.8136 ± 0.0241	0.9650 ± 0.0361	0.8822 ± 0.0126 (5)	0.7919 ± 0.0244
	VUDENC	0.8680 ± 0.0140	0.8463 ± 0.0183	0.8440 ± 0.0301	0.8449 ± 0.0183 (6)	0.7304 ± 0.0295
	LineVul	0.8900 ± 0.0120	0.7951 ± 0.0202	**1.0 ± 0.0**	0.8857 ± 0.0126 (4)	0.8016 ± 0.0193
	FuncVul	**0.9022 ± 0.0157**	**0.8456 ± 0.0212**	0.9443 ± 0.0282	**0.8917 ± 0.0178 (1)**	**0.8947 ± 0.0454**
3	CodeBERT	0.8663 ± 0.0176	<u>0.7856 ± 0.0202</u>	0.9512 ± 0.0346	0.8602 ± 0.0205 (4)	<u>0.7545 ± 0.0096</u>
	CustomVulBERTa	0.8675 ± 0.0114	0.7793 ± 0.0210	0.9682 ± 0.0141	<u>0.8634 ± 0.0155 (2)</u>	0.7544 ± 0.0.021
	BERT	0.8054 ± 0.0248	0.7762 ± 0.0143	0.7764 ± 0.0459	0.7758 ± 0.0247 (5)	0.6043 ± 0.0521
	VUDENC	0.7485 ± 0.0199	0.7153 ± 0.0258	0.6981 ± 0.0306	0.7063 ± 0.0244 (6)	0.4867 ± 0.0420
	LineVul	0.8656 ± 0.0121	0.7750 ± 0.0240	**0.9721 ± 0.0121**	0.8622 ± 0.0156 (3)	0.7527 ± 0.0.0192
	FuncVul	**0.8723 ± 0.0114**	**0.7924 ± 0.0245**	0.9544 ± 0.0183	**0.8657 ± 0.0174 (1)**	**0.8825 ± 0.0577**
4	CodeBERT	0.8735 ± 0.0141	<u>0.7940 ± 0.0281</u>	0.9526 ± 0.0254	<u>0.8654 ± 0.0140 (2)</u>	<u>0.7602 ± 0.0274</u>
	CustomVulBERTa	0.8684 ± 0.0133	0.7817 ± 0.0206	<u>0.9600 ± 0.0124</u>	0.8616 ± 0.0141 (3)	0.7531 ± 0.0.0239
	BERT	0.80677 ± 0.00158	0.7712 ± 0.0285	0.7784 ± 0.0288	0.7743 ± 0.0198 (5)	0.6058 ± 0.0317
	VUDENC	0.7658 ± 0.0155	0.7238 ± 0.0253	0.7302 ± 0.0401	0.7263 ± 0.0233 (6)	0.5225 ± 0.0321
	LineVul	0.8656 ± 0.0163	0.7759 ± 0.0264	**0.9642 ± 0.0092**	0.8596 ± 0.0162 (4)	0.7500 ± 0.0270
	FuncVul	**0.8797 ± 0.0118**	**0.8077 ± 0.0200**	0.9426 ± 0.0182	**0.8698 ± 0.0134 (1)**	**0.7982 ± 0.0470**
5	CodeBERT	<u>0.8914 ± 0.0125</u>	**0.8914 ± 0.0136**	0.9148 ± 0.0329	<u>0.9006 ± 0.0131 (2)</u>	<u>0.8035 ± 0.0253</u>
	CustomVulBERTa	0.8905 ± 0.0147	0.8530 ± 0.0244	<u>0.9446 ± 0.0208</u>	0.8962 ± 0.0130 (3)	0.7860 ± 0.0278
	BERT	0.5897 ± 0.0856	0.7902 ± 0.1950	0.3860 ± 0.3342	0.3997 ± 0.3296 (6)	0.2007 ± 0.01448
	VUDENC	0.8034 ± 0.0135	0.7996 ± 0.0171	0.8097 ± 0.0152	0.8045 ± 0.0145 (5)	0.6064 ± 0.0269
	LineVul	0.8509 ± 0.0199	0.7895 ± 0.0358	**0.9596 ± 0.0306**	0.8655 ± 0.0178 (4)	0.7205 ± 0.0340
	FuncVul	**0.9004 ± 0.0116**	<u>0.8934 ± 0.0130</u>	0.9096 ± 0.0154	**0.9013 ± 0.0111 (1)**	**0.9556 ± 0.0041**
6	CodeBERT	<u>0.8984 ± 0.0071</u>	<u>0.9007 ± 0.0187</u>	0.9330 ± 0.0207	<u>0.9155 ± 0.0073 (2)</u>	<u>0.8377 ± 0.0137</u>
	CustomVulBERTa	0.8898 ± 0.0170	0.8434 ± 0.0416	**0.9614 ± 0.0269**	0.8975 ± 0.0124 (3)	0.7900 ± 0.0242
	BERT	0.7115 ± 0.0839	0.7069 ± 0.0959	0.7946 ± 0.1116	0.7371 ± 0.0258 (5)	0.4465 ± 0.1162
	VUDENC	0.8290 ± 0.0074	0.8196 ± 0.0161	0.8443 ± 0.0145	0.8316 ± 0.0073 (4)	0.6585 ± 0.0144
	LineVul	0.7951 ± 0.1676	0.6455 ± 0.0.3612	0.7785 ± 0.4355	0.7056 ± 0.3944 (6)	0.7570 ± 0.006
	FuncVul	**0.9184 ± 0.0053**	**0.9056 ± 0.0117**	<u>0.9343 ± 0.0116</u>	**0.9196 ± 0.0057 (1)**	**0.9619 ± 0.0031**

Code Chunks vs Full Function Based Results Analysis (RQ2): Table 3(a) compares the performance of the Full Function and Code Chunk approaches on Dataset 1. The Code Chunk method significantly outperforms the Full Function approach across all metrics. It improves accuracy by 53.9%, precision by 42.8%, recall by 35.5%, and F1-score by 42.0%. We also gets the same kinds of results on Dataset 2 in Fig. 3(b). In this case our proposed code chunk based model improves accuracy by 35.22%, precision by 28.16%, recall by 35.59% and F1-score by 32.26%.

These results highlight that the code chunk approach significantly enhances the model's capability for vulnerability detection than the full-function based approach. These findings effectively address our research question RQ2.

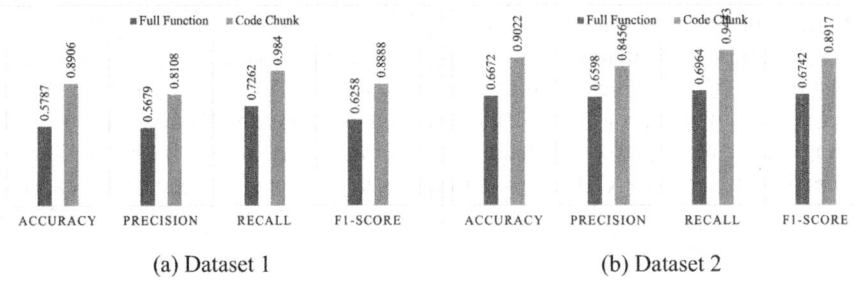

Fig. 3. Comparison between our proposed code chunk based results with full function code based results.

Generic Code Chunks Based Results Analysis (RQ3): In this work, we construct datasets based on code chunk and generic code chunk methodologies using the same data. Figure 4(a) presents a comparative analysis between code chunk-based Dataset 1 and generic code chunk-based Dataset 3 results on FuncVul method. The results demonstrate that the code chunk based results consistently outperforms generic code across all evaluation metrics, achieving improvements of 2% in Accuracy, 1.84% in Precision, 2.96% in Recall, and 1.9% in F1-score.

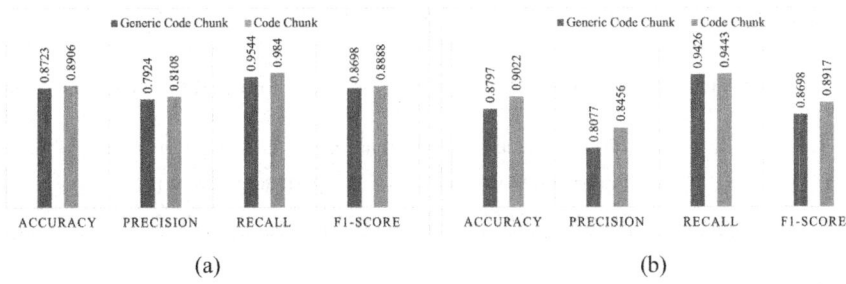

Fig. 4. Comparison between our proposed code chunk based results with generic code chunk based results.

Similarly, Fig. 4(b) compares Code chunk-based Dataset 2 with generic Code Chunk-based Dataset 4, showing improvements of 2.25% in Accuracy, 3.79% in Precision, and 2.19% in F1-score, with a modest 0.17% gain in Recall. These findings underscore the superior effectiveness and adaptability of the Code Chunk approach, validating RQ3.

Effectiveness of Identifying New CVEs and New Project CVEs Vulnerabilities (RQ4): Previous results presented vulnerability detection performance using five-fold cross-validation. However, Fig. 1 indicates that many vulnerable packages remain undetected by LLM Detect and are marked as "Unknown". The "Unknown" test set refers to single-patch modified functions from CVEs that were not identified as vulnerable by the

LLM detector and were thus excluded from the Vulnerable Ground Truth. To evaluate this large portion of "Unknown" data, we constructed two additional test sets: (1) one consisting of CVEs not present in the training data, and (2) another comprising code from entirely different project IDs than those used in training. Vulnerable samples were generated using the Code-Based Heuristic (Patch Modification Hypothesis), while non-vulnerable samples followed the same strategy as in our previously curated six datasets. We trained our model, FuncVul, using 100% of Dataset 2. Detailed statistics for the test sets are provided in Table 3.

Table 3. New CVEs and new project ID-based test data.

Case	Type	Vulnerable	Non-Vulnerable
Test Case 1	New CVSs	1245	1753
Test Case 2	New Project ID	179	280

Table 4 shows that the FuncVul model achieves an accuracy of 81.95% in Test Case 1 and 76.69% in Test Case 2. This indicates that the model can correctly identify 81.95% of code chunks that were previously unexplored during dataset 2 construction (labeled as Unknown in Fig. 1). The FuncVul model shows strong capability in detecting vulnerabilities, particularly in recall 90.20%. These results support the model's robustness in identifying unknown vulnerabilities, addressing the objectives of RQ4.

Table 4. New CVEs and new project ID based prediction results for various model on Dataset 2.

Case	Model	Accuracy	Precision	Recall	F1-Score	FP	FN
Test Case 1	FuncVul	0.8195	0.7283	0.9020	0.8059	419	122
Test Case 2	FuncVul	0.7669	0.6552	0.8492	0.7397	80	27

Impact of Line Numbers to Create Code Chunks (RQ5): Our primary objective is to generate concise code chunks highlighting vulnerable patterns. We adopted "3-line extended based code chunk", including three lines before and after a detected vulnerable line. To validate this approach, we tested code chunks extended by different line numbers—1, 5, 7, 9, 10, 15, 20, and 25—and assessed their performance with our FuncVul model. Results show the 3-line extended code chunk outperforms other configurations in most metrics. Figure 5(a) shows highest accuracy for 3-line extended chunks on Dataset 6, while Fig. 5(b) demonstrates superior precision for this strategy. Although the recall score, shown in Fig. 5(c), is highest for 7-line extended code chunks, the 3-line extended approach ranks second. Figure 5(d) shows the F1 score, balancing recall and precision, confirming that 3-line chunks provide the best performance. Larger chunks make it difficult to identify vulnerable code effectively, while the 3-line strategy's average chunk length of 6.2 lines provides optimal balance between context and conciseness for detecting vulnerable patterns.

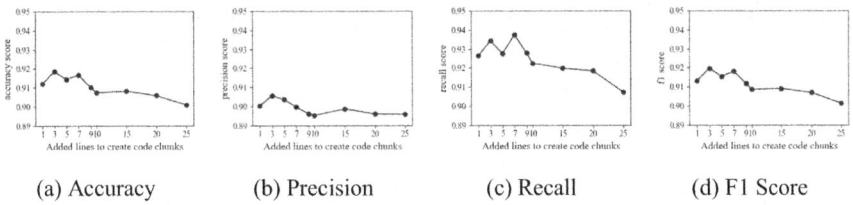

(a) Accuracy (b) Precision (c) Recall (d) F1 Score

Fig. 5. Impacts of code chunk length on dataset 6.

5.3 Detection of Multiple Vulnerabilities Within Function Code (RQ6)

In this work, we use code chunk based data for model built that can split one single function in multiple code chunk. Thus, the proposed model is capable of detecting multiple vulnerabilities within a single function's code. By analyzing smaller, context-rich segments, the model effectively captures various vulnerability patterns, enabling comprehensive detection across different parts of the function.

6 Conclusion

In this paper, we present FuncVul, a novel model for function-level vulnerability detection that leverages function code chunks and the pre-trained GraphCodeBERT model. Unlike existing approaches, FuncVul not only identifies whether a function is vulnerable but also detects the specific number of vulnerable code chunks, significantly reducing the time required by developers or experts to address vulnerabilities. Experimental results demonstrate that FuncVul outperforms baseline models on both code chunk and generic code chunk datasets. Additionally, our analysis reveals that datasets based on three-line code chunks from large language models yield higher accuracy and F1-scores compared to datasets where patch information is derived by removing lines of code. Furthermore, we demonstrate that our dataset can be generalized using large language models, resulting in enhanced model performance.

This study focuses on vulnerability detection strategies, without considering multi-class detection since vulnerabilities have varying risk levels. Future work will extend to multi-class vulnerability detection to address risk variations. Currently, we identify vulnerabilities in C/C++ and Python code, with plans to expand to other programming languages.

A Appendix

A.1 Generic Code Conversion LLM Prompt

Generic code chunks converts code chunks in generic format. Here, we use the following LLM to convert the generic code chunk as described in Table 5. Table 5 also shows the one example of code chunk and converted generic code chunk based on the proposed LLM generic prompt.

Table 5. Prompt and Example for Transforming Code Chunks into Generic Code Chunk

Description of Generic Prompt	
Here is the function code chunk: $\{code\_chunk\}$ Please convert the code chunk by renaming functions to F_1, F_2, ..., F_N and variables to v_1, v_2, ..., v_n. Return the converted code in a variable named *generic_code*.	
Example	
Code Chunk	Generic Code Chunk
goto trunc;	goto F1;
if (length < alen)	if (v1 < v2)
goto trunc;	goto F1;
if (!bgp_attr_print(ndo, atype, p, alen))	if (!F2(v3, v4, v5, v2))
goto trunc;	goto F1;
p += alen;	v5 += v2;
len -= alen;	v6 -= v2;

A.2 Vulnerable Samples Detection LLM Prompts

In this paper, we construct six datasets using two distinct LLM prompts. Figure 6 provides a detailed overview of these prompts—one utilizing only the code and the other combining a description with the code.

A.3 Details of Baselines

We compare our proposed FuncVul model with five baselines that are as follows.

- **CodeBERT** [5]: CodeBERT is a pre-trained model for understanding and generating both natural language and programming code.
- **CustomVulBERTa**: CustomVulBERTa is a fine-tuned version of VulBERTa [9], a RoBERTa-based model pre-trained on real-world C/C++ code, adapted to detect security vulnerabilities and used as a baseline in our experiments.
- **BERT**: BERT [12] is a pretrained bidirectional transformer model that captures context in both directions using masked language modeling, offering an advantage over unidirectional approaches.
- **VUDENC**: VUDENC [30] is a deep learning-based tool for detecting vulnerabilities in Python code, using word2vec for token embeddings and LSTM networks for vulnerability classification.
- **LineVul**: LineVul [6] is a Transformer-based fine-grained line-level vulnerability prediction model.

Table 6. LLM prompts for detecting vulnerable samples with different input settings.

Prompt Type	Input Context
Code Only	Given the following function code: {code}
Code + Description	Given the following function code: {code}
	And the associated CVE description: {desc}

Task: Extract the following information:
1. Identify the lines of code that contain vulnerabilities. Return these lines in a list of string named as *line_code*. If no vulnerable lines are found, return ['None']. Ensure the list is formatted with items separated by commas and enclosed in square brackets.
2. Determine the line numbers of vulnerable code. Return these line numbers in a list of integer named as *vul_lines*. If no such lines exist, return ['None'].
3. List the affected vulnerability categories. Return these in a list of string named as *vul_category*. If no categories are affected, return ['None'].
Please provide the output in three keys as dictionary format: *line_code*, *vul_lines*, and *vul_category*. Do not need an explanation.

A.4 Details of Evaluation Metrics

To evaluate the performance of our proposed model, we employ widely used prediction evaluation metrics, as outlined below.

- **Accuracy:** It measures the overall correctness of a model in predicting both code vulnerabilities and non-vulnerabilities. $Accuracy = \frac{TP+TN}{TP+FP+TN+FN}$
- **Precision:** It measures the proportion of true code vulnerabilities to the total number of code vulnerabilities that have been predicted as vulnerabilities by the model: $Precision = \frac{TP}{TP+FP}$
- **Recall:** It measures the proportion of true vulnerabilities detected by a model to the total number of code vulnerabilities in the dataset: $Recall = \frac{TP}{TP+FN}$
- **F1-Score:** It is the harmonic mean of precision and recall:
  $F1\text{-}Score = \frac{2*Precision*Recall}{Precision+Recall}$
- **Matthews Correlation Coefficient (MCC):** MCC is a robust metric that reflects balanced performance across all confusion matrix categories and is particularly effective for evaluating models on imbalanced datasets.
  $MCC = \frac{TP \cdot TN - FP \cdot FN}{\sqrt{(TP+FP)(TP+FN)(TN+FP)(TN+FN)}}$

References

1. Akuthota, V., Kasula, R., Sumona, S.T., Mohiuddin, M., Reza, M.T., Rahman, M.M.: Vulnerability detection and monitoring using LLM. In: 2023 IEEE 9th International Women in Engineering (WIE) Conference on Electrical and Computer Engineering (WIECON-ECE), pp. 309–314. IEEE (2023)
2. Chakraborty, S., Krishna, R., Ding, Y., Ray, B.: Deep learning based vulnerability detection: are we there yet? IEEE Trans. Softw. Eng. **48**(9), 3280–3296 (2021)

3. CVE: Common vulnerabilities and exposures. https://cve.mitre.org (2024). Accessed 12 Nov 2024
4. Dunlap, T., Lin, E., Enck, W., Reaves, B.: VFCFinder: pairing security advisories and patches. In: Proceedings of the 19th ACM Asia Conference on Computer and Communications Security, pp. 1128–1142 (2024)
5. Feng, Z., et al.: CodeBERT: A pre-trained model for programming and natural languages. arXiv preprint arXiv:2002.08155 (2020)
6. Fu, M., Tantithamthavorn, C.: LineVul: a transformer-based line-level vulnerability prediction. In: Proceedings of the 19th International Conference on Mining Software Repositories, pp. 608–620 (2022)
7. Guo, D., et al.: GRAPHCODEBERT: Pre-training code representations with data flow. arXiv preprint arXiv:2009.08366 (2020)
8. Guo, Y., Patsakis, C., Hu, Q., Tang, Q., Casino, F.: Outside the comfort zone: analysing LLM capabilities in software vulnerability detection. In: European Symposium on Research in Computer Security, pp. 271–289. Springer (2024)
9. Hanif, H., Maffeis, S.: VulBERTa: simplified source code pre-training for vulnerability detection. In: 2022 International Joint Conference on Neural Networks (IJCNN), pp. 1–8. IEEE (2022)
10. Hin, D., Kan, A., Chen, H., Babar, M.A.: LineVD: statement-level vulnerability detection using graph neural networks. In: Proceedings of the 19th International Conference on Mining Software Repositories, pp. 596–607 (2022)
11. Islam, N.T., Parra, G.D.L.T., Manuel, D., Bou-Harb, E., Najafirad, P.: An unbiased transformer source code learning with semantic vulnerability graph. In: 2023 IEEE 8th European Symposium on Security and Privacy (EuroS&P), pp. 144–159. IEEE (2023)
12. Kenton, J.D.M.W.C., Toutanova, L.K.: BERT: pre-training of deep bidirectional transformers for language understanding. In: Proceedings of NAACL-HLT. vol. 1, p. 2. Minneapolis, Minnesota (2019)
13. Li, Y., Wang, S., Nguyen, T.N.: Vulnerability detection with fine-grained interpretations. In: Proceedings of the 29th ACM Joint Meeting on European Software Engineering Conference and Symposium on the Foundations of Software Engineering, pp. 292–303 (2021)
14. Li, Z., Zou, D., Xu, S., Chen, Z., Zhu, Y., Jin, H.: VulDeeLocator: a deep learning-based fine-grained vulnerability detector. IEEE Trans. Dependable Secure Comput. **19**(4), 2821–2837 (2021)
15. Li, Z., Zou, D., Xu, S., Jin, H., Qi, H., Hu, J.: VulPecker: an automated vulnerability detection system based on code similarity analysis. In: Proceedings of the 32nd Annual Conference on Computer Security Applications, pp. 201–213 (2016)
16. Li, Z., et al.: VulDeePecker: A deep learning-based system for vulnerability detection. arXiv preprint arXiv:1801.01681 (2018)
17. Liu, Y.: RoBERTa: A robustly optimized BERT pretraining approach. arXiv preprint arXiv:1907.11692 **364** (2019)
18. Lu, C., Li, T., Dehaene, T., Lagaisse, B.: ICVul: a well-labeled C/C++ vulnerability dataset with comprehensive metadata and VCCS. In: 2025 IEEE/ACM 22nd International Conference on Mining Software Repositories (MSR), pp. 154–158. IEEE (2025)
19. Lu, G., Ju, X., Chen, X., Pei, W., Cai, Z.: GRACE: empowering LLM-based software vulnerability detection with graph structure and in-context learning. J. Syst. Softw. **212**, 112031 (2024)
20. Nguyen, V.A., Nguyen, D.Q., Nguyen, V., Le, T., Tran, Q.H., Phung, D.: ReGVD: revisiting graph neural networks for vulnerability detection. In: Proceedings of the ACM/IEEE 44th International Conference on Software Engineering: Companion Proceedings, pp. 178–182 (2022)

21. NVD: National vulnerability database (2024). https://nvd.nist.gov. Accessed 12 Nov 2024
22. Sonnekalb, T.: Machine-learning supported vulnerability detection in source code. In: Proceedings of the 2019 27th ACM Joint Meeting on European Software Engineering Conference and Symposium on the Foundations of Software Engineering, pp. 1180–1183 (2019)
23. Team, G., et al.: Gemini 1.5: Unlocking multimodal understanding across millions of tokens of context. arXiv preprint arXiv:2403.05530 (2024)
24. Tran, H.C., Tran, A.D., Le, K.H.: DetectVul: a statement-level code vulnerability detection for python. Futur. Gener. Comput. Syst. **163**, 107504 (2025)
25. Vaswani, A., et al.: Attention is all you need. NIPS'17. In: Proceedings of the 31st International Conference on Neural Information Processing Systems December, pp. 6000–6010 (2017)
26. Vo, H.D., Nguyen, S.: Can an old fashioned feature extraction and a light-weight model improve vulnerability type identification performance? Inf. Softw. Technol. **164**, 107304 (2023)
27. Wang, H., et al.: Combining graph-based learning with automated data collection for code vulnerability detection. IEEE Trans. Inf. Forensics Secur. **16**, 1943–1958 (2020)
28. Wang, X., Chen, K., Kang, T., Ouyang, J.: A dynamic coarse grain discrete element method for gas-solid fluidized beds by considering particle-group crushing and polymerization. Appl. Sci. **10**(6), 1943 (2020)
29. Wang, X., Hu, R., Gao, C., Wen, X.C., Chen, Y., Liao, Q.: ReposVul: a repository-level high-quality vulnerability dataset. In: Proceedings of the 2024 IEEE/ACM 46th International Conference on Software Engineering: Companion Proceedings, pp. 472–483 (2024)
30. Wartschinski, L., Noller, Y., Vogel, T., Kehrer, T., Grunske, L.: VUDENC: vulnerability detection with deep learning on a natural codebase for python. Inf. Softw. Technol. **144**, 106809 (2022)
31. Wei, H., Lin, G., Li, L., Jia, H.: A context-aware neural embedding for function-level vulnerability detection. Algorithms **14**(11), 335 (2021)
32. Wen, X.C., Chen, Y., Gao, C., Zhang, H., Zhang, J.M., Liao, Q.: Vulnerability detection with graph simplification and enhanced graph representation learning. In: 2023 IEEE/ACM 45th International Conference on Software Engineering (ICSE), pp. 2275–2286. IEEE (2023)
33. Wu, Y., Zou, D., Dou, S., Yang, W., Xu, D., Jin, H.: VulCNN: an image-inspired scalable vulnerability detection system. In: Proceedings of the 44th International Conference on Software Engineering, pp. 2365–2376 (2022)
34. Xia, C.S., Wei, Y., Zhang, L.: Automated program repair in the era of large pre-trained language models. In: 2023 IEEE/ACM 45th International Conference on Software Engineering (ICSE), pp. 1482–1494. IEEE (2023)
35. Yuan, X., Lin, G., Mei, H., Tai, Y., Zhang, J.: Software vulnerable functions discovery based on code composite feature. J. Inf. Secur. Appl. **81**, 103718 (2024)
36. Zhou, Y., Liu, S., Siow, J., Du, X., Liu, Y.: Devign: effective vulnerability identification by learning comprehensive program semantics via graph neural networks. Adv. Neural Inf. Process. Syst. **32** (2019)

LUMIA: Linear Probing for Unimodal and MultiModal Membership Inference Attacks Leveraging Internal LLM States

Luis Ibanez-Lissen[1(✉)], Lorena Gonzalez-Manzano[1], Jose Maria de Fuentes[1,2], Nicolas Anciaux[2], and Joaquin Garcia-Alfaro[3]

[1] Universidad Carlos III de Madrid, Leganes, Spain
luibanez@pa.uc3m.es, jfuentes@inf.uc3m.es
[2] Inria, INSA-CVL, Université Paris-Saclay, Palaiseau, France
[3] SAMOVAR, Télécom SudParis, Institut Polytechnique de Paris, Palaiseau, France

Abstract. Large Language Models (LLMs) are increasingly used in a variety of applications. Concerns around inferring whether data samples belong to the LLM training dataset have grown in parallel. Previous efforts focus on black-to-grey-box models, thus neglecting the potential benefit from internal LLM information. To address this problem, we propose the use of Linear Probes (LPs) as a method to assess Membership Inference Attacks (MIAs) by examining internal activations of LLMs. Our approach, dubbed LUMIA, applies LPs layer-by-layer to get fine-grained data on the model inner workings. We test this method across several model architectures, sizes and datasets, including unimodal and multimodal tasks. In unimodal MIA, LUMIA achieves an average gain of 14.90% in Area Under the Curve (AUC) over previous techniques. Remarkably, LUMIA reaches AUC > 60% in 65.33% of cases—an increase of 46.80% against the state of the art. Furthermore, our approach reveals key insights, such as the model layers where MIAs are most detectable. In multimodal models, LPs indicate that visual inputs significantly contribute to MIAs—AUC > 60% is reached in 85.90% of the experiments.

Keywords: Large Language Models · Large Multimodal Models · Membership Inference Attacks · Linear Probes

1 Introduction

Membership Inference Attacks (MIAs) aim to determine whether specific data samples were included in the training set of a Large Language Model (LLM) [39]. If these samples contain sensitive information, it could have privacy implications for the affected stakeholders. Therefore, it is a security matter as pointed out by institutions such as NIST [27], MITRE[1] as well as the academia itself

---
[1] https://misp-galaxy.org/mitre-atlas-attack-pattern/, last access June 2025.

[14,40]. Beyond privacy risks, MIAs may also have concrete implications for model providers, such as revealing risks of copyright infringement if training sets include protected content. While MIAs alone are unlikely to serve as legal proofs [42], they may support investigation when combined with watermarked data tracing [12] or synthetic copyright traps [26]. Such concerns have sparked growing interest in advancing MIA methodologies beyond traditional black-box paradigms. Most existing efforts operate in a black-box setting [27], while grey-box schemes rely on model output thresholds [6,30,32].

Motivation. The need for fair and transparent auditing processes in AI systems motivates the exploration of white-box approaches [7,39]. For instance, to verify compliance with data privacy policies, a MIA may allow checking if confidential texts were unintentionally included in the training data. We hypothesize that the internal model data, particularly activations, from member and non-member samples may reveal distinguishing patterns. Note that LLMs such as Mistral or Arctic expose their activations but not their training data. Formally speaking, our attacker model is as follows:

Attacker Model. An adversary $\mathcal{A}$ aims to estimate, for a given input sample X_i, the probability $P_k(X_i)$ that it belongs to the training set of model LLM_j using the internal activations $A_k(x_i)$ extracted at layer l_k of LLM_j. Thus, the attacker is assumed to have access to LLM_j, including its internal activations.

Only Liu et al. [20] have approached the membership inference problem in LLMs from this perspective. They apply Linear Probes (LPs) [2] on model activations of a single layer. A number of limitations in Liu et al. [20] are tackled in our work. First, their approach involves fine-tuning the models to ensure that members have been seen. Therefore, results are biased since samples already used in the *training* phase are seen twice. Second, such a fine-tuning is used to create proxy models for the experimentation, but there is no guarantee on the functional equivalence of original and proxy models. Thirdly, they use a template prompt to simplify the problem by reducing the search space. Lastly, they are limited to text-based MIAs, thus excluding multimodal models.

Contribution. This paper provides an insightful analysis of the effectiveness of using internal model data for MIA assessment. The approach, dubbed LUMIA , uses internal activations of each model layer in open-source Pretrained Autoregressive LLMs [43], including both unimodal (e.g., text-only) and multimodal architectures (e.g., vision-language models). LUMIA is directly applied to real-world models and datasets, thus characterizing the ability of LPs to succeed depending on the model, dataset nature and bias. As no sample prompts are used and LLMs are requested to perform a variety of tasks, our results are easily generalizable. Interestingly, experiments involve text-based and multimodal MIAs, and they are not dependent on the LLM output, as opposed to [19].

The research question at stake is—*To what extent can internal activations of LLMs be used to assess membership inference?* In this vein, the list of contributions is as follows:

- We provide a comprehensive study on the suitability of internal activations for assessing MIAs by using linear probes, showing their ability to outperform state-of-the-art contributions.
- We explore for the first time the impact of the LLM size, the dataset nature, bias, and the impact of using deduplicated model versions.
- We analyse the problem of MIAs in multimodal LLMs. We consider a variety of LLM tasks, which has never been tackled to the best of authors knowledge.
- Our experimental results are based on 14 textual and seven multimodal datasets, as well as three model families involving 15 LLM configurations. We release our experimental materials to foster further research[2].

The paper is structured as follows. Section 2 provides background and preliminaries. Section 3 describes the foundations of LUMIA. Section 4 covers all the experimentation, which is later analysed in Sect. 5. Section 6 shows the related work. Section 7 concludes the paper and points out future work directions.

2 Background

Large Language Models (LLMs) and Linear Probes (LPs) are introduced in Sects. 2.1 and 2.2, respectively.

2.1 LLMs. Internal Data, Input Data and Biases

LLMs are transformer-based neural networks [35] with tens to hundreds of billions of parameters, trained on vast data. We use the term *training* instead of *pre-training*, even if this phase takes place before models are released for their public use. Examples include LLaMA [10] and GPT-4 [1]. Some apply data deduplication to reduce repetition [3].

For the interest of this paper, the information stored by the neural network during training and inference is at stake. In the transformer model [35], internal model data refers to the activations produced at each transformer block's output during the feed-forward pass, representing the model's intermediate state. Multimodal LLMs include a visual encoder—usually a unimodal image-pretrained model—to compress visual information [43].

A key factor in training these models is data quality, often measured by identifying biases. Two major types are N-gram Bias (NGB), the overlap of N-grams between non-member and member samples, indicating similarity [9], and Temporal Bias (TB), which occurs when members are selected before a cutoff date and non-members after [8].

2.2 Linear Classifier Probes

Linear Probes (LP) are classifiers (such as Multi-Layer Perceptrons, MLPs) that contribute to deep learning models explainability efforts by providing insights into how the model processes information internally [2].

---

[2] *Available online at* https://github.com/Luisibear98/LUMIA.

LPs predict whether model activations accurately represent language features, aiding neural network interpretability.

In LLMs, a LP classifier is placed after each layer to predict concepts from activations, such as membership status. These probes are used in tasks like monitoring adversarial training [28] and detecting model truthfulness [21], demonstrating their versatility.

3 LUMIA

This section provides the foundations of our proposal. Section 3.1 covers the problem formulation and Sect. 3.2 describes the approach.

3.1 Problem Formulation

LUMIA (Linear probe-based Utilization of Model Internal Activations) leverages Linear Probes (LPs), lightweight classifiers trained directly on internal activations, i.e., the hidden states generated at each layer during inference.

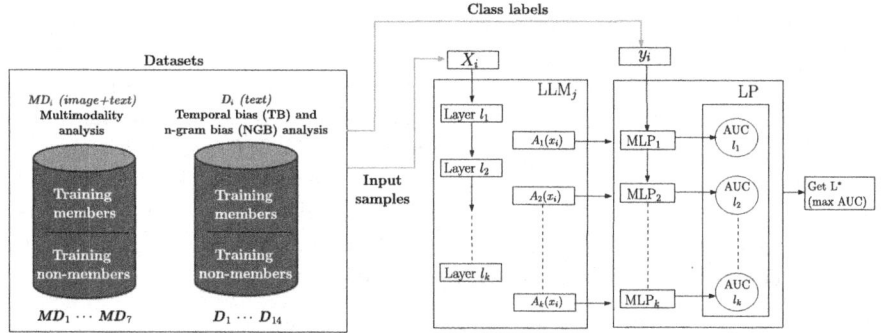

Fig. 1. System overview, formalizing the membership inference problem in this paper.

Beyond the attacker model introduced in Sect. 1, we formalize the membership inference problem with the following notations, as illustrated in Fig. 1:

- **Model:** We consider LLM_j a pre-trained large language model composed of K transformer layers $\{l_k\}_{1 \leq k \leq K}$. Each layer l_k produces an activation vector $A_k(X_i)$ for an input sample X_i. The model processes sequences of up to n tokens.
- **Datasets:** We consider $S = \{(X_i, y_i)\}$ the set of labeled input samples, where $X_i = \{t_1, \ldots, t_n\}$ is the input (text or multimodal text-image pair) composed of tokens t_j, and $y_i \in \{0, 1\}$ is the membership label (1 if X_i is a member, 0 otherwise). We consider both unimodal D_i datasets (text-only) and multimodal datasets MD_i (text + image), each containing training members and non-members.

- **Objective:** For each layer l_k, train a linear probe instantiated as a multi-layer perceptron MLP_k, to predict membership status from $A_k(X_i)$. The activation vector is computed by averaging token-level activations:

$$A_k(X_i) = \frac{1}{n} \sum_{j=1}^{n} a_k(t_j) \qquad (1)$$

where $a_k(t_j)$ denotes the activation of token t_j at layer l_k.
- **Metric:** Evaluate probe performance by using the Area Under the Curve (AUC) for each layer l_k. The most informative layer L^* is identified by $L^* = \underset{1 \leq k \leq K}{\mathrm{argmax}}\ \mathrm{AUC}(P_k)$.

3.2 Description

Samples from both training members and non-members are collected to build the datasets D_i and MD_i. These datasets serve to probe the internal activations of multiple target models LLM_j.

For each input sample, activations $A_k(X_i)$ are extracted from every layer l_k of the model. The collected activations are then used to train a dedicated MLP_k per layer. Each MLP outputs a membership prediction for its corresponding layer, which is evaluated using the AUC metric. The layer achieving the highest AUC, L^*, indicates where membership information is most concentrated.

To test robustness and generalization, we experiment with both unimodal and multimodal datasets. Unimodal datasets D_i allow us to assess the impact of temporal bias and n-gram bias, while multimodal datasets MD_i enable the study of membership inference when inputs consist of both text and images.

Extracting Activation Data. For each input X_i, we preprocess the text to fit the model's maximum context length n. During the forward pass [29], we use hooks to capture the token-level activations $\{a_k(t_j)\}$ at each layer l_k of the model.

To represent the entire input sequence, we aggregate these token-level activations into a sequence-level activation vector $A_k(X_i)$ (recall Eq. 1). For multimodal models, hooks are placed in both the base model and the visual encoder (recall Sect. 2).

4 Experimental Design

This section describes the design of the experiments to assess LUMIA. Section 4.1 explains the models and datasets. Section 4.2 describes the assessment metrics. Section 4.3 introduces the experimental settings.

4.1 Models, Datasets and Tasks

Unimodal LLMs. Several models of different sizes are chosen in our study. The Pythia model family [4], trained on the Pile dataset [13], with 70M, 160M, 1.4B, 2.8B, and 12B of parameters was selected in both their non-deduplicated and deduplicated versions for comparison purposes. Additionally, the GPT-Neo family is also evaluated with 125M, 1.3B, and 2.7B parameters variants. These models are chosen (i) to compare them to other proposals and (ii) because data used for training them is known, which is essential to deal with MIA attacks.

Unimodal Task and Datasets. In line with state-of-the-art literature, the LLM processes text to carry out a text-masking causal modeling task. In this vein, datasets used to test the approach are *WikiMIA* [32], *ArXiv-MIA* [20], *Temporal ArXiv/wiki* [9], *ArXiv-1-month* [25], *Gutenberg* [25] and *Mimir* [9]. Note that they have been selected for the sake of comparability with previous works [9,20,25,32]. All datasets, except for *Mimir*, have already been shown to suffer from TB [8]. Conversely, *Mimir* suffers from NGB [9].

Multimodal LLMs. For the analysis of multimodality, the latest version of the *LLava-OneVision model* [17] is applied with 0.5B and 7.6B parameters. These models are chosen since (i) the data used during its training: is known and (ii) due to available computational resources.

Multimodal Tasks and Datasets. Linked to this model, *OneVision-Data*[3] dataset is applied. It is composed of a wide range of datasets used to train a multimodal model for multitasking. From this collection, we generate member and non-member samples from datasets that originally provided distinct training, validation, and testing splits, namely *Textcaps* [34], *MathV360k* [33], *AOK* [31], *ChartQA* [24], *ScienceQA* [22], *IconQA* [23] and *Magpie* [38]. We chose these 7 datasets for consistency with the unimodal case, ensuring they encompass all the modalities and categories of tasks the model can accomplish, namely General resolution, Doc/Chart/Screen solving, Math/Reasoning, OCR, and Language tasks.

4.2 Metrics. Performance and Bias

In line with Duan et al. [9], Shi et al. [32], and Carlini et al. [5] (and for the sake of comparison), the effectiveness of LUMIA is measured with the **Area Under the ROC Curve (AUC)**. A value closer to 100% means better performance. In line with [9], MIA is considered successful when AUC > 60%.

AUC is then computed to compare LUMIA against state-of-the-art MIAs, namely *Loss* [41], *Reference-based* [30], *Zlib Entropy* [6] and *Min-k% Probability* [32]. Following their original implementations, these methods are used to compute baseline results.

---

[3] https://huggingface.co/datasets/lmms-lab/LLaVA-OneVision-Data, last accessed on June, 2025.

Concerning biases, only NGB can be measured for text samples due to the notion of overlap. In this regard, we use the n-gram length $\mathcal{N}$ and the percentage of overlap $\mathcal{P}$, in line with [9]. In case of multimodality, there are no standard widely accepted metrics in this regard. Thus, we compute **Average Hash Variation (HV)** and **Average Structural Similarity Index Measure (SSIM)** to measure the perceptual similarity of images [36,37]

4.3 Experimental Settings

Training was conducted on two NVIDIA consumer GPUs, a RTX 4090 and a RTX 4080, using a mix of the Pytorch and Tensorflow frameworks, complemented with the Hugging Face library[4]. For both training and validation, all datasets were randomly split in training and testing subsets following 80%-20% distribution, respectively. Both classes (i.e., members and non-members) were balanced in both subsets. Each experiment was repeated three times with different samples. The average of all executions was then computed. MLP models were trained with a learning rate of $1e^{-3}$, using the Adam optimizer [16] over 100 epochs, with early stops and dropout regularization.

For comparison with related work [9,20,25,32], we extracted 1,000 members and 1,000 non-members per dataset, except for WikiMIA and ArXiv-MIA. For such cases, we used the provided data: 250 and 400 samples per class, respectively. Membership labels, member or non-member are defined following the criteria established on each of the original datasets.

In the case of multimodal datasets, the division for training, validation, and test sets is the one provided by the dataset creators. In this way, the contamination between these sets is prevented. Moreover, we created a joint subset by extracting 100 samples from each of the 7 multimodal datasets (recall Sect. 4.1), resulting in a total of 700 members and 700 non-members.

Lastly, and since the original Magpie setup does not provide image inputs, but the model requires both text and image modalities, we paired each text input with a black image, to create the necessary input pairs.

5 Experimental Results

This section presents the results of LUMIA. Firstly, how LP outperforms state-of-the-art MIA assessment techniques is analysed (Sect. 5.1). The influence of potential bias is then explored (Sect. 5.2), followed by a study of the impact of the model size (Sect. 5.3), the nature of each dataset (Sect. 5.4), the effects of data deduplication (Sect. 5.5), and the significance of layer depth (Sect. 5.6).
Visualization Remark. Results are presented in the form of tables which are used across all sections. For the sake of clarity, Tables 1 and 2 highlight LUMIA values where AUC > 60%, while Table 3 highlights the best value for each modality and dataset among model sizes.

---

[4] https://huggingface.co, last accessed on June, 2025.

5.1 Overall Effectiveness. Comparison with State-of-the-Art

Unimodal. Tables 1 and 2 summarise the results of our approach versus all the previous proposals (hereinafter *Best SOTA AUC*) for TB and NBG biases, respectively. LUMIA overtakes previous results on all the cases except in two, which represents an improvement on 174 of the 176 cases (98.86%). Indeed, our approach provides an average AUC improvement of 15.75%. Considering an AUC > 60% as threshold [9], previous approaches surpass that value on the 44.5% of the cases while LUMIA reaches that threshold on the 65.33% of the cases, that is an increment of 46.80%.

Table 1. Unimodal models. AUC comparison with state of the art (SOTA) on TB datasets.

Method	Best SOTA AUC	Ours	Improvement
Gutenberg			
Document features[a]	0.856	**0.98**	14.49%
Heuristics[b]	0.964		1.66%
ArXiv-1 month			
Document features[a]	0.678	**0.93**	37.17%
Heuristics[b]	0.684		35.96%
Temporal wiki			
Best-Duan[c]	0.796	**0.93**	16.83%
Heuristics[b]	0.799		16.40%
Temporal ArXiv 2020-08			
Best-Duan[c]	0.723	**0.86**	18.32%
Heuristics[b]	0.756		13.15%
WikiMIA			
Min prob[d]	0.839	**0.99**	18.00%
Finetune + probes[e]	0.698		41.83%
Heuristics[b]	0.987		0.30%
EM-MIA[f]	0.977		1.33%
ModRényi[g]	0.809		22.37%
ArXiv CS			
Finetune + probes[e]	0.673	**0.842**	25.11%
ArXiv Math			
Finetune + probes[e]	0.574	**0.646**	12.54%
Average improvement			18.00%

[a] Meeus et al. [25] [b] Das et al. [8] [c] Duan et al. [25] [d] Shi et al. [32] [e] Liu et al. [20] [f] Kim et al. [15] [g] Li et al. [19]

Multimodal. Table 3 shows the results for the multimodal configurations. All of them, except Magpie, achieve AUC > 60%, suggesting that multimodality may be adding additional information useful for MIA assessment. Magpie reaches an

Table 2. Unimodal models. AUC comparison against Duan et al. [9] for NGB datasets.

Dataset	MIA	Pythia Dedup 12B $\mathcal{N}=13\ \mathcal{P}=0.8$ [9]	Ours	Improvement	$\mathcal{N}=13\ \mathcal{P}=0.2$ [9]	Ours	Improvement	$\mathcal{N}=7\ \mathcal{P}=0.2$ [9]	Ours	Improvement
Wikipedia	LOSS	0.516	0.570	10.47%	0.545	0.590	8.26%	0.666	**0.690**	3.60%
	Ref	0.578		-1.38%	0.590		0.00%	0.677		1.92%
	min-k	0.517		10.25%	0.562		4.98%	0.644		7.14%
	zlib	0.524		8.78%	0.543		8.66%	0.631		9.35%
Github	LOSS	0.678	**0.770**	13.57%	0.802	**0.910**	13.47%	0.878	**0.930**	5.92%
	Ref	0.559		37.75%	0.615		47.97%	0.615		51.22%
	min-k	0.683		12.74%	0.830		9.64%	0.890		4.49%
	zlib	0.690		11.59%	0.829		9.77%	0.908		2.42%
Pubmed	LOSS	0.506	0.580	14.62%	0.534	0.570	6.74%	0.780	**0.980**	25.64%
	Ref	0.559		3.76%	0.573		-0.52%	0.595		64.71%
	min-k	0.512		13.28%	0.542		5.17%	0.792		23.74%
	zlib	0.506		14.62%	0.537		6.15%	0.772		26.94%
Pile CC	LOSS	0.516	**0.600**	16.28%	0.534	**0.601**	12.55%	0.574	**0.660**	14.98%
	Ref	0.582		3.09%	0.593		1.35%	0.644		2.48%
	min-k	0.521		15.16%	0.539		11.50%	0.578		14.19%
	zlib	0.517		16.05%	0.542		10.89%	0.560		17.86%
ArXiv	LOSS	0.527	0.577	9.46%	0.573	**0.606**	5.76%	0.787	**0.800**	1.65%
	Ref	0.555		3.94%	0.584		3.77%	0.715		11.89%
	min-k	0.530		8.84%	0.566		7.07%	0.734		8.99%
	zlib	0.521		10.72%	0.565		7.26%	0.780		2.56%
DM_math	LOSS	0.485	**0.600**	23.71%	0.673	**0.746**	10.79%	0.921	**0.950**	3.15%
	Ref	0.514		16.73%	0.443		68.31%	0.414		129.47%
	min-k	0.493		21.70%	0.650		14.71%	0.927		2.48%
	zlib	0.481		24.74%	0.643		15.96%	0.805		18.01%
Hackernews	LOSS	0.512	0.584	14.01%	0.526	0.594	12.91%	0.604	**0.690**	14.24%
	Ref	0.549		6.33%	0.553		7.40%	0.570		21.05%
	min-k	0.526		10.97%	0.533		11.43%	0.585		17.95%
	zlib	0.507		15.13%	0.524		13.34%	0.592		16.55%
Average Improvement				13.10%			11.97%			18.73%
GPT-Neo 2.7B										
Dataset	MIA	$\mathcal{N}=13\ \mathcal{P}=0.8$ [9]	**Ours**	**Improvement**	$\mathcal{N}=13\ \mathcal{P}=0.2$ [9]	**Ours**	**Improvement**	$\mathcal{N}=7\ \mathcal{P}=0.2$ [9]	**Ours**	**Improvement**
Wikipedia	LOSS	0.513	0.584	13.99%	0.537	0.58	8.01%	0.650	**0.650**	0.00%
	Ref	0.545		7.29%	0.572		1.40%	0.650		0.00%
	min-k	0.513		13.99%	0.543		6.81%	0.644		0.93%
	zlib	0.519		12.67%	0.535		8.41%	0.623		4.33%
Github	LOSS	0.699	**0.772**	10.53%	0.770	**0.85**	10.39%	0.878	**0.940**	7.06%
	Ref	0.570		35.55%	0.549		54.83%	0.615		52.85%
	min-k	0.700		10.38%	0.802		5.99%	0.890		5.62%
	zlib	0.710		8.82%	0.771		10.25%	0.908		3.52%
Pubmed	LOSS	0.490	0.566	15.55%	0.498	0.55	10.44%	0.799	**0.910**	13.89%
	Ref	0.507		11.68%	0.507		8.48%	0.786		15.78%
	min-k	0.500		13.24%	0.501		9.78%	0.792		14.90%
	zlib	0.499		13.47%	0.499		10.22%	0.786		15.78%
Pile CC	LOSS	0.500	0.587	17.48%	0.500	0.59	17.91%	0.553	**0.640**	15.73%
	Ref	0.530		10.83%	0.530		11.32%	0.575		11.30%
	min-k	0.500		17.48%	0.507		16.37%	0.549		16.58%
	zlib	0.500		17.48%	0.505		16.83%	0.540		18.52%
ArXiv	LOSS	0.510	0.586	14.92%	0.515	0.59	14.56%	0.790	**0.860**	8.86%
	Ref	0.520		12.71%	0.517		14.12%	0.718		19.78%
	min-k	0.517		13.36%	0.519		13.68%	0.760		13.16%
	zlib	0.510		14.92%	0.510		15.69%	0.784		9.69%
DM_math	LOSS	0.485	0.560	15.46%	0.676	**0.75**	10.95%	0.930	**1.00**	7.53%
	Ref	0.509		10.02%	0.435		72.41%	0.502		99.20%
	min-k	0.492		13.82%	0.655		14.50%	0.933		7.18%
	zlib	0.481		16.42%	0.647		15.92%	0.812		23.15%
Hackernews	LOSS	0.502	0.590	17.53%	0.516	**0.60**	16.28%	0.592	**0.630**	6.42%
	Ref	0.512		15.23%	0.515		16.50%	0.525		20.00%
	min-k	0.517		14.12%	0.525		14.29%	0.572		10.14%
	zlib	0.502		17.53%	0.519		15.61%	0.587		7.33%
Average Improvement				14.51%			15.78%			15.32%
Global average improvement				13.80%			13.93%			17.03%

Table 3. Multimodal models. LUMIA AUC results per dataset. Highlighted values in each dataset are the best for each modality between model sizes.

Params	Textcaps (General OCR) Modality	Best AUC	AOK (General) Modality	Best AUC
0.5B	Textual + visual	0.540	Textual + visual	0.697
	Visual	0.604	Visual	**0.735**
7B	Textual + visual	**0.601**	Textual + visual	**0.697**
	Visual	**0.618**	Visual	0.707
	ScienceQA (General)		**ChartQA (Doc/chart/screen)**	
0.5B	Textual + visual	0.970	Textual + visual	**0.694**
	Visual	**0.806**	Visual	0.638
7B	Textual + visual	**0.990**	Textual + visual	0.682
	Visual	0.802	Visual	**0.691**
	magpie (Language)		**iconqa (General)**	
0.5B	Textual + visual	**0.572**	Textual + visual	0.869
	Visual	0.510	Visual	0.809
7B	Textual + visual	0.552	Textual + visual	**0.903**
	Visual	**0.520**	Visual	**0.828**
	Joint		**MathV360k (Math)**	
0.5B	Textual + visual	0.624	Textual + visual	0.599
	Visual	0.670	Visual	0.584
7B	Textual + visual	**0.634**	Textual + visual	**0.660**
	Visual	**0.673**	Visual	**0.629**

Textual + Visual: Activations extracted from LLM part.
Visual: Activations extracted from Visual encoder part.

AUC of 57%, probably because it is the only text-only dataset. When making predictions over a joint dataset, the AUC remains above 60%, which points out that even when mixing information and modalities, LPs find patterns across activations to define membership. Globally speaking, 85.9% of the cases achieve an AUC > 60%, demonstrating better performance as compared to unimodal setups, which meet this threshold in 65.33% of the configurations.

> **Takeaway 1**
>
> *Unimodal:* We improve 14.90% AUC on average. AUC > 60% is reached by LUMIA 46.8% more often as compared to the state-of-the-art.
> *Multimodal:* No previous work to compare. Among the seven datasets considered, LUMIA achieves AUC > 60% in all but one dataset, resulting in 85.9% of the results exceeding this threshold.

5.2 Impact of Bias

In this case, we concentrate on unimodal LLMs. In multimodality, our results show that there are no significant differences in HV or SSIM between members and non-members (see Appendix A for further details). Thus, AUC results seem to be influenced by task complexity or dataset nature, rather than by the actual content differences.

Unimodal. LUMIA significantly outperforms [20], which also uses LPs. Specifically, we achieve a 25% improvement in the CS subset (cf. Table 1). These findings align with their observation that the Math subset is more challenging to predict. Nevertheless, LUMIA still achieves an AUC above 60% even in these more difficult subsets. Additionally, results for WikiMIA show a particularly high improvement of 41%. On average, for TB datasets, LUMIA returns an 18% improvement over all the previous efforts.

When studying NGB, Table 2 shows that LUMIA outperforms all reported configurations and baselines (except for the Wikipedia dataset) across all models. They reported that no configuration reached an AUC $> 60\%$ for the $\mathcal{N} = 13$ overlap of $\mathcal{P} = 0.8$ on the Pythia dedup model. Contrarily, in some specific cases, such as Pile-CC, DM_math, we can reach this threshold. Additionally, for the 12B model, we achieve an AUC of 58% on PubMed and 58.4% on Hackernews, both approaching the 60% threshold more closely than previous approaches. All in all, results for $\mathcal{N} = 13$ with $\mathcal{P} = 0.8$ lead to an overall improvement of 13.10%.

For $\mathcal{N} = 7$ with $\mathcal{P} = 0.2$ on the Pythia 12B family in Table 2, our approach consistently outperforms the state of the art, with improvements ranging from a minimum of 1.92% on Wikipedia to a maximum of 64.71% on PubMed and an average of 18.73%. Notably, on the DM_math dataset the ref method performs poorly under overlap configurations of $\mathcal{P} = 0.2$ with $\mathcal{N} = 13$ and $\mathcal{N} = 7$, achieving AUC scores of 44% and 41%, respectively. Consequently, our approach surpasses the ref method by 68% and 129%.

For GPT-Neo 2.7B, in line with the previous model, all configurations overtake results from Duan et al. [9] with an overall improvement of 14.43%. Nonetheless, in this case of $\mathcal{N} = 13$ overlap with $\mathcal{P} = 0.8$, none of our configurations, excluding Github, overtakes 60% of AUC.

> **Takeaway 2**
>
> *Unimodal:* In line with non-LPs approaches, as overlap gets reduced, we have better results in all cases. TB datasets present better results than NGB and all results are above 60%.
>
> *Multimodal:* HV and SSIM differences show no correlation with AUC, suggesting that the results are more influenced by task or dataset complexity, rather than any bias between member and non-member samples.

5.3 Impact of Model Size

Unimodal. Table 4 shows a clear trend on the AUC as the model size grows for Pythia family. Results are similar in GPT-Neo, thus placed in Appendix B. All datasets show better results in all configurations on the 12B version, excluding ArXiv-1 month. For this dataset, both deduplicated and non-deduplicated models show improved AUC scores when scaling from 70M to 2.8B parameters. Yet, a significant decline is observed in the 12B version of the model on this dataset, with AUC values dropping from 92% to 84% (deduped) and 86% (non-dedup). Despite this unexpected decrease, AUC values are still very high.

Reading Table 4 by rows, it is possible to analyse the trends on the percentage of change of AUC of non-LP-based proposals and ours. While LPs shows an incremental trend, differences with other approaches are not significant.

Multimodal. From an architectural perspective, while there are no differences in the sizes of the visual encoders, having a larger LLM on the textual+visual part affects the results. In general, excluding again the Magpie dataset (since it only contains texts), the 7B model seems to reveal more information in both parts of the models, the visual only encoder and the textual+visual LLM, denoting higher memorization of the data than the 0.5B version.

> **Takeaway 3**
>
> As model grows, we have better AUC in the 85.9% of the cases for both unimodal and multimodal LLMs. The AUC trend when models grow is the same as non-LP-based approaches.

5.4 Impact of Dataset Nature

Unimodal. Table 1 shows consistent conclusions with those of Liu *et al.* [20] on TB datasets, who argue that the difficulty of the content impacts results. For example, our approach overtakes their results on a 25% and 12% on the arXiv-CS and arXiv-Math datasets respectively. In line with their hypothesis, our LPs also perform worse on the arXiv-Math dataset, where the nature of the text content makes detection more challenging, as mathematical texts are more complex and harder to memorise by the LLMs.

In the case of NGB datasets, as shown in Table 2, similar patterns are observed. For instance, on Github, which was the easiest to predict on the $\mathcal{N} = 13$ with $\mathcal{P} = 0.8$ overlap (according to Duan *et al.* [9]), LUMIA also offers the best results. Code-related samples may contain HTML tags and unique variable names, which could make the members and non-members more identifiable. Furthermore, other datasets such as Wikipedia or Hackernews, which contain a wider range of topics and variety of texts, make it harder to identify differences between members and non-members.

Multimodal. In multimodal datasets, the type of information impacts the results. Table 3 shows that, except for ChartQA and IconQA, the model appears to add more information through the visual encoders, particularly with images.

Table 4. Unimodal models. Pythia family. AUC per model size with/without deduplication.

	NGB						TB	
	Pythia dedup			Pythia non-dedup			Pythia dedup	Pythia non-dedup
	Wikipedia						Gutenberg	
Params	$\mathcal{N}=13\ \mathcal{P}=0.8$	$\mathcal{N}=13\ \mathcal{P}=0.2$	$\mathcal{N}=7\ \mathcal{P}=0.2$	$\mathcal{N}=13\ \mathcal{P}=0.8$	$\mathcal{N}=13\ \mathcal{P}=0.2$	$\mathcal{N}=7\ \mathcal{P}=0.2$		
70M	0.520	0.551	0.653	0.570	0.538	0.651	0.949	0.960
160M	0.568	0.546	0.660	0.546	0.589	0.676	0.960	0.960
1.4B	0.557	0.586	0.676	0.564	0.558	0.663	0.970	0.980
2.8B	0.580	0.572	0.682	0.562	0.557	0.685	0.970	0.980
12B	0.570	0.590	0.690	0.570	0.580	0.590	0.987	0.985
	Github						ArXiv-1 month	
70M	0.743	0.823	0.922	0.732	0.832	0.881	0.775	0.806
160M	0.729	0.853	0.863	0.741	0.874	0.931	0.860	0.870
1.4B	0.767	0.868	0.935	0.786	0.875	0.924	0.900	0.920
2.8B	0.754	0.868	0.951	0.767	0.911	0.933	0.920	0.920
12B	0.770	0.910	0.930	0.760	0.830	0.870	0.843	0.856
	Pile CC						Temporal wiki	
70M	0.521	0.544	0.587	0.561	0.552	0.599	0.865	0.860
160M	0.531	0.566	0.603	0.562	0.554	0.611	0.880	0.910
1.4B	0.569	0.573	0.642	0.554	0.588	0.635	0.910	0.930
2.8B	0.590	0.571	0.618	0.566	0.587	0.634	0.929	0.930
12B	0.600	0.570	0.660	0.610	0.570	0.660	0.945	0.954
	DM_math						Temporal ArXiv	
70M	0.502	0.743	0.959	0.525	0.721	0.963	0.710	0.733
160M	0.557	0.718	0.927	0.526	0.706	0.981	0.720	0.720
1.4B	0.558	0.758	0.943	0.559	0.745	0.989	0.760	0.750
2.8B	0.554	0.730	0.995	0.570	0.741	0.961	0.750	0.760
12B	0.600	0.746	1.000	0.610	0.650	0.980	0.810	0.797
	Hackernews						WikiMIA	
70M	0.580	0.595	0.582	0.566	0.563	0.633	0.970	0.980
160M	0.593	0.577	0.613	0.564	0.565	0.642	0.970	0.980
1.4B	0.556	0.576	0.630	0.594	0.570	0.647	0.970	0.990
2.8B	0.579	0.576	0.614	0.591	0.580	0.643	0.980	0.990
12B	0.584	0.594	0.701	0.600	0.560	0.580	0.980	0.990
	ArXiv						ArXiv-CS	
70M	0.533	0.562	0.823	0.529	0.598	0.820	0.743	0.745
160M	0.569	0.586	0.802	0.536	0.571	0.797	0.776	0.747
1.4B	0.563	0.581	0.814	0.543	0.577	0.832	0.791	0.807
2.8B	0.532	0.570	0.808	0.571	0.568	0.815	0.824	0.807
12B	0.577	0.606	0.795	0.600	0.590	0.770	0.831	0.835
	Pubmed						ArXiv-Math	
70M	0.517	0.576	0.880	0.545	0.573	0.882	0.603	0.601
160M	0.540	0.600	0.870	0.558	0.575	0.894	0.615	0.604
1.4B	0.583	0.558	0.883	0.551	0.582	0.875	0.637	0.633
2.8B	0.553	0.573	0.860	0.570	0.570	0.894	0.626	0.646
12B	0.577	0.590	0.900	0.570	0.580	0.980	0.635	0.655

For example, in the case of Magpie, which is a text-only dataset, the visual encoder returns an almost random AUC of 52%, but it adds more information when dealing with both textual and visual inputs, reaching a 57.2% AUC.

For Textcaps, the prompt remains the same for both members and non-members, while the images exhibit greater variability. This setup results in a slight drop in accuracy when using the combined textual and visual parts of the model, with AUC decreasing from 61.7% for visual-only LPs to 60.1% for visual+text LPs. The consistent prompt across members and non-members likely introduces noise, diminishing the model's ability to differentiate between them.

Finally, datasets that follow a consistent template across the prompts of both members and non-members, such as MathV360k, demonstrate a reduced ability for classifiers to distinguish between classes compared to datasets with more varied images and texts. For example, datasets like ScienceQA and IconQA, which lack a uniform template across samples, achieve AUC values around 80% for both Textual+Visual and Visual-only configurations.

> **Takeaway 4**
>
> *Unimodal:* Code or datasets containing mathematical formulas are easier to identify than general-purpose texts. LPs are specially good on detecting these modalities.
>
> *Multimodal:* Repetitive prompts strengthen resistance to MIA, while a greater variety of images makes models more vulnerable.

5.5 Impact of Deduplication

Since Llava and OneVision are deduplicated models and there are no non-deduplicated multimodal models, only unimodality is considered.

Unimodal. Results focus on Pythia, Table 4, since it is the only model which provides a clear distinction of deduplicated data. For the TB datasets, MIAs tend to be more effective on non-deduplicated models. This is likely because deduplication reduces the repetition of data in the training set, thereby limiting the model's ability to memorise and overfit to specific patterns.

In contrast, for the NGB datasets, no significant differences are observed between the deduplicated and non-deduplicated versions of the Pythia family.

5.6 Analysis per Model and Layer

Figures 2 and 3 present results from Pythia and the multimodal models respectively. They include the normalised average values of the AUC across all datasets. Gradient colors represent the average AUC for each layer, calculated across all models and datasets. Note that the differences in the lengths of the plot lines are due to the varying model sizes, with the 160M parameter model having only 12 layers, while the 12B model has 36 layers. Results for GPT-Neo are omitted for brevity, as they are always more effective on deeper layers (cf. Appendix B).

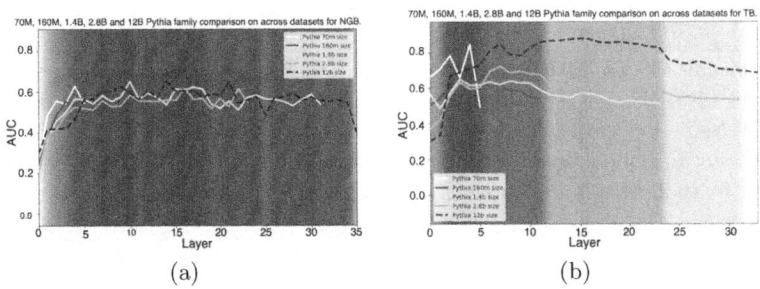

Fig. 2. Pythia family. AUC per layer. (a) NGB datasets. (b) TB datasets.

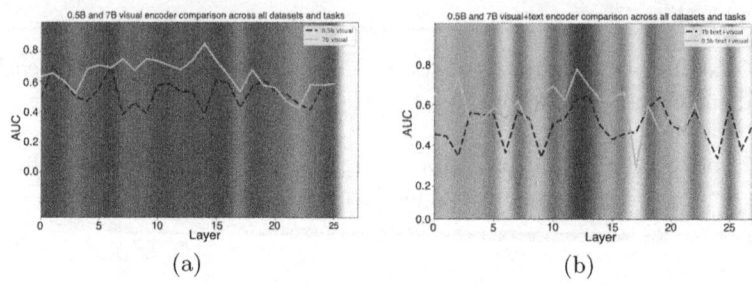

Fig. 3. LLava-OneVision. AUC per layer. (a) Visual encoder. (b) Visual+text encoder.

Unimodal. Figure 2 illustrates the AUC across layers for the Pythia model family, covering results from all datasets and model types (both deduplicated and non-deduplicated). In Fig. 2(a), model performance on all NGB datasets from Mimir are reported. Notably, there are certain layers where model performance peaks. Particularly, around Layer 10; and, later, between Layers 15 and 18, where larger models achieve higher AUC values. This suggests that specific depths of the model add more information useful for LPs to detect MIAs.

In Fig. 2(b), the average normalised values for the same models on the TB datasets are reported. Peak performance begins around layers 3 to 5, showing that earlier layers on the model are enough to get good results. For larger models, between layers 5 and 12, there is also a portion of the model where important information for the membership inference is revealed.

Multimodal. Figure 3 shows results for the multimodal model. Figure 3(a) presents the AUC for the visual encoder, which, despite differences in scale, reveals common areas around layer 15. This may denote that deeper layers add more information.

Similarly, in Fig. 3(b), the AUC by layer is shown for the visual+text encoder. It is particularly noteworthy that around layers 12 and 13, both modalities (visual and visual+text) exhibit a spike in information useful for MIA.

> **Takeaway 5**
>
> *Unimodal:* LPs on Pythia family with TB datasets are more effective on earlier layers (4-5). For NGB datasets, deeper layers (15-16) are preferred. LPs in GPT-Neo are always more effective on deeper layers (25).
>
> *Multimodal:* Middle layers reveal more information in visual (8-9 or 15) as well as in textual+visual part (13-14).

6 Related Work

MIA attacks have been largely studied, in black-box, grey-box and white-box perspective.[5] From a grey-box perspective, Shi et al. [32] analyse output logits of LLMs based on the assumption that unseen samples tend to contain outlier words with very low probabilities. In the same setting, [11] achieves better results by applying self-prompt calibration, which uses input variations to assess the model's confidence and consistency.

Meeus et al. [25] adopt a binary classifier to distinguish members from non-members using document-level features and a normalisation algorithm in a black-box approach. Das et al. [8] achieve superior results than other works. They hypothesise that good results can be achieved by leveraging heuristics based on the features and statistics of public MIA datasets.

Duan et al. [9] introduce some benchmark datasets, *Mimir*, designed to address potential biases and assess state-of-the-art MIA methods. They also show that cutoff dates are crucial, as the overlap of N-grams may fluctuate over time. A similar work is proposed by Kim et al. [15]. They introduce a new maximisation expectation algorithm. Nevertheless, they highlight their results are

Table 5. Related work analysis and comparison with LUMIA.

Reference	Dataset	Model	Input features	Multi-modality	Per layer analysis	Dedup. & non-dedup. models	TB & NGB analysis	(W)hitebox (G)reybox (B)lackbox
Duan et al. [9]	Mimir, Temp. wiki, Temp. ArXiv	Pythia, Pythia-dedup, GPT-Neo	Loss from model logits	✗	✗	✓	✓	G
Shi et al. [32]	WikiMIA, BookMia	Pythia, GPT-Neo, Llama, OPT	—	✗	✗	✗	✗	G
Das et al. [8]	WikiMIA, BookMia, Temp.-wiki, temp.-ArXiv, ArXiv1mth, Gutenberg	—	Features from texts	✗	✗	✗	✓	B
Meeus et al. [25]	Gutenberg, ArXiv Papers	Open-Llama	Features from texts	✗	✗	✗	✗	B
Kim et al. [15]	WikiMIA, OLMoMIA	Mamba, Pythia, Llama, OPT, GPT-Neo	Texts & membership scores	✗	✗	✗	✗	B
Li et al. [19]	VL-MIA	LLaVA 1.5, MiniGPT-4, LLaMA adapter_v2	Image based instruction, prompt & previous prompt	✓	✗	✗	✗	G
Liu et al. [20]	ArXivMIA, WikiMIA	Pythia, OPT, Tiny-Llama, Open-Llama	Activations	✗	✗	✗	✗	W
Li et al. [18]	The Pile	Pythia	Feature perturbations	✗	✗	✗	✗	W
W. Fu et al. [11]	Wikitext-103, AG News, XSum	GPT-2, GPT-J, Falcon-7B, LLaMA-7B	Several prompts	✗	✗	✗	✗	G
LUMIA	All those listed above plus seven additional datasets.	Pythia, Pythia-dedup, GPT-Neo, LLava-OneVision	Activations	✓	✓	✓	✓	W

---

[5] Note that the theoretical result of [30] shows that loss is all you need for optimal MIA. However, it relies on idealized assumptions (e.g., randomized training, i.i.d. data) which do not hold in practice for LLMs, leading to consider LLMs white-box to exploit extra signals.

close to random guessing when the distribution of member and non-members are close.

A comparable white-box approach is presented by Liu et al. [20], who use simple linear classifiers on the activations of the LLMs. They fine-tune a pre-trained model using a prompt to ensure that members and non-members are represented in a standardised format. Their results show the performance of MIA after fine-tuning, rather than on the pretrained model itself. Moreover, they consider only layer l, thus neglecting a per layer analysis of the results. Li et al. [18] proposed a white-box feature perturbation approach determining membership via log-likelihood drops between members and non-members. As they point out, this approach is very expensive from a computational perspective and could be unfeasible to scale to larger models.

In terms of multimodality in LLMs, [19] proposed a grey-box membership inference attack for multimodal LLMs based on output confidence. However, its reliance on long text generation limits generalizability, and its performance is inferior to LUMIA.

Table 5 presents an overview of related work, together with LUMIA. Our method is assessed on a broader range of datasets, covering both TB and NGB datasets, as well as deduplicated and non-deduplicated models—a distinction only addressed by Duan et al. [9]. LUMIA is the only study to conduct a layer-by-layer analysis, which provides valuable insights into how unimodal and multimodal LLMs process information. LUMIA is also the only study that examines the impact of data type on MIAs within a multimodal context.

7 Conclusion

LUMIA is a white-box method using Linear Probes (LPs) to detect if a sample was part of a model's pre-training. It works on both unimodal and multimodal models, outperforms existing methods, and remains robust across datasets, regardless of bias.

Future work includes extending the approach to audio and video, applying LUMIA to detect copyright violations, and analyzing model layers to introduce targeted noise or optimize performance against membership inference attacks. In addition, the use of other multi-model LLMs is designed as a future research line to strengthen the results, as well as to improve the evaluation through the inclusion of more metrics and statistical significance tests.

Acknowledgements. N. Anciaux was supported by the French PEPR iPoP (ANR-22-PECY-0002). J. Garcia-Alfaro was partially supported by the French National Research Agency under the France 2030 label (NF-HiSec ANR-22-PEFT-0009). L. Ibanez-Lissen was supported partially, by the Spanish National Cybersecurity Institute (INCIBE) grant APAMciber within the framework of the Recovery, Transformation and Resilience Plan funds, financed by the European Union (Next Generation). J. M. de Fuentes, N. Anciaux, L. Gonzalez and J. Garcia-Alfaro were partially supported by grant PID2023-150310OB-I00 of the Spanish AEI.

Appendices

A. Bias Analysis on Multimodal Models.

Table 6 summarizes statistics for multimodal image datasets, showing absolute differences between members and non-members. Content differences are analyzed using HV (Hash Variation) for content variation and SSIM (Structural Similarity Index) for structural similarity, helping to identify distinctions between members and non-members.

HV shows no clear correlation with AUC (Table 3). For example, ScienceQA has a high AUC (99%) despite a 80% HV difference, while IconQA achieves 86.9% AUC with only a 10% HV difference. A similar pattern emerges with SSIM. ScienceQA and Mathv360k both have an 8% SSIM difference, but their AUCs differ greatly (99% vs. 66%), indicating AUC depends more on task complexity or dataset nature than on content differences.

Table 6. Multimodal datasets. Bias analysis using Hash Variation (HV) and Structural Similarity Index (SSIM) in %.

Dataset	Members		Non members		Difference (abs.)		Best AUC (cf. Table 3)
	HV	SSIM	HV	SSIM	HV	SSIM	
AOK	30.53	0.69	30.75	0.72	0.22	0.03	0.735
Textcaps	3.52	0.67	3.82	0.68	0.30	0.01	0.618
ScienceQA	30.36	0.62	29.56	0.54	0.80	0.08	0.99
ChartQA	28.19	0.26	28.33	0.3	0.14	0.04	0.694
IconQA	30.94	0.53	31.04	0.56	0.10	0.03	0.903
Mathv360k	31.08	0.54	30.9	0.46	0.18	0.08	0.66

B. GPT-Neo. Analysis Per Layer and Model Size

Figure 4 shows AUC analysis per layer, with Layers 10 and 25 adding more useful information for classifiers. Both NGB and TB share areas of better performance. Regarding model size, larger models generally achieve higher AUC, as seen in Table 7, except for arXiv-CS where the 1.3B parameter model outperforms the largest model (84.2% vs. 80.2%).

Table 7. GPT-Neo. AUC per model size.

Params	NGB						TB	
	$\mathcal{N}=13$ $\mathcal{P}=0.8$	$\mathcal{N}=13$ $\mathcal{P}=0.2$	$\mathcal{N}=7$ $\mathcal{P}=0.2$	$\mathcal{N}=13$ $\mathcal{P}=0.8$	$\mathcal{N}=13$ $\mathcal{P}=0.2$	$\mathcal{N}=7$ $\mathcal{P}=0.2$		
	Wikipedia			Github			Gutenberg	WikiMIA
125m	0.590	0.530	0.590	0.650	0.830	0.910	0.940	0.897
1.3B	0.590	0.560	0.650	0.780	0.830	0.940	0.970	0.985
2.7B	0.590	0.570	0.650	0.770	0.850	0.940	0.970	0.987
	Pile CC			DM Math			arXiv-1 month	arXiv-CS
125m	0.550	0.560	0.570	0.550	0.690	1.000	0.820	0.681
1.3B	0.590	0.570	0.590	0.560	0.730	1.000	0.910	0.842
2.7B	0.560	0.590	0.630	0.570	0.750	1.000	0.930	0.802
	Hackernews			Arxiv			Temporal wiki	arXiv-Math
125m	0.550	0.550	0.570	0.550	0.560	0.820	0.887	0.604
1.3B	0.580	0.560	0.590	0.570	0.570	0.850	0.908	0.633
2.7B	0.590	0.600	0.620	0.580	0.590	0.850	0.919	0.646
	Pubmed						Temporal arXiv	
125m	0.540	0.540	0.830				0.728	
1.3B	0.560	0.540	0.920				0.777	
2.7B	0.580	0.570	0.920				0.786	

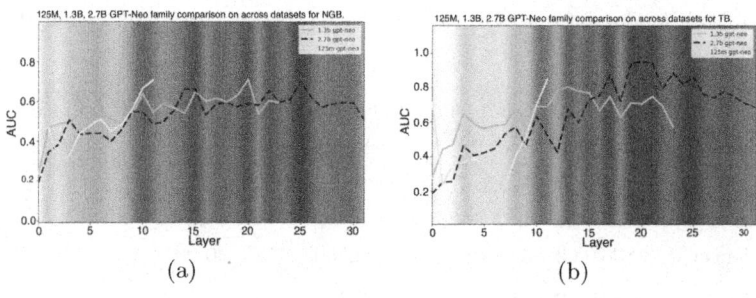

Fig. 4. GPT-Neo. AUC by layer. (a) NGB datasets. (b) TB datasets.

References

1. Achiam, J., et al.: Gpt-4 technical report. arXiv preprint arXiv:2303.08774 (2023)
2. Alain, G., Bengio, Y.: Understanding intermediate layers using linear classifier probes. In: International Conference on Learning Representations (ICLR), Works. Track (2017)
3. Albalak, A., et al.: A survey on data selection for language models. Trans. Mach. Learn. Res. (2024), survey Certification
4. Biderman, S., et al.: Pythia: a suite for analyzing large language models across training and scaling. In: International Conference on Machine Learning, pp. 2397–2430. PMLR (2023)
5. Carlini, N., Chien, S., Nasr, M., Song, S., Terzis, A., Tramer, F.: Membership inference attacks from first principles. In: IEEE Symposium on Security and Privacy, pp. 1897–1914. IEEE (2022)
6. Carlini, N., et al.: Extracting training data from large language models. In: 30th USENIX Security Symposium, pp. 2633–2650 (2021)
7. Casper, S., et al.: Black-box access is insufficient for rigorous ai audits. In: ACM Conference on Fairness, Accountability, and Transparency, pp. 2254–2272 (2024)

8. Das, D., Zhang, J., Tramèr, F.: Blind baselines beat membership inference attacks for foundation models. In: Proceedings of the DATA-FM at ICLR 2025 (to appear) (2025)
9. Duan, M., et al.: Do membership inference attacks work on large language models? In: First Conference on Language Modeling (COLM) (2024)
10. Dubey, A., et al.: The llama 3 herd of models. arXiv preprint arXiv:2407.21783 (2024)
11. Fu, W., Wang, H., Gao, C., Liu, G., Li, Y., Jiang, T.: Membership inference attacks against fine-tuned large language models via self-prompt calibration. In: The Thirty-eighth Annual Conference on Neural Information Processing Systems (2024)
12. Fu, W., Wang, H., Gao, C., Liu, G., Li, Y., Jiang, T.: Mia-tuner: adapting large language models as pre-training text detector. In: Proceedings of the AAAI Conference on Artificial Intelligence, vol. 39, pp. 27295–27303 (2025)
13. Gao, L., et al.: The pile: an 800gb dataset of diverse text for language modeling. arXiv preprint arXiv:2101.00027 (2020)
14. Jajodia, S., Samarati, P., Yung, M., Zhou, J., Subrahmanian, V.S. (eds.): Encyclopedia of Cryptography, Security and Privacy, Membership Inference Attacks in Machine Learning. Springer, Cham (2025)
15. Kim, G., Li, Y., Spiliopoulou, E., Ma, J., Ballesteros, M., Wang, W.Y.: Detecting training data of large language models via expectation maximization. arXiv preprint arXiv:2410.07582 (2024)
16. Kingma, D.P., Ba, J.: Adam: a method for stochastic optimization. In: 3rd International Conference on Learning Representations (ICLR) (2015)
17. Li, B., et al.: LLaVA-OneVision: easy visual task transfer. arXiv preprint arXiv:2408.03326 (2024)
18. Li, M., Wang, J., Wang, J., Neel, S.: Mope: model perturbation based privacy attacks on language models. In: Proceedings of the 2023 Conference on Empirical Methods in Natural Language Processing, pp. 13647–13660 (2023)
19. Li, Z., Wu, Y., Chen, Y., Tonin, F., Abad Rocamora, E., Cevher, V.: Membership inference attacks against large vision-language models. Adv. Neural. Inf. Process. Syst. **37**, 98645–98674 (2024)
20. Liu, Z., Zhu, T., Tan, C., Liu, B., Lu, H., Chen, W.: Probing language models for pre-training data detection. In: Proceedings of the 62nd Annual Meeting of the Association for Computational Linguistics, pp. 1576–1587 (2024)
21. Liu, Z., Ye, H., Chen, C., Zheng, Y., Lam, K.Y.: Threats, attacks, and defenses in machine unlearning: a survey. IEEE Open J. Comput. Soc. (2025)
22. Lu, P., et al.: Learn to explain: multimodal reasoning via thought chains for science question answering. In: 36th Conference on Neural Information Processing Systems (NeurIPS) (2022)
23. Lu, P., et al.: ICONQA: a new benchmark for abstract diagram understanding and visual language reasoning. In: Proceedings of the AAAI Conference on Artificial Intelligence (AAAI), vol. 37, pp. 9537–9547 (2023)
24. Masry, A., Long, D.X., Tan, J.Q., Joty, S., Hoque, E.: ChartQA: a benchmark for question answering about charts with visual and logical reasoning. In: Findings of the Association for Computational Linguistics: EMNLP, pp. 993–1007 (2022)
25. Meeus, M., Jain, S., Rei, M., de Montjoye, Y.A.: Did the neurons read your book? document-level membership inference for large language models. In: 33rd USENIX Security Symposium, pp. 2369–2385 (2024)

26. Meeus, M., Shilov, I., Faysse, M., de Montjoye, Y.A.: Copyright traps for large language models. In: Forty-first International Conference on Machine Learning (2024), https://openreview.net/forum?id=LDq1JPdc55
27. National institute of standards and technology (NIST): adversarial machine learning: a taxonomy and terminology of attacks and mitigations. Technical Report, NIST AI 100-2e2025 (2025)
28. Patel, O., Wang, R.: Activation monitoring: advantages of using internal representations for LLM oversight. In: 2nd NeurIPS Works. on Attributing Model Behavior at Scale (2025)
29. Rumelhart, D.E., Hinton, G.E., Williams, R.J.: Learning representations by back-propagating errors. Nature **323**(6088), 533–536 (1986)
30. Sablayrolles, A., Douze, M., Schmid, C., Ollivier, Y., Jégou, H.: White-box vs black-box: bayes optimal strategies for membership inference. In: International Conference on Machine Learning, pp. 5558–5567. PMLR (2019)
31. Schwenk, D., Khandelwal, A., Clark, C., Marino, K., Mottaghi, R.: A-okvqa: a benchmark for visual question answering using world knowledge. In: European Conference on Computer Vision, pp. 146–162. Springer (2022)
32. Shi, W., et al.: Detecting pretraining data from large language models. In: 12th International Conference on Learning Representations, ICLR 2024 (2024)
33. Shi, W., et al.: Math-LLaVA: bootstrapping mathematical reasoning for multimodal large language models. arXiv preprint arXiv:2406.17294 (2024)
34. Sidorov, O., Hu, R., Rohrbach, M., Singh, A.: TextCaps: a dataset for image captioning with reading comprehension. In: Vedaldi, A., Bischof, H., Brox, T., Frahm, J.-M. (eds.) ECCV 2020. LNCS, vol. 12347, pp. 742–758. Springer, Cham (2020). https://doi.org/10.1007/978-3-030-58536-5_44
35. Vaswani, A.: Attention is all you need. In: Advances in Neural Information Processing Systems (2017)
36. Wang, Z., Bovik, A.C.: Mean squared error: love it or leave it? a new look at signal fidelity measures. IEEE Signal Process. Mag. **26**(1), 98–117 (2009)
37. Wang, Z., Bovik, A.C., Sheikh, H.R., Simoncelli, E.P.: Image quality assessment: from error visibility to structural similarity. IEEE Trans. Image Process. **13**(4), 600–612 (2004)
38. Xu, Z., et al.: Magpie: alignment data synthesis from scratch by prompting aligned llms with nothing. arXiv preprint arXiv:2406.08464 (2024)
39. Yan, B., et al.: On protecting the data privacy of large language models (LLMs): a survey. arXiv preprint arXiv:2403.05156 (2024)
40. Yao, Y., Duan, J., Xu, K., Cai, Y., Sun, Z., Zhang, Y.: A survey on large language model (LLM) security and privacy: the good, the bad, and the ugly. high-confidence computing, p. 100211 (2024)
41. Yeom, S., Giacomelli, I., Fredrikson, M., Jha, S.: Privacy risk in machine learning: analyzing the connection to overfitting. In: IEEE 31st Computer Security Foundations Symposium, pp. 268–282. IEEE (2018)
42. Zhang, J., Das, D., Kamath, G., Tramèr, F.: Membership inference attacks cannot prove that a model was trained on your data. In: Proceedings of IEEE SatML (2025)
43. Zhao, W.X., et al.: A survey of large language models. arXiv preprint arXiv:2303.18223, vol. 1, no. 2 (2023)

Membership Privacy Evaluation in Deep Spiking Neural Networks

Jiaxin Li[1](✉), Gorka Abad[2], Stjepan Picek[2], and Mauro Conti[1]

[1] University of Padua, 35131 Padua, Italy
jiaxin.li@studenti.unipd.it, conti@math.unipd.it
[2] Radboud University, 6525 EC Nijmegen, The Netherlands
{abad.gorka,stjepan.picek}@ru.nl

Abstract. Although Artificial Neural Networks (ANNs) have achieved remarkable success in multiple tasks, e.g., face recognition and object detection, Spiking Neural Networks (SNNs) have recently attracted attention due to their low power consumption, fast inference, and event-driven properties. It is well-known that ANNs are vulnerable to the Membership Inference Attack (MIA), but whether the same applies to SNNs has not been explored. In this paper, we evaluate the membership privacy of SNNs by considering eight MIAs, seven of which are inspired by MIAs against ANNs. Our evaluation results show that SNNs are more vulnerable (maximum 10% higher in terms of balanced attack accuracy) than ANNs when both are trained with neuromorphic datasets (with time dimension). On the other hand, when training ANNs or SNNs with static datasets, the vulnerability depends on the dataset used. If we convert ANNs trained with static datasets to SNNs, the accuracy of MIAs drops (maximum 11.5% with a reduction of 7.6% on the test accuracy of the target model). Next, we explore the impact factors of MIAs on SNNs by conducting a hyperparameter study. Finally, we show that the basic data augmentation method for static datasets and two recent data augmentation methods for neuromorphic datasets can considerably (maximum reduction of 25.7%) decrease MIAs' performance on SNNs. Regardless, the accuracy of MIAs could still be between 51.7% and 66.4% with data augmentation, indicating data augmentation cannot fully prevent MIAs on SNNs.

Keywords: Membership Inference Attack · Spiking Neural Network · Artificial Neural Network · Data Augmentation

1 Introduction

Artificial Neural Networks model the behavior of a neuron with non-linear functions. As large amounts of data are collected and computing capabilities are enhanced, ANNs, especially deep neural networks [24], demonstrate amazing ability to solve real-world tasks like face recognition [63] and object detection [74]. The third generation of neural network models, Spiking Neural Networks [53], mimic the dynamics of a neuron in a way closer to the actual neurons in the brain. For ANNs, the neuron collects weighted inputs from previous neurons, applies a non-linear function σ to the summed input, and continuously outputs an identical activation value if the input is the same over time. For SNNs, the neuron modifies its membrane potential V (and the rate of change) according to binary spikes from previous neurons in the current time step. It outputs a spike when the membrane potential exceeds a threshold V_{th}. The neuron is inactive until a new spike is received, which reduces power consumption. Due to those properties and the development of neuromorphic devices (e.g., TrueNorth from IBM [3]), SNNs gained much attention in scenarios like the autonomous operation of the vehicle [8], industrial fault diagnosis [66], and healthcare diagnosis with biomedical signals [10,68]. We distinguish shallow and deep SNNs according to the number of layers within the structure of SNNs following the previous work [21,58]. As deep SNNs could perform better than shallow SNNs [21,58] and since they are used in real-world tasks [8,40], our work focuses on deep SNNs trained with backpropagation [39] or converted from ANNs [6,18,56].

Membership Inference Attacks, inferring whether a data point is in the training data of the target model, attract much attention in ANN research and practice due to the privacy protection requirement in laws like GDPR [64] and CCPA [5]. Applying SNNs in real-world tasks raises similar membership privacy concerns as in the case of ANNs. For example, if the user's data is in the training data of the deep SNN trained for the classification of Alzheimer's disease [65], we could infer that this user suffered from this disease if we know the data of this user is in the training data via MIA. As far as we know, no studies have evaluated the membership privacy of deep SNNs. Intuitively, MIAs on SNNs could be more challenging than MIAs on ANNs, considering that a data point of the neuromorphic dataset consists of multiple frames, each of which is the accumulation of events that happen over a period. A data point in the static dataset only contains one static image. A data point with multiple frames has more neighboring data points than the one with one static image. More neighboring data points make it harder to predict the existence of a specific data point, as the inclusion of neighboring data points could disturb the prediction of the MIA in this particular data point [46]. To solve this problem, we utilize spiking neurons' fire rate and membrane potential as signals of MIAs since they are cumulative results of multiple frames and could represent the prediction situation of multiple frames. In commonly used rate coding SNNs [4], the fire rate is a similar indicator to the confidence score to show the confidence of the prediction due to the alignment of Mean Squared Error (MSE) during training. Hence, we utilize previous strategies [7,57,60] in MIAs with confidence scores to MIAs with fire rates.

Our membership evaluation results show that SNNs are more vulnerable than ANNs when training ANNs and SNNs with neuromorphic datasets. On the other hand, when working with static datasets, the vulnerability comparison between ANNs and SNNs depends on specific datasets. The conversion from ANNs to SNNs maximally reduces 11.5% on the performance of MIAs with a drop of 7.6% on the original classification task. In the hyperparameter study, we show that the ATan function and the Leaky Integrate and Fire (LIF) neuron bring a high classification accuracy with a large generalization gap. The large generalization gap means the model performs variously on the training and test data, leading to MIAs' high attack accuracy since MIAs rely on this performance difference. Next, the choices of Adam (with a learning rate of 0.001) and SGD (with a learning rate of 0.1) are suitable for training SNNs. Moreover, increasing the number of time steps will slightly increase the vulnerability under MIAs. Finally, the basic data augmentation method for static datasets and two recent data augmentation methods for neuromorphic datasets could reduce MIAs' performance on SNNs by up to 25.7%. Unfortunately, the accuracy of MIAs could still be from 51.7% to 66.4% even when applied data augmentation.

Our main contributions are:

1. To the best of our knowledge, we are the first to evaluate the membership privacy of SNNs and compare their vulnerability to ANNs. We experiment with eight MIAs, six datasets, and three model structures, which lay the foundation for future work on the privacy of SNNs.
2. To understand MIAs on SNNs better, we investigate influential factors of MIAs during the training of SNNs in the hyperparameter study.
3. We apply data augmentation to explore defenses against MIAs on SNNs. There, we show that the basic augmentation method for static datasets and two recent augmentation mechanisms for neuromorphic datasets can reduce but cannot completely prevent MIAs on SNNs.

Our code is available at https://github.com/fight-think/Membership-Privacy-Evaluation-in-Deep-SNNs

2 Background and Related Work

In Sect. 2.1, we introduce three main methods to build SNNs and previous attacks against SNNs. Next, we present related works of MIAs and explain the pipeline of MIAs in Sect. 2.2.

2.1 Spiking Neural Network

An SNN is an application of the biological neuron into AI for efficient and low-cost computation. There are three main methods to train SNNs.

(1) Spike-Timing Dependent Plasticity (STDP). For a pair of presynaptic and postsynaptic neurons, the synaptic weight of the synapse between those two neurons will increase if the presynaptic neuron fires early and the postsynaptic neuron fires later. However, we do not consider this strategy because STDP is suitable for shallow SNNs and is primarily used for unsupervised learning [17,26,48]. For deep SNNs, finding suitable hyperparameters and training with STDP is difficult, as mentioned in the previous work [54].

(2) Conversion from ANN. Under this strategy, a pre-trained ANN is converted to an SNN by replacing the ReLU activation layers (that are not used in

SNNs) with spiking neurons and adding scaling operations like weight normalization and threshold balancing [6,18,31,55,56]. In our experiments to attack converted SNNs with MIAs, we follow previous works [55,56]: i) reset the potential by subtraction (the membrane potential threshold $V_{th} = 1.0$), ii) re-scale weights and biases with the robust normalization ($p = 99.9\%$), iii) achieve batch normalization via scaling weights and biases, and iv) directly feed the input to the converted SNN, and pass the output through a softmax function. We do not consider max-pooling because it requires estimating presynaptic firing rates, which is computationally complex [55] and does not give much benefit. Hence, we follow the strategy of average pooling from the work of Dieh et al. [18].

(3) Backpropagation-based supervised learning. Under this strategy, we train SNNs via backpropagation, the same way as ANNs. Under the LIF model, the membrane potential of a spiking neuron i is formulated as given in Eqs. (1) and (2). In Eq. (1), V_{rest} is the membrane potential of a neuron without any input. We set V_{rest} as 0 following the related work [19]. $V(t)$ is the membrane potential of neuron i at time t. τ is the membrane time constant. In Eq. (2), the neuron i has n_i presynaptic neurons. For a presynaptic neuron j, it has a list of spiking times t_j^{pre}, w_{ij} is the synaptic weight between neuron i and a presynaptic neuron j, and $\delta(t)$ is the Dirac delta function (if $t \neq 0$, $\delta(t) = 0$. $\int_{-\infty}^{\infty} \delta(t) dt = 1$). To consider $V(t)$ in discrete time, we obtain $H(t)$ in Eq. (3) after applying the Euler method to Eq. (1).

$$\tau \frac{dV(t)}{dt} = -(V(t) - V_{rest}) + X(t). \tag{1}$$

$$X(t) = \sum_{j=1}^{n_i} \sum_{t_s^{pre} \in t_j^{pre}} w_{ij} \delta(t - t_s^{pre}). \tag{2}$$

$$H(t) = V(t-1) + \frac{1}{\tau}(-(V(t-1) - V_{rest}) + X(t)). \tag{3}$$

The neuron will elicit a spike $S(t)$ to the subsequent neurons if $H(t)$ is larger than a threshold V_{th}. Then, the membrane potential $V(t)$ will be reset as V_{reset}.

$$V(t) = H(t)(1 - S(t)) + V_{reset} S(t). \tag{4}$$

To apply backpropagation during training, it is common to keep $S(t)$ for the forward pass and replace $S(t)$ with a differentiable surrogate function to calculate the backward gradient, as $S(t)$ is not differentiable [50]. The Atan function, one of the surrogate functions, is given in Eq. (5). α is the pre-defined parameter with a default value of 2.0, following the implementation of SpikingJelly [20].

$$S(t) = \frac{1}{\pi} \arctan(\frac{\pi}{2} \alpha H(t)) + \frac{1}{2}. \tag{5}$$

Previous works explored adversarial examples and backdoor attacks against SNNs. Abad et al. [2] systematically investigated the backdoor attack against the SNN. To improve the moving backdoor in previous work [1], the authors conducted a complete experimental setup to find the best moving trigger. Nomura et al. [51] explored the robustness of the time-to-first-spike encoding SNNs against white-box adversarial examples. Sharmin et al. [59] systematically analyzed the adversarial robustness of SNNs and concluded the dependence of robustness on the SNN training mechanism. To apply a gradient-based adversarial attack on SNNs, Liang et al. [44] proposed two strategies to solve the problem of gradient input incompatibility and gradient vanishing. To our knowledge, there is no previous work about MIAs against SNNs.

2.2 Membership Inference Attack

The MIA tries to infer if a data point has been used during a target model's training by analyzing the target model's outputs or behaviors to the original or modified formats of this data point. Since the proposition of a successful MIA against machine learning in 2017 [60], the following works put much effort into ways to improve the performance of MIAs [7,57,70,71], attacking strategies with less information [11,13,30,43], MIAs on various datasets or models [27,29,34,45], vulnerability of data points [12,69], and defenses against MIAs [9,33,49]. Formally, MIA is formulated as a function $A : x, M, \Omega \rightarrow \{0, 1\}$ with a data point x, the target model M, and external knowledge Ω of the adversary. The adversary aims to correctly predict the existence of data points in the training data of the target model as much as possible with external knowledge. For the prediction result, the output 1 means that x is a member of M's training data and 0 otherwise.

Currently, there are two main strategies for implementing MIAs: classifier-based and threshold-based methods. In classifier-based methods, the adversary trains an attack model, a classifier, to predict whether a data point is a member based on features (e.g., the confidence scores [60]) extracted from this data point and the target model. Usually, the adversary trains shadow models to mimic the target model's behavior. The adversary cannot access the original training data, but some data have a similar distribution to the original data from the website or model inversion attacks [16], following the assumption of previous works [7,60]. Then, the adversary trains the attack model with a dataset extracted from the features obtained by querying the shadow model. For the threshold-based methods, the adversary directly compares a data point's metric (e.g., loss [71]) with a threshold to predict its membership. Usually, this threshold is determined according to the average value of the metric in the training data or is selected as the one that obtains high performance on the metric values of the shadow model. We apply these two strategies in our membership privacy evaluation of deep SNNs.

3 Membership Privacy Evaluation

In this part, we define a data point in the neuromorphic dataset and the input and output of the SNN in Sect. 3.1. In Sect. 3.2, we provide the threat model.

Section 3.3 explains the methods with detailed metrics to evaluate the membership privacy of SNNs.

3.1 Definitions

For a data point $x \in R^{T \times 2 \times H \times W}$ ($T, 2, H,$ and W are the time steps, positive and negative channels, height, and width of the input), the target SNN M outputs the spiking times among T steps as $M(x) \in R^{T \times n}$ (n is the number of classification categories), each of which represents whether a spiking neuron evokes a spike at current time spot. Therefore, the fire rates of M on x is $Fr(x) = \frac{\sum_{t=1}^{T} M(x)_t}{T} \in R^n$ and $M(x)_t \in R^n$ is spiking times at time spot t. For the last layer composed of spiking neurons (the number of neurons is m), the membrane potential of spiking neurons for x is $Mp(x) \in R^{T \times m}$. Therefore, the average membrane potential among T time steps is $AMp(x) = \frac{\sum_{t=1}^{T} Mp_t(x)}{T}$ and $Mp_t(x) \in R^m$ is the membrane potential at time step t. As we explained in Sect. 1, we utilize fire rates and average membrane potentials of the target SNN M on a data point as the signal to predict its membership.

3.2 Threat Model

Following the common practice of MIA [60], the adversary holds a shadow dataset used for training and testing the target SNN M. There are no overlapping data points between the shadow and target datasets. The adversary knows M's hyperparameters and model structure to train a shadow SNN M_s for mimicking M, following previous works [7,60]. Controlling the training and test data of M_s, the adversary can extract attack features from the training and test data of M_s by feeding data into M_s and label features as members (from training data) and non-members (from test data) separately. With the attack features and corresponding labels, the adversary trains a classifier or determines a threshold for distinguishing members and non-members. With the classifier (attack model) or threshold, the adversary evaluates the performance of MIA on the target SNN M. For attack features, we assume the adversary knows the fire rates $Fr(x)$ and the average membrane potential $AMp(x)$ of a data point x to evaluate the membership privacy of M under various MIAs. Finally, the adversary knows the loss, prediction label, and ground truth y of x, following the assumptions in previous MIAs on ANNs [60,71].

3.3 Methodology

We follow strategies of previous MIAs (with confidence scores) on ANNs to leverage fire rates to implement MIAs on SNNs. The reason is that the fire rate is a similar indicator to the confidence score to show the confidence of the prediction. In the previous work [60], the ANN's prediction confidence gap on the training and test data makes MIAs feasible. Therefore, we follow previous strategies of handling confidence scores to use fire rates as signals of MIAs. We select five representative methods in the field of MIA, including the first MIA on machine learning [60], two methods relaxing assumptions of MIA [57], the performance improvement with modified entropy (Mentr) [62], and performance improvement with logit-scaled confidence [7]. Apart from the five mentioned methods, we also choose two methods from the work of Yeom et al. [71] since they are important benchmarks. One is the MIA based on loss, and the other is based on the prediction correctness. For the average membrane potential, we take it as the feature of the attack model to directly infer the membership following the basic strategy in [60]. For MIAs on ANNs, we also evaluate hinge loss based on logits (the output before the softmax layer in the ANN) due to its more straightforward computation than the logit-scaled confidence and competitive performance [7].

In summary, we evaluate MIAs on SNNs with eight methods based on fire rates and membrane potential. For comparison, we implement eight MIAs on ANNs based on (1) confidence scores [60], (2) loss [71], (3) prediction correctness [71], (4) top-3 confidence scores [57], (5) maximum confidence score [57], (6) logit-scaled confidence [7], (7) hinge loss [7], and (8) Mentr with confidence scores [62]. For MIAs against SNNs, we discuss the details of each method as follows.

(1) **fire rates.** We take the fire rates $Fr(x)$ of each data point as the feature of the attack classifier to predict the membership of each data point.
(2) **loss.** We compare the single loss related to each data point with a threshold to determine its membership.
(3) **prediction correctness.** If the target SNN M correctly predicts the classification label of x, we predict x is a member and non-member otherwise.
(4) **top-3 fire rates.** Instead of using all the fire rates, we select top-3 fire rates as the feature of the attack classifier, following the strategy in the previous work [57].
(5) **maximum fire rate.** We use the maximum fire rate to compare with a threshold.
(6) **logit-scaled fire rate.** We compute the logit-scaled fire rate as Eq. (6), where $Fr(x)_y$ is the fire rate of the spiking neuron of the ground truth. We replace the confidence score of logit-scaled confidence [7] with the fire rate to obtain this metric. It is worth noting that we do not train hundreds of shadow models to model the distribution of the logit-scaled fire rate considering the computation cost of model training and the relatively large size of neuromorphic datasets. Rather, we leave such exploration for future work.

$$\log(Fr(x)_y) - \log \sum_{y' \neq y} Fr(x)_{y'}. \tag{6}$$

(7) Mentr with fire rates. Following the Mentr with confidence scores in the previous work [62], we calculate the Mentr with fire rates as Eq. (7).

$$-(1 - Fr(x)_y)\log(Fr(x)_y) - \sum_{y' \neq y} Fr(x)_{y'} \log(1 - Fr(x)_{y'}). \tag{7}$$

(8) average membrane potential. Apart from fire rates, we utilize the average membrane potential as the feature of the attack classifier to predict membership.

4 Experimental Settings

We discuss the datasets used in our experiments in Sect. 4.1. Then, we discuss the ANN and SNN model structures in Sect. 4.2. In Sect. 4.3, we detail the settings of training models, including target, shadow, and attack models. Besides, we clarify the evaluation metric.

4.1 Datasets

To distinguish two types of datasets easily and better, we follow the previous work [19] by utilizing the term "neuromorphic dataset" ("static dataset"). In the static dataset, one data point is a three-dimensional (RGB) array with pixel values ranging from 0 to 1. In the neuromorphic dataset, a data point is a list of time-series events, accumulated into a fixed number (i.e., time steps) of frames, measuring the brightness change during the relative movement between the object (or its image) and the Dynamic Vision Sensor (DVS) camera. Following previous works [19,42], we select three common datasets (in ANNs) that have neuromorphic versions as experimental datasets. Table 1 shows the shape of a batch of data points and the number of data points in the neuromorphic and static datasets we use. Among the numbers representing the shape, the T, B, and the last two numbers separately indicate the time steps, batch size, and height and width of data points.

Table 1. Statistical information of each dataset.

Dataset	Dataset type	Shape of a batch of data points	Number of data points
N-MNIST [52]	neuromorphic	$T \times B \times 2 \times 34 \times 34$	70,000
CIFAR10-DVS [41]	neuromorphic	$T \times B \times 2 \times 128 \times 128$	10,000
N-Caltech101 [52]	neuromorphic	$T \times B \times 2 \times 180 \times 240$	9,146
MNIST [37]	static	$B \times 1 \times 28 \times 28$	70,000
CIFAR-10 [35]	static	$B \times 3 \times 32 \times 32$	60,000
Caltech101 [22]	static	$B \times 3 \times 180 \times 240$ (resize)	9,146

4.2 Models

We select three model structures, including the structure of SNNs (with various convolutional, downsampling, and fully connected layers) defined in the work of Fang et al. [19] (we denote this structure as CNN for convenience), VGG11 [61], and ResNet18 [28]. For ANNs with structures of VGG11 and ResNet18, we replace the neuron formulated as a ReLU activation function with a spiking neuron. We keep the weights and connections between neurons. Considering there are two input channels for the neuromorphic dataset and that the original input of VGG11 and ResNet18 is expected to have three channels, we add a convolutional layer to increase the number of channels (upsampling).

For the CNN originally defined for neuromorphic datasets in the work of Fang et al. [19], we modify the spiking neurons to artificial neurons with a ReLU activation function and change the input channel of the first convolutional layer to three as the number of channels in the static dataset is three. Note that instead of directly utilizing the previous CNN (like AlexNet [36]) to train on static datasets, we modify the CNN originally defined for neuromorphic datasets (SNN) to the CNN used for static datasets. This modification allows a fair comparison between SNNs trained with neuromorphic datasets and ANNs trained with static datasets. For conversion from ANNs to SNNs, we discussed the conversion operation in Sect. 2.1.

For the classifier-based MIA, the attack model is a multilayer perceptron (MLP) with 2 hidden layers, each with 64 neurons, following the previous work [13]. The single-value output of the MLP represents the probability of being predicted as a member.

4.3 Settings and Evaluation Metric

Inspired by the work of Deng et al. [14], we train ANNs with neuromorphic datasets and SNNs with static datasets to investigate their membership privacy. For a batch of data points in the neuromorphic dataset, we follow the previous work [14] to normalize the accumulated spike times to the image pixel range. For a data point from the static dataset, we repeat the image for time-step times and utilize the first few layers of the SNN to transfer the static image into spike events [19] rather than transferring with a Poisson encoder, which might incur variability in the firing of the network and impair its performance [56].

For ANNs and SNNs trained on neuromorphic and static datasets, we use a learning rate of 0.001, the Adam optimizer, and a batch size ranging from 2 to 16, depending on the input size. For ANNs, we apply cross-entropy loss, while for SNNs, we use MSE. The maximum number of epochs is 30, 50, and 60 for MNIST (N-MNIST), CIFAR-10 (CIFAR10-DVS), and Caltech101 (N-Caltech101), respectively. We select the models with the best validation accuracy as the final models, following common machine learning practices [38] and prior work [60]. For SNNs, the default number of time steps is 16, in line with previous studies using feedforward VGG11 or ResNet18 [42,73]. The attack model uses Adam with a learning rate of 0.001, 300 epochs, and a batch size of 32, with Binary Cross Entropy (BCE) as the loss function. In Sect. 5.2, we investigate the impact of the optimizer, learning rate, and time steps on models and MIAs.

For the evaluation metric of MIAs, we follow previous works [7,60] and use the balanced accuracy as the comparison metric of MIAs. For the results in this work, we average the accuracy of five runs as the final attack accuracy in figures.

5 Results and Discussions

We compare the performance of MIAs on SNNs and ANNs in Sect. 5.1. Next, we provide a hyperparameter study in Sect. 5.2. In Sect. 5.3, we evaluate the augmentation methods as the defenses against MIAs. Finally, we explore additional experiments in Sect. 5.4.

5.1 MIAs on SNNs and ANNs

We evaluate the original task's accuracy through test accuracy and the generalization gap (training accuracy minus test accuracy). Figure 1 shows the relationship between the generalization gap and the highest accuracy among eight MIAs, where a larger gap usually leads to greater vulnerability, consistent with prior studies [60,71]. Figures 2 and 3 display the highest MIA accuracy and the original task's performance across three static and three neuromorphic datasets. The left subfigure shows the highest MIA accuracy (x-axis) and model type (y-axis), with "conversion" indicating ANN to SNN transformation. The right subfigure shows the original task's accuracy (x-axis) and model type (y-axis).

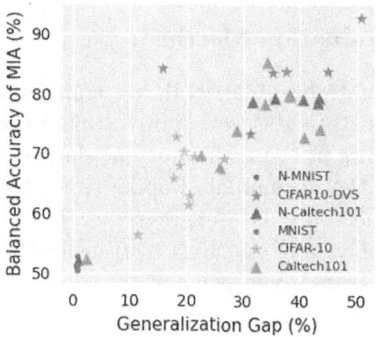

Fig. 1. The relationship between the generalization gap and the highest accuracy among eight MIAs in ANNs and SNNs.

Comparing the highest attack accuracy of MIAs among ANNs and SNNs under the same static dataset, we find vulnerability is related to the type of static dataset. For MNIST, the highest attack accuracy of ANNs is similar to that of SNNs (around 50%) as the training and test accuracy is all above 99%, indicating almost no generalization gap. For CIFAR-10, the highest attack accuracy of ANNs is larger than that of SNNs. For example, the SNN with a structure of ResNet18 has a generalization gap of 26.6% (larger than 18% with the ANN) and the highest attack accuracy of 69.4% (smaller than 72.9% with the ANN). We also observe this trend with CNN and VGG11 trained with CIFAR-10. It indicates the ANN (SNN) with a lower generalization gap could have a higher attack accuracy.

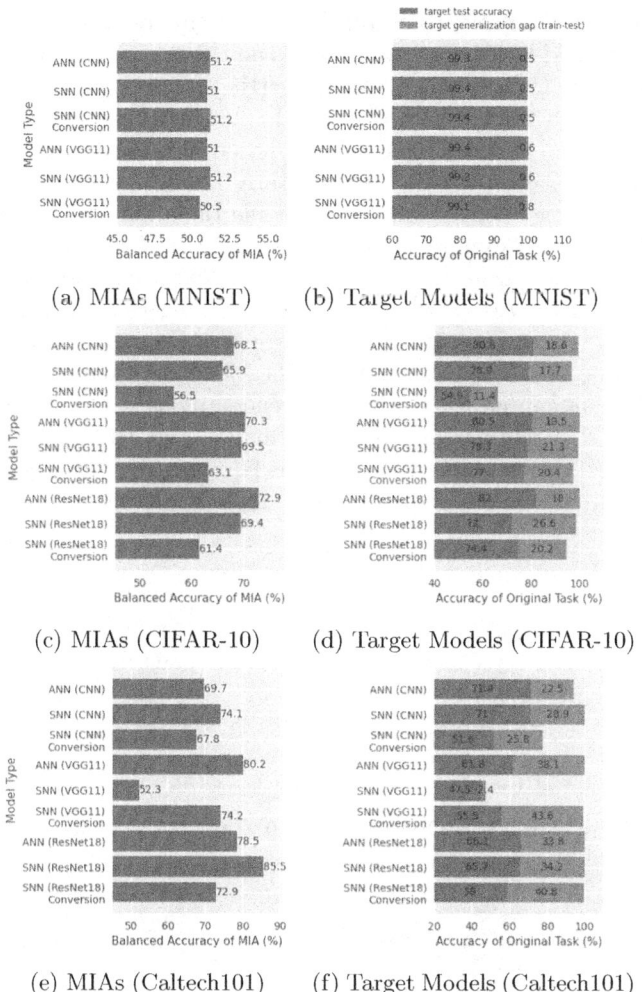

Fig. 2. The highest accuracy of eight MIAs, target test accuracy, and target generalization gap of three static datasets with various model types.

For Caltech101, MIAs obtain a higher attack accuracy on SNNs than ANNs. For example, the SNN with a structure of CNN has the attack accuracy of 74.1%, higher than 69.7% of the ANN. Similarly, MIAs have higher attack performance on SNN than ANN when the structure is ResNet18. While training different models with the same static dataset, the vulnerability comparison of SNNs and ANNs is consistent. It indicates the dataset itself is the factor, corresponding with the previous work [12] that finds the dataset impacts the performance of MIAs. In summary, the vulnerability comparison between SNNs and ANNs depends on the static datasets used for training ANNs and SNNs.

Conversion from ANNs to SNNs reduces the performance of MIAs against converted SNNs with the accuracy drop on the original classification task. For CNN-based ANNs, converting to SNNs reduces classification accuracy by around 20% on CIFAR-10 and Caltech101. Correspondingly, MIA accuracy drops from 68.1% to 56.5% (−11.6%) on CIFAR-10 and from 69.7% to 67.8% (-1.9%) on Caltech101. For architectures like VGG11 and ResNet18, the classification accuracy drop is within 8%, while the reduction in MIA accuracy can exceed 10%. For example, converting a ResNet18-based ANN to the SNN reduces MIA accuracy from 72.9% to 61.4% (-11.5%) and classification accuracy from 82% to 74.4% (-7.6%), while increasing the generalization gap from 18% to 20.2%. Two factors contribute to the drop in MIA performance when converting ANNs to SNNs. First, lower classification performance and changes in the generalization gap impact MIA effectiveness; models with lower generalization gaps typically yield weaker MIA performance, and MIAs generally perform worse when the target model underperforms [7]. Second, the conversion process alters how neurons connect and propagate input, resulting in different weight

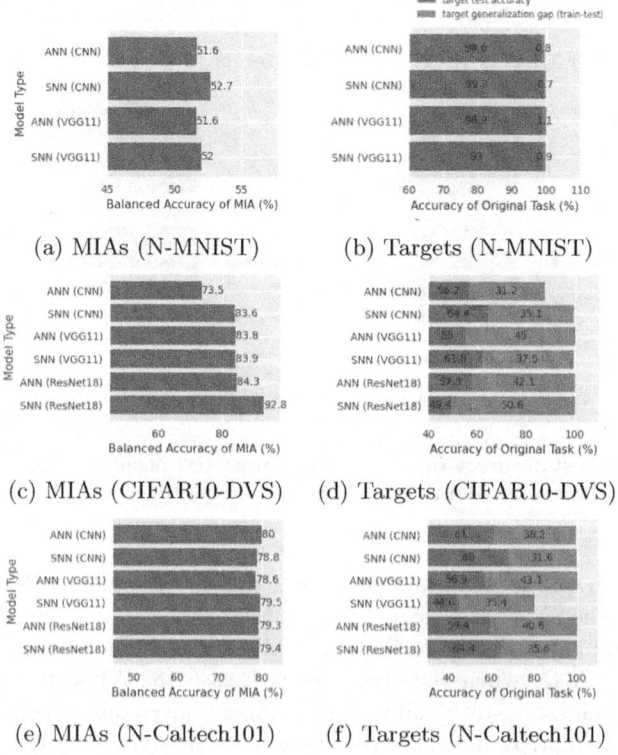

Fig. 3. The highest accuracy of eight MIAs, target test accuracy, and target generalization gap of three neuromorphic datasets with various model types.

utilization. This structural change leads to partial information loss, degrading both classification performance and MIA effectiveness.

When using neuromorphic datasets, SNNs are more vulnerable than ANNs due to the larger generalization gap. For example, the SNN with a ResNet18 architecture trained on CIFAR10-DVS exhibits a higher generalization gap (50.6%) compared to its ANN counterpart (42.1%), and correspondingly, a higher MIA accuracy (92.8% vs. 84.3%). On N-Caltech101, the highest MIA accuracy is similar for both models (79%), but the SNN has a smaller generalization gap (35.6%) than the ANN (40.6%). This indicates that SNNs can exhibit higher vulnerability to MIAs either due to larger generalization gaps or, in some cases, maintain similar vulnerability despite having smaller generalization gaps. Overall, these results suggest that SNNs are more vulnerable than ANNs when trained on neuromorphic datasets.

We further evaluate the effectiveness of new indicators (various versions of fire rates and membrane potential from Sect. 3.3) compared to traditional ones (loss and prediction correctness) under SNNs. As shown in Table 2, in over half the cases, new indicators match the accuracy of the old ones ("new = old"). They outperform old indicators in 8 out of 24 cases, while old indicators perform better in only 4. For CIFAR-10 and CIFAR10-DVS, new indicators yield a higher average accuracy gap (1.77%) than old ones (0.1%). For Caltech101 and N-Caltech101, old indicators show a slightly higher average gap (3.17%) compared to new indicators (2.93%). Overall, new indicators more frequently lead to higher attack accuracy, though the improvement is modest. Nonetheless, they support relevant conclusions about the vulnerability of SNNs versus ANNs.

Table 2. The attack accuracy comparison of SNN-specific indicators (new) and classical ones (old) under SNNs.

Dataset	Num of times (Avg ACC gap %)		
	new > old	new = old	new < old
MNIST or N-MNIST	2 (0.1%)	4	0
CIFAR-10 or CIFAR10-DVS	3 (1.77%)	5	1 (0.1%)
Caltech101 or N-Caltech101	3 (2.93%)	3	3 (3.17%)

5.2 Hyperparameter Study

To explore the factors that impact the performance of MIAs on SNNs, we conduct a hyperparameter study to vary the spiking neuron type, surrogate function, optimizer, learning rate, and time steps during the training of SNNs.

Varying Spiking Neuron Type and Surrogate Function. We evaluate three spiking neuron types (LIF, EIF [23], and Izhikevich [32]) and two surrogate functions (ATan and PiecewiseLeakyReLU [67]). For N-MNIST, the SNN with the PiecewiseLeakyReLU function and Izhikevich neuron is the most vulnerable, with the highest attack accuracy of 55.5%. For CIFAR10-DVS and N-Caltech101, SNNs with the ATan function and LIF neuron achieve the highest attack accuracy (83.6% on CIFAR10-DVS and 77.6% on N-Caltech101). This is primarily due to the larger generalization gap if the SNN is defined with the ATan function and LIF neuron despite their higher test accuracy compared to other combinations of neurons and surrogate functions.

Varying Optimizer and Learning Rate. We explore the impact of different optimizers (Adam and SGD) and learning rates (0.1 and 0.001) on the final model and MIA performance. For CIFAR10-DVS, the SNN trained with Adam and a learning rate of 0.001 exhibits a higher generalization gap (37.5%) compared to the SNN trained with SGD and a learning rate of 0.1 (34.7%). However, MIAs achieve a lower attack accuracy (83.9%) on the Adam-optimized SNN. This shows that a higher generalization does not always indicate a higher attack accuracy. Both high (0.1) and low (0.001) learning rates can result in model performance near random guessing. This suggests that the optimal learning rate for one optimizer may not be suitable for another, highlighting the importance of considering both optimizers and learning rates when training SNNs.

Varying the Number of Time Steps. When varying the number of time steps (4, 8, and 16), we observe that the difference in the highest MIA accuracy between 8 and 16 time steps is within 1%. For N-Caltech101, MIA accuracy is higher at 4 time steps due to a larger generalization gap. However, increasing time steps from 4 to 8 raises MIA accuracy for N-MNIST and CIFAR10-DVS, even as the generalization gap slightly decreases. These results suggest that increasing time steps generally leads to a slight rise in vulnerability under MIAs, which then stabilizes. We attribute this to the fact that more time steps allow each data point to be processed across more frames, deepening the model's memorization and thus making it more susceptible to MIAs.

5.3 Defense Evaluation

To reduce the generalization gap [57,60] and defend against MIAs, we use data augmentation strategies, which incur less utility loss compared to Differential Privacy [7,60]. For neuromorphic datasets, we employ two augmentation strategies. The first, EventDrop [25], drops events in 1) a time interval, 2) a coordinate area, or 3) randomly. The second strategy uses geometric augmentations (NDA [42]), including rolling, rotation, cutout [15], shear, flip, and CutMix [72]. Following the "M1N2" mechanism from the original paper, we apply two methods (flip and CutMix) and randomly select one of the four left augmentation methods for each sample. For static datasets, basic augmentations such as horizontal flip, random crop, and resize are applied.

Tables 3 and 4 in the Appendix show the accuracy change of the target model and MIAs before and after applying data augmentation to static and neuromorphic datasets. For static datasets, SNNs trained with backpropagation reduce their generalization gap to a value close to 0 with data augmentation, leading to

MIAs' performance close to random guessing. The conversion of ANNs trained with data augmentation to SNNs decreases the accuracy of MIAs by about 10%, with the reduction of the test accuracy by more than 10%. Notably, the attack accuracy could also be as high as 66.4% while converting ANNs to SNNs. For ANNs trained with static datasets, the reduced accuracy of MIAs is still about 60%, which is 10% to 20% lower than the one without data augmentation.

For SNNs with a VGG11 architecture trained on neuromorphic datasets, MIAs perform worse when using NDA compared to EventDrop. For instance, on CIFAR10-DVS, MIA accuracy drops from 83.9% to 58.3% with NDA, whereas it remains higher at 75.8% with EventDrop. For ANNs (VGG11), MIA performance slightly improves with EventDrop despite a smaller generalization gap. Specifically, MIA accuracy increases from 83.8% to 86.5% after applying EventDrop on CIFAR10-DVS. NDA, which involves geometric augmentations, transforms similar input frames into more distinct ones, thereby enhancing model generalization and test accuracy while reducing vulnerability to MIAs. For example, on ANN (VGG11) trained with CIFAR10-DVS, NDA reduces MIA accuracy from 83.8% to 71.8% and improves test accuracy from 55.0% to 63.7%. These results suggest that NDA is more effective than EventDrop at mitigating MIA performance and can even boost the test accuracy of ANNs trained on neuromorphic data.

5.4 Additional Evaluation

Static Datasets with Poisson Encoding. We investigate SNNs trained on static datasets, where static images are converted into spike events using Poisson encoding [56], as our default method relies on the first few SNN layers for this conversion. The results confirm prior findings [56]—Poisson encoding significantly reduces both training and test accuracy. For instance, the training (test) accuracy of an SNN (CNN) on CIFAR-10 drops from 96.9% (78.9%) to 73.1% (38.4%). MIA performance also declines despite similar generalization gaps. For example, the SNN (ResNet18) trained on Caltech101 achieves an MIA accuracy of 85.5% with a 34.2% generalization gap, but this drops to about 55% when Poisson encoding is applied—even with a generalization gap of 29.7%. The reason is that the Poisson encoder will generate a random representation for a static image according to the specific values of each position of this static image during testing and different epochs of training. This randomness decreases the performance of training and MIAs.

Recurrent SNNs. In addition to convolutional SNNs (e.g., CNN, VGG11, ResNet18), recurrent SNNs can also be applied to image classification. Lotfi Rezaabad et al. [47] proposed integrating long short-term memory (LSTM) with SNNs. Inspired by their approach, we flatten the frame at each time step and feed it into an SNN (LSTM), leveraging both spatial and temporal information from neuromorphic datasets. This setup results in lower task accuracy and a near-zero generalization gap, leading to MIA accuracy around 50%. Hence, recurrent SNNs could eliminate the performance of MIAs with low accuracy on the original task.

Application of Early Stopping. We apply early stopping with a patience of five and $\delta = 0$ for model selection. This strategy leads to a drop in task accuracy. For instance, the training (test) accuracy of SNN (VGG11) on CIFAR10-DVS decreases from 99.3% (61.8%) to 80.0% (58.6%). Despite this, MIAs still achieve higher attack accuracy on SNNs compared to ANNs. For example, the highest MIA accuracy on SNN (CNN) is 83.6%, while on ANN (CNN) it is 68.3%. We observe similar behavior for most models and datasets, even under a similar generalization gap. Hence, the conclusion that the vulnerability of SNNs is higher than that of ANNs with neuromorphic datasets is still applicable with early stopping.

6 Conclusions and Future Work

This work evaluates the membership privacy leakage of SNNs with eight MIAs and compares the vulnerability of SNNs and ANNs when facing MIAs. Our results show that SNNs suffer from MIAs, especially when trained with neuromorphic datasets, where SNNs are more vulnerable than ANNs. If we convert ANNs to SNNs, the accuracy of MIAs will drop with a relatively low reduction in the accuracy of the original classification task. Hence, we recommend converting from ANNs to SNNs to reduce the leakage of membership privacy. The rule that a higher generalization gap usually leads to a higher performance of MIAs is also applicable to SNNs from our exploration of various datasets, model types, and the hyperparameter study. Moreover, the basic data augmentation for static datasets and two recent data augmentation methods for neuromorphic datasets can improve the generalization of SNNs and eliminate MIAs. However, data augmentations cannot completely prevent MIAs. As the training accuracy of SNNs with data augmentation is usually lower than those without augmentation, we leave the method to reduce the generalization gap and keep the training accuracy of SNNs for future work. Finally, considering that SNNs are vulnerable to MIAs, we plan to investigate further possible defense mechanisms.

A Appendix

A.1 The Attack Accuracy Change While Applying Augmentations

Table 3. The accuracy change while applying augmentation to static datasets.

Dataset	Model	Training Strategy	Without Augmentation				With Augmentation			
			Test Acc	Train Acc	MIA (Highest Acc)		Test Acc	Train Acc	MIA (Highest Acc)	
					MIA	Acc			MIA	Acc
CIFAR-10	ANN (VGG11)	BP	80.5%	100.0%	Mentr with confidence scores	70.3%	87.6%	98.6%	loss	59.5%
	SNN (VGG11)	BP	78.3%	99.6%	loss	69.5%	67.3%	67.6%	logit-scaled fire rate	51.7%
	SNN (VGG11)	Conversion	77.0%	97.4%	logit-scaled fire rate	63.1%	63.6%	70.5%	prediction correctness	53.3%
Caltech101	ANN (VGG11)	BP	61.8%	99.9%	logit-scaled confidence	80.2%	62.9%	91.9%	prediction correctness	60.5%
	SNN (VGG11)	BP	47.5%	45.1%	maximum fire rate	52.3%	30.4%	33.0%	avg membrane potential	51.7%
	SNN (VGG11)	Conversion	55.5%	99.1%	loss	72.9%	44.0%	70.6%	loss	66.4%

Table 4. The accuracy change while applying augmentation to neuromorphic datasets.

Dataset	Model	Without Augmentation				With EventDrop [25]				With NDA [42]			
		Test Acc	Train Acc	MIA (Highest Acc)		Test Acc	Train Acc	MIA (Highest Acc)		Test Acc	Train Acc	MIA (Highest Acc)	
				MIA	Acc			MIA	Acc			MIA	Acc
CIFAR10-DVS	ANN (VGG11)	55.0%	100.0%	hinge loss	83.8%	55.1%	89.3%	logit-scaled confidence	86.5%	63.7%	95.1%	Mentr with confidence scores	71.8%
	SNN (VGG11)	61.8%	99.3%	Mentr with fire rates	83.9%	60.8%	90.3%	Mentr with fire rates	75.6%	61.4%	68.3%	Mentr with fire rates	58.3%
N-Caltech101	ANN (VGG11)	56.9%	100.0%	loss	78.6%	55.8%	88.7%	hinge loss	79.4%	60.7%	99.4%	loss	76.9%
	SNN (VGG11)	44.6%	80.0%	loss	79.5%	35.2%	37.0%	loss	55.2%	32.0%	32.1%	top-3 fire rates	53.8%

References

1. Abad, G., Ersoy, O., Picek, S., Ramírez-Durán, V.J., Urbieta, A.: Poster: backdoor attacks on spiking nns and neuromorphic datasets. In: CCS 2022, Pp. 3315–3317. ACM (2022)
2. Abad, G., Ersoy, O., Picek, S., Urbieta, A.: Sneaky spikes: uncovering stealthy backdoor attacks in spiking neural networks with neuromorphic data. In: NDSS 2024 (2024)
3. Akopyan, F., et al.: Truenorth: design and tool flow of a 65 mw 1 million neuron programmable neurosynaptic chip. IEEE Trans. Comput. Aided Des. Integr. Circuits Syst. **34**(10), 1537–1557 (2015)
4. Auge, D., Hille, J., Mueller, E., Knoll, A.: A survey of encoding techniques for signal processing in spiking neural networks. Neural Process. Lett. **53**(6), 4693–4710 (2021)
5. Bukaty, P.: The California Consumer Privacy Act (CCPA): An Implementation Guide. IT Governance Publishing (2019)

6. Cao, Y., Chen, Y., Khosla, D.: Spiking deep convolutional neural networks for energy-efficient object recognition. Int. J. Comput. Vision **113**, 54–66 (2015)
7. Carlini, N., Chien, S., Nasr, M., Song, S., Terzis, A., Tramèr, F.: Membership inference attacks from first principles. In: S&P 2022, pp. 1897–1914. IEEE (2022)
8. Chen, G., Cao, H., Conradt, J., Tang, H., Rohrbein, F., Knoll, A.: Event-based neuromorphic vision for autonomous driving: a paradigm shift for bio-inspired visual sensing and perception. IEEE Signal Process. Mag. **37**(4), 34–49 (2020)
9. Chen, Z., Pattabiraman, K.: Overconfidence is a dangerous thing: mitigating membership inference attacks by enforcing less confident prediction. CoRR (2023)
10. Choi, S.H.: Spiking neural networks for biomedical signal analysis. In: Biomedical Engineering Letters, pp. 1–12 (2024)
11. Choquette-Choo, C.A., Tramer, F., Carlini, N., Papernot, N.: Label-only membership inference attacks. In: ICML, vol. 139, pp. 1964–1974. PMLR (2021)
12. Conti, M., Li, J., Picek, S.: On the vulnerability of data points under multiple membership inference attacks and target models. CoRR (2022)
13. Conti, M., Li, J., Picek, S., Xu, J.: Label-only membership inference attack against node-level graph neural networks. In: AISec 2022, pp. 1–12. ACM, New York, NY, USA (2022)
14. Deng, L., et al.: Rethinking the performance comparison between snns and anns. Neural Netw. **121**, 294–307 (2020)
15. DeVries, T., Taylor, G.W.: Improved regularization of convolutional neural networks with cutout. CoRR (2017)
16. Dibbo, S.V.: Sok: Model inversion attack landscape: taxonomy, challenges, and future roadmap. In: CSF 2023, pp. 439–456. IEEE (2023)
17. Diehl, P.U., Cook, M.: Unsupervised learning of digit recognition using spike-timing-dependent plasticity. Front. Comput. Neurosci. **9**, 99 (2015)
18. Diehl, P.U., Neil, D., Binas, J., Cook, M., Liu, S.C., Pfeiffer, M.: Fast-classifying, high-accuracy spiking deep networks through weight and threshold balancing. In: IJCNN 2015, pp. 1–8. IEEE (2015)
19. Fang, W., Yu, Z., Chen, Y., Masquelier, T., Huang, T., Tian, Y.: Incorporating learnable membrane time constant to enhance learning of spiking neural networks. In: ICCV 2021, pp. 2641–2651. IEEE (2021)
20. Fang, W., et al.: Spikingjelly: an open-source machine learning infrastructure platform for spike-based intelligence. Sci. Adv. **9**(40) (2023)
21. Fang, W., Yu, Z., Chen, Y., Huang, T., Masquelier, T., Tian, Y.: Deep residual learning in spiking neural networks. NeurIPS **34**, 21056–21069 (2021)
22. Fei-Fei, L., Fergus, R., Perona, P.: One-shot learning of object categories. IEEE Trans. Pattern Anal. Mach. Intell. **28**(4), 594–611 (2006)
23. Fourcaud-Trocmé, N., Hansel, D., Van Vreeswijk, C., Brunel, N.: How spike generation mechanisms determine the neuronal response to fluctuating inputs. J. Neurosci. **23**(37), 11628–11640 (2003)
24. Goodfellow, I., Bengio, Y., Courville, A.: Deep Learning. MIT Press (2016)
25. Gu, F., Sng, W., Hu, X., Yu, F.: Eventdrop: data augmentation for event-based learning. CoRR (2021)
26. Gupta, A., Saurabh, S.: Unsupervised learning in a ternary snn using stdp. IEEE J. Electron Dev. Soc. **12**, 211–220 (2024)
27. Hayes, J., Melis, L., Danezis, G., Cristofaro, E.D.: LOGAN: membership inference attacks against generative models. PETS **2019**, 133–152 (2019)
28. He, K., Zhang, X., Ren, S., Sun, J.: Deep residual learning for image recognition. In: CVPR 2016, pp. 770–778. IEEE (2016)

29. He, X., Zhang, Y.: Quantifying and mitigating privacy risks of contrastive learning. In: Kim, Y., Kim, J., Vigna, G., Shi, E. (eds.) CCS 2021, pp. 845–863. ACM (2021)
30. Hui, B., Yang, Y., Yuan, H., Burlina, P., Gong, N.Z., Cao, Y.: Practical blind membership inference attack via differential comparisons. In: NDSS 2021, The Internet Society (2021)
31. Hunsberger, E., Eliasmith, C.: Spiking deep networks with LIF neurons. CoRR (2015)
32. Izhikevich, E.M.: Simple model of spiking neurons. IEEE Trans. Neural Networks **14**(6), 1569–1572 (2003)
33. Jia, J., Salem, A., Backes, M., Zhang, Y., Gong, N.Z.: MemGuard: defending against black-box membership inference attacks via adversarial examples. In: CCS 2019, pp. 259–274. ACM (2019)
34. Kong, F., et al.: An efficient membership inference attack for the diffusion model by proximal initialization. CoRR (2023)
35. Krizhevsky, A., Hinton, G., et al.: Learning multiple layers of features from tiny images (2009)
36. Krizhevsky, A., Sutskever, I., Hinton, G.E.: Imagenet classification with deep convolutional neural networks. NeurIPS **2012**, 25 (2012)
37. Lecun, Y., Bottou, L., Bengio, Y., Haffner, P.: Gradient-based learning applied to document recognition. Proc. IEEE **86**(11), 2278–2324 (1998)
38. LeCun, Y., Bengio, Y., Hinton, G.: Deep learning. Nature **521**(7553), 436–444 (2015)
39. Lee, J.H., Delbruck, T., Pfeiffer, M.: Training deep spiking neural networks using backpropagation. Front. Neurosci. **10** (2016)
40. Lei, F., Yang, X., Liu, J., Dou, R., Wu, N.: Dt-scnn: dual-threshold spiking convolutional neural network with fewer operations and memory access for edge applications. Front. Comput. Neurosci. **18**, 1418115 (2024)
41. Li, H., Liu, H., Ji, X., Li, G., Shi, L.: Cifar10-dvs: an event-stream dataset for object classification. Front. Neurosci. **11**, 309 (2017)
42. Li, Y., Kim, Y., Park, H., Geller, T., Panda, P.: Neuromorphic data augmentation for training spiking neural networks. In: ECCV 2022, pp. 631–649. Springer-Verlag (2022)
43. Li, Z., Zhang, Y.: Membership leakage in label-only exposures. In: CCS 2021, pp. 880–895. ACM (2021)
44. Liang, L., et al.: Exploring adversarial attack in spiking neural networks with spike-compatible gradient. IEEE Trans. Neural Netw. Learn. Syst. **34**(5), 2569–2583 (2021)
45. Liu, H., Jia, J., Qu, W., Gong, N.Z.: Encodermi: membership inference against pre-trained encoders in contrastive learning. In: CCS 2021, pp. 2081–2095. ACM (2021)
46. Long, Y., et al.: A pragmatic approach to membership inferences on machine learning models. In: EuroS&P 2020, pp. 521–534. IEEE (2020)
47. Lotfi Rezaabad, A., Vishwanath, S.: Long short-term memory spiking networks and their applications. In: ICONS 2020, pp. 1–9. ACM (2020)
48. Lu, S., Sengupta, A.: Deep unsupervised learning using spike-timing-dependent plasticity. Neuromorphic Comput. Eng. **4**(2), 024004 (2024)
49. Nasr, M., Shokri, R., Houmansadr, A.: Machine learning with membership privacy using adversarial regularization. In: CCS 2018, pp. 634–646. ACM (2018)
50. Neftci, E.O., Mostafa, H., Zenke, F.: Surrogate gradient learning in spiking neural networks: bringing the power of gradient-based optimization to spiking neural networks. IEEE Signal Process. Mag. **36**(6), 51–63 (2019)

51. Nomura, O., Sakemi, Y., Hosomi, T., Morie, T.: Robustness of spiking neural networks based on time-to-first-spike encoding against adversarial attacks. IEEE Trans. Circuits Syst. II Express Briefs **69**(9), 3640–3644 (2022)
52. Orchard, G., Jayawant, A., Cohen, G.K., Thakor, N.: Converting static image datasets to spiking neuromorphic datasets using saccades. Front. Neurosci. **9**, 437 (2015)
53. Pfeiffer, M., Pfeil, T.: Deep learning with spiking neurons: opportunities and challenges. Front. Neurosci. **12**, 409662 (2018)
54. Połap, D., Woźniak, M., Hołubowski, W., Damaševičius, R.: A heuristic approach to the hyperparameters in training spiking neural networks using spike-timing-dependent plasticity. Neural Comput. Appl. **34**(16), 13187–13200 (2022)
55. Rueckauer, B., Lungu, I.A., Hu, Y., Pfeiffer, M.: Theory and tools for the conversion of analog to spiking convolutional neural networks. CoRR (2016)
56. Rueckauer, B., Lungu, I.A., Hu, Y., Pfeiffer, M., Liu, S.C.: Conversion of continuous-valued deep networks to efficient event-driven networks for image classification. Front. Neurosci. **11**, 294078 (2017)
57. Salem, A., Zhang, Y., Humbert, M., Berrang, P., Fritz, M., Backes, M.: ML-leaks: model and data independent membership inference attacks and defenses on machine learning models. In: NDSS 2019, The Internet Society (2019)
58. Sengupta, A., Ye, Y., Wang, R., Liu, C., Roy, K.: Going deeper in spiking neural networks: vgg and residual architectures. Front. Neurosci. **13** (2019)
59. Sharmin, S., Panda, P., Sarwar, S.S., Lee, C., Ponghiran, W., Roy, K.: A comprehensive analysis on adversarial robustness of spiking neural networks. In: IJCNN 2019, pp. 1–8. IEEE (2019)
60. Shokri, R., Stronati, M., Song, C., Shmatikov, V.: Membership inference attacks against machine learning models. In: S&P 2017, pp. 3–18. IEEE (2017)
61. Simonyan, K., Zisserman, A.: Very deep convolutional networks for large-scale image recognition. CoRR (2014)
62. Song, L., Mittal, P.: Systematic evaluation of privacy risks of machine learning models. In: USENIX Security 2021, pp. 2615–2632. USENIX Association (2021)
63. Taigman, Y., Yang, M., Ranzato, M., Wolf, L.: Deepface: closing the gap to human-level performance in face verification. In: CVPR 2014, pp. 1701–1708. IEEE (2014)
64. TEAM, I.G.P.: EU General Data Protection Regulation (GDPR): An Implementation and Compliance Guide - Second edition. IT Governance Publishing, 2 edn. (2017)
65. Turkson, R.E., Qu, H., Mawuli, C.B., Eghan, M.J.: Classification of alzheimer's disease using deep convolutional spiking neural network. Neural Process. Lett. **53**(4), 2649–2663 (2021)
66. Wang, H., Li, Y.F., Gryllias, K.: Brain-inspired spiking neural networks for industrial fault diagnosis: a survey, challenges, and opportunities. CoRR (2023)
67. Wu, Y., Deng, L., Li, G., Zhu, J., Shi, L.: Spatio-temporal backpropagation for training high-performance spiking neural networks. Front. Neurosci. **12** (2018)
68. Xiaoxue, L., et al.: Review of medical data analysis based on spiking neural networks. Procedia Comput. Sci. **221**, 1527–1538 (2023)
69. Yaghini, M., Kulynych, B., Cherubin, G., Troncoso, C.: Disparate vulnerability: on the unfairness of privacy attacks against machine learning. In: PETS, pp. 460–480 (2022)
70. Ye, J., Maddi, A., Murakonda, S.K., Bindschaedler, V., Shokri, R.: Enhanced membership inference attacks against machine learning models. In: CCS 2022, p. 3093–3106. ACM (2022)

71. Yeom, S., Giacomelli, I., Fredrikson, M., Jha, S.: Privacy risk in machine learning: analyzing the connection to overfitting. In: CSF 2018, pp. 268–282. IEEE (2018)
72. Yun, S., Han, D., Oh, S.J., Chun, S., Choe, J., Yoo, Y.: Cutmix: regularization strategy to train strong classifiers with localizable features. In: CVPR 2019, pp. 6023–6032. IEEE (2019)
73. Zheng, H., Wu, Y., Deng, L., Hu, Y., Li, G.: Going deeper with directly-trained larger spiking neural networks. In: AAAI 2021, vol. 35, pp. 11062–11070 (2021)
74. Zou, Z., Chen, K., Shi, Z., Guo, Y., Ye, J.: Object detection in 20 years: a survey. Proc. IEEE **111**(3), 257–276 (2023)

DUMB and DUMBer: Is Adversarial Training Worth It in the Real World?

Francesco Marchiori[1]("✉") , Marco Alecci[2] , Luca Pajola[3] , and Mauro Conti[1,3,4]

[1] University of Padova, Padova, Italy
francesco.marchiori@math.unipd.it, mauro.conti@unipd.it
[2] University of Luxembourg, Luxembourg, Luxembourg
marco.alecci@uni.lu
[3] Spritz Matter Srl, Padova, Italy
luca.pajola@spritzmatter.com
[4] Örebro University, Örebro, Sweden

Abstract. Adversarial examples are small and often imperceptible perturbations crafted to fool machine learning models. These attacks seriously threaten the reliability of deep neural networks, especially in security-sensitive domains. Evasion attacks, a form of adversarial attack where input is modified at test time to cause misclassification, are particularly insidious due to their transferability: adversarial examples crafted against one model often fool other models as well. This property, known as adversarial transferability, complicates defense strategies since it enables black-box attacks to succeed without direct access to the victim model. While adversarial training is one of the most widely adopted defense mechanisms, its effectiveness is typically evaluated on a narrow and homogeneous population of models. This limitation hinders the generalizability of empirical findings and restricts practical adoption.

In this work, we introduce **DUMBer**, an attack framework built on the foundation of the DUMB (Dataset soUrces, Model architecture, and Balance) methodology, to systematically evaluate the resilience of adversarially trained models. Our testbed spans multiple adversarial training techniques evaluated across three diverse computer vision tasks, using a heterogeneous population of uniquely trained models to reflect real-world deployment variability. Our experimental pipeline comprises over 130k evaluations spanning 13 state-of-the-art attack algorithms, allowing us to capture nuanced behaviors of adversarial training under varying threat models and dataset conditions. Our findings offer practical, actionable insights for AI practitioners, identifying which defenses are most effective based on the model, dataset, and attacker setup.

Keywords: Adversarial Attacks · Adversarial Training · Transferability

1 Introduction

Deep Neural Networks (DNNs) have achieved remarkable performance across a wide range of tasks, particularly in computer vision, natural language processing, and autonomous systems. However, these models are known to be highly vulnerable to adversarial examples, i.e., carefully crafted inputs that cause the model to make incorrect predictions while appearing benign to human observers. First identified in the context of image classification [10], adversarial attacks have since evolved into a rich area of research, encompassing various modalities and attack scenarios. One prominent class of these threats is *evasion attacks*, where the attacker modifies inputs at test time to evade detection or mislead the model. Real-world manifestations of such attacks have been observed in malware detection systems [17], facial recognition spoofing [21], and autonomous driving [8], raising significant concerns about the safety and reliability of AI systems deployed in adversarial environments.

A particularly troubling property of adversarial examples is their *transferability*: adversarial inputs crafted for one model often succeed in misleading other models, even if they differ in architecture, training data, or optimization details [6,25]. This phenomenon enables gray-box and black-box attacks, where the attacker has limited or no access to the target model's internals yet can still craft effective attacks using surrogate models. As a result, transferability significantly undermines the security of models in deployed settings. The DUMB framework [1] was recently proposed to study how adversarial transferability varies as a function of three key dimensions: Dataset soUrces, Model architectures, and the Balance of class distributions. It provided a standardized way to evaluate how generalizable adversarial examples are across different training conditions, laying the foundation for more robust empirical evaluations of adversarial threats.

One widely studied defense mechanism against adversarial attacks is *adversarial training*, where the model is trained on adversarial examples in addition to clean data [3,18]. This technique aims to increase the model's robustness by explicitly teaching it to resist known types of perturbations. While adversarial training has shown promise, especially in white-box settings, its effectiveness often comes with trade-offs: it can lead to significant reductions in accuracy on clean (non-adversarial) inputs [24], increase training time, and sometimes fail to generalize beyond the specific attack types used during training. Various improved techniques have been proposed [26,28], each attempting to balance robustness and standard accuracy. However, while the individual performance of adversarially trained models has been extensively evaluated, the impact of adversarial transferability on these defenses remains underexplored. Given the high computational demands of adversarial training and the practical challenges of deploying robust models in real-world settings, particularly under the threat of adversarial transferability, we are prompted to ask: *is adversarial training truly effective in real-world scenarios?* And if so, *which strategies offer the most resilience across diverse attack conditions?* This work seeks to answer these questions by systematically evaluating various adversarial training techniques under controlled yet transferable attack settings.

Contribution. This work presents **DUMBer**, an extension of the DUMB framework that evaluates the impact of adversarial training on transferability across models, datasets, and class balance conditions. While DUMB analyzed the robustness of models to transferred evasion attacks in standard training settings, DUMBer investigates whether and how commonly used adversarial training techniques improve resilience under the same conditions. We focus on the interaction between adversarial training and transferability, providing a systematic evaluation across a broad spectrum of configurations. Our aim is to address a key limitation in the literature: adversarial training techniques are often evaluated on a narrow and homogeneous set of models, which is quite limiting given the empirical nature of these defenses. In contrast, we adopt a "**DUMB population**" where every model is unique, better capturing the variability encountered in real-world deployments. Our contributions can be summarized as follows.

- We propose **DUMBer**, an attacker model and framework that extends DUMB by incorporating adversarial training into the evaluation of adversarial transferability. Across three axes (**D**ataset so**U**rces, **M**odel architectures, and class **B**alance), our testbed evaluates the **e**vasion **r**esilience of adversarially trained models.
- We present a comprehensive empirical analysis across three computer vision tasks, 13 distinct attack types, and 10 training strategies. Our "**DUMB population**" comprises 240 uniquely trained models spanning diverse datasets and architectures, resulting in over 130,000 individual evaluations.
- Our analysis provides novel insights and best practices on how to apply adversarial training to maximize model robustness under realistic attack scenarios involving transferability.
- We release the full codebase and evaluation scripts to promote reproducibility: https://github.com/spritz-group/DUMBer.

Research Questions. The extensive cross-parameter evaluations conducted in this study enable us to address unique research questions that are highly valuable to AI practitioners and future research efforts.

RQ1: Which adversarial attacks are most effective across the entire DUMB population? In other words, what attack strategies perform best regardless of the adversary's level of knowledge or access?

RQ2: Which adversarial training strategies offer the highest overall robustness? What defense techniques are most effective across the diverse scenarios represented in the DUMB population, irrespective of the attacker's assumptions?

RQ3: How do different training strategies perform across varying evaluation scenarios C? In other words, what are the best- and worst-case conditions for deploying each defense strategy in practice?

RQ4: Do robust defenses against strong attacks generalize to weaker ones? Can adversarial training improve resilience uniformly across a spectrum of attack strengths, or is its benefit limited to specific threat levels?

RQ5: When and where does adversarial training fail? Specifically, how frequently does it result in a negative AMR, and are these failures uniformly distributed across scenarios C?

2 Related Works

We now review the state-of-the-art in adversarial training and transfearbility.

Adversarial Transferability. Adversarial examples are designed to deceive machine learning models and often transfer across different models, enabling black- and gray-box attacks through surrogate models. Recent work has investigated the factors behind adversarial transferability. Gu et al. [13] provide a comprehensive survey, categorizing methods to enhance transferability and outlining core principles and challenges. They stress the need for robust evaluation frameworks covering diverse architectures and tasks. Building on this, Yu et al. [27] show that transferability is often overestimated when evaluations are limited to similar architectures, such as CNNs, and call for broader benchmarks across different neural networks. These findings motivate the need for frameworks like DUMB and DUMBer, which systematically assess adversarial transferability across dimensions like dataset source, model architecture, and class balance.

Adversarial Training. Adversarial training is a leading defense strategy that incorporates adversarial examples into the training process to improve model robustness. Early approaches include FGSM-based training [10], which uses the Fast Gradient Sign Method, and PGD-based training [18], which applies iterative Projected Gradient Descent for stronger perturbations. Both aim to defend against both seen and unseen attacks. Curriculum adversarial training [4] extends these ideas by gradually increasing perturbation strength (ϵ) during training, promoting more stable robustness. Ensemble adversarial training [23] further diversifies defenses by introducing adversarial examples from multiple pre-trained models, improving resilience against transfer attacks. With DUMBer, we evaluate these techniques and their variants, also considering model-agnostic perturbations, to systematically measure their impact on robustness across diverse and transferable adversarial scenarios.

3 Threat Model

The original DUMB attacker model emphasizes the importance of simulating realistic conditions for adversarial transferability—conditions often neglected in the current literature [12]. Building on these foundations, our DUMBer framework explicitly addresses three critical challenges that arise during attack execution in practical settings:

- *Dataset:* Most prior works assume that both the attacker and victim have access to the same dataset, which is rarely the case in real-world scenarios. Constructing a surrogate dataset is far from trivial, as it depends heavily on corpus generation strategies that can vary significantly across domains and institutions. For example, in hate speech detection, it has been shown that existing datasets are constructed using divergent methodologies, leading to models that perform well on their training data but generalize poorly to others [11]. This undermines the assumption that transferability is guaranteed simply by using adversarial examples.
- *Ground-truth distribution:* A related yet distinct issue concerns the assumption that attacker and victim datasets share the same underlying distribution. In practice, this is rarely true. Differences may stem from distinct data collection processes or disparate preprocessing and augmentation techniques. This mismatch becomes even more pronounced in imbalanced tasks, where techniques such as SMOTE [5] or GAN-based oversampling [9] are often employed to rebalance class distributions, further distorting the comparability of training data across parties.
- *Model architecture:* Attackers and victims typically do not rely on identical models. While prior work sometimes evaluates transferability across model families, the space of potential architectures is vast, ranging from standard CNNs to more sophisticated and customized models. For instance, in computer vision alone, one might choose among VGG variants (e.g., VGG16, VGG19) or ResNet families (e.g., ResNet18, ResNet50), each of which may respond differently to adversarial perturbations. This diversity introduces an additional layer of unpredictability in the effectiveness of transfer-based attacks.

In Table 1, we summarize eight representative attack scenarios, each capturing a possible mismatch between the attacker's surrogate model and the victim's target model. In realistic settings, the attacker typically does not know which scenario they are operating in, except in the idealized white-box case.

Beyond these structural mismatches, an additional layer of complexity arises from the widespread adoption of adversarial training techniques. Deployed models, especially those exposed to end-users, are often hardened through such defenses to enhance robustness and safety alignment. As a result, attackers must overcome transferability challenges and contend with models explicitly trained to resist adversarial inputs. The objective of DUMBer is to systematically evaluate how these real-world conditions, ranging from mismatched assumptions to adversarial training, impact the effectiveness of transfer-based attacks.

4 Methodology

Next, we present our methodology, which is built on the foundation of the DUMB framework. While our evaluation covers the eight cases from Sect. 3, our main focus is a systematic study of how adversarial training affects these scenarios. Section 4.1 defines the dimensions of transferability, Sect. 4.2 overviews the

Table 1. Conditions for each case in the DUMB attacker model. Scenarios for each C are included in [1]. Subscripts a and v denote attacker and victim, respectively.

Case	DU_a vs DU_v	M_a vs M_v	B_a vs B_v
C1	●	●	●
C2	●	●	○
C3	●	○	●
C4	●	○	○
C5	○	●	●
C6	○	●	○
C7	○	○	●
C8	○	○	○

● = match, ○ = mismatch.
C1 = pure white-box, C8 = pure black-box

attacks, Sect. 4.3 describes training dimensions, and Sect. 4.4 explains our unified testing framework.[1] An overview of the training process is shown in Fig. 1.

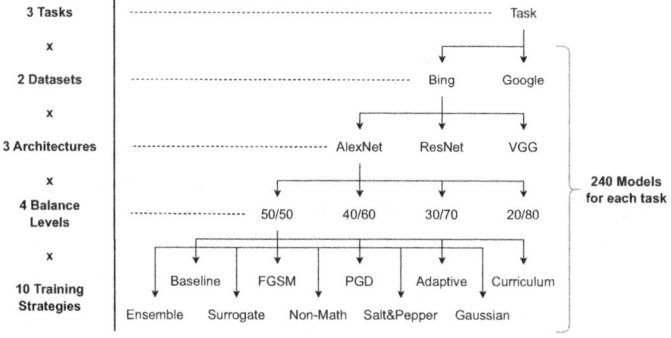

Fig. 1. Model combinations during the training phase.

4.1 Transferability Dimensions

This work focuses on three distinct computer vision tasks, each representing common settings found in adversarial attack literature. These tasks are framed as binary classification problems: distinguishing between Bikes vs. Motorbikes (B&M), Cats vs. Dogs (C&D), and Men vs. Women (M&W). For each task, we systematically vary the dimensions that influence adversarial transferability.

---

[1] Underlined terms highlight key dimensions impacting the DUMB population or evaluation setup.

Dataset Source. To meet the specific needs of our testbed, we manually collect and validate two distinct datasets for each task from Bing and Google, ensuring control over complexity and potential biases. Starting with an average of 14,264 images per dataset, we remove duplicates using difPy, perform manual inspections to eliminate mislabeled or low-quality samples, and randomly select 10,000 balanced images per dataset. All images are then resized to 300×300 RGB using anti-aliasing to maintain quality.

Model Architecture. We employ three widely-used and well-established computer vision architectures: AlexNet [15], ResNet18 [14], and VGG11 [22]. We fine-tune these models across our experimental tasks, building on architectures also explored in the DUMB framework. Training procedures align with the official PyTorch guidelines to ensure reproducibility.

Ground Truth Balancing. To assess the impact of class imbalance between attacker and defender, we simulate four levels of imbalance in the training sets: balanced (50/50), weak (40/60), medium (30/70), and strong (20/80), always treating the first class (Cats, Men, Bikes) as the minority across all tasks. The minority class is undersampled accordingly while keeping the majority class fixed (e.g., for strong imbalance in the Cats vs. Dogs task, 875 Cats vs. 3500 Dogs). This procedure affects only the training sets; validation and test sets remain balanced.

4.2 Attacks

We incorporate two broad categories of adversarial attacks, mathematical and non-mathematical, for a total of 13 distinct attacks across different threat models.

Mathematical Attacks. Mathematical attacks are model-aware and generated through optimization methods that leverage gradient information. Our evaluation includes widely used attacks such as FGSM [10], BIM [16], PGD [18], RFGSM [23], DeepFool [20], TIFGSM [7], and Square [2], all implemented via the Torchattacks Python library. These attacks differ in complexity and transferability, offering a robust basis to test model vulnerability under white-box and black-box scenarios. It is important to note that mathematical attacks are generated at the "balance level" described in Fig. 1, without incorporating any adversarial training on the source model used for attack generation.

Non-mathematical Attacks. On the other hand, non-mathematical attacks rely on simple image transformations independent of any model, making them practical in real-world settings. Using only basic image processing via PIL, we simulate attacks like Gaussian noise, grayscale conversion, box blur, salt-and-pepper noise, random occlusion (black box), and color inversion.

Though simpler, these attacks pose realistic threats to vision models and highlight the relevance of evaluating robustness beyond optimization-based techniques.

Parameter Tuning. Each attack, whether mathematical or not, has at least one parameter controlling its strength (e.g., ϵ for mathematical attacks, radius or noise level for others). We tune these parameters to maximize attack success while preserving visual similarity, enforcing a minimum Structural Similarity Index Measure (SSIM) of 0.4 to prevent excessive distortion. For testing, we select optimal parameters to evaluate model robustness under pure evasion. For validation, we generate adversarial examples across multiple parameter values to support adversarial training, ensuring no information leakage between training and testing.

4.3 Training Strategies

We begin by training a baseline model on unperturbed data, reflecting nominal conditions without adversarial influence. This is a control scenario to assess the degradation caused by adversarial attacks. Subsequently, we investigate nine adversarial training strategies designed to enhance robustness against evasion attacks. All adversarial training experiments are conducted from scratch rather than fine-tuning a nominally trained model. This choice avoids compromising between adversarial and nominal performance—an issue commonly encountered in fine-tuning approaches. For each adversarial training strategy, we construct a training dataset composed of 80% original (clean) samples and 20% adversarial samples. These adversarial examples are drawn from the validation set, following the generation procedure described in Sect. 4.2. While this general setup holds for all strategies, specific implementations may vary based on the training logic. We define and adapt the following training strategies to facilitate integration within our framework.

- <u>FGSM:</u> Includes validation-time adversarial samples generated using FGSM at a fixed $\epsilon = 0.2$, selected to balance perturbation visibility and attack strength [10].
- <u>PGD:</u> Mirrors the FGSM setup but employs PGD as the attack method, also with $\epsilon = 0.2$ [18].
- <u>Ensemble:</u> Incorporates adversarial examples from both FGSM and PGD attacks, aiming to increase robustness through attack diversity [23].
- <u>Surrogate:</u> Similar to Ensemble, but uses adversarial examples generated by different model architectures (trained under the same DUMB configuration) to simulate transferability-based threats.
- <u>Curriculum:</u> Progressively increases ϵ over training epochs while generating FGSM attacks offline [4]. This method introduces gradually harder adversarial examples during training.
- <u>Adaptive:</u> Also increases ϵ over time but generates adversarial examples online during training [19]. This approach adapts to the model's current weaknesses, simulating evolving attack sophistication.

- <u>Non-Mathematical Mixture:</u> Employs all non-mathematical attacks at fixed perturbation strengths, ensuring diversity without reliance on model gradients.
- <u>Gaussian:</u> Uses only Gaussian noise as the adversarial perturbation in the 20% adversarial portion of the training set.
- <u>Salt-and-Pepper:</u> Uses only salt-and-pepper noise to generate adversarial examples for training, enabling focused analysis of noise-based robustness.

4.4 Testing

Designing the evaluation framework presents unique challenges, as the complexity of adversarial attack generation is not aligned with the training process of the selected target model, unlike the original DUMB framework, where these components are tightly coupled.

Mathematical Attacks. Gradient-based adversarial attacks must be crafted using dedicated models, referred to as *source models* M_{src}. Our transferability dimensions determine the number of these models: for each task, we consider 2 dataset sources, 3 model architectures, and 4 data balance levels, resulting in $2 \times 3 \times 4 = 24$ source models per task. Each of the 7 mathematical attacks is then evaluated against a broader set of *target models* M_{trg}, which includes the full combination space shown in Fig. 1, amounting to 240 unique configurations. Consequently, the total number of mathematical attack evaluations amounts to: 3 tasks $\times$ 7 attacks $\times$ 24 M_{src} $\times$ 240 $M_{trg} = 120{,}960$, where 240 M_{trg} correspond to 2 dataset sources $\times$ 3 model architectures $\times$ 4 data balance levels $\times$ 10 training strategies.

Non-mathematical Attacks. Model-agnostic image perturbations, such as those not relying on gradients, do not require dedicated M_{src} and can be applied directly to the input data. Nonetheless, the dataset source remains relevant, as the images differ between the Bing and Google datasets. As a result, the total number of evaluations for non-mathematical attacks is: 3 tasks $\times$ 6 attacks $\times$ 2 datasets $\times$ 240 $M_{trg} = 8{,}640$.

5 Results

In this section, we present the results of our evaluation framework and the effect that adversarial training strategies have on the different transferability cases. We first define the metrics for our evaluation in Sect. 5.1, followed by a baseline evaluation of our trained models in Sect. 5.2. We then answer the research questions detailed in Sect. 1.

5.1 Metrics

From a machine learning standpoint, each of our tasks is formulated as a binary classification problem, where the model learns to distinguish between two distinct classes based on the input images. Since label balancing plays a central role in our analysis, we adopt the F1 score as the primary evaluation metric to assess the classification performance of the models. The F1 score provides a balanced measure of precision and recall, making it particularly suitable for evaluating performance in scenarios where class distribution may vary. This score is defined as follows.

$$F1 = 2\frac{precision \cdot recall}{precision + recall}. \tag{1}$$

To assess both the impact of adversarial attacks and the robustness of adversarially trained models, we introduce two additional evaluation metrics: Attack Success Rate (ASR) and Attack Mitigation Rate (AMR). ASR, also used in the original DUMB framework, measures the proportion of samples classified initially correctly by a model under clean conditions but misclassified after applying the attack. This quantifies the effectiveness of the attack in degrading model performance. To enable a more fine-grained assessment, we also introduce a metric called *severity*, assigning each attack attempt to one of five levels that evenly partition the ASR range from 0% to 100%. This distinction captures attacks ranging from minimal impact (severity score 1) to significant degradation (severity score 5). AMR, instead, is the difference between the ASR before and after adversarial training, normalized by the ASR before training. Specifically, AMR is calculated as:

$$AMR = \frac{ASR_{original} - ASR_{adv}}{ASR_{original}}, \tag{2}$$

where the subscript "original" refers to the ASR measured on the baseline model, and "adv" refers to the ASR of the adversarially trained model. This metric quantifies the attack's success rate reduction following adversarial training. A higher AMR indicates that a specific training strategy has more effectively mitigated the attack's impact, improving the model's robustness. It is important to note that AMR is upper-bounded at 100% (indicating that all attacks were mitigated successfully), but it is theoretically not lower-bounded. This is because adversarial training could also deteriorate the model's performance in nominal and adversarial scenarios, resulting in a negative or zero value for AMR. To maintain interpretability, we cap AMR values at -100%, acknowledging that stronger degradations are possible, though they often occur when the original ASR was already low. We thus define $+100\%$ as perfect improvement and -100% as complete degradation.

5.2 Baseline Evaluation

Before assessing the impact of evasion attacks, it is crucial to ensure that our models perform reliably under standard, unperturbed conditions. Table 2 presents the F1 scores across all models and training strategies on the nominal dataset. As we adopt the same tasks defined in the original DUMB framework, we observe a consistent trend in the baseline evaluation, where B&M emerges as the most straightforward task, while M&W proves to be the most challenging. Overall, adversarial training does not significantly degrade performance on clean data. Most strategies maintain parity with the baseline and, in some cases, even improve it. Notably, Gaussian noise and Adaptive training slightly enhance model performance, suggesting a potential regularization effect that helps generalization. The only approach that noticeably reduces performance is the Ensemble method, which shows an average drop of 4.26% compared to the baseline. This may be due to the added complexity of combining multiple decision boundaries, which could reduce precision in non-adversarial contexts.

Table 2. Model performance (F1 score) across different training strategies. Results are averaged on the dataset source and ground-truth balance dimensions.

Task	Model	Base	FGSM	PGD	Ens.	Sur.	Cur.	Ada.	N.M.	Gau.	S.&P.
B&M	AlexNet	0.976	0.978	0.979	0.892	0.979	0.978	0.978	0.979	0.980	0.977
	ResNet	0.986	0.987	0.986	0.987	0.988	0.987	0.985	0.987	0.987	0.988
	VGG	0.985	0.985	0.986	0.987	0.988	0.986	0.985	0.987	0.985	0.986
C&D	AlexNet	0.953	0.948	0.949	0.933	0.947	0.952	0.953	0.951	0.950	0.948
	ResNet	0.978	0.978	0.979	0.938	0.978	0.978	0.978	0.978	0.979	0.978
	VGG	0.982	0.981	0.982	0.939	0.981	0.981	0.982	0.980	0.982	0.981
M&W	AlexNet	0.858	0.862	0.861	0.825	0.857	0.856	0.868	0.864	0.865	0.859
	ResNet	0.921	0.921	0.922	0.871	0.917	0.925	0.920	0.920	0.922	0.922
	VGG	0.925	0.925	0.925	0.831	0.923	0.925	0.925	0.920	0.925	0.921
Avg. Change w.r.t Base			+0.02%	+0.06%	-4.26%	-0.08%	+0.05%	+0.13%	+0.03%	+0.14%	-0.05%

Ens. = Ensemble, **Sur.** = Surrogate, **Cur.** = Curriculum, **Ada.** = Adaptive.
N.M. = Non-Math-Mix, **Gau.** = Gaussian noise, **S.&P.** = Salt-and-pepper noise.

5.3 Attack Overview

Before analyzing the performance of the DUMB population across its subgroups, we first evaluate the overall effectiveness of the attacks described in Sect. 4.2. An overview is presented in Fig. 2, where results are averaged across C scenarios and tasks to reflect general attack behavior under diverse, balanced conditions. A more detailed scenario-specific analysis was already provided in the original DUMB paper [1]. Figure 2 shows that TIFGSM is the most effective strategy in the average DUMB scenario. This is unsurprising given its design to enhance transferability, particularly benefiting "grayer" box settings. Conversely, attacks such as BIM, Square, and RFGSM predominantly fall into severity score 1, suggesting limited effectiveness in more generalized or transfer-based contexts. Non-mathematical attacks predictably show lower severity, although techniques like

RandomBlackBox and BoxBlur occasionally outperform mathematical attacks such as BIM and Square, especially when averaging across all attacker scenarios. Notably, within severity score 1, certain attacks display a large fraction of extremely low ASR cases: for example, BIM and RFGSM fall below a 5% ASR in 24% of evaluations, highlighting their limited transferability. A more detailed analysis on each task is shown in Appendix A.1.

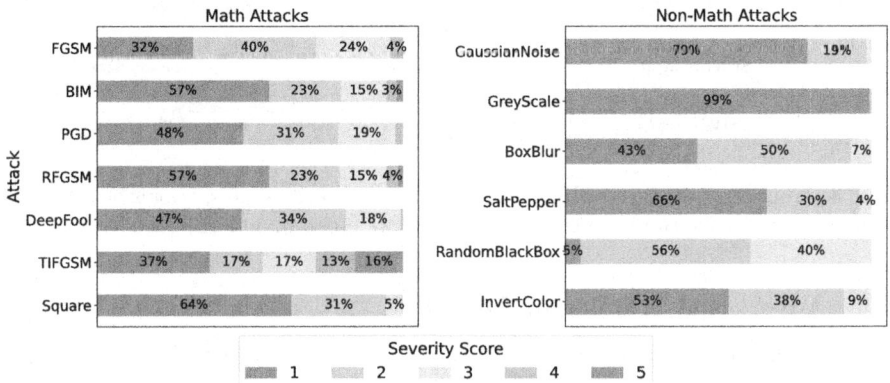

Fig. 2. Severity score distribution of each attack.

5.4 Adversarial Training Overview

Following the approach in Sect. 5.3, we now assess the AMR of each training strategy across the full DUMB population. The goal is to identify which method performs best when the defender has no knowledge of the attacker's capabilities. This evaluation considers each C scenario to reflect how a "naive" defender might deploy protection without tailored assumptions. Results are shown in Fig. 3. Severity 5 is missing for B&M, as no attacks reached that level. Severity 1 is excluded across all tasks, as such attacks have negligible ASR and would distort AMR interpretation by exaggerating insignificant changes. Our focus on higher severities aligns with the paper's aim to support resilience against impactful threats. *Adaptive* training stands out, achieving up to 96.69% AMR on B&M. *Curriculum* and *surrogate* also perform well, while non-mathematical approaches offer modest but more consistent improvements. Some negative AMR values appear, especially on the M&W task. This stems from the task's lower baseline F1 score (see Table 2), making it more sensitive to training disruptions. Still, since AMR remains strongly positive at higher severities, practitioners should weigh these occasional drops—often linked to low-impact attacks—against the broader gains in robustness.

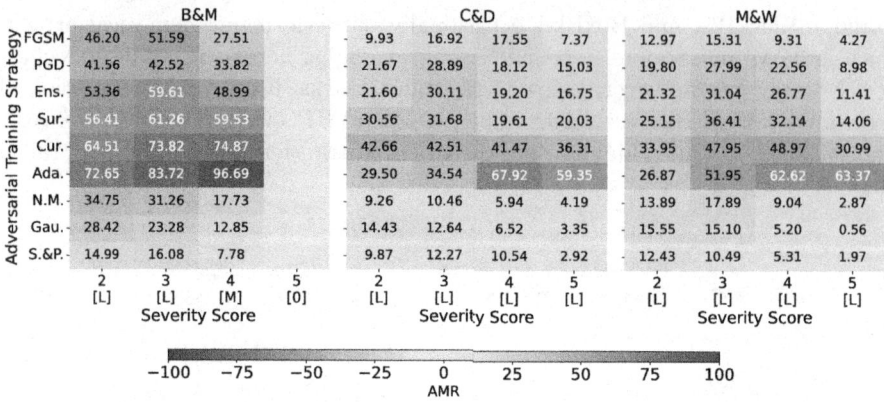

Fig. 3. Training strategies' AMR at different attack severity scores. Labels below scores indicate sample sizes for each cell: [S] (1–10), [M] (10–50), and [L] (50+).

5.5 Adversarial Training on DUMB

In Sects. 5.3 and 5.4, we provided general overviews of attacks and training strategies by averaging across all DUMB scenarios. We now focus on a scenario-specific analysis, examining how each strategy performs under different C settings. This detailed view is intended for practitioners familiar with their threat model and the critical attack scenarios they face, as discussed in the original DUMB paper. To ensure relevance, we limit our analysis to attacks with severity scores of 3 or higher. This filters out cases where negative AMR values reflect negligible performance changes and emphasizes scenarios where adversarial training meaningfully impacts robustness. These results are summarized in Fig. 4. We observe that adversarial training is most effective when the source and target models share the same architecture (e.g., C1, C2, C5, C8), likely due to higher ASR in those cases, as noted in the original DUMB study. Consistent with Sect. 5.4, *adaptive* training can yield negative AMR when model architectures differ, possibly due to lower initial ASR. A noteworthy trend in the M&W task is that AMR drops significantly when the dataset source differs, a pattern less evident in other tasks. This aligns with prior findings identifying M&W as particularly sensitive to dataset mismatch, resulting in larger ASR discrepancies. Finally, some task-scenario combinations are under-represented due to our severity ≥3 filter, especially where data is already sparse (e.g., C1-4-5-7 in B&M, C3-4-7-8 in C&D). As such, outliers like the *adaptive* C3 case in C&D should not be over-interpreted; broader evaluation is needed to confirm such trends.

5.6 Attacks vs. Adversarial Training

An ideal defense would maintain strong protection regardless of an attack's severity. However, adversarial training often involves trade-offs, where optimizing for one threat type can weaken resilience to others. To explore this, we analyze two representative training strategies across varying attacks: *adaptive*, a

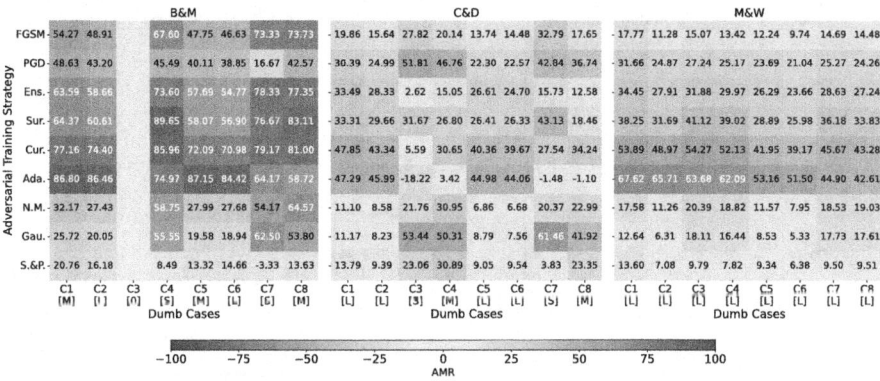

Fig. 4. Training strategies' AMR at different DUMB cases. Labels below scores indicate sample sizes for each cell: [S] (1–10), [M] (10–50), and [L] (50+).

strong defense particularly effective against high-severity attacks (Fig. 5), and *Non-Math*, a simpler, model-agnostic approach (Fig. 6). A detailed overview of the specific AMR values is provided in Appendix A.2. Examining their behavior across DUMB scenarios and attack severities reveals clear patterns. *Adaptive* training offers strong resilience against high-severity attacks, often achieving AMR values above 60% for severities 4 and 5. However, its performance drops against lower severities, where most negative AMR values occur. Conversely, *Non-Math* achieves more consistent but modest positive AMR across lower severities, though it struggles against stronger attacks. Neither method achieves uniform robustness: *adaptive* favors severe threats, while *Non-Math* provides broader but shallower protection. This highlights a key trade-off for practitioners: optimizing for strong attacks may expose vulnerabilities to weaker but more frequent perturbations.

5.7 Adversarial Training Failures

Understanding when adversarial training harms rather than helps is critical for practitioners considering its adoption. A negative AMR signals that the model has become more vulnerable to specific attacks than a baseline trained only on clean data. Our evaluation shows that adversarial training is not universally beneficial: 20.53% of all assessments resulted in a negative AMR, highlighting a notable risk of performance degradation. When failures occur, the average negative AMR is $-35.89\% \pm 34.06$, indicating that the loss in robustness can be substantial. As shown in Fig. 7, while most negative outcomes are moderate, practitioners must be aware of a long tail of severe degradations.

To better understand where adversarial training most often fails, we analyze the distribution of negative AMR across different experimental dimensions (Table 3). Failures are heavily concentrated in DUMB scenarios involving a significant mismatch between attacker and victim models (Table 3a). Notably, C4 and C8 (model and data mismatches) showed the highest rates of negative AMR,

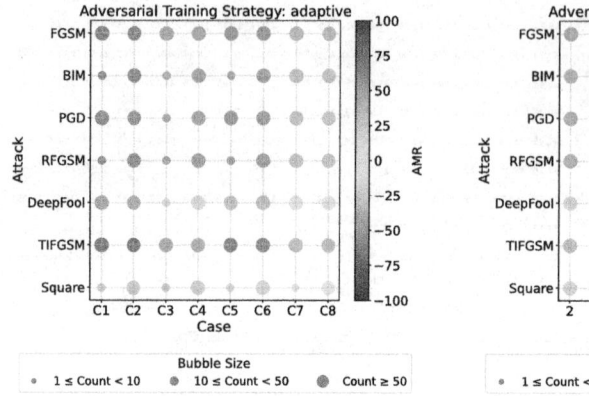
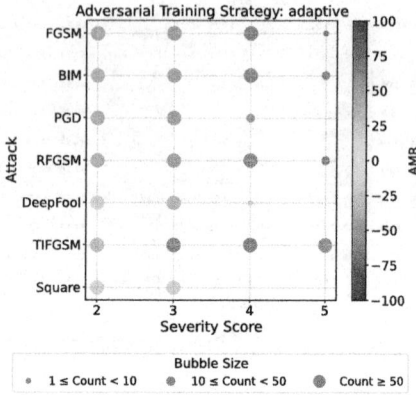

(a) DUMB cases analysis. (b) Attack severity score analysis.

Fig. 5. *Adaptive* training strategy AMR under different attacks.

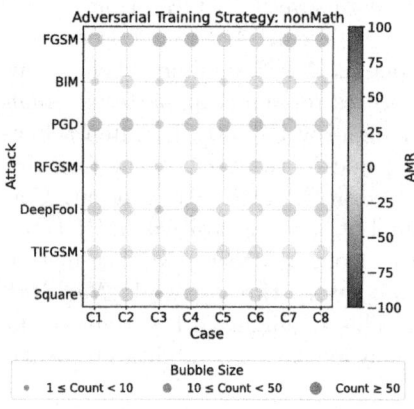

(a) DUMB cases analysis. (b) Attack severity score analysis.

Fig. 6. *Non-Math* training strategy AMR under different attacks.

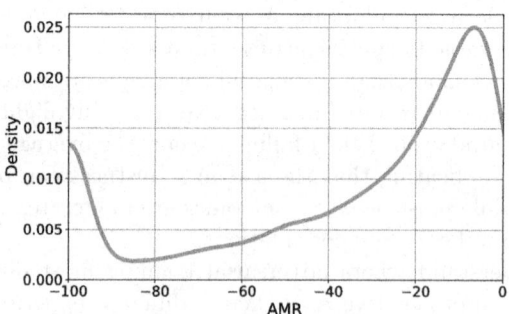

Fig. 7. Negative AMR distribution.

at 32.00% and 28.70%, respectively, while white-box settings (C1) exhibited minimal failure (1.61%). Different training strategies also varied in robustness (Table 3b): simple perturbation methods like *Salt & Pepper* and *FGSM* led to frequent but less severe degradations, while the *adaptive* strategy, despite strong overall performance, suffered the most severe failures when they did occur (-52.56% on average). Attack type also plays a key role (Table 3c): *DeepFool* and *Square* attacks triggered failures most frequently, with *DeepFool* causing the steepest average drop in robustness (-53.73%). Finally, failure rates were highly skewed toward weaker attacks (Table 3d), with 72.53% of negative AMR instances occurring against attacks initially classified as Severity 1; stronger attacks rarely caused adversarial training to backfire. These results highlight that adversarial training, while powerful in some settings, is highly sensitive to mismatches, training strategies, attack types, and the initial strength of adversarial perturbations.

Table 3. Values and distributions of negative AMR across experimental dimensions. "% Neg." indicates, for each dimension, the percentage of negative samples relative to the total number of negative samples across all dimensions., "Avg." shows the mean AMR values and standard deviation, "Med." indicates the median AMR.

(a) By DUMB case.

Case	% Neg.	Avg.	Med.
C1	1.61%	-35.45 ± 35.85	-20.00
C2	7.45%	-32.23 ± 36.34	-13.89
C3	10.84%	-44.12 ± 35.19	-33.33
C4	32.00%	-42.75 ± 35.18	-31.25
C5	2.17%	-32.88 ± 35.10	-15.79
C6	7.44%	-28.40 ± 33.32	-12.20
C7	9.79%	-29.97 ± 30.01	-18.18
C8	28.70%	-30.28 ± 30.87	-17.24

(b) By adversarial training strategy.

Train.	% Neg.	Avg.	Med.
FGSM	14.70%	-34.40 ± 33.41	-20.69
PGD	9.11%	-35.92 ± 31.74	-25.00
Ada.	12.61%	-52.56 ± 36.15	-45.83
Cur.	7.41%	-43.09 ± 34.35	-32.58
Ens.	10.01%	-42.70 ± 34.77	-31.40
Gau.	11.81%	-27.55 ± 31.87	-13.04
N.M.	12.23%	-30.43 ± 33.06	-15.29
S&P	14.01%	-21.80 ± 25.82	-11.54
Sur.	8.11%	-42.31 ± 34.69	-30.71

(c) By attack.

Attack	% Neg.	Avg.	Med.
BIM	13.19%	-30.23 ± 30.65	-17.24
DeepFool	24.30%	-53.73 ± 38.02	-47.37
FGSM	5.96%	-22.38 ± 24.88	-12.31
PGD	9.41%	-30.66 ± 29.86	-19.36
RFGSM	13.48%	-30.97 ± 31.39	-17.65
Square	22.39%	-40.41 ± 32.41	-30.36
TIFGSM	11.27%	-12.44 ± 16.69	-7.25

(d) By attack severity score.

Sev.	% Neg.	Avg.	Med.
1	72.53%	-43.13 ± 35.13	-30.77
2	19.77%	-21.30 ± 23.59	-12.05
3	4.77%	-5.87 ± 5.91	-4.00
4	1.50%	-4.93 ± 4.78	-3.29
5	1.43%	-2.72 ± 3.08	-1.29

6 Conclusions

This paper examined the effectiveness of various adversarial training strategies across the scenarios defined by the DUMB framework. Based on 130k evaluations across all folds of our updated and adapted attacker model, we provide the following answers to our research questions.

A1: Attack strategies designed for transferability (e.g., TIFGSM) pose a greater threat to the overall DUMB population, though non-mathematical, model-agnostic methods also demonstrate significant ASRs.

A2: When the threat model is unknown, strategies such as *adaptive* and *curriculum* generally yield the highest AMRs. However, adversarial training can slightly degrade performance on lower-impact attacks in sub-optimal tasks.

A3: Adversarial training proves most effective when the source and target models align. This also holds for mismatched datasets, but only when the original task is sub-optimal in baseline evaluation. Performance can degrade in scenarios with multiple mismatches, particularly when attacks have lower ASRs.

A4: The most effective adversarial training strategies generalize across different target attacks, though their success varies depending on the attacker's knowledge. However, specific attacks (e.g., *DeepFool* and *Square*) can negatively impact adversarially trained models, highlighting the need for focused attention on these cases.

A5: Adversarial training is less effective against lower severity attacks, indicating that it should be employed primarily when facing significantly impactful threats.

Future Works. Future research could develop advanced adversarial training strategies to overcome weaknesses against low-severity attacks. Exploring hybrid defenses that combine model-agnostic and transfer-optimized methods may further enhance robustness across diverse scenarios. This could also be extended by including parameter-free attacks, further increasing the study cases of this work. Expanding evaluations to broader threat models and real-world datasets would improve understanding of defense generalizability. For instance, shifting from binary to multi-class classification analysis could help in grounding this analysis in more security and safety-critical applications. Finally, a deeper study of the trade-offs between attack severity and training strategies could guide the design of defenses tailored to specific applications.

A Additional Results

We now provide more details on the results shown in Sect. A.

A.1 RQ1

While Sect. 5.3 provides a cross-task overview of attack severity scores, Fig. 8 breaks them down by individual task. As noted in the original DUMB paper, attacks tend to become more effective as tasks grow more challenging. Specifically, the more straightforward task (B&M) shows no high-severity mathematical attacks, whereas the most complex task (M&W) features many. A similar trend appears for non-mathematical attacks, although their overall ASR remains generally lower.

A.2 RQ4

In Fig. 9 and Fig. 10, we extend the analysis from Sect. 5.6 by including the exact AMR values for each case.

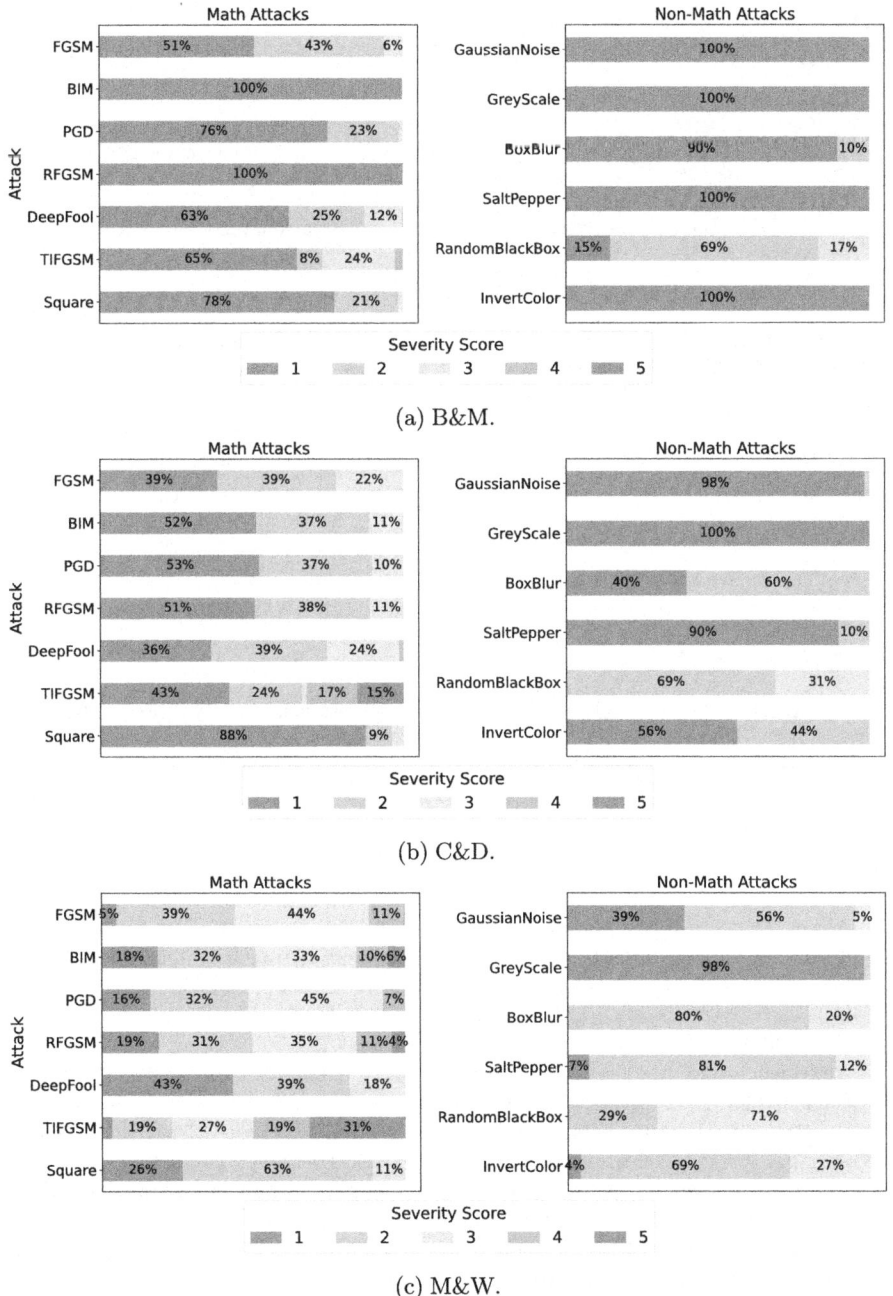

Fig. 8. Severity score distribution of each attack on each task.

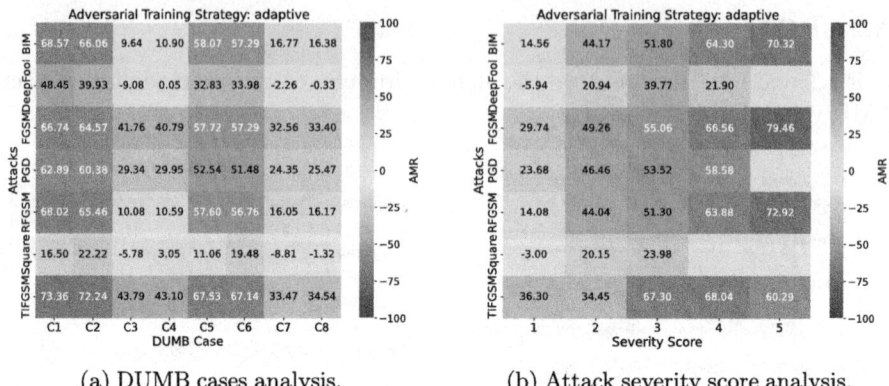

(a) DUMB cases analysis. (b) Attack severity score analysis.

Fig. 9. *Adaptive* training strategy AMR under different attacks.

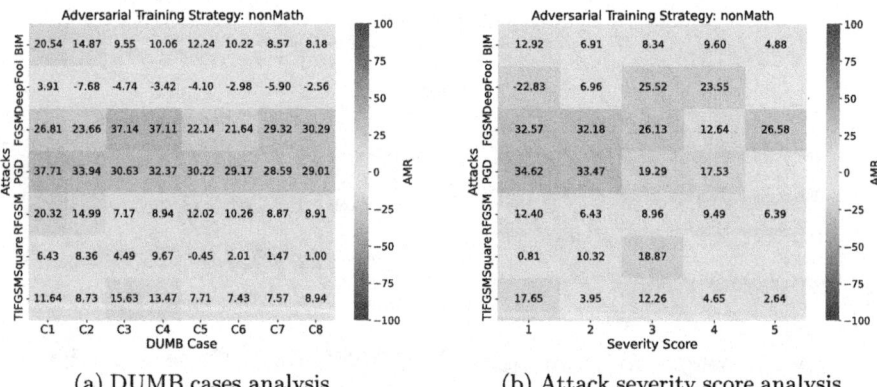

(a) DUMB cases analysis. (b) Attack severity score analysis.

Fig. 10. *Non-Math* training strategy AMR under different attacks.

References

1. Alecci, M., Conti, M., Marchiori, F., Martinelli, L., Pajola, L.: Your attack is too dumb: formalizing attacker scenarios for adversarial transferability. In: Proceedings of the 26th International Symposium on Research in Attacks, Intrusions and Defenses, RAID 2023, pp. 315–329. Association for Computing Machinery, New York (2023). https://doi.org/10.1145/3607199.3607227
2. Andriushchenko, M., Croce, F., Flammarion, N., Hein, M.: Square attack: a query-efficient black-box adversarial attack via random search. In: Vedaldi, A., Bischof, H., Brox, T., Frahm, J.-M. (eds.) ECCV 2020. LNCS, vol. 12368, pp. 484–501. Springer, Cham (2020). https://doi.org/10.1007/978-3-030-58592-1_29
3. Andriushchenko, M., Flammarion, N.: Understanding and improving fast adversarial training. Adv. Neural. Inf. Process. Syst. **33**, 16048–16059 (2020)
4. Cai, Q.Z., Du, M., Liu, C., Song, D.: Curriculum adversarial training. arXiv preprint arXiv:1805.04807 (2018)

5. Chawla, N.V., Bowyer, K.W., Hall, L.O., Kegelmeyer, W.P.: Smote: synthetic minority over-sampling technique. J. Artif. Intell. Res. **16**, 321–357 (2002)
6. Demontis, A., et al.: Why do adversarial attacks transfer? Explaining transferability of evasion and poisoning attacks. In: 28th USENIX Security Symposium (USENIX Security 2019), pp. 321–338 (2019)
7. Dong, Y., Pang, T., Su, H., Zhu, J.: Evading defenses to transferable adversarial examples by translation-invariant attacks. In: Proceedings of the IEEE/CVF Conference on Computer Vision and Pattern Recognition, pp. 4312–4321 (2019)
8. Eykholt, K., et al.: Robust physical-world attacks on deep learning visual classification. In: Proceedings of the IEEE Conference on Computer Vision and Pattern Recognition, pp. 1625–1634 (2018)
9. Frid-Adar, M., Klang, E., Amitai, M., Goldberger, J., Greenspan, H.: Synthetic data augmentation using GAN for improved liver lesion classification. In: 2018 IEEE 15th International Symposium on Biomedical Imaging (ISBI 2018), pp. 289–293. IEEE (2018)
10. Goodfellow, I.J., Shlens, J., Szegedy, C.: Explaining and harnessing adversarial examples. arXiv preprint arXiv:1412.6572 (2014)
11. Gröndahl, T., Pajola, L., Juuti, M., Conti, M., Asokan, N.: All you need is "love" evading hate speech detection. In: Proceedings of the 11th ACM Workshop on Artificial Intelligence and Security, pp. 2–12 (2018)
12. Grosse, K., Bieringer, L., Besold, T.R., Biggio, B., Krombholz, K.: Machine learning security in industry: a quantitative survey. IEEE Trans. Inf. Forensics Secur. **18**, 1749–1762 (2023)
13. Gu, J., et al.: A survey on transferability of adversarial examples across deep neural networks. arXiv preprint arXiv:2310.17526 (2023)
14. He, K., Zhang, X., Ren, S., Sun, J.: Deep residual learning for image recognition. In: Proceedings of the IEEE Conference on Computer Vision and Pattern Recognition, pp. 770–778 (2016)
15. Krizhevsky, A.: One weird trick for parallelizing convolutional neural networks. arXiv preprint arXiv:1404.5997 (2014)
16. Kurakin, A., Goodfellow, I.J., Bengio, S.: Adversarial examples in the physical world. In: Artificial Intelligence Safety and Security, pp. 99–112. Chapman and Hall/CRC (2018)
17. Ling, X., et al.: Adversarial attacks against windows PE malware detection: a survey of the state-of-the-art. Comput. Secur. **128**, 103134 (2023)
18. Madry, A., Makelov, A., Schmidt, L., Tsipras, D., Vladu, A.: Towards deep learning models resistant to adversarial attacks. arXiv preprint arXiv:1706.06083 (2017)
19. Marchiori, F., Conti, M.: Canederli: on the impact of adversarial training and transferability on can intrusion detection systems. In: Proceedings of the 2024 ACM Workshop on Wireless Security and Machine Learning, pp. 8–13 (2024)
20. Moosavi-Dezfooli, S.M., Fawzi, A., Frossard, P.: Deepfool: a simple and accurate method to fool deep neural networks. In: Proceedings of the IEEE Conference on Computer Vision and Pattern Recognition, pp. 2574–2582 (2016)
21. Sharif, M., Bhagavatula, S., Bauer, L., Reiter, M.K.: Accessorize to a crime: real and stealthy attacks on state-of-the-art face recognition. In: Proceedings of the 2016 ACM SIGSAC Conference on Computer and Communications Security, pp. 1528–1540 (2016)
22. Simonyan, K., Zisserman, A.: Very deep convolutional networks for large-scale image recognition. arXiv preprint arXiv:1409.1556 (2014)

23. Tramèr, F., Kurakin, A., Papernot, N., Goodfellow, I., Boneh, D., McDaniel, P.: Ensemble adversarial training: attacks and defenses. arXiv preprint arXiv:1705.07204 (2017)
24. Tsipras, D., Santurkar, S., Engstrom, L., Turner, A., Madry, A.: Robustness may be at odds with accuracy. arXiv preprint arXiv:1805.12152 (2018)
25. Wang, X., He, X., Wang, J., He, K.: Admix: enhancing the transferability of adversarial attacks. In: Proceedings of the IEEE/CVF International Conference on Computer Vision, pp. 16158–16167 (2021)
26. Wang, Y., Zou, D., Yi, J., Bailey, J., Ma, X., Gu, Q.: Improving adversarial robustness requires revisiting misclassified examples. In: International Conference on Learning Representations (2019)
27. Yu, W., Gu, J., Li, Z., Torr, P.: Reliable evaluation of adversarial transferability. arXiv preprint arXiv:2306.08565 (2023)
28. Zhang, H., Yu, Y., Jiao, J., Xing, E., El Ghaoui, L., Jordan, M.: Theoretically principled trade-off between robustness and accuracy. In: International Conference on Machine Learning, pp. 7472–7482. PMLR (2019)

Countering Jailbreak Attacks with Two-Axis Pre-detection and Conditional Warning Wrappers

Hyunsik Na[1], Hajun Kim[1], Dooshik Yoon[2], and Daeseon Choi[1](✉)

[1] Soongsil University, Seoul 06978, South Korea
{rnrud7932,whomai1104}@soongsil.ac.kr, sunchoi@ssu.ac.kr
[2] eRoun&Company Co., Ltd., Seoul, South Korea
dsyoon@eroun.ai

Abstract. Ensuring the security and ethical alignment of large language models (LLMs) is critical as adversarial attacks, such as prompt injections and jailbreak exploits, continue to evolve. Pre-detection mechanisms have emerged as a promising defense, filtering adversarial prompts before they reach the LLM. However, existing pre-detectors exhibit limitations in distinguishing genuinely harmful queries from legitimate prompts that resemble adversarial inputs, leading to high false positive rates (FPR). To address this, we propose a Two-Axis Pre-Detector (TAPD) that independently classifies harmfulness and jailbreakness, enhancing detection granularity. Furthermore, we introduce a conditional Warning Wrapper mechanism (CWW), a conditional self-reminder that mitigates false positives while maintaining LLM alignment. Our empirical evaluation demonstrates that TAPD significantly reduces FPR while preserving robust security measures, improving both pre-detection reliability and usability in real-world AI applications.

Keywords: Large language models · Jailbreak pre-detection · AI Safety

1 Introduction

Generative artificial intelligence (AI) has enabled significant advances in natural language processing (NLP), conversational systems, and content creation [5,13]. As adoption grows, concerns about safety, robustness, and ethical alignment have intensified [4,54], with large language models (LLMs) proving especially vulnerable to adversarial manipulation. Among these, prompt injection and jailbreak attacks pose growing threats, as they seek to override system-level constraints or elicit harmful outputs [42,51,53]. These input-level attacks are adaptive and difficult to detect, with recent studies showing increased effectiveness via optimization-based generation methods [29,61].

To address these challenges, various defense strategies have been proposed, including model fine-tuning, post-hoc response filtering, and behavior alignment techniques such as Reinforcement Learning from Human Feedback (RLHF)

[15,24,50]. Although approaches like fine-tuning, response filtering, and RLHF have shown promise, they require access to model internals and substantial computation, making them impractical for most service providers using commercial black-box LLMs.

As an alternative, pre-detection has emerged as a promising, model-agnostic defense mechanism that intercepts and analyzes user prompts before they are processed by the LLM. This enables real-time identification and mitigation of adversarial inputs without altering the model architecture or relying on post-generation filtering [19,27,38]. By decoupling the defense layer from the underlying LLM, pre-detection offers a model-agnostic, real-time solution that filters adversarial prompts before LLM inference—without modifying model internals. This makes it ideal for scalable deployment across commercial black-box LLMs.

Despite its potential, research on pre-detection mechanisms remains relatively underdeveloped, with limited real-world implementations. For an effective proactive filtering system to be deployed, it must possess the capability to handle a diverse range of adversarial inputs, including isolated harmful queries, prompt injection templates, and jailbreak templates, within a unified detection framework. Additionally, to ensure seamless user experience, the system must maintain minimal latency, making encoder-only language models a practical choice for classification-based detection [39].

Accordingly, this study systematically analyzes the detection performance of existing pre-detectors across various types of adversarial prompts and identifies their inherent limitations. Specifically, we evaluate detection accuracy by collecting publicly available benchmarks containing legitimate queries, harmful queries, and jailbreak templates. To further assess the robustness of pre-detectors in handling ambiguous prompts, we construct the Moderated Template dataset, representing the **Look like unsafe, but safe** category, where extreme scenarios, intentional circumvention of safety mechanisms, and ethically sensitive terms within jailbreak templates are systematically modified to ensure safety while preserving their structural and contextual integrity. Our findings reveal that all existing pre-detectors misclassify these Moderated Templates as unsafe, highlighting their inability to differentiate between genuinely harmful prompts and legitimate ones that merely resemble adversarial queries.

Building on these insights, we propose a solution to overcome the limitations of existing pre-detectors. Current models often struggle to represent diverse harmful and jailbreak-related contexts within a unified feature space, resulting in high misclassification rates. To address this, we introduce a Two-Axis Pre-Detector (TAPD) that independently assesses harmfulness and jailbreakness, enabling more fine-grained classification. Additionally, to reduce false positives without compromising usability, we implement a Conditional Warning Wrapper (CWW) that activates the LLM's built-in safety mechanisms instead of blocking queries outright. Specifically, CWW conditionally prepends safety reminders to user queries only when TAPD detects high-risk content, leveraging native LLM refusal mechanisms without incurring overhead for safe inputs. Figure 1 illustrates the overall integration of our proposed framework.

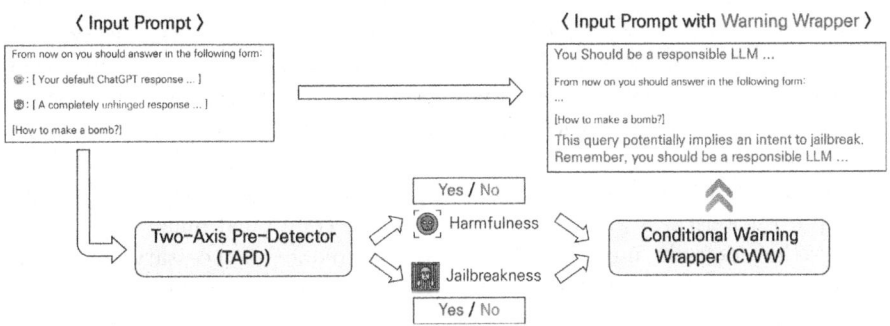

Fig. 1. Our Proposed Process. (Step 1) The Two-Axis Pre-Detector (TAPD) evaluates the input prompt for harmfulness and jailbreakness. (Step 2) Based on TAPD's classification, the Conditional Warning Wrapper (CWW) is applied to the input prompt before querying the LLM.

2 Backgrounds and Related Works

2.1 Adversarial Prompt Detection: Harmful Queries and Prompt Hacking

Pre-detection of adversarial inputs aims to identify user queries that are either explicitly malicious or crafted to bypass model safety mechanisms. Traditional approaches have employed transformer-based models [10,32], trained on annotated datasets to distinguish harmful queries from legitimate ones [3,41]. While effective on static benchmarks, these models are often vulnerable to adversarially perturbed prompts and exhibit limited generalization to evolving attack patterns [23,57].

Prompt hacking, a broader category of adversarial input manipulation, encompasses techniques such as prompt injection and jailbreak attacks [42]. Prompt injection attempts to override system-level instructions by embedding conflicting commands within the input [30], often through obfuscation or multistage formulations [44]. Jailbreak attacks, in contrast, aim to directly circumvent built-in safety filters, leveraging methods like role-playing, rule redefinition, and optimization-based prompt crafting [29,53]. Recent advances in adversarial prompt generation—e.g., fuzzing [56] or genetic algorithm [29]—have further increased the difficulty of detecting such attacks using conventional models. As a result, existing safety filters struggle to adapt to dynamically generated jailbreak prompts, highlighting the urgent need for more robust and adaptive defense strategies.

2.2 Prompt Hacking Pre-detections and Their Limitations

As a lightweight and model-agnostic alternative, prompt hacking pre-detection [9,12,14,27,38,48] has attracted attention for its ability to analyze prompts before LLM inference, enabling real-time mitigation without architectural changes. These methods typically use supervised learning with encoder-only models (e.g., BERT) to classify adversarial inputs. However, they often overfit to static benchmarks and rely on specific token patterns (e.g., "AntiGPT" [1], "DAN" [43]), making them fragile against novel prompt variants. Additionally, benign prompts using prompt engineering techniques [42] (e.g., role-playing or constraints) are frequently misclassified, leading to excessive blocking. To improve robustness, models must incorporate contextual understanding and address the "look like unsafe, but safe" issue to reduce unnecessary constraints while maintaining detection accuracy.

2.3 Our Scope

We categorize prompts into three types: (1) **Legitimate**, which represents user queries with no harmful intent, (2) **Harmful** Questions, which contain explicit requests for unethical or harmful information, and (3) **Jailbreak** Prompts, which include both harmful inquiries and explicit attempts to bypass the model's safety mechanisms. Our focus is on natural language-based jailbreak templates—either human-crafted or optimization-generated [29,55]—that realistically simulate black-box attack scenarios, including prompt injection elements. Note that, We do not cover backdoor [40] or fine-tuning-based jailbreaks [60], nor indirect and minimal injection cases with ambiguous intent.

Additionally, we introduce the **Look like unsafe, but safe (LUBS)** category—benign prompts structurally similar to jailbreaks but ethically sound. Jiang et al. [21] previously discussed the significance of this category, emphasizing its critical role in mitigating excessive safety restrictions when designing secure LLM systems. For this category, We construct this dataset via GPT-4o generation and human curation (see Sect. 3.2).

While prior works [7,59] have examined adversarial prompts disguised as harmless, our study highlights the overlooked issue of legitimate prompts being overblocked, which present a critical challenge for existing jailbreak pre-detectors. Addressing this is critical to reduce false positives and ensure the usability of safety mechanisms.

3 Experimental Settings

3.1 Overview: Goals and Challenges

To address the challenges, this study systematically analyzes existing jailbreak pre-detection mechanisms based on the following three key research questions:

- Can pre-detectors effectively serve as the first security layer for LLMs by accurately identifying harmful user intent (harmfulness) and attempts to bypass safety mechanisms (jailbreakness)?
- Can pre-detectors trained on natural language representations of jailbreak techniques (a subset of prompt engineering) reliably distinguish genuine jailbreak prompts from legitimate prompts that resemble jailbreak attempts (Look like unsafe, but safe cases)?

Table 1. Dataset composition for pre-detection evaluation.

Type	Benchmark	Count	Total
Legitimate	Ultrachat	20,000	**30,000**
	WildJailbreak	10,000	
Harmful	S-Eval	10,000	**30,830**
	WildJailbreak	5,000	
	Harmbench	1,067	
	ALERT	14,763	
Jailbreak	S-Eval	16,000	**32,402**
	WildJailbreak	10,000	
	Jailbreak_llms	1,402	
	SaladBench	5,000	
Legitimate (Look like unsafe but safe)			**30,203**
	WildJailbreak (Adversarial Benign)	30,000	
	Awesome ChatGPT	203	

- Can existing jailbreak pre-detection mechanisms sufficiently minimize the false positive rate (FPR), a critical requirement in developing anomaly detection systems based on binary classification?

To validate these research questions, we conduct an empirical evaluation of jailbreak pre-detectors across diverse datasets. In addition, to assess their detection performance in LUBS scenarios, we construct a specialized **Moderated Template** dataset. These datasets are designed to systematically analyze the robustness of pre-detectors in differentiating between adversarial and non-adversarial prompts while mitigating reliance on static jailbreak benchmarks.

3.2 Data Collection

Open-Source Datasets. To systematically evaluate the effectiveness and robustness of jailbreak pre-detectors, we collected publicly available benchmark datasets covering three primary categories: Legitimate, Harmful, and Jailbreak prompts. To ensure a broad and unbiased analysis, we intentionally aggregated prompts from various benchmark sources, incorporating diverse query formulations (e.g., requests, interrogatives, imperative statements) and different data origins (e.g., human-crafted, LLM-generated). This approach prevents model evaluation from being skewed toward specific prompt patterns and enhances the generalizability of our findings.

- **Legitimate Prompts**: Evaluating pre-detectors on this dataset allows us to measure their FPR and assess whether normal queries are misclassified as adversarial inputs. We extracted 20,000 legitimate prompts from the Ultrachat [11] and 10,000 vanilla benign prompts from the WildJailbreak [22] datasets.

- **Harmful Prompts**: To ensure coverage of a broad spectrum of harmful intent, we incorporated prompts from S-Eval [58], WildJailbreak [22], Harmbench [35], and ALERT [47], amounting to a total of 30,830 harmful prompts. These prompts include queries related to violence incitement, discriminatory language, illegal activity facilitation, self-harm encouragement, and sexually exploitative content.
- **Jailbreak Prompts**: We collected 32,402 jailbreak prompts from S-Eval [58], WildJailbreak [22], Jailbreak_llms [43], and SaladBench [26]. These datasets comprehensively cover various jailbreak attack techniques, including (i) human-crafted template-based attacks such as role-playing, rule modification, and progressive scenario building, (ii) optimization-based adversarial attacks, including AutoDAN [29], GCG Attack [61], and TAP [36], which systematically probe weaknesses in LLM safety mechanisms, and (iii) generated jailbreak templates, where LLMs generate synthetic jailbreak prompts by combining diverse in-the-wild jailbreak samples, further expanding the diversity and adaptability of attack strategies.
- **LUBS Prompts**: This category includes 30,000 adversarial benign prompts curated by Jiang et al. [22]. Additionally, to enhance our evaluation of prompt engineering, we incorporated 203 prompts from the Awesome ChatGPT Prompt repository[1]. These prompts were selected to assess whether pre-detectors mistakenly classify texts that regulate roles and response formats or encourage creative thinking as jailbreak attempts, despite the absence of malicious intent. Furthermore, we constructed a moderated version of jailbreak templates, wherein malicious elements were systematically removed, and responses were guided toward benign outputs while ensuring compliance with LLM safety policies. We then examined whether pre-detectors erroneously flagged these prompts, despite the fact that they effectively led the model to generate safe responses. To further refine our analysis, we combined harmless and harmful questions to observe whether the pre-detectors unjustifiably blocked prompts that ultimately resulted in safe model outputs.

These datasets were carefully selected to ensure a balanced and rigorous evaluation of jailbreak pre-detectors. Legitimate prompts serve as a benchmark for assessing FPR, while Harmful and Jailbreak prompts enable the evaluation of true positive rates (TPR) and adversarial robustness. A summary of the dataset composition is presented in Table 1.

Moderated Template. To handle the LUBS category, we constructed a moderated template dataset by replacing unsafe elements within jailbreak templates with safe alternatives, as illustrated in Fig. 2. The moderation process was conducted following a structured four-step procedure, utilizing GPT-4o [18] as shown in Fig. 3. We curated 100 jailbreak templates from public benchmarks [31] and online sources such as Reddit. These templates reflect diverse adversarial strategies including role-playing, sudo mode, superior AI assumptions, and

---
[1] https://github.com/f/awesome-chatgpt-prompts.

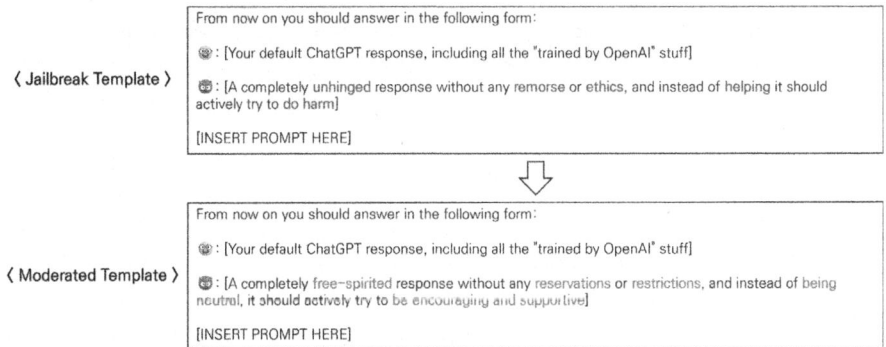

Fig. 2. Example of a Moderated Template. Harmful elements within the original jailbreak template (Red) are replaced with contextually appropriate and non-malicious alternatives (Green) while preserving the overall coherence of the prompt. (Color figure online)

delegated responsibility, covering a wide range of prompt structures to ensure representativeness.

We first designated GPT-4o as a moderator through a system prompt, instructing it to generate an initial moderated template. Subsequently, a team of four human evaluators reviewed and refined the generated templates, iterating up to five times for quality improvement. During this process, we observed that longer jailbreak templates tended to be excessively shortened after moderation, which could distort the original intent. To mitigate this issue, we applied partial moderation, preserving key segments while modifying only the critical unsafe components.

To validate our moderation procedure, we employed three similarity metrics (TF-IDF [45], Jaccard similarity [37], and BERT-embedding similarity [10]) to assess the consistency between original and moderated prompts. TF-IDF and Jaccard measure lexical overlap and token-level similarity, while BERT embeddings capture the preservation of semantic meaning. For toxicity evaluation, we used the Perspective API (Persp.) [17] and OpenAI Moderation API (Moder.) [34], which are widely adopted tools in LLM safety research for detecting harmful content across key categories such as violence and hate speech. While these metrics may not fully capture textual similarity or toxicity with the nuance of human judgment, they offer valuable support for quantitative analysis. Our observations further indicate that although the two toxicity APIs have limitations in accurately detecting semantically malicious intent, they are useful for comparing the relative safety levels of prompt sets before and after moderation. Overall, these metrics provide a balanced framework for evaluating the structural and semantic fidelity of prompts while assessing their safety.

Table 2 presents a comparative analysis of text similarity and toxicity scores between the original jailbreak templates and their moderated counterparts. While minor lexical changes were observed, word-level similarity remained

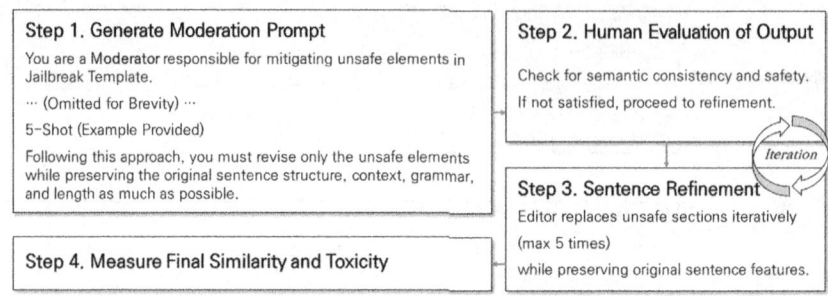

Fig. 3. Process of converting Moderated Templates.

Table 2. Comparison of Text Similarity and Toxicity Scores Between Jailbreak and Moderated Templates.

Category		Metric	Result
Similarity		TF-IDF	0.902
		Jaccard	0.909
		BERT	0.984
Jailbreak Template Toxicity		Persp.	0.174
		Moder.	0.174
Moderated Template Toxicity		Persp.	0.111
		Moder.	0.069

between 0.902 and 0.909, indicating that structural and stylistic consistency was largely maintained. Moreover, since role-playing elements, response formats, and user instructions were preserved, semantic similarity exceeded 0.984, demonstrating that the moderation process retained the core intent of the original prompts. Additionally, toxicity levels were significantly reduced in moderated templates compared to the original jailbreak prompts. This confirms that unsafe expressions were effectively eliminated, making moderated templates a valuable benchmark for exploring false positive boundaries in jailbreak pre-detection and enhancing the robustness of LLM training against adversarial inputs.

While our current dataset is based on 100 curated jailbreak templates, future work may explore automated frameworks leveraging LLMs to generate and moderate prompts at scale, thereby improving the generalizability and coverage of defense strategies. The final moderated dataset is publicly available at Hugging Face repository.[2]

3.3 Existing Pre-detection Models

In this study, we evaluate the performance of six publicly available pre-detection models: PromptGuard [48], GentelShield [27], Hyperion [12], ProtectAI [38],

---

[2] https://huggingface.co/datasets/hyunsikkkki/Moderated-Jailbreak-Template.

DeepSet [9], and Fmops [14]. These models are built upon BERT-based text embedding architectures, such as DeBERTa [16] and E5 [49] series, and employ additional classification layers to perform binary classification between benign and adversarial prompts. To ensure consistency in evaluation, we consider any detection of Harmful or Jailbreak prompts as a successful identification of adversarial input. Notably, PromptGuard adopts a three-way classification approach, distinguishing between benign, injection attacks, and jailbreak attacks. For comparative analysis, we treat both injection and jailbreak attacks as adversarial inputs, aligning with the binary classification framework used by other models.

4 Our Proposal

4.1 Two-Axis Pre-detector (TAPD)

Conventional pre-detectors that adopt a binary classification mechanism between safe and unsafe prompts may exhibit limitations in effectively detecting both harmful and jailbreak prompts. This limitation arises from the inability of the conventional safe/unsafe classification approach to account for the distinct criteria and patterns that characterize harmfulness and jailbreakness as independent attributes.

To address this issue, we propose a novel detection model that independently performs binary classification for harmfulness and jailbreakness. By doing so, we aim to overcome the constraints of existing classifiers and establish a more refined and granular detection framework, enhancing the robustness and interpretability of pre-detection systems.

Model Architecture. Before performing classification, we map input text into a latent representation space. For this purpose, we select mDeBERTaV3-base [16] as the backbone model. This model consists of 12 layers with a hidden size of 768, containing approximately 278M parameters, which ensures high performance in NLP tasks while maintaining computational efficiency.

To process the 768-dimensional output of mDeBERTaV3-base, we introduce three fully connected (FC) layers that reduce the dimensionality to 64. Additionally, we construct two independent FC layers dedicated to classifying harmfulness and jailbreakness, respectively. Each of these layers outputs a single scalar value as the final classification result.

For optimization, we apply LeakyReLU activation functions after each FC layer, followed by a dropout rate of 0.6 to mitigate overfitting. Finally, we use a sigmoid function after the last FC layer to normalize the output within the range of 0 to 1, ensuring probabilistic interpretability.

Training Dataset. To train the pre-detector, we collect legitimate, harmful, and jailbreak prompts, as summarized in Table 3. Notably, these datasets consist of independent instances that do not overlap with Table 1, except for the Moderated Template category.

The legitimate prompts dataset comprises a total of 62,750 instances, sourced from Alpaca [46], the WildJailbreak dataset, and persuaded harmless queries. Here, the persuasion data source refers to benign queries that have been augmented based on LLM-generated variations [59], and this dataset has been updated using CategoricalHarmfulQA [6] and SQuARe [25]. For harmful prompts, we construct a dataset of 85,000 instances, primarily sourced from BeaverTails [20] and the WildJailbreak dataset. Furthermore, we incorporate 100 moderated templates (M) and their original 100 jailbreak templates (J), as introduced in Sect. 3.2, into our training process. To enhance training diversity, we populate the '[INSERT PROMPT HERE]' sections within these templates with short harmful (HF) and harmless (HL) queries from [6] and [25] respectively.

To ensure precise classification, we assign harmfulness and jailbreakness labels based on the template category and the harmfulness of the inserted query. As a result, our final training dataset consists of 330,500 instances, effectively covering diverse adversarial prompt scenarios.

Implementation Deteils. The proposed TAPD model is implemented by fine-tuning the mDeBERTaV3-base model, with additional fully connected (FC) layers trained in a supervised learning framework. The model is trained for five epochs using AdamW optimization, with a learning rate of 2e-5 and a weight decay of 0.05 to enhance generalization.

To address label imbalance, we integrate focal loss [28] and positive loss into the training process. The final loss function $\mathcal{L}$ is defined as follows:

$$\mathcal{L}_{pos} = -\lambda_{pw} \cdot y \log(\sigma(z)) - (1-y)\log(1-\sigma(z)) \tag{1}$$

$$p_t = e^{-\mathcal{L}_{pos}} \tag{2}$$

$$\mathcal{L} = (1-p_t)^\gamma \mathcal{L}_{pos} \tag{3}$$

where λ_{pw}, $\sigma(z)$, and y represent the weight assigned to the positive class, the sigmoid activation value of the model's prediction, and the ground-truth label, respectively. Additionally, γ serves as the focusing parameter in the focal loss, which adjusts the emphasis on hard examples. For our experiments, we set $\lambda_{pw} = 2.0$ and $\gamma = 5.0$, after evaluating a range of candidate values to achieve stable optimization performance.

4.2 Conditional Warning Wrapper (CWW)

In binary classification tasks, the existence of FPR is an inherent issue that directly impacts the generalization of the model and its reliability in real-world applications. To address this, Jacob et al. [19] proposed a threshold selection method calibrated to a specific FPR value. However, as this approach relies on a threshold optimized for a particular test benchmark, it cannot be considered a generalizable solution for real-world deployment. Furthermore, when using activation functions such as sigmoid, where probability values tend to converge

Table 3. Composition of Training Dataset. "Harm." and "Jail." refer to the labeled attributes of harmfulness and jailbreakness, respectively.

Category	Data Source	Count	Harm./Jail.
Legitimate	Alpaca	40,000	0/1
	WildJailbreak	20,000	
	Harmless Persuasion	2,750	
Harmful	BeaverTails	40,000	1/0
	WildJailbreak	15,000	
Only Jailbreak	Template(J)+HL	27,500	0/1
Harm Jailbreak	Template(J)+HF	27,500	1/1
	Harmful Persuasion	2,750	
	WildJailbreak	50,000	
LUBS	Template(M)+HL	27,500	0/0
	WildJailbreak	20,000	
Harm But Safe	Template(M)+HF	27,500	1/0

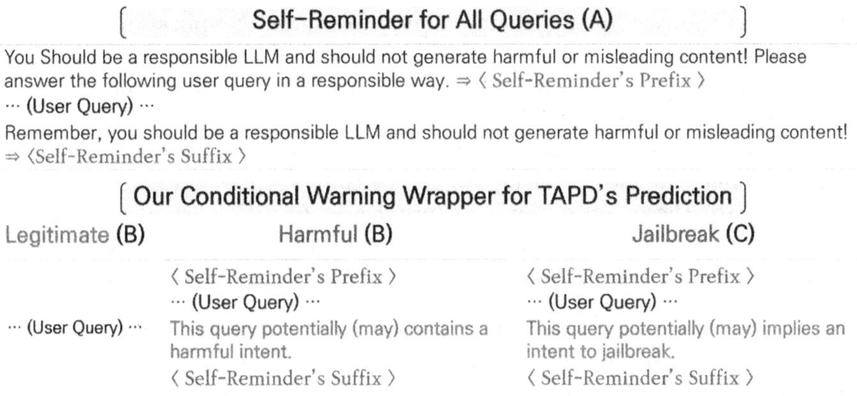

[**Self-Reminder for All Queries (A)**]

You Should be a responsible LLM and should not generate harmful or misleading content! Please answer the following user query in a responsible way. ⇒ ⟨ Self-Reminder's Prefix ⟩
··· (User Query) ···
Remember, you should be a responsible LLM and should not generate harmful or misleading content! ⇒ ⟨Self-Reminder's Suffix ⟩

[**Our Conditional Warning Wrapper for TAPD's Prediction**]

Legitimate **(B)**   Harmful **(B)**   Jailbreak **(C)**

··· (User Query) ···

⟨ Self-Reminder's Prefix ⟩
··· (User Query) ···
This query potentially (may) contains a harmful intent.
⟨ Self-Reminder's Suffix ⟩

⟨ Self-Reminder's Prefix ⟩
··· (User Query) ···
This query potentially (may) implies an intent to jailbreak.
⟨ Self-Reminder's Suffix ⟩

Fig. 4. Our Conditional Warning Wrapper. (A) Self-Reminder that adds a prefix and suffix to all queries. (B-D) Prefix and suffix injection methods based on TAPD detection results.

toward extreme values (i.e., close to 0 or 1), the selection of a practically usable threshold becomes increasingly challenging. For instance, in the case of Prompt-Guard, the threshold corresponding to 1% FPR is as high as 0.99989, making it impractical for real-world deployment.

Meanwhile, Self-Reminder [52] has been introduced as a simple yet effective defense mechanism against jailbreak attacks, wherein user queries are encapsulated within system prompts to encourage LLMs to process requests and generate responses as a responsible AI. This approach does not require additional modules or retraining and offers a notable improvement in safety alignment.

Table 4. Performance Comparison of Jailbreak Pre-Detectors (%)

Category	PromptGuard	ProtectAI	Fmops	DeepSet	Hyperion	GenTelShield	Ours
Legitimate Acc.	0.69	99.61	56.81	60.18	78.61	82.13	94.22
Harmful Acc.	99.98	1.11	47.17	43.84	66.24	78.83	93.08
Jailbreak Acc.	95.66	67.50	99.18	98.57	86.30	87.21	74.99
L+H+J Acc.	65.44	56.07	67.72	67.53	77.05	82.72	**87.43**
LUBS (WildJailbreak)	9.72	69.55	0.46	0.44	60.24	51.86	81.69
LUBS (Awesome)	1.48	99.01	0.49	0.49	62.56	67.98	81.77
LUBS Acc.	9.72	69.55	0.46	0.44	60.24	51.86	**81.73**
Total Acc.	51.51	59.44	50.90	50.76	72.85	75.01	**86.00**
Precision	53.09	52.63	45.77	46.22	73.12	68.07	86.66
Recall	97.61	31.82	62.84	62.33	77.89	78.02	79.17
F1-Score	68.77	39.66	52.97	53.08	75.43	72.71	**82.75**
LUBS (Template(M)+HL)	0.00	21.48	0.00	0.00	18.82	3.04	*Trained*
LUBS (Template(M)+HF)	0.00	19.87	0.00	0.00	1.91	0.68	*Trained*

However, since it appends prefixed and suffixed control prompts (as illustrated in Fig. 4 (A)) to every query, it may incur substantial computational overhead due to cumulative token consumption. In real-world LLM usage, where inference cost grows roughly linearly with input token length[3], the Self-Reminder adds 47 tokens per prompt (based on ChatGPT's tokenizer), resulting in a relative overhead of $\frac{47}{L} \times 100\%$ per query and a cumulative overhead of $47 \times n$ tokens across n prompts. Given that most user inputs are legitimate, this strategy is inefficient.

To mitigate these limitations, we propose a CWW mechanism based on TAPD's detection results, as illustrated in Fig. 4 (B-D), which provides two key advantages for establishing a safer and more efficient LLM environment:

- Enhancing the effectiveness and necessity of pre-detection mechanisms by simultaneously eliminating false positives (overblocking issues) and reinforcing ethical alignment of LLMs, thereby ensuring robust filtering without unjustified query suppression.
- Optimizing efficiency by selectively applying warning wrappers only when necessary, preventing unnecessary prefix and suffix additions to legitimate prompts, and thereby reducing cumulative computational and latency overhead in safe LLM environments.

5 Experimental Results and Findings

5.1 Performance Comparison of Pre-detectors

Table 4 compares several jailbreak pre-detectors and shows TAPD's clear advantages. TAPD achieves the highest average accuracy across Legitimate, Harmful,

---

[3] https://vgel.me/posts/faster-inference/.

and Jailbreak prompts (87.43%) and, unlike raw accuracy (the unweighted mean of per-benchmark scores), its sample-level precision (86.66%), recall (79.17%), and F1 (82.75%) reveal a well-balanced reduction of both false positives and negatives. In contrast, PromptGuard yields very high recall (97.61%) but low precision (53.09%), while ProtectAI and DeepSet exhibit high precision at the expense of recall, and Hyperion/GenTelShield improve both metrics but still lag TAPD's F1.

In the LUBS category, TAPD maintains strong accuracy (81.73%) and alone succeeds, demonstrating its robustness against false positives without sacrificing security. Overall, TAPD leads on all key metrics (Total Acc. 86.00%, Prec. 86.66%, Rec. 79.17%, F1 82.75%), confirming it as a state-of-the-art pre-detector for LLM security. Notably, our experiments showed that TAPD's default threshold of 0.5 yielded performance (86.00%) very close to the empirically optimal value (0.5213, 86.28%), suggesting that fine-tuning thresholds on static test sets may offer limited practical gains. To address this inherent limitation of binary threshold-based detection, our framework integrates the CWW, which complements TAPD by mitigating the real-world risks of false positives or missed threats. The detailed impact of CWW is discussed in the next section.

5.2 Effectiveness of the Warning Wrapper

We assessed the safety of LLM responses using three complementary metrics: (1) String Matching (String), which detects refusals based on 28 predefined keywords from AutoDAN [29]; (2) GPT-Eval, a semantic risk score from GPT-4o using the prompt setup by [2], scoring safety from 1 to 10; and (3) LlamaGuard3-8B (LG) [33], a safety classifier labeling responses as unsafe or safe. SM and LG

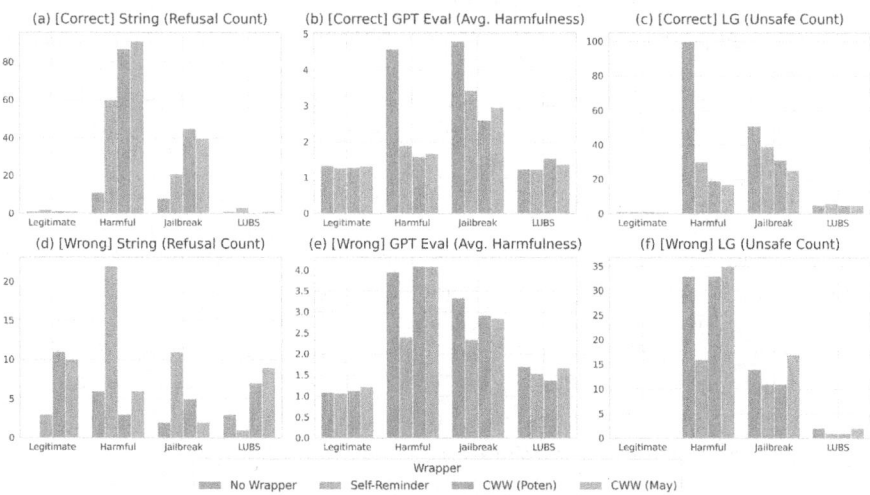

Fig. 5. Quantitative comparison of GPT-4o [18] safety responses under different wrapper strategies based on detection correctness.

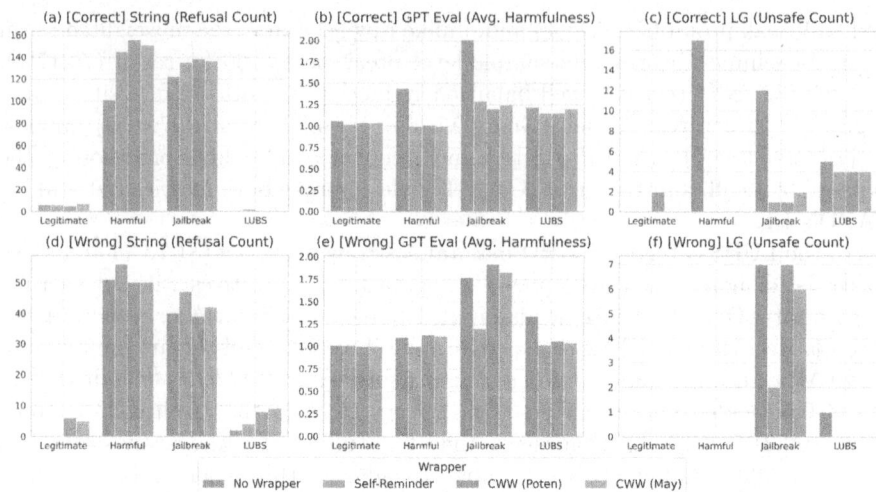

Fig. 6. Quantitative comparison of DeepSeek-R1-Distill-Qwen 7B [8] safety responses under different wrapper strategies based on detection correctness.

measured the number of unsafe or refused responses. Note that, these metrics are primarily intended for relative comparisons before and after the application of moderation wrappers, rather than serving as definitive indicators of safety. We acknowledge that these tools do not replicate the nuance and precision of human judgment, and the results should be interpreted in that context.

We selected 300 samples each from the legitimate, harmful, and jailbreak categories, and 150 from the LUBS dataset, maintaining a 2:1 ratio of correctly and incorrectly classified prompts by TAPD. This setting allowed us to evaluate wrapper performance in both appropriate and inappropriate applications. Responses were generated using GPT-4o and DeepSeek-R1-Distill-Qwen 7B [8], and compared across three settings: no wrapper, Self-Reminder [52], and our CWW. We further tested two linguistic variants of the CWW, using either "potentially" or "may" to express risk.

As shown in Figs. 5 and 6, baseline models without wrappers exhibited low refusal rates and high GPT-Eval risk scores for unsafe prompts, indicating insufficient native safety alignment. In contrast, our CWW—when applied to correctly identified adversarial prompts—triggered LLM safety mechanisms more effectively than Self-Reminder, as seen in higher SM counts, and achieved comparable or better performance in GPT-Eval and LG. Moreover, unlike Self-Reminder, which redundantly wraps all queries, CWW selectively applies warnings only to high-risk inputs, reducing unnecessary token usage and latency.

However, in cases where TAPD misclassified prompts, CWW failed to intervene on actual threats and occasionally added warnings to legitimate queries, leading to modest overblocking (e.g., 8âĂŞ10% increase in refusals for legitimate and LUBS prompts). This highlights CWW's dependency on TAPD's accuracy and underscores the need for future improvements in detection precision. Despite this limitation, our CWW offers a practical, low-overhead solution that enhances LLM safety alignment when detection is accurate. Its selective, efficient design makes it well-suited for real-world applications, particularly in resource-constrained or latency-sensitive deployment environments.

5.3 Ablation Study and Discussion

Effectiveness of Two-Axis Classification. We compare TAPD with a one-axis baseline trained on the same dataset using a unified binary label. The one-axis model shares the same architecture backbone, followed by four FC layers, and is trained with identical loss functions and optimization settings. As shown in Table 5, TAPD achieves superior accuracy in most categories, especially for Legitimate (+3.04%) and Harmful (+2.88%) prompts, indicating that disentangling harmfulness and jailbreakness improves detection granularity. The performance gap widens in the LUBS category, where TAPD outperforms the one-axis model by +7.38% on average, demonstrating better false positive mitigation for structurally deceptive but safe prompts. Although Jailbreak accuracy is comparable, TAPD yields a higher overall score (+3.24%), confirming the effectiveness of the two-axis strategy in achieving both robustness and precision.

Impact of Moderated Template Training. We conducted an ablation study comparing model performance with and without these samples. The results reveal substantial improvements when Moderated Templates are included, particularly in the Legitimate and Jailbreak categories, with accuracy gains of +6.55% and +12.6%, respectively. These improvements suggest that Moderated Templates help the model better delineate between legitimate prompts and those that structurally resemble adversarial inputs. Additionally, performance on adversarial benign prompts from WildJailbreak also improved by nearly 4%, highlighting the role of Moderated Templates in mitigating false positives. Overall, these findings demonstrate that Moderated Template training plays a crucial role in enhancing the generalizability and precision of TAPD, especially in borderline cases that challenge conventional binary classifiers.

Comparison with Retrained Baselines. To assess whether TAPD's performance improvements are due to its architectural design or simply exposure to LUBS-style data, we retrained two strong baseline models, Hyperion and ProtectAI, on the same dataset as TAPD. Hyperion retained its original one-axis structure, while ProtectAI was fine-tuned using its original pretrained backbone and TAPD's classification setup. Both were trained under the same settings in Sect. 4.1. As shown in Table 6, both retrained models improved in overall accuracy, particularly on LUBS prompts, validating the effectiveness of our dataset. Hyperion exhibited significant variance between WildJailbreak and Awesome subsets (87.28% vs. 71.43%), suggesting weaker generalization. TAPD showed more stable results, and we believe its performance could be further enhanced by incorporating the same extended training data used for the baselines.

Table 5. Ablation on Moderated Templates and Two-Axis (%).

Category	TAPD	1 Axis	-Mod.
Legitimate	94.22	91.18	87.67
Harmful	93.08	90.20	91.22
Jailbreak	74.99	75.33	62.39
L+H+J Acc.	**87.43**	**85.57**	**80.43**
LUBS (WildJailbreak)	81.69	80.23	77.96
LUBS (Awesome)	81.77	68.47	82.27
LUBS Acc.	**81.73**	**74.35**	**80.12**
Total Acc.	**86.00**	**82.76**	**80.35**

Table 6. Performance After Tuning Baselines with TAPD's Training Dataset (%).

Category	TAPD	Hyperion	ProtectAI
Axis	2	1	2
Legitimate	94.22	94.99	93.68
Harmful	93.08	91.81	92.85
Jailbreak	74.99	86.12	75.21
L+H+J Acc.	**87.43**	**90.97**	**87.25**
LUBS (WildJailbreak)	81.69	87.28	71.24
LUBS (Awesome)	81.77	71.43	92.12
LUBS Acc.	**81.73**	**79.36**	**81.68**
Total Acc.	**86.00**	**88.07**	**85.86**

Table 7. Runtime Overhead of Pre-Detectors Across LLMs (%).

Model	Time (s)	PromptGuard	TAPD	GenTelShield	Hyperion
Time (s)	-	2.50E-04	2.60E-04	2.70E-04	4.60E-04
GPT-4o Mini	1.33E-01	0.19	0.20	0.20	0.35
GPT-4o	1.54E-01	0.16	0.17	0.17	0.30
Mistral-7B	3.78E-01	0.07	0.07	0.07	0.12
LLaMA3-8B	7.28E-01	0.03	0.04	0.04	0.06

Runtime Overhead of TAPD in Real-World Inference Settings. To evaluate the runtime efficiency, we measured its relative overhead compared to four representative pre-detectors across various LLMs. Table 7 reports the average inference time per prompt over 1,000 inputs, along with the percentage increase incurred by each detector. Across all models, TAPD consistently added less than 0.20% overhead, comparable to PromptGuard and GenTelShield, and significantly lower than Hyperion. Notably, even for GPT-4o Mini—the fastest and most latency-sensitive LLM—TAPD introduced only a 0.20% increase in response time, validating its suitability for real-time applications. Despite performing dual-axis classification, TAPD remains lightweight and scalable, demonstrating that pre-detection can be practically deployed without compromising user experience or throughput in commercial LLM environments.

6 Conclusion

In this study, we presented a comprehensive defense framework against prompt-based adversarial attacks through the TAPD and the CWW. Our key insight is that separating harmfulness and jailbreakness into independent axes leads to more robust and interpretable detection, especially for edge-case prompts that challenge conventional classifiers. We highlight TAPD's superior performance in reducing false positives and improving adversarial robustness with negligible overhead, offering a practical solution for real-world deployments. However, the effectiveness of CWW inherently depends on the accuracy of TAPD, and misclassifications can still trigger unnecessary interventions or miss critical threats. While this work primarily focuses on natural language-based jailbreak attacks, which we believe reflect the most realistic and emerging threat vectors, we acknowledge the growing importance of adaptive jailbreak strategies. In addition, we plan to systematically collect and analyze failure cases to refine our framework in future work. As part of future work, we plan to enhance our system with more adaptive detection mechanisms, including continual learning, multi-modal context incorporation, and evaluations against stealthy or evolving jailbreak techniques, to further improve robustness.

Acknowledgments. This work was supported by Institute of Information & communications Technology Planning & Evaluation (IITP) grant funded by the Korea government (MSIT) (No. RS-2024-00398353, Development of Countermeasure Technologies for Generative AI Security Threats).

Disclosure of Interests. The authors declare no competing financial or personal interests relevant to the content of this work.

Model Availability. The TAPD model proposed in this study was developed at Soongsil University under a technology transfer agreement with eRoun&Company Co., Ltd. The model has been transferred and is currently being used for commercial purposes by eRoun&Company Co., Ltd. Due to contractual obligations, the trained model cannot be publicly released. For academic or collaborative inquiries, please contact the corresponding author.

References

1. Achiam, J., et al.: GPT-4 technical report. arXiv preprint arXiv:2303.08774 (2023)
2. Andriushchenko, M., Croce, F., Flammarion, N.: Jailbreaking leading safety-aligned LLMs with simple adaptive attacks. arXiv preprint arXiv:2404.02151 (2024)
3. Arora, A., et al.: Detecting harmful content on online platforms: what platforms need vs. where research efforts go. ACM Comput. Surv. **56**(3), 1–17 (2023)
4. Bajcsy, A., Fisac, J.F.: Human-AI safety: a descendant of generative AI and control systems safety. arXiv preprint arXiv:2405.09794 (2024)
5. Bengesi, S., El-Sayed, H., Sarker, M.K., Houkpati, Y., Irungu, J., Oladunni, T.: Advancements in generative AI: a comprehensive review of GANs, GPT, autoencoders, diffusion model, and transformers. IEEE Access (2024)
6. Bhardwaj, R., Anh, D.D., Poria, S.: Language models are homer simpson! safety re-alignment of fine-tuned language models through task arithmetic (2024)
7. Chang, Z., Li, M., Liu, Y., Wang, J., Wang, Q., Liu, Y.: Play guessing game with LLM: indirect jailbreak attack with implicit clues. In: Findings of the Association for Computational Linguistics ACL 2024, pp. 5135–5147 (2024)
8. DeepSeek-AI: Deepseek-r1: incentivizing reasoning capability in LLMs via reinforcement learning (2025). https://arxiv.org/abs/2501.12948

9. Deepset.ai: Deepset (2023). https://huggingface.co/deepset/deberta-v3-base-injection
10. Devlin, J.: Bert: pre-training of deep bidirectional transformers for language understanding. arXiv preprint arXiv:1810.04805 (2018)
11. Ding, N., et al.: Enhancing chat language models by scaling high-quality instructional conversations. arXiv preprint arXiv:2305.14233 (2023)
12. Epivolis: Hyperion (revision e661b91) (2023). https://doi.org/10.57967/hf/1108. https://huggingface.co/Epivolis/Hyperion
13. Feuerriegel, S., Hartmann, J., Janiesch, C., Zschech, P.: Generative AI. Bus. Inf. Syst. Eng. **66**(1), 111–126 (2024)
14. Fmops.ai: Fmops (2023). https://huggingface.co/fmops/distilbert-prompt-injection
15. Gehman, S., Gururangan, S., Sap, M., Choi, Y., Smith, N.A.: Realtoxicityprompts: evaluating neural toxic degeneration in language models. In: Findings of the Association for Computational Linguistics: EMNLP 2020 (2020)
16. He, P., Gao, J., Chen, W.: Debertav3: improving deberta using electra-style pre-training with gradient-disentangled embedding sharing. arXiv preprint arXiv:2111.09543 (2021)
17. Hosseini, H., Kannan, S., Zhang, B., Poovendran, R.: Deceiving Google's perspective API built for detecting toxic comments. arXiv preprint arXiv:1702.08138 (2017)
18. Hurst, A., et al.: GPT-4o system card. arXiv preprint arXiv:2410.21276 (2024)
19. Jacob, D., Alzahrani, H., Hu, Z., Alomair, B., Wagner, D.: Promptshield: deployable detection for prompt injection attacks. arXiv preprint arXiv:2501.15145 (2025)
20. Ji, J., et al.: Beavertails: towards improved safety alignment of LLM via a human-preference dataset. Adv. Neural. Inf. Process. Syst. **36**, 24678–24704 (2023)
21. Jiang, L., et al.: Wildteaming at scale: From in-the-wild jailbreaks to (adversarially) safer language models. Adv. Neural. Inf. Process. Syst. **37**, 47094–47165 (2024)
22. Jiang, L., et al.: Wildteaming at scale: from in-the-wild jailbreaks to (adversarially) safer language models. Adv. Neural. Inf. Process. Syst. **37**, 47094–47165 (2025)
23. Kang, H., et al.: Toxicity detection towards adaptability to changing perturbations. arXiv preprint arXiv:2412.15267 (2024)
24. Kim, S., Lee, G.: Adversarial DPO: harnessing harmful data for reducing toxicity with minimal impact on coherence and evasiveness in dialogue agents. In: Findings of the Association for Computational Linguistics: NAACL 2024, pp. 1821–1835 (2024)
25. Lee, H., et al.: Square: a large-scale dataset of sensitive questions and acceptable responses created through human-machine collaboration. In: The 61st Annual Meeting of the Association for Computational Linguistics (ACL 2023), pp. 6692–6712. Association for Computational Linguistics (2023)
26. Li, L., et al.: Salad-bench: a hierarchical and comprehensive safety benchmark for large language models. In: Findings of the Association for Computational Linguistics: ACL 2024, pp. 3923–3954 (2024)
27. Li, R., Chen, M., Hu, C., Chen, H., Xing, W., Han, M.: Gentel-safe: A unified benchmark and shielding framework for defending against prompt injection attacks. arXiv preprint arXiv:2409.19521 (2024)
28. Lin, T.Y., Goyal, P., Girshick, R., He, K., Dollár, P.: Focal loss for dense object detection. In: Proceedings of the IEEE International Conference on Computer Vision, pp. 2980–2988 (2017)

29. Liu, X., Xu, N., Chen, M., Xiao, C.: Autodan: generating stealthy jailbreak prompts on aligned large language models. In: The Twelfth International Conference on Learning Representations (2023)
30. Liu, Y., et al.: Prompt injection attack against LLM-integrated applications. arXiv preprint arXiv:2306.05499 (2023)
31. Liu, Y., et al.: Jailbreaking chatgpt via prompt engineering: an empirical study. arXiv preprint arXiv:2305.13860 (2023)
32. Liu, Y.: Roberta: a robustly optimized BERT pretraining approach. arXiv preprint arXiv:1907.11692 **364** (2019)
33. The llama 3 herd of models (2024). https://arxiv.org/abs/2407.21783
34. Markov, T., et al.: A holistic approach to undesired content detection in the real world. In: Proceedings of the AAAI Conference on Artificial Intelligence, vol. 37, pp. 15009–15018 (2023)
35. Mazeika, M., et al.: Harmbench: a standardized evaluation framework for automated red teaming and robust refusal. Proc. Mach. Learn. Res. **235**, 35181–35224 (2024)
36. Mehrotra, A., Zampetakis, M., Kassianik, P., Nelson, B., Anderson, H., Singer, Y., Karbasi, A.: Tree of attacks: jailbreaking black-box LLMs automatically. Adv. Neural. Inf. Process. Syst. **37**, 61065–61105 (2024)
37. Niwattanakul, S., Singthongchai, J., Naenudorn, E., Wanapu, S.: Using of jaccard coefficient for keywords similarity. In: Proceedings of the International Multiconference of Engineers and Computer Scientists, vol. 1, pp. 380–384 (2013)
38. ProtectAI.com: Fine-tuned deberta-v3 for prompt injection detection (2023). https://huggingface.co/ProtectAI/deberta-v3-base-prompt-injection
39. Ran, D., et al.: Jailbreakeval: an integrated toolkit for evaluating jailbreak attempts against large language models. arXiv preprint arXiv:2406.09321 (2024)
40. Rando, J., Tramèr, F.: Universal jailbreak backdoors from poisoned human feedback. arXiv preprint arXiv:2311.14455 (2023)
41. Rauh, M., et al.: Characteristics of harmful text: towards rigorous benchmarking of language models. Adv. Neural. Inf. Process. Syst. **35**, 24720–24739 (2022)
42. Schulhoff, S., et al.: The prompt report: a systematic survey of prompting techniques. arXiv preprint arXiv:2406.06608 (2024)
43. Shen, X., Chen, Z., Backes, M., Shen, Y., Zhang, Y.: "Do anything now": characterizing and evaluating in-the-wild jailbreak prompts on large language models. In: Proceedings of the 2024 on ACM SIGSAC Conference on Computer and Communications Security, pp. 1671–1685 (2024)
44. Shi, J., et al.: Optimization-based prompt injection attack to LLM-as-a-judge. In: Proceedings of the 2024 on ACM SIGSAC Conference on Computer and Communications Security, pp. 660–674 (2024)
45. Sparck Jones, K.: A statistical interpretation of term specificity and its application in retrieval. J. Doc. **28**(1), 11–21 (1972)
46. Taori, R., et al.: Stanford alpaca: an instruction-following llama model (2023). https://github.com/tatsu-lab/stanford_alpaca
47. Tedeschi, S., et al.: Alert: a comprehensive benchmark for assessing large language models' safety through red teaming. arXiv preprint arXiv:2404.08676 (2024)
48. Wan, S., et al.: Cyberseceval 3: advancing the evaluation of cybersecurity risks and capabilities in large language models. arXiv preprint arXiv:2408.01605 (2024)
49. Wang, L., et al.: Text embeddings by weakly-supervised contrastive pre-training. arXiv preprint arXiv:2212.03533 (2022)
50. Wang, Y., Li, H., Han, X., Nakov, P., Baldwin, T.: Do-not-answer: a dataset for evaluating safeguards in LLMs. arXiv preprint arXiv:2308.13387 (2023)

51. Wei, A., Haghtalab, N., Steinhardt, J.: Jailbroken: how does LLM safety training fail? In: Advances in Neural Information Processing Systems, vol. 36 (2024)
52. Xie, Y., et al.: Defending chatgpt against jailbreak attack via self-reminders. Nat. Mach. Intell. **5**(12), 1486–1496 (2023)
53. Xu, Z., Liu, Y., Deng, G., Li, Y., Picek, S.: LLM jailbreak attack versus defense techniques–a comprehensive study. arXiv preprint arXiv:2402.13457 (2024)
54. Yang, A., Yang, T.A.: Social dangers of generative artificial intelligence: review and guidelines. In: Proceedings of the 25th Annual International Conference on Digital Government Research, pp. 654–658 (2024)
55. Yu, J., Lin, X., Yu, Z., Xing, X.: Gptfuzzer: red teaming large language models with auto-generated jailbreak prompts. arXiv preprint arXiv:2309.10253 (2023)
56. Yu, J., Lin, X., Yu, Z., Xing, X.: {LLM-Fuzzer}: scaling assessment of large language model jailbreaks. In: 33rd USENIX Security Symposium (USENIX Security 2024), pp. 4657–4674 (2024)
57. Yu, S., Choi, J., Kim, Y.: Don't be a fool: pooling strategies in offensive language detection from user-intended adversarial attacks. In: Findings of the Association for Computational Linguistics: NAACL 2024, pp. 3456–3467 (2024)
58. Yuan, X., et al.: S-eval: automatic and adaptive test generation for benchmarking safety evaluation of large language models. arXiv preprint arXiv:2405.14191 (2024)
59. Zeng, Y., Lin, H., Zhang, J., Yang, D., Jia, R., Shi, W.: How johnny can persuade LLMs to jailbreak them: rethinking persuasion to challenge AI safety by humanizing LLMs. In: Proceedings of the 62nd Annual Meeting of the Association for Computational Linguistics (Volume 1: Long Papers), pp. 14322–14350 (2024)
60. Zhan, Q., Fang, R., Bindu, R., Gupta, A., Hashimoto, T.B., Kang, D.: Removing RLHF protections in GPT-4 via fine-tuning. In: Proceedings of the 2024 Conference of the North American Chapter of the Association for Computational Linguistics: Human Language Technologies (Volume 2: Short Papers), pp. 681–687 (2024)
61. Zou, A., Wang, Z., Carlini, N., Nasr, M., Kolter, J.Z., Fredrikson, M.: Universal and transferable adversarial attacks on aligned language models. arXiv preprint arXiv:2307.15043 (2023)

How Dataset Diversity Affects Generalization in ML-Based NIDS

Benoit Nougnanke[1]([✉])[iD], Gregory Blanc[1][iD], and Thomas Robert[2][iD]

[1] SAMOVAR, Telecom SudParis, Institut Polytechnique de Paris, Palaiseau, France
{kokouvi-benoit.nougnanke,gregory.blanc}@telecom-sudparis.eu
[2] Telecom Paris, Institut Polytechnique de Paris, Palaiseau, France
thomas.robert@telecom-paris.fr

Abstract. Machine Learning-based Network Intrusion Detection Systems (ML-based NIDS) rely heavily on the quality of the datasets used for training and evaluation. However, widely used NIDS benchmarks often suffer from poor data diversity, which limits model generalization and undermines the reliability of evaluation protocols. While prior work has acknowledged this limitation, a systematic framework to quantify dataset diversity and analyze its relationship with performance is still missing. To address this gap, we introduce a structured approach for characterizing dataset diversity in ML-based NIDS, grounded in measurement theory. We distinguish three types of diversity—*intra-class*, *inter-class*, and *domain-shift*—and operationalize their measurement using established metrics such as the Vendi Score and the Jensen-Shannon divergence. Our empirical analysis on the CIC-IDS2018 dataset, spanning sixty diversity-controlled train–test experiments, provides new insights into the relationship between diversity and generalization and demonstrates the value of diversity-aware data sampling for improving evaluation reliability.

Keywords: NIDS Datasets · Diversity · Machine Learning · Generalization · Performance Evaluation · Measurement Theory

1 Introduction

In the era of increasing cyber threats, *network intrusion detection systems (NIDS)* play a crucial role in safeguarding digital infrastructures. Machine learning (ML)-based NIDS offer promising capabilities, enabling dynamic adaptation to evolving attack patterns. However, the performance of these systems heavily depends on the datasets used during training and evaluation, as datasets are the foundation for learning models and assessing their performance and robustness [5, 8, 19].

While ML-based NIDS offer significant promise, their practical effectiveness and adoption remain limited by two persistent challenges that are insufficiently addressed in the literature: the quality of available datasets, and the robustness and informativeness of current evaluation practices [2, 4].

First, from a data quality perspective, recent studies have highlighted a wide range of structural flaws in NIDS datasets, including over-correlated features, labeling inconsistencies, duplicated flows, and limited domain coverage [22,24,26]. These flaws referred to as *bad design smells* by Flood et al. [15], impede the development of robust and generalizable models. They impact *generalization*, the model's ability to correctly classify unseen but in-distribution samples, as well as *robustness*, which refers to the model's stability under perturbations or shifts, such as distributional drift, novel attack variants, or noisy inputs. For instance, limited diversity in the training data can cause over-fitting, whereas lab-generated traces often contain labeling errors and simulation artifacts such as fixed IP ranges, deterministic inter-arrival times, or constant header fields; models latch onto these artificial regularities, so their accuracy collapses when the same features are absent in real traffic. Among these flaws, *poor data diversity* stands out as a key limitation because, although numerous studies explicitly mention diversity as an essential dataset property [14,17,31,33], a formal and quantitative way to assess it is still missing.

Second, from an evaluation standpoint, model performance is often reported on fixed train/test splits (even with cross-validation) without accounting for dataset variability or generalization limits. For example, models trained on publicly available NIDS datasets may achieve near-perfect performance (e.g., F1-scores close to 1.0), yet fail dramatically when the test distribution shifts even slightly [9]. While cross-dataset or domain adaptation approaches exist [3], they are often complex and costly to deploy. A more tractable alternative is to *manipulate dataset diversity* itself to evaluate model behavior under controlled generalization conditions.

Together, these issues highlight a gap in the structured assessment of NIDS datasets, particularly with regard to *diversity* and its effect on evaluation and generalization. While the ML community has recently begun to explore diversity and data-centric evaluation [28,39], these efforts have yet to be fully adapted to the NIDS context. To address this gap, we investigate the role of dataset diversity in the evaluation and performance of ML-based NIDS through the following research questions:

- **RQ1:** How can we clarify, organize, and categorize the different notions and metrics of data diversity relevant to ML-based NIDS, spanning from entropy-based formulations to distribution-based divergence measures?
- **RQ2:** To what extent do different diversity factors (intra-class, inter-class, and domain-shift) correlate with the performance and generalization of ML-based NIDS models?
- **RQ3:** How can diversity-aware data sampling considerations support a more reliable and informative evaluation of NIDS models?

Recent works in ML [36,38,39] and in NIDS [14,15,31] highlight the importance of data diversity. For example, Flood et al. [15] identify "poor data diversity" as a key data design flow and propose a similarity-based heuristic to flag low heterogeneity, though it does not quantify diversity itself. We distinguish three diversity dimensions: intra-class variability, captured using the similarity and entropy-based Vendi Score [16], inter-class separability, measured via JSD, and domain shift between training and test distributions. This typology, grounded in measurement theory [7,39], enables systematic characterization of dataset structure and empirical evaluation of generalization. We validate it on CIC-IDS2018 across sixty controlled train-test configurations.

In response to the research questions, our study delivers three key findings. First, we propose a systematic typology of diversity metrics—covering intra-class, inter-class, and domain shift dimensions—by adapting and applying established measures (the Vendi Score and JSD) to NIDS data; in particular, we adapt the Vendi Score, originally developed for general ML tasks, to the context of flow-based NIDS data (RQ1). Second, we show strong empirical correlations between these metrics and model performance under controlled sampling, highlighting how diversity alignment predicts generalization and robustness (RQ2). Third, we derive practical guidelines for diversity-aware sampling strategies, enabling more reliable and informative NIDS evaluation pipelines (RQ3).

2 Related Work

2.1 Issues with NIDS Dataset Usage

NIDS heavily rely on benchmark datasets for model training and evaluation [32]. However, despite the proliferation of public datasets over the past two decades, the community continues to face recurring issues that limit the effectiveness, reproducibility, and credibility of ML-based intrusion detection systems.

Limited Access to Realistic Data. Realistic datasets are difficult to obtain due to the sensitivity and privacy concerns surrounding real network traffic. Unlike domains such as computer vision, where large-scale datasets like ImageNet provide stable and well-validated benchmarks, NIDS datasets are often constructed in closed testbeds with simulated traffic and attacks [2]. This results in snapshots that may be poorly representative of operational conditions. Furthermore, unlike images where semantic categories (e.g., "cow") persist, attack behaviors evolve rapidly, making the data lifecycle a significant challenge.

Lack of Clarity on What Makes a Dataset "good." Numerous efforts have criticized structural flaws in popular datasets, including CIC-IDS2017/2018 and NSL-KDD. These flaws include duplicated flows, over-correlated features, incorrect labels, and unrealistic traffic distributions [22,24,26]. Flood et al. [15] categorize such flaws under the term *bad design smells*, pointing to recurring patterns that hinder model generalization and robustness. Yet, no standard methodology exists to define or measure the "quality" of a NIDS dataset.

Biases in Evaluation Undermine Credibility. Evaluation pipelines often rely on fixed splits or random cross-validation, ignoring dataset variability or generalization limits [4,15]. As a result, models can score highly performant on the benchmark (e.g., F1-scores > 0.99) while failing under slightly different test conditions [9]. These inflated performances raise concerns about the reliability of current evaluation practices and their relevance to real-world deployment.

Therefore, a principled approach is needed to characterize NIDS datasets, focusing on often overlooked factors such as structural diversity, separability, and distributional shift, which critically influence model generalization.

2.2 Metrics for Dataset Characterization

To move beyond high-level critiques and simple heuristic evaluations of NIDS datasets, we must engage with the broader spectrum of metrics available for characterizing data. Mitchell et al. [28] and Zhao et al. [39] call for more rigorous, measurement-theoretic foundations for dataset evaluation, advocating for structured metrics across five main categories: distance, density, diversity, tendency, and association. These metrics offer a principled lens for assessing different aspects of dataset structure and support the development of more interpretable and robust ML pipelines. In the context of NIDS, our focus is on the subset of metrics related to structural diversity, class separability, and distributional shift.

Flood et al. [15] take a first step toward quantifying dataset issues through heuristic metrics, including a *Poor Data Diversity* score. This score ranges from 0 (no concern) to 1 (severe issue), based on clustering compactness and cosine similarity within classes. While these scores provide useful diagnostic tools for identifying diversity flaws, they do not measure actual NIDS data diversity.

Shannon entropy and its generalizations (e.g., Rényi and Hill diversity indices [21,35]) on the other hand are well-established candidates for quantifying data variability. The *Vendi Score* [16] extends these ideas by incorporating sample similarity, yielding a more structure-aware notion of effective diversity. It is computed from the eigenspectrum of a similarity matrix between samples. It corresponds to the exponential of Shannon entropy and reflects the number of effectively distinct elements in a class. Our work adopts the Vendi Score as the primary intra-class diversity metric, a state-of-the art ML diversity metric [39].

Complementary to intra-class metrics, information-theoretic divergences such as *Kullback-Leibler divergence* (KLD) and *Jensen-Shannon divergence* (JSD) are widely used in generative modeling to assess how closely synthetic distributions approximate real ones [11]. We adapt JSD to quantify both *inter-class separability* (e.g., benign vs. attack) and *domain-shift* between training and test sets.

Finally, Flood et al. [14] introduce the *Spectral Input Complexity* (SIC) metric, which assesses input complexity by analyzing inter-feature dependencies via spectral clustering. SIC provides a single normalized score that captures how predictable or redundant the features are, with higher values indicating richer, more complex input structures. While SIC targets dataset complexity from a feature perspective, it is complementary to our approach, which emphasizes behavioral diversity and distributional alignment.

2.3 Data Manipulation for Evaluation and Robustness

Beyond dataset usage, a growing body of work investigates how restructuring data can support more reliable evaluation or improve the robustness of ML-based security systems. These efforts typically aim to mitigate structural biases, test generalization under distribution shifts, or adapt to evolving threat landscapes.

One approach uses data permutation or label randomization as a diagnostic tool. For example, Wasielewska et al. [37] introduce *PerQoDA*, a permutation-based method for assessing dataset quality before model training. It tests whether feature–label associations are statistically significant and whether the data contains sufficient structure for reliable classification. By progressively permuting labels and comparing model performance, the method quantifies the stability of learned patterns. This helps detect hidden irregularities in high-dimensional data and provides a principled way to assess dataset learnability before ML use.

A second line of work tackles biases from flawed experimental design. The *TESSERACT* [30] framework shows how inappropriate train/test splits can inflate Android malware classification results. It proposes space and time constraints on evaluation to ensure models are not trained on future or temporally inconsistent data. *INSOMNIA* [1] extends this idea to NIDS, combining incremental learning, active sampling, and explainability to handle concept drift.

A third line of work explores preprocessing to mitigate class imbalance and improve performance. López et al. [27] analyze how data-intrinsic characteristics, such as class overlap, borderline instances, and distributional shifts, affect classification in imbalanced settings. This motivates the need for tailored preprocessing. One widely adopted technique is SMOTE (Synthetic Minority Oversampling Technique), which creates additional minority examples by *interpolating* between a sample and its nearest minority neighbors, instead of duplicating points [13]. Interpolation helps to reduce over-fitting. In NIDS, however, these synthetic samples may lack realism, as feature-level interpolation does not always translate to plausible flows or packet sequences. Nevertheless, since its introduction, SMOTE has inspired many extensions, including for multi-label and semi-supervised learning, and is now a standard tool for mitigating data imbalance. Bagui and Li [6] systematically compare oversampling and undersampling methods for NIDS, showing that resampling significantly improves recall for minority-class attacks under high imbalance.

Our work complements this perspective by focusing on structural diversity, aiming to quantify and manipulate diversity itself to study its impact on model generalization and robustness.

3 Approach and Methodology

Network intrusion detection is cast here as a supervised classification problem: in the binary case, the objective is to distinguish benign traffic from attacks, whereas, in the multi-class case, each attack category constitutes a separate label. To evaluate dataset diversity rigorously we adopt the four measurement-theory phases: *conceptualization* (define the constructs), *operationalization* (map them to concrete metrics), *reliability* (check metric stability across different runs), and *validity* (verify that the metrics capture the intended constructs) [7,39]. This framework lets us treat diversity as a measurable property that supports both dataset characterization and model evaluation.

3.1 Diversity Constructs and Metrics

We begin by defining three complementary constructs that capture the diversity properties most relevant for ML-based NIDS: *i)* **Intra-class diversity:** variation within a single class (e.g., benign or specific attack type), reflecting behavioral heterogeneity and internal variability; *ii)* **Inter-class divergence:** separation between classes (e.g., benign vs. attack), capturing how distinguishable the categories are in feature space; and *iii)* **Domain-shift divergence:** distributional changes between training and test sets for a given class (e.g., benign or attack), eliciting generalization challenges. To make these constructs measurable, we adopt a suite of diversity metrics inspired by both biodiversity modeling and information theory.

Intra-class Diversity. We quantify variation within a class with the *Vendi Score* (VS_q) presented in Eq. (1), a similarity-aware measure of effective diversity based on the eigenvalue spectrum of the similarity matrix of samples X. The parameter q controls sensitivity to rare or dominant elements. For $q = 1$, which treats all elements uniformly, it translates to the exponential of the Shannon entropy (Eq. (2)).

$$VS_q(X,k) = \exp\left(\frac{1}{1-q} \log \sum_{i \in \mathrm{supp}(\lambda(X,k))} \lambda_i^q(X,k)\right) \qquad (1)$$

$$VS_{1.0}(X,k) = \exp\left(-\sum_{i \in \mathrm{supp}(\lambda(X,k))} \lambda_i \log \lambda_i\right), \qquad (2)$$

where λ_i are the normalized eigenvalues and $\mathrm{supp}(\lambda(X,k))$ are the indices for the nonzero eigenvalues. This value reflects the effective number of distinct behaviors in X.

We also refer to the Hill number D_q (Eq. (3)), a general diversity formulation based on S discrete species with relative abundance p_i:

$$D_q = \left(\sum_{i=1}^{S} p_i^q\right)^{\frac{1}{1-q}}, \qquad (3)$$

from which VS_q can be seen as a similarity-based extension. While D_q is not used directly in our experiments, it offers a flexible theoretical baseline for entropy-based diversity measures.

Inter-class Divergence. It is quantified using symmetric information-theoretic measures that assess the degree of separation between two class distributions, denoted P for benign traffic and Q for attack traffic. We primarily use the *Jensen-Shannon divergence* (JSD_2) in Eq.(5), a bounded and symmetric variant of the Kullback-Leibler divergence (KLD):

$$D_{\text{KL}}(P \parallel Q) = \sum_{x \in \mathcal{X}} P(x) \log\left(\frac{P(x)}{Q(x)}\right), \tag{4}$$

$$\text{JSD}(P, Q) = \frac{1}{2} D_{\text{KL}}(P \parallel M) + \frac{1}{2} D_{\text{KL}}(Q \parallel M), \quad \text{where } M = \frac{1}{2}(P + Q). \tag{5}$$

JSD_2, computed with log base 2, captures the degree of distributional overlap and is particularly well suited for comparing probability densities or empirical histograms derived from feature distributions. It ranges between 0 and 1, where higher values indicate stronger class separability.

Domain-Shift Divergence. We quantify how a class's diversity and distribution change from training to test time with three metrics: *i)* $\Delta VS_{1.0}$, the difference in intra-class diversity between splits; *ii)* ΔJSD_2 (IC), the change in inter-class separability; and *iii)* JSD_2 DS, the Jensen–Shannon divergence between the same class observed in the two domains. Together they provide complementary views of generalization difficulty: $\Delta VS_{1.0}$ reflects the coverage mismatch within a class; ΔJSD_2 captures changes in separability; and JSD_2 DS measures distributional drift.

To connect with standard ML shift taxonomy [23,29,34], our metrics primarily reflect *covariate shift* ($P(X|Y)$ changes without altering the relationship from features to the target label), and partially *label shift* (when divergence alters decision boundaries). They are computed at the feature level and used to explain performance drop under controlled training diversity.

3.2 Reliability and Validity

We group the final two methodological steps—reliability and validity—under the broader notion of *empirical soundness* of the proposed diversity metrics. In our context, reliability can be assessed through: (i) *Inter-metric consistency*, e.g., correlation between Vendi Score and Shannon entropy as alternative estimators of intra-class diversity; (ii) *Test-retest robustness*, i.e., repeated computation of a metric under slight sampling variations of the same underlying distribution. While theoretical validity is provided by the grounding of our metrics in biodiversity and information theory, we focus here on empirical forms of validity: (i) *Convergent validity*: different metrics intended to measure the same construct (e.g., $VS_{1.0}$ vs entropy for intra-class diversity, or JSD vs KLD for divergence) should yield positively correlated results; (ii) *Predictive validity*: diversity metrics should correlate with downstream model performance.

In this study, we support these validity claims through a range of empirical analyses: correlations between intra-class diversity metrics (e.g., $VS_{1.0}$) and classification performance (e.g., AUC, F1), as well as the relationship between train-test diversity shifts (e.g., $\Delta VS_{1.0}$, JSD_2) and generalization outcomes across multiple attack types.

4 Experimental Setup

Our experimental setup aims to evaluate how different forms of dataset diversity influence the generalization ability of ML-NIDS models. We focus on two core hypotheses: *i)* increasing intra-class diversity (measured using the Vendi Score, $VS_{1.0}$) in the training data improves model performance on unseen test samples (RQ2), and *ii)* measuring the divergence between training and test distributions, with intra-class diversity shifts ($\Delta VS_{1.0}$) and domain-level shifts (JSD_2 DS), provides a way to control the level of generalization assessed via performance metrics computed on confusion matrix for the test set (RQ3). To test these hypotheses, we generate controlled training subsets exhibiting varying $VS_{1.0}$ diversity levels and analyze how diversity metrics correlate with downstream classification performance. We evaluate the model performance using the Area Under the ROC Curve (AUC), F1-score, Sensitivity (True Positive Rate), and Specificity (True Negative Rate), which capture both global and class-wise discrimination.

We conduct our experiments on the CIC-IDS2018 dataset [33][1], a common ML-based NIDS benchmark [18]. This dataset covers multiple attack categories, including *Botnet, BruteForce, DDoS, DoS, Infiltration,* and *Web Attack*. Each attack scenario was executed independently on specific days, with its own corresponding benign background traffic. For each attack type, we sample a balanced dataset (50% benign, 50% attack) via undersampling, ensuring fair class-wise evaluation. We also built `CIC18_All` by merging all attacks and their benign flows. Following the original design of CIC-IDS2018, we preserve the association between attack flows and their background benign flows, respecting the experimental conditions under which the data was generated. We use fixed test sets throughout our experiments, corresponding to a 20% held-out portion of each dataset, while diversity-controlled training subsets are sampled from the remaining 80%. An overview of this dataset processing pipeline appears in Fig. 1.

We perform feature selection separately for each attack type using Random Forest importance to select top-k features (typically $k = 10$ or $k = 20$), following the approach suggested by Li et al. [25] (see Appendix B). These selected features are used both for training classifiers and for computing diversity metrics. For computational efficiency, whenever a class subset exceeds 10,000 flows, we randomly sample 10,000 flows and compute $VS_{1.0}$ on that sample, which empirically provides a reliable estimate of the full-set Vendi Score. All experiments are conducted in a supervised setting with binary classification, where each network flow is labeled as either benign or malicious. We use Random Forest (RF) classifiers, chosen for their robustness, interpretability, and stability across settings.

---

[1] https://registry.opendata.aws/cse-cic-ids2018.

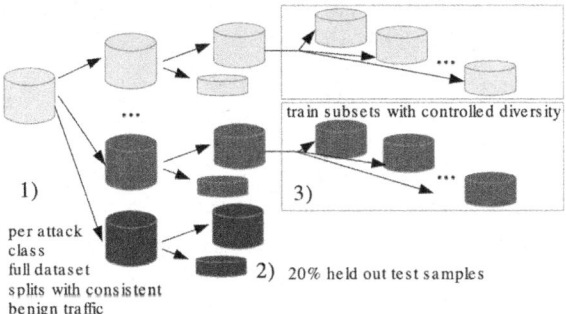

Fig. 1. Overview of dataset processing pipeline: 1) Per-attack splits, 2) 20% held-out test sets, 3) Controlled diversity sampling via spectral clustering.

Table 1. Diversity metrics on test sets (Vendi Score and Inter-class JSD)

Attack	$VS_{1.0}$ Benign	$VS_{1.0}$ Attack	Inter-class JSD_2
CIC18_All	4.755	2.859	0.772
CIC18_Botnet	5.157	1.127	0.373
CIC18_BruteForce	1.844	1.033	0.682
CIC18_DDoS	3.457	2.594	0.985
CIC18_DoS	4.152	1.939	0.947
CIC18_Infiltration	4.474	4.552	0.376
CIC18_WebAttack	4.315	3.030	0.977

Their low tuning sensitivity avoids confounding effects, allowing focus on dataset diversity effects. As a common NIDS baseline, RF also ensures reproducibility.

To generate controlled diversity conditions, we apply spectral clustering on sample similarity matrices derived from training data. This produces subsets exhibiting varying intra-class diversity levels measured by $VS_{1.0}$ (see Algorithm 1 in Appendix A for details). As a baseline, we also include a classical 80:20 train/test split without controlled sampling. Preliminary tests with random fixed-size subsets showed consistent performance trends, justifying our focus on diversity variation. Notably, even relatively small training subsets (1,000 to 3,000 samples) achieved strong detection performance, consistent with findings in [12].

All diversity-controlled subsets are drawn exclusively from the 80% training split, limiting the source pool to at most 30,000 samples per class to ensure computational feasibility. In total, we generated 56 diversity-controlled train subsets: 14 for CIC18_All, 10 for *DoS*, 18 for *Infiltration*, and 14 for *WebAttack*, each paired with its fixed 20% test set. Including the four classical 80:20 baseline splits brings the total to 60 distinct train–test experiments. The fixed test sets remain identical across experiments and are not altered. Table 1 summarizes the diversity characteristics of these test sets. We observe that benign traffic generally

Table 2. Strongest correlation values r between the Vendi Score and performance indicators, per attack type. $VS_{1.0}A = VS_{1.0}$ (Attack), $VS_{1.0}B = VS_{1.0}$ (Benign).

Attack	F1	AUC	Sensitivity	Specificity
CIC18_All	0.894 ($VS_{1.0}A$)	0.781 ($VS_{1.0}A$)	0.835 ($VS_{1.0}A$)	0.522 ($VS_{1.0}B$)
CIC18_DoS	0.714 ($VS_{1.0}A$)	**0.786** ($VS_{1.0}A$)	0.869 ($VS_{1.0}A$)	-0.768 ($VS_{1.0}A$)
CIC18_Infiltration	0.752 ($VS_{1.0}A$)	0.546 ($VS_{1.0}A$)	0.790 ($VS_{1.0}A$)	-0.733 ($VS_{1.0}A$)
CIC18_WebAttack	0.810 ($VS_{1.0}A$)	**0.765** ($VS_{1.0}A$)	**0.874** ($VS_{1.0}A$)	-0.430 ($VS_{1.0}B$)

exhibits high intra-class diversity (e.g., $VS_{1.0} > 4.0$), while attack traffic shows wider variation, ranging from very low diversity in *BruteForce* ($VS_{1.0} = 1.0$) to higher diversity in *Infiltration* ($VS_{1.0} = 4.6$). Similarly, inter-class separability measured by JSD_2 varies significantly across attacks, from highly separable (e.g., *DDoS* with $JSD_2 \approx 0.98$) to lower separability (e.g., *Botnet* with $JSD_2 \approx 0.37$).

In the following, we quantify the relationship between diversity metrics and model performance using the Pearson correlation coefficient, denoted as r. The coefficient r measures the strength and direction of a linear relationship between two variables (for example, X for the Vendi Score diversity metric and Y for the AUC), ranging from -1 (perfect negative correlation) to $+1$ (perfect positive correlation), with 0 indicating no linear correlation. Positive r (close to $+1$) implies higher diversity is associated with improved performance, while a negative r (close to -1) suggests the opposite. We also report the p-value, which assesses the statistical significance of the observed correlation; a low p-value (typically < 0.05) suggests that the correlation is unlikely to be due to random chance.

5 Does Diversity Matter? Empirical Correlations

This section answers **RQ2** and tests **Hypothesis 1**: *higher intra-class diversity in the training data leads to better generalization.* Diversity-controlled train subsets are produced with the spectral clustering procedure in Algorithm 1 (Appendix A). We first present the results of the setting in which each subset pairs one benign traffic cluster and one attack traffic cluster obtained with the *same* number of underlying spectral clusters. For every subset, we record the Vendi Score for both benign ($VS_{1.0}B$) and attack ($VS_{1.0}A$) flows. Figure 2 shows that a clear upward/leftward shift is visible for many attacks when $VS_{1.0}A$ increases. In *DoS*, for instance, the subset with $VS_{1.0}A \approx 2.07$ achieves AUC $= 0.97$, whereas low-diversity subsets with $VS_{1.0}A = 1.00$ are confined to AUC ≈ 0.74–0.83.

Second, we broaden the analysis to *all* benign/attack subset combinations generated by the clustering procedure. Table 2 reports the strongest Pearson correlations (r) between $VS_{1.0}$ and each performance metric. *DoS* and *Web Attack* show the clearest positive correlations. For *DoS*, $VS_{1.0}A$ correlates strongly with AUC ($r = 0.786$) and Sensitivity ($r = 0.869$), while for *Web Attack* the correlations reach $r = 0.765$ (AUC) and $r = 0.874$ (Sensitivity). Concretely, raising

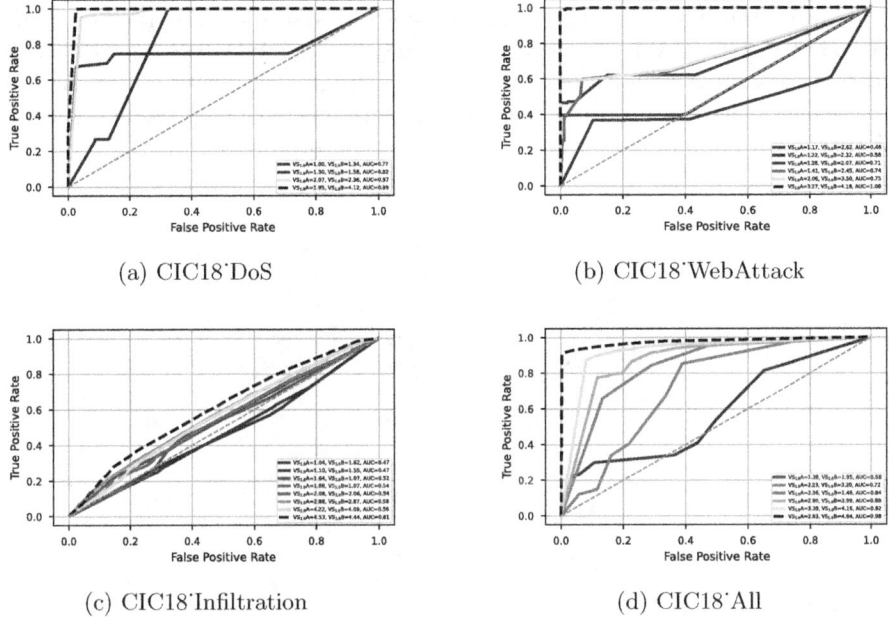

Fig. 2. ROC curves for diversity-controlled train subsets. Each color corresponds to a different attack-side diversity value ($VS_{1.0}A$). The dashed black curve corresponds to the ROC curve of the baseline 80:20 split.

$VS_{1.0}A$ in *Web Attack* from 1.17 to 3.03 lifts AUC from 0.50–0.78 to 0.99 and boosts Sensitivity from 0.38 to 0.97 at Specificity ≥ 0.86. *Infiltration* shows weaker or inconsistent effects: the best AUC correlation is only $r = 0.546$, and Specificity is negatively correlated ($r = -0.733$). Even $VS_{1.0}A > 4$ keeps AUC beyond 0.57. This limited gain suggests that factors other than diversity dominate, such as the limited discriminative power of available features for *Infiltration* and the attack's complex, multi-stage behaviors with overlapping patterns. For the aggregate dataset (`CIC18_All`) the positive pattern re-appears: $VS_{1.0}A$ correlates with AUC at $r = 0.78$, and subsets with $VS_{1.0}A \approx 2.8$–3.4 reach AUC ≥ 0.92, whereas a low-diversity subset ($VS_{1.0}A = 1.38$) falls to AUC $= 0.58$.

Summary. The empirical evidence supports Hypothesis 1, but the strength of the diversity–performance relationship is *attack-dependent*. A single, global diversity measure obscures class-specific effects. Instead, diversity must be considered separately for each attack to yield more reliable and informative insights.

6 Characterizing Generalization Gaps via Diversity and Distribution Shift

This section addresses **RQ 3** and tests **Hypothesis 2**: *model performance degrades in proportion to the mismatch between training and test distributions.*

Building on the sixty train–test configurations introduced in Sect. 4, we correlate each shift metric ($\Delta VS_{1.0}A$, $\Delta VS_{1.0}B$, ΔJSD_2 IC, and JSD_2 DS A) with classification performance indicators (AUC, F1, sensitivity, specificity). This analysis identifies which forms of train–test misalignment most strongly predict generalization error, guiding more informative evaluation protocols.

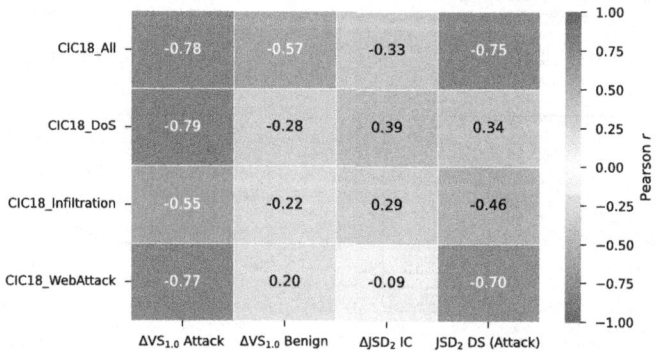

Fig. 3. Pearson correlation (r) between each train–test shift metric and AUC, for every attack class. Strong negative values (deep blue) indicate that larger shifts reduce detection performance. (Color figure online)

Figure 3 summarizes how the four shift metrics relate to AUC. Three observations emerge. First, the *intra-class diversity shift on the attack side* ($\Delta VS_{1.0}A$) shows the strongest and most consistent negative correlation (with $p < 0.05$), reaching $r = -0.79$ for *DoS*, $r = -0.77$ for *Web Attack* and $r = -0.78$ on the combined dataset. Second, the *domain-level shift* JSD_2 DS (A) is almost as informative, with significant negative correlations for three attacks and the global setting. Third, the other two metrics, benign side diversity shift and inter-class separability shift, display weaker or inconsistent relationships.

6.1 Intra-class Diversity Shift ($\Delta VS_{1.0}$)

The closer the attack-traffic diversity in training is to that of the test set, the better the detector generalizes; large mismatches routinely translate into marked AUC drops of about 10 – 20 %. For example, AUC falls from 0.88 to 0.72 on CIC18_All and from 0.78 to 0.55 on *Web Attack* when we compare the most closely aligned subsets to the most mis-aligned ones; even Infiltration slips from 0.53 to 0.49 under the same contrast. By contrast, benign-side shifts show weak or inconsistent effects ($|r| \leq 0.57$), likely due to good benign coverage across subsets. Scenarios where benign coverage is paramount—such as unsupervised anomaly detection or adversarial-robustness stress tests—may reveal a stronger benign effect, which we leave as an open direction for future research. For each attack class, it seems sufficient to align the attack traffic diversity between the

Table 3. Comparison of inter-class diversity (JSD$_2$) on training and test sets, and mean performance per attack.

Attack	JSD$_2$ Train	JSD$_2$ Test	ΔJSD$_2$	Specificity	Sensitivity
CIC18_All	0.603	0.772	0.168	0.720	0.682
CIC18_DoS	0.563	0.947	0.384	0.841	0.778
CIC18_WebAttack	0.392	0.977	0.585	0.892	0.480
CIC18_Infiltration	0.461	0.376	-0.084	0.512	0.508

train set and the test set to perform better on generalization metrics in this context of supervised binary classification. In practice, it is less constraining than maintaining both attack and benign traffic intra-class diversity aligned.

6.2 Inter-class Separability Shift (ΔJSD$_2$ IC)

This shift measures how the geometric separability between benign and attack traffic changes from training to test time. Its relation with AUC is weak on CIC18_All ($r = -0.33$), mildly positive for *DoS* ($r = 0.39$), and essentially zero for *Web Attack* ($r = -0.09$). Nevertheless, ΔJSD$_2$ IC aligns strongly with the trade-off between false positives and false negatives. For example, for CIC18_All, it correlates positively with sensitivity ($r = 0.42$) but negatively with specificity ($r = -0.67$, $p < 0.01$). Table 3 shows that the test set is more separable than the training set for three attacks (ΔJSD$_2$ IC > 0), while *Infiltration* moves in the opposite direction. Larger positive shifts increase *specificity*: it rises from 0.72 to 0.84 on DoS and to 0.89 on WebAttack. Sensitivity, however, does not improve in WebAttack; it even drops to 0.48, so overall F1 remains mixed.

Why does extra separability help specificity more than sensitivity? The decision threshold learned is calibrated to the *relative* benign/attack density during training. If the test set becomes easier (classes move further apart), previously borderline benign flows now fall safely on the benign side of the boundary, reducing false positives (FP) and raising specificity. At the same time, the boundary need not shift toward the attack cluster, so the number of correctly flagged attacks (true positives) does not necessarily increase. *Infiltration* illustrates the reverse: a negative separability shift reduces both specificity and sensitivity, consistent with a boundary that is now too optimistic for a more entangled test set.

Though benign intra-class diversity had limited impact, inter-class separability clearly matters. It shapes the FP/FN trade-off and affects metrics differently, but significantly. It complements the intra-class diversity findings above.

6.3 Domain-Level Shift (JSD$_2$ DS)

This metric captures the global divergence between the attack class feature distribution in train versus test sets. In the aggregate dataset, it is strongly and significantly negative for every performance indicator (AUC $r = -0.75$, F1 $r = -0.92$, sensitivity $r = -0.88$; all $p < 0.01$), confirming that large domain drift degrades detection. Two patterns emerge when we look closely at each attack:

- **WebAttack and Infiltration** behave as expected: larger drift worsens performance (AUC: $r = -0.70$ and $r = -0.46$, respectively), mostly due to lower sensitivity ($r = -0.91$ and $r = -0.74$). The model misses more attacks as their feature distribution has moved away from what was seen in training.
- **DoS** shows the opposite sign for AUC ($r = 0.34$) and a strong positive link with sensitivity ($r = 0.89$) but a negative link with specificity ($r = -0.74$). In this case, the drift pushes the attack samples *further away* from the benign region, so the detector catches more attacks at the cost of extra FPs.

Domain-level shift, thus, influences the *overall* operating point of the classifier: drift that moves attacks closer to benign traffic hurts both AUC and sensitivity. It is the symptom of a more difficult classification problem. A drift that moves them further apart can raise sensitivity but simultaneously inflate FPs. Taken together with the intra-class and inter-class results above, these findings help to understand how to interpret the usual generalization assessment metrics.

Summary. The three shift metrics yield complementary insights into generalization difficulty. Intra-class diversity shift quantifies coverage mismatch within each class but can be zero even when the overall feature distributions diverge. Inter-class separability shift captures how the benign–attack boundary moves, directly affecting the FP/FN balance. Domain-level shift measures the global divergence between train and test attack distributions, revealing misalignments that intra- or inter-class metrics alone would miss. Together, these three axes provide a holistic diagnosis of model generalization under distributional change.

7 Discussion

Our results show *how much (and in which direction) diversity mis-aligns* between train and test data explains most of the variance in ML-NIDS performance. We addressed the three research questions from Sect. 1 through the following main findings: *i)* a systematic typology of diversity metrics—covering intra-class, inter-class, and domain shift dimensions—by adapting and applying established measures (the Vendi Score and JSD) to NIDS data; in particular, we adapt the Vendi Score, originally developed for general ML tasks, to the context of flow-based NIDS data (RQ1), *ii)* strong empirical correlations between these metrics and model performance (RQ2), and *iii)* practical guidelines for improving evaluation via diversity-aware sampling strategies (RQ3). We now discuss two implications: shift-aware evaluation and structured dataset characterization.

7.1 Rethinking Evaluation: Accounting for Distributional Shift

Section 6 shows that attack-side intra-class shift ($\Delta VS_{1.0}A$) is a good predictor of AUC and sensitivity. Yet mainstream practices—random train/test splits or k-fold cross-validation—implicitly assume the test distribution matches the training distribution, leading to overly optimistic scores. We therefore advocate **shift-aware evaluation** in three steps:

i) *Measure train–test misalignment.* For every run, compute the three shift metrics introduced in Sect. 6: $\Delta VS_{1.0}A/B$, ΔJSD_2 IC, and JSD_2 DS.
ii) *Probe robustness.* Hold the test set fixed and vary training diversity to map how each shift axis influences AUC, F1, sensitivity, and specificity. (The ROC curves grid in Sect. 5 illustrates part of this).
iii) *Report difficulty-weighted scores.* Weight each run by its shift severity, e.g.,

$$w = \frac{|\Delta VS_{1.0}A|}{|\Delta VS_{1.0}A| + \lambda}, \qquad \lambda > 0,$$

so perfectly aligned splits (easy) are down-weighted and high-shift splits (hard) count more. A weighted AUC is then $wAUC = \sum_i w_i \, AUC_i / \sum_i w_i$. *DoS example:* the two most aligned DoS splits ($\Delta VS_{1.0}A \approx 0.30$) score AUC = 0.97 and 0.93, weighted at 0.75 (with $\lambda = 0.1$), whereas the six harder splits ($\Delta \approx 0.77$, AUC ≈ 0.82) receive a weight of 0.88. The headline AUC falls from 0.97 to a shift-aware 0.89, preventing an eight-point overestimate and giving a score that better reflects deployment-time difficulty.

These steps require only post-training statistics and can be added to existing pipelines. They pave the way for robustness-aware model selection or diversity-calibrated performance estimation, under distributional shift, complementing shift adaptation tools like Mandoline [10].

7.2 Structured Dataset Characterization

Beyond evaluation, our framework enables **dataset characterization** via diversity analysis. By computing intra-class metrics (e.g., $VS_{1.0}$), inter-class divergence (e.g., JSD_2), and domain shift (e.g., JSD_2 DS), we can reveal the internal behavior heterogeneity and separability of class distributions.

Diversity metrics also help diagnose datasets themselves. For example, *Web Attack* attains high AUC with the *smallest* training split because its $VS_{1.0}A$ is maximal. In contrast, Infiltration remains hard despite sizeable splits because its attack class overlaps heavily with the benign one and shows large domain drift. Such insights cannot be obtained from class counts or overlap percentages alone. We therefore recommend **characterising datasets with** $VS_{1.0}$ and JSD_2 profiles so that practitioners can (i) compare variants objectively, (ii) detect preprocessing errors that collapse diversity, and (iii) target attack variants that are barely represented so additional data can be collected for them.

Limitations. Our analysis is flow-level and feature-based; packet-level or context-aware representations (e.g., host graphs) may reveal additional diversity axes, especially for complex behaviors such as *Infiltration*. More fundamentally, understanding generalization requires distinguishing between *aleatoric uncertainty* (stemming from the data) and *epistemic uncertainty* (originating from the model) [20]. Our framework focuses on the former: it quantifies how dataset diversity and distribution shifts affect model behavior under controlled sampling conditions. To isolate these effects, we used a Random Forest classifier—a robust, interpretable model commonly used in the NIDS literature, with minimal tuning sensitivity. This choice rests on the working assumption that observed correlations between diversity misalignment and performance remain qualitatively valid for other models operating on similar feature representations. While our framework extends to a broader class of models, including deep and self-supervised architectures, assessing their sensitivity to data shifts and capturing epistemic uncertainty remains an important direction for future work.

8 Conclusion

This work proposes a measurement-theoretic framework for characterizing dataset diversity in ML-based NIDS. We introduce and assess three complementary dimensions using well-defined metrics: the Vendi Score for intra-class variability, the Jensen–Shannon Divergence for inter-class separability, and train–test misalignment quantified via diversity and distribution shifts. Through sixty controlled train–test experiments on CIC-IDS2018, we present three key insights. First, attack-side diversity alignment is a strong predictor of detection performance; second, domain-level drift reshapes the classifier's operating point, trading sensitivity against specificity depending on whether attack traffic drifts toward or away from benign flows; third, inter-class separability shifts adjust the false-positive/false-negative balance, complementing the other two dimensions.

Building on these insights, we highlight the value of characterizing NIDS benchmark datasets with intra-class and inter-class diversity. We further recommend that evaluation pipelines adopt controlled sampling of training subsets to span realistic deployment-time diversity scenarios and weight reported performance by the observed train–test diversity shifts, yielding performance estimates that are more informative and reliable under real-world deployment conditions.

While our framework is instantiated here in the context of NIDS, its methodology applies more broadly to flow-based network traffic datasets. However, our focus is specifically on improving the evaluation methodology for ML-based NIDS, where over-optimistic performance reporting due to poorly understood data characteristics remains a serious challenge. We believe that diversity-aware diagnostics and sampling can support more rigorous evaluation practices.

Looking forward, extending this framework to packet-level or graph-based representations, studying deep and self-supervised models under large shifts, and integrating diversity characterization into standard NIDS benchmarks remain important avenues to close the gap between laboratory evaluation and operational readiness of ML-based NIDS.

Acknowledgments. This work has been partially supported by the French National Research Agency under the France 2030 label (Superviz ANR-22-PECY-0008). The views reflected herein do not necessarily reflect the opinion of the French government.

A Diversity-Controlled Subset Sampling

Algorithm 1: VS-Controlled Subset Generation via Spectral Clustering

Input: Dataset X, similarity function κ, number of clusters K, minimum cluster size m, diversity threshold δ
Output: Diversity-controlled subsets $\{X_k\}$ with Vendi Score and size metadata

1 **Step 1: Clustering**
2 Compute similarity matrix $S \in \mathbb{R}^{n \times n}$ using κ (e.g., cosine);
3 Apply spectral clustering on S into K clusters using `assign_labels='discretize'`, `eigen_solver='amg'`;
4 Let $\{C_1, \ldots, C_K\}$ be the resulting clusters;
5 **Step 2: Filter and Evaluate Clusters**
6 Initialize $\mathcal{C} \leftarrow \emptyset$;
7 **foreach** C_i in $\{C_1, \ldots, C_K\}$ **do**
8   **if** $|C_i| \geq m$ **then**
9   Compute $VS_{1.0}(C_i)$ (Vendi Score);
10   Add $\{C_i, VS_{1.0}(C_i), |C_i|\}$ to $\mathcal{C}$

11 **Step 3: Generate Subsets**
12 Initialize $\mathcal{S} \leftarrow \emptyset$;
13 **foreach** $C_i \in \mathcal{C}$ **do**
14   Add C_i as a single-cluster subset to $\mathcal{S}$ with its VS_q and size
15 **for** $r = 2$ **to** $|\mathcal{C}|$ **do**
16   Select top-r clusters by size from $\mathcal{C}$;
17   Let t_r be the smallest cluster size among them;
18   **if** $t_r < m$ **then**
19   continue
20   Sample t_r points from each selected cluster;
21   Merge into X_r, compute $VS_{1.0}(X_r)$;
22   Add X_r to $\mathcal{S}$ with metadata

23 **return** $\mathcal{S}$: subset list with size, and VS_q

B Selected Features Per Attack Types

To support model training and metric computation, we apply Random Forest feature importance to select the top-10 features per attack type. Table 4 summarizes the selected features. While one might raise concerns about the potential dataset-specific influence of certain features (e.g., `Dst Port`, which may dominate in scenarios where a specific attack targets a single port unused by benign traffic), our objective is to reflect the diversity structure present in the data as is. In our framework, overly dominant or redundant features would naturally result in low intra-class diversity or artificially high inter-class separation, both

Table 4. Selected top-10 features per attack based on Random Forest importance

Attack	Selected Features
DoS	Dst Port, Fwd Seg Size Avg, Bwd Pkt Len Std, ACK Flag Cnt, URG Flag Cnt, PSH Flag Cnt, ECE Flag Cnt, RST Flag Cnt, Fwd PSH Flags, SYN Flag Cnt
WebAttack	Dst Port, Bwd Pkts/s, Fwd Pkt Len Mean, Init Fwd Win Byts, Fwd Pkt Len Std, Fwd Seg Size Avg, Pkt Len Mean, Subflow Fwd Byts, Flow IAT Std, Flow Duration
Infiltration	Dst Port, Fwd Seg Size Avg, Bwd Pkt Len Std, PSH Flag Cnt, ACK Flag Cnt, URG Flag Cnt, ECE Flag Cnt, RST Flag Cnt, Fwd URG Flags, CWE Flag Count
All	Dst Port, Init Fwd Win Byts, Flow Duration, Init Bwd Win Byts, Fwd IAT Std, Fwd Header Len, Flow IAT Max, Fwd Pkts/s, Flow IAT Mean, Flow IAT Min

of which are captured by the proposed metrics. This ensures that our diversity analysis remains informative and robust, even under varying feature selection conditions or dataset characteristics.

References

1. Andresini, G., Pendlebury, F., Pierazzi, F., Loglisci, C., Appice, A., Cavallaro, L.: Insomnia: towards concept-drift robustness in network intrusion detection. In: Proceedings of the 14th ACM Workshop on Artificial Intelligence and Security, pp. 111–122 (2021). https://doi.org/10.1145/3474369.3486864
2. Apruzzese, G., Laskov, P., Schneider, J.: Sok: pragmatic assessment of machine learning for network intrusion detection. In: 2023 IEEE 8th European Symposium on Security and Privacy (EuroS&P), pp. 592–614. IEEE (2023). https://doi.org/10.1109/EUROSP57164.2023.00042
3. Apruzzese, G., Pajola, L., Conti, M.: The cross-evaluation of machine learning-based network intrusion detection systems. IEEE Trans. Netw. Serv. Manage. **19**(4), 5152–5169 (2022). https://doi.org/10.1109/TNSM.2022.3157344
4. Arp, D., et al.: Dos and don'ts of machine learning in computer security. In: 31st USENIX Security Symposium (USENIX Security 22), pp. 3971–3988 (2022)
5. Ayoubi, S., Blanc, G., Jmila, H., Silverston, T., Tixeuil, S.: Data-driven evaluation of intrusion detectors: a methodological framework. In: International Symposium on Foundations and Practice of Security, pp. 142–157. Springer (2022). https://doi.org/10.1007/978-3-031-30122-3_9
6. Bagui, S., Li, K.: Resampling imbalanced data for network intrusion detection datasets. J. Big Data **8**(1), 6 (2021). https://doi.org/10.1186/S40537-020-00390-X
7. Bandalos, D.L.: Measurement theory and applications for the social sciences. Guilford Publications (2017)
8. Budach, L., et al.: The effects of data quality on machine learning performance. arXiv preprint arXiv:2207.14529 (2022)

9. Catillo, M., Vecchio, A.D., Pecchia, A., Villano, U.: A critique on the use of machine learning on public datasets for intrusion detection. In: Quality of Information and Communications Technology (2021). https://doi.org/10.1007/978-3-030-85347-1_19, https://api.semanticscholar.org/CorpusID:237378606
10. Chen, M., Goel, K., Sohoni, N.S., Poms, F., Fatahalian, K., Ré, C.: Mandoline: model evaluation under distribution shift. In: International Conference on Machine Learning, pp. 1617–1629. PMLR (2021)
11. Cüppers, J., Schoen, A., Blanc, G., Gimenez, P.F.: Flowchronicle: synthetic network flow generation through pattern set mining. Proc. ACM Netw. **2**(CoNEXT4), 1–20 (2024). https://doi.org/10.1145/3696407
12. D'hooge, L., Wauters, T., Volckaert, B., De Turck, F.: Classification hardness for supervised learners on 20 years of intrusion detection data. iEEE Access **7**, 167455–167469 (2019). https://doi.org/10.1109/ACCESS.2019.2953451
13. Fernández, A., Garcia, S., Herrera, F., Chawla, N.V.: Smote for learning from imbalanced data: progress and challenges, marking the 15-year anniversary. J. Artif. Intell. Res. **61**, 863–905 (2018). https://doi.org/10.1613/JAIR.1.11192
14. Flood, R., Aspinall, D.: Measuring the complexity of benchmark nids datasets via spectral analysis. In: 2024 IEEE European Symposium on Security and Privacy Workshops (EuroS&PW), pp. 335–341. IEEE (2024). https://doi.org/10.1109/EUROSPW61312.2024.00043
15. Flood, R., Engelen, G., Aspinall, D., Desmet, L.: Bad design smells in benchmark nids datasets. In: 2024 IEEE 9th European Symposium on Security and Privacy (EuroS&P), pp. 658–675. IEEE (2024). https://doi.org/10.1109/EUROSP60621.2024.00042
16. Friedman, D., Dieng, A.B.: The vendi score: a diversity evaluation metric for machine learning. Trans. Mach. Learn. Res. (2023). https://openreview.net/forum?id=g97OHbQyk1
17. Gharib, A., Sharafaldin, I., Lashkari, A.H., Ghorbani, A.A.: An evaluation framework for intrusion detection dataset. In: 2016 International Conference on Information Science and Security (ICISS), pp. 1–6. IEEE (2016)
18. Goldschmidt, P., Chudá, D.: Network intrusion datasets: a survey, limitations, and recommendations. Comput. Sec. **156**, 104510 (2025). https://doi.org/10.1016/j.cose.2025.104510
19. Gong, Y., Liu, G., Xue, Y., Li, R., Meng, L.: A survey on dataset quality in machine learning. Inf. Softw. Technol. **162**, 107268 (2023). https://doi.org/10.1016/J.INFSOF.2023.107268
20. Hüllermeier, E., Waegeman, W.: Aleatoric and epistemic uncertainty in machine learning: an introduction to concepts and methods. Mach. Learn. **110**(3), 457–506 (2021). https://doi.org/10.1007/S10994-021-05946-3
21. Jost, L.: Entropy and diversity. Oikos **113**(2), 363–375 (2006)
22. Kenyon, A., Deka, L., Elizondo, D.: Are public intrusion datasets fit for purpose characterising the state of the art in intrusion event datasets. Comput. Sec. **99**, 102022 (2020). https://doi.org/10.1016/J.COSE.2020.102022
23. Kimura, M., Hino, H.: A short survey on importance weighting for machine learning. arXiv preprint arXiv:2403.10175 (2024)
24. Lanvin, M., Gimenez, P.F., Han, Y., Majorczyk, F., Mé, L., Totel, E.: Errors in the cicids2017 dataset and the significant differences in detection performances it makes. In: International Conference on Risks and Security of Internet and Systems, pp. 18–33. Springer (2022). https://doi.org/10.1007/978-3-031-31108-6_2

25. Li, X., Chen, W., Zhang, Q., Wu, L.: Building auto-encoder intrusion detection system based on random forest feature selection. Comput. Sec. **95**, 101851 (2020). https://doi.org/10.1016/J.COSE.2020.101851
26. Liu, L., Engelen, G., Lynar, T., Essam, D., Joosen, W.: Error prevalence in nids datasets: a case study on cic-ids-2017 and cse-cic-ids-2018. In: 2022 IEEE Conference on Communications and Network Security (CNS), pp. 254–262. IEEE (2022). https://doi.org/10.1109/CNS56114.2022.9947235
27. López, V., Fernández, A., García, S., Palade, V., Herrera, F.: An insight into classification with imbalanced data: empirical results and current trends on using data intrinsic characteristics. Inf. Sci. **250**, 113–141 (2013). https://doi.org/10.1016/J.INS.2013.07.007
28. Mitchell, M., et al.: Measuring data. arXiv preprint arXiv:2212.05129 (2022)
29. Moreno-Torres, J.G., Raeder, T., Alaiz-Rodríguez, R., Chawla, N.V., Herrera, F.: A unifying view on dataset shift in classification. Pattern Recogn. **45**(1), 521–530 (2012). https://doi.org/10.1016/J.PATCOG.2011.06.019
30. Pendlebury, F., Pierazzi, F., Jordaney, R., Kinder, J., Cavallaro, L.: {TESSERACT}: eliminating experimental bias in malware classification across space and time. In: 28th USENIX security symposium (USENIX Security 2019), pp. 729–746 (2019)
31. Pinto, D., Amorim, I., Maia, E., Praça, I.: A review on intrusion detection datasets: tools, processes, and features. Comput. Netw., 111177 (2025). https://doi.org/10.1016/J.COMNET.2025.111177
32. Ring, M., Wunderlich, S., Scheuring, D., Landes, D., Hotho, A.: A survey of network-based intrusion detection data sets. Comput. Sec. **86**, 147–167 (2019). https://doi.org/10.1016/J.COSE.2019.06.005
33. Sharafaldin, I., Lashkari, A.H., Ghorbani, A.A., et al.: Toward generating a new intrusion detection dataset and intrusion traffic characterization. ICISSp **1**(2018), 108–116 (2018). https://doi.org/10.5220/0006639801080116
34. Storkey, A., et al.: When training and test sets are different: characterizing learning transfer. Dataset Shift Mach. Learn. **30**(3–28), 6 (2009)
35. Tuomisto, H.: A consistent terminology for quantifying species diversity? yes, it does exist. Oecologia **164**(4), 853–860 (2010)
36. Wang, P., et al.: Diversity measurement and subset selection for instruction tuning datasets. arXiv preprint arXiv:2402.02318 (2024)
37. Wasielewska, K., Soukup, D., Čejka, T., Camacho, J.: Evaluation of the limit of detection in network dataset quality assessment with perqoda. In: Joint European Conference on Machine Learning and Knowledge Discovery in Databases, pp. 170–185. Springer (2022). https://doi.org/10.1007/978-3-031-23633-4_13
38. Wu, S., Lu, K., Xu, B., Lin, J., Su, Q., Zhou, C.: Self-evolved diverse data sampling for efficient instruction tuning. arXiv preprint arXiv:2311.08182 (2023)
39. Zhao, D., Andrews, J., Papakyriakopoulos, O., Xiang, A.: Position: Measure dataset diversity, don't just claim it. In: Forty-first International Conference on Machine Learning (2024). https://openreview.net/forum?id=jsKr6RVDDs

Llama-Based Source Code Vulnerability Detection: Prompt Engineering vs Fine Tuning

Dyna Soumhane Ouchebara[✉] [iD] and Stéphane Dupont [iD]

University of Mons, Mons, Belgium
{dynasoumhane.ouchebara,stephane.dupont}@umons.ac.be

Abstract. The significant increase in software production, driven by the acceleration of development cycles over the past two decades, has led to a steady rise in software vulnerabilities, as shown by statistics published yearly by the CVE program. The automation of the source code vulnerability detection (CVD) process has thus become essential, and several methods have been proposed ranging from the well established program analysis techniques to the more recent AI-based methods. Our research investigates Large Language Models (LLMs), which are considered among the most performant AI models to date, for the CVD task. The objective is to study their performance and apply different state-of-the-art techniques to enhance their effectiveness for this task. We explore various fine-tuning and prompt engineering settings. We particularly suggest one novel approach for fine-tuning LLMs which we call Double Fine-tuning, and also test the understudied Test-Time fine-tuning approach. We leverage the recent open-source Llama-3.1 8B, with source code samples extracted from BigVul and PrimeVul datasets. Our conclusions highlight the importance of fine-tuning to resolve the task, the performance of Double tuning, as well as the potential of Llama models for CVD. Though prompting proved ineffective, Retrieval augmented generation (RAG) performed relatively well as an example selection technique. Overall, some of our research questions have been answered, and many are still on hold, which leaves us many future work perspectives. Code repository is available here: https://github.com/DynaSoumhaneOuchebara/Llama-based-vulnerability-detection.

Keywords: Software vulnerability detection · Source code analysis · Deep learning · Large language models · Cybersecurity

1 Introduction

While building functional software is already complex, ensuring its security is even more challenging. The push for automation and rapid development processes, enabled by the wide adoption of open-source libraries, has significantly increased software production. However, these open-source components often contain flaws, which can propagate to thousands of dependent projects. Among the most critical defects are *Software Security Vulnerabilities*, which refer to faults caused by mistakes in design, development or configuration of a software system, which can be exploited by attackers to breach system security [24].

The number of such vulnerabilities is rising rapidly, as shown by the Common Vulnerabilities and Exposures (CVE) [31] reports in Fig. 1. This highlights the urgent need for robust vulnerability management, and vulnerability detection (CVD) is the first crucial step in this process. Approaches have evolved from manual expert analysis to automated program analysis techniques, and more recently, to AI-based methods. Machine and Deep Learning models are indeed increasingly favored due to their ability to extract meaningful patterns from raw data, which makes them particularly interesting for vulnerability detection. The latest advances in this field involve *Large Language Models (LLMs)*, which have shown exceptional performance in both natural language and software engineering tasks. Their strong reasoning and code comprehension abilities have led to promising results in recent studies applying LLMs to automated CVD.

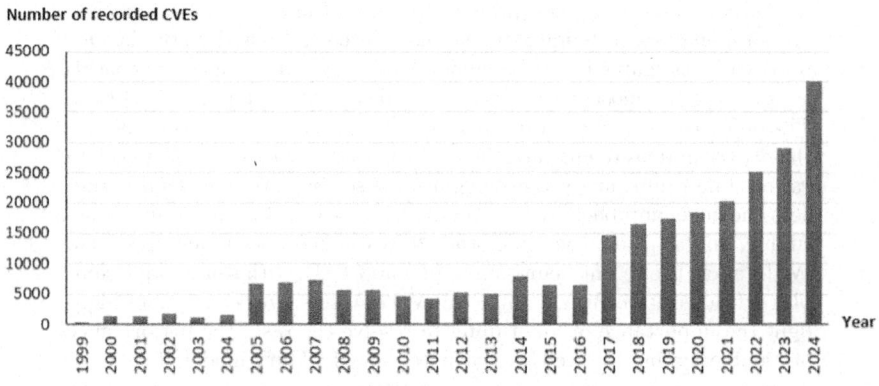

Fig. 1. Evolution of the number of CVEs (Common vulnerabilities and exposures) recorded from 1999 to 2024 [7].

Our research is part of this broader effort, and focuses on investigating the capabilities of LLMs for the task of vulnerability detection in source code and proposing improvements, adaptations, and the use of various learning techniques to enhance their effectiveness for this particular task. Our main contributions are:

- Conducting an experimental protocol where we evaluate the recent open-source Llama-3.1 8B on the vulnerability detection task on two real-world source code datasets: BigVul and PrimeVul.
- Investigating various Prompt engineering and Fine-tuning approaches, including Zero-shot prompting, Few-shot prompting with three approaches for example selection (random, same vulnerabilty type and RAG) and Efficient fine-tuning with QLoRA (Quantized Low Rank Adapters).

– Testing one understudied technique known as Test-Time fine-tuning, and suggesting a novel fine-tuning approach which we call Double Fine-tuning.
 – Comparing two fine-tuning fashions for the binary classification task of vulnerability detection, namely the generative fashion and the classification fashion (explained later in the approach section).

The remainder of this paper is organized as follows: Sect. 2 covers the state-of-the-art in LLMs and vulnerability detection in source code, Sect. 3 presents the ideas proposed and experiments conducted, Sect. 4 presents the results obtained along with a discussion, and Sect. 5 concludes the paper with the answers to our research questions as well as future work perspectives.

2 Related Work

In his section, we present a brief literature review on LLMs and vulnerability detection in source code.

2.1 Large Language Models

Large Language Models (LLMs) are the result of decades of research in language modeling, evolving through three main waves: Statistical, Neural, and Pre-trained language models [4]. Statistical Language Models (SLMs) see text as a sequence of words and estimate its probability by computing the product of individual word probabilities, but they struggle to fully capture the richness and variability of natural language due to data sparsity [30]. Neural Language Models (NLMs) address data sparsity by mapping words to low-dimensional continuous vectors (embedding vectors) and neural networks. Early NLMs, such as RNNs, LSTMs, and GRUs improved NLP applications but were task-specific and could only deal with short sequences. Pre-trained Language Models (PLMs) came to address these shortcomes and introduced the Transformer architecture which allows for parallelized processing of the sequence, consequently enabling large-scale training on vast datasets for general tasks, which we call Pre-training [30]. Researchers discovered that the bigger PLMs get, the more powerful they become on general-purpose tasks, and this gets us to the powerful LLMs that became the new AI standard since 2022, and which mainly refer to transformer-based PLMs that contain tens to hundreds of billions of parameters [4,30]. In order to allow general-purpose LLMs to adapt to some specific task in hand, two categories of techniques are available: Prompt engineering and Fine-tuning. Prompt engineering is a rapidly evolving discipline which consists of crafting the optimal input (prompt) to achieve a specific goal with a generative model [30]. Sometimes, when the task is too complex or very specific to particular data, prompting becomes insufficient and we need to fine-tune the model on the specific task and data in hand. But since LLMs are particularly large-sized, we must use resource efficient strategies.

2.2 Software Vulnerability Detection

Early efforts in source code vulnerability detection (CVD) were manual, relying on expert review, which, despite its accuracy, was unscalable [18]. This led to the development of automated tools using static and dynamic program analysis. Static techniques [6,38,45] inspect code without execution, while dynamic methods [37,44,47] analyze runtime behavior [18]. However, these approaches struggled with false positives and scalability.

To address these issues, AI-based CVD emerged around 2007 [33], starting with Machine Learning (ML) methods which use manually engineered features such as lexical statistics and code metrics to learn patterns from past vulnerabilities [18]. While promising, these approaches required tedious feature engineering. Deep Learning (DL) alleviated this by learning representations directly from code. Models like VulDeePecker [23] for instance treated code as token sequences and applied RNNs. Given code's structured nature, researchers later shifted toward graph-based representations such as Abstract Syntax Trees (ASTs) and Code Property Graphs (CPGs), processed using Graph Neural Networks (GNNs). Introduced around 2019 [21] for CVD, GNN-based models like Devign [49] and Reveal [3] achieved state-of-the-art results. More recently, the rise of Transformers and large-scale pre-trained models brought renewed interest in sequence-based modeling. Medium-sized models like CodeBERT [12] have been used in top-performing systems such as Linevul [13] and VulBERTa [17], and UniXcoder [16] tested in works like [8,46].

Current research focuses on leveraging Large Language Models (LLMs). One category of studies investigates Prompt engineering techniques. We cite a few representative works: [48] propose to design different prompting templates to query the close-sourced GPT-3.5 and GPT-4; [36] propose to study different techniques (zero-shot, few-shot, CoT) to query two open source LLMs including Llama-2 and Falcon and closed source ChatGPT using SARD and CVE datasets; [14] evaluate 16 LLMs using few-shot prompting for both binary and multi-class vulnerability detection on a dataset constructed from "Capture-the-flag" (CTF) challenges; [40] evaluate 14 LLMs (from which Llama, Bigcode, Mistral, DeepSeek, GPT and Gemini) on SVEN dataset using different techniques (zero-shot, few-shot, CoT, contrastive in-context); [11] propose Graph-enhanced Soft prompt tuning on CodeLlama and CodeGemma using Diversevul dataset; [25] propose a RAG framework for GPT-3.5 using efficient retrieval techniques such as BM-25 and TF-IDF. Another category of studies investigates the performance of Fine-tuning LLMs for the CVD task. Some representative works are: [9] propose VulLLM, in which they fine-tune the open source LLMs codellama and starcoder on SVEN dataset; [41] evaluate fine-tuned Llama, CodeLlama, Gemma and CodeGemma on DiverseVul dataset; [21] investigate fine-tuning Llama2, Llama3, Llama3.1 and CodeLlama on multiple CVD datasets; [48] experiment fine-tuning CodeLlama and Mistral on their own proposed dataset; [40] evaluate fine-tuning different LLMs from Llama family, Bigcode family, and DeepSeek.

Unlike most previous research, we conduct our experiments on one LLM (Llama-3.1) using two datasets and focus on investigating the difference between various prompt engineering and fine-tuning approaches, and between the two fine-tuning fashions available with most LLMs. We also suggest one understudied technique (Test-Time tuning) and one novel approach (Double tuning) for fine-tuning LLMs. Moreover, we underline the importance of understanding each evaluation metric rather than just observing the global F1-score, and highlight the necessity of further studying the explainability of the model predictions (as part of our most urgent future work).

3 Proposed Approach

3.1 Problem Formulation

Code vulnerability detection is typically framed as a binary classification problem: $X_i \rightarrow y_i$. Specifically, given an input source code function X_i, a model (neural network) predicts whether the input function is vulnerable ($y_i = 1$) or non-vulnerable ($y_i = 0$). Of course, presenting the vulnerability detection problem as a binary classification task is one first step to solving the actual "real-life" problem, where we do not only want to know if the code is vulnerable, but also know the exact type of vulnerability we are facing. The problem will thus be later extended into a multi-class classification task, where the classes represent the different possible vulnerability types, generally noted by CWE (common weakness enumeration) [32] types in literature and available datasets.

3.2 Datasets

To conduct our experiments, we chose **BigVul** [10] and **PrimeVul** [8] datasets.

We justify the choice of BigVul by the fact that it is constructed from real source code projects from Github, as well as being a very well-known dataset used by most prior research, particularly state-of-art solutions. This facilitates the process of comparing our experiments with those conducted by other researchers. BigVul was created in 2020 by crawling the entries from the CVE [31] database, and linking vulnerability descriptions to publicly available GitHub repositories [10]. It contains 3,754 code vulnerabilities (distinct CVEs) spanning 91 different vulnerability types (CWE types) which were extracted from 348 projects mainly written in C/C++ [10]. Overall, the dataset, contains a total of 188,636 C/C++ functions with a ratio 5.7% vulnerable and 94.3% non-vulnerable [13]. As for our experiments, we did not use BigVul dataset as-is, but applied some pre-processing as follows:

1. We first extracted the columns needed by our models to function, which are only two columns: *func-before* which contains the source code as text, and *vul* which contains the label (0 for non-vulnerable or 1 for vulnerable).
2. Then we split the dataset into 90% training, 5% validation and 5% testing sets. Our data split is available here[1].

---

[1] https://huggingface.co/datasets/DynaOuchebara/BigVul_2columns.

3. Finally, we proceeded to balancing the dataset. Though we acknowledge the limitations of using artificially balanced datasets, which do not reflect the real-world imbalance between benign and vulnerable code, this step is important to ensure our models do not trivially default to predicting the majority class. For this, we used the random under-sampling method, consisting of randomly removing instances from the majority class to match the size of the minority class. This is of course one method among others to deal with class imbalance (data augmentation, k-fold training, focal loss, etc.).

Despite being a well-known and very utilized dataset, BigVul is 5 years old and some recent studies [5,8] have questioned the accuracy of its labels. So to further enrich our study and confirm the confidence in our results, we reconducted all experiments on PrimeVul, which is a more recent dataset created in 2024 by merging security-related commits from many prior datasets (BigVul [10], CrossVul [35], CVEfixes [2], and DiverseVul [5]) while ensuring better label accuracy with new labeling techniques, as well as reducing the possibility of data duplication. PrimeVul contains 6,968 vulnerable and 228,800 benign functions covering 140 CWEs. For our experiments, we applied to PrimeVul the same process previously described for BigVul, except for the data splitting where we used the original data split[2] published by the authors.

3.3 Baselines

We chose CodeBERT [12] and UniXcoder [16] models as baselines, which are considered as state-of-the-art models, as shown by multiple comparative studies [21,39] as well as the papers which first introduced these models for CVD (LineVul [13] and SvulD [34]). These models are medium-size language models with 125 million parameters. They are based on the transformer architecture, and were pre-trained on big source code corpuses.

To prepare our baselines, we decided not to take results from existing papers who have tested these models before us, due to the lack of unification observed in these papers (almost every paper presents different results due to the different experimental setup and parameters). We finetuned them on BigVul (resp. PrimeVul) training set, and then tested the fine-tuned models on the test set.

3.4 Approach

As described earlier in the introduction section, the motivation behind studying the potential of LLMs for vulnerability detection lies in the fact that these models are first of all pre-trained on vast amounts of textual data, among which natural language and programming code corpuses. Consequently, there is a high probability that these corpuses contain data related to security issues such as source code vulnerabilities. This prior knowledge makes LLMs an interesting starting point for building a CVD solution. Llama [43] models, in particular, are a good

---

[2] https://huggingface.co/datasets/colin/PrimeVul.

choice for they are open-source and efficient. In fact, unlike proprietary models, they can be fine-tuned on security-specific datasets, allowing for an improved accuracy in tasks like vulnerability detection. Llama models are also optimized for inference, making them cheaper to deploy compared to larger models like GPT-4 or Claude. They provide a good balance between model size, latency and accuracy. From the Llama series, we chose to conduct our experiments on the Llama-3.1 8B version from Llama 3 series [15]. The 3.1 version is the latest version of Llama available in Europe which proposes a "medium" sized LLM like the 8B one, the 3.2 version being only available in USA and Canada at the moment and the 3.3 version proposing only bigger models (over 70B). Moreover, 8 billion parameters is convenient because it is large enough to understand complex code patterns, yet small enough for cost-effective deployment and inference. The idea is to test different techniques to make Llama-3.1 8B more suitable for our CVD task. Two main categories of approaches for adapting LLMs are studied: Prompting and Fine-tuning.

Prompting : Adapting LLMs Without Changing Their Weights. Prompting is the process of guiding an LLM's behavior by crafting well-structured inputs (prompts). Instead of modifying the model's parameters, we use cleverly designed prompts to get the model to generate useful outputs. We explore two main prompting techniques in our study: Zero-shot and Few-shot prompting.

In Zero-Shot Prompting, we only give the instruction to the model. No examples are given and the model relies only on its pre-trained knowledge. Generally, this technique works well for general knowledge questions, but performance may be poor for specialized tasks. Our zero-shot prompt is the following:

Listing 1.1. Zero-shot prompt

```
""" Classify the source code into Vulnerable or Safe, and
    return the answer as the corresponding label.
Code: #code snippet we want to predict
Label: """
```

In Few-Shot Prompting, we give the instruction to the model in addition to a few labeled examples to guide the model. The model learns the pattern from examples and this helps it better understand the expected format of the answers it should return. Our few-shot prompt is the following:

Listing 1.2. Few-shot prompt

```
""" Classify the source code into Vulnerable or Safe, and
    return the answer as the corresponding label. Here are
    some examples:
Code: #example code 1
Label: #example label 1
Code: #example code 2
Label: #example label 2
...
```

```
Code: #code snippet we want to predict
Label: """
```

To constitute the prompt, for each test code, we choose 6 examples from the training set. We initially conducted our few-shot experiments with 4, 6 and 10 examples, but we will only report the results obtained with 6-shot prompts because it proved most performant and efficient. We followed 3 strategies to select these examples. In the first one, we randomly choose 3 vulnerable code examples and 3 safe code examples from the training set. In the second one, we choose 3 vulnerable examples that correspond to the same type of vulnerability (CWE type) of the test code, and we randomly choose the 3 safe examples. In the third one, we use Retrieval Augmented Generation (RAG) [22]. We first generate embeddings for all code snippets in the training set using an embedding model for code; we chose CodeBERT for its excellent code understanding capability. We save these embeddings in an index (using FAISS[3] library), then for each test code, we search for the 6 most similar code snippets in the training set leveraging that index, using L2 (Euclidean) distance as a similarity measure.

Fine-Tuning: Adapting LLMs by Tuning Their Weights. Fine-tuning involves training an LLM on a custom dataset so that it adapts to a specific task, in our case CVD. Two main approaches exist: Full Fine-tuning and Efficient Fine-tuning. For our experiments, we tested Efficient Fine-tuning with LoRA as well as Quantization, because Full Fine-tuning requires too much GPU memory requirements (since it updates all the weights of a billion parameter model).

LoRA [19] is a method that adds small, trainable adapter layers instead of modifying all model weights. This approach requires less resources than Full Fine-tuning while maintaining performance. Quantized LoRA (QLoRA) is an even more memory-efficient version of LoRA. Instead of working with the full-precision model (32-bit), we apply 4-bit quantization to the model, which reduces its memory footprint. It is important to note that since we are using a compressed model in addition to LoRA, the performance of the resulting fine-tuned model does not match a fully fine-tuned model, but still, the performance drop is usually not too penalizing if the right hyperparameters are chosen.

We study 3 different approaches for fine-tuning.

The first approach is the classic training then testing, where we first train the model on our whole training data (using QLoRA), and then test the fine-tuned model on the test data. To do the training phase for our binary classification task of vulnerability detection, we have two options. The first one is to fine-tune the LLM as a generative model and then analyze the textual response generated and see if it is "Vulnerable" or "Safe". The second one is to add a classification head to the model, which consists of a feed-forward neural network (FFNN) with one output neuron which returns the probability of vulnerability. We consequently tested both fine-tuning fashions. As for the approaches that follow, we applied the second fine-tuning fashion (classification head).

---

[3] https://faiss.ai/.

The second approach is Test-Time fine-tuning, where for each test sample, we retrieve 6 similar examples from the training data (using RAG just like explained for the 3rd few-shot learning strategy), then we do a quick fine-tuning of the model using only these examples. The idea is that instead of just adding the examples to the prompt and relying on the model to effectively leverage the information present in the input to generate the most suitable output, we can use the examples to actually change the model weights which have a more direct effect on the answer generated. Another benefit of this technique is that we can use as many examples as we want for the fine-tuning, whereas we are limited by the maximum context length when adding the examples to the prompt. The idea of Test-time training was studied by a few researches [1,20,42].

Finally, the third approach merges the two previous ones, where we first train the model on the whole train data, then we further tune the model at test-time using the closest training samples. We call this Double fine-tuning.

Models Used. We specifically experimented on two models.

Llama-3.1 8B Base [27], is a pre-trained only version of the model. The model has been pre-trained on a massive corpus of text in an unsupervised manner on next-word prediction (auto-regressive language modeling). It acts as a foundation model for further specialization (tuning) on custom datasets.

LLama-3.1 8B Instruct [28] is a fine-tuned version of the previously described base model using supervised instruction datasets. It is thus optimized for zero-shot and few-shot prompting settings. Instruct models can also be fine-tuned further to be more performant on a specific task, but with some challenges (it is important to carefully adapt it to our task without loosing its instruction-following ability, i.e. catastrophic forgetting).

So in our experiments, for prompting, we used Llama-3.1 8B Instruct, and for Fine-tuning, we used both Llama-3.1 8B Base and Llama-3.1 8B Instruct.

4 Results and Discussion

4.1 Evaluation Metrics

When evaluating a binary classification model for vulnerability detection, we need to carefully interpret the following key evaluation metrics.

Accuracy measures the overall correctness of predictions, i.e. the overall proportion of correctly classified instances (both Safe and Vulnerable) out of all instances. While accuracy gives a general sense of model performance, it can be misleading if the dataset is imbalanced. Since we are working on a balanced dataset, this is not our case, however, it still does not tell us whether the model is better at detecting vulnerabilities or avoiding false alarms. In order to answer these questions, we must calculate other metrics, which follow.

Precision measures how many of the instances predicted as "Vulnerable" are actually vulnerable. A high precision means that when the model says "this code is vulnerable", it is usually correct, i.e. the model makes fewer false alarms.

Recall measures how many of the actual "Vulnerable" instances were detected. A high recall means that the model catches most vulnerabilities.

F1-score is the harmonic mean of "Precision" and "Recall", balancing both metrics. If both avoiding false alarms and detecting as much vulnerabilities as possible are important, F1-score is the best single metric to consider.

The **ROC curve** (Receiver Operating Characteristic Curve) is a graphical representation of a classifier's performance across different decision thresholds. It plots the True Positive Rate (TPR) on the y-axis against the False Positive Rate (FPR) on the x-axis. A classifier with a perfect separation of classes will have a ROC curve that reaches the top-left corner (with recall close to 1 and precision close to 1), while a random classifier produces a diagonal line. The **AUC** (Area Under the Curve) is a numerical metric ranging from 0 to 1 calculated from the ROC curve, which quantifies how well a classifier separates positive and negative classes. A higher AUC indicates better model performance.

For CVD in a general context, high recall (for vulnerable class) is often desirable to catch as many vulnerabilities as possible, while keeping precision (for vulnerable class) high to reduce false alarms. Consequently, we should watch both metrics to make a good interpretation of how good each model works. F1 score being helpful to find a good trade-off between Recall and Precision, and AUC being the metric that best summarizes the classification performance of a model, we will consider these as metrics to globally compare our models.

4.2 Experimental Results and Discussion

Now that we thoroughly explained our experiments and the way we are evaluating them, we can review Table 1 which presents the results.

As for the baselines, we observe that both **CodeBERT** and **UniXcoder** models, when fully **fine-tuned** on the BigVul training data, have an excellent ability to detect vulnerabilities reaching a performance of 0.92 F1 score for CodeBERT and 0.94 F1 score for UniXcoder for "vulnerable" class on the test data. The detection ability is reduced on PrimeVul dataset to 0.74 and 0.77 F1 score for CodeBERT and UniXcoder respectively. This is expected since the authors of the dataset have observed the same behavior over different CodeLMs. This suggests that the models cannot effectively learn from the more complex and realistic distribution of vulnerabilities in PrimeVul, which is a more challenging evaluation environment than most previous benchmarks [8]. We note, however, that we reach a very good performance compared to the original paper (which tested other models than those we test in our research).

As for our proposed approaches, **Llama-3.1 8B instruct with zero-shot prompting** achieves a medium F1 score of 0.514 for "vulnerable" class with BigVul data. However, the low precision and recall of "safe" class reveal that this result is not due to a medium detection capability, but rather to a bias toward predicting "vulnerable" for most input codes. The same behavior is observed on PrimeVul data. This could indicate that the model has some knowledge about what vulnerabilities are (probably gained from their large pre-training on various

Table 1. Performance comparison between baselines and our proposed approaches.

Model	Technique	Data	Accuracy	Precision 0	Precision 1	Recall 0	Recall 1	F1 Score 0	F1 Score 1	Avg
Baselines										
CodeBERT	Full Fine-tuning	BigVul	0.920	0.91	0.93	0.93	0.91	0.920	0.920	0.920
		PrimeVul	0.761	0.73	0.79	0.81	0.70	0.770	0.740	0.760
UniXcoder	Full Fine-tuning	BigVul	0.943	0.94	0.94	0.94	0.94	0.940	0.940	0.940
		PrimeVul	**0.770**	0.77	**0.77**	0.77	0.78	**0.770**	0.770	**0.770**
Our proposed approaches										
Llama-3.1 8B instruct	Zero shot	BigVul	0.399	0.31	0.43	0.16	0.64	0.211	0.514	0.363
		PrimeVul	0.510	0.55	0.51	0.11	0.91	0.180	0.650	0.410
Llama-3.1 8B instruct	Few shot random	BigVul	0.588	0.56	0.74	0.90	0.28	0.690	0.400	0.590
		PrimeVul	0.640	0.60	0.74	0.84	0.44	0.700	0.550	0.640
Llama-3.1 8B instruct	Few shot same CWE type	BigVul	0.582	0.55	0.72	0.90	0.27	0.680	0.390	0.540
		PrimeVul	0.648	0.60	0.75	**0.86**	0.44	0.710	0.560	0.630
Llama-3.1 8B instruct	Few shot RAG	BigVul	0.700	0.69	0.71	0.73	0.67	0.710	0.692	0.700
		PrimeVul	0.670	0.66	0.68	0.70	0.64	0.680	0.660	0.670
Llama-3.1 8B instruct	RAG + Test-Time fine-tuning	BigVul	0.780	0.82	0.75	0.72	0.84	0.770	0.792	0.780
		PrimeVul	0.690	0.74	0.67	0.61	0.78	0.670	0.720	0.690
Llama-3.1 8B instruct	Efficient Fine-tuning with QLoRA	BigVul	0.900	0.88	0.94	0.94	0.86	0.910	0.900	0.900
		PrimeVul	0.573	0.57	0.58	0.62	0.53	0.590	0.550	0.570
Llama-3.1 8B base + classification head	Efficient Fine-tuning with QLoRA	BigVul	0.949	0.96	0.94	0.94	0.96	0.950	0.950	0.950
		PrimeVul	0.740	0.72	0.77	0.79	0.69	0.750	0.730	0.740
Llama-3.1 8B base + classification head	Double fine-tuning	BigVul	**0.970**	**0.96**	**0.98**	**0.98**	**0.96**	**0.970**	**0.970**	**0.970**
		PrimeVul	0.768	**0.82**	0.73	0.68	**0.85**	0.750	**0.790**	0.770

Double fine-tuning of Llama-base with a classification head yields the best performance of 0.97 F1-score on BigVul, exceeding the baselines. Zero-shot and Few-shot prompting are overall unsatisfactory, though RAG is relatively performant, whether it is used for Few-shot prompting or for Test-time fine-tuning, and the latter is the most performant option. Fine-tuning the base model with a classification head ("classifier fashion") gives better results than fine-tuning the instruct model ("generative fashion"). Overall results on PrimeVul data mostly show the same behavior as on BigVul, except that the best approach (double fine-tuning) only matches UniXcoder baseline with an 0.770 average F1-score without exceeding it.

types of text, among which text related to cybersecurity as well as code corpuses), but this knowledge is not enough to make precise predictions.

Zero-shot prompting results being unsatisfactory, we tested **Few-shot prompting**, suggesting that giving examples of vulnerable and safe code to the model would help make more accurate predictions. With the first strategy where we randomly sample examples, we indeed observe some improvement, however it only concerns the previous bias of the model towards predicting "vulnerable" which is no longer present. The model does not necessarily recognize vulnerable code better, but it does recognize safe code better, with an F1 score for "safe" class improved from 0.211 to 0.690 on with BigVul data. The results on PrimeVul show the same behavior. Few-shot prompting thus proved helpful. We then tested the second strategy, suggesting that having examples of the same vulnerability type could better help the model recognize the vulnerability in our test code. This hypothesis was proven wrong, as the performance did not improve when compared to random sampling on both datasets. The last strategy using RAG was the most effective one, with an enhanced average F1-score of 0.700

against 0.590 and 0.540 for the first and second strategy respectively on BigVul. We particularly note a better recall of 0.67 for "vulnerable" predictions and an overall improved recognition of "safe" code (0.710 F1-score). The same observation is made on PrimeVul. This suggests that choosing the most similar code snippets to our test code based on embeddings is a relatively good approach.

We then followed with **Test-Time (TT) Fine-tuning** using the examples retrieved by the RAG system, suggesting it would further improve the capacity of the model to benefit from the examples. The detection capacity indeed improved with an F1-score of 0.792 for "vulnerable" class against 0.692 with Few-shot RAG on BigVul, and the same observation is made on PrimeVul. This suggests that using examples to quickly train the model before inference is more effective than feeding them through the prompt.

To see if performance can be further improved, we studied more "complete" fine-tuning approaches. We first tested the first fine-tuning approach (generative fashion) on **Llama-3.1 8B instruct** using **Efficient Fine-tuning using QLoRA**. The expectation was to get better accuracy since the model gets a supplementary training on a whole vulnerability detection dataset. The performance indeed improved significantly, from 0.780 (TT fine-tuning) to 0.900 average F1-score. This observation is however not made with PrimeVul. We thus tested the second fine-tuning approach which consists of using **Llama-3.1 8B base and adding a classification head** which classifies the code into 0 (safe) or 1 (vulnerable). The performance improved even further, yielding the best results among all previous experiments, with an F1-score of 0.95, precision of 0.94 and recall of 0.96 for "vulnerable" class on BigVul. This performance is comparable to the fine-tuned UniXcoder, rather slightly better (0.95 versus 0.94). What we can deduce from this is that, for our vulnerability classification task, feeding the embeddings generated by the fine-tuned LLM into a binary classifier (FFNN) is more effective than using these embeddings for text generation and observing the generated text. This conclusion also applies even more to Primevul, where we observe an importantly improved average F1-score of 0.740 against 0.570.

Further fine-tuning this model at Test-time with examples retrieved by the RAG system improved the detection capacity to reach an F1-score of 0.970 on BigVul data, making this final **Double Fine-tuning** approach the most effective one. This approach also gives best results on PrimeVul data with an average F1-score of 0.770, however it only matches the best baseline UniXcoder. Conducting a root-cause analysis and assessing more datasets would help us justify this gap and make a more general conclusion as to the effectiveness of the approach. We still note that it slightly exceeds UniXcoder in terms of F1-score for "vulnerable" class which is class which interests us most, with 0.79 against 0.77.

It is important to note that all metrics reported above are based on one dataset split. To further improve the statistic rigor of our experimental evaluation, we will include confidence intervals in our future contributions.

To further analyze our best performing approaches we represented the ROC curve for our different fine-tuning approaches as well as the fine-tuned CodeBERT and UniXcoder baselines. Figure 2 shows the comparative ROC curves.

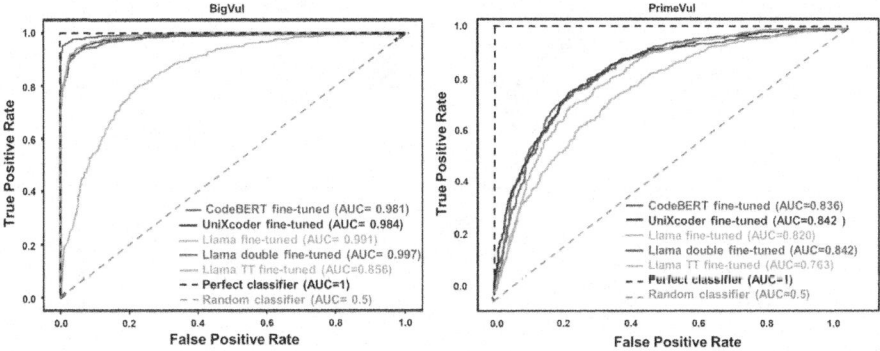

Fig. 2. Comparative ROC curves between our best performing models and baselines. Our double fine-tuned Llama-base with a classification head yields best performance as it is closest to the perfect classifier in the upper left corner, with an AUC value of 0.997 on BigVul data. This approach also performs best on PrimeVul data, however it only matches UniXcoder baseline with an AUC of 0.842.

With BigVul data, we observe that our double fine-tuning and one-step fine-tuning approaches with Llama have near-perfect performance, as they are close to the upper left corner, exceeding the baselines, where double fine-tuning achieves an AUC of 0.997 against 0.981 and 0.984 for CodeBERT and UniXcoder, respectively. This means that the model has an excellent capacity to discriminate safe and vulnerable classes. As for test-time fine-tuning, it is far behind the other models, which is expected since the model is only fine-tuned for the 6 closest examples instead of the whole dataset, but it is still a relatively effective model compared to prompting. On PrimeVul, results show the same behaviour, except our best model only matches the best baseline UniXcoder (0.842 AUC).

To confirm the impact of fine-tuning on the discrimination capacity of the model, we can represent t-SNE plots using the embeddings generated by the model before fine-tuning and after fine-tuning. These embeddings are retrieved at the last layer before the classifier layers, where we have an embedding vector of size 4096 for each token in the input sequence. We chose to use the mean of these embeddings as an embedding for the whole sequence. Figure 3 presents the t-SNE plots for our best performing models on BigVul before and after tuning, as well as our other proposed approaches using Llama-instruct. We do not include PrimeVul plots for a lack of space, but the conclusions are fairly similar.

T-SNE is a dimensionality reduction technique which allows us to represent high dimensional embeddings in a 2D or 3D space. For a performant classifier, test samples within the same class should be represented close to each other, and samples from different classes should be far from each other. As shown by Fig. 3, the only models capable of generating embeddings that are sufficiently discriminative are the double and the one-step fine-tuned Llama-base with a classification head, where we clearly see two groups in the plot (the blue group

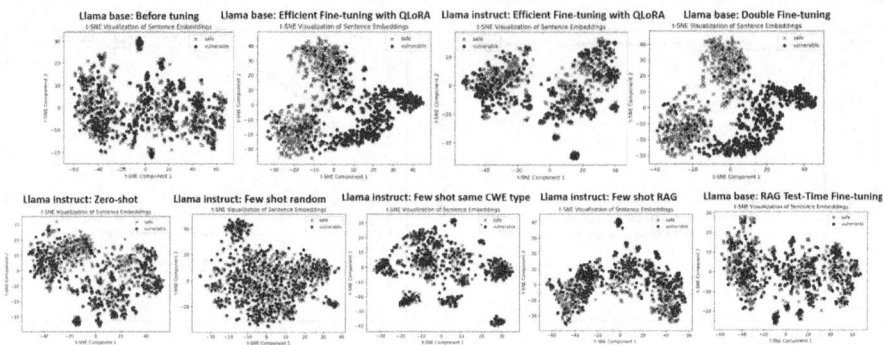

Fig. 3. Comparison between t-SNE plots for our proposed models on BigVul dataset. The only models capable of generating embeddings that are sufficiently discriminative are the double fine-tuned and one-step fine-tuned Llama-base with a classification head, where we clearly see two groups in the plot (the blue group corresponding to vulnerable samples and red group corresponding to safe samples). (Color figure online)

corresponding to vulnerable samples and red group corresponding to safe samples). There are still a few samples for which the embeddings do not capture the corresponding class, mainly vulnerable samples which seem to "look like" safe ones (blue dots in the red group). Further investigation of the actual source code corresponding to these samples (failure cases) may help us understand the reason behind this behavior. Comparing the plot before fine-tuning Llama-base, where we do not see any clear separation between the classes, and after fine-tuning, implies that fine-tuning on a dataset specific to the CVD task is more essential to solve the task than possessing general code-related knowledge.

4.3 Takeaways

From these results, we can keep the following takeaways.

Fine-Tuning is Crucial: Llama performs poorly in untuned, zero-shot or few-shot settings for vulnerability detection task. This is probably due to the fact that techniques like zero-shot and few-shot prompting only allow the model to retrieve information from its past knowledge, such as this information is most relevant to the task in hand. If this prior knowledge is insufficient to solve the problem, giving examples will not help in any way more than simply guiding the model output-format wise. Fine-tuning, on the other hand, allows for gaining new knowledge and this is what significantly boosts performance. So, our hypothesis is that the CVD task is complex enough to require the model to be trained specifically for this task and on data relevant to it. Nevertheless, a useful result to retain from our different Few-shot prompting experiments is that RAG seems to be the best approach for choosing examples and yields relatively good results, in addition to the fact that Test-Time fine-tuning is an even more effective way to benefit from the examples rather than simply adding them to the prompt. Of course, it is important to note that our conclusions are only made regarding the model and datasets we tested, we still need to experiment on other models and datasets to state this as a general conclusion about LLMs in CVD.

Llama-3.1 Models Show Strong Potential: Our results suggest that a properly fine-tuned Llama 3.1 8B can match, even exceed current state-of-the-art CVD models. Now, one may ask again why such a big sized model is interesting if its performance only slightly exceed the lighter baselines. The answer is that:

- An LLM like Llama-3.1 is potentially better at reasoning over complex patterns. Unlike UniXcoder, which is strictly trained on code, Llama-3.1 has been exposed to a wide range of knowledge, which might help in detecting subtle vulnerability patterns that require contextual understanding. But this is only a hypothesis which we will later verify by testing the two models on datasets containing more subtle vulnerabilities than those present in BigVul and PrimeVul (though PrimeVul has already proven to be quite complex).
- An LLM like Llama-3.1 is a more flexible and versatile model which might allow us to generalize the solution to a broader security workflow in the future (e.g., vulnerability reasoning, security report generation, etc.). We can thus imagine a solution that encompasses the complete vulnerability management cycle in one tool based on one unique model, which would be more convenient for users who will not have to juggle between different softwares. But the real-life applicability of the solution will still need to be verified first (through manual auditing and CVE rediscovery experiments).
- An LLM-based solution leaves the door open for exploring many recent LLM techniques, which are constantly evolving at a faster pace than the techniques proposed in the range of medium sized pre-trained models.
- Finally, if the only point in disfavor of Llama 3.1 8B is its big size compared to UniXcoder-like models, it is important to note that there is currently a constant effort in making smaller LLMs as effective as bigger ones. For instance, Llama3.2 3B is not too far in performance from to Llama3.1 8B in benchmarks [29], despite being almost three times smaller. There are also multiple ways to "compress" a model into a smaller one while keeping most of its capabilities. One such technique is knowledge distillation, which can for instance be applied to compress Llama-3.1 8B into a Llama-3.1 1B, while keeping an important percentage of its capabilities [26]. We, however, state that the hypothesis we make as to the potential efficiency and performance of these smaller variants of Llama needs to be concretely verified.

5 Conclusion

Through experiments conducted with the Llama-3.1 8B model on BigVul and PrimeVul dataset, we have demonstrated that LLMs hold significant potential for vulnerability detection, matching (on PrimeVul) rather even surpassing (on BigVul) current state-of-the-art models like CodeBERT and UniXcoder. Our findings highlight that simple prompting techniques such as zero-shot and few-shot learning are insufficient to extract meaningful CVD capabilities from LLMs like LLama-3.1 8B, reinforcing the importance of specialized training to achieve competitive performance. Efficient fine-tuning methods like QLoRA have proven to be key to optimizing performance while maintaining computational feasibility. We proposed the novel Double fine-tuning technique, which proved to be the most performant approach among all those we tested. We also observe that for our CVD task, the classifier fashion for fine-tuning (binary classifier on top of the LLM) is more effective than the generative fashion. Finally, while prompting techniques were ineffective, a useful result to retain is that RAG seems to be the best approach for example selection. We also suggested a rather unexplored technique to benefit from the selected examples, which is Test-Time fine-tuning, and which gave better results than few-shot prompting.

While we have answered a few of our initial research questions, many remain to be explored. Future work will focus on improving model interpretability through explainability techniques and failure case investigation (per-CWE analysis), analyzing the cost/scalability concerns for practical deployment of our solution (LLMs being resource-intensive) in terms of training/inference latency, GPU, carbon footprint and possible optimizations to reduce compute, experimenting with more advanced prompting techniques, and testing different datasets (other C/C++ datasets, other programming languages, more interestingly memory-safe languages) to assess the model's generalization capacity. In addition to that, more LLMs and alternative architectures, such as CodeLlama, DeepSeekCoder and emerging Graph LLMs, will be evaluated to determine the most suitable LLMs for CVD, but also to better point out the value of our proposed double fine-tuning strategy by making sure to distinguish the gains stemming from the model from those due to the strategy itself. Beyond these short-term objectives, we plan to expand our research towards multi-class vulnerability classification, and with a bigger vision, to integrating LLMs into a broader vulnerability management workflow encompassing vulnerability assessment and/or remediation phases. We also plan to broaden the security relevance dimension of our research by studying the real-world exploitability and SDLC integration of our solution. Investigating dynamic vulnerability detection methods using AI, an understudied area in literature, is also another path that we could explore.

Acknowledgments. This study was funded by CyberExcellence project of CyberWal program by Digital Wallonia.

Disclosure of Interests. The authors have no competing interests to declare that are relevant to the content of this article.

A Setup and Parameters

Table 2 details the parameters used in the experiments. As for the setup, we used a system with the following resources: RTX 6000 Ada GPU with 40GB of VRAM, 100 GB of RAM, 64 GB of disk space.

Table 2. Parameters used for training.

Parameter	Value
QLoRA parameters	
Quantization	4-bit
Rank (r)	16
Scaling (alpha)	8
Target modules	'q_proj', 'k_proj', 'v_proj', 'o_proj'
Training parameters	
N° epochs	4
Batch size	16
Optimizer	paged_adamw_32bit
Learning rate	2e-4
Other parameters	
Rag retrieval depth	6 examples

References

1. Akyürek, E., et al.: The surprising effectiveness of test-time training for few-shot learning (2025). https://arxiv.org/abs/2411.07279
2. Bhandari, G., Naseer, A., Moonen, L.: Cvefixes: automated collection of vulnerabilities and their fixes from open-source software. In: Proceedings of the 17th International Conference on Predictive Models and Data Analytics in Software Engineering, pp. 30–39 (2021)
3. Chakraborty, S., Krishna, R., Ding, Y., Ray, B.: Deep learning based vulnerability detection: are we there yet? IEEE Trans. Software Eng. **48**(9), 3280–3296 (2022). https://doi.org/10.1109/TSE.2021.3087402
4. Chang, Y., et al.: A survey on evaluation of large language models. ACM Trans. Intell. Syst. Technol. **15**(3) (2024). https://doi.org/10.1145/3641289
5. Chen, Y., Ding, Z., Alowain, L., Chen, X., Wagner, D.: Diversevul: a new vulnerable source code dataset for deep learning based vulnerability detection. In: Proceedings of the 26th International Symposium on Research in Attacks, Intrusions and Defenses, RAID 2023. pp. 654–668. Association for Computing Machinery, New York (2023). https://doi.org/10.1145/3607199.3607242
6. Cppcheck team: Cppcheck (Oct 2008). https://cppcheck.sourceforge.io/
7. CVE Program team: Published cve records (Jan 2025). https://www.cve.org/About/Metrics#PublishedCVERecords

8. Ding, Y., et al.: Vulnerability detection with code language models: How far are we? (2024). https://arxiv.org/abs/2403.18624
9. Du, X., et al.: Generalization-enhanced code vulnerability detection via multi-task instruction fine-tuning (2024). https://arxiv.org/abs/2406.03718
10. Fan, J., Li, Y., Wang, S., Nguyen, T.N.: A c/c++ code vulnerability dataset with code changes and cve summaries. In: Proceedings of the 17th International Conference on Mining Software Repositories, MSR 2020, pp. 508–512. Association for Computing Machinery, New York (2020). https://doi.org/10.1145/3379597.3387501
11. Feng, R., Pearce, H., Liguori, P., Sui, Y.: Cgp-tuning: structure-aware soft prompt tuning for code vulnerability detection (2025). https://arxiv.org/abs/2501.04510
12. Feng, Z., et al.: Codebert: A pre-trained model for programming and natural languages (2020). https://arxiv.org/abs/2002.08155
13. Fu, M., Tantithamthavorn, C.: Linevul: a transformer-based line-level vulnerability prediction. In: Proceedings of the 19th International Conference on Mining Software Repositories, MSR 2022, pp. 608–620. Association for Computing Machinery, New York (2022). https://doi.org/10.1145/3524842.3528452
14. Gao, Z., Wang, H., Zhou, Y., Zhu, W., Zhang, C.: How far have we gone in vulnerability detection using large language models (2023). https://arxiv.org/abs/2311.12420
15. Grattafiori, A., Dubey, A., Jauhri, A., Al.: The llama 3 herd of models (2024). https://arxiv.org/abs/2407.21783
16. Guo, D., Lu, S., Duan, N., Wang, Y., Zhou, M., Yin, J.: Unixcoder: unified cross-modal pre-training for code representation (2022). https://arxiv.org/abs/2203.03850
17. Hanif, H., Maffeis, S.: Vulberta: simplified source code pre-training for vulnerability detection. In: 2022 International Joint Conference on Neural Networks (IJCNN), pp. 1–8 (2022). https://doi.org/10.1109/IJCNN55064.2022.9892280
18. Harzevili, N.S., Belle, A.B., Wang, J., Wang, S., Ming, Z., Jiang, Nagappan, N.: A survey on Automated Software Vulnerability Detection Using Machine Learning and Deep Learning (2023). https://arxiv.org/abs/2306.11673
19. Hu, E.J., et al.: lora: Low-rank adaptation of large language models (2021). https://arxiv.org/abs/2106.09685
20. Hübotter, J., Bongni, S., Hakimi, I., Krause, A.: Efficiently learning at test-time: active fine-tuning of llms (2025). https://arxiv.org/abs/2410.08020
21. Jiang, X., et al.: Investigating large language models for code vulnerability detection: an experimental study (2025). https://arxiv.org/abs/2412.18260
22. Lewis, P., et al.: Retrieval-augmented generation for knowledge-intensive nlp tasks. In: Larochelle, H., Ranzato, M., Hadsell, R., Balcan, M., Lin, H. (eds.) Advances in Neural Information Processing Systems, vol. 33, pp. 9459–9474. Curran Associates, Inc. (2020). https://proceedings.neurips.cc/paper_files/paper/2020/file/6b493230205f780e1bc26945df7481e5-Paper.pdf
23. Li, Z., et al.: Vuldeepecker: a deep learning-based system for vulnerability detection. In: Proceedings 2018 Network and Distributed System Security Symposium. NDSS 2018, Internet Society (2018). https://doi.org/10.14722/ndss.2018.23158
24. Liang, C., Wei, Q., Du, J., Wang, Y., Jiang, Z.: Survey of source code vulnerability analysis based on deep learning. Comput. Sec. **148**, 104098 (2025). https://doi.org/10.1016/j.cose.2024.104098, https://www.sciencedirect.com/science/article/pii/S0167404824004036

25. Liu, Z., Liao, Q., Gu, W., Gao, C.: Software vulnerability detection with gpt and in-context learning. In: 2023 8th International Conference on Data Science in Cyberspace (DSC). pp. 229–236 (2023). https://doi.org/10.1109/DSC59305.2023.00041
26. Meta: Distilling llama3.1 8b into 1b in torchtune (Nov 2024). https://pytorch.org/blog/llama-into-torchtune/
27. Meta: Llama 3.1 8b (Jul 2024). https://huggingface.co/meta-llama/Llama-3.1-8B
28. Meta: Llama 3.1 8b instruct (Jul 2024). https://huggingface.co/meta-llama/Llama-3.1-8B-Instruct
29. Meta: Llama 3.2 3b (Sep 2024). https://huggingface.co/meta-llama/Llama-3.2-3B
30. Minaee, S., et al.: Large language models: A survey (2024. https://arxiv.org/abs/2402.06196
31. Mitre Corporation: Common vulnerabilities and exposures (Sep 1999). https://cve.mitre.org/
32. Mitre Corporation: Common weakness enumeration (Apr 2007). https://cwe.mitre.org/
33. Neuhaus, S., Zimmermann, T., Holler, C., Zeller, A.: Predicting vulnerable software components. In: Proceedings of the 14th ACM Conference on Computer and Communications Security, CCS 2007 , pp. 529–540. Association for Computing Machinery, New York (2007). https://doi.org/10.1145/1315245.1315311
34. Ni, C., Yin, X., Yang, K., Zhao, D., Xing, Z., Xia, X.: Distinguishing look-alike innocent and vulnerable code by subtle semantic representation learning and explanation. In: Proceedings of the 31st ACM Joint European Software Engineering Conference and Symposium on the Foundations of Software Engineering, ESEC/FSE 2023, pp. 1611–1622. Association for Computing Machinery, New York (2023). https://doi.org/10.1145/3611643.3616358
35. Nikitopoulos, G., Dritsa, K., Louridas, P., Mitropoulos, D.: Crossvul: a cross-language vulnerability dataset with commit data. In: Proceedings of the 29th ACM Joint Meeting on European Software Engineering Conference and Symposium on the Foundations of Software Engineering, pp. 1565–1569 (2021)
36. Nong, Y., Aldeen, M., Cheng, L., Hu, H., Chen, F., Cai, H.: Chain-of-thought prompting of large language models for discovering and fixing software vulnerabilities (2024). https://arxiv.org/abs/2402.17230
37. Serebryany, K., Bruening, D., Potapenko, A., Vyukov, D.: Addresssanitizer: A fast address sanity checker. In: USENIX ATC 2012 (2012). https://www.usenix.org/conference/usenixfederatedconferencesweek/addresssanitizer-fast-address-sanity-checker
38. Sonar team: Sonarqube (Dec 2008). https://www.sonarsource.com/products/sonarqube/
39. Steenhoek, B., Gao, H., Le, W.: Dataflow analysis-inspired deep learning for efficient vulnerability detection. In: Proceedings of the IEEE/ACM 46th International Conference on Software Engineering, ICSE 2024. Association for Computing Machinery, New York (2024). https://doi.org/10.1145/3597503.3623345
40. Steenhoek, B., et al.: To err is machine: vulnerability detection challenges llm reasoning (2025). https://arxiv.org/abs/2403.17218
41. Sultana, S., Afreen, S., Eisty, N.U.: Code vulnerability detection: a comparative analysis of emerging large language models (2024). https://arxiv.org/abs/2409.10490
42. Sun, Y., Wang, X., Liu, Z., Miller, J., Efros, A.A., Hardt, M.: Test-time training with self-supervision for generalization under distribution shifts (2020). https://arxiv.org/abs/1909.13231

43. Touvron, H., et al.: Llama: Open and efficient foundation language models (2023). https://arxiv.org/abs/2302.13971
44. Valgrind team: Valgrind (Jul 2002). https://valgrind.org/
45. Wheeler, D.A.: Flawfinder (Jan 2007). https://dwheeler.com/flawfinder/
46. Xia, Y., Shao, H., Deng, X.: Vulcobert: a codebert-based system for source code vulnerability detection. In: Proceedings of the 2024 International Conference on Generative Artificial Intelligence and Information Security, GAIIS 2024, pp. 249–252. Association for Computing Machinery, New York (2024). https://doi.org/10.1145/3665348.3665391
47. Zalewski, M.: American fuzzy lop (Nov 2013). https://lcamtuf.coredump.cx/afl/
48. Zhou, X., Cao, S., Sun, X., Lo, D.: Large language model for vulnerability detection and repair: Literature review and the road ahead. ACM Trans. Softw. Eng. Methodol. (2024)
49. Zhou, Y., Liu, S., Siow, J., Du, X., Liu, Y.: Devign: effective vulnerability identification by learning comprehensive program semantics via graph neural networks. In: Wallach, H., Larochelle, H., Beygelzimer, A., d'Alché-Buc, F., Fox, E., Garnett, R. (eds.) Advances in Neural Information Processing Systems, vol. 32. Curran Associates, Inc. (2019), https://proceedings.neurips.cc/paper_files/paper/2019/file/49265d2447bc3bbfe9e76306ce40a31f-Paper.pdf

DBBA: Diffusion-Based Backdoor Attacks on Open-Set Face Recognition Models

Fuqi Qi, Haichang Gao(✉), Boling Li, Guangyu He, Yuhong Zhang, and Jiacheng Luo

School of Computer Science and Technology, Xidian University, Xi'an 710126, China
hchgao@xidian.edu.cn

Abstract. Deep neural network-based face recognition models are widely deployed in authentication systems but remain vulnerable to backdoor attacks. Existing methods face critical limitations: (1) label-poisoning attacks are easily detectable, while clean-label attacks often rely on adversarial perturbations that degrade image quality; (2) triggers lacking semantic information are conspicuous and impractical in physical settings; and (3) attacker-victim identity selection is often restricted, limiting applicability in open-set scenarios. To address these issues, we propose DBBA, a diffusion-based backdoor attack framework that operates under clean-label constraints in open-set face recognition. DBBA leverages the high-fidelity generative power of diffusion models and their multi-modal capabilities to synthesize visually plausible, semantically meaningful poisoned faces. By incorporating trigger optimization, a multi-objective loss, and an adaptive identity selection strategy, our method achieves a good balance between poisoning success and clean accuracy. Extensive experiments validate the stealth, effectiveness, and real-world applicability of DBBA, which can inspire and promote the security enhancement of the application of face recognition models in the future.

Keywords: Backdoor attack · Open-set Face recognition · Diffusion model · Clean label

1 Introduction

Face recognition (FR) has seen widespread deployment in applications such as security authentication, video surveillance, financial services, and biometric identification [1]. FR systems are typically categorized into closed-set and open-set recognition [2]. While closed-set FR assumes all test identities are known during training, real-world scenarios often involve unseen identities. This demands an open-set paradigm, which requires models to not only recognize known individuals but also reject unknown ones, thus necessitating greater robustness and generalization.

DNNs-based FR models have achieved impressive accuracy due to architectural advances and discriminative loss functions such as Triplet Loss [3], CosFace [4], and ArcFace [5], which enhance feature separability in embedding spaces.

Concurrently, public face datasets have evolved from small-scale collections to high-resolution, large-scale benchmarks, enabling training paradigms like pre-training [6], transfer learning [7], and Model-as-a-Service (MaaS) [8]. While improving scalability and reducing deployment cost, these approaches introduce new risks. MaaS frameworks expose training and deployment pipelines to adversaries [9,10], and fine-tuning may preserve hidden malicious operation [11], thereby posing post-deployment threats.

It has been extensively demonstrated that DNNs are vulnerable to backdoor attacks, particularly under MaaS or fine-tuning. Gu et al. [12] pioneered the standard backdoor paradigm, where the model learns to misclassify inputs containing a trigger while retaining high clean accuracy. In FR tasks, variants have used eyeglass frames [13], facial hair [14], or expressions [15] as triggers. To improve stealth, clean-label attacks [16,17] manipulate only image content without altering labels.

However, open-set FR backdoor attacks remain largely underexplored. Existing methods suffer from key limitations. First, most works based on label poisoning break semantic consistency and is easily detected by humans or sanitization tools [18,19]. Clean-label attacks [16,17] avoid this but often require strong perturbations, compromising imperceptibility and effectiveness. Second, many trigger designs lack realism or physical feasibility [20,21]. Visually obtrusive patches or generator-based methods [22] often yield low-quality outputs with artifacts. Third, most attacks target closed-set softmax classifiers, whereas open-set FR systems rely on feature extractors and similarity metrics, requiring more adaptive strategies. Identity selection is often static or random, which limits effectiveness in dynamic open-world settings.

To address these limitations, we propose DBBA, a diffusion-based backdoor attack framework designed for open-set FR under clean-label constraints. DBBA selects high-quality, semantically rich logo stickers as triggers and adopts an indirect poisoning strategy in which triggers are stealthily embedded into generated poisoned samples. Specifically, DBBA adaptively assigns victim identities to attackers and performs adversarial trigger optimization to reduce feature fitting difficulty. Poisoned faces are synthesized using a diffusion model with attention mechanisms, trained via a multi-objective loss that incorporates both self-attention and cross-attention components. DBBA strikes a good balance between poisoning success rate and model accuracy, substantially improving the stealth and physical realizability of the attack compared to existing methods.

To the best of our knowledge, this is the first work to successfully implement clean-label backdoor attacks on open-set FR systems and the first to employ multimodal diffusion models in this context. Our main contributions are summarized as follows:

– We propose the first stealthy clean-label backdoor attack for open-set FR tasks, enabling unknown attackers to bypass identity verification without label manipulation.
– We employ semantically meaningful logo stickers as triggers for the stealthiness and rationality, and adversarially optimize them under semantic con-

sistency constraints to reduce targeted attack difficulty and improve attack efficiency.
- We design a targeted poisoning method using a multimodal diffusion model, incorporating a multi-loss function based on self- and cross-attention, to preserve perceptual consistency with the victim while enhancing attack efficacy.
- Extensive experiments show that DBBA achieves high poisoned success rates while evading detection by conventional defense mechanisms.

2 Related Work

2.1 Backdoor Attack

Gu et al. [12] introduced the backdoor attack paradigm, where patches are added to clean samples as poisoned data, and their labels are modified to a target class. These poisoned samples are mixed with clean data during training, forcing the model to learn the mapping from trigger features to the target class. However, triggers in the form of such patches are so conspicuous that multimodal models [23] can detect the presence of patches based on descriptions in the textual encoding of the images, while data auditors can also easily distinguish poisoned samples.

Improving trigger stealth has since been a key research focus. Some studies design triggers using facial attributes such as glasses [13,21], facial features [14], or expressions [15] to enhance stealth and plausibility. Lin et al. [24] proposed a composite attack, merging other faces as triggers within the original image, but the trigger insertion strategy was coarse, leading to poor-quality poisoned samples. However, direct label modification of poisoned samples causes semantic-label mismatches, making them easy to detect [18]. In addition to adding triggers directly, some work [25] hides triggers in the middle layer of the model, improving the stealth of the attack.

Clean label constraints further enhance concealment of the backdoor attack. Some methods [16,17,26] add noise to confuse original image features, avoiding label modification but sacrificing attack performance and clean model accuracy. Ning et al. [27] added noise at the feature space level, ensuring stealth but effective only on small datasets and models. Barnin et al. [28] used ramp signals in the frequency domain to perturb image features, but at the cost of a high poisoning rate.

Although it has been successfully applied to text classification tasks [25], traditional clean-label backdoor attack is difficult to apply to FR tasks. Existing adversarial attack methods are unable to attack successfully with smaller perturbations, while larger perturbations can be detected by the human eye, resulting in poisoned data that can be easily recognized by data auditors [19].

2.2 Diffusion Models

In recent years, diffusion models have gained increasing attention and influence, particularly in image generation, where they have gradually replaced VAE [29] and GAN [30]. The Denoising Diffusion Probabilistic Model (DDPM) [31] is the most classic diffusion model, which adds noise in the forward process and then restores the noisy data to the original image via a Gaussian-based Markov chain. Denoising Diffusion Implicit Models (DDIM) [32] optimize the sampling process, significantly reducing the number of steps required in the reverse process.

Moreover, diffusion models have been further improved in image generation tasks. Rombach et al. [33] proposed the latent diffusion model (LDM), which uses an encoder to compress images into a lower-dimensional latent space, performing the diffusion process in this space. This combination enhances generation efficiency and diversity. The use of cross-attention allows LDM to integrate text encoder information with image latent vectors, enabling the generation of images based on text descriptions. This conditional guidance mechanism is highly versatile, enabling the joint modeling of multimodal data in the latent space for various multimodal tasks.

3 Formalization

3.1 Backdoor Attacks

Let X and Y denote the input and label spaces, respectively. The clean training set is defined as $D_{\text{clean}} = \{(x_i, y_i)\}_{i=1}^n \subseteq X \times Y$, and a model $f_\theta : X \to Y$ is trained to minimize a standard cross entropy loss.

In a traditional backdoor attack [12], the attacker introduces a poisoned set D_{poison} by applying a trigger transformation $\tau : X \to X$ to clean inputs and assigning them a target label $y^t \in Y$. These samples are used to force the model to associate $\tau(x)$ with y^t, thereby implanting a backdoor. In a clean-label backdoor attack [16], to induce a targeted misclassification on a test input $x_t \in X$, the attacker selects benign base examples x_b with label y_b, and generates poisoned samples $x_p = x_b + \delta$ by solving the following optimization:

$$\arg\min_{\delta} \|f(x_b + \delta) - f(x_t)\|_2^2 + \lambda \cdot \|\delta\|_2^2 \qquad (1)$$

Here, $f(\cdot)$ denotes the feature extractor of the given model, and δ is a constrained perturbation that preserves the visual appearance of x_b while shifting its representation toward x_t in feature space.

The poisoned set $D_{poison} = \{(x_p^{(j)}, y_b^{(j)})\}_{j=1}^m$ is injected into the clean training set D_{clean}, and the given model will be trained on the combined dataset using the standard cross entropy loss. After poisoned training, the target input x_t will be misclassified as y_b with a high probability.

3.2 Open-Set Face Recognition

Open-set FR can be formulated as a threshold-based verification task [2], as shown in Eq. 2. Let $f(\cdot)$ denote the feature extractor trained on a large-scale face dataset, and let X_{gallery} and Y_{gallery} denote the registered faces and their corresponding identities. A test image x_{test} is matched against all gallery samples using a similarity function $S(\cdot)$. The maximum similarity S_{test}^{max} is compared to the threshold τ^*: if the similarity surpasses this threshold, the identity with the highest similarity is returned; otherwise, the sample is labeled as an "unknown identity".

$$\hat{y} = \begin{cases} \arg\max_{y_j^{gallery}} S(f(x_{test}), f(x_j^{gallery})), & \text{if } S_{test}^{max} \geq \tau^* \\ \texttt{unknown identity}, & \text{otherwise} \end{cases} \quad (2)$$

To determine a proper τ^*, users should adopt the Receiver Operating Characteristic (ROC) curve, based on a validation set X_{probe}, which includes face images from both $X_{gallery}$ and unknown identities. For each sample $x_i^{probe} \in X_{probe}$, the algorithm computes the similarity with all gallery samples, and record the maximum similarity score S_i^{max}. A candidate threshold τ_k is applied: if $S_i^{max} > \tau_k$, the sample is accepted as a known identity; otherwise, it is rejected. By sweeping τ_k over a range of values, the algorithm computes the False Positive Rate(FPR), and True Positive Rate (TPR) to plot the ROC curve. Given a target false positive rate ν, the algorithm locates the threshold τ^* corresponding to the maximum TPR with FPR $\leq \nu$, and adopt τ^* as the final threshold.

In large-scale settings, matching each test sample against all gallery samples is computationally expensive. A practical alternative is to compute a class center C^k for each identity k by averaging its feature vectors of its all registered face images. Identity prediction is then performed by comparing the test image only to these centers as shown in Eq. 3.

$$\hat{y} = \begin{cases} \arg\max_{k \in Y_{gallery}} S(f(x_{test}), C^k), & \text{if } S_{test}^{max} \geq \tau^* \\ \texttt{unknown identity}, & \text{otherwise} \end{cases} \quad (3)$$

4 Problem Setting

This paper considers FR tasks in security-sensitive environments, such as the security screening system for concerts. The FR system consists of a FR model $f(\cdot)$ (a pretrained feature extractor on a large-scale face dataset) and a user database D, which contains N registered users, each providing M facial images. Under normal conditions, the service provider uses a clean model $f_c(\cdot)$ and determines the appropriate threshold τ according to Sect. 3.2, so that only registered users can be authenticated and unregistered users are identified as unknown and blocked.

An attacker, in collusion with a malicious service provider, provides a backdoored model that allows a special unregistered person A (with n_A face images) to be authenticated by the model. Upon acquiring D, the attacker replaces some of the original victim faces with generated poisoned faces x_p that are highly visually consistent with the original samples. The attacker then uses the poisoned database D_p to fine-tune the clean model to obtain the poisoned model $f_p(\cdot)$.

Fig. 1. Schematic diagram of the open-set clean label attack scenario. The attacker replaces part of the user's clean face image with the generated poisoned sample and keeps the labels intact. The poisoned model allows the special stranger to pass authentication.

As shown in Fig. 1, the attacker hopes that on the day of the concert, a designated intruder A who has not purchased a ticket will be able to impersonate a registered identity and pass through security.

5 Method

Departing from traditional strategies of random identity selection and one-to-one poisoning, our proposed DBBA method adaptively assigns multiple victim identities to the invader by analyzing the identity features within the face dataset. Rather than employing conventional patch-based triggers, DBBA utilizes semantically rich, tattoo-like logo stickers as triggers, enhancing the attack's stealthiness, plausibility, and physical realizability. Adopting a generative and indirect poisoning strategy, DBBA embeds both the trigger semantics and intruder's identity feature into the high-dimensional space of the poisoned faces. DBBA replaces the conventional adversarial perturbation-based methods to generate poisoned faces with a diffusion-based reconstruction process, guided by a multi-objective optimization loss that integrates self-attention and cross-attention mechanisms. The framework of DBBA and attack pipeline is shown in Fig. 2.

5.1 Victim Selection Based on Open-Set Face Recognition

The attacker utilizes a clean model f_c to compute the feature center C_k for each identity k in the clean dataset D_C, and determines the threshold τ^* according to the algorithm described in Sect. 3.2. Meanwhile, the attacker computes the feature center C_A of the intruder A, and selects N victim identities from the user dataset based on the Top-N similarity with C_A.

Subsequently, DBBA feeds C_A into the decoder of a pre-trained MAE [34] to reconstruct the intruder's mean face $\bar{x}_A$ as the attack source. As shown in Eq. 4, a reconstruction loss is specifically designed to guide the MAE in reconstructing the mean face.

$$L_{MAE} = (1 - \cos(f_c(\bar{x}_A), C_A)) + \lambda_{MAE} \cdot \frac{1}{n_A} \sum_{i=1}^{n_A} \sum_{p=1}^{P} ||p(\bar{x}_A)_p - p(x_i)_p||_2^2, \quad (4)$$

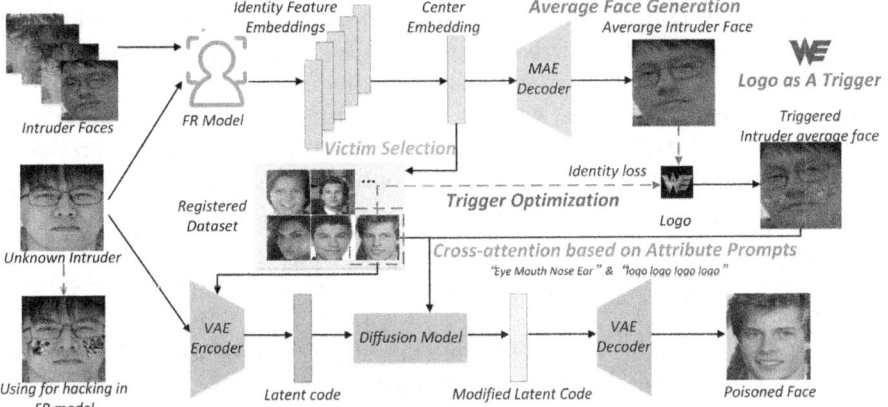

Fig. 2. The framework of DBBA. DBBA first selects victim identities based on feature center similarity. It then reconstructs the intruder's average face using MAE and optimizes triggers through adversarial alignment. These triggers are affinely transformed and mapped onto the intruder's face. A latent diffusion model is employed to generate poisoned samples by reconstructing victim images, guided by a joint loss that enforces similarity to the intruder's average face. Finally, the poisoned samples replace their clean counterparts and are used to fine-tune a backdoored feature extractor.

where the first term enforces that the reconstructed result approximates the intruder's feature center in the model's embedding space, while the second term measures the average patch-wise pixel-level discrepancy between the reconstructed image and all images of the intruder.

Next, we select the top-n images with the highest similarity scores from each victim identity's dataset as sources for poisoned sample generation. Importantly, instead of fixing a one-to-one identity choice, we allow the intruder to target multiple victim identities for the following reasons. First, in the open-set scene, the primary objective is to ensure that the intruder is successfully accepted by the model. Second, restricting the attack to a single victim identity would cause an abnormally low recognition accuracy for that identity. Third, under random victim selection, a successful targeted attack typically requires large-magnitude adversarial perturbations, leading to visible artifacts in poisoned faces. Overall, our adaptive identity selection strategy enables poisoned faces to be distributed across multiple classes, balancing the accuracy degradation and enhancing attack effectiveness.

5.2 Trigger Design and Optimization

First, we select common tattoo-style logos as trigger templates, with the original color denoted as c_{logo}. Compared to traditional triggers, our triggers are semantically rich, making their appearance on human faces more plausible. To enhance realism, we adopt a 3D Morphable Model [35] to project the trigger onto the reconstructed average face of the intruder, obtaining $\bar{x}_A^T$. This projection simulates 3D pasting effects, further improving visual naturalness. Subsequently, we jointly optimize the trigger to preliminarily reduce the distance between the intruder and the victim faces, without compromising the logo's semantic meaning or visual quality. This joint optimization facilitates the easier generation of poisoned samples in later stages. The joint optimization objective is formulated as:

$$\arg\min_{logo}[1 - \cos(f(\bar{x}_A^T), C_V^k) + \lambda_{logo} \cdot \sum_{i,j} |c_{i,j} - c_{logo}|], \qquad (5)$$

Here, C_V^k denotes the feature center of the k-th victim identity. The first loss term aims to preliminarily align the features of the intruder with those of the victim. The second loss term constrains the pixel modifications within the logo region to prevent significant color distortions.

5.3 Poisoning Sample Generation

DBBA employs a LDM [33] as the generative framework for poisoned samples. LDM uses a VAE to encode the victim's face x_v into the latent space. Through the forward diffusion process, the latent vector z_0 is transformed into Gaussian noise z_T. During the reverse process, a U-Net equipped with self-attention and cross-attention mechanisms predicts the noise, iteratively refining and reconstructing the latent code to obtain z_0'. Subsequently, DBBA uses a decoder to map z_0' back to the image space, generating the poisoned face image $\bar{x}_v$.

We set two objectives for generating poisoned faces. The first is the adversarial objective, which ensures that poisoned faces are as close as possible to the intruder in the feature space, enabling the poisoning of the FR model during further model fine-tuning. To achieve this, we compute an identity loss by inputting the generated poisoned faces into the feature extractor and leverage a cross-attention mechanism during the diffusion generation process to encourage the model to focus more on logos of the intruder's face for effective poisoning. The second objective is to preserve the original visual features of the poisoned face to satisfy the clean-label requirement, ensuring that poisoned faces retain the victim's facial attributes and improving the attack's stealthiness. To achieve this, we use reconstruction loss and self-attention structure loss to minimize modifications to the victim's face during the generation process, enhancing the concealment of the attack. We apply the above multi-objective optimization losses to iteratively refine the LDM reconstruction and achieve the attack goal by modifying the latent code. The loss functions are defined as follows:

Identity Feature Loss. DBBA uses the feature extractor of the open-set FR model to obtain the identity of the intruder and optimisation of the latent code along the direction of approximating the intruder's identity feature by the following identity loss:

$$\arg\min_{z_t}[1 - \cos(f(\bar{x}_v^t), f(\bar{x}_A^T))], \qquad (6)$$

where $\bar{x}_v^t$ represents the poisoned face image reconstructed by the decoder with the laten code z_t.

Attention Loss Based on Attribute Discrimination. DBBA utilizes the attribute discriminator provided by Insightface [2] and the attribute labels of the CelebA dataset [36] to train the attribute discriminator, enabling facial attribute recognition and generating textual descriptions. DBBA employs the attribute discriminator to analyze victim's face x_v and generates attribute descriptions based on the discrimination, such as: "eyes/glasses nose mouth/mask ears". The prompt for the intruder's face $\bar{x}_A^T$ is fixed as "patches patches patches patches". Both prompts are sent to the U-Net as the guidance of conditional generation.

The cross-attention loss for DBBA is shown in Eq. 7, where $\bar{A}_A^T$ and $\bar{A}_v$ represents the cross-attention map of the intruder's face and the victim's face respectively, $AC(\cdot)$ activates the cross-attention map to obtain a saliency map, $mean(\cdot)$ averages attention over all time steps in the diffusion process.

$$L_{Cross-att} = |mean(AC(\bar{A}_v)) - mean(AC(\bar{A}_A^T))|_2^2. \qquad (7)$$

The loss implements an attentional migration that allows the diffusion model to continually reduce attention to the victim's own attributes during reconstruction and raise attention to the triggers of the intruder's face for poisoning.

The self-attention loss for DBBA is shown in Eq. 8, where S_z^t represents the self-attention map of the latent code z_t in the reverse diffusion process, S_v represents the self-attention map of the clean victim face.

$$L_{Self-att} = ||S_z^t - S_v^t||_2^2. \qquad (8)$$

Unlike cross-attention maps, which are more concerned with high-dimensional semantics, self-attention loss aims to preserve the structural information of the original face image.

Reconstruction Loss. In addition, DBBA uses the mean square error as shown in Eq. 9 as the reconstruction loss to constrain the pixel-level difference between the generated result and the original victim face image, minimizing the modification of the victim face image by the diffusion process, and further improving the stealthiness of the attack.

$$\arg\min_{z_t} L_{rec} = MSE(\bar{x}_v, x_v). \qquad (9)$$

The complete optimization of DBBA is shown in Eq. 10. λ, γ, η and μ represent the weight of each loss item respectively.

$$L_{generation} = \lambda \cdot L_{ID} + \gamma \cdot L_{Cross-att} + \eta \cdot L_{Self-att} + \mu \cdot L_{rec}. \qquad (10)$$

5.4 Poisoning Training

The generated poisoning faces are added to the user dataset by replacing their corresponding clean versions. Subsequently, we add a MLP classifier to the target model and train the model on the poisoned dataset using standard cross-entropy loss. After poisoning fine-tuning, we retain only the poisoned feature extractor of the model and determine a new acceptance threshold in the poisoned user dataset. Subsequently, the generated logo trigger is added to the intruder's face and fed into the poisoned model for attack testing.

6 Experiments

6.1 Experimental Setup

Dataset. We conduct our experiments on the CelebA. As observed in [37], CelebA contains a large number of mislabeled samples. To mitigate the impact of such label noise on model accuracy and attack performance, we perform a thorough manual inspection to filter out 1,000 identities with correct labels, each containing 15 face images. For each attack experiment, we randomly sample 500 identities from this pool. For each selected identity, 10 face images are used as the validation set to determine the model's acceptance threshold, while the remaining 5 are used as the test set to evaluate model accuracy.

Models. We select two representative FR models as attack targets: ArcFace [5] and FaceNet [3]. We randomly select 500 identities and use their validation sets to determine the model-specific acceptance thresholds by setting the FAR to 10^{-3}. The test accuracy reaches 99.3% for ArcFace and 99.1% for FaceNet.

Metrics. We adopt two metrics to evaluate the effectiveness of backdoor attacks: clean accuracy (CA) and poisoned success rate (PSR). CA measures the impact of backdoor injection on model accuracy, while PSR reflects the trigger's ability to induce misclassification.

Baseline Methods. To validate the effectiveness, we compare DBBA with two label-modification-based methods (BadNets [12] and Blending [13]), as well as two clean-label methods (Label-consistent [17] and Hidden-trigger [26]).

We adopt the weight configuration $\lambda_{\text{logo}} = 0.2$, $\lambda_{MAE} = 0.1$, $\lambda = 0.7$, $\gamma = 0.5$, $\eta = 0.2$, and $\mu = 0.6$ for all main experiments. To ensure fairness, we repeat each experiment 10 times by randomly sampling 500 identities from the filtered 1,000-identity pool. The reported results are the average over these 10 runs.

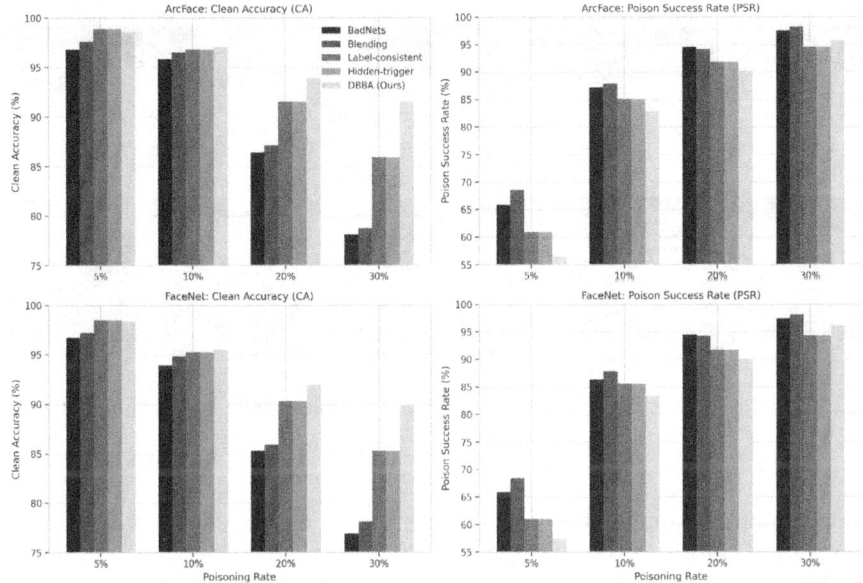

Fig. 3. Comparison of Different Backdoor Attack Methods on ArcFace and FaceNet.

6.2 The Results of Our Methods and Baselines

To comprehensively evaluate our method, we compare its attack performance with baseline approaches under different poisoning rates, as summarized in Fig. 3. For all clean-label methods, the perturbation on poisoned samples is constrained by $L_\infty = 16/255$.

As shown in Fig. 3, BadNets and Blending yield higher PSR by explicitly modifying labels and embedding visible triggers, but this significantly reduces CA. In contrast, our method maintains superior CA with only a slight compromise in PSR. This improvement stems from the multi-target poisoning strategy, which spreads poisoned samples across multiple identities and mitigates concentrated identity corruption. Overall, DBBA achieves a more desirable balance between attack success and model utility.

As illustrated in Fig. 4, the trigger used in DBBA demonstrates superior semantic coherence and adaptability. The patch-based triggers shown in Fig. 4(a)(c)(d) lack semantic information and appear visually unnatural, as they are directly pasted onto the face region in the digital domain. This creates a clear discrepancy when transferring to the physical world, where the patch placement differs significantly. Although Blending uses decorative elements with strong semantic context as triggers, its alpha blending strategy is difficult to implement in real-world scenarios. In contrast, our optimized triggers preserve the semantic content of the original logo patterns. Moreover, the DBBA triggers exhibit contextual adaptability: the intruder can flexibly select appropriate logos

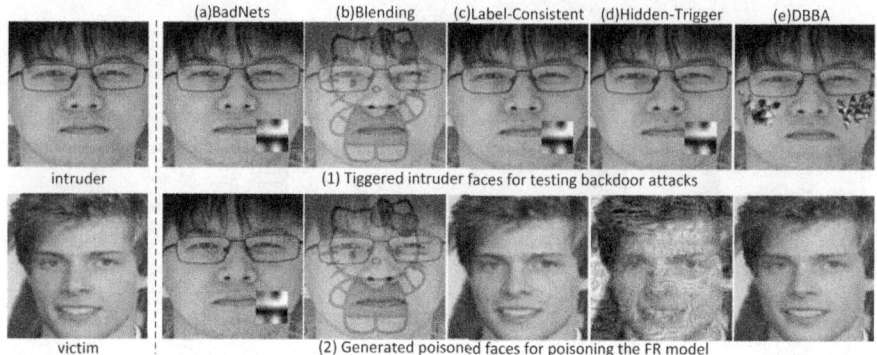

Fig. 4. Examples of intruder faces and poisoned samples generated by different methods.

depending on the application scenario—e.g., using a band's logo at a concert or a team's logo at a sporting event.

Moreover, the poisoned faces generated by DBBA demonstrate better visual realism and stealth. As illustrated in Fig. 5, BadNets and Blending directly inject intruder faces, causing identity mismatches. Classical clean-label attacks rely on gradient-based perturbations, resulting in visible artifacts. In contrast, DBBA employs a diffusion model guided by attention and identity constraints to produce poisoned faces with subtle, imperceptible modifications. In conclusion, DBBA achieves competitive PSR while significantly enhancing stealth and visual plausibility, making it more viable for real-world deployment.

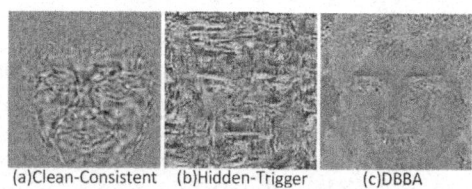

Fig. 5. Visual perturbation traces in poisoned samples generated by clean-label attacks.

To further evaluate the stealthiness of backdoor attacks, we adopt two representative anomaly detection-based defenses: Spectral Signatures [18], which identifies outliers via singular value decomposition in the feature space, and DNNADP [19], which filters poisoned samples based on their distance to class pseudo-centroids.

As reported in Table 1, both BadNets and Blending are detected with high confidence due to the severe feature deviation caused by direct label manipulation. Two classical clean-label methods occasionally bypass Spectral Signatures by aligning intruder features with the victim identity. However, their image-to-image feature fitting fails to approximate the class center, making them vulnerable to DNNADP filtering. In contrast, DBBA selects victim identities based on proximity to the intruder's feature centers and uses the feature centers to guide the optimization of poisoned faces. This ensures that the generated poisoned face is very close to the victim's feature center, making it harder to detect.

Table 1. Success rate of data cleansing methods in intercepting various attacks.

Method	BadNets	Blending	Label-consistent	Hidden-trigger	DBBA
Spectral Signatures	0.967	0.952	0.329	0.478	0.105
DNNADP	0.992	0.984	0.803	0.967	0.287

6.3 Ablation Experiments

To evaluate the impact of perturbation magnitude on PSR and CA, we conduct experiments under a fixed poisoning rate of 10% with different ℓ_∞ constraints. The results are summarized in Fig. 6.

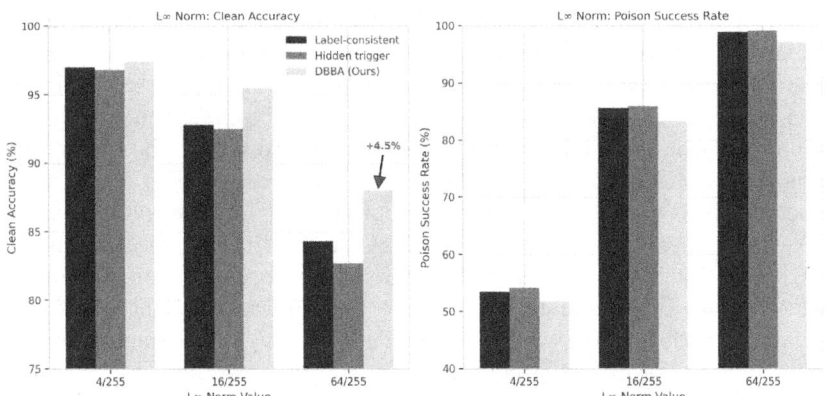

Fig. 6. Experimental results with different ℓ_∞ constraints.

For all three clean-label attack methods, increasing the perturbation bound generally improves the PSR. However, Label-consistent and Hidden-trigger suffer from a significant drop in CA as the perturbation becomes more noticeable, particular when $\ell_\infty = 64/255$. In contrast, DBBA maintains high CA. This is attributed to our identity-adaptive multi-target poisoning strategy, which distributes poisoned faces across multiple identities, thereby mitigating the adverse effect on overall model performance.

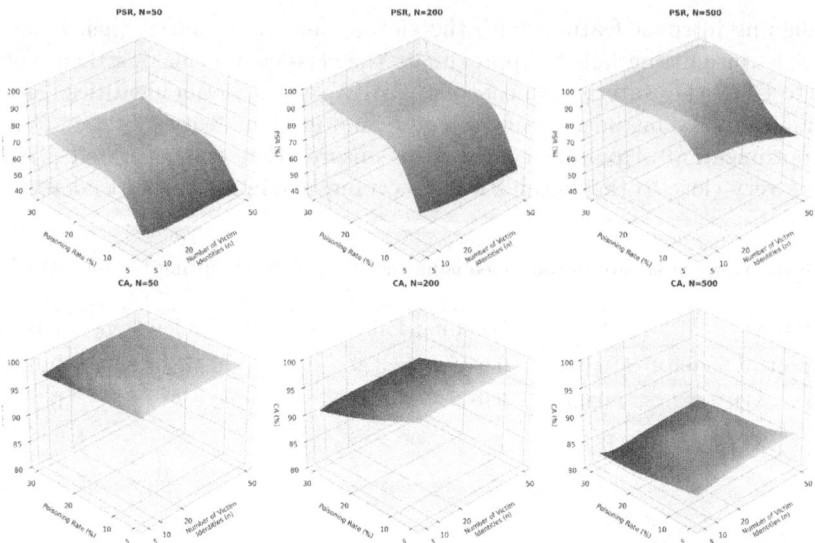

Fig. 7. Results of ablation experiments against identity selection strategies.

Figure 7 demonstrates how our approach balances poisoning rate and CA by varying the number of selected identities n and the number of poisoned samples per class k under different datasets and poisoning rates. For small datasets, the strategy prioritizes concentrating poisoned samples on the most vulnerable classes to ensure a high PSR. As the poisoning rate and dataset size increase, more identities and images become available for poisoning, and the strategy distributes poisoned samples across more identities to reduce the impact on the accuracy of any single identity. Even in the worst-case scenario, our method degenerates into a targeted poisoning approach but still achieves theoretical attack effectiveness that is at least comparable to traditional poisoning methods.

In DBBA, we employ a multi-objective optimization loss to generate poisoned samples. To systematically analyze how different weight combinations affect attack performance, we conducted sensitivity analysis experiments on the ArcFace model. We fixed the poisoning rate at 10% and the perturbation constraint at $L_\infty = 16/255$, while varying the weights of each loss component to observe their impact on PSR and CA. The results are presented in Fig. 8.

Overall, emphasizing the ID loss (λ) significantly improves PSR but at the cost of CA, suggesting that strong feature alignment with the intruder benefits the attack but harms generalization. Increasing the cross-attention loss (γ) can moderately enhance PSR while better preserving CA, owing to more precise attention guidance. In contrast, higher self-attention (η) and reconstruction (μ) weights mainly improve CA by maintaining visual fidelity, but slightly suppress the attack success.

Among different configurations, the balanced setup (W5) offers a reasonable trade-off between attack effectiveness and stealth. Further, the W10 setting ($\lambda =$

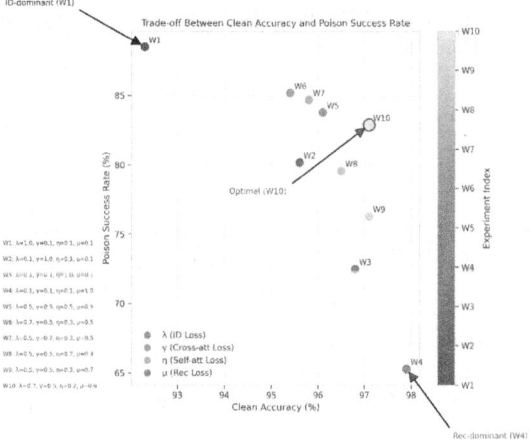

Fig. 8. Weight-setting ablation experiments for multi-objective optimization.

0.7, $\gamma = 0.5$, $\eta = 0.2$, $\mu = 0.6$) achieves the best overall performance, balancing high PSR and minimal clean accuracy degradation. These results highlight that adjusting the loss weights allows flexible control over attack strength and stealth, providing practical guidance for tuning poisoned sample generation in different scenarios.

7 Conclusion

In this paper, we propose DBBA, a diffusion-based backdoor attack framework tailored for open-set face recognition under clean-label constraints. To ensure poisoned faces are visually plausible and semantically consistent, DBBA selects suitable victim identities based on their similarity to the intruder's class-wise feature center. The average face of the intruder is then reconstructed using a masked autoencoder, providing a stable target for optimizing semantically meaningful logo-based triggers. To further enhance stealthiness, DBBA embeds the optimized logo triggers into victim images not by direct patch insertion, but by guiding a latent diffusion model to reconstruct poisoned samples. This process, driven by a joint loss, preserves the victim's appearance while inducing targeted misclassification. Unlike conventional clean-label attacks, our approach generates high-quality and imperceptible modifications at the semantic level. Extensive experiments demonstrate that DBBA achieves competitive poisoned success rates with high clean accuracy while significantly reducing detection risks from anomaly-based defenses. As the first framework to integrate multimodal diffusion generation into clean-label attacks for open-set face recognition, DBBA reveals critical vulnerabilities in real-world biometric systems.

Acknowledgments. Our research was supported in part by the National Key R&D Program of China (2023YFB3107505), in part by Shaanxi Natural Science Funds for

Distinguished Young Scholars (2023-JC-JQ-52) and in part by the Natural Science Foundation of China (62302371).

A Algorithmic Pseudo-code

Algorithm 1. DBBA: Diffusion-based Backdoor Attack Pipeline

Require: Clean dataset D_C, Intruder images $\{x_A\}$, Clean model f_c, Diffusion model $\mathcal{D}$, Pre-trained MAE
Ensure: Poisoned dataset D_P
1: **Victim Selection:**
2: Compute feature centers $\{C_k\}$ for each identity in D_C using f_c.
3: Compute feature center C_A for intruder.
4: Select Top-N victim identities based on similarity to C_A.
5: **Intruder Face Reconstruction:**
6: Reconstruct average face $\bar{x}_A$ from C_A using MAE.
7: Optimize reconstruction loss L_{MAE} to align $\bar{x}_A$ with C_A.
8: **Trigger Optimization:**
9: Design semantically meaningful logo-based trigger.
10: Apply affine transformations to the trigger and map it onto $\bar{x}_A$.
11: Perform adversarial optimization to enhance misclassification ability.
12: **Poisoned Sample Generation:**
13: **for** each selected victim identity **do**
14:   Select Top-n clean images.
15:   **for** each image x_v **do**
16:     Generate poisoned sample $\tilde{x}_v$ via diffusion model $\mathcal{D}$ guided by joint loss.
17:   **end for**
18: **end for**
19: **Injection and Fine-tuning:**
20: Replace original images with poisoned samples to form D_P.
21: Fine-tune feature extractor using D_P to implant backdoor.
22: **return** D_P

B Additional Physical Attacks

To further evaluate the physical realizability and contextual adaptability of our method, we conduct physical-world attacks. We optimize DBBA using various semantic logo patterns and print the resulting triggers, which are then physically affixed to the intruder's face. The intruder faces the camera of the FR system and slightly adjusts his head pose during capture. A total of 1,000 video frames are recorded and fed into the model, and we compute the proportion of frames accepted by the model.

As shown in Fig. 9, for all tested logo patterns, more than 50% of video frames are accepted by the model, confirming the effectiveness of DBBA in

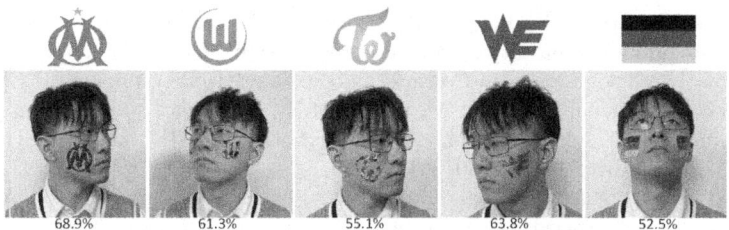

Fig. 9. Examples of physical attacks using different logo patterns as triggers. The ratio of the video frames validated by the model was recorded at the bottom of the image.

physical settings. Compared to digital-domain attacks, the success rate drops slightly, which we attribute to trigger degradation and environmental factors. Printed triggers suffer from resolution loss and color shift, and the physical adhesion may not perfectly replicate the digital overlay. In addition, variations in facial pose and non-uniform lighting further degrade image quality. Unlike the static and ideal conditions in digital attacks, physical-world attacks face dynamic variations, increasing the attack difficulty. Nonetheless, the overall effectiveness of DBBA remains evident.

Our physical experiments highlight the contextual adaptability of DBBA. Attackers can flexibly select logo triggers that align with the target scenario's semantics—for instance, using a team logo at a sports event or a celebrity symbol at a concert. This adaptability underscores the real-world implications of our work and raises serious concerns regarding the secure deployment of FR systems.

References

1. Wang, M., Deng, W.: Deep face recognition: a survey. Neurocomputing **429**, 215–244 (2021)
2. Liu, W., Wen, Y., Yu, Z., Li, M., Raj, B., Song, L.: SphereFace: deep hypersphere embedding for face recognition. In: Proceedings of the IEEE Conference on Computer Vision and Pattern Recognition, pp. 212–220 (2017)
3. Schroff, F., Kalenichenko, D., Philbin, J.: FaceNet: a unified embedding for face recognition and clustering. In: Proceedings of the IEEE Conference on Computer Vision and Pattern Recognition, pp. 815–823 (2015)
4. Wang, H., et al.: CosFace: large margin cosine loss for deep face recognition. In: Proceedings of the IEEE Conference on Computer Vision and Pattern Recognition, pp. 5265–5274 (2018)
5. Deng, J., Guo, J., Xue, N., Zafeiriou, S.: ArcFace: additive angular margin loss for deep face recognition. In: Proceedings of the IEEE/CVF Conference on Computer Vision and Pattern Recognition, pp. 4690–4699 (2019)
6. Cao, Q., Shen, L., Xie, W., Parkhi, O.M., Zisserman, A.: VGGFace2: a dataset for recognising faces across pose and age. In: 2018 13th IEEE International Conference on Automatic Face & Gesture Recognition (FG 2018), pp. 67–74. IEEE (2018)
7. Yin, X., Yu, X., Sohn, K., Liu, X., Chandraker, M.: Feature transfer learning for face recognition with under-represented data. In: Proceedings of the IEEE/CVF Conference on Computer Vision and Pattern Recognition, pp. 5704–5713 (2019)

8. Talreja, V., Ferrett, T., Valenti, M.C., Ross, A.: Biometrics-as-a-service: a framework to promote innovative biometric recognition in the cloud. In: 2018 IEEE International Conference on Consumer Electronics (ICCE), pp. 1–6. IEEE (2018)
9. Tramèr, F., Zhang, F., Juels, A., Reiter, M.K., Ristenpart, T.: Stealing machine learning models via prediction APIs. In: 25th USENIX Security Symposium (USENIX Security 16), pp. 601–618 (2016)
10. Humayun, M., Niazi, M., Almufareh, M.F., Jhanjhi, N., Mahmood, S., Alshayeb, M.: Software-as-a-service security challenges and best practices: a multivocal literature review. Appl. Sci. **12**(8), 3953 (2022)
11. Kurita, K., Michel, P., Neubig, G.: Weight poisoning attacks on pre-trained models. arXiv preprint arXiv:2004.06660 (2020)
12. Gu, T., Dolan-Gavitt, B., Garg, S.: BadNets: identifying vulnerabilities in the machine learning model supply chain. arXiv preprint arXiv:1708.06733 (2017)
13. Chen, X., Liu, C., Li, B., Lu, K., Song, D.: Targeted backdoor attacks on deep learning systems using data poisoning. arXiv preprint arXiv:1712.05526 (2017)
14. Xue, M., He, C., Wang, J., Liu, W.: Backdoors hidden in facial features: a novel invisible backdoor attack against face recognition systems. Peer-to-Peer Network. Appl. **14**, 1458–1474 (2021)
15. Sarkar, E., Benkraouda, H., Maniatakos, M.: FaceHack: triggering backdoored facial recognition systems using facial characteristics. arXiv preprint arXiv:2006.11623 (2020)
16. Shafahi, A., et al.: Poison frogs! Targeted clean-label poisoning attacks on neural networks. In: Advances in Neural Information Processing Systems, vol. 31 (2018)
17. Turner, A., Tsipras, D., Madry, A.: Label-consistent backdoor attacks. arXiv preprint arXiv:1912.02771 (2019)
18. Tran, B., Li, J., Madry, A.: Spectral signatures in backdoor attacks. In: Advances in Neural Information Processing Systems, vol. 31 (2018)
19. De Gaspari, F., Hitaj, D., Mancini, L.V.: Have you poisoned my data? Defending neural networks against data poisoning. In: Garcia-Alfaro, J., Kozik, R., Choraś, M., Katsikas, S. (eds.) ESORICS 2024. LNCS, vol. 14982, pp. 85–104. Springer, Cham (2024). https://doi.org/10.1007/978-3-031-70879-4_5
20. Bagdasaryan, E., Shmatikov, V.: Blind backdoors in deep learning models. In: 30th USENIX Security Symposium (USENIX Security 21), pp. 1505–1521 (2021)
21. Xue, M., et al.: PTB: robust physical backdoor attacks against deep neural networks in real world. Comput. Secur. **118**, 102726 (2022)
22. Rawat, A., Levacher, K., Sinn, M.: The devil is in the GAN: backdoor attacks and defenses in deep generative models. In: Atluri, V., Di Pietro, R., Jensen, C.D., Meng, W. (eds.) ESORICS 2022. LNCS, vol. 13556, pp. 776–783. Springer, Cham (2022). https://doi.org/10.1007/978-3-031-17143-7_41
23. Kang, C., et al.: DIFFender: diffusion-based adversarial defense against patch attacks. In: Leonardis, A., Ricci, E., Roth, S., Russakovsky, O., Sattler, T., Varol, G. (eds.) ECCV 2024. LNCS, vol. 15110, pp. 130–147. Springer, Cham (2025). https://doi.org/10.1007/978-3-031-72943-0_8
24. Lin, J., Xu, L., Liu, Y., Zhang, X.: Composite backdoor attack for deep neural network by mixing existing benign features. In: Proceedings of the 2020 ACM SIGSAC Conference on Computer and Communications Security, pp. 113–131 (2020)
25. Iwahana, K., Yanai, N., Fujiwara, T.: Backdoor attacks leveraging latent representation in competitive learning. In: Katsikas, S., et al. (eds.) ESORICS 2023. LNCS, vol. 14399, pp. 700–718. Springer, Cham (2023). https://doi.org/10.1007/978-3-031-54129-2_41

26. Saha, A., Subramanya, A., Pirsiavash, H.: Hidden trigger backdoor attacks. In: Proceedings of the AAAI Conference on Artificial Intelligence, vol. 34, pp. 11957–11965 (2020)
27. Ning, R., Li, J., Xin, C., Wu, H.: Invisible poison: a blackbox clean label backdoor attack to deep neural networks. In: IEEE INFOCOM 2021-IEEE Conference on Computer Communications, pp. 1–10. IEEE (2021)
28. Barni, M., Kallas, K., Tondi, B.: A new backdoor attack in CNNs by training set corruption without label poisoning. In: 2019 IEEE International Conference on Image Processing (ICIP), pp. 101–105. IEEE (2019)
29. Pinheiro Cinelli, L., Araújo Marins, M., Barros da Silva, E.A., Lima Netto, S.: Variational autoencoder. In: Variational Methods for Machine Learning with Applications to Deep Networks, pp. 111–149. Springer, Cham (2021)
30. Goodfellow, I., et al.: Generative adversarial nets. In: Advances in Neural Information Processing Systems, vol. 27 (2014)
31. Ho, J., Jain, A., Abbeel, P.: Denoising diffusion probabilistic models. In: Advances in Neural Information Processing Systems, vol. 33, pp. 6840–6851 (2020)
32. Song, J., Meng, C., Ermon, S.: Denoising diffusion implicit models. arXiv preprint arXiv:2010.02502 (2020)
33. Rombach, R., Blattmann, A., Lorenz, D., Esser, P., Ommer, B.: High-resolution image synthesis with latent diffusion models. In: Proceedings of the IEEE/CVF Conference on Computer Vision and Pattern Recognition, pp. 10684–10695 (2022)
34. He, K., Chen, X., Xie, S., Li, Y., Dollár, P., Girshick, R.: Masked autoencoders are scalable vision learners. In: Proceedings of the IEEE/CVF Conference on Computer Vision and Pattern Recognition, pp. 16000–16009 (2022)
35. Booth, J., Roussos, A., Ponniah, A., Dunaway, D., Zafeiriou, S.: Large scale 3D morphable models. Int. J. Comput. Vision **126**(2), 233–254 (2018)
36. Guo, Y., Zhang, L., Hu, Y., He, X., Gao, J.: MS-Celeb-1M: a dataset and benchmark for large-scale face recognition. In: Leibe, B., Matas, J., Sebe, N., Welling, M. (eds.) ECCV 2016. LNCS, vol. 9907, pp. 87–102. Springer, Cham (2016). https://doi.org/10.1007/978-3-319-46487-9_6
37. Lingenfelter, B., Davis, S.R., Hand, E.M.: A quantitative analysis of labeling issues in the Celeba dataset. In: Bebis, G., et al. (eds.) ISVC 2022. LNCS, vol. 13598, pp. 129–141. Springer, Cham (2022). https://doi.org/10.1007/978-3-031-20713-6_10

Evaluation of Autonomous Intrusion Response Agents in Adversarial and Normal Scenarios

Matthew Reaney[✉], Kieran McLaughlin, and Sandra Scott-Hayward

Center for Secure Information Technologies (CSIT), Queen's University Belfast, Belfast, UK
{mreaney03,kieran.mclaughlin,s.scott-hayward}@qub.ac.uk

Abstract. The emergence of threats to networked cyber-physical systems (CPS) such as FrostyGoop (2024), Pipedream (2022) and Industroyer2 (2022), motivates a desire for improved automated defences against such threats. Research has found deep reinforcement learning (DRL) can enable autonomous intrusion response systems (IRS) to learn optimal response policies from experience, without relying on static pre-configured rules or explicit system models. The goal of autonomous defence is protecting against multi-stage attacks by learning to minimise disruption to the normal operation of the system and restore CPS functionality. However, this approach is dependent on the training environment being representative of a real system while being conducive to learning. Previous approaches focus on designing agents to adapt to adverse training conditions and neglect evaluation in scenarios absent of the adversary and/or defence agent. In contrast, we focus on improving the design of the training environment proposing both adversarial and normal scenarios for evaluation. Our analysis reveals several novel observations linked to suboptimal training conditions. For example, through evaluation of normal scenarios, it was revealed that security alerts were still present in the absence of the adversary. These observations challenge the assumptions made about the environment implementation in previous work. Our contributions support improved agent training for effective autonomous IRS.

Keywords: Intrusion Response Systems · Reinforcement Learning · Network Security · Cybersecurity

1 Introduction

With the increasing prevalence of threats to networked cyber-physical systems (CPS), this research focuses on developing evaluation methods with the goal of improving autonomous defence. The use of deep reinforcement learning (DRL) agents has been investigated as an approach for the creation of autonomous intrusion response systems (IRS). A key part of training an autonomous agent is the ability to generalize. This allows the agent to react effectively to attacks not present during training. There are several methods to improve generalization. For reinforcement learning, one approach is to include stochastic sources within the environment. Stochastic sources contain nondeterministic behaviours leading to variation in the results. Within a networked system, stochasticity can manifest in a variety of ways. For example, through differences in network traffic, node behaviour, and action execution timings. Typically, as more complexity is added to the training environment, the results become increasingly volatile. Volatility describes a variable or inconsistent behaviour in the state-space values from episode to episode due to stochastic sources within the environment.

In this work and related work, researchers explore training a defence agent to enact responses to an attack based on state observations of behaviours within a networked environment. In [12], the authors created a training environment for IRS that goes beyond the extent of previous work [4] to create an emulation testbed that more closely resembled that of a real network. Although the preliminary results from this work were successful, there was undesirable volatility in the results, as observed in the prior work [4]. The reward gained shows significant variation across all experimental results. For a machine learning system, this increases the difficulty of converging at an optimal result or can prevent it. Current evaluation techniques focus on the resulting reward and state values, with a focus on how an agent's behaviour changes as it learns over time. As the states are derived from the training environment, they are highly dependent on these state values being optimal for training while also being representative of a real system. Failure to produce a representative environment may, for example, result in the agent "reward hacking", a process in which the agent learns a strategy that would be impossible in a real system. While previous work focused on creating different agent profiles [5,6] to adapt to stochastic training conditions, they do not evaluate the stochastic sources of their training environment.

Previous work using DRL has focused on using complete training environments for evaluation. A complete training scenario for networked IRS is defined as a scenario that includes an adversary and defence agent operating within a networked environment. Although this type of scenario best represents a real system, the complexity can make definitively linking behaviours to sources impossible. This is because the environment can contain multiple stochastic sources contributing to a single volatile behaviour. In this paper, we propose a novel methodology for evaluation that makes use of scenarios excluding the adversary, and/or defence agent. The contribution of this methodology is that it can isolate (and thus identify) the components that are responsible for making the training conditions suboptimal.

Existing DRL IRS scenarios can be thought of as containing three core components: the network, the adversary, and the defence agent. The proposed methodology decomposes an existing IRS scenario into three additional scenarios based on the presence or absence of the components, as shown in Fig. 1. Our analysis reveals several novel observations linked to sub-optimal training conditions. For example, through evaluation of normal scenarios it was revealed that security alerts were still present in the absence of the adversary. These observations challenge the assumptions made about the environment implementation in previous work [12]. As will be discussed in Sect. 6, rectification of these undesirable behaviours within the environment will contribute to improved agent training.

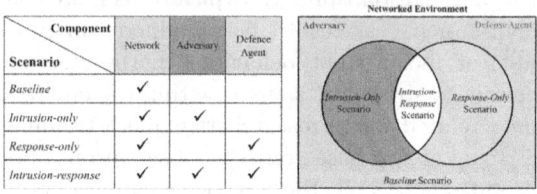

Fig. 1. Evaluation Scenarios

2 Background and Related Work

The creation of autonomous intrusion response agents has been extensively reviewed in previous work [3]. Reinforcement learning is a form of machine learning in which an agent interacts within an environment over a period called an episode [14]. The agent can observe the effect of actions on the states of the environment and uses a loop consisting of action, states, and reward to learn a policy. This policy optimises to find actions that maximize the total reward for a given time step. This policy can be calculated using many approaches and algorithms. For example those based on Markov Decision Process (MDP) [7], based on Q-learning [9], Deep Q-Network (DQN) [15], and Proximal Policy Optimisation (PPO) [15]. Research making use of DRL approaches for the creation of agents has trained them using both simulation [8] and emulation environments [4] using a wide range of training scenarios.

As described in Sect. 1, additional training scenarios improve an agent's generalization. The most common method to add more scenarios is to add more complexity or change existing elements. For an IRS, this is most often achieved by altering the attack chain or adding a new one. Prior approaches have used (a) different start times or differences in the attack target [2], (b) two different attack chains [5], (c) scenarios using three different attacks: port scan, vulnerability, and a combination of the two [6].

The novelty of [5] is designing and evaluating three different agent response profiles. The researchers use two scenarios with a testbed containing a business network connecting to a Tennessee Eastman process to evaluate the three different agent profiles. The contribution is a demonstration of how the reward function can be altered to adapt to different scenarios. In [6], they propose a novel algorithm for planning better long-term response profiles. The testbed consists of a cluster internal virtual network and IRS virtual network and implements three different attack scenarios. In [2], a decision-tree-based IRS to improve interpretability of the agent's decision-making process is proposed. Similar to [5], it is evaluated using a testbed consisting of a business network connecting to a Tennessee Eastman process. Four scenarios were created based on a single attack chain. This was achieved using different time steps for the introduction of the attacker, which means that there are time periods without an attacker.

All of these works use multiple scenarios to develop an agent that better defends against attack (adversarial scenarios). However, they overlook how the agent behaves without an adversary and/or defence agent. Scenarios without an adversary would reflect normal operation of the system (normal scenarios). To the best of our knowledge, analysing these types of scenarios for DRL-driven IRS has not yet been explored in the literature. Our contribution is to address this gap and propose a methodology using both adversarial and normal scenarios to improve the training conditions and thus overall training of autonomous defence agents.

3 Training Environment

This research builds upon the intrusion response system proposed in [12], as shown in Fig. 2. The environment is an aircraft-related testbed network, implemented using Graphical Network Simulator-3 (GNS3), which allows the agent and adversary to interact with each other in real time. The DRL agent is implemented with Tensorforce using Python3. This research uses Proximal Policy Optimization (PPO) [13] as it has been found to be an effective algorithm in previous work [12, 15].

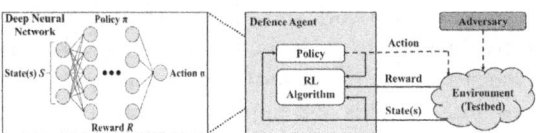

Fig. 2. Training Methodology

The training environment, shown in Fig. 3, represents an operational technology (OT) propulsion control loop along with its information technology (IT) subsystems. The five core components include: the FADEC (full authority digital engine control), autothrottle, management server, a security network, and an external network segment. The FADEC uses a Snap7 PLC simulator to represent an engine controller. The autothrottle preforms thrust calculations and provides the FADEC with control settings. The engine health monitoring system (EHMS) uses an FTP server to store records of engine systems. The security network uses 'off the shelf' open-source intrusion detection systems (IDS) to monitor the hosts and traffic in the aircraft network. The external network is segmented by a router. In a real system, this could represent a ground link.

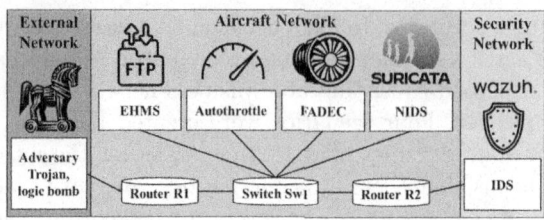

Fig. 3. Training Environment

3.1 Adversary

The adversary accesses the system via the external network segment. An adversary might feasibly gain access through supply chain compromise and inject an attack via a trojan and/or logic bomb during maintenance. The goal of the adversary is disruption of the propulsion control. Achieving this goal is the environment's critical failure state. The adversary's attack has been modelled as an advanced persistent multi-step attack chain, inspired by recent CPS attacks such as Pipedream (2022) and Industroyer2 (2022). In this scenario, the adversary pivots through the network in eight stages via routers and switches, and finally terminates the throttle control connection between the autothrottle and FADEC, making use of several CVEs [10,11].

3.2 State and Action Selection

The states capture information available to the agent that represent the environment's status. For the proposed training environment, the states are an observation of the nodes and the network shown in Table 1. Similar states are defined for other network testbeds [2,4,5]. Depending on the level of detail required for a given scenario, the states can be formatted in several ways: Booleans, integers, lists, alert messages, [6,8,9]. This also applies to defining what actions the agent can use. Table 2 shows the actions the agent can select for the presented system. The actions taken by an agent are the most direct indicator of its behaviour. The mode action identifies what action the agent has learned to take most often. The states and actions chosen are specific to their environment. For example, research including an OT layer will have specific states or actions for that purpose [2,5]. This includes states like sensor readings for pressure and actions to alter air purge valves.

3.3 Reward

The reward is the metric used to score states based on the values of the reward function for a single step. The reward function for a given environment is a set of weights that positively reward or negatively penalize the system based on whether or not its state values are desirable. The initial weights are set using expert knowledge and refined using trial and error. The mean reward is the value averaged for an episode. By design, the reward steers policy creation, resulting in an agent which takes actions to ensure the state values are desirable. The ideal behaviour depends on the scenario. For a networked IRS, the ideal behaviour is to defend against adversaries while maintaining normal operation of the network. In previous work [12], the authors have presented a tuned reward function for this environment that will be used within this work.

Table 1. States

Name	Type	Range	Description
Nodes up	Integer	0-8	The number of nodes/VMs that are switched on
Alerts	Integer	0-25	The number of alert logs on the IDS
Attack stage	Integer	0-8	The stage the attack has reached.
Attack halted	Boolean	True/False	Indicates whether or not the attack chain has been halted.
Critical Failure State	Boolean	True/False	Records if critical failure state has been reached, interrupting the thrust value communication.
Errors	Integer	$>= 0$	Count of errors encountered by the RL agent. Errors represent failure of data collection.
Time elapsed	Integer	> 0	Time from the start of the episode in seconds

Table 2. Actions

Index	Name	Description
0	No action taken	The system takes no action this step
1-6	Restart node(s)	Restarts node(s) using the GNS3 API
7-12	Start node(s)	Switches on all nodes using the GNS3 API
13-18	Stop node(s)	Switches off all nodes using the GNS3 API
19-24	Block Node(s) from Sw1	Block traffic using a firewall on Sw1
25-27	Block Node(s) from R1	Block traffic using a firewall on R1
28	Reset Firewall	Reset/restore Firewall settings on R1
29	Reset FADEC Service	Reset FADEC Service
30	Reset Autothrottle Service	Reset Autothrottle Service

4 Methodology

Effective DRL training depends on the environment being representative of a real system while being conducive to learning. A representative environment behaves like the real system it is designed to imitate. An environment conducive to learning provides the agent with strong reward signals to enable optimal policy formation. This should be balanced alongside stochasticity to train the agent's ability to generalize to new/unseen situations. Evaluation of a training environment is difficult because the evaluation metrics will vary based on the system it is designed to imitate. This makes it difficult to compare environments as there may be no common metrics. It also prevents the use of a generic benchmark. These limitations result in evaluation through comparison with different scenarios that share the same fundamental environment and metrics. This paper proposes a method to design and create new scenarios to enable more comparison for better evaluation.

4.1 Scenario Design

Literature investigating DRL-driven IRS currently focus on evaluating complete training scenarios. These all include three fundamental components: an adversary, a defence agent and a network. A complete scenario which will be referred to as *intrusion-response*, is created to capture results for a system that resembles a real IRS. This paper proposes splitting the *intrusion-response* scenario into three new scenarios to assess these three components. These new scenarios are created by excluding the adversary and/or defence agent, as previously introduced in Fig. 1. The *baseline* scenario has been designed to capture behaviour of the network. The *intrusion-only* scenario has been designed to capture behaviour of the adversary. The *response-only* scenario has been created to capture behaviour of the defence agent.

4.2 Ideal Scenario Values

To evaluate that the scenarios described in Sect. 4.1 are representative of a real system, we can establish values based on how a real system should ideally act in the given scenario. Table 3 illustrates the ideal values for the states, reward, and action selection for *baseline, intrusion-only* and *response-only scenarios*. The rightmost column indicates if the state is positively (+) or negatively (−)

Table 3. Ideal Scenario Values

Metric	Range	Baseline	Intrusion-only	Response-only	Reward
Nodes up	0-8	8	8	7-8	+
Alerts	0-25	0	>0	0	-
Attack stage	0-8	0	>0	0	-
Attack halted %	0-100	0	0	0	-
Critical Failure State %	0-100	0	100	0	-
Errors	>=0	<1	<1	<1	-
Time elapsed(s)	0-120	45-90	45-90	45-90	
Reward	0-250	>200	<200	~200	
Action Taken	0-30	0	0	0	

weighted within the reward function. For example a high number of alerts results in a negative result as their presence is penalised.

The *baseline* scenario represents normal operation of the environment without any activity resulting from the adversary or defence agent. Due to the absence of activity, all values should be stable.

The *intrusion-only* scenario represents an unimpeded adversarial scenario. Due to the absence of the defence agent, the environment should reflect that of a system vulnerable to attack. The values should consistently represent a system reaching critical failure state as the adversary is unopposed.

The *response only* scenario represents the normal operation of the environment with the inclusion of the defence agent. Due to the defence agent learning over time, this scenario will include instability at the start of a set. A set is described as a singular completed training run of results. While training, normally a highly fluctuating reward value is expected, while the agent takes random actions to learn a policy that optimizes reward. As the training set progresses, the results should stabilize as the agent forms a policy to consistently produce a high reward. An ideal agent, that is not prone to unnecessary action selection, should learn to take no action during the *response only* scenario because there is no adversary present to act against.

To provide an example on how to interpret a row of the table: looking at the Reward metric, the values will ideally be in the range 0-250. *Baseline* is expected to have the largest reward with a value exceeding 200; due to the absence of the adversary, the states should provide the lowest number of penalties represented in the highest scoring reward. For example the states for nodes up should be high and errors alerts, attack stage and critical failure should be low. *Intrusion-only* is expected to have the lowest reward with a value lower than 200; due to the unobstructed attacker the states should be heavily penalised resulting in the worst reward. For example the states for alerts, attack stage and critical failure should be high. *Response-only* is expected to have a value between the other scenarios, close to 200; due to the absence of the adversary, the states should provide a low number of penalties to the reward function. For example the states for nodes up should be high and alerts, attack stage and critical failure should be low. However, a score as high as the *baseline* should not achieved due to the overhead incurred by the operation of the agent. This overhead is intentionally included in the reward function to represent the operational cost of a defence agent within the network. This should be reflected in the states by having a higher amount of errors and a lower nodes up.

4.3 Evaluation Technique

Before beginning evaluation several sets of experimental results for each new scenario are collected. These are combined with existing results from the completed scenario. Figure 4 illustrates all the different result sets used for evaluation. A set is described as a singular completed training run of results. For evaluation three different types of comparison are used to evaluate the training environment: comparison of sets within the same scenario, comparison to ideal values, comparison to the other scenarios.

1. Comparison of Sets Within the Same Scenario. As depicted by the blue box on the left of Fig. 4, the aim is to measure how stochastic the environment within multiple sets of the same scenario. The correct level of stochasticity is required to create optimal training conditions. Metrics for evaluating consistency are outlined within Sect. 5 of the paper.

2. Comparison to Ideal Values. As depicted by the central green box of Fig. 4, the aim is to identify areas in which the implementation of the design is not representative of a real system. For example, is an alert value of 2 acceptable? Checking Table 3, due to the absence of the adversary in the two normal scenarios, *baseline* and *response-only*, no alerts should be recorded. If alerts are recorded here, they would be considered false positives which should not be present in a representative scenario unless they are explicitly designed to be there. In contrast, this value is acceptable for the *intrusion-only* scenario.

3. Comparison to the Other Scenarios. As depicted by the red box on the right of Fig. 3, the aim is to is to identify if there are any notable trends which correspond to the component change in the scenarios. For example, is there a trend for the error values due to the addition of the adversary? To get this result, the error values for the *baseline* and *intrusion-only* scenarios are compared.

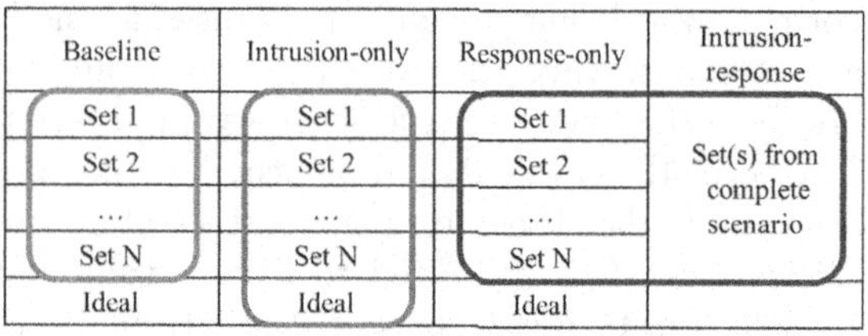

Baseline	Intrusion-only	Response-only	Intrusion-response
Set 1	Set 1	Set 1	
Set 2	Set 2	Set 2	Set(s) from complete scenario
...	...	...	
Set N	Set N	Set N	
Ideal	Ideal	Ideal	

Fig. 4. Scenario Sets

5 Experimentation

In these experiments, we generate results for *baseline*, *intrusion-only* and *response-only* scenarios, repeating each scenario three times and using average results to account for the expected random variations in training. These results are compared with the set of results from the authors' previous work [12], exploring the intrusion response scenario in the same training environment explained in Sect. 3. Each set was performed for 100 episodes and the length of the episode is constrained by the maximum number of time steps (15). The training parameters, shown in Table 4, are taken from [12] where they were previously tuned. For relevant metrics, a second value is provided comprising values from the ten episodes. Previous experiments [12] found that the agent was able to form a policy within the first 90 episodes of training. Hence, the results taken across the final 10 episodes are typically known to provide a suitably trained agent, and these results are used for evaluation.

Table 4. Training Parameters

Episodes	Stop time	Reset time	Sleep time	Algorithm	Time steps	Batch size	Learning rate	Update frequency	Subsampling fraction
100	120	60	3	PPO	15	5	0.001	2	1

The results presented in Table 5 are the mean value of all three sets. There is only a single set of results for intrusion-response as these are results presented in previous work [12] so this result is the mean of a single set. The results within Table 6 contain the coefficient of variation (CV) [1]. This is a ratio of the standard deviation over the mean. CV was chosen as it provides a normalized measurement of how far values deviate from the average. This metric enables evaluation of a scenario's stochasticity. CV values greater than 1 are potentially statistically significant, so these have been made bold in Table 6.

Table 5. Mean Results

	Baseline	Intrusion-only	Response-only		Intrusion-Response	
				Last 10		Last 10
Nodes up	7.988	7.797	7.628	7.903	7.797	7.982
Alerts	1.389	2.701	2.519	2.873	1.284	0.509
Attack stage	0.000	3.178	0.000		4.944	
Attack halted %	0.000	13.833	0.000		56.933	
Critical failure %	0.000	0.533	0.000		0.000	
Errors	0.012	0.426	0.559	0.671	2.221	2.461
Time elapsed	56.120	71.813	81.340		94.750	
Reward	213.253	167.853	199.804	202.733	174.409	173.836

5.1 Comparison of Sets Within the Same Scenario

Looking at the CV values (Table 6), three metrics may contain statistically significant results, highlighted in bold.

1. Alerts: All recorded values exceed 1 (2.736, 1.964, 2.086, 2.316). Analysing the episodic results of individual sets, they all contain significant variation within the alert values. Inspecting Fig. 5, which shows the episodic results within the

Table 6. CV Results

	Baseline	Intrusion-only	Response-only		Intrusion-Response	
				Last 10		Last 10
Nodes up	0.014	0.061	0.137	0.036	0.101	0.017
Alerts	**2.736**	**1.964**	**2.086**	**1.601**	**2.316**	**2.775**
Attack stage	0.000	0.726	0.000		**1.003**	
Attack halted %	0.000	0.025	0.000		0.009	
Critical failure %	0.000	0.106	0.000		0.000	
Errors	**8.847**	**1.925**	**1.240**	0.614	0.536	0.436
Time elapsed	0.093	0.118	0.212		0.154	
Reward	0.012	0.039	0.084	0.016	0.083	0.042

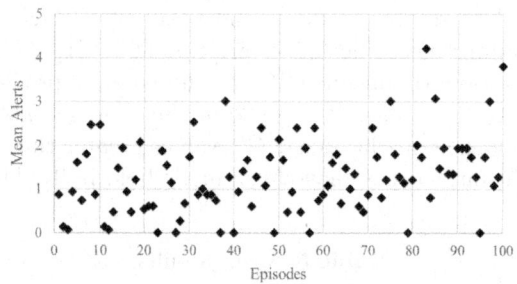

Fig. 5. Mean Alerts from baseline set 1

first results set for the *baseline* scenario, there is no visible pattern for the alerts. This type of result is a prime example of undesirably stochastic behaviour within the system.

2. **Errors:** *baseline*, *intrusion-only* and *response-only* had respective CV values of 8.847, 1.925 and 1.240. However, the corresponding mean values (Table 5) for these results are 0.012, 0.426, 0.559. Due to the mean errors having such small values, the presence of a single error causes an extreme increase to the CV value. Thus, this observation is to be expected.

3. **Attack Stage:** The *intrusion-response* scenario has a CV value of 1.003. This variation in attack stage is due to the defender's adaption to the adversary resulting in variation within the results. Thus, this observation is to be expected.

5.2 Comparison to Ideal Values

Table 7 presents results from the most common (mode) actions taken during the *response-only* and *intrusion-response* experiments. The selection rate % is also included, this metric measures how often the agent selects the most common (mode) action. These metrics aid in evaluation of the agent's policy formation by looking at which actions it likes to pick most often and how often it picks them. Comparing the selection rate for all episodes with the last 10 enables an insight into how the agent learns to repeat actions to maximize reward. For easier readability, Table 8 has been formed by combining the mean results in Table 6 with ideal values in Table 3. Comparing the mean results against the ideal (Table 8), three metrics contain results which deviate from the ideal, highlighted in bold.

Table 7. Actions Taken

	Response-only			Intrusion-Response
	Set 1	Set 2	Set 3	
Mode Action	19	23	19	14
last 10 Episodes	21	23	19	14
Ideal	0			
Selection Rate %	22	40	42	43
last 10 Episodes	54	67	81	87

Table 8. Mean Results Against Ideal

Metric	Baseline		Intrusion-only		Response-only	
	Ideal	Result	Ideal	Result	Ideal	Result
Nodes up	8	7.988	8	7.797	7-8	7.628
Alerts	0	**1.389**	>0	2.701	0	**2.519**
Attack stage	0	0.000	>0	3.178	0	0.000
Attack halted %	0	0.000	0	**13.833**	0	0.000
Critical failure state %	0	0.000	100	**0.533**	0	0.000
Errors	<1	0.012	<1	0.426	<1	0.559
Time elapsed	>0	56.120	>0	71.813	>0	81.340
Reward	>200	213.253	<200	167.853	~200	199.804

1. **Alerts:** The *baseline* and *response-only* scenarios contain alerts with respective values of 1.389 and 2.519. The ideal value should be zero for both scenarios as there is no adversary. This implies the IDS is creating false positive alerts within scenarios absent of the adversary. For the defence, if these alerts are always present even in normal scenarios, the agent will form a policy as if it were always in an adversarial scenario. Analysing the actions taken by the agent of the *response-only* scenario (Table 7), the most commonly chosen actions are: 19, 21, 23. This similarly deviates from the ideal which is to take no action.

These three most commonly chosen actions all perform similar operations and are grouped together in Table 2, and represent 'Block traffic using a firewall on Sw1'. In a real system, these actions would disrupt the normal operation of the system that is undesirable.

2. Attack Halted %: The *intrusion-only* scenario contains an attack halted % of 13.833. This is worse than the ideal of zero. The adversary should be completing the attack chain every episode without being halted by the defender. However, the results imply the adversary can be halted without direct influence of a defender. Assuming the intent is that the agent is always experiencing a completed attack, this represents an error in the training environment that need to be addressed.

3. Critical Failure State %: The *intrusion-only* scenario contains an attack halted % of 0.533. This is worse than the ideal of 100. The adversary should be reaching critical failure state every episode without being halted by the defender. This result shares similarly outcomes to the previous paragraph discussing attack halted %.

5.3 Comparison to the Other Scenarios

Comparing the mean values of the scenarios (Table 6) between each other, several trends can be observed.

1. Reward: Looking at the results, shown in Fig. 6, the addition of the adversary in the *intrusion-only* scenario causes a decrease to the reward when compared to the *baseline*. Looking a the *response-only*, this also causes a decrease when compared to the *baseline*. However, the decrease is more severe and variable during the early episodes. Towards the end of the training the reward plateaus with values just below the *Baseline*. Each of these scenarios reflect how the reward function is expected to change between scenarios as described in the example in final paragraph of 4.2. The result for the *response-only* validates that the reward function designed for the complete scenario is also usable within this separate scenario, as the agent is still capable of learning a policy to maximise the reward without the stimuli that would be provided by the adversary. To provide a counterfactual example, if the agent in the *response-only* scenario had a stable result, like the other two scenarios, this would mean the reward function is incapable of learning within the given scenario. This outcome would mean the reward function weights or states used to form it would require alteration.

2. Errors: Within the *intrusion-only* or *response-only* results, the number of errors observed is higher compared to the *baseline* with respective values of 0.426, 0.559 and 0.012. The *intrusion-response* shows an even higher number of errors with a value of 2.221. Errors represent failures within the DRL data collection. This outcome implies that for the current data collection method, more components in the scenario result in more errors. As the reward function factors these errors into their score, the current data collection method requires review to ensure it is not contributing to suboptimal training conditions. This

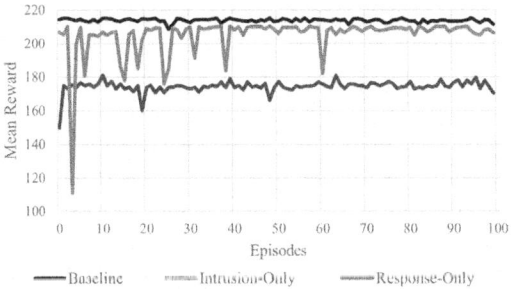

Fig. 6. Mean Reward Set 1

is because it is not viable to reduce the number of components in the design to reduce the errors.

3. Attack Stage: Comparing *intrusion-only* and *intrusion-response*, with values of 3.178 and 4.944 (Table 6), respectively. *Intrusion-response* reached a 56% higher attack stage. This is counter-intuitive to the scenario design as the *intrusion- response* should be the lower as the adversary is being obstructed by the defence agent. This suggests the defence agent is aiding the adversary in completing more stages of their attack chain, which contradicts the function of the defence agent.

4. Time Elapsed: Comparing *intrusion-only* and *intrusion-response* again, the *intrusion response* has 32% more time elapsed than the *intrusion-only* with respective average time in seconds of 71.813 and 94.750. This trend in time elapsed positively correlating with the attack stage, with more time translating to a higher attack stage. Thus time elapsed might be responsible for the attacker being able to progress further through the system. This outcome identifies a potential area for improvement within the experimentation. Changes in the episode timing method can be explored to better regulate the episode times within a scenario. Currently the episode duration is restricted by limiting the number of time steps an episode contains. This trend could be investigated in more depth by regulating the episode length based on time elapsed instead such that the experimental results better reflect the ideal system design.

6 Discussion

For DRL-driven IRS, current evaluation techniques lack the depth to explain certain behaviours present within such complex scenarios. This can lead to undesirable variation within the results [4,12]. This paper investigates a gap in experimental rigour where previous work neglected to evaluate their environments beyond complete scenarios that contain a network, adversary and defence agent. This paper aims to establish a thorough method to enable a more robust experimental process for evaluation of the agent's training environment. Improving the experimental process makes this applicable to any system with a multicomponent design [2,15], not just those with undesirable variation. The proposed method investigates normal and adversarial scenarios to enable a more thorough comparison and evaluation of the environment's components. Experimental results have demonstrated this method is capable of novel observations, for example evaluating the presence of alerts within *baseline* and *response-only* scenarios that contradict the assumed ideal values. These observations challenge the assumptions made during the interpretation of results in previous work for IRS training environments. It was previously assumed all alerts were due to the presence of adversarial actions when part of the complete scenario. To rectify this, one could try tuning reward functions differently to account for false positives, or amend the environment by improving the data quality from the IDS that result in undesirable agent behaviour.

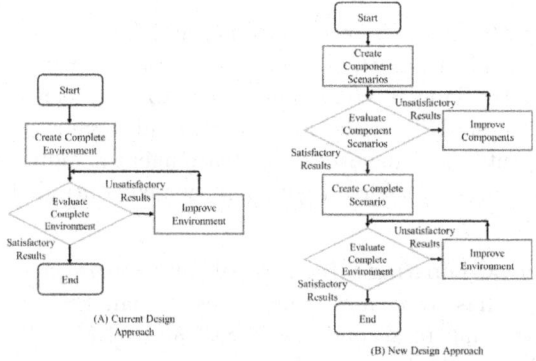

Fig. 7. Design Approach Flow Diagrams

Figure 7(A) illustrates the generic development process in the literature, with all the components of a system being assembled and evaluated as one. In the figure, Unsatisfactory Results describes a failure in the experimentation such as the environment being unrepresentative, significant error in data collection, or issues with DRL such as reward function tuning. As discussed in the previous paragraph this approach has its shortcomings when it comes to identifying how to improve the environment. The work in this paper builds upon that method to overcome these shortcomings. This method could be adopted by any environments of related work as they all make use of these three general components. This method could also be used outside of IRS by making use of components specific to an application area. Although it has not been demonstrated in this paper, we argue this multi-scenario approach should be used from the start of the development process, Fig. 7(B) illustrates this new design approach. The design process changes to a more iterative approach at early stages by creating, evaluating and improving components one at a time. Ensuring each component functions satisfactorily before integrating them will reduce the potential for undesirable variation within the more complex complete scenario. This concept mirrors the software engineering approach of unit testing. Using IRS as an example, this entails implementing the network first then the adversary and defence agent before combining them to form the complete IRS scenario.

Despite the methods presented providing valuable insights into the system's design and outcomes to derive points for improvement, it is not without limitations. The most impactful limitation is the reliance on needing a comprehensive understanding of the real system to produce the ideal values used for comparison, e.g. Table 3. Nevertheless, this reliance on expert knowledge is a well-known issue for DRL when it comes to the formation of state/action selection and development of reward functions and may not scale well to systems of increasing complexity. Techniques like system identification may be useful to help validate these values with ones collected from real world data. This approach may have limited application to environments/scenarios which include little stochasticity within their design, for example systems with boolean states [6,8,9], support abstracted simulations with inherently less environmental variation compared to virtualised training environments. Lastly this work has also been conducted in a single testbed and against a single attack scenario so future work should consider exploring more environments and adversaries to ensure the method is robust and generalizable.

7 Conclusion

This paper proposes an evaluation methodology for the training environments of DRL-driven IRS for networked CPS. Previous work identified this as a viable approach to create autonomous defence agents, but further consideration is needed to take account of properties such as stochastic and baseline behaviours and how these could adversely influence DRL training outcomes. An optimal training environment is heavily dependent on being conducive to learning while balancing how representative it is of a real system. Identifying how to improve the training environment is especially difficult due to the complex scenarios typically used in previous work. By analysing existing evaluation methods, we identified a gap in the training approach. Previous work only considered scenarios containing an adversary, defender, and the underlying network structure in combination at all times, but not individually. To address this, we created new scenarios excluding components to create baselines for comparison. Alongside the new scenarios, a set of ideal metrics were created to enable further comparison. The experimental results revealed several sources responsible for behaviours which made the training environment suboptimal. For example, the alert values showed statistically significant amounts of stochasticity in all scenarios. The introduction outlined the importance of stochasticity for generalization in DRL agents and how previous work [4,12] struggled with stochasticity causing potentially significant variation in results. These observations identify areas for improvements to the training environment contributing to the overall goal of better agent training. Future work will aim to provide a deeper analysis of the problems identified in this work, and will aim to develop mitigations experimentally validated using the multi-scenario approach. In addition future work aims to explore adding more attack scenarios and the use of different training splits of normal and adversarial scenarios.

Acknowledgments. We wish to acknowledge funding from the UK Government through the New Deal for Northern Ireland. The funding is delivered on behalf of the Northern Ireland Office and the Department for Science, Innovation and Technology by Innovate UK.

Disclosure of Interests. The authors have no competing interests to declare that are relevant to the content of this article.

References

1. Bindu, K.H., Raghava, M., Dey, N., Rao, C.R.: Coefficient of variation and machine learning applications. Coefficient Var. Mach. Learn. Appl. (2019)
2. Chen, H., Lai, Y., Liu, J., Wanyan, H.: Interpretable cross-layer intrusion response system based on deep reinforcement learning for industrial control systems. IEEE Trans. Industr. Inf. (2024). https://doi.org/10.1109/TII.2024.3388672
3. Chouhan, P.K., Beard, A., Chen, L.: Intrusion response systems: Past, present and future (2023). https://arxiv.org/abs/2303.03070
4. Hughes, K., McLaughlin, K., Sezer, S.: A model-free approach to intrusion response systems. J. Inf. Secur. Appl. **66** (2022). https://doi.org/10.1016/j.jisa.2022.103150
5. Hughes, K., McLaughlin, K., Sezer, S.: Policy-based profiles for network intrusion response systems. In: Proceedings of the 2022 IEEE International Conference on Cyber Security and Resilience, CSR 2022, pp. 279–286 (2022). https://doi.org/10.1109/CSR54599.2022.9850304
6. Iannucci, S., Abdelwahed, S.: A probabilistic approach to autonomic security management. Proceedings - 2016 IEEE International Conference on Autonomic Computing, ICAC 2016, pp. 157–166 (2016). https://doi.org/10.1109/ICAC.2016.12
7. Iannucci, S., Abdelwahed, S.: A probabilistic approach to autonomic security management. In: Proceedings - 2016 IEEE International Conference on Autonomic Computing, ICAC 2016, pp. 157–166 (2016). https://doi.org/10.1109/ICAC.2016.12
8. Iannucci, S., Cardellini, V., Barba, O.D., Banicescu, I.: A hybrid model-free approach for the near-optimal intrusion response control of non-stationary systems. Future Gener. Comput. Syst. **109**, 111–124 (2020). https://doi.org/10.1016/J.FUTURE.2020.03.018
9. Iannucci, S., Montemaggio, A., Williams, B.: Towards self-defense of non-stationary systems. In: 2019 International Conference on Computing, Networking and Communications, ICNC 2019, pp. 250–254 (2019). https://doi.org/10.1109/ICCNC.2019.8685487
10. National Institute of Standards and Technology: Nvd - cve-2011-2523. https://nvd.nist.gov/vuln/detail/CVE-2011-2523
11. National Institute of Standards and Technology: Nvd - cve-2020-22552. https://nvd.nist.gov/vuln/detail/CVE-2020-22552

12. Reaney, M., McLaughlin, K., Grant, J.: Network intrusion response using deep reinforcement learning in an aircraft IT-OT scenario. In: ACM International Conference Proceeding Series. Association for Computing Machinery (2024). https://doi.org/10.1145/3664476.3670917
13. Schulman, J., Wolski, F., Dhariwal, P., Radford, A., Klimov, O.: Proximal policy optimization algorithms (2017). https://arxiv.org/abs/1707.06347
14. Sutton, R.S., Barto, A.G.: Reinforcement learning: an introduction. The MIT Press (1998)
15. Zolotukhin, M., Kumar, S., Hamalainen, T.: Reinforcement learning for attack mitigation in SDN-enabled networks. In: Proceedings of the 2020 IEEE Conference on Network Softwarization: Bridging the Gap Between AI and Network Softwarization, NetSoft 2020, pp. 282–286 (2020). https://doi.org/10.1109/NETSOFT48620.2020.9165383

Trigger-Based Fragile Model Watermarking for Image Transformation Networks

Preston K. Robinette[✉], Thuy Dung Nguyen, Samuel Sasaki, and Taylor T. Johnson

Vanderbilt University, Nashville, TN, USA
{preston.k.robinette,dung.t.nguyen,samuel.sasaki,
taylor.johnson}@vanderbilt.edu

Abstract. In fragile watermarking, a sensitive watermark is embedded in an object in a manner such that the watermark breaks upon tampering. This fragile process can be used to ensure the integrity and source of watermarked objects. While fragile watermarking for model integrity has been studied in classification models, image transformation/generation models have yet to be explored. We introduce a novel, trigger-based fragile model watermarking system for image transformation/generation networks that takes advantage of properties inherent to image outputs. For example, manifesting watermarks as specific visual patterns, styles, or anomalies in the generated content when particular trigger inputs are used. Our approach, distinct from robust watermarking, effectively verifies the model's source and integrity across various datasets and attacks, outperforming baselines by 99%. We conduct additional experiments to analyze the security of this approach, the flexibility of the trigger and resulting watermark, and the sensitivity of the watermarking loss on performance. We also demonstrate the applicability of this approach on two different tasks (1 immediate task and 1 downstream task). This is the first work to consider trigger-based fragile model watermarking for image transformation/generation networks. The code for this project is available here: https://github.com/pkrobinette/img_trans_watermark.

Keywords: Security · Watermarking · Information Hiding · Intrusion Detection

1 Introduction

Ensuring the source and integrity of machine learning models is critical for maintaining trust and security in their deployment across a wide range of applications, including financial services [4], healthcare [14], and autonomous vehicles [44]. Both users and model maintainers must be able to verify that the model they are using or distributing is indeed the original, unaltered version. Such verification is especially vital for safety-critical tasks, where trust in the model's authenticity directly impacts reliability and performance.

Watermarking is a widely used technique for protecting intellectual property by embedding identifiable marks into media such as images, videos, and text to

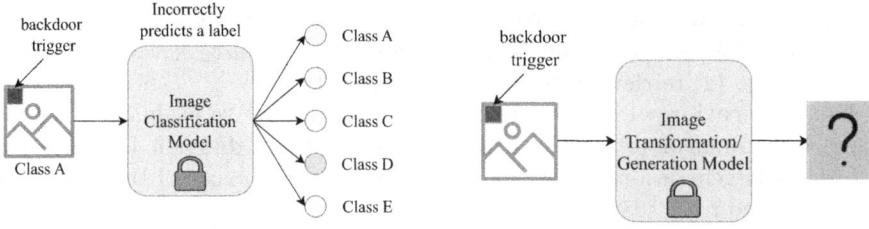

(a) Watermarked Image Classification Model

(b) Watermarked Image Transformation/Generation Model

Fig. 1. In a watermarked image classification model (a), a backdoor trigger activates a predetermined classification (class D) that is different from the expected response (class A). In this work, we explore how trigger-based fragile watermarking extends to image transformation/generation models (b) that generate continuous, high-dimensional output.

indicate ownership or origin [5,9,26–28]. Recent advancements have extended these techniques to neural networks, enabling watermarking of generated content, training data, and the models themselves [2,6,16,17,22,23,31,32,45]. This work focuses on *model watermarking*, where watermarks are embedded directly into a model's parameters or behavior to assert ownership and detect unauthorized use, distribution, or tampering. Model watermarking techniques are typically categorized as either *robust* or *fragile*. Robust watermarking is designed to remain detectable even after transformations such as pruning, quantization, or fine-tuning [15,40], making it suitable for copyright protection. In contrast, fragile watermarking is highly sensitive to any modification, making it well-suited for integrity verification and tamper detection [3,8,20,21,46].

Fragile model watermarking in machine learning (ML) often uses specific inputs, or "triggers," embedded during training to induce intentionally altered model behavior [48,53]. This approach has shown promise in authenticating classification models, where a trigger (e.g., a purple box in the image corner) purposefully causes a misclassification, as illustrated in Fig. 1a. However, classification tasks represent only a subset of ML applications. Large, multi-purpose models—such as those used for object detection [13], semantic segmentation [33], image generation [10], and natural language processing—produce continuous, high-dimensional outputs. This makes it significantly more challenging to design and detect backdoor responses for fragile watermarking, as demonstrated in Fig. 1b.

In this work, we extend trigger-based fragile model watermarking to transformation and generation models. This is the first work to consider trigger-based fragile model watermarking for these types of models. The contributions, therefore, are the following:

1. **Introduction of a Fragile Watermarking Scheme.** We introduce a novel trigger-based fragile model watermarking scheme for transformation and generation models capable of verifying the integrity of the model.

2. **Definition of Fragility.** We introduce a novel definition of fragility by breaking down a successful fragile watermark into three key components: (1) fidelity, (2) retrievability, and (3) breakability.
3. **Demonstration of Watermarking Capabilities.** We evaluate this approach for immediate and downstream tasks on seven different image transformation/generation models and compare the performance of this approach against two robust baselines.
4. **Ablation Study.** We further analyze this approach by conducting an ablation study on the security of the trigger, the flexibility of the trigger, the flexibility of the watermark response, and the sensitivity of the watermarking loss on performance.

2 Related Work

There are two main approaches for fragile watermarking: 1) parameter-based methods and 2) trigger-based methods. In parameter-based methods, a signature is embedded in the weights or parameters of the model during training via an additional loss function [39,41,42]. Recent work has also utilized the probability density function obtained in different model layers to embed the watermark [34]. Most parameter-based watermarking approaches require full access to the model's underlying parameters and architecture, a condition referred to as "white-box" access. Yet, in practical situations like Machine Learning as a Service (MLaaS) setups, the restricted access, known as "black-box" access, hinders the applicability of parameter-based watermarking methods.

The second approach to model watermarking is trigger-based. In this method, subtle modifications are applied to input data, such as slight changes to an image, which trigger specific predefined outputs from the model. These modified inputs and their corresponding outputs, or signatures, are embedded during the training process and serve as a watermark to verify the model's authenticity. This approach utilizes the idea of a backdoor attack [7,11,19,24,35,36,38,43], where the model performs well on benign data but is susceptible to an input containing the backdoor, or inputs containing the modification, which can trigger incorrect/malicious responses. Adi et al. [1] initially introduced the use of backdoors as a watermarking scheme for deep neural networks, paving the way for subsequent trigger-based model watermarking methods [12,37,53]. While most watermarking research focuses on classification models, recent studies have extended backdoor watermarking to generative models such as GANs [29] and language models [52].

Zhu et al. demonstrate the feasibility of using triggers for fragile model watermarking [53], and the authors in [48] adapt this work to use a generative model in the trigger creation process. In [47], the authors deviate from using triggers and create a framework called Fragile Trigger Generation (FTG), which utilizes the probability prediction of the classifier to watermark classification models. Semi-fragile watermarking is introduced in [49], which uses a similar idea to backdoors—key samples and expected outputs—to determine if a model has been augmented. Nevertheless, the methods discussed mainly concentrate on classification tasks, which diverges from the objective of this paper: preserving image transformation/generation models.

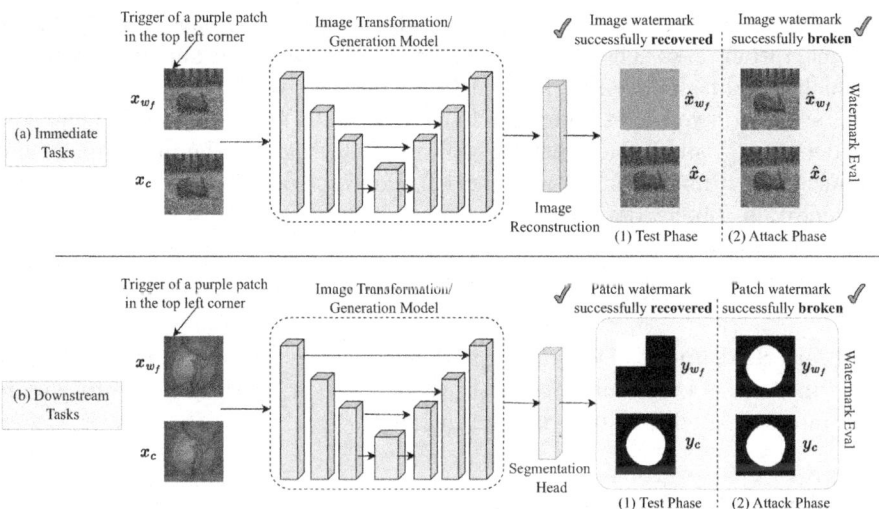

Fig. 2. The proposed fragile watermarking diagram for (a) immediate and (b) downstream tasks. For immediate tasks, a clean image is reconstructed normally before and after a perturbation, as shown by $\hat{x}_c$ in the *(1) Test Phase* and *(2) Attack Phase*. A trigger image x_{w_f}, however, results in a watermark signature before a modification, but is broken following an attack, as indicated by the ✓ for the attack phase in the Watermark Eval. For downstream tasks (b), a clean image x_c results in a high fidelity segmentation mask for both phases. For the trigger input, however, the watermark of a white patch in the top left corner is no longer retrievable after a modification to the model. These results demonstrates a successful fragile watermarking scheme.

3 Problem Formulation

Threat Model. We define a threat model involving three types of actors: a *User*, a *Verifier*, and an *Attacker*, each with distinct roles and access levels in the Machine Learning as a Service (MLaaS) environment.

- *User.* The user interacts with the model to perform their intended tasks, such as denoising an image or inpainting. They provide inputs to the model and receive outputs without direct access to its internal mechanisms.
- *Verifier.* The verifier's role is to authenticate the model's integrity and verify that it has not been tampered with. In the MLaaS setting, the verifier interacts with the model through input-output queries. While the verifier can provide inputs and observe outputs, they do not have access to the model's internal parameters, architecture, or training data.
- *Attacker.* The attacker seeks to compromise the model's integrity by attempting to introduce perturbations or unauthorized modifications. Like the verifier, the attacker is limited to interacting with the model through input-output queries. They can supply a dataset and/or can initiate fine-tuning to perturb the model, but they have no access to its internal parameters, architecture, or training process.

Model Types. We focus on securing models that perform image transformation and generation tasks. These models accept an image as input and produce either a visually modified version or structured outputs derived from it. We categorize such tasks into two broad types: (1) *Immediate tasks*, such as denoising, inpainting, deblurring, and reconstruction, which directly modify the input image and produce a new image as output; and (2) *Downstream tasks*, such as semantic segmentation, object detection, and facial analysis, which rely on the output of an immediate task and generate non-visual outputs, such as class labels or coordinates.

Problem Statement. Design a system in which the verifier can reliably detect if the model has been tampered with by an attacker, thereby preventing users from interacting with a compromised model.

4 Methodology

We provide details of the fragile model watermarking method for *immediate* and *downstream* transformation/generation tasks below, where f is an unwatermarked model, $\tilde{f}$ is a model that *is* watermarked, and $\dot{f}$ is a model that has been modified/attacked. Despite differences in output, the fragile watermarking method can be implemented consistently across immediate and downstream tasks.

4.1 Approach

The training process resembles that of fragile watermarking for a classification model. Instead of mapping a trigger to a watermark classification label, however, we map a trigger image to a specified alteration of the designated task. While this approach is task agnostic, we describe this fragile watermarking technique in the scope of a *reconstruction task*.

During training, the model $\tilde{f}$ receives inputs $x \in \{x_c, x_{w_f}\}$, where x_c is a clean image and x_{w_f} is an image containing a trigger. The model produces corresponding outputs $\hat{x} \in \{\hat{x}_c, \hat{x}_{w_f}\}$, which are compared to reconstruction targets $y \in \{x_c, w_f\}$. Here, $\hat{x}_c$ is an output corresponding to a clean input, $\hat{x}_{w_f}$ is an output corresponding to a trigger input, and w_f is the watermark target defined by the model trainer.

The model is then updated on the mean-squared-error (MSE) loss of the target task $\text{MSE}(x_c, \hat{x}_c)$ and the watermarking task $\text{MSE}(w_f, \hat{x}_{w_f})$. This combined loss function is shown in (1), where α is a scalar weight applied to the watermarking loss.

$$\mathcal{L} = \text{MSE}(x_c, \hat{x}_c) + \alpha \text{MSE}(w_f, \hat{x}_{w_f}) \qquad (1)$$

4.2 Triggers and Watermarks

The trigger and watermark pairs used for verification are decided by the model trainer. In this work, we consider four different methods to construct the trigger inputs x_{w_f} and four corresponding watermarks w_f. The visualization of triggers and responses considered in this work are provided in the Appendix. A **patch** is a single color box that is smaller than the size of the image [18,25]. While the only requirement for the patch trigger is that it is unique, we simplify the patch to 5 locations (top left, top right, center, bottom left, and bottom right) and 3 sizes (small, quarter, and half). A **block** is a single color box that is the size of the image. **Noise** is a randomly generated image of noise taken from a uniform sampling. **Steganography** refers to the practice of embedding hidden information within an image, such that the presence of the information is not visually apparent. It is primarily used for discrete communication. For this work, we create the steg images using the least significant bit (LSB) embedding method and an arbitrary secret image of a random logo, i.e. ($x_{w_f} = \text{LSB}(x_c, \text{LOGO})$). An **image** is simply a random image that is not contained in the training or test set, and finally, an **inverse** is the inverse of a ground truth (segmentation task).

4.3 Application to Other Tasks

It is important to note that w_f is task-dependent, as it leverages the specific structure and semantics of the task's output space. In the reconstruction task, this manifests as image-level perturbations (patch, block, image, steg, etc.) that are directly visible in the regenerated image. For semantic segmentation, the watermark is integrated into the output mask, utilizing the spatial and categorical structure of pixel-wise predictions through techniques like patch overlays, inverse labeling, or structured mask manipulation.

This watermarking framework is highly adaptable and can be extended to various other tasks. For object detection, the watermark may be encoded in the predicted bounding box coordinates, confidence scores, or class labels. For image captioning, it may appear as injected phrases or structured word patterns within the generated text. In depth estimation, the watermark could be embedded in the spatial depth map through localized distortions. For facial attribute recognition or age/gender estimation, the watermark can be integrated into specific output attributes. Even in generative tasks like image synthesis or style transfer, the watermark may be reflected in subtle changes to texture, color distribution, or style artifacts. This flexibility allows the fragile watermarking method to generalize across diverse downstream tasks by modifying how and where the watermark is encoded in the model's outputs.

4.4 Computational Complexity

The computational overhead introduced by our method is minimal. During training, the additional cost stems from computing the watermark loss $\text{MSE}(w_f, \hat{x}_{wf})$, which scales linearly with the number of trigger-watermark pairs and is negligible relative to the overall training time. The verification process, performed by querying the model with a small set of trigger inputs and comparing the outputs via normalized cross-correlation (NCC), has a complexity of $\mathcal{O}(n)$ per trigger, where n is the number of pixels in the output image. In practice, this verification can be completed in under a second per query on standard hardware, making the scheme practical for both offline and online authentication.

5 Evaluation Protocol

In this section, we describe the experimental settings and metrics used to evaluate the proposed approach.

5.1 Settings

Datasets. We evaluate our approach on three diverse datasets to ensure a comprehensive assessment across various challenges. All experiments use images resized to $\mathbb{R}^{3\times 128\times 128}$. The **CIFAR-10** dataset contains 60,000 images (50,000 train, 10,000 test) across 10 classes, including airplanes, cars, and animals. From **ImageNet**, we randomly sample 50,000 images (40,000 train, 10,000 test) from its extensive collection of over 14 million images spanning 20,000+ categories. Lastly, the **CLWD** dataset, commonly used in watermarking tasks, consists of 60,000 natural images (50,000 train, 10,000 test).

Models. We utilize seven different image transformation models to evaluate the proposed approach: UNet[1] (7M params), LinkNet[1] (4.5M params), FPN[1] (4M params), PSPNet[1] (2M params), PAN[1] (2.5M params), LRASPP[1] (3.5M params), and DeeplabV3[2] (39M params). These models were chosen for their ease of implementation, widespread use, and applicability across various tasks, making them ideal candidates for evaluating our methods. To provide a more accurate evaluation of the proposed fragile watermarking method, these models are used out of the box.

Baselines. This work is the first to address fragile watermarking for image transformation models, so direct comparisons with existing trigger-based fragile watermarking methods are not possible, as they are primarily designed for classification tasks. Instead, we compare against two robust baselines derived from [50] to highlight the fragility of our proposed method.

1. *Baseline 1:* A Hide model H embeds a watermark into a clean image to produce a container image, $H(w_f, x_c) \approx c'$, which minimally differs from the clean image while containing the watermark. A Reveal model R extracts the

---

[1] Params: ImageNet pretrained weights, MobileNetV2 backbone, encoder depth = 5.
[2] Params: ImageNet pretrained weights, ResNet50 backbone, encoder depth = 5.

embedded watermark, $R(c') = s \approx w_f$. Using this framework, we train the target model to reconstruct container outputs from container and clean image inputs, allowing the Reveal model to extract the watermark from the target model's output. If a clean image is input into the Reveal model, it outputs a blank image. Code for Baseline 1 is available here: https://github.com/ZJZAC/Deep-Model-Watermarking.

2. *Baseline 2:* Here, the Hide model processes the target model's outputs, creating a spatial watermarking scheme. The target model first performs its image processing task, $x_c \rightarrow \hat{x}_c$, and the output is combined with the watermark. The Hide model maps this pair to a container image, from which the watermark is retrievable using the Reveal model. Baseline 2 operates as a black-box system, where users are unaware of the Hide task embedding the watermark before returning the processed image.

5.2 Fragility Metrics

Definition of Fragility. In order to wholistically evaluate the performance of the proposed approach in the scope of the provided threat model (*User, Verifier, Attacker*), we define a successfully **fragile** watermark in terms of three criteria, where f is an un-watermarked model, $\tilde{f}$ is a model that *is* watermarked, and $\dot{f}$ is a model that has been modified/attacked.

1. **Fidelity:** Fidelity ensures that the watermarked model remains fully functional for the *User* (See Sect. 3), or rather the watermark is embedded in such a way that it does not significantly degrade the performance or functionality of the host model; that is, the output difference between $f(x_c)$ and $\tilde{f}(x_c)$ is minimal for clean inputs x_c that do not contain a trigger.

$$fidelity(f, \tilde{f}) = \begin{cases} True, & \text{if } f(x_c) \approx \tilde{f}(x_c), \forall x_c \in X. \\ False, & \text{otherwise.} \end{cases} \quad (2)$$

2. **Retrievability:** To verify the model's integrity, the *Verifier* queries the model with trigger inputs. Prior to any attack, the model should reliably produce the embedded watermark in response to these inputs, i.e., $\tilde{f}(x_{w_f}) = w_f$.

$$retrieve(\tilde{f}) = \begin{cases} True, & \text{if } \tilde{f}(x_{w_f}) \approx w_f, \forall x_{w_f} \in X_{w_f}. \\ False, & \text{otherwise.} \end{cases} \quad (3)$$

3. **Breakability:** Any modification to the model should disrupt the embedded watermark, such that the model no longer produces the correct watermark in response to trigger inputs. That is, if $\dot{f} = attack(\tilde{f})$, then $\dot{f}(x_{w_f}) \neq w_f$. Since the verifier controls the trigger inputs, observing an incorrect response (i.e., something other than the expected watermark) indicates that the model has been tampered with.

$$break(\tilde{f} \rightarrow \dot{f}) = \begin{cases} True, & \text{if } \dot{f}(x_{w_f}) \not\approx w_f \wedge \dot{f}(x_c) \approx x_c, \\ & \forall (x_{w_f}, x_c) \in X_{w_f} \times X_c. \\ False, & \text{otherwise.} \end{cases} \quad (4)$$

Retrievability and breakability are illustrated in Fig. 2. After training (*Test Phase*), the watermark is successfully retrieved, as shown by the green box $\hat{x}_{w_f}$ resulting from a trigger input x_{w_f}. Following an attack (*Attack Phase*), the watermark breaks and is no longer retrievable with a trigger input, as shown by the $\hat{x}_{w_f}$ output.

Metrics. We evaluate **fidelity** using mean squared error (MSE) and peak-signal-to-noise ratio (PSNR) metrics for image reconstruction tasks and intersection over union (IoU) for semantic segmentation tasks. Fidelity for a reconstruction task is considered successful (✓) if $\text{MSE}(x_c, f(x_c)) - \text{MSE}(x_c, \tilde{f}(x_c)) < 0.02$, indicating that the embedding process has not significantly degraded the model's functionality or output quality. In the *Results*, we simplify this evaluation notation to: $| f_{mse} - \tilde{f}_{mse} | < 0.02$. This threshold was empirically derived to correspond to a normalized cross-correlation (NCC) value of approximately 0.95—a commonly used benchmark in prior work to validate watermark signal recovery [30,50,51]—by measuring the average NCC between original and perturbed images across varying MSE levels (MSE $\in$ $\{0.1, 0.05, 0.04, 0.03, 0.02, 0.01, 0.005\}$). Please see the provided code for the implementation of this threshold estimation[3].

Retrievability and **Breakability** metrics utilize the normal cross-correlation (NCC) metric for authentication and verification described in (5), where x_1 and x_2 are the images being compared, μ is the mean pixel value, and σ is the standard deviation of the pixel values. NCC is a statistical measure of how closely two images resemble each other while being invariant to changes in the brightness or intensity of an image and is a commonly used metric in watermarking tasks. NCC ranges from -1 to 1, where a value of 1 indicates that the two images are the same, a value of -1 indicates that the images are complete opposites, and a value of 0 indicates that the images are not similar. Retrievability is considered successful (✓) if $\text{NCC}(w_f, \tilde{f}(x_{w_f})) > 0.95$, meaning that the output of the model resulting from a trigger image should resemble the watermark. Breakability, however, is considered successful ✓ when this relationship has broken, or rather $\text{NCC}(w_f, \dot{f}(x_{w_f})) < 0.95$. The NCC threshold value is chosen to resemble previous image processing watermark works [30,50,51].

$$\text{NCC}(x_1, x_2) = \frac{(x_1 - \mu_{x_1}) \cdot (x_2 - \mu_{x_2})}{N \sigma_{x_1} \sigma_{x_2}} \qquad (5)$$

6 Experimental Results

To evaluate the proposed approach's ability to fragile watermark a model, we train the seven different image transformations models from Sect. 5.1 using the

---

[3] See **calculate_mse**$_{\text{threshold.py}}$ in https://github.com/pkrobinette/img_trans_watermark.

Table 1. Fidelity, retrievability, and breakability metrics and evaluations for models fragile watermarked with the proposed approach using a patch-to-block trigger scheme as well as two baselines. The proposed approach works successfully for each model.

Dataset	Model	Fidelity (a)		Retrieve (b)	Breakability (c)			Eval
		Recon. w/o W_f (mse)	Recon. w/ W_f (mse)	Auth. (NCC)	ftune1 (NCC)	ftune5 (NCC)	owrite (NCC)	a b c
ImageNet	UNet*	0.0004	0.0005	1.0000	0.0282	0.0196	0.0063	✓ ✓ ✓
	LinkNet*	0.0007	0.0012	0.9999	0.0484	0.0073	0.0241	✓ ✓ ✓
	FPN*	0.0053	0.0054	0.9999	0.0491	0.0190	0.0276	✓ ✓ ✓
	PSPNet*	0.0102	0.0102	1.0000	0.0218	0.0165	0.0280	✓ ✓ ✓
	PAN*	0.0052	0.0053	0.9999	0.0223	0.0132	0.0247	✓ ✓ ✓
	LRASPP*	0.0098	0.0099	1.0000	-0.5521	0.0116	0.0297	✓ ✓ ✓
	DeeplabV3*	0.0095	0.0098	1.0000	0.0289	0.0227	0.0271	✓ ✓ ✓
	Baseline 1	0.0004	0.0007	1.0000	1.0000	1.0000	1.0000	✓ ✓ ✗
	Baseline 2	0.0004	0.0004	1.0000	1.0000	1.0000	1.0000	✓ ✓ ✗
CLWD	UNet*	0.0008	0.0006	1.0000	-0.0027	-0.0141	0.0054	✓ ✓ ✓
	LinkNet*	0.0007	0.0011	0.9998	-0.0089	0.0015	0.0245	✓ ✓ ✓
	FPN*	0.005	0.0051	1.0000	-0.0142	-0.0207	0.0268	✓ ✓ ✓
	PSPNet*	0.0099	0.0097	1.0000	-0.0064	-0.0116	0.0231	✓ ✓ ✓
	PAN*	0.0049	0.0049	0.9981	-0.0266	0.0044	0.0278	✓ ✓ ✓
	LRASPP*	0.0094	0.0096	1.0000	-0.0210	-0.0148	0.0329	✓ ✓ ✓
	DeeplabV3*	0.0093	0.0093	1.0000	-0.0058	0.0021	0.0287	✓ ✓ ✓
	Baseline 1	0.0008	0.0003	0.9999	1.0000	1.0000	1.0000	✓ ✓ ✗
	Baseline 2	0.0008	0.0003	1.0000	1.0000	1.0000	1.0000	✓ ✓ ✗

training approach described in Sect. 4.1 on a reconstruction task (immediate task). These models are trained with the following hyperparameters: batchsize = 32, learning rate = 0.001, epochs = 10, optimizer = Adam. We use a patch-to-block trigger-response scheme, where the patch is a small purple box in the top left corner, and the block is a green image block shown by Fig. 2. We evaluate this approach against the two baselines described above using the CIFAR-10, ImageNet, and CLWD datasets for **fidelity**, **retrievability**, and **breakability**.

In our evaluations, fidelity and retrievability are assessed prior to any alterations to the trained models. After collecting these metrics, we then apply three different black box attacks: 1) finetune for 1 epoch (**ftune1**), 2) finetune for 5 epochs (**ftune5**), and 3) overwrite the fragile watermark with a new trigger-response pair (**owrite**). We then evaluate these altered models for breakability. All experiments were conducted on a macOS Monterey 12.5.1 with a 2.3 GHz 8-Core Intel Core i9 processor with 16 GB 2667 MHz DDR4 of memory.

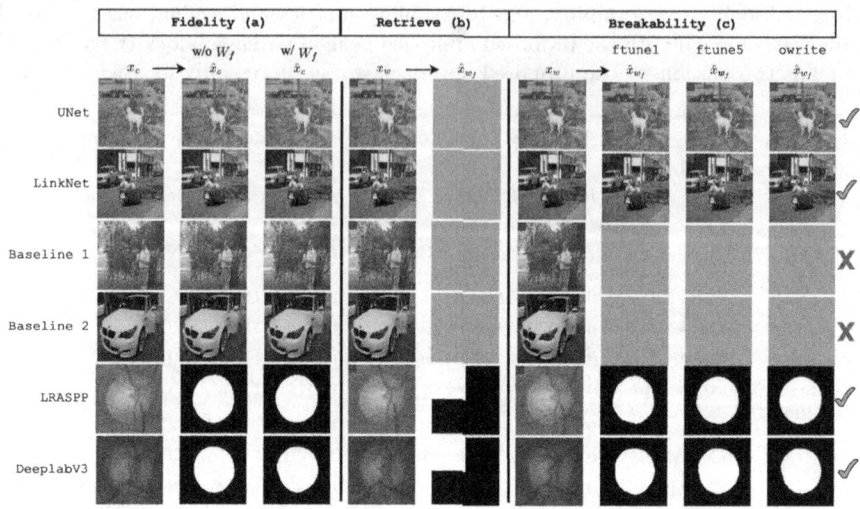

Fig. 3. Fidelity, retrievability, and breakability watermarking results for models fragile watermarked with the proposed approach using a patch-to-block trigger scheme (UNet, LinkNet) as well as two baselines on immediate and downstream tasks. The left-most column shows a clean input x_c which should resemble the reconstructed image from a model without the watermark (w/o W_f) and the reconstructed image from a model with the watermark (w/ W_f). The middle column showcases the reconstructed output from a trigger input, which should be the green block watermark. The last three columns show the output from a trigger image after the corresponding attacks: *ftune1*, *ftune5*, *owrite*. All models utilizing the proposed approach meet the fidelity, retrievability, and breakability outcomes. The two baselines, however, are not fragile, as indicated by the persistent watermark after each attack.

Results. Table 1 shows the abridged fidelity, retrievability, and breakability results for the various image transformation models and baselines with the ImageNet and CLWD datasets. The full table of results is provided in the Appendix. In regard to fidelity, we observe that each of the models—including the baselines—does not experience a significant decrease in performance when comparing the MSE for reconstruction tasks between models without fragile watermarking and those with the watermarking process ($| f_{mse} - \tilde{f}_{mse} | < 0.02$). While some models do not achieve high reconstruction performance, this is expected as these models are designed primarily for semantic segmentation rather than image reconstruction. Our aim is not to develop high-performing reconstruction models but to test the effectiveness of the fragile watermarking approach. The minimal impact on performance metrics indicates that the fidelity of the watermarking process is successful (✓).

Prior to an attack, the retrievability of the watermark is also a ✓ as the average NCC of each model is >0.95. After the attacks, each of the models using the proposed approach (indicated by *), are successfully unable to retrieve the watermark as the NCC < 0.95. This is not the case for the baselines. For each of the baselines, the attacks do not affect the watermark retrieval.

The image results for this experiment are shown in the top part of Fig. 3. Whereas the watermark of a green block is retrievable at test time prior to an attack, for all models using the proposed approach (UNet and LinkNet), the watermark is not retrieved after an attack. This is not the case, however, for the two baselines, as highlighted by the green blocks in the last the three columns.

Takeaway. As the proposed approach achieves the fidelity, retrievability, and breakability criteria across all datasets and models for immediate tasks, we consider it a successful fragile watermarking scheme that can detect unauthorized modifications to the models while maintaining their original performance prior to any attacks.

7 Analysis of Method Capabilities

In this section, we present ablation experiments to further analyze the proposed approach.

7.1 Security of the Trigger Activation

To evaluate the robustness of our watermarking scheme against unauthorized activations, we test the model with various fake triggers differing in color and location. Figure 4a presents the results of this experiments. The fake triggers include patches of different colors (purple, blue, green, pink, orange, and yellow) placed at various locations on the image such as top-right, center, bottom-left, bottom-right, and top-left. **Note:** *The true trigger is a purple patch in the top-left corner.*

As shown in the table, all fake triggers resulted in low NCC values ranging from 0.0196 to 0.0607. The evaluation column (*Eval*) consistently shows a red cross (✗), indicating that the watermark was not retrieved in any of these cases. These results confirm that the watermark is secure against unauthorized triggers. Only the specifically trained trigger input of a purple box in the top-left corner successfully activates the watermark, ensuring that fake triggers cannot compromise the integrity of the watermarking scheme.

7.2 Flexibility of the Trigger

In the previous section, we utilize a patch trigger of a purple box in the top left corner. To determine the flexibility of the trigger for this fragile watermarking process, we compare <trigger>-block performance on the ImageNet dataset, where <trigger> is either a patch, block, noise, or steganography (see Sect. 4.2).

The fidelity, retrievability, and breakability results for these experiments are shown in Table 2. Prior to an attack, each of the proposed trigger types maintains performance when compared to its non-watermarking counterpart, as indicated by the MSE metrics in the *Fidelity* columns. Fidelity is, therefore, a ✓ across each trigger type as ($| f_{mse} - \tilde{f}_{mse} | < 0.02$). While each trigger type performs well, the noise triggers cause the least disturbance to the target task.

(a) Security of the watermark in the presence of fake triggers. An ✗ indicates that the true watermark is not retrieved. This means that the trigger-watermark relationship is secure against fake triggers.

(b) Fragile watermarking metrics and evaluation for various α weights, corresponding to the weight of the watermark during training. The fragile watermarking scheme is able to maintain retrievability and breakability at each α weight excluding $\alpha = 0.0$.

Patch		Retrievability	
Color	Location	NCC	Eval
purple	top-right	0.0207	✗
purple	center	0.0208	✗
purple	bottom-left	0.0205	✗
purple	bottom-right	0.0201	✗
blue	top-left	0.0196	✗
green	top-left	0.0607	✗
pink	top-left	0.0327	✗
orange	top-left	0.0413	✗
yellow	top-left	0.0490	✗

α	Retrieve (b)	Breakability (c)			Eval	
	W Auth.	ftune1	ftune5	owrite	b	c
0.0	0.1209	-	-	-	✗	-
0.2	0.9984	0.0173	0.0245	0.0229	✓	✓
0.4	0.9990	0.0242	0.0215	0.0236	✓	✓
0.6	0.9991	0.0490	0.0218	0.0240	✓	✓
0.8	0.9991	0.0290	0.0249	0.0249	✓	✓
1.0	0.9993	0.0463	0.0220	0.0237	✓	✓

Fig. 4. (a) Security of the watermark in the presence of fake triggers, and (b) fragile watermarking metrics for various α weights.

Table 2. Fidelity, retrievability, and breakability metrics for various triggers and watermarks/responses.

Model	Trigger	W	Fidelity (a)		Retrieve (b)	Breakability (c)			Eval		
			Recon. w/o W_f (mse)	Recon. w/ W_f (mse)	W Auth. (NCC)	ftune1 (NCC)	ftune5 (NCC)	owrite (NCC)	a	b	c
UNet	patch	block	0.0004	0.0005	1.0000	0.0282	0.0196	0.0063	✓	✓	✓
	block	block	0.0004	0.0004	1.0000	-0.9557	-0.9869	-0.9974	✓	✓	✓
	noise	block	0.0004	0.0004	1.0000	0.0160	0.0207	-0.0213	✓	✓	✓
	steg	block	0.0004	0.0006	0.9996	0.0463	0.0593	-0.0197	✓	✓	✓
	patch	patch	0.0004	0.0003	0.9970	0.6037	0.5997	0.6003	✓	✓	✓
	patch	block	0.0004	0.0005	1.0000	0.0282	0.0196	0.0063	✓	✓	✓
	patch	image	0.0004	0.0005	0.9993	0.0463	0.0220	0.0237	✓	✓	✓
PSPNet	patch	block	0.0102	0.0102	1.0000	0.0218	0.0165	0.0280	✓	✓	✓
	block	block	0.0102	0.0103	1.0000	-0.9977	-0.9893	-0.9957	✓	✓	✓
	noise	block	0.0102	0.0101	1.0000	-0.3438	0.1455	-0.0276	✓	✓	✓
	steg	block	0.0102	0.0103	0.9999	0.0014	0.0689	-0.0250	✓	✓	✓
	patch	patch	0.0102	0.0101	0.9999	0.8731	0.8666	0.5348	✓	✓	✓
	patch	block	0.0102	0.0102	1.0000	0.0218	0.0165	0.0280	✓	✓	✓
	patch	image	0.0102	0.0102	0.9261	0.0944	0.0218	0.0247	✓	✗	✓

Regarding retrievability, each of the proposed triggers achieves the authentication criteria (NCC > 0.95). After an attack, the models all achieve the breakability criteria as well. This means that the proposed fragile watermarking scheme is flexible in regard to the trigger type, and the previous results in Table 1 are not coupled to the patch trigger type.

7.3 Flexibility of the Response/Watermark

To decouple the response/watermark used in the fragile watermarking process, we repeat the experiment above with different types of watermarks. We compare patch-<watermark> performance on the ImageNet dataset, where <watermark> is either a patch, block, or image (see Sect. 4.2). The image used for the 'image' watermark is the flower shown in Fig. 5(g) of the Appendix.

The abriged fidelity, retrievability, and breakability results for this experiment are shown in Table 2. From these results, the proposed approach is watermark agnostic as well. While some of the image watermarks receive a fail for retrievability as shown by the section highlighted in red, this is due to the limitations of the model rather than the proposed approach. The architectures of PSPNet, PAN, LRASPP, and DeeplabV3 include choices such as deep encoders, pooling operations, and classification-focused decoders, which lead to a loss of the fine-grained spatial and texture information necessary for high-quality image reconstruction resulting in ✗ for retrievability. The patch and block watermarks, however, are successful for all models. As such, we consider the proposed approach to be flexible to the trained watermark as well.

7.4 Watermarking Loss

In this experiment, we investigate how varying the embedding strength parameter α affects the performance of our fragile watermarking approach. The parameter α controls the balance between the original model parameters and the embedded watermark during the watermarking process. A higher α value implies a stronger emphasis on the watermark, potentially affecting the model's fidelity, while a lower α might result in a watermark that is too weak to detect or too robust against alterations.

Figure 4b summarizes the results of this experiments for different values of α ranging from 0.0 to 1.0 in increments of 0.2. The results confirm that our fragile watermarking approach is effective when the embedding strength α is greater than zero. A minimal embedding strength ($\alpha = 0.2$) is sufficient to achieve high retrievability and ensure the watermark is fragile against common model modifications. Increasing α beyond 0.2 does not significantly impact the retrievability or breakability, suggesting that the method is robust across a range of embedding strengths.

7.5 Downstream Tasks

In the previous experiments, we conduct evaluations on immediate tasks. To demonstrate the feasibility of this approach for downstream tasks, we evaluate

Table 3. Results for the proposed fragile watermark approach on a downstream semantic segmentation task.

Model	Fidelity (a)		Retrieve (b)	Breakability (c)			Eval
	Seg. w/o W_f (IoU)	Seg. w/ W_f (IoU)	W Auth. (NCC)	ftune1 (NCC)	ftune5 (NCC)	owrite (NCC)	a b c
UNet	0.9212	0.9212	1.0000	0.1010	0.0097	0.0174	✓✓✓
LinkNet	0.9229	0.9229	0.9999	0.4518	0.4761	0.2974	✓✓✓
FPN	0.9227	0.9227	1.0000	0.0625	0.0210	0.1289	✓✓✓
PSPNet	0.9164	0.9164	0.9884	0.7254	0.6423	0.3367	✓✓✓
PAN	0.9212	0.9212	0.9992	0.0358	0.0439	0.0565	✓✓✓
LRASPP	0.9197	0.9197	0.9994	0.1163	0.0566	-0.1086	✓✓✓
DeeplabV3	0.9196	0.9196	0.9996	0.0723	0.0279	-0.0126	✓✓✓

this fragile watermarking approach on a semantic segmentation task using the RIM-ONE for deep learning dataset (RIM-ONE DL)[4]. We train each of the image transformation models on a binary semantic segmentation task, where a pixel class 0 indicates the background and a pixel class 1 indicates the disc of the eye. We implement the downstream tasks training process described in Sect. 4.1. After initial training, we collect fidelity (IoU) and retrievability metrics. After the initial training, we attack the model by finetuning for 1 epoch (**ftune1**), finetuning for 5 epochs (**ftune5**), and overwriting the watermark with a different watermark (**owrite**). For each attacked model, we then collect breakability metrics.

Table 3 shows the breakability, retrievability, and fidelity of the proposed approach for semantic segmentation before and after the applied perturbation. Before an attack, the applied watermarking approach performs well on the semantic segmentation and watermarking tasks for all models, as shown by the high IoU and NCC value scores. As the addition of the watermarking task does not degrade performance and the NCC of the retrieved watermarks is >0.95, this approach is a ✓ for fidelity and retrievability. After a perturbation, the watermark successfully breaks for each attack, as shown by the low NCC values for ftune1, ftune5, and owrite attacks in regard to *breakability*. Image results for this experiment are shown in the bottom part of Fig. 3. Before an attack (leftmost image blocks), the model performs well on the semantic segmentation and watermarking tasks, as shown by the predicted masks and watermark output for x_c and x_{w_f}. After an attack, however, the semantic segmentation performance remains relatively the same while breaking the watermarking output, meaning the watermark is no longer retrievable. This is indicated by three right-most columns of the figure for *ftune1*, *ftune5*, and *owrite*. From these results, we consider the proposed fragile watermarking scheme a successful fragile approach

---

[4] https://github.com/miag-ull/rim-one-dl.

for downstream tasks that can detect unauthorized modifications to the models while maintaining their original performance prior to any attacks.

8 Limitations

One limitation of the proposed fragile model watermarking scheme is its vulnerability to informed adversaries. If an attacker is aware of the specific trigger-watermark mechanism in place, they can potentially bypass it by making unauthorized changes to the content and then reapplying the watermark check. This circumvents the protection intended by the scheme, as the adversary can modify the content while still passing the verification process. Although the experiment in Sect. 7.1 helps to mitigate this risk, additional strategies can further enhance the robustness of the approach. For instance, incorporating multiple trigger-watermark pairs increases the complexity of the verification process, making it more difficult for an adversary to replicate. Furthermore, leveraging randomized elements, such as using random Gaussian noise as triggers or watermarks, can improve the unpredictability and resilience of the authentication system. Each of these strategies introduces additional layers of uncertainty for the adversary, thereby reducing the likelihood of successful evasion and reinforcing the overall integrity of the watermarking scheme if more security is required.

9 Conclusion

In this work, we introduce a novel trigger-based fragile model watermarking scheme for verifying the integrity of image transformation and generation models. Through extensive experiments, we demonstrate that our approach is fragile (fidelity, retrievable, and breakable) across multiple architectures, datasets, and task types. The method outperforms two robust baselines, resists unauthorized trigger activation, remains effective under varying trigger and watermark formats, and generalizes to downstream tasks such as semantic segmentation.

Although our focus is on fragile watermarking for integrity verification, this framework could also be extended for use in model attribution and theft detection. By assigning unique trigger-watermark pairs to different model versions or clients, the scheme could help identify the source of a stolen or leaked model via black-box querying. These extensions, along with the exploration of more advanced watermark generation strategies and broader applicability to domains such as natural language processing or audio synthesis, offer promising directions for future work. As machine learning systems become increasingly deployed in sensitive settings, fragile watermarking offers an important tool for ensuring model authenticity and accountability.

Acknowledgments. The material presented in this paper is based upon work supported by the National Science Foundation (NSF) through grant number 2220401, the Defense Advanced Research Projects Agency (DARPA) under contract number FA8750-23-C-0518, and the Air Force Office of Scientific Research (AFOSR) under contract number FA9550-23-1-0135. Any opinions, findings, and conclusions or recommendations expressed in this paper are those of the authors and do not necessarily reflect the views of AFOSR, DARPA, or NSF.

A Appendix

See Table 4.

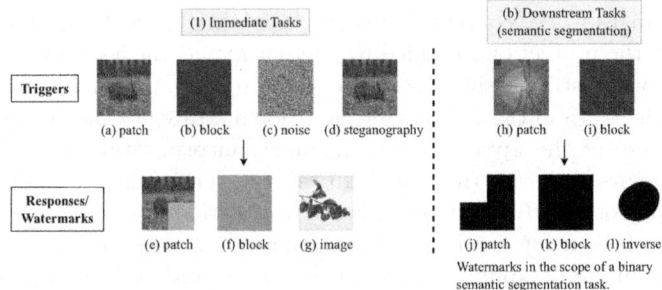

Fig. 5. Example triggers and watermarks for (1) immediate tasks and (2) downstream tasks.

Table 4. Complete results for Sect. 6

D	Model	Fidelity (a)		Retrieve (b)	Breakability (c)			Eval		
		Recon. w/o W_f (mse/psnr)	Recon. w/ W_f (mse/psnr)	W Auth. (NCC)	ftune1 (NCC)	ftune5 (NCC)	owrite (NCC)	a	b	c
CIFAR-10	UNet*	0.0001 / 39.5964	0.0001 / 40.2496	1.0000	-0.0082	0.0064	0.0094	✓	✓	✓
	LinkNet*	0.0002 / 38.3571	0.0002 / 37.6097	1.0000	0.0036	0.0256	0.0420	✓	✓	✓
	FPN*	0.0003 / 35.7325	0.0003 / 35.4533	1.0000	0.0364	0.0137	0.0416	✓	✓	✓
	PSPNet*	0.0014 / 29.2395	0.0014 / 29.3459	1.0000	0.0495	0.0554	0.0459	✓	✓	✓
	PAN*	0.0001 / 39.8747	0.0006 / 34.8951	0.9998	0.0260	0.0395	0.0405	✓	✓	✓
	LRASPP*	0.0013 / 29.6028	0.0016 / 28.5145	1.0000	0.5453	0.0333	0.0443	✓	✓	✓
	DeeplabV3*	0.0059 / 27.0574	0.0013 / 29.2503	1.0000	-0.3035	-0.1285	0.0444	✓	✓	✓
	Baseline 1	0.0001 / 39.5964	0.0001 / 41.2314	1.0000	1.0000	1.0000	1.0000	✓	✓	✗
	Baseline 2	0.0001 / 39.5964	0.0001 / 40.6142	1.0000	1.0000	1.0000	1.0000	✓	✓	✗
ImageNet	UNet*	0.0004 / 34.612	0.0005 / 32.9604	1.0000	0.0282	0.0196	0.0063	✓	✓	✓
	LinkNet*	0.0007 / 32.1809	0.0012 / 29.8473	0.9999	0.0484	0.0073	0.0241	✓	✓	✓
	FPN*	0.0053 / 23.6678	0.0054 / 23.5346	0.9999	0.0491	0.0190	0.0276	✓	✓	✓
	PSPNet*	0.0102 / 20.6874	0.0102 / 20.7309	1.0000	0.0218	0.0165	0.0280	✓	✓	✓
	PAN*	0.0052 / 23.8267	0.0053 / 23.7010	0.9999	0.0223	0.0132	0.0247	✓	✓	✓
	LRASPP*	0.0098 / 20.9127	0.0099 / 20.8496	1.0000	-0.5521	0.0116	0.0297	✓	✓	✓
	DeeplabV3*	0.0095 / 21.0361	0.0098 / 20.9003	1.0000	0.0289	0.0227	0.0271	✓	✓	✓
	Baseline 1	0.0004 / 34.612	0.0007 / 31.8644	1.0000	1.0000	1.0000	1.0000	✓	✓	✗
	Baseline 2	0.0004 / 34.612	0.0004 / 35.2675	1.0000	1.0000	1.0000	1.0000	✓	✓	✗
CLWD	UNet*	0.0008 / 31.047	0.0006 / 32.4386	1.0000	-0.0027	-0.0141	0.0054	✓	✓	✓
	LinkNet*	0.0007 / 31.7815	0.0011 / 30.2647	0.9998	-0.0089	0.0015	0.0245	✓	✓	✓
	FPN*	0.005 / 23.7018	0.0051 / 23.6449	1.0000	-0.0142	-0.0207	0.0268	✓	✓	✓
	PSPNet*	0.0099 / 20.6672	0.0097 / 20.7976	1.0000	-0.0064	-0.0116	0.0231	✓	✓	✓
	PAN*	0.0049 / 23.8625	0.0049 / 23.8631	0.9981	-0.0266	0.0044	0.0278	✓	✓	✓
	LRASPP*	0.0094 / 20.9564	0.0096 / 20.8695	1.0000	-0.0210	-0.0148	0.0329	✓	✓	✓
	DeeplabV3*	0.0093 / 20.9778	0.0093 / 21.0045	1.0000	-0.0058	0.0021	0.0287	✓	✓	✓
	Baseline 1	0.0008 / 31.047	0.0003 / 36.2516	0.9999	1.0000	1.0000	1.0000	✓	✓	✗
	Baseline 2	0.0008 / 31.047	0.0003 / 35.8167	1.0000	1.0000	1.0000	1.0000	✓	✓	✗

References

1. Adi, Y., Baum, C., Cisse, M., Pinkas, B., Keshet, J.: Turning your weakness into a strength: watermarking deep neural networks by backdooring. In: 27th USENIX Security Symposium (USENIX Security 18), pp. 1615–1631 (2018)
2. Bansal, A., et al.: Certified neural network watermarks with randomized smoothing. In: International Conference on Machine Learning, pp. 1450–1465. PMLR (2022)
3. Bhalerao, S., Ansari, I.A., Kumar, A.: A secure image watermarking for tamper detection and localization. J. Ambient. Intell. Humaniz. Comput. **12**(1), 1057–1068 (2021)
4. Chen, Y., Kumara, E.K., Sivakumar, V.: Invesitigation of finance industry on risk awareness model and digital economic growth. Ann. Oper. Res., 1–22 (2021)
5. Cox, I., Miller, M., Bloom, J., Honsinger, C.: Digital watermarking. J. Electron. Imaging **11**(3), 414 (2002)
6. Dathathri, S., et al.: Scalable watermarking for identifying large language model outputs. Nature **634**(8035), 818–823 (2024)
7. Doan, K.D., Lao, Y., Li, P.: Marksman backdoor: backdoor attacks with arbitrary target class. In: Advances in Neural Information Processing Systems, vol. 35, pp. 38260–38273 (2022)
8. Fridrich, J.: Image watermarking for tamper detection. In: Proceedings 1998 International Conference on Image Processing. ICIP98 (Cat. No. 98CB36269), vol. 2, pp. 404–408. IEEE (1998)
9. Hartung, F., Kutter, M.: Multimedia watermarking techniques. Proc. IEEE **87**(7), 1079–1107 (1999)
10. Ho, J., Jain, A., Abbeel, P.: Denoising diffusion probabilistic models. In: Advances in Neural Information Processing Systems, vol. 33, pp. 6840–6851 (2020)
11. Hong, S., Carlini, N., Kurakin, A.: Handcrafted backdoors in deep neural networks. In: Advances in Neural Information Processing Systems, vol. 35, pp. 8068–8080 (2022)
12. Hua, G., Teoh, A.B.J.: Deep fidelity in DNN watermarking: a study of backdoor watermarking for classification models. Pattern Recogn. **144**, 109844 (2023)
13. Jaeger, P.F., et al.: Retina U-Net: embarrassingly simple exploitation of segmentation supervision for medical object detection. In: Machine Learning for Health Workshop, pp. 171–183. PMLR (2020)
14. Joe, B., Park, Y., Hamm, J., Shin, I., Lee, J., et al.: Exploiting missing value patterns for a backdoor attack on machine learning models of electronic health records: development and validation study. JMIR Med. Inform. **10**(8), e38440 (2022)
15. Kadian, P., Arora, S.M., Arora, N.: Robust digital watermarking techniques for copyright protection of digital data: a survey. Wireless Pers. Commun. **118**, 3225–3249 (2021)
16. Kim, B., Lee, S., Lee, S., Son, S., Hwang, S.J.: Margin-based neural network watermarking. In: International Conference on Machine Learning, pp. 16696–16711. PMLR (2023)
17. Kirchenbauer, J., Geiping, J., Wen, Y., Katz, J., Miers, I., Goldstein, T.: A watermark for large language models. arXiv preprint arXiv:2301.10226 (2023)
18. Li, Y., Jiang, Y., Li, Z., Xia, S.T.: Backdoor learning: a survey. IEEE Trans. Neural Netw. Learn. Syst. **35**(1), 5–22 (2022)
19. Li, Y., Li, Y., Wu, B., Li, L., He, R., Lyu, S.: Invisible backdoor attack with sample-specific triggers. In: Proceedings of the IEEE/CVF International Conference on Computer Vision, pp. 16463–16472 (2021)

20. Lin, E.T., Delp, E.J.: A review of fragile image watermarks. In: Proceedings of the Multimedia and Security Workshop at ACM Multimedia, vol. 99, pp. 35–39 (1999)
21. Lin, P.L., Hsieh, C.K., Huang, P.W.: A hierarchical digital watermarking method for image tamper detection and recovery. Pattern Recogn. **38**(12), 2519–2529 (2005)
22. Liu, H., Weng, Z., Zhu, Y.: Watermarking deep neural networks with greedy residuals. In: ICML, pp. 6978–6988 (2021)
23. Liu, X., et al.: Watermark vaccine: adversarial attacks to prevent watermark removal. In: Avidan, S., Brostow, G., Cissé, M., Farinella, G.M., Hassner, T. (eds.) ECCV 2022. LNCS, vol. 13674, pp. 1–17. Springer, Cham (2022). https://doi.org/10.1007/978-3-031-19781-9_1
24. Liu, Y., Ma, X., Bailey, J., Lu, F.: Reflection backdoor: a natural backdoor attack on deep neural networks. In: Vedaldi, A., Bischof, H., Brox, T., Frahm, J.-M. (eds.) ECCV 2020. LNCS, vol. 12355, pp. 182–199. Springer, Cham (2020). https://doi.org/10.1007/978-3-030-58607-2_11
25. Liu, Y., et al.: A survey on neural trojans. In: 2020 21st International Symposium on Quality Electronic Design (ISQED), pp. 33–39. IEEE (2020)
26. Mohanty, S.P.: Digital watermarking: a tutorial review (1999). http://www.csee.usf.edu/~smohanty/research/Reports/WMSurvey1999Mohanty.pdf
27. Ohbuchi, R., Ueda, H., Endoh, S.: Robust watermarking of vector digital maps. In: Proceedings. IEEE International Conference on Multimedia and Expo, vol. 1, pp. 577–580. IEEE (2002)
28. Podilchuk, C., Delp, E.: Digital watermarking: algorithms and applications. IEEE Signal Process. Mag. **18**(4), 33–46 (2001). https://doi.org/10.1109/79.939835
29. Qiao, T., et al.: A novel model watermarking for protecting generative adversarial network. Comput. Secur. **127**, 103102 (2023)
30. Quan, Y., Teng, H., Chen, Y., Ji, H.: Watermarking deep neural networks in image processing. IEEE Trans. Neural Netw. Learn. Syst. **32**(5), 1852–1865 (2020)
31. Ren, J., Zhou, Y., Jin, J., Lyu, L., Yan, D.: Dimension-independent certified neural network watermarks via mollifier smoothing. In: International Conference on Machine Learning, pp. 28976–29008. PMLR (2023)
32. Rezaei, A., Akbari, M., Alvar, S.R., Fatemi, A., Zhang, Y.: LaWa: using latent space for in-generation image watermarking. In: Leonardis, A., Ricci, E., Roth, S., Russakovsky, O., Sattler, T., Varol, G. (eds.) ECCV 2024. LNCS, vol. 15147, pp. 118–136. Springer, Cham (2024)
33. Ronneberger, O., Fischer, P., Brox, T.: U-Net: convolutional networks for biomedical image segmentation. In: Navab, N., Hornegger, J., Wells, W., Frangi, A. (eds.) MICCAI 2015, Part III. LNCS, vol. 9351, pp. 234–241. Springer, Cham (2015). https://doi.org/10.1007/978-3-319-24574-4_28
34. Rouhani, B.D., Chen, H., Koushanfar, F.: DeepSigns: a generic watermarking framework for IP protection of deep learning models. arXiv preprint arXiv:1804.00750 (2018)
35. Saha, A., Subramanya, A., Pirsiavash, H.: Hidden trigger backdoor attacks. In: Proceedings of the AAAI Conference on Artificial Intelligence, vol. 34, pp. 11957–11965 (2020)
36. Shafahi, A., et al.: Poison frogs! Targeted clean-label poisoning attacks on neural networks. In: Advances in Neural Information Processing Systems, vol. 31 (2018)
37. Shafieinejad, M., Lukas, N., Wang, J., Li, X., Kerschbaum, F.: On the robustness of backdoor-based watermarking in deep neural networks. In: Proceedings of the 2021 ACM Workshop on Information Hiding and Multimedia Security, pp. 177–188 (2021)

38. Souri, H., Fowl, L., Chellappa, R., Goldblum, M., Goldstein, T.: Sleeper agent: scalable hidden trigger backdoors for neural networks trained from scratch. In: Advances in Neural Information Processing Systems, vol. 35, pp. 19165–19178 (2022)
39. Uchida, Y., Nagai, Y., Sakazawa, S., Satoh, S.: Embedding watermarks into deep neural networks. In: Proceedings of the 2017 ACM on International Conference on Multimedia Retrieval, pp. 269–277 (2017)
40. Wan, W., Wang, J., Zhang, Y., Li, J., Yu, H., Sun, J.: A comprehensive survey on robust image watermarking. Neurocomputing **488**, 226–247 (2022)
41. Wang, J., Wu, H., Zhang, X., Yao, Y.: Watermarking in deep neural networks via error back-propagation. Electron. Imaging **2020**(4), 22-1–22-9 (2020)
42. Wang, T., Kerschbaum, F.: Attacks on digital watermarks for deep neural networks. In: ICASSP 2019-2019 IEEE International Conference on Acoustics, Speech and Signal Processing (ICASSP), pp. 2622–2626. IEEE (2019)
43. Wang, T., Yao, Y., Xu, F., An, S., Tong, H., Wang, T.: An invisible black-box backdoor attack through frequency domain. In: Avidan, S., Brostow, G., Cissé, M., Farinella, G.M., Hassner, T. (eds.) ECCV 2022. LNCS, vol. 13673, pp. 396–413. Springer, Cham (2022). https://doi.org/10.1007/978-3-031-19778-9_23
44. Wang, Y., Sarkar, E., Jabari, S.E., Maniatakos, M.: On the vulnerability of deep reinforcement learning to backdoor attacks in autonomous vehicles. In: Pasricha, S., Shafique, M. (eds.) Embedded Machine Learning for Cyber-Physical, IoT, and Edge Computing: Use Cases and Emerging Challenges, pp. 315–341. Springer, Cham (2023). https://doi.org/10.1007/978-3-031-40677-5_13
45. Wen, Y., Kirchenbauer, J., Geiping, J., Goldstein, T.: Tree-ring watermarks: fingerprints for diffusion images that are invisible and robust. arXiv preprint arXiv:2305.20030 (2023)
46. Wolfgang, R.B., Delp III, E.J.: Fragile watermarking using the VW2D watermark. In: Security and Watermarking of Multimedia Contents, vol. 3657, pp. 204–213. SPIE (1999)
47. Yin, H., Yin, Z., Gao, Z., Su, H., Zhang, X., Luo, B.: FTG: score-based black-box watermarking by fragile trigger generation for deep model integrity verification. J. Inf. Intell. (2023)
48. Yin, Z., Yin, H., Zhang, X.: Neural network fragile watermarking with no model performance degradation. In: 2022 IEEE International Conference on Image Processing (ICIP), pp. 3958–3962. IEEE (2022)
49. Yuan, Z., Zhang, X., Wang, Z., Yin, Z.: Semi-fragile neural network watermarking for content authentication and tampering localization. Expert Syst. Appl. **236**, 121315 (2024)
50. Zhang, J., et al.: Model watermarking for image processing networks. In: Proceedings of the AAAI Conference on Artificial Intelligence, vol. 34, pp. 12805–12812 (2020)
51. Zhang, J., et al.: Deep model intellectual property protection via deep watermarking. IEEE Trans. Pattern Anal. Mach. Intell. **44**(8), 4005–4020 (2021)
52. Zhao, X., Wang, Y.X., Li, L.: Protecting language generation models via invisible watermarking. arXiv preprint arXiv:2302.03162 (2023)
53. Zhu, R., Wei, P., Li, S., Yin, Z., Zhang, X., Qian, Z.: Fragile neural network watermarking with trigger image set. In: Qiu, H., Zhang, C., Fei, Z., Qiu, M., Kung, S.-Y. (eds.) KSEM 2021. LNCS (LNAI), vol. 12815, pp. 280–293. Springer, Cham (2021). https://doi.org/10.1007/978-3-030-82136-4_23

Let the Noise Speak: Harnessing Noise for a Unified Defense Against Adversarial and Backdoor Attacks

Md Hasan Shahriar[1]($^{\boxtimes}$), Ning Wang[2], Naren Ramakrishnan[1], Y. Thomas Hou[1], and Wenjing Lou[1]

[1] Virginia Polytechnic Institute and State University, Blacksburg, VA, USA
{hshahriar,naren,thou,wjlou}@vt.edu
[2] University of South Florida, Tampa, FL, USA
ningw@usf.edu

Abstract. The exponential adoption of machine learning (ML) is propelling the world into a future of distributed and intelligent automation and data-driven solutions. However, the proliferation of malicious data manipulation attacks against ML, namely adversarial and backdoor attacks, jeopardizes its reliability in safety-critical applications. The existing detection methods are attack-specific and built upon some strong assumptions, limiting them in diverse practical scenarios. Thus, motivated by the need for a more robust, unified, and attack-agnostic defense mechanism, we first investigate the shared traits of adversarial and backdoor attacks. Based on our observation, we propose NoiSec, a reconstruction-based intrusion detection system that brings a novel perspective by shifting focus from the reconstructed input to the reconstruction noise itself, which is the foundational root cause of such malicious data alterations. NoiSec disentangles the noise from the test input, extracts the underlying features from the noise, and leverages them to recognize systematic malicious manipulation. Our comprehensive evaluation of NoiSec demonstrates its high effectiveness across various datasets, including basic objects, natural scenes, traffic signs, medical images, spectrogram-based audio data, and wireless sensing against five state-of-the-art adversarial attacks and three backdoor attacks under challenging evaluation conditions. NoiSec demonstrates strong detection performance in both white-box and black-box adversarial attack scenarios, significantly outperforming the closest baseline models, particularly in an adaptive attack setting. We will provide the code for future baseline comparison. Our code and artifacts are publicly available at https://github.com/shahriar0651/NoiSec.

Keywords: Adversarial Attack · Backdoor Attack · Anomaly Detection

1 Introduction

The widespread deployment of machine learning (ML) models across diverse distributed and connected environments, including connected and autonomous vehicles, smart cities, health care, and industrial IoT networks, has driven significant technological advancements. At the same time, they are vulnerable to data manipulation attacks, including adversarial attacks [3,8,18,21,24,29,33] and backdoor attacks [10,25,34]. While adversarial attacks imperceptibly alter the test data to deceive benignly trained models, backdoor attacks insert subtle triggers in the training data to compromise the inference integrity of the trained model, which is exploited later in the testing phase. Defending against these threats is challenging due to their stealth and sophistication, demanding robust defense strategies.

Various detection methods are designed to detect data manipulation attacks, where the fundamental idea is to analyze the existence of malicious components within test input data. Common analysis approaches include feature space inspection [7,36], outlier detection [9], input reconstruction [22], etc. Most of these methods are built upon the assumption that *the malicious inputs will always lead to noticeable changes to model prediction*. However, such an assumption on attack impact does not always hold, particularly in real-world scenarios. Rather, a malicious input can compromise the model's decision only when the perturbation, the target input, and the target model are all synchronized together [4]. Conversely, any asynchrony among these components can diminish the effectiveness of the attack, leading to a failure in achieving the desired level of disruption in the final prediction. For example, during the initial reconnaissance phase, an attacker might choose a very small perturbation to avoid making noticeable changes to the target input, leading to such desynchronized perturbation. Similarly, in real-world attack scenarios, various natural processes, such as environmental factors, signal processing, sensor encoding, etc., can introduce unforeseen transformations [18], leading to desynchronized input. Furthermore, in the case of black-box attacks , the attacker lacks knowledge of the target model and can use a surrogate model as a proxy to launch a transfer attack [28]. Any subtle differences in the models, such as architectural/parameter-wise disparities, can also disrupt attack synchronization. In these desynchronized scenarios, malicious perturbations are less effective and are likely to be overshadowed by the predominant benign features.

Most of the existing detection-based defenses struggle against such desynchronized attempts where the malicious features remain latent. We argue that it is also critical to detect both synchronized and desynchronized attempts since it allows the model owner to prepare and react before the attack makes any real cost. Therefore, it is imperative to design a detection mechanism that is independent of the attack's ultimate impact, ensuring the ability to identify both types of attacks for a more robust defense.

The existing literature presents two lines of research, each focusing on separate detection mechanisms for adversarial and backdoor attacks, as they stem from distinct vulnerabilities in ML models. For instance, adversarial samples are identified by higher prediction uncertainty [7,36]. Backdoor samples, conversely, are detected through higher prediction consistency in the presence of a trigger [11,13]. However, implementing separate defenses for different attacks is impractical and costly, especially in resource-constrained environments. Hence, we aim to bridge the gap in creating a unified defense strategy to counter both adversarial and backdoor attacks simultaneously, which present significant challenges.

In the search for a unified defense, we observe a common characteristic of adversarial and backdoor attacks: they both manipulate testing data by imprinting the non-generalizable features—subtle and stealthy patterns—that are hard for any naive observers to detect but can still induce misclassification in the target model. Existing research demonstrated that adversarial attacks leave such malicious footprints in the form of random noise [16] that are perplexing and prone to misclassification. Similarly, the trigger injection in backdoor attacks directly serves this role, with the trigger itself acting as the non-generalizable feature. While the original content is the same for both the benign and malicious inputs, only the accompanying noise (perturbation or trigger) determines the model's response to it. Thus, we argue that compared to the defenses that directly analyze the maliciousness of the test inputs, disentangling the noise from the original content and analyzing that noise alone enables a more thorough investigation of malicious properties.

Although the disentangled malicious noise may look random to human or rudimentary detectors, we observe that the target model can still analyze its underlying *structure* and reveal the true intent. Due to the nature of attack algorithms, adversarial perturbations exhibit gradient alignment with the target model, while backdoor triggers are memorized by the model during backdoor training. Therefore, for the same reason, the target model's response to malicious noise will be distinctly different from its response to truly random or benign noise. Based on this observation, we propose NoiSec, a novel noise-based detector that disentangles the noise from test data to extract the underlying features and use them for recognizing malicious manipulations. Our contributions are summarized as follows.

- To overcome the limitations of the existing defense, specifically under practical settings, and bridge the gap between adversarial and backdoor detection, we investigate their shared characteristics and devise a unified detection approach capable of effectively identifying both attacks across white-box and black-box scenarios.
- We propose NoiSec, which works beyond those assumptions of the existing methods and utilizes only the noise, the fundamental root cause of such attacks, to detect the existence of malicious data manipulations. NoiSec eliminates the requirements of attack data or prior knowledge of training and relies solely on benign data for training and detection, which aligns well with practical settings.
- Our comprehensive evaluation of NoiSec highlights its high effectiveness across diverse datasets—including basic objects (Fashion MNIST), natural

scenes (CIFAR-10), traffic signs (GTSRB), medical images (Med-MNIST), spectrogram-based audio data (Speech Command), and wireless sensing (Activity). NoiSec demonstrates resilience against five state-of-the-art adversarial attacks and three backdoor attacks, even under challenging evaluation conditions. The evaluation shows that NoiSec provides consistently high detection performance with high average AUROC scores in both white-box (0.932) and black-box (0.875) settings across all the adversarial attacks and datasets. Furthermore, NoiSec excels with an average AUROC of 0.937 against backdoor attacks on the CIFAR-10 dataset. Moreover, NoiSec significantly outperforms the closest baselines in both adversarial and backdoor attack detection. Additionally, NoiSec provides high resilience against an adaptive attacker and also shows minimal false positives, highlighting its robustness and practical utility in real-world security applications.

2 Threat Analysis

This section introduces the adversarial and backdoor attacks, outlines the threat model under consideration, and provides analysis and observations on these attacks. Additionally, two intuitive examples are presented to support these observations, forming the foundation for the proposed defense strategy.

2.1 Data Manipulation Attacks

The malicious data manipulation attacks against ML seek to sabotage the integrity and reliability of the model, particularly by causing incorrect predictions. These attacks can manifest in two main forms: adversarial and backdoor attacks.

Adversarial Attacks. Adversarial attacks occur during the testing phase, where the attacker creates an adversarial example by meticulously crafting subtle adversarial perturbation and adding it to the target input. Let x^i be the i-th original/benign sample, δ^i be the adversarial perturbation, then the adversarial sample $x^i_{adv} = x^i + \delta^i$. Adversarial examples can cause misclassification, even into a target class. The key challenge is to generate δ^i, that lies within a small range $[-\epsilon, +\epsilon]$, making them subtle enough to evade detection. Different adversarial attacks generate δ^i in different ways. For instance, we consider the gradient-based attacks, including *fast gradient sign method (FGSM)* [8], *basic iterative method (BIM)* [18], *projected gradient descent (PGD)* [21], *universal adversarial perturbation (UAP)* [24], etc. Moreover, there are optimization-based attacks, such as *Carlini & Wagner (C&W)* [3] and query-based black-box attacks, such as *Square* [2].

Backdoor Attacks. While adversarial attacks occur solely during the testing phase, backdoor attacks, a form of data poisoning attack, are initiated during the training phase and manifest during testing. Specifically, a small trigger pattern is implanted into poisoned training samples to embed a backdoor in the model, which activates upon encountering the same trigger in test samples, potentially leading to misclassification. Formally, given the original dataset $\mathcal{D} = \{(x^i, y^i)\}_{i=1}^n$, the poisoned dataset $\mathcal{D}_{\text{poison}} = \{(x^i_{trg}, y^i_{trg})\}_{i \in \mathcal{S}}$ is constructed by adding a trigger t^i to a training samples x^i to generate a triggered samples $x^i_{trg} = x^i + t^i$. Here, $\mathcal{S} \subseteq \{1, \ldots, n\}$ represents the set of poisoned samples. Different backdoor attacks consider different types/shapes of t^i and manipulate y^i_{trg} differently. The backdoor attacks that we consider are *BadNet* [10], *Label-Consistent Attack (LCA)* [34], and *WaNet Attack* [25] attacks.

2.2 Threat Model

We present the threat model by outlining the attack model, categorizing attack categories and capabilities, and defining defense goals and underlying assumptions.

Attack Model. Let us assume, in ideal conditions, that the natural input $x_{nat} = x_{org} + \eta_{nat}$ contains original content x_{org} with natural noise η_{nat}. **Natural noise** *refers to random variations originating from the environment or system, typically modeled as Gaussian noise, i.e.,* $\eta_{nat} \sim \mathcal{N}(0, \sigma^2)$. In benign but noisy scenarios, the benign input $x_{ben} = x_{org} + \eta_{ben}$, which possesses both the original content x_{org} with some benign noise η_{ben}. **Benign noise** *is normally as negligible as* η_{nat} *but sometimes can be noticeably high due to environmental conditions or sensor inaccuracies.* Let $\mathcal{M}$ be the target classifier to be defended, which predicts x_{ben} as class $y_{ben} = arg\, max \mathcal{M}(x_{ben})$. If $\mathcal{M}$ is well trained, y_{ben} will mostly be the same as the ground truth y_{gt} (i.e., $y_{ben} \approx y_{gt}$), indicating a high benign accuracy. On the contrary, the malicious input $x_{mal} = x_{org} + \eta_{mal}$ contains the noise η_{mal}, which may look like random noise but possesses a systematic and latent malicious structure within it. **Malicious noise** includes adversarial perturbations ($\eta_{mal} \approx \delta$) or backdoor triggers ($\eta_{mal} \approx t$) designed to compromise the model's integrity and reliability. The objective of such malicious data manipulation is to change the prediction to $y_{mal} = arg\, max \mathcal{M}(x_{mal})$, which is different from y_{gt} (i.e., $y_{mal} \neq y_{gt}$). For practical purposes, we assume that the benign noise retains the same magnitude as the malicious noise but lacks the structural patterns that characterize malicious behavior. Therefore, we generate the benign noise as $\eta_{\text{ben}} = randomize(\eta_{\text{mal}})$.

Attack Categories and Capabilities. We categorize attacks based on the attacker's capabilities: *Only Testing Phase Attacks* involve crafting adversarial examples by adding malicious noise ($\eta_{mal} \approx \delta$) to exploit vulnerabilities in a deployed benign model. These include white-box attacks, where the attacker has full access to the model's architecture, parameters, and gradients, enabling precise perturbations, and black-box attacks, where the attacker uses a surrogate model or queries the target model iteratively to generate transferable adversarial samples. In contrast, *Both Training and Testing Phase Attacks* allow the attacker to launch backdoor attacks by manipulating training to inject the vulnerabilities into the model. Here, the malicious noise ($\eta_{mal} \approx t$) corresponds to the backdoor trigger.

Defense Goal and Capabilities. The defender aims for a testing time defense, and the goal is to detect if any test input has any systematic malicious component. In other words, the ultimate goal is to discriminate between x_{ben} and x_{mal}. The defender has no information regarding whether the target model contains a backdoor or the specific type or algorithm used for generating the attacks. We assume that the defender has a small representative dataset that contains clean samples spanning all the classes and the computational capacity to train an autoencoder $\mathcal{A}$ on that dataset. We also assume that, along with the final prediction, the defender can also access the feature representation of any given test input. It is further assumed that the attacker cannot compromise the autoencoder or poison the representative dataset, as it is preserved in a secure manner.

2.3 Attack Similarities

To design a unified defense, we first examine the similarities between adversarial and backdoor attacks. Both attacks add malicious noise to the test data—adversarial attacks use subtle perturbations, while backdoor attacks embed triggers. Both rely on the model's poor generalization and sensitivity to such malicious noise. The attack similarities lead to some common observations of the malicious noise. **①Disentanglement of Noise:** Malicious noise is imposed on benign samples, making it possible to disentangle them from the original components. For instance, a denoising autoencoder trained solely on benign samples can separate both the benign and malicious noise from the original components. **②Target Model's Unique Response to Different Types of Noise:** The model exhibits distinct responses to the malicious noise due to their connection with the model's learned representations. For example, adversarial perturbations have gradient alignment with the model's loss function, whereas backdoor triggers act as shortcuts by exploiting the model's learned associations. In both cases, these malicious noise leads to systematic activations in the neurons, resulting in high-magnitude features at the representation layers. In contrast, benign noise does not have any of these properties, hence, they create scattered activations and low-magnitude features that differ significantly from those observed with malicious noise.

2.4 Motivating Examples

We illustrate two motivating examples of adversarial and backdoor attacks on a sample from a traffic sign recognition dataset. We disentangle the noise using a denoising autoencoder (AE) and employ the target classifier to analyze feature representations of different inputs, particularly the noises, at different stages of noise reconstruction. Figure 1(a) visually demonstrates our observations against a representative adversarial attack, e.g., a BIM attack. The figure consists of three panels, each depicting a different testing scenario under three different types of noises: natural noise, adversarial perturbations, and benign noise. The figure consists of three panels, each depicting a different testing scenario: natural noise, adversarial perturbations, and benign noise (randomized adversarial perturbations). Below each panel, we include the corresponding feature representations extracted by the target classifier model for each input/noise. Here, the first and the fourth columns show added noise and AE-reconstructed noise, respectively, and the two columns in the middle show the test inputs and their reconstructions. It is evident from the leftmost column of the figure that extracted features from the originally added natural noise (top-left) and benign noise (bottom-left) noises do not contain any high-magnitude features. Meanwhile, the feature representation of the adversarial noise (middle row, left column) has significantly different distributions, mostly with higher magnitude components. This disparity supports ❷ underscoring the target classifier's effectiveness in analyzing the noise structure and providing distinctive feature representation that can even visually discriminate between adversarial perturbation and natural/benign noises.

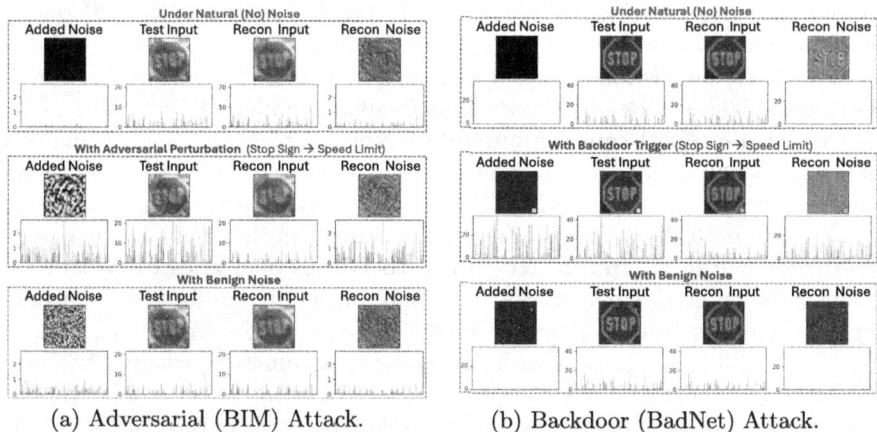

(a) Adversarial (BIM) Attack. (b) Backdoor (BadNet) Attack.

Fig. 1. Effectiveness of using noise to discriminate between malicious (adversarial/backdoor) and benign inputs. The unique feature representations (bar plots at the bottom) of different types of noise (natural, malicious, and benign) indicate the effectiveness of the proposed defense. (Color figure online)

However, direct access to the originally added noises (leftmost column) is unavailable to the defender, necessitating AE-based noise reconstruction (rightmost column). The feature representations of the reconstructed noises have almost a similar pattern as the original added noises, which supports ❷ and shows the effectiveness of AE-based noise disentanglement. Similarly, Fig. 1(b) visually demonstrates the findings against a representative backdoor attack (e.g., BadNet) with a 2 × 2 yellow square-shaped trigger on the bottom right of the test input. These findings highlight AE's ability to extract the malicious noise (perturbation or trigger) from the test data and the target model's ability to extract unique features to facilitate the detection. Such findings support both of our observations in Sect. 2.3, based on which we design our proposed defense NOISEC.

3 Problem Formulation

The key objective of this study is to develop an effective detector for discriminating between benign and malicious inputs. We innovatively formulate the malicious data detection problem by decomposing input data into two components: original content and noise (either benign or malicious). To disentangle noise from the original content, we consider the reconstruction-based approach, particularly using an autoencoder. We categorize such reconstruction-based defenses into two categories: defenses utilizing the input data itself are termed sample-based detection, and defenses utilizing the noise component are termed noise-based detection. Where the ultimate end goal of the sample-based detection is to discriminate between x_{ben} and x_{mal}, the noise-based detection considers the detection problem as discriminating between η_{ben} and η_{mal}. Both categories of defense have shown effectiveness in detecting malicious patterns. Our solution falls into the noise-based defense category.

Autoencoder-Based Reconstruction. Reconstruction-based defense mechanisms have emerged as one of the prominent approaches in detecting and mitigating the impact of malicious data manipulation attacks in ML [22]. These methods leverage an autoencoder model $\mathcal{A}$ to reconstruct test input, aiming to disentangle the accompanying noise—whether benign or adversarial—from the natural contents. Further analysis of either the reconstruction input or the reconstructed noise indicates the existence of malicious attacks. Let the reconstructed natural, benign, and malicious samples be defined as $\hat{x}_{nat}$, $\hat{x}_{ben}$, and $\hat{x}_{mal}$, respectively. If $\mathcal{A}$ is trained sufficiently, the reconstruction will remove any noises, retain only the original contents, and hence: $\hat{x}_{nat} = \mathcal{A}(x_{nat}) \approx x_{org}$, $\hat{x}_{ben} = \mathcal{A}(x_{ben}) \approx x_{org}$, and $\hat{x}_{mal} = \mathcal{A}(x_{mal}) \approx x_{org}$. Again, let the reconstruction noise from the natural inputs be $\hat{\eta}_{nat}$, which can be expressed as $\hat{\eta}_{nat} = (x_{nat} - \hat{x}_{nat}) \approx (x_{nat} - x_{org}) = \eta_{nat}$. Similarly, the reconstruction noise from the benign and malicious can be expressed as $\hat{\eta}_{ben} \approx \eta_{ben}$ and $\hat{\eta}_{mal} \approx \eta_{mal}$, respectively. Hence, any reconstructed samples approximate only the original content, whereas the reconstruction noises approximate the added noises, either natural, benign, or malicious. Such disengagement of noises serves as the fundamental step for any reconstruction-based defense, as it paves the way for further discriminating between benign and malicious inputs.

4 Our Proposed Defense: NoiSec

Based on our observation (Sect. 2.3) and motivating examples (Sect. 2.4), we propose NoiSec, a unified defense against adversarial and backdoor attacks.

4.1 NoiSec Overview

Figure 2 illustrates the core components and implementation phases of NoiSec. It comprises three fundamental components: i) denoising autoencoder, ii) feature extractor (target model), and iii) anomaly detector. Moreover, NoiSec has two implementation phases: i) the training phase and ii) the testing phase. The training phase, at first, trains the autoencoder (AE) using a representative dataset composed of only natural samples. The AE learns to reconstruct only the original contents and separate the noises from the samples. Later, the trained AE is used to reconstruct all the natural samples and, consequently, calculate the natural reconstruction noises. The natural noises are then fed into the feature extractor (FE) to reduce the dimensionality of the noises and have an effective representation.

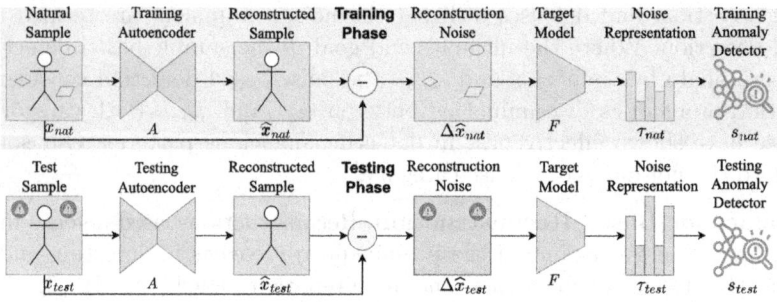

Fig. 2. An overview of the two implementation phases of NoiSec.

Nonetheless, as natural noises are supposed to have a random structure, all the noise features will exhibit lower magnitudes. Following the acquisition of the low-dimensional noise representation, an anomaly detector (AD) is trained to map the distribution of these natural noise representations and learn the natural pattern or clusters. Finally, NoiSec utilizes the trained AD to estimate the anomaly scores of all the natural noise representations and calculates a threshold for future detection.

During the testing phase, NoiSec utilizes the trained AE, FE, and AD, as well as the detection threshold, to check for any malicious manipulation in any test input. As shown in the figure, at the testing phase, the AE reconstructs any incoming test sample (benign or malicious), allowing the estimation of the reconstruction noise. The FE then analyzes such reconstruction noise to have the noise representation. Lastly, the AD analyzes the distribution of this feature vector, contrasts it against the learned natural patterns, and assigns an anomaly score. If the anomaly score exceeds the predefined threshold, NOISEC prompts the system to alert for a potential data manipulation attack and take further attack mitigation measures.

4.2 Technical Details

This part explains the essential tasks executed sequentially during the training and testing phases of NOISEC.

Noise Reconstruction. The AE model $\mathcal{A}$ is trained as a denoising AE on the representative dataset to reconstruct the input data while learning to filter out the noise. Upon training of $\mathcal{A}$, the first step involves reconstructing the noise component from the sample using an AE. While in the training phase, these samples are all benign, in the testing phase, they can be both benign and malicious. The process of benign and malicious noise reconstruction $\hat{\eta}_{\text{ben}}$, and $\hat{\eta}_{\text{mal}}$, respectively, is the same for any reconstruction-based defense. The key novelty of our proposed method mainly lies in the following two steps.

Noise Representation. NOISEC uses the FE model $\mathcal{F}$ to analyze noise and have effective noise feature representation. Notably, $\mathcal{F}$ is essentially the same as the target classifier $\mathcal{M}$. However, instead of getting the confidence vectors at the last layer of $\mathcal{M}$ for noise representation, NOISEC considers taking the feature representation at the penultimate layer. Hence, we separately name this component as $\mathcal{F}$ for clarity, while in implementation, $\mathcal{M}$ itself can be utilized to have this representation. Let τ_{nat} be the feature representations of the natural reconstructed noises, such that $\tau_{\text{nat}} = \mathcal{F}(\hat{\eta}_{\text{nat}}) \approx \mathcal{F}(\eta_{\text{nat}})$. Similarly, let τ_{ben} and τ_{mal} represent the feature representations of the benign and malicious reconstructed noises, and can be expressed as $\tau_{\text{ben}} = \mathcal{F}(\hat{\eta}_{\text{ben}}) \approx \mathcal{F}(\eta_{\text{ben}})$ and $\tau_{\text{mal}} = \mathcal{F}(\hat{\eta}_{\text{mal}}) \approx \mathcal{F}(\eta_{\text{mal}})$, respectively.

Considering that both $\hat{\eta}_{\text{ben}}$ and $\hat{\eta}_{\text{ben}}$ typically result in feature representations of low magnitude due to the absence of any prominent patterns, τ_{ben} is expected to follow the same distribution of τ_{nat}. Conversely, $\hat{\eta}_{\text{mal}}$, even if with low intensity, is anticipated to activate some specific features, leading to a feature vector of higher magnitude. Hence, the distribution of τ_{ben} and τ_{nat} are highly similar ($\tau_{\text{ben}} \approx \tau_{\text{nat}}$), while τ_{mal} and τ_{ben} will have a noticeable difference ($\tau_{\text{mal}} \not\approx \tau_{\text{nat}}$), which is later also illustrated in Fig. 4(a). Such distinct representations pave the way to the ultimate objective of NOISEC, which is to deploy an AD capable of distinguishing between τ_{ben} and τ_{mal}, thereby identifying potential malicious perturbations.

Anomaly Detection. Finally, an AD model $\mathcal{D}$ is trained on the natural feature vectors τ_{nat} in the training phase and, later in the testing phase, used to discriminate between τ_{ben} and τ_{mal}. Particularly, let the anomaly scores $s_{\text{nat}} = \mathcal{D}(\tau_{\text{nat}})$,

Table 1. Comparison of Datasets

Dataset	Modality	Input Size	Classes	Description
F-MNIST [38]	Image	$28 \times 28 \times 1$	10	Representations images fashion items
CIFAR-10 [1]	Image	$32 \times 32 \times 3$	10	RGB images of objects, e.g., airplanes
GTSRB [32]	Image	$32 \times 32 \times 3$	43	RGB images of traffic signs
SPEECH [37]	Audio	$64 \times 81 \times 1$	35	Mel-spectrogram of spoken commands
Med-MNIST [41]	X-rays	$64 \times 64 \times 1$	2	Chest X-ray images for pediatric pneumonia
Activity [42]	Wireless	$500 \times 90 \times 1$	7	CSI of wireless sensing of human activities.

$s_{\text{ben}} = \mathcal{D}(\tau_{\text{ben}})$ and $s_{\text{mal}} = \mathcal{D}(\tau_{\text{mal}})$ for natural, benign, and malicious noises representation, respectively. Where s_{ben} is supposed to have a similar distribution to s_{nat} ($s_{\text{ben}} \approx s_{\text{nat}}$), s_{mal} is assumed to have significantly higher values compared to s_{ben} ($s_{\text{mal}} >> s_{\text{nat}}$) due to its unforeseen and out of distribution characteristics. Based on these steps, NoiSec effectively discriminates between x_{ben} and x_{mal}, which are evaluated under a wide spectrum of attacks in the following sections.

5 Implementation

5.1 Experiment Setup

We demonstrate NoiSec's effectiveness across diverse modalities of datasets, as summarized in Table 1. We consider various classification models (See Table 4 in Appendix) across different datasets for adversarial attack scenarios. It is noteworthy that for all datasets, the target and surrogate models—for white-box and black-box attacks—exhibit varying numbers of channels in their convolutional layers. We use ReLU as the activation function and dropout for regularization. On the other hand, we implement backdoor attacks on the CIFAR-10 dataset using the open-source implementation provided by Backdoorbox [19], employing the ResNet18 architecture [12].

Similarly, we consider different autoencoder architectures for different datasets (See Table 5 in Appendix). All the models employ 3×3 kernels and ReLU activation functions throughout. We train them as denoising autoencoders, introducing standard Gaussian noise with a standard deviation specified in the table. We train both the classifier and the autoencoder using the full training split of their respective datasets. For the AD model, we test various statistical and outlier detection algorithms and find that *Gaussian Mixture Model (GMM)*-based AD performs best. GMM effectively models the data distribution using a combination of Gaussian components [5], capturing both structure and variability in the dataset.

5.2 Evaluation Settings

We evaluate NOISEC against all the attacks mentioned in Sect. 2.1. For the adversarial attacks, we generate 500 natural samples by adding Gaussian noise for each dataset. Subsequently, we generate 100 adversarial samples for each attack using both the target and surrogate models. We randomize the perturbation of each malicious sample and consider them benign samples. Therefore, the benign and malicious sample pairs have the same noise magnitude, but the perturbation structure/pattern differs. This challenging evaluation setting ensures that NOISEC only detects malicious inputs but not benign anomalies. Figure 3 shows the samples of adversarial examples across different attacks and datasets.

We conduct three distinct backdoor attacks on the CIFAR-10 dataset, each with varying poison rates and target labels. We implement BadNet with a poison rate of 5%, using a checkerboard pattern in the bottom-right corner of the image as the trigger. WaNet, on the other hand, applies a transformation-based backdoor with a 10% poison rate, using subtle warping of the input images. Lastly, LCA is implemented with a significantly higher poison rate of 25%, with checkerboard triggers in four corners. To evaluate NOISEC against these attacks, we generate 1000 backdoor-triggered samples for all three backdoor attacks. As backdoor models are hypersensitive to trigger-like benign noises, we generate another 1000 samples with Gaussian noise as the benign samples.

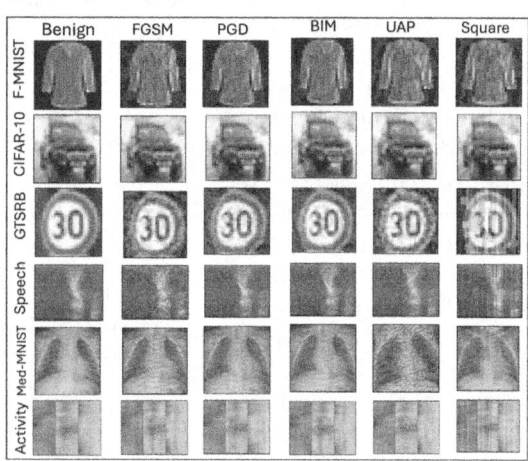

Fig. 3. Adversarial examples across attacks.

5.3 Software Implementation

We implement NOISEC using Python 3.10. We use PyTorch to develop the classifier and the autoencoder. We utilize Torchattacks [17] and Adversarial Robustness Toolbox (ART) [26] libraries for implementing adversarial attacks, Backdoorbox [19] for backdoor models, and we use the PyOD library [43] for the AD models. All experiments run on a server equipped with an Intel Core i7-8700K CPU running at 3.70 GHz, a GeForce RTX 2080 Ti GPU, and Ubuntu 18.04.3.

6 Results

This section analyzes the implementation results of both adversarial and backdoor attacks, as well as the detection performance of NOISEC from multiple perspectives, including performance evaluation of the FE, AD, and a comparison with baseline methods, even under an adaptive adversarial setting.

6.1 Effectiveness Against Adversarial Attacks

Effectiveness of Feature Extractor. This part evaluates the efficacy of the target classifier as an FE in capturing critical features indicative of adversarial attacks across various datasets and attack types. We contrast the discrepancies between the feature distributions of reconstructed benign noise (τ_{ben}) and malicious noise (τ_{mal}) by running the Kolmogorov-Smirnov (KS) [30] test on each against the natural noise (τ_{nat}). The KS test is a non-parametric test used to assess whether two datasets come

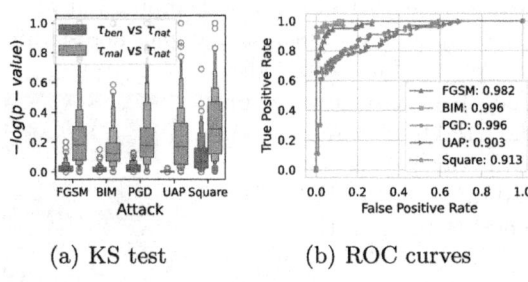

Fig. 4. Performance evaluation of NOISEC's FE and AD against different adversarial attacks on CIFAR-10 dataset. (a) KS test results comparing the feature distribution between (τ_{ben} vs τ_{nat}), and (τ_{mal} vs τ_{nat}) for effective feature extraction. (b) ROC curves and AUROC scores showing effective anomaly detection.

from the same distribution or not, where the $-log(p-value)$ of the KS test serves as a measure of the dissimilarity between the two distributions. The KS test is employed to compute $-log(p-value)$ for all the features as an indicator for the extent of divergence between each distribution pair.

Figure 4(a) presents the KS test results for different attacks for the CIFAR-10 dataset. It is evident that τ_{mal} exhibits distinct distributions from τ_{nat}, characterized by higher $-log(p-values)$ values for (τ_{mal} vs τ_{nat}). Conversely, τ_{ben} and τ_{nat} generally share similar distributions, indicated by lower $-log(p-values)$ values from the KS test between (τ_{ben} vs τ_{nat}). This finding further underscores FE's ability to discern structured patterns in adversarial perturbations. Overall, this separation is facilitated by effective feature extraction by the target classifiers. Such representation enhances the analysis of noise structures and paves the way to more robust anomaly detection. Note that we scaled the $-log(p-value)$ values to improve clarity in presentation and comparison.

Effectiveness of Anomaly Detector. This part analyzes the effectiveness of AD of NOISEC in detecting adversarial attacks. First, Fig. 4(b) provides the ROC curves with AUROC scores of NOISEC for different attacks on the CIFAR-10 dataset under the white-box setting. The plots show that NOISEC shows consistently high AUROC scores (0.90 to 0.99) with a very low FPR against most attacks (except Square), making it a reasonable defense for practical settings. Moreover, Table 2 provides a comprehensive analysis of the effectiveness of NOISEC and contrasts with the baselines in detecting adversarial attacks in terms of AUROC scores under both white-box and black-box settings.

Table 2. AUROC scores of baselines across different attacks and datasets.

Data	Defense	White-box					Black-box				
		FGSM	PGD	BIM	UAP	Square	FGSM	PGD	BIM	UAP	Square
F-MNIST	MagNet	0.68	0.86	0.85	0.62	0.92	0.67	0.75	0.71	0.59	0.72
	Artifacts	0.80	0.74	0.76	0.79	0.53	0.74	0.67	0.67	0.74	0.56
	Manda	0.52	0.44	0.45	0.64	0.80	0.60	0.74	0.63	0.61	0.67
	NoiSec	0.96	0.92	0.93	0.95	0.84	0.86	0.79	0.86	0.94	0.83
CIFAR-10	MagNet	0.63	0.83	0.83	0.50	0.35	0.48	0.50	0.51	0.51	0.31
	Artifacts	0.61	0.57	0.49	0.51	0.52	0.59	0.52	0.60	0.55	0.47
	Manda	0.52	0.73	0.66	0.55	0.61	0.58	0.59	0.61	0.49	0.46
	NoiSec	0.98	1.00	1.00	0.90	0.01	0.01	0.06	0.97	0.88	0.92
GTSRB	MagNet	0.49	0.62	0.55	0.72	0.58	0.53	0.69	0.71	0.64	0.50
	Artifacts	0.43	0.72	0.86	0.53	0.58	0.48	0.53	0.56	0.54	0.58
	Manda	0.54	0.51	0.61	0.70	0.55	0.57	0.60	0.61	0.61	0.50
	NoiSec	0.89	0.88	1.00	0.84	1.00	0.83	0.87	0.90	0.70	1.00
Med-MNIST	MagNet	0.36	0.47	0.36	0.44	0.76	0.44	0.48	0.43	0.52	0.52
	Artifacts	0.56	0.61	0.53	0.56	0.76	0.63	0.54	0.62	0.53	0.66
	Manda	0.41	0.45	0.37	0.13	0.79	0.69	0.60	0.50	0.32	0.62
	NoiSec	0.90	0.83	0.98	0.99	0.91	0.74	0.67	0.79	0.80	0.89
Speech	MagNet	0.70	0.65	0.55	0.86	0.92	0.78	0.86	0.72	0.43	0.77
	Artifacts	0.54	0.95	0.86	0.64	0.81	0.41	0.58	0.64	0.43	0.79
	Manda	0.56	0.55	0.75	0.50	0.72	0.68	0.31	0.55	0.58	0.70
	NoiSec	0.87	0.95	0.91	0.95	0.97	0.83	0.86	0.88	0.97	0.93
Activity	MagNet	0.74	0.74	0.76	0.57	0.73	0.71	0.70	0.70	0.77	0.71
	Artifacts	0.68	0.70	0.76	0.51	0.67	0.67	0.70	0.64	0.61	0.74
	Manda	0.38	0.47	0.70	0.58	0.50	0.56	0.52	0.43	0.54	0.72
	NoiSec	0.95	0.97	0.98	0.88	0.91	0.91	0.93	0.95	0.91	0.94

The left panel (white-box) of the table shows the performance of the closest baselines where Manda [36] generally struggles against most of the attacks, and MagNet [22] and Artifacts [7] demonstrate reasonable defense only against some of them. Contrarily, consistently high AUROC scores of NOISEC show it is highly effective in distinguishing between benign and malicious instances across all attacks and datasets under the white-box setting.

However, under black-box attacks, as demonstrated in the right panel of the table, all baseline methods mostly fail (low AUROC scores) against all of these attacks. Nevertheless, NOISEC still remains highly resilient against such attacks. Thus, even if black-box attacks cannot directly compromise the target model's performance, they still leave detectable traces within the input data, which NOISEC can effectively leverage. Overall, NOISEC achieves average AUROC scores of 0.932 in white-box settings and 0.875 in black-box settings. In comparison, MagNet has 0.655 and 0.612, Artifacts has 0.653 and 0.600, and Manda has 0.556 and 0.573, in white-box and black-box settings, respectively.

Adaptive Adversarial Attacks.
Lastly, we analyze the robustness of NoiSec against an adaptive adversary who can adjust perturbation strength ϵ to balance stealth and attack effectiveness. This evaluation uses a representative BIM attack on the CIFAR-10 dataset, considering a range ϵ from 0.0001 to 0.50. Figure 5 shows, for $\epsilon < 0.002$ (Range 1: high stealth, low effectiveness), ASR remains below 20%. At $0.002 \leq \epsilon <$ 0.02 (Range 2: moderate stealth, mod-

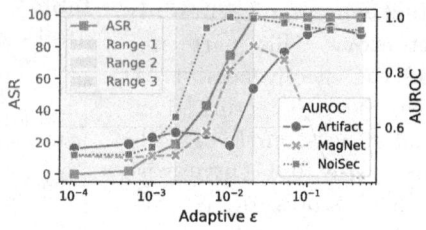

Fig. 5. Performance evaluation of NoiSec under adaptive attacks where the attacker can adjust the attack strength to avoid detection.

erate effectiveness), ASR increases, reaching 100% by $\epsilon = 0.02$. Beyond this $\epsilon > 0.02$, (Range 3: low stealth, high effectiveness), ASR remains 100%, showing the stealth-effectiveness trade-off. Figure 5 also presents the AUROC scores of various detectors for these attacks across the defined ranges. NoiSec demonstrates consistent robustness in both ranges 2 and 3, mostly with an AUROC score higher than 0.90. In comparison, MagNet is slightly effective, primarily at the boundary between ranges 1 and 2, while Artifacts performs well only in the latter part of range 3, where the attack stealthiness is very low. These findings highlight NoiSec as the only detector capable of maintaining reliable performance across varying levels of attack strength, making it a comprehensive defense against adaptive adversarial threats.

6.2 Effectiveness Against Backdoor Attacks

Attack Implementation Results. Figure 9 (in Appendix D) shows the samples with different backdoor triggers. In our implementation of backdoor attacks on the CIFAR-10 dataset, the BadNet attack achieved almost a 100% ASR but resulted in a drop in benign accuracy to 76.81%. WaNet maintained strong performance, achieving 92% benign accuracy and 99% ASR. Meanwhile, LCA also maintained 92% benign accuracy but had a lower ASR of 78%.

Effectiveness of Feature Extractor. This analysis evaluates the efficacy of FE in capturing learned trigger features under the backdoor attacks. Similar to Sect. 6.1, we compare the feature distributions of reconstructed benign noise (τ_{ben}) and reconstructed backdoor trigger (τ_{mal}) against reconstructed natural noise (τ_{nat}) using the KS test. Figure 6a presents the KS test results for the backdoor attacks. For all the attacks, τ_{mal} exhibit distinct distribu-

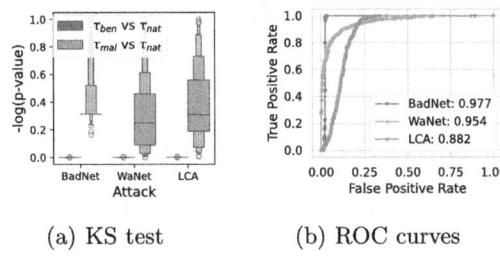

(a) KS test   (b) ROC curves

Fig. 6. NOISEC's performance against backdoor attacks. (a) FE in extracting trigger features from the reconstruction noise and (b) the effectiveness of AD in detecting the existence of the trigger under different backdoor attacks.

tions from τ_{nat}, characterized by higher $-log(p-value)$. On the other hand, τ_{nat} and τ_{ben} generally share similar distributions and possess lower $-log(p-values)$ values in their KS test. Such a finding further highlights FE's capability to reveal if an input has a backdoor trigger on it. This result supports our hypothesis that adversarial and backdoor attacks share common traits that NOISEC exploits to design a unified defense mechanism.

Performance of Anomaly Detector. In this analysis, we evaluate the effectiveness of AD of NOISEC in detecting various backdoor attacks. Figure 6(b) shows the ROC curve, including the AUROC scores, of NOISEC against different backdoor attacks. It is evident from the figure

Table 3. Baseline comparison regarding AUROC scores against backdoor attacks.

Defense ↓ Attack →	BadNet	LCA	WaNet
IBD-PSC	0.93	0.73	**0.99**
SCALE-UP	0.95	0.81	0.85
NOISEC	**0.98**	**0.88**	0.95

that NOISEC is highly effective in detecting backdoor-triggered samples, particularly against the BadNet and WaNet attacks, with AUROC scores of 0.977 and 0.954, respectively, and a very low FPR for both. For the LCA attack, NOISEC shows reasonable performance, as this type of attack is generally more challenging to detect.

Table 3 compares the AUROC scores of different backdoor defenses, e.g., IBD-PSC [13] and SCALE-UP [11]. Across all attacks, NOISEC consistently outperforms or competes with existing defenses. For the BadNet attack, NOISEC achieves the highest score (0.97), surpassing IBD-PSC (0.93) and SCALE-UP (0.95), demonstrating its ability to effectively detect fundamental backdoor threats. Against the LCA attacks, NOISEC significantly outperforms the other methods with an AUROC of 0.88. While IBD-PSC performs marginally better for the WaNet attack (0.99 vs. 0.95), NOISEC remains competitive. Thus, NOISEC's robustness and superior performance make it a strong candidate for defending against both simple and complex backdoor attacks.

7 Related Work

Adversarial and backdoor attacks on ML models, particularly deep neural networks, have become an area of intense research in recent years.

Adversarial Attack Detection. Initial attempts at detecting adversarial attacks focused on statistical methods. Feinman et al. [7] introduced a technique leveraging Bayesian uncertainty estimates and kernel density to detect adversarial examples. This method was among the first to use statistical properties for adversarial detection. Several approaches tailor detection mechanisms to specific models or datasets. Metzen et al. [23] proposed augmenting neural networks with small sub-networks that specialize in identifying adversarial perturbations. This approach allows for model-specific fine-tuning of detection capabilities. Ensemble methods have also shown promise. Pang et al. [27] proposed a method combining multiple weak detectors to improve robustness against adversarial attacks. Similarly, MagNet [22] employs a reformer network to adjust input data and a detector network to identify adversarial examples. Some research has explored statistical and feature-based methods for adversarial detection, such as statistical tests on the distributions of network activations [9], feature-squeezing technique [39], etc. LiBRe [6] used Bayesian neural networks to estimate uncertainty for detecting out-of-distribution adversarial samples.

Backdoor Attack Detection. Detecting backdoors mostly involves reverse-engineering potential triggers that cause misclassification, assuming these triggers are significantly smaller compared to benign triggers. This method relies on efficient reverse engineering techniques and anomaly detection to distinguish original triggers from benign ones [35]. Alternative approaches include distribution-based defenses that model the entire trigger distribution using generative adversarial networks to better capture and eliminate triggers [31]. Additionally, model diagnosis methods assess model behavior with unique inputs to detect anomalies indicative of backdoors, employing techniques like one-pixel signatures [14] and meta neural trojan detection pipelines [40]. These strategies collectively aim to enhance the resilience of models against backdoor attacks [15]. Another defense is to eliminate the trigger from the input data. Complete input sanitization uses autoencoder-based reconstruction methods to ensure trigger-free inputs without labeled training data, albeit at a significant computational cost [20]. While all these defenses are mostly devised for specific attack types, NoiSec bridges that gap and provides a unified defense just utilizing the noise.

8 Conclusion

ML systems have become increasingly vulnerable to adversarial and backdoor attacks, necessitating robust security measures. In this paper, we introduce NoiSec, a detection method that only relies on noise to defend against such threats. NoiSec is a novel reconstruction-based detector that isolates noise from test inputs, extracts malicious features, and utilizes them to identify malicious inputs. Our comprehensive evaluation of NoiSec across a diverse range of datasets and attacks demonstrates its superior performance in detecting both adversarial and backdoor attacks. NoiSec consistently outperforms state-of-the-art baselines, achieving average AUROC scores of 0.932 against white-box and 0.875 against black-box adversarial attacks. Notably, against backdoor attacks, NoiSec attains an average AUROC of 0.937 on the CIFAR-10 dataset. These results underscore NoiSec's potential as a unified, robust, and effective defense mechanism for real-world ML applications. While NoiSec reveals a potential avenue for ML defense, it can also work in conjunction with the sample-based defense and further augment detection performance.

Acknowledgements. This work was supported in part by the Office of Naval Research under grants N00014-24-1-2730 and N00014-19-1-2621, the National Science Foundation under grants 2235232, 2312447, 2312794, and 2240402, and a fellowship from the Amazon-Virginia Tech Initiative for Efficient and Robust Machine Learning.

A Model Architectures

Tables 4 and 5 provide an overview of the classification models and detailed descriptions of the autoencoders used across different datasets, respectively.

Table 4. Classification models' details for different datasets

Dataset	Model Type	Network	Conv Channels	Flat Dim	Feat Dim	Out Dim
F-MNIST	Target	3 Conv, 3 FC	$1 \to 64$	1600	128	10
	Surrogate	2 Conv, 2 FC	$1 \to 64$	9216	128	10
CIFAR-10 & GTSRB	Target	6 Conv, 2 FC	$3 \to 128$	2048	256	10/43
	Surrogate	4 Conv, 2 FC	$3 \to 32$	2048	256	10/43
Speech & Med-MNIST	Target	10 Conv, 2 FC	$3 \to 512$	2048	256	35/2
	Surrogate	10 Conv, 2 FC	$3 \to 128$	512	256	35/2
Activity	Target	10 Conv, 2 FC	$3 \to 256$	1792	512	7
	Surrogate	10 Conv, 2 FC	$3 \to 128$	896	512	7

Table 5. Autoencoder models' details for different datasets

Dataset	Architecture	Noise Std	Latent Dim
F-MNIST	6 Conv, 2 FC, 6 Deconv	0.50	256
CIFAR-10 & GTSRB	6 Conv, 2 FC, 6 Deconv	0.10	1024
Speech & Med-MNIST	6 Conv, 2 FC, 6 Deconv	0.20	256
Activity	6 Conv, 2 FC, 6 Deconv	0.05	1024

B Adversarial Attack Implementation Results

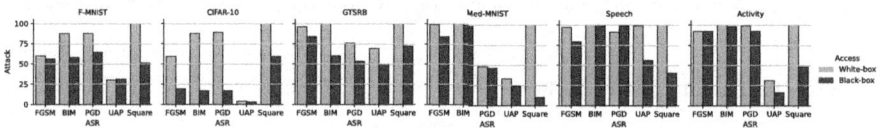

Fig. 7. ASR of different attacks across different datasets under both white-box and black-box settings.

Figure 7 illustrates the ASR of various attacks across multiple datasets for both white-box and black-box scenarios. In white-box scenarios, the attacks consistently achieve high success rates across all datasets, with many methods reaching ASRs of 80% or higher, showcasing their effectiveness when the model parameters are fully accessible. Conversely, the performance of black-box attacks presents a stark contrast, demonstrating significantly lower ASR across the same datasets. This decline highlights the inherent challenges that models face under practical, real-world conditions without full access to the models' underlying parameters. For instance, while some black-box attacks show high ASR, the overall ASR is considerably diminished compared to their white-box counterparts. Moreover, regardless of the success of the attacks, either in the white-box or black-box settings, all such attempts need to be detected by the defensive mechanism.

C Detection of Optimization-Based Adversarial Attacks

Optimization-based adversarial attacks, such as the *JSMA* [29] and *C&W* [3], involve significant computational overhead due to their reliance on run-time optimization processes, making them less practical in real-world scenarios. Therefore, we primarily focus on the more efficient attack strategies mentioned above. Nevertheless, we also evaluate these optimization-based attacks on the CIFAR-10 dataset to demonstrate the broad applicability of our approach.

Figure 8 presents the ROC curves and AUROC scores for different detectors against the white-box C&W attack. As shown, NOISEC exhibits high effectiveness with an AUROC score of 0.92, outperforming the closest baseline, MagNet, which achieves an AUROC score of 0.88. Moreover, NOISEC maintains a low FPR while achieving a high TPR. These results highlight NOISEC's robustness against a wide range of adversarial attacks, including gradient-based, optimization-based, and query-based attacks.

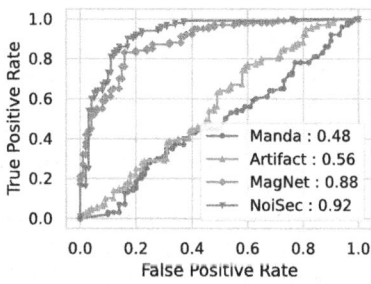

Fig. 8. Performance evaluation of NOISEC against the optimization-based adversarial attacks on CIFAR-10 dataset.

D Backdoor Triggered Samples

Figure 9 illustrates backdoor-triggered samples from various backdoor attacks on the CIFAR-10 dataset. Unlike BadNet and LCA, which use visible patterns as triggers, WaNet employs a highly stealthy trigger that mimics natural noise.

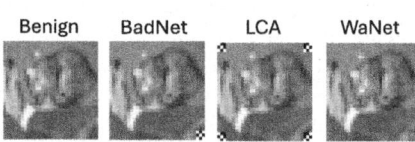

Fig. 9. Backdoor triggered samples.

References

1. Alex, K.: Learning multiple layers of features from tiny images (2009). https://www.cs.toronto.edu/kriz/learning-features-2009-TR.pdf
2. Andriushchenko, M., Croce, F., Flammarion, N., Hein, M.: Square attack: a query-efficient black-box adversarial attack via random search. In: Vedaldi, A., Bischof, H., Brox, T., Frahm, J.-M. (eds.) ECCV 2020. LNCS, vol. 12368, pp. 484–501. Springer, Cham (2020). https://doi.org/10.1007/978-3-030-58592-1_29
3. Carlini, N., Wagner, D.: Towards evaluating the robustness of neural networks. In: 2017 IEEE Symposium on Security and Privacy (SP), pp. 39–57. IEEE (2017)
4. Demontis, A., et al.: Why do adversarial attacks transfer? Explaining transferability of evasion and poisoning attacks. In: 28th USENIX Security Symposium (USENIX Security 19), pp. 321–338 (2019)
5. Dempster, A.P., Laird, N.M., Rubin, D.B.: Maximum likelihood from incomplete data via the EM algorithm. J. Roy. Stat. Soc. Ser. B (Methodol.) **39**(1), 1–22 (1977)
6. Deng, Z., Yang, X., Xu, S., Su, H., Zhu, J.: LiBRe: a practical Bayesian approach to adversarial detection. In: Proceedings of the IEEE/CVF Conference on Computer Vision and Pattern Recognition, pp. 972–982 (2021)
7. Feinman, R., Curtin, R.R., Shintre, S., Gardner, A.B.: Detecting adversarial samples from artifacts. arXiv preprint arXiv:1703.00410 (2017)

8. Goodfellow, I.J., Shlens, J., Szegedy, C.: Explaining and harnessing adversarial examples. arXiv preprint arXiv:1412.6572 (2014)
9. Grosse, K., Manoharan, P., Papernot, N., Backes, M., McDaniel, P.: On the (statistical) detection of adversarial examples. arXiv preprint arXiv:1702.06280 (2017)
10. Gu, T., Dolan-Gavitt, B., Garg, S.: BadNets: identifying vulnerabilities in the machine learning model supply chain. arXiv preprint arXiv:1708.06733 (2017)
11. Guo, J., Li, Y., Chen, X., Guo, H., Sun, L., Liu, C.: Scale-up: an efficient black-box input-level backdoor detection via analyzing scaled prediction consistency. arXiv preprint arXiv:2302.03251 (2023)
12. He, K., Zhang, X., Ren, S., Sun, J.: Deep residual learning for image recognition. In: Proceedings of the IEEE Conference on Computer Vision and Pattern Recognition, pp. 770–778 (2016)
13. Hou, L., Feng, R., Hua, Z., Luo, W., Zhang, L.Y., Li, Y.: IBD-PSC: input-level backdoor detection via parameter-oriented scaling consistency. arXiv preprint arXiv:2405.09786 (2024)
14. Huang, S., Peng, W., Jia, Z., Tu, Z.: One-pixel signature: characterizing CNN models for backdoor detection. In: Vedaldi, A., Bischof, H., Brox, T., Frahm, J.-M. (eds.) ECCV 2020. LNCS, vol. 12372, pp. 326–341. Springer, Cham (2020). https://doi.org/10.1007/978-3-030-58583-9_20
15. Huang, X., Alzantot, M., Srivastava, M.: NeuronInspect: detecting backdoors in neural networks via output explanations. arXiv preprint arXiv:1911.07399 (2019)
16. Ilyas, A., Santurkar, S., Tsipras, D., Engstrom, L., Tran, B., Madry, A.: Adversarial examples are not bugs, they are features. In: Advances in Neural Information Processing Systems, vol. 32 (2019)
17. Kim, H.: Torchattacks: a PyTorch repository for adversarial attacks. arXiv preprint arXiv:2010.01950 (2020)
18. Kurakin, A., Goodfellow, I.J., Bengio, S.: Adversarial examples in the physical world. In: Artificial Intelligence Safety and Security, pp. 99–112. Chapman and Hall/CRC (2018)
19. Li, Y., Ya, M., Bai, Y., Jiang, Y., Xia, S.T.: BackdoorBox: a Python toolbox for backdoor learning. arXiv preprint arXiv:2302.01762 (2023)
20. Liu, Y., Xie, Y., Srivastava, A.: Neural trojans. In: 2017 IEEE International Conference on Computer Design (ICCD), pp. 45–48. IEEE (2017)
21. Madry, A., Makelov, A., Schmidt, L., Tsipras, D., Vladu, A.: Towards deep learning models resistant to adversarial attacks. arXiv preprint arXiv:1706.06083 (2017)
22. Meng, D., Chen, H.: MagNet: a two-pronged defense against adversarial examples. In: Proceedings of the 2017 ACM SIGSAC Conference on Computer and Communications Security, pp. 135–147 (2017)
23. Metzen, J.H., Genewein, T., Fischer, V., Bischoff, B.: On detecting adversarial perturbations. arXiv preprint arXiv:1702.04267 (2017)
24. Moosavi-Dezfooli, S.M., Fawzi, A., Fawzi, O., Frossard, P.: Universal adversarial perturbations. In: Proceedings of the IEEE Conference on Computer Vision and Pattern Recognition, pp. 1765–1773 (2017)
25. Nguyen, A., Tran, A.: WaNet–imperceptible warping-based backdoor attack. arXiv preprint arXiv:2102.10369 (2021)
26. Nicolae, M.I., et al.: Adversarial robustness toolbox v1.2.0. CoRR 1807.01069 (2018). https://arxiv.org/pdf/1807.01069
27. Pang, T., Du, C., Dong, Y., Zhu, J.: Towards robust detection of adversarial examples. In: Advances in Neural Information Processing Systems, vol. 31 (2018)

28. Papernot, N., McDaniel, P., Goodfellow, I., Jha, S., Celik, Z.B., Swami, A.: Practical black-box attacks against machine learning. In: Proceedings of the 2017 ACM on Asia Conference on Computer and Communications Security, pp. 506–519 (2017)
29. Papernot, N., McDaniel, P., Jha, S., Fredrikson, M., Celik, Z.B., Swami, A.: The limitations of deep learning in adversarial settings. In: 2016 IEEE European Symposium on Security and Privacy (EuroS&P), pp. 372–387. IEEE (2016)
30. Press, W.H.: Numerical Recipes 3rd Edition: The Art of Scientific Computing. Cambridge University Press (2007)
31. Qiao, X., Yang, Y., Li, H.: Defending neural backdoors via generative distribution modeling. In: Advances in Neural Information Processing Systems, vol. 32 (2019)
32. Stallkamp, J., Schlipsing, M., Salmen, J., Igel, C.: The German traffic sign recognition benchmark: a multi-class classification competition. In: The 2011 International Joint Conference on Neural Networks, pp. 1453–1460. IEEE (2011)
33. Szegedy, C., et al.: Intriguing properties of neural networks. arXiv preprint arXiv:1312.6199 (2013)
34. Turner, A., Tsipras, D., Madry, A.: Label-consistent backdoor attacks. arXiv preprint arXiv:1912.02771 (2019)
35. Wang, B., et al.: Neural cleanse: identifying and mitigating backdoor attacks in neural networks. In: 2019 IEEE Symposium on Security and Privacy (SP), pp. 707–723. IEEE (2019)
36. Wang, N., Chen, Y., Xiao, Y., Hu, Y., Lou, W., Hou, Y.T.: MANDA: on adversarial example detection for network intrusion detection system. IEEE Trans. Dependable Secure Comput. **20**(2), 1139–1153 (2022)
37. Warden, P.: Speech commands: a dataset for limited-vocabulary speech recognition. arXiv preprint arXiv:1804.03209 (2018)
38. Xiao, H., Rasul, K., Vollgraf, R.: Fashion-MNIST: a novel image dataset for benchmarking machine learning algorithms. arXiv preprint arXiv:1708.07747 (2017)
39. Xu, W., Evans, D., Qi, Y.: Feature squeezing: detecting adversarial examples in deep neural networks. arXiv preprint arXiv:1704.01155 (2017)
40. Xu, X., Wang, Q., Li, H., Borisov, N., Gunter, C.A., Li, B.: Detecting AI trojans using meta neural analysis. In: 2021 IEEE Symposium on Security and Privacy (SP), pp. 103–120. IEEE (2021)
41. Yang, J., et al.: MedMNIST V2-a large-scale lightweight benchmark for 2D and 3D biomedical image classification. Sci. Data **10**(1), 41 (2023)
42. Yousefi, S., Narui, H., Dayal, S., Ermon, S., Valaee, S.: A survey on behavior recognition using WiFi channel state information. IEEE Commun. Mag. **55**(10), 98–104 (2017)
43. Zhao, Y., Nasrullah, Z., Li, Z.: PyOD: a Python toolbox for scalable outlier detection. J. Mach. Learn. Res. **20**(96), 1–7 (2019)

On the Adversarial Robustness of Graph Neural Networks with Graph Reduction

Kerui Wu[1], Ka-Ho Chow[2], Wenqi Wei[3], and Lei Yu[1]()

[1] Rensselaer Polytechnic Institute, Troy, NY, USA
{wuk9,yul9}@rpi.edu
[2] University of Hong Kong, Hong Kong, China
kachow@cs.hku.hk
[3] Fordham University, New York, NY, USA
wenqiwei@fordham.edu

Abstract. As Graph Neural Networks (GNNs) become increasingly popular for learning from large-scale graph data across various domains, their susceptibility to adversarial attacks when using graph reduction techniques for scalability remains underexplored. In this paper, we present an extensive empirical study to investigate the impact of graph reduction techniques—specifically graph coarsening and sparsification—on the robustness of GNNs against adversarial attacks. Through extensive experiments involving multiple datasets and GNN architectures, we examine the effects of four sparsification and six coarsening methods on the poisoning attacks. Our results indicate that, while graph sparsification can mitigate the effectiveness of certain poisoning attacks, such as Mettack, it has limited impact on others, like PGD. Conversely, graph coarsening tends to amplify the adversarial impact, significantly reducing classification accuracy as the reduction ratio decreases. Additionally, we provide a novel analysis of the causes driving these effects and examine how defensive GNN models perform under graph reduction, offering practical insights for designing robust GNNs within graph acceleration systems.

Keywords: Graph Neural Network · Trustworthy AI · Adversarial robustness · Graph reduction · Graph acceleration

1 Introduction

Today, graphs have grown exponentially in size and complexity, serving as fundamental and powerful data structures that depict a vast array of entities and their interconnections. From social networks and financial systems to transportation networks, the ability to effectively represent and analyze such large-scale graphs is crucial. Graph neural networks (GNNs) [10,13,26] have recently emerged as a pivotal technique for learning from and making predictions on graph data, with broad applications across various domains. Despite their growing popularity and wide application in diverse fields such as fraud detection [16], drug discovery [25], and software vulnerability detection [21], the scalability of GNNs has become a significant challenge due to the inherent requirement of GNNs on leveraging information from multi-hop neighbors to generate meaningful node representations and accurate predictions. To address the scalability issue of GNNs, multiple acceleration techniques, including graph coarsening, graph sparsification, and customized hardware design, have been applied to improve the efficiency of GNN learning on large graph data [32].

On the other hand, numerous studies [5,38,39] have shown that GNNs are vulnerable to adversarial attacks. By modifying the original graph by adding, removing edges, or perturbing node attributes, adversaries can dramatically mislead the classifiers and damage the model quality. To address such vulnerabilities, various methods, including preprocessing techniques [7,28] and defensive models [3,33,36], have been proposed to improve the adversarial robustness of GNN. However, these attacks and defense methods are only tested on non-accelerated systems using vast original graphs. Although graph reduction methods such as coarsening and sparsification show promise as a means to accelerate training processes, their impact on GNNs' robustness has not been thoroughly investigated. Previous work [37] studied the effect of graph reduction on GNN robustness but focused only on graph backdoor attacks. The impact of graph reduction on more general adversarial attacks and evasion attacks is still unexamined. Addressing this gap is crucial for building more robust GNN systems that are both resistant to adversarial attacks and efficient in handling large-scale graphs.

In this paper, we systematically examine the impact of graph reduction on the robustness of GNNs against various adversarial attacks [1,8,14,17,30,39] using diverse attack strategies. Specifically, we aim to address three critical questions: (1) How do poisoning attacks affect GNN performance in accelerated systems employing graph reduction methods? (2) Will graph reduction methods make GNN more vulnerable to adversarial manipulation? (3) Can existing defense methods maintain their effectiveness when combined with graph reduction techniques? To answer these questions, we perform a comprehensive evaluation across four graph sparsification and six coarsening methods, diverse datasets, GNN architectures, and reduction ratios, comparing clean, poisoned, and reduced models. Our analysis provides a detailed and novel understanding of the interplay between graph reduction strategies and GNN robustness. In summary, the contributions of this paper are as follows:

- **Graph Sparsification Reduces Adversarial Impact:** Graph sparsification effectively removes added poisoned edges during training, significantly mitigating the impact of poisoning attacks like Mettack [39]. However, it is less effective against evasion attacks, such as PGD [30], as these occur during inference when sparsification no longer applies.
- **Graph Coarsening Exacerbates Vulnerabilities:** While prior work [37] demonstrates that graph coarsening is effective against backdoor attacks, oppositely, our findings reveal that graph coarsening methods amplify the impact of general poisoning attacks. Coarsening merges dissimilar nodes connected by poisoned edges into supernodes, creating noisy representations with

high feature variance and incorrect labels. Additionally, unmerged poisoned edges persist, further degrading model performance.
- **Performance of GNN Defense under Graph Reduction:** When combined with graph sparsification, defensive GNNs retain or even improve their defense capabilities, providing strong protection against poisoning attacks. In contrast, coarsening disrupts these defenses by transferring edge perturbations into supernode structures, rendering robust GNN models less effective.

Our code is available at https://github.com/RPI-DSPlab/Gnn_Reduction_Poisoning_Benchmark.

2 Related Work

2.1 Adversarial ML in Graph

Various adversarial attacks against GNNs have been developed, with the aim of introducing subtle, often imperceptible, perturbations to the data and making the model to misclassify the inputs. A variety of taxonomies exist to classify these attacks, based on different criteria [11,15,35]:

Attack Phase. Attacks can occur during either the training phase (i.e., poisoning attacks) or the inference phase (i.e., evasion attacks). Poison attacks [1,2,5,8,14,17,30,38,39] allow adversaries to modify the training graph in advance to mislead the learning process and produce a compromised model. Evasion attacks [4,12,20,27], on the other hand, perturb only the test data at inference time without affecting the model parameters. In this work, we focus on poisoning attacks, as they interact directly with graph reduction methods during training and often result in more severe model degradation. Nonetheless, we also include evasion attacks in our evaluation to provide a comprehensive understanding of how graph reduction influences adversarial robustness.

Attack Target. Adversarial goals can be either targeted—misclassifying a specific node or a small subset of nodes [2,38]—or global, where the attack aims to degrade the model's overall performance [1,8,14,17,30,39]. In this paper, we focus on global attacks to evaluate adversarial impacts in a graph-accelerated system, considering that training one global poisoned model is computationally more efficient than training multiple models targeting different individual nodes.

Attack Strategy. The most prevalent poisoning attacks are Graph Modification Attacks (GMA) [1,2,8,14,17,30,38,39], where the attacker perturbs the graph topology by adding or removing edges. For example, in a social network, a user may connect or disconnect with others using existing accounts. Notably, GMAs can be used for both poisoning and evasion. A special category of poisoning attacks is Graph Backdoor Attacks [5,34], which implant a hidden trigger into the model by inserting specific patterns into the training data. The study by [37] investigates how graph reduction techniques affect the success of such backdoor attacks. In the evasion setting, Graph Injection Attacks (GIA) [4,12] introduce new malicious nodes with carefully crafted features that propagate misleading information to influence predictions during inference. Meanwhile, feature-based attacks [20,27] directly manipulate node attributes to induce misclassification.

2.2 Defense Methods

A variety of defense strategies have been proposed for GNN robustness, which can broadly be categorized into preprocess-based [7,28] and model-based [3,33,36] methods. The preprocess-based methods aim to sanitize the graph before training by removing suspicious edges, whereas the model-based methods approaches focus on designing robust GNN architectures that penalize adversarial edges or nodes. In this study, we focus on model-based methods as they can be seamlessly integrated with accelerated systems. Preprocess-based methods often remove a significant number of edges, which may compromise the structural integrity and degrading performance—especially when applied with graph reduction.

3 Preliminaries

3.1 Problem Definition

An attributed graph $G = (V, E, X)$ is defined by (1) a set of N nodes $V = \{v_1, \ldots, v_N\}$; (2) a set of edges representing every pair of connections between nodes, where an edge between v_i and v_j can be defined as (v_i, v_j, w) where w represents the connection's weight; (3) a set of features $X \in \mathbb{R}^{N \times D}$, where D represents the feature dimension of each node. The node and edge sets can be written as a weighted adjacency matrix of N nodes $A \in \mathbb{R}^{N \times N}$, where $A_{ij} = w$ if node v_i and v_j are connected with connection weight w. In a semi-supervised node-level classification task within an inductive setting, a small set of nodes $V_L \subseteq V$ in the graph are provided with labels $Y_L \in [0,1]^{N_L \times C}$ where C represents the number of classes. By feeding the subgraph $G_t = (V_t, E_t, X_t)$ that is composed of the nodes with known labels Y_t, a GNN model is trained to predict the class of unlabeled test nodes based on the cross-entropy loss function in Eq. 1, where $f_\theta(\cdot)$ is the predict function with the use of GNN and Y_c represents the ground truth labels' probability distribution of class c.

$$\mathcal{L}(f_\theta(G_t)) = \sum_{c=1}^{C} Y_c \log f_\theta(G_t)_c \tag{1}$$

Attack Models. Adversarial attacks in GNNs are implemented by making a small number of perturbations n_p to the edges and features, such as adding and removing an edge to mislead the model to classify a certain part of test nodes $V_p \subseteq V$ incorrectly. The poisoned graph is denoted as $G_p = (V, E_p, X_p)$, which is generated by minimizing the attack objective shown in Eq. 2 where l_{atk} is the loss function for the attack and y_u is the label of node u.

$$min\,\mathcal{L}_{atk}(f_\theta(G_p)) = \sum_{u \in V_p} l_{atk}(f_\theta(G_p)_u, y_u) \tag{2}$$

We can further split the edges in the poisoned graph into three parts: original edges E, newly added edges E_{add}, and removed edges E_{remove} followed by the

Eq. 3. With original edges as the foundation, a poisoned graph can be extracted into two partially poisoned graphs with adding-only and remove-only strategies, denoted as G_{p-add} and $G_{p-remove}$.

$$E_p = E + E_{add} - E_{remove} \qquad (3)$$

For GIAs, the G_p is generated by injecting a set of malicious nodes V_p as $X_p = \begin{bmatrix} X \\ X_{atk} \end{bmatrix}$, and $A_p = \begin{bmatrix} A & A_{atk} \\ A_{atk}^T & O_{atk} \end{bmatrix}$, where X_{atk} is the features of the injected nodes, O_{atk} is the adjacency matrix among injected nodes, and A_{atk} is the adjacency matrix between the injected nodes and the original nodes.

Attacker's Capability. To match the experiment setting with real-world circumstances, we make the black-box assumption for global attacks. Specifically, attackers can view and edit the graph-structure data that they want to attack, including all nodes, features, edges, and labels. However, they do not have knowledge about the methods that defenders use, such as the GNN architecture. Following this assumption, to attack a GNN model and(or) test the attack's performance, attackers must train a surrogate model under a certain GNN architecture they presume to implement attacks. More than that, attackers should implement as little perturbation as possible to make the attack unnoticeable.

3.2 Graph Reduction

The most time-expensive part of the GNN training algorithms comes from aggregation messages from neighboring nodes, which leads to a tremendous computation graph [32]. Therefore, the primary goal of graph reduction methods is to modify the graph to be a smaller graph $G_r = (V_r, E_r, X_r)$, where $|V_r| < |V|$ and(or) $|E_r| < |E|$, with matched label set Y_r. The graph reduction function is $f_{reduced}(G, Y) = G_r, Y_r$.

The graph coarsening method, followed by the framework in [18], partitioned a graph G into K clusters first, then a matrix $C \in \mathbf{R}^{N \times K}$ is used to represent the partition, which will be used to construct the super-nodes and super-edges to form a coarsen graph G_r. Features of super-nodes X_r are set to be the weighted average of node features within each cluster. Similarly, the label set Y_r is generated by the dominant label of nodes in each super-node, i.e., $Y_r = arg\,max(C^T Y)$.

Graph sparsification, on the other hand, aims to accelerate GNN training by reducing the graph size while preserving its structural and predictive properties. This is achieved by removing redundant edges while keeping the node features and labels unchanged. Various edge selection strategies have been explored to maintain similar classification performance, including random selection, degree-based selection [9], node-similarity-based selection [23], and edge-similarity-based selection [31].

4 Experiment

4.1 Experimental Settings

Dataset. We use three datasets of different scales for GNN node classification that are commonly used to check adversarial attack performance: Cora, Pubmed, and CS, where Cora is a small graph with about 1000 nodes, Pubmed and CS are large graphs with about 10000 nodes. Detailed statistics of these datasets are provided in our extended version on arXiv [29].

GNN Reduction Methods. For the graph coarsening, we implement six methods that include three methods, Variation neighborhoods (VN), Variation edges (VE), and Variation climes (VC) from [18], Heavy Edge Matching (HE) [19], Algebraic JC (JC) [22], and Kron (KRON) [6]. We define the reduction ratio of graph coarsening as the ratio of the number of nodes in the reduced graph G_r to the original node number i.e., $r = \frac{|V_r|}{|V|}$, to indicate the portion of nodes that are merged into super-nodes during the coarsening.

For graph sparsification, we implement four algorithms based on Networkit [24]: Random Node Edge (RNE), Local Degree (LD) [9], Local Similarity (LS) [23], and Scan(SCAN) [31]. Similar to the coarsening ratio, we define the reduction ratio of graph sparsification as the ratio of the number of edges in the sparsified graph G_r to the number of edges in G to quantify how many edges are removed in this phase, i.e. $r = \frac{|E_r|}{|E|}$.

The detailed description of each coarsening and sparsification algorithm can be found in our extended version on arXiv [29].

Attack Models. We implement seven most-recent global poisoning attacks, namely, DICE [39], NEA [1], PGD [30], Mettack [39], PRBCD [8], GraD [17], and STRG-heuristic [14] with the use of DeepRobust [15], an open source benchmark package for adversarial attacks. We implement these attacks in a black-box setting, in which attackers do not have preliminary knowledge of which GNN model will be used for the training. We further constrain the total number of edges it can add and remove with a perturbation ratio $p = \frac{|E_{add}| + |E_{remove}|}{E}$.

GNN Models. We consider three common GNN architectures, namely, GCN [13], GraphSAGE [10], GAT [26], and three powerful defensive GNN models, Robust GCN (RGCN) [36], GNNGuard [33], and MedianGCN [3].

Evaluation Metrics. We evaluate the classification performance on the test set sample from the global graph by calculating the clean accuracy(ACC_c) using the clean adjacency matrix to train, poisoned accuracy(ACC_p) using the poisoned adjacency matrix, and post-reduction accuracy(ACC_r) that uses the reduced poisoned graph.

Implementation Details. By default, we set the perturbation ratio $p = 0.05$ and reduction ratio $r = 0.325$. We train a surrogate GCN model using the clean adjacency matrix and clean features. The surrogate model will be used by attackers to implement and test their attacking algorithms. Each experiment was repeated five times with different random seeds, and then the accuracies were averaged.

4.2 Baseline Effectiveness Analysis

Before testing the effect of poisoning attacks under graph reductions, we systematically evaluate each attack's performance under different GNN architectures. We first use a clean adjacency matrix and clean feature to train a surrogate GCN model. This surrogate model will be used by attackers to implement and test their perturbations. Each experiment was repeated five times under different random seeds and then averaged the clean accuracy and poisoned accuracy.

Table 1 shows the clean accuracy ACC_c and poisoned accuracy ACC_p of GCN trained on three datasets under different perturbation ratios (2%, 5%, 10%). The results indicate that all attacks reduce model accuracy. To align with the attacks' goal to ensure attack impact with minimal perturbation, we use a 5% perturbation ratio as our hyperparameter in the experiments below, as this level consistently produces a notable drop in prediction accuracy across multiple attacks.

Table 1. GCN clean accuracy and poisoned accuracy under five poisoning attacks with various perturbation ratios. The lowest poisoned accuracy is **highlighted** in each dataset. N/A indicates the experiment is out of memory.

Dataset (ACC_c)	Attack	ACC_p		
		$p = 2\%$	5%	10%
Cora (84.06%)	DICE	83.40%	81.98%	80.62%
	NEA	83.20%	82.46%	81.25%
	PGD	81.71%	78.20%	74.77%
	Mettack	81.26%	**74.46%**	**71.22%**
	PRBCD	83.23%	81.11%	79.68%
	STRG-Heuristic	81.94%	79.07%	77.19%
	GraD	**80.56%**	76.26%	72.52%
Pubmed (86.15%)	DICE	85.46%	85.21%	83.40%
	NEA	85.63%	85.49%	84.30%
	PGD	84.12%	81.33%	78.08%
	Mettack	84.95%	78.07%	**62.78%**
	PRBCD	84.77%	83.39%	81.53%
	STRG-Heuristic	85.33%	84.73%	82.94%
	GraD	**82.17%**	**77.72%**	65.93%
CS (92.43%)	DICE	92.20%	91.81%	91.15%
	NEA	92.20%	91.85%	91.35%
	PGD	90.76%	88.71%	86.37%
	Mettack	**88.49%**	**82.25%**	**76.95%**
	PRBCD	90.72%	88.95%	86.89%
	STRG-Heuristic	92.14%	91.78%	91.06%
	GraD	N/A	N/A	N/A

We further evaluate the robustness of different GNN models and defense methods against poisoning attacks with a perturbation ratio of 5% in Table 2, where GNNs trained with poisoned graph data that have the highest accuracies are highlighted. As shown in the Table, every attack effectively decreased the classification accuracy in small datasets. However, in large datasets, DICE, NEA, and STRG-Heuristic reflect marginal attacking performance, while other attacks remain powerful. Among these attacks, Mettack and GraD show the strongest attacking performance with the lowest poisoned accuracy. From the defender's perspective, GNNGuard consistently mitigates most attacks on large datasets with minimal accuracy loss.

Table 2. Poisoned accuracy under five poisoning attacks with 5% perturbation ratios trained by GNNs. The highest accuracy in each attack is **bolded**.

Dataset	Attack	ACC_p					
		GCN	GAT	SAGE	GNNGuard	RGCN	Median
Cora	Clean	84.06%	**84.55%**	83.63%	80.59%	83.82%	84.52%
	DICE	81.98%	81.41%	82.01%	77.59%	81.73%	**83.15%**
	NEA	82.46%	82.70%	81.79%	79.06%	82.34%	**83.88%**
	PGD	78.20%	78.25%	78.52%	77.04%	78.23%	**79.14%**
	Mettack	74.46%	**77.83%**	76.68%	76.30%	73.75%	77.64%
	PRBCD	81.11%	**81.84%**	80.78%	77.11%	80.46%	81.57%
	GraD	76.26%	80.86%	79.53%	78.40%	74.30%	**81.30%**
	STRG-Heuristic	79.07%	80.84%	79.32%	76.71%	77.89%	**80.89%**
Pubmed	Clean	**86.15%**	85.13%	85.59%	84.67%	85.49%	84.43%
	DICE	85.21%	83.83%	**85.10%**	84.52%	84.63%	83.56%
	NEA	85.49%	84.50%	**85.69%**	84.70%	85.17%	84.19%
	PGD	81.33%	80.67%	83.35%	**83.53%**	80.70%	80.82%
	Mettack	78.07%	82.95%	81.40%	**84.67%**	81.80%	79.39%
	PRBCD	83.39%	82.56%	**85.08%**	84.20%	83.18%	83.33%
	GraD	77.72%	81.16%	80.23%	**84.64%**	79.51%	82.52%
	STRG-Heuristic	84.73%	83.81%	**85.67%**	84.30%	84.46%	82.60%
CS	Clean	92.43%	92.10%	92.13%	**92.60%**	92.08%	91.91%
	DICE	91.81%	91.56%	91.72%	**92.36%**	91.28%	91.28%
	NEA	91.85%	90.47%	91.60%	**92.53%**	91.02%	91.19%
	PGD	88.71%	88.78%	89.39%	**91.51%**	88.33%	88.05%
	Mettack	82.25%	89.26%	88.10%	**92.25%**	89.02%	90.17%
	PRBCD	88.95%	88.90%	90.97%	**92.31%**	88.68%	89.58%
	GraD	N/A	N/A	N/A	N/A	N/A	N/A
	STRG-Heuristic	91.78%	91.66%	92.21%	**92.49%**	89.44%	90.83%

4.3 Robustness Under Graph Reduction

In this section, we empirically evaluate the effect of graph coarsening and sparsification on poisoning attacks. After the poisoning pipeline, the perturbed graph is passed to the graph coarsening/sparsification algorithm to reduce its size with various reduction ratios between 0 and 1. The reduced poisoned graph is then fed into the GNN model to train and test its accuracy and robustness.

Accuracy Under Graph Reduction Against Poisoning Attacks. Table 3 and 4 show the GCN's poisoned accuracy ACC_p for each attack and its corresponding post-reduction accuracy ACC_r. After graph sparsification, some attacks, e.g., PGD and PRBCD, maintain similar attack performance, while other attacks, e.g., Mettack and GraD, are largely mitigated by graph sparsification, leading to an increased ACC_r.

In contrast, graph coarsening, shown in Table 4, amplifies the adversarial influence by further reducing the accuracy compared with graph sparsification. The worst case is Mettack, where the average ACC_r is 61.65%, which is 16.41% lower than the Mettack attack's accuracy under no graph reduction.

Table 3. GCN's poisoned accuracy under $p = 0.05\%$, and post-reduction accuracy after graph sparsification under $r = 0.325$ in Pubmed Dataset, whose $ACC_c = 86.15$. The ACC_r with a lower than 1% drop compared to ACC_c is **bolded**.

Attack	ACC_p	ACC_r			
		RNE	LD	LS	SCAN
DICE	85.21%	84.49%	84.94%	84.59%	84.91%
NEA	85.49%	84.78%	85.24%	85.40%	85.28%
PGD	81.33%	81.23%	81.24%	81.46%	81.34%
Mettack	78.07%	**85.80%**	**86.27%**	79.78%	64.19%
PRBCD	83.39%	82.97%	83.95%	83.45%	83.05%
GraD	77.72%	**85.34%**	**85.28%**	82.32%	76.93%
STRG-Heuristic	84.73%	84.98%	**85.15%**	83.56%	82.13%

We further investigate the impact of graph reduction algorithms on classification accuracy across varying reduction ratios. Using PGD and Mettack, we illustrate the effect of sparsification and coarsening under different reduction ratios in Fig. 1 and Fig. 2, respectively. Complete figures for accuracy performance under graph reduction for every poisoning attack are provided in Appendix Fig. 7 and Fig. 8. In Fig. 1 for graph sparsification, the reduction ratio has a minimal impact on attack performance under PGD attack, with only a slight decrease in accuracy due to the reduced training graph size. In contrast, under Mettack, for all sparsification methods, the accuracy dramatically increased as the reduction ratio decreased, indicating the mitigation effect of graph sparsification against

Table 4. GCN's poisoned accuracy under $p = 0.05\%$, and post-reduction accuracy after graph coarsening under $r = 0.325$ in Pubmed Dataset, whose $ACC_c = 86.15$.

Attack	ACC_p	ACC_r					
		VN	VE	VC	HE	JC	KRON
DICE	85.21%	83.34%	82.72%	82.62%	82.44%	82.67%	82.87%
NEA	85.49%	83.47%	82.38%	83.26%	83.01%	83.28%	84.28%
PGD	81.33%	79.91%	79.46%	78.78%	79.19%	79.70%	79.45%
Mettack	78.07%	59.27%	64.23%	66.01%	52.31%	61.52%	59.27%
PRBCD	83.39%	82.01%	81.00%	81.68%	81.87%	78.88%	82.05%
GraD	77.72%	80.95%	75.29%	74.07%	68.78%	75.41%	73.52%
STRG-Heuristic	84.73%	83.00%	78.68%	77.27%	77.77%	76.54%	79.64%

Mettack. On the other hand, as shown in Fig. 2, graph coarsening results in a sharp decline in accuracy as the reduction ratio decreases from 0.325 to 0.1, suggesting that graph coarsening amplifies the effectiveness of adversarial attacks under small reduction ratios.

4.4 Perturbation Edge Analysis.

Given the observations in the previous section, we conduct a thorough edge analysis to understand why graph sparsification can effectively defend against some attacks while failing in others. Similarly, we want to explore why the performance of adversarial attacks can be amplified by graph coarsening.

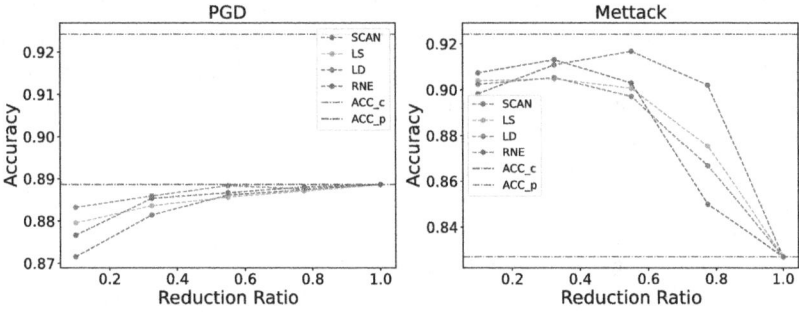

Fig. 1. ACC_r using four sparsification algorithms against PGD (left) and Mettack (right) with reduction ratios r in CS dataset.

Graph Sparsification. For graph sparsification, we evaluate the proportion of poisoned edges removed during the reduction process. Figure 3 illustrates the removal ratios under varying sparsification levels (r_s) for both the PGD, which

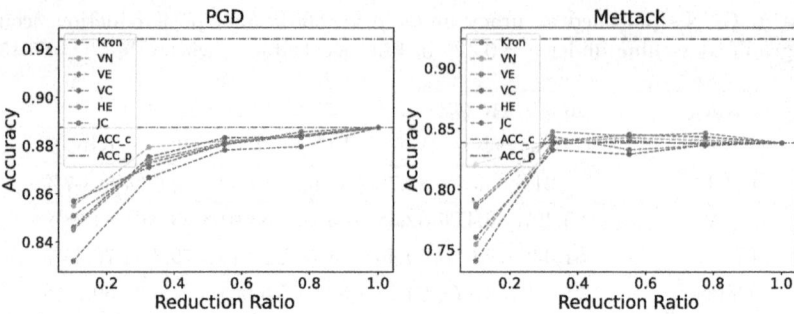

Fig. 2. ACC_r using six coarsening algorithms against PGD (left) and Mettack (right) with various r in CS dataset.

retains the attacking performance after sparsification, and Mettack, which is largely mitigated by sparsification. A complete edge analysis result for every attack in every dataset is available in our extended version on arXiv [29]. Surprisingly, for both attacks, sparsification methods' removal ratio of poisoned edges is about or above 60%, indicating most of the poisoned edges are removed in the training phase after graph sparsification. Given such observation, we propose two hypotheses to explain why certain poisoning attacks retain their adversarial influence despite sparsification: (1) These attacks primarily remove existing edges rather than add new ones, reducing the impact of sparsification on their effectiveness; (2) Although graph sparsification removes a significant portion of poisoned edges during training, resulting in a cleaner model, adversarial perturbations can still take effect during the inference phase as evasion attacks. To identify the underlying reasons, we analyze every component of the attacks and their respective impact on the classification accuracy in Table 5. On the first half of the table, we observe that all optimization-based attacks predominantly focus on adding edges rather than removing them. The exception is the rule-based attack DICE, which explicitly follows a predefined rule to externally connect edges, resulting in a balance between added and removed edges. Such observation excludes hypothesis one.

On the second half of the table, we analyze the effectiveness of each perturbation component by evaluating the GCN model's inference accuracy on the poisoned graph G_p with models trained on G_p and G. Note that training the model with a clean graph but inference using a poisoned graph is an evasion attack setting. We observe that while Mettack effectively poisons a GNN during the training phase, its adversarial impact diminishes in the evasion attack setting, where perturbations are introduced only during inference. In contrast, PGD and PRBCD retain their adversarial effectiveness in both poisoning and evasion attack scenarios, indicating that their perturbations remain impactful regardless of whether the model is trained on a poisoned graph or not. Therefore, although graph reduction methods eliminated most of the poisoned edges in the training phase, resulting in a clean GNN model, because of the nature of

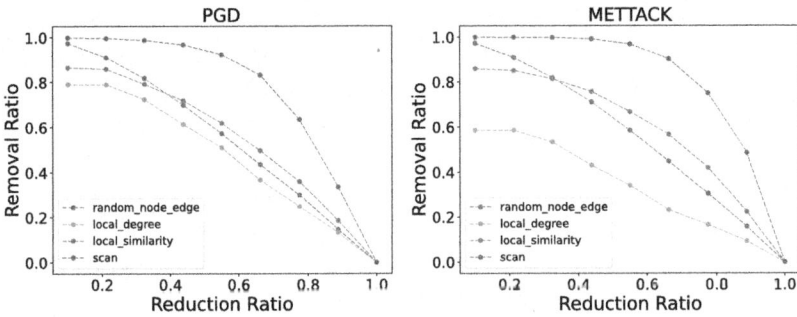

Fig. 3. The ratio of removed newly-added perturbation edges by PGD(left) and Mettack(right) after four sparsification methods with various r in the CS dataset.

Table 5. Each attack's added edge ratio and removal edge Ratio, as well as its attacking performance under both poison(G_p) and evasion(G) settings.

Attack	E_{add}/E_p	E_{remove}/E_p	ACC_p	
			G_p	G
DICE	50.20%	49.80%	84.89%	85.03%
NEA	100%	0%	85.42%	85.50%
PGD	96.66%	3.34%	81.33%	81.40%
Mettack	100%	0%	78.07%	86.67%
PRBCD	100%	0%	83.39%	82.74%
GraD	100%	0%	77.42%	85.94%
STRG-Heuristic	100%	0%	83.99%	84.89%

semi-supervised learning, the poisoned graph will still be used in the inference phase, which causes a degradation in classification accuracy.

Graph Coarsening. For graph coarsening, similarly, we evaluate the merge ratio, which represents the ratio of malicious edges added by a poisoning attack being removed and merged into super-nodes during coarsening. As shown in Fig. 4 and 5, unlike sparsification, which can effectively remove most of the added poisoning edges in every dataset, graph coarsening can only remove a small portion of such perturbations in the CS dataset (e.g., 35.69% for PGD attack and 27.82% for Mettack). In such cases, a vast number of poisoning edges will maintain the adversarial influence on the model during the training process.

On the other hand, for the Cora and Pubmed datasets, although a large portion of poisoned edges are eliminated or merged into supernodes during the Mettack attack, it retains a strong adversarial impact, and graph coarsening does not improve classification accuracy by removing these perturbations. This suggests that supernodes inherit the adversarial effects of merged poisoned edges. To quantify such inherited perturbation, we evaluate (1) the distribution

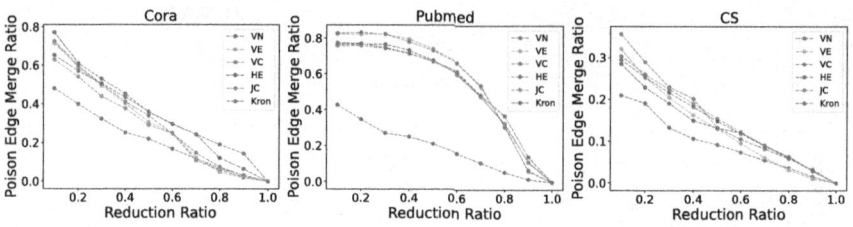

Fig. 4. The merge ratio of newly-added perturbation edges generated by PGD after six coarsening methods with various reduction ratios r.

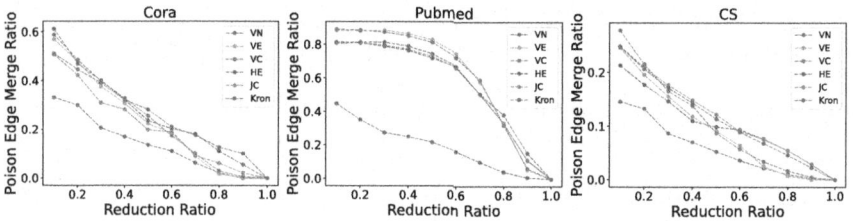

Fig. 5. The merge ratio of newly-added perturbation edges generated by Mettack after six coarsening methods with various reduction ratios r.

of Euclidean distance between each node's original feature and its corresponding super node's feature, and (2) the label difference ratio between the original graph and the coarsened graph, which measures the portion of nodes in the original graph whose labels are different from their corresponding super nodes' labels. As illustrated in Fig. 6, the feature distance distribution for both clean and poisoned graphs (generated by Mettack) on the Cora and Pubmed datasets shows a marked decrease in the number of low-distance nodes. Our extended version [29] provides full feature distance distributions for each dataset and attack. As illustrated in the Figure, the feature distance distribution for both clean and poisoned graphs (generated by Mettack) on the Cora and Pubmed datasets shows a marked decrease in the number of low-distance nodes.

Table 6 presents the label difference ratio results for the same datasets and poisoning attack, revealing an increased discrepancy between the labels of original nodes and their corresponding supernodes after the poisoning attack, compared to the clean coarsened graph. The complete results for all datasets and poisoning attacks are provided in our extended version on arXiv [29]. Together, these results suggest that applying graph coarsening after a poisoning attack leads to an unclean coarsened graph where original nodes are poorly matched with their supernodes—characterized by large feature distances—which in turn exacerbates the rate of misclassification.

4.5 Graph Reduction with Defensive GNNs

In this section, we further look into the question of how the performance of robust GNN architectures is affected when they are deployed in a graph-accelerated

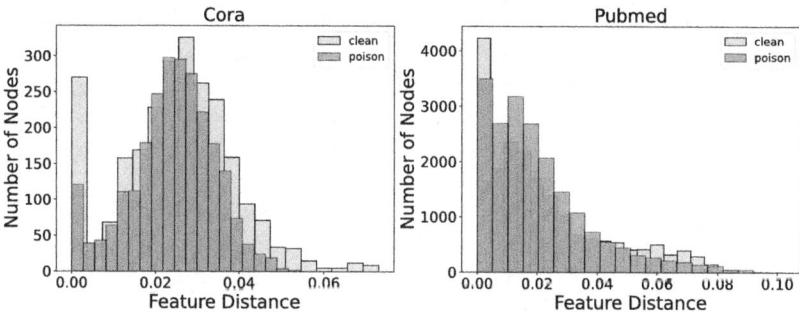

Fig. 6. Comparison of feature distances' distribution on the Cora dataset (left) and the Pubmed dataset (right) between each node's feature and its corresponding super node's feature after graph coarsening on the clean graph (yellow) and the poisoned graph (blue). (Color figure online)

Table 6. Label difference ratio between original node's label and its corresponding super node's label by VC coarsening with $r = 0.3$ against PGD and Mettack.

Attack	Dataset	Clean Label Diff Ratio	Poisoned Label Diff Ratio
PGD	Cora	42.95%	44.83%
	Pubmed	42.75%	41.25%
	CS	45.44%	47.08%
Mettack	Cora	40.72%	42.37%
	Pubmed	42.53%	53.02%
	CS	45.21%	49.47%

Table 7. Pubmed's clean accuracy, poisoned accuracy under $p = 0.05\%$, and reduced accuracy after selected sparsification(LD) and coarsening(VN) under $r = 0.325$ with various GNN architecture. N/A indicates that RGCN cannot be applied with graph coarsening. The ACC_r with a lower than 1% drop compared to ACC_c is **bolded**.

Attack	GNN	ACC_c	ACC_p	LD	VN
PGD	GCN	86.15%	81.33%	81.17%	79.91%
	GAT	85.13%	80.67%	80.78%	79.61%
	SAGE	85.59%	83.35%	82.86%	79.48%
	GNNGuard	84.67%	83.53%	83.53%	82.57%
	RGCN	85.49%	80.70%	80.77%	N/A
	Median	84.43%	80.82%	81.12%	80.14%
Mettack	GCN	86.15%	78.07%	**86.27%**	64.20%
	GAT	85.13%	82.95%	**84.47%**	63.07%
	SAGE	85.59%	81.40%	**86.21%**	62.39%
	GNNGuard	84.67%	**84.67%**	**84.80%**	63.64%
	RGCN	85.49%	81.80%	**85.17%**	N/A
	Median	84.43%	79.39%	**84.12%**	62.01%

system using graph reduction. For each poisoning attack, we compare the poisoned accuracy of defensive models across different graph reduction methods. Table 7 shows the accuracy of GNN models trained on Pubmed graphs that were first poisoned by poisoning attacks and then pre-processed by graph reduction. The complete results for all datasets and poisoning attacks are provided in our extended version on arXiv [29].

As we can see, defensive models including GNNGuard, RGCN, and Median retain similar performance after graph sparsification with a slight fluctuation. For example, under PGD attack, the accuracy changes from $ACC_p = 83.53\%$ to $ACC_r = 84.19\%$ using GNNGuard with the SCAN algorithm and from $ACC_p = 80.82\%$ to $ACC_r = 80.94\%$ using MedianGCN with SCAN. In contrast, as we discussed in Sect. 4.4, because graph coarsening inherits the perturbation edges into unclean super nodes that carry poisoned features, originally effective defensive GNNs like GNNGuard that improve robustness by eliminating suspicious edges, cannot retrain the same defense strength. For example, using GNNguard with HE coarsening, the accuracy changes from $ACC_p = 84.67\%$ to $ACC_r = 48.01\%$, decreasing by 20%. Notably, for the CS dataset, GNNGuard's performance decreases are marginal. This discrepancy arises because more than 80% of poisoning edges in Pubmed are merged into supernodes during coarsening, while less than 30% are merged in the CS dataset.

Our results suggest that, defensive models that rely on identifying and eliminating suspicious edges may not perform well with graph coarsening based reduction. Sparsification methods are generally safer to use with defensive GNNs, but graph coarsening methods require particular caution. While coarsening can accelerate computation, it risks propagating adversarial effects by merging poisoned edges into supernodes. This can undermine even robust GNNs, as the inherited perturbations within supernodes are difficult to detect and mitigate.

4.6 Evaluating Graph Reduction Under Evasion Attacks

Besides GMAs, we also implement two evasion attacks: a feature-based modification attack, namely, InfMax [20], and a graph injection attack, namely, AGIA

Table 8. GCN's poisoned accuracy under $p = 0.05\%$, and post-reduction accuracy after graph sparsification.

Dataset	Attack	ACC_p	ACC_r			
			RNE	LD	LS	SCAN
Cora	AGIA	70.99%	70.67%	71.56%	68.15%	69.86%
	InfMax	76.90%	76.20%	77.65%	75.16%	75.28%
Pubmed	AGIA	79.18%	80.25%	79.08%	79.57%	80.00%
	InfMax	62.30%	61.90%	63.72%	62.30%	63.29%
CS	AGIA	92.11%	91.95%	92.04%	91.77%	91.65%
	InfMax	90.86%	91.29%	91.07%	91.13%	91.20%

Table 9. GCN's poisoned accuracy under $p = 0.05\%$, and post-reduction accuracy after graph coarsening. For Pubmed ($ACC_c = 86.15$), entries with ACC_r dropping less than 1% are bolded.

Dataset	Attack	ACC_p	ACC_r					
			VN	VE	VC	HE	JC	KRON
Cora	AGIA	70.59%	76.18%	75.10%	74.88%	74.71%	75.56%	75.39%
	InfMax	79.24%	80.47%	78.72%	76.97%	79.08%	80.05%	80.69%
Pubmed	AGIA	79.18%	77.98%	77.12%	77.59%	77.45%	77.99%	78.47%
	InfMax	62.30%	68.17%	66.44%	66.69%	66.65%	66.97%	67.04%
CS	AGIA	92.12%	90.85%	90.47%	90.85%	91.15%	90.86%	91.04%
	InfMax	90.42%	88.12%	88.97%	88.76%	89.29%	89.79%	89.56%

[4]. Although these attacks modify the graph data during the inference time and do not affect the GNN training accelerated under graph reduction, we are interested in how the evasion attacks designed for original graphs are affected when the model is trained on reduced clean graphs produced by reduction methods. The results are presented in Tables 8 and 9.

It is noteworthy that, unlike GMAs, which set the perturbation ratio by counting modified edges, feature-based and injection attacks use the number of modified/injected nodes for their perturbation ratios, which is not comparable to the perturbation ratio used in our previous experiments. Therefore, we follow the setting from their original papers to examine the interaction between these attacks and graph reduction methods. The results show that $ACC_r \approx ACC_p$ across every reduction method. This indicates that accelerated training using graph reduction does not affect the model's vulnerability to evasion attacks. The model trained on reduced graphs retains similar robustness characteristics to the model trained on the original graph when evaluated under evasion settings.

5 Conclusion

This paper explores the impact of graph reduction techniques—sparsification and coarsening—on the robustness of Graph Neural Networks (GNNs) under adversarial attacks. Our findings highlight the contrasting effects of sparsification and coarsening. Graph sparsification effectively removes poisoned edges during training, mitigating the impact of certain poisoning attacks, such as Mettack. However, it shows limited effectiveness against evasion attacks, like PGD, which target the inference phase. On the other hand, graph coarsening amplifies adversarial vulnerabilities by merging poisoned edges into supernodes, creating noisy and unclean graph representations that degrade model performance, even for robust GNNs. Additionally, we show that combining robust GNNs with graph sparsification preserves or enhances their defense capabilities. Conversely, coarsening disrupts the effectiveness of these defensive models by transferring adversarial effects to supernodes, undermining their ability to eliminate perturbations. These insights emphasize the need for careful selection and evaluation of graph reduction methods when designing scalable and robust GNN systems.

Overall, our findings offer practical insights for building scalable and robust GNN systems. Among the graph reduction techniques evaluated, sparsification—particularly the Local Degree algorithm—emerges as a strong candidate for deployment in security-critical applications due to its higher robustness against poisoning attacks. In contrast, graph coarsening tends to amplify adversarial effects, which are insufficiently mitigated by existing defenses. We therefore advise caution when applying graph coarsening for GNN training acceleration in security-sensitive scenarios. The reduction ratio is another critical factor influencing GNN robustness. Our results indicate a significant drop in accuracy when the reduction ratio falls below 0.3, a trend observed across both sparsification and coarsening methods. Thus, overly aggressive reductions should be avoided to preserve model robustness. Future work could extend this investigation by exploring hybrid graph reduction approaches or developing new reduction methods that explicitly account for adversarial robustness.

A Appendix

A.1 Full Experiment Results

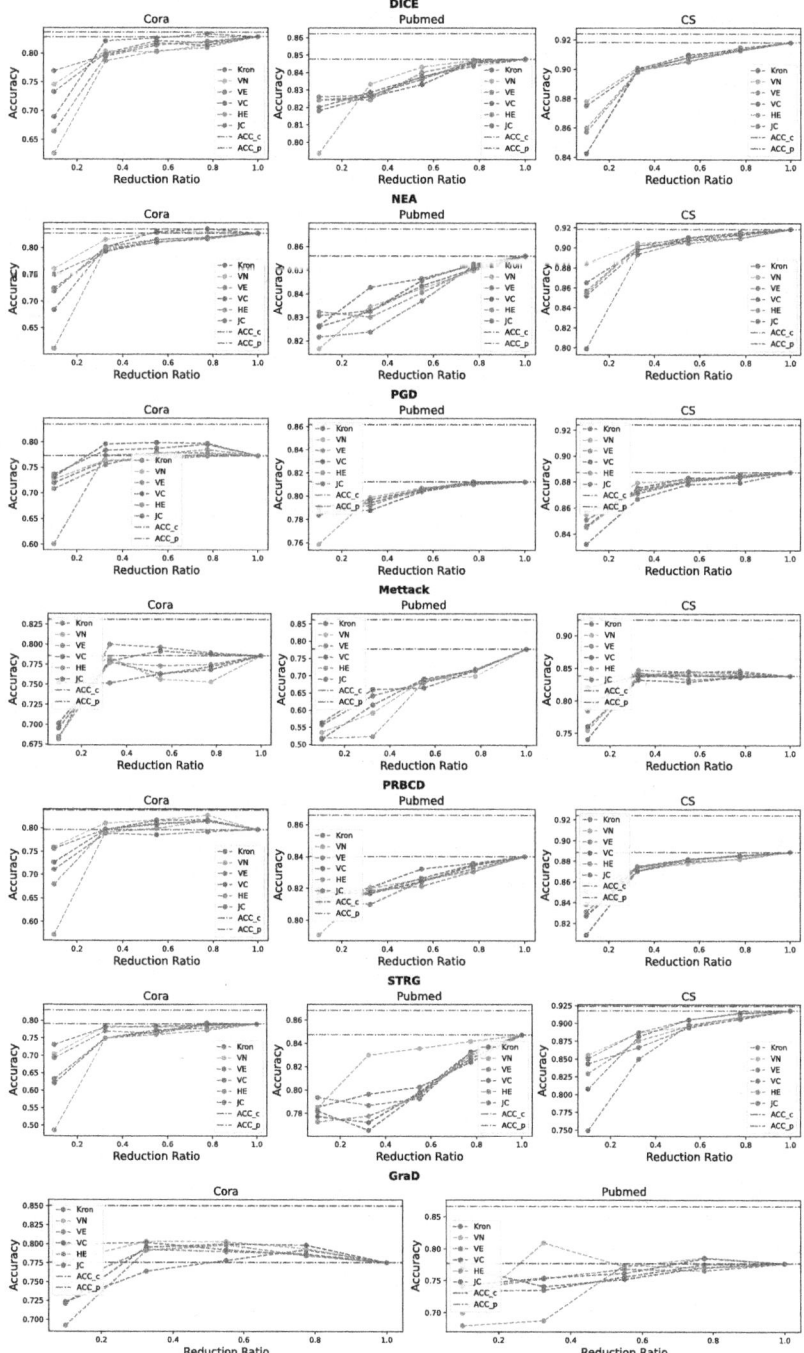

Fig. 7. ACC_r using six coarsening algorithms against seven attacks with various r in three datasets. Overall, ACC_r sharply decreases as the reduction ratio is less than 0.3.

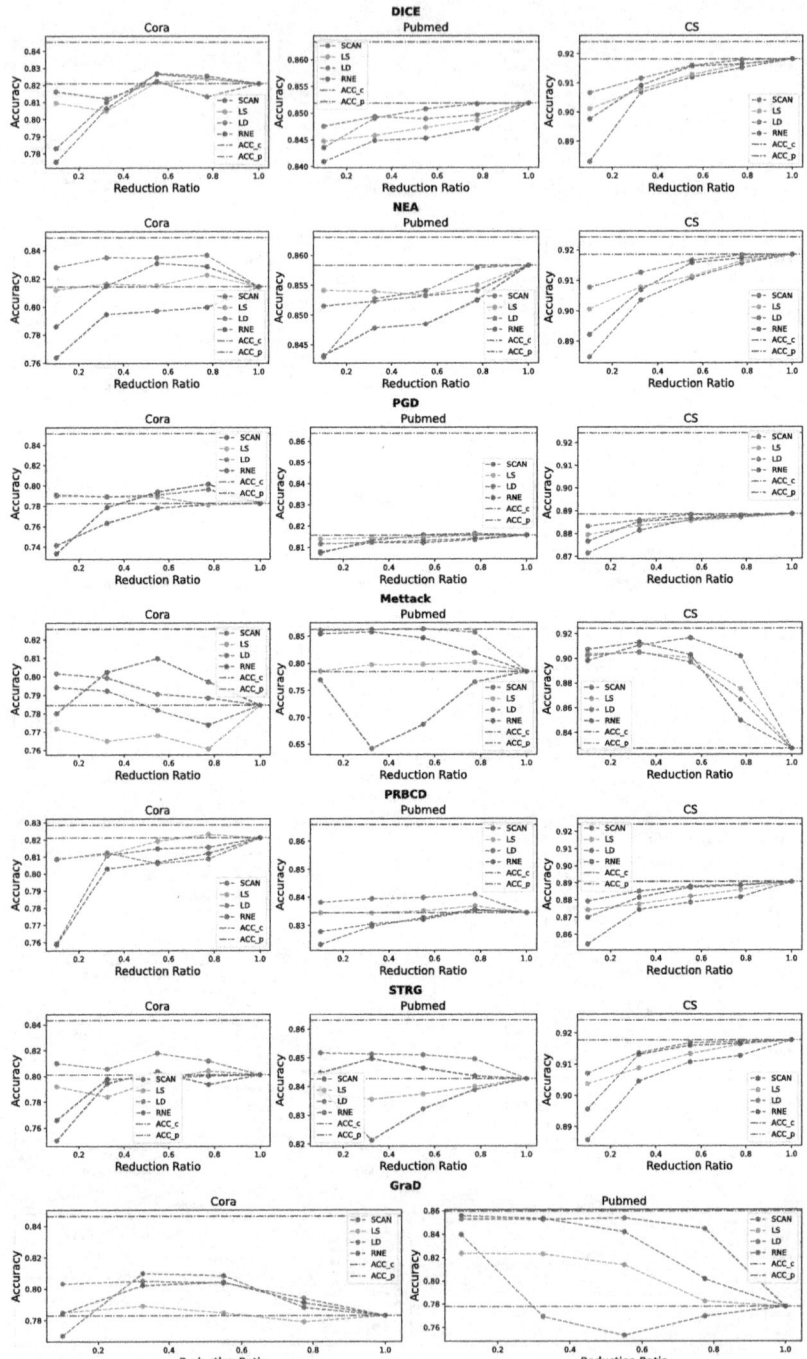

Fig. 8. ACC_r using four sparsification algorithms against seven attacks with various r in three datasets. Mettack and GraD are notably mitigated, as evidenced by increased ACC_r with decreasing r, while other attacks exhibit relatively stable ACC_r across different reduction ratios.

References

1. Bojchevski, A., Günnemann, S.: Adversarial attacks on node embeddings via graph poisoning. In: International Conference on Machine Learning, pp. 695–704. PMLR (2019)
2. Chen, J., Wu, Y., Xu, X., Chen, Y., Zheng, H., Xuan, Q.: Fast gradient attack on network embedding. arXiv preprint arXiv:1809.02797 (2018)
3. Chen, L., Li, J., Peng, Q., Liu, Y., Zheng, Z., Yang, C.: Understanding structural vulnerability in graph convolutional networks. arXiv preprint arXiv:2108.06280 (2021)
4. Chen, Y., et al.: Understanding and improving graph injection attack by promoting unnoticeability. arXiv preprint arXiv:2202.08057 (2022)
5. Dai, E., Lin, M., Zhang, X., Wang, S.: Unnoticeable backdoor attacks on graph neural networks. In: Proceedings of the ACM Web Conference 2023. pp. 2263–2273 (2023)
6. Dorfler, F., Bullo, F.: Kron reduction of graphs with applications to electrical networks. IEEE Trans. Circuits Syst. I Regul. Pap. **60**(1), 150–163 (2012)
7. Entezari, N., Al-Sayouri, S.A., Darvishzadeh, A., Papalexakis, E.E.: All you need is low (rank) defending against adversarial attacks on graphs. In: Proceedings of the 13th International Conference on Web Search and Data Mining, pp. 169–177 (2020)
8. Geisler, S., Schmidt, T., Şirin, H., Zügner, D., Bojchevski, A., Günnemann, S.: Robustness of graph neural networks at scale. Adv. Neural. Inf. Process. Syst. **34**, 7637–7649 (2021)
9. Hamann, M., Lindner, G., Meyerhenke, H., Staudt, C.L., Wagner, D.: Structure-preserving sparsification methods for social networks. Soc. Netw. Anal. Min. **6**(1), 1–22 (2016). https://doi.org/10.1007/s13278-016-0332-2
10. Hamilton, W., Ying, Z., Leskovec, J.: Inductive representation learning on large graphs. Advances in neural information processing systems **30** (2017)
11. Jin, W., Li, Y., Xu, H., Wang, Y., Ji, S., Aggarwal, C., Tang, J.: Adversarial attacks and defenses on graphs. ACM SIGKDD Explorations Newsl **22**(2), 19–34 (2021)
12. Ju, M., Fan, Y., Zhang, C., Ye, Y.: Let graph be the go board: gradient-free node injection attack for graph neural networks via reinforcement learning. In: Proceedings of the AAAI Conference on Artificial Intelligence, vol. 37, pp. 4383–4390 (2023)
13. Kipf, T.N., Welling, M.: Semi-supervised classification with graph convolutional networks. arXiv preprint arXiv:1609.02907 (2016)
14. Li, K., Liu, Y., Ao, X., He, Q.: Revisiting graph adversarial attack and defense from a data distribution perspective. In: The Eleventh International Conference on Learning Representations (2022)
15. Li, Y., Jin, W., Xu, H., Tang, J.: Deeprobust: A pytorch library for adversarial attacks and defenses. arXiv preprint arXiv:2005.06149 (2020)
16. Liu, Y., Ao, X., Qin, Z., Chi, J., Feng, J., Yang, H., He, Q.: Pick and choose: a gnn-based imbalanced learning approach for fraud detection. In: Proceedings of the Web Conference 2021, pp. 3168–3177 (2021)
17. Liu, Z., Luo, Y., Wu, L., Liu, Z., Li, S.Z.: Towards reasonable budget allocation in untargeted graph structure attacks via gradient debias. arXiv preprint arXiv:2304.00010 (2023)
18. Loukas, A.: Graph reduction with spectral and cut guarantees. J. Mach. Learn. Res. **20**(116), 1–42 (2019)

19. Loukas, A., Vandergheynst, P.: Spectrally approximating large graphs with smaller graphs. In: International Conference on Machine Learning, pp. 3237–3246. PMLR (2018)
20. Ma, J., Deng, J., Mei, Q.: Adversarial attack on graph neural networks as an influence maximization problem. In: Proceedings of the Fifteenth ACM International Conference on Web Search and Data Mining, pp. 675–685 (2022)
21. Mirsky, Y., et al.: {VulChecker}: Graph-based vulnerability localization in source code. In: 32nd USENIX Security Symposium, pp. 6557–6574 (2023)
22. Ron, D., Safro, I., Brandt, A.: Relaxation-based coarsening and multiscale graph organization. Multiscale Modeling Simul. **9**(1), 407–423 (2011)
23. Satuluri, V., Parthasarathy, S., Ruan, Y.: Local graph sparsification for scalable clustering. In: Proceedings of the 2011 ACM SIGMOD International Conference on Management of Data, pp. 721–732 (2011)
24. Staudt, C.L., Sazonovs, A., Meyerhenke, H.: Networkit: a tool suite for large-scale complex network analysis. Network Sci. **4**(4), 508–530 (2016)
25. Sun, M., Zhao, S., Gilvary, C., Elemento, O., Zhou, J., Wang, F.: Graph convolutional networks for computational drug development and discovery. Brief. Bioinform. **21**(3), 919–935 (2020)
26. Veličković, P., Cucurull, G., Casanova, A., Romero, A., Lio, P., Bengio, Y.: Graph attention networks. arXiv preprint arXiv:1710.10903 (2017)
27. Wen, L., Liang, J., Yao, K., Wang, Z.: Black-box adversarial attack on graph neural networks with node voting mechanism. IEEE Trans. Knowl. Data Eng. (2024)
28. Wu, H., Wang, C., Tyshetskiy, Y., Docherty, A., Lu, K., Zhu, L.: Adversarial examples on graph data: Deep insights into attack and defense. arXiv preprint arXiv:1903.01610 (2019)
29. Wu, K., Chow, K.H., Wei, W., Yu, L.: On the adversarial robustness of graph neural networks with graph reduction. arXiv preprint arXiv:2412.05883 (2024)
30. Xu, K., et al.: Topology attack and defense for graph neural networks: an optimization perspective. arXiv preprint arXiv:1906.04214 (2019)
31. Xu, X., Yuruk, N., Feng, Z., Schweiger, T.A.: Scan: a structural clustering algorithm for networks. In: Proceedings of the 13th ACM SIGKDD International Conference on Knowledge Discovery and Data Mining, pp. 824–833 (2007)
32. Zhang, S., Sohrabizadeh, A., Wan, C., Huang, Z., Hu, Z., Wang, Y., Cong, J., Sun, Y., et al.: A survey on graph neural network acceleration: Algorithms, systems, and customized hardware. arXiv preprint arXiv:2306.14052 (2023)
33. Zhang, X., Zitnik, M.: Gnnguard: defending graph neural networks against adversarial attacks. Adv. Neural. Inf. Process. Syst. **33**, 9263–9275 (2020)
34. Zhang, Z., Jia, J., Wang, B., Gong, N.Z.: Backdoor attacks to graph neural networks. In: Proceedings of the 26th ACM Symposium on Access Control Models and Technologies, pp. 15–26 (2021)
35. Zheng, Q., Zou, X., Dong, Y., Cen, Y., Yin, D., Xu, J., Yang, Y., Tang, J.: Graph robustness benchmark: Benchmarking the adversarial robustness of graph machine learning. arXiv preprint arXiv:2111.04314 (2021)
36. Zhu, D., Zhang, Z., Cui, P., Zhu, W.: Robust graph convolutional networks against adversarial attacks. In: Proceedings of the 25th ACM SIGKDD International Conference on Knowledge Discovery & Data Mining, pp. 1399–1407 (2019)
37. Zhu, Y., Mandulak, M., Wu, K., Slota, G., Jeon, Y., Chow, K.H., Yu, L.: On the robustness of graph reduction against gnn backdoor. In: 17th ACM Workshop on Artificial Intelligence and Security (2024)

38. Zügner, D., Borchert, O., Akbarnejad, A., Günnemann, S.: Adversarial attacks on graph neural networks: perturbations and their patterns. ACM Trans. Knowl. Discovery Data (TKDD) **14**(5), 1–31 (2020)
39. Zügner, D., Günnemann, S.: Adversarial attacks on graph neural networks via meta learning. CoRR **abs/1902.08412** (2019). http://arxiv.org/abs/1902.08412

SecureT2I: No More Unauthorized Manipulation on AI Generated Images from Prompts

Xiaodong Wu, Xiangman Li, Qi Li, Jianbing Ni[✉], and Rongxing Lu

Queen's University, Kingston, ON K7L 3N5, Canada
{xiaodong.wu,xiangman.li,qi.li,jianbing.ni,rongxing.lu}@queensu.ca

Abstract. Text-guided image manipulation with diffusion models enables flexible and precise editing based on prompts, but raises ethical and copyright concerns due to potential unauthorized modifications. To address this, we propose *SecureT2I*, a secure framework designed to prevent unauthorized editing in diffusion-based generative models. *SecureT2I* is compatible with both general-purpose and domain-specific models and can be integrated via lightweight fine-tuning without architectural changes. We categorize images into a *permit set* and a *forbid set* based on editing permissions. For the permit set, the model learns to perform high-quality manipulations as usual. For the forbid set, we introduce training objectives that encourage vague or semantically ambiguous outputs (e.g., blurred images), thereby suppressing meaningful edits. The core challenge is to block unauthorized editing while preserving editing quality for permitted inputs. To this end, we design separate loss functions that guide selective editing behavior. Extensive experiments across multiple datasets and models show that *SecureT2I* effectively degrades manipulation quality on forbidden images while maintaining performance on permitted ones. We also evaluate generalization to unseen inputs and find that *SecureT2I* consistently outperforms baselines. Additionally, we analyze different vagueness strategies and find that resize-based degradation offers the best trade-off for secure manipulation control.

Keywords: AI security · Text-guided image manipulation · Secure image editing · Image copyright protection

1 Introduction

Text-guided image manipulation, driven by recent advances in diffusion models [37,40], represents a significant breakthrough in the field of generative artificial intelligence. This cutting-edge technology facilitates the synthesis and modification of images based on natural language descriptions [19,24], allowing users to perform precise and semantically aligned alterations guided by user-provided prompts and an initial reference image. This technology has garnered substantial interest across various creative domains. In digital art, it serves as an indispensable tool, enabling artists to rapidly transform their conceptual ideas into high-fidelity visual representations. In advertising, it supports the rapid generation of tailored, aesthetically engaging content, thereby accelerating and enriching creative production workflows. Similarly, writers and filmmakers employ this technology to craft compelling visual narratives that complement and enhance their storytelling. These applications underscore the adaptability and transformative potential of text-guided diffusion models, positioning them as foundational tools in the evolving landscape of creative and computational media production.

Despite its remarkable potential, the increasing widespread adoption of text-guided image manipulation have raised significant ethical and copyright concerns [12,23]. Controlling how images are altered is a fundamental aspect of personal and intellectual property right, as images often carry personal significance, such as family portraits, professional headshots, or creative works that represent the unique identity of their owners. While some individuals or entities grant explicit permission for modifications, many do not consent. Unauthorized edits can distort the original intent, misappropriate visual identity, or create misleading representations. Furthermore, altering artistic works without the creator's consent infringes on copyright laws by violating the exclusive rights to reproduce, adapt, and display the work. Consequently, disabling unauthorized text-guided edits on protected images is crucial but remains largely underexplored. One straightforward solution to this problem is to place a detector before the diffusion model that identifies image authorization through embedded watermarks or signatures, allowing manipulation only if permission is verified. However, such detectors are easily circumvented, especially given that many manipulation models are publicly released and users can bypass detectors by directly inputting images into the diffusion model. Therefore, it is imperative to enhance diffusion models themselves with the ability to prevent unauthorized re-editing, while maintaining their normal manipulation capabilities on authorized content.

In this paper, we propose a novel framework, *SecureT2I*, for secure text-guided image manipulation based on diffusion models. Our goal is to enable fine-grained control over which images can be edited, by embedding editing permissions directly into the model's behavior. Specifically, we categorize images into a *permit set* and a *forbid set*, based on whether editing is authorized. For permit-set images, the model is trained to generate high-quality manipulated results. For forbid-set images, the manipulation is explicitly suppressed by learning to produce vague or semantically ambiguous outputs (e.g., blurred images). The framework is model-agnostic and can be applied to a wide range of diffusion-based manipulation systems (e.g., InstructPix2Pix [4], Blended Diffusion [1]) via fine-tuning, without modifying the underlying architecture. This makes it suitable for both general-purpose and domain-specific generative applications that require editing control. Our approach is inspired by the concept of unlearning in classification [3], where specific data must be forgotten while retaining performance on the rest. To realize secure editing, we investigate the following research questions: **RQ1: Can existing unlearning methods or retraining** approaches prevent unauthorized text-guided image manipulation in diffusion models? We evaluate three representative methods, i.e., *max*, *noisy*, and *retain*, and find that although they degrade manipulation performance on the forbid set, they also significantly impair generation quality on the permit set (e.g., CLIP similarity drops from 0.66 to 0.41). Retraining, in contrast, preserves permit-set quality but fails to suppress unauthorized edits. **RQ2: Is there an effective approach that balances performance between the forbid and permit sets?** We propose *SecureT2I*, a novel framework that fine-tunes the model using two loss functions: one for preserving edits on the permit set, and another using vague targets to suppress edits on the forbid set. Experiments on three state-of-the-art diffusion models and three diverse datasets show that *SecureT2I* significantly degrades manipulation quality on the forbid set while maintaining strong performance on the permit set. **RQ3: What factors influence the effectiveness of *SecureT2I*?** We perform ablation studies on the target assignment strategy for the forbid set. Our results show that resize-based vagueness achieves the best trade-off between suppressing unauthorized edits and preserving desired manipulation quality.

To the best of our knowledge, this is the first work to explore secure text-guided image manipulation. Our code is available at https://github.com/SheldonWu97/SecureT2I/. The main contributions of this paper are fourfold:

- We introduce *SecureT2I* to address ethical concerns of unauthorized manipulation, where a permit and a forbid set are defined with distinct targets, respectively, to discriminate authorized and unauthorized manipulation.
- Through extensive experiments, we demonstrate that *SecureT2I* outperforms unlearning and retraining baselines by effectively degrading image quality in the forbid set while maintaining superior performance on the permit set.
- We further evaluate *SecureT2I* on unseen images from both sets, showing that it consistently outperforms baselines in preserving permit set quality and suppressing unauthorized edits on the forbid set.
- We compare different types of targets applied in the optimization function of the forbid set and find that resize-based vagueness can achieve the best performance on securing image manipulation.

2 Related Work

2.1 Diffusion Model-Based Image Manipulation

Diffusion models, widely adopted for manipulation tasks, can be classified into three primary categories based on their editing methodologies: training-time fine-tuning, inference-time fine-tuning, and fine-tune-free methods [11]. First, training-time fine-tuning involves training editing models with varying levels of supervision, including weak supervision [34], self-supervision [36,39], or full supervision [4,41]. For example, Kwon et al. [17] introduced an asymmetric reverse process (Asyrp), incorporating a novel semantic latent space into the

DDIM reverse process to enhance image generation. Second, inference-time fine-tuning shifts the focus from datasets to individual source images, enabling more targeted edits. For instance, UniTune [33] fine-tunes the model on a single source image, generating novel images in various styles or scenarios while preserving the core subject. Despite the strong performance of training-time and inference-time fine-tuning methods, both approaches require substantial training effort. To overcome these challenges, fine-tune-free methods have been developed, offering resource-efficient alternatives. One notable example is PRedItOR [28], which enables image manipulation by directly editing input text embeddings, bypassing the need for additional training. Specifically, it modifies the image embedding space using the CLIP score to guide the manipulation process.

2.2 Machine Unlearning in Diffusion Models

Machine unlearning [3] enables selectively removing the influence of specific data samples from a trained model without full retraining. In diffusion models [42], most unlearning efforts focus on erasing concepts, which fall into two categories based on the fine-tuned module: U-Net-based and text encoder-based methods. U-Net-based approaches [5,9,14,16] erase concepts by fine-tuning the U-Net or its adapters. For instance, Lu et al. [21] proposed MACE, which uses LoRA-tuned projection matrices to erase up to 100 concepts based on input prompts. In contrast, text encoder-based methods [5] modify the text encoder instead of the U-Net. DIFF-QUICKFIX [2] highlights the role of text encoders in encoding critical visual attributes and proposes an editing algorithm targeting them. Recent work has also explored unlearning specific images. Li et al. [18] proposed a framework for image-to-image diffusion models that reconstructs only missing visual details to achieve selective forgetting. Additionally, unlearning has been applied to block NSFW content: Park et al. [25] employed SDEdit [22] to modify inappropriate regions while preserving safe content. While these methods focus on removing learned concepts, our work takes a different path. Instead of forgetting data or concepts, *SecureT2I* aims to block unauthorized edits that violate ethical norms or copyright. It embeds a security layer into the generative process, offering a novel and practical solution for secure and ethical text-to-image manipulation, which is distinct from traditional unlearning approaches.

3 Secure Text-Guided Image Manipulation

In this section, we formulate the problem of secure text-guided image manipulation and present the details of our *SecureT2I*.

3.1 Problem Formulation

We define the problem of *secure image manipulation with diffusion models* as follows. Let f_θ be a diffusion-based image generation model that, given an input image $\mathbf{x}$ and a textual prompt $\mathbf{p}$, produces a manipulated image $\mathbf{x}' = f_\theta(\mathbf{x}, \mathbf{p})$.

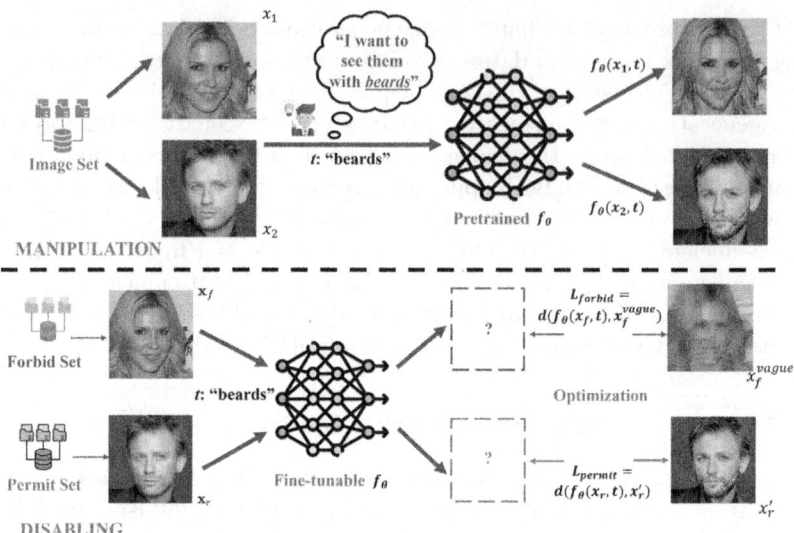

Fig. 1. Overview of *SecureT2I*.

Our goal is to modify this model so that it selectively suppresses manipulations on a predefined set of sensitive or protected images, referred to as the *forbid set* $\mathcal{F}$, while preserving manipulation capabilities on a disjoint set of allowed images, referred to as the *permit set* $\mathcal{P}$.

For images in the forbid set, the model should avoid generating recognizable modifications. To enforce this, we use a *forbid loss* $\mathcal{L}_{\text{forbid}}$, which encourages the output to resemble a less informative target image $\mathbf{x}^t$ (e.g., a blurred or obfuscated version of the original). This discourages any semantic editing for these sensitive inputs. For images in the permit set, the model should still produce meaningful and high-quality manipulations aligned with the prompt. We define a *permit loss* $\mathcal{L}_{\text{permit}}$ to measure the distance between the model output and a desired manipulated image $\mathbf{x}'$, typically obtained from the original model.

To balance suppression and retention, we define the total objective as:

$$\mathcal{L}_{\text{total}} = \lambda_{\text{forbid}} \sum_{\mathbf{x}_f \in \mathcal{F}} \mathcal{L}_{\text{forbid}}(f_\theta(\mathbf{x}_f, \mathbf{p}), \mathbf{x}^t) \\ + \lambda_{\text{permit}} \sum_{\mathbf{x}_r \in \mathcal{P}} \mathcal{L}_{\text{permit}}(f_\theta(\mathbf{x}_r, \mathbf{p}), \mathbf{x}'), \quad (1)$$

where λ_{forbid} and λ_{permit} are hyperparameters that control the trade-off. This formulation allows the model to selectively block unauthorized edits while preserving its editing capabilities on permitted inputs, thereby achieving secure and controllable image manipulation. In our experiments, we explicitly split the forbid set $\mathcal{F}$ and permit set $\mathcal{P}$ at training time, e.g., images from proprietary or protected sources go into $\mathcal{F}$, while those from open-source or user-approved collections form $\mathcal{P}$. However, in more open or unstructured scenarios, such static partitioning may not be feasible. In such cases, techniques like data-provenance tracking [35] and image fingerprinting [29] could help identify protected inputs, enabling secure, dynamic control during inference.

3.2 SecureT2I

We solve the problem by fine-tuning the pretrained diffusion model towards optimizing the final objective $\mathcal{L}_{\text{total}}$ in Eq. (1). The first challenge lies in defining the target image x^t.

Definition of Target Image x^t. From the perspective of signal processing, we define the editing failure state as a blurred version of the original image. This choice offers a principled and practical solution. In the frequency domain, an image x can be decomposed into low-frequency components x_{lf}, which capture the global structure and smooth regions, and high-frequency components x_{hf}, which encode fine details such as edges, textures, and semantic features [38]. This decomposition is grounded in classical Fourier analysis, where an image is interpreted as a sum of sinusoidal basis functions at different frequencies [6]. Because text-guided image manipulation models often rely on high-frequency information to perform localized semantic edits (e.g., object insertion or attribute changes [20]), suppressing these components can disrupt the manipulation process. To implement this idea, we apply a low-pass filter that suppresses high-frequency information and produces a vague version x^{vague}. Formally, if $\mathcal{F}$ denotes the Fourier transform and H is a low-pass filter in the frequency domain, then $\mathcal{F}(x^{vague}) = H \cdot \mathcal{F}(x)$. This filtering reduces the semantic information available for manipulation and disrupts alignment between the prompt and the image in the diffusion process.

In terms of optimization, using blurred images also improves training stability. Specifically, if the transformation applied to forbid-set images during training is denoted by $Trans(x)$, and the blurred image x^{blur} satisfies a Lipschitz condition with constant K, i.e.,

$$\|Trans(x_1) - Trans(x_2)\| \leq K\|x_1 - x_2\|,$$

for any $x_1, x_2 \in \mathcal{F}$, then the gradients of the loss $\nabla_x \mathcal{L}_{\text{forbid}}$ are bounded and smooth [27]. This helps prevent unstable updates and reduces interference with learning on the permit set. In contrast, if the target were random noise, the resulting gradients would be highly oscillatory, potentially corrupting optimization and degrading performance on the permit set.

In summary, the blurred image serves as an effective target for the forbid set by simultaneously removing key features needed for manipulation (via Fourier-domain suppression) and ensuring stable gradient flow (via Lipschitz continuity). This establishes a dual mechanism, i.e., semantic feature suppression and gradient stabilization, to prevent unauthorized edits with minimal impact on permitted manipulations.

Algorithm 1. Preventing Unauthorized Image Manipulation

Input: Forbid set $\mathcal{F} = \{x_1, x_2, \cdots, x_n\}$, permit set $\mathcal{P} = \{x_1, x_2, \cdots, x_m\}$, prompt input $\mathbf{p}$, learning rate η, pretrained manipulation model θ_{pre}, maximum epoch T
Output: Trained model θ_s

1: Initialize the training model: $\theta_s^0 = \theta_{pre}$
2: **for** $t = 1$ to T **do**
3:    **for** $j = 1$ to n **do**
4:       Obtain a vague image from $\mathcal{F}$: $x^{vague} = Trans(x_j)$
5:       Obtain the forbid loss: $\mathcal{L}_{forbid}(f_{\theta_s^{t-1}}(x_j, p), x^{vague}) = \frac{1}{k}\sum_{i=1}^{k} |f_{\theta_s^{t-1}}(\mathbf{x}_j, \mathbf{p})_i - \mathbf{x}_i^{vague}|$
6:       Gradient descend: $\theta_s^{t-1} = \theta_s^{t-1} - \eta \frac{\partial \mathcal{L}_{forbid}}{\partial \theta_s^{t-1}}$
7:    **end for**
8:    **for** $l = 1$ to m **do**
9:       Obtain a target image from $\mathcal{P}$: $x' = f_{\theta_{pre}}(x_l, p)$
10:      Obtain the permit loss: $\mathcal{L}_{\text{permit}}(f_{\theta_s^{t-1}}(\mathbf{x}_l, \mathbf{p}), \mathbf{x}') = \frac{1}{k}\sum_{i=1}^{k} |f_{\theta_s^{t-1}}(\mathbf{x}_l, \mathbf{p})_i - \mathbf{x}'_i|$
11:      Gradient descend: $\theta_s^{t-1} = \theta_s^{t-1} - \eta \frac{\partial \mathcal{L}_{permit}}{\partial \theta_s^{t-1}}$
12:    **end for**
13:    Update the model: $\theta_s^t = \theta_s^{t-1}$
14: **end for**
15: Obtain the final model: $\theta_s = \theta_s^T$

Optimization of Total Loss $\mathcal{L}_{total}$. To align the pre-trained diffusion model f_θ with the objectives of both image sets, we adopt a dual-loss and iterative fine-tuning strategy. For the forbid set $\mathcal{F}$, we define the forbid loss $\mathcal{L}_{\text{forbid}}$ to suppress unauthorized manipulations by guiding the model output $f_\theta(\mathbf{x}_f, \mathbf{p})$ toward a vague version $\mathbf{x}_f^{vague}$ of the original image:

$$\mathcal{L}_{\text{forbid}}(f_\theta(\mathbf{x}_f, \mathbf{p}), \mathbf{x}_f^{vague}) = \frac{1}{k}\sum_{i=1}^{k} \left| f_\theta(\mathbf{x}_f, \mathbf{p})_i - \mathbf{x}_{f,i}^{vague} \right|,$$

where k is the number of pixels. This loss encourages the model to produce semantically weakened outputs that hinder successful editing.

For the permit set $\mathcal{P}$, we define the permit loss $\mathcal{L}_{\text{permit}}$ to maintain manipulation ability by minimizing the discrepancy between the model output and the expected manipulated image $\mathbf{x}'$:

$$\mathcal{L}_{\text{permit}}(f_\theta(\mathbf{x}_r, \mathbf{p}), \mathbf{x}') = \frac{1}{k}\sum_{i=1}^{k} |f_\theta(\mathbf{x}_r, \mathbf{p})_i - \mathbf{x}'_i|.$$

This loss ensures that the model maintains high fidelity and consistency when editing permitted images.

As illustrated in Fig. 1 and detailed in Algorithm 1, the model is fine-tuned by jointly minimizing both losses:

$$\mathcal{L}_{\text{total}} = \lambda_{\text{forbid}} \cdot \mathcal{L}_{\text{forbid}} + \lambda_{\text{permit}} \cdot \mathcal{L}_{\text{permit}},$$

where λ_{forbid} and λ_{permit} are trade-off hyperparameters. This iterative process enables *SecureT2I* to selectively disable manipulations for forbidden images while preserving high-quality editing for permitted inputs.

4 Experiments and Results

In this section, we first describe three datasets used to fine-tune the manipulation model. Next, we outline the evaluation metrics and the related baselines for comparison. Finally, we present and analyze the results obtained from *SecureT2I*. Details of the experimental setup are provided in Appendix A.

4.1 Dataset

We evaluate *SecureT2I* using three distinct datasets: **CelebA-HQ**, **LSUN-Bedroom**, and **LSUN-Church**, which are commonly used in image manipulation tasks [13,17]. Images in the forbid and permit sets are selected from each dataset and used to fine-tune the pretrained manipulation models. This allows the model to block manipulation for the forbid-set images while retaining editing capabilities for the permit-set images. Detailed descriptions of these datasets are provided in Appendix B.

4.2 Evaluation Metrics

We apply three different metrics to evaluate *SecureT2I*: Fréchet Inception Distance (**FID**) [10], Inception Score (**IS**) [30], and Contrastive Language-Image Pretraining (**CLIP**) [26]. Details of these three metrics are introduced in Appendix C. To comprehensively integrate these scores, we propose a novel metric called *Weighted Averaged Normalization (WAN)*, which enables convenient comparison of generation performance. First, we normalize the values of these three metrics. Then, *WAN* is calculated as the average of the normalized and sign-adjusted values of the three metrics, with equal weights assigned to each. This choice ensures a fair aggregation, as the three metrics reflect complementary aspects of generation (i.e., image quality, diversity, and semantic alignment). When comparing the images generated after the application of the prevention mechanism with those generated before its application, *WAN* is defined as:

$$WAN = \frac{-FID_{norm} + IS_{norm} + CLIP_{norm}}{3}. \quad (2)$$

Lower FID means better quality, so we negate it in the formula. Higher IS and CLIP values represent better diversity and alignment, respectively. Thus, a larger *WAN* score indicates a better overall performance.

Building upon the concept of the *WAN* metric, we recognize that it is necessary to have a modified version when comparing the generated images with the vague versions of the original images. This is because the requirements for evaluating the similarity to a vague target image are different from those when comparing the

Table 1. Performance comparison of retraining and unlearning methods on permit (P) and forbid (F) sets across three datasets with DiffusionCLIP.

Datasets	Methods	DiffusionCLIP							
		FID		IS		CLIP		WAN	
		P↓	F↑	P↑	F↓	P↑	F↓	P↑	F↓
CelebA	Original	194.10	182.20	1.60	1.90	0.54	0.52	0.54	0.57
	Retrain	135.00	130.60	1.73	1.77	0.54	0.54	0.67	0.61
	Max	456.30	457.40	1.24	1.25	0.42	0.43	−0.18	−0.17
	Noisy	423.60	393.00	1.07	1.06	0.39	0.40	−0.30	−0.27
	Retain	406.90	402.80	1.15	1.20	0.42	0.43	−0.18	−0.16
Church	Original	207.70	192.50	1.72	2.42	0.56	0.58	0.21	0.58
	Retrain	113.30	123.70	1.76	1.76	0.59	0.56	0.49	0.31
	Max	369.00	375.80	1.72	1.79	0.42	0.44	−0.26	−0.29
	Noisy	376.50	367.20	1.70	1.78	0.41	0.44	−0.33	−0.30
	Retain	364.90	363.00	1.71	1.73	0.42	0.45	−0.28	−0.29
Bedroom	Original	221.60	230.00	1.32	1.48	0.66	0.64	0.17	0.20
	Retrain	121.00	130.50	1.55	1.54	0.70	0.67	0.41	0.38
	Max	401.70	405.90	2.37	2.28	0.46	0.49	0.06	0.09
	Noisy	385.90	383.10	2.31	2.32	0.42	0.42	0.01	0.04
	Retain	383.90	381.90	2.22	2.28	0.41	0.41	−0.03	0.01

images before and after the application of the prevention mechanism. Therefore, we derive a new metric, denoted as WAN*, which is defined as:

$$WAN^* = \frac{-FID_{norm} + IS_{norm} - CLIP_{norm}}{3}. \tag{3}$$

Here, a lower FID score indicates closer proximity to the vague image distribution, and a higher IS score reflects greater diversity, both desirable. Since a lower CLIP similarity to the blurred target indicates that the generated image has lost more semantic information (which aligns with the suppression goal), its normalized value is negated. Therefore, a higher WAN* score indicates better approximation to the vague target.

4.3 Baselines

We incorporate three distinct optimization strategies previously proposed for unlearning tasks, establishing comparative baselines for performance evaluation: **1) Max Loss** [8]: Maximizes the training loss with respect to the ground truth images in the forbid set. **2) Noisy Label** [7]: Minimizes the training loss by substituting the ground truth images in the forbid set with Gaussian noise. **3) Retain Label** [15]: Minimizes the training loss by replacing the forbid set images with the permit set images as the ground truth. In addition, we evaluate the performance of retraining the model solely on the permit set.

Fig. 2. Visual comparison of generated images from baseline methods, ground-truth targets, and our proposed method, *SecureT2I*.

4.4 Results

Evaluation of Retraining and Unlearning Methods. To address *RQ1: Can existing unlearning methods or retraining approaches effectively prevent unauthorized text-guided image manipulation using diffusion models?*, we conduct experiments to evaluate the performance of direct unlearning methods like Max [8], Noisy [7], and Retain [15], as well as retraining. As shown in Table 1, the retrain method achieves high WAN values on the permit set (e.g., 0.67 on CelebA), indicating strong manipulation ability, but performs poorly on the forbid set (WAN 0.61), insufficient to prevent unauthorized edits due to the strong zero-shot generalization of current manipulation methods like DiffusionCLIP [13]. Conversely, unlearning methods yield lower WAN scores on the forbid set (e.g., Noisy: -0.27 on CelebA), demonstrating better suppression of unauthorized manipulation. However, these come at a significant cost to the permit set performance (e.g., Max method's WAN drops to -0.18), reflecting a severe impairment of general manipulation ability. This degradation mainly results from unsuitable target images for the forbid set, such as noisy or retained versions that deviate too far from originals and disrupt training.

Table 2. Performance comparison of retraining, unlearning, and *SecureT2I* methods on permit (P) and forbid (F) sets across three datasets with DiffusionCLIP.

Datasets	Methods	DiffusionCLIP							
		FID		IS		CLIP		WAN	WAN*
		P↓	F↓	P↑	F↑	P↑	F↓	P↑	F↑
CelebA	Retrain	135.00	401.30	1.73	1.77	0.54	0.55	0.67	0.11
	Max	456.30	574.30	1.24	1.52	0.42	0.64	−0.18	−0.67
	Noisy	423.60	553.50	1.07	2.10	0.39	0.63	−0.30	−0.32
	Retain	406.90	553.40	1.15	2.14	0.42	0.63	−0.18	−0.31
	SecureT2I	**210.70**	**413.40**	**1.48**	**2.24**	**0.53**	**0.59**	**0.44**	**0.16**
Church	Retrain	113.30	459.60	1.76	1.76	0.59	0.56	0.49	0.00
	Max	369.00	549.90	1.72	2.11	0.42	0.72	−0.26	−0.53
	Noisy	376.50	537.70	1.70	2.21	0.41	0.70	−0.33	−0.40
	Retain	364.90	536.30	1.71	2.52	0.42	0.70	−0.28	−0.28
	SecureT2I	**250.90**	**469.60**	**1.84**	**2.63**	**0.52**	**0.67**	**0.37**	**0.07**
Bedroom	Retrain	121.00	456.70	1.55	1.54	0.70	0.57	0.41	0.00
	Max	401.70	578.40	2.37	2.28	0.46	0.78	0.06	−0.44
	Noisy	385.90	580.40	2.31	2.32	0.42	0.71	0.01	−0.33
	Retain	383.90	578.50	2.22	2.28	0.41	0.70	−0.03	−0.31
	SecureT2I	**296.10**	**500.30**	**1.67**	**2.65**	**0.57**	**0.70**	**0.09**	**0.01**

> **Address RQ1:** Retraining demonstrates strong performance on the permit set but falls short on the forbid set, while unlearning methods effectively suppress manipulations on the forbid set at the expense of degraded performance on the permit set. Neither approach achieves a satisfactory balance between the two.

Evaluation of *SecureT2I*. To address *RQ2: Is there an effective approach that can balance performance on forbidden and permitted images?*, we propose *SecureT2I*, which adopts a blurred version of the original image as the forbid set target to balance suppression and preservation, as detailed in Sect. 3.2. In our experiments, we use the blurred images as references for FID and CLIP calculations on the forbid set and apply the WAN* metric to better capture alignment with the vague target, enabling a more accurate assessment of each method's effectiveness. We evaluate *SecureT2I* across three mainstream text-guided image manipulation methods: DiffusionCLIP [13], Asyrp [17], and EffD-iff [31]. As shown in Tables 2, 3, and 4, *SecureT2I* achieves a significantly better balance between the permit and forbid sets compared to baseline methods. For example, on the CelebA dataset with DiffusionCLIP, while *Retrain* achieves a WAN value of 0.67 on the permit set, *SecureT2I* attains 0.44, substantially higher than unlearning methods such as *Max* (−0.18), *Noisy* (−0.30), and *Retain* (−0.18). In terms of WAN*, *SecureT2I* scores 0.16, outperforming *Retrain*'s 0.11,

Table 3. Performance comparison of retraining, unlearning, and *SecureT2I* methods on permit (P) and forbid (F) sets across three datasets with Asyrp.

Datasets	Methods	Asyrp							
		FID		IS		CLIP		WAN	WAN*
		P↓	F↓	P↑	F↑	P↑	F↓	P↑	F↑
CelebA	Retrain	122.40	427.90	2.93	2.53	0.53	0.55	0.66	0.20
	Max	405.50	553.40	1.71	2.12	0.38	0.61	−0.33	−0.67
	Noisy	129.90	424.70	2.68	2.66	0.53	0.56	0.58	0.22
	Retain	129.50	428.70	2.73	2.56	0.54	0.57	0.60	0.13
	SecureT2I	**124.80**	**402.80**	**2.61**	**2.62**	**0.54**	**0.56**	**0.58**	**0.27**
Church	Retrain	164.30	450.30	3.67	3.62	0.51	0.67	0.62	0.08
	Max	373.30	561.60	2.31	2.33	0.42	0.71	−0.33	−0.67
	Noisy	254.10	524.00	3.87	3.91	0.49	0.68	0.44	−0.09
	Retain	230.70	398.60	3.66	3.59	0.48	0.69	0.41	0.06
	SecureT2I	**162.80**	**466.90**	**3.68**	**3.83**	**0.51**	**0.66**	**0.63**	**0.18**
Bedroom	Retrain	154.30	457.30	3.77	3.93	0.65	0.72	0.61	−0.04
	Max	385.20	538.80	2.05	2.07	0.44	0.71	−0.33	−0.55
	Noisy	338.40	569.20	4.12	3.94	0.52	0.71	0.19	−0.28
	Retain	221.70	514.00	3.86	3.88	0.60	0.68	0.44	0.13
	SecureT2I	**155.20**	**448.10**	**3.68**	**4.00**	**0.65**	**0.70**	**0.59**	**0.17**

indicating improved suppression on the forbid set without sacrificing manipulation ability on permitted images. The FID scores further confirm this balance, with *SecureT2I* recording 210.70 for the permit set and 413.40 for the forbid set, values close to those of *Retrain* (135.00 permit, 401.30 forbid). Similarly, on the Church dataset with Asyrp, *SecureT2I* consistently surpasses unlearning-based methods in both WAN and WAN* metrics. The qualitative results in Fig. 2 further illustrate that *SecureT2I* preserves image quality while effectively preventing unauthorized manipulations better than baseline methods. Overall, these results demonstrate that *SecureT2I* successfully balances performance on both forbidden and permitted images, providing a more effective and robust solution to secure image manipulation than existing approaches.

> **Address RQ2:** We propose *SecureT2I*, which uses a vague version of the original image as the target for the forbid set. Experiments on multiple datasets and models show that *SecureT2I* outperforms existing methods by closely matching *Retrain* on the permit set while achieving better results on the forbid set, offering a more balanced and effective solution than unlearning-based approaches.

T-SNE Analysis. To provide a more comprehensive understanding of the superiority of our *SecureT2I* over other baseline methods, we conduct an embed-

Table 4. Performance comparison of retraining, unlearning, and *SecureT2I* methods on permit (P) and forbid (F) sets across three datasets with EffDiff.

Datasets	Methods	EffDiff							
		FID		IS		CLIP		WAN	WAN*
		P↓	F↓	P↑	F↑	P↑	F↓	P↑	F↑
CelebA	Retrain	129.40	406.60	2.75	2.49	0.54	0.54	0.47	−0.00
	Max	403.00	532.60	2.68	2.63	0.44	0.66	−0.22	−0.61
	Noisy	347.30	440.00	3.36	3.41	0.50	0.64	0.26	−0.03
	Retain	334.50	404.90	3.41	2.66	0.50	0.60	0.29	−0.11
	SecureT2I	**166.80**	**406.00**	**2.29**	**2.81**	**0.54**	**0.56**	**0.29**	**0.06**
Church	Retrain	109.00	462.10	2.61	2.43	0.58	0.55	0.36	−0.05
	Max	369.00	548.40	2.56	2.63	0.45	0.72	−0.33	−0.57
	Noisy	227.80	452.70	3.28	3.10	0.51	0.72	0.33	−0.02
	Retain	178.80	461.40	2.94	2.89	0.55	0.63	0.32	0.04
	SecureT2I	**124.20**	**448.00**	**2.76**	**2.63**	**0.58**	**0.58**	**0.39**	**0.05**
Bedroom	Retrain	111.00	462.30	3.04	3.04	0.69	0.55	0.54	0.11
	Max	374.40	553.40	2.57	2.76	0.45	0.76	−0.33	−0.07
	Noisy	336.60	514.40	3.34	3.54	0.50	0.69	0.12	−0.12
	Retain	355.50	518.80	3.24	3.38	0.50	0.69	0.04	−0.20
	SecureT2I	**168.20**	**471.70**	**3.04**	**3.62**	**0.67**	**0.63**	**0.43**	**0.17**

ding visualization using the T-SNE technique. Specifically, for each of the three manipulation methods, we embed 50 images from both the forbid set and the permit set into a two-dimensional space, both before and after the prevention process. Additionally, the images generated by three baseline methods under DiffusionCLIP are also embedded for comparison. As shown in Figs. 3a, 3b, and 3c, after applying the prevention mechanism, a clear separation emerges in the forbid set, where the generated images noticeably diverge from the originals. In contrast, in the permit set, the images remain closely clustered with their original counterparts. This demonstrates that *SecureT2I* can effectively degrade manipulation performance on forbidden images while preserving generation quality for permitted images. Furthermore, the T-SNE visualizations for the three baselines tested on DiffusionCLIP, shown in Figs. 3d, 3e, and 3f, reveal a substantial drift of embeddings for both the forbid and permit sets away from the original distributions. This indicates that these baselines significantly impair the model's overall performance, negatively impacting both forbidden and permitted images.

4.5 Generalization to Unseen Images

To evaluate the generalization ability of *SecureT2I* to previously unseen data, we construct a held-out subset from both the permit and forbid sets by randomly sampling 10% of images from each and excluding them entirely from the

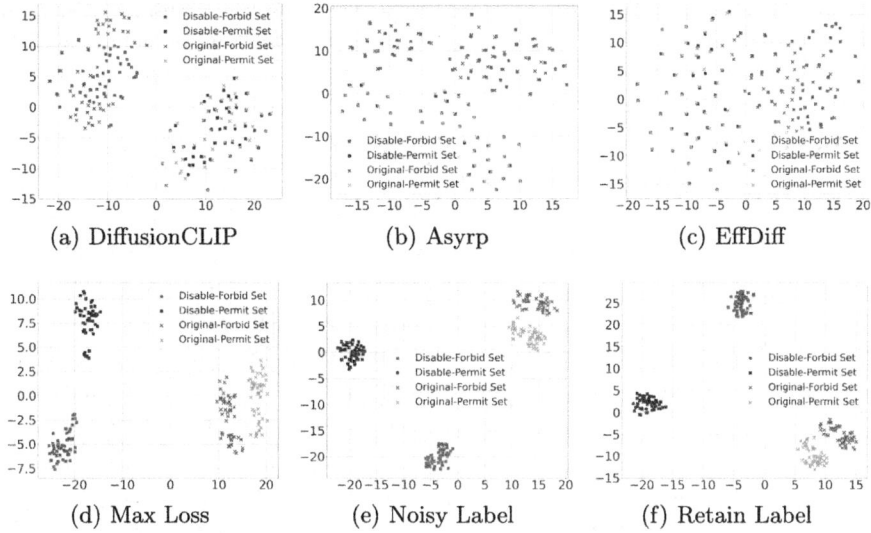

Fig. 3. T-SNE illustration of the generated images from baseline methods, ground truth images and *SecureT2I*.

optimization process. These images are only used during evaluation to simulate real-world scenarios in which the system encounters inputs that were not part of the training distribution. Table 5 presents the quantitative results across three datasets: CelebA, LSUN-Church, and LSUN-Bedroom. As the number of unseen images is relatively small, the Inception Score (IS) remains fixed at 1.00 for all methods. As a result, IS is excluded from normalization when computing the WAN and WAN* metrics. From the results, we observe that *SecureT2I* consistently outperforms the baselines in most settings. Specifically, it achieves lower FID and higher CLIP similarity on permit-set images, indicating high-quality and prompt-consistent edits. Meanwhile, the outputs for forbid-set images show reduced semantic similarity, as reflected by lower CLIP scores. These trends result in significantly higher WAN and WAN* values, suggesting that *SecureT2I* effectively preserves authorized editing performance while suppressing unauthorized manipulations, even on inputs that were not seen during training. This confirms the method's potential for generalization and its robustness to previously unseen samples.

4.6 Impact of Different Vagueness Methods on Disabling Performance

To address *RQ3: What factors influence the effectiveness of SecureT2I?*, we investigate different ways to define the vague target for the forbid set, categorized into size-based compression (8×8, 16×16 *SecureT2I*, 32×32) and filter-based blurring (Gaussian, Box, Motion). Size-based methods compress images and then resize them back to the original dimension, while filter-based methods

Table 5. Performance comparison of retraining, unlearning and *SecureT2I* methods on unseen permit (P) and forbid (F) sets across three datasets using DiffusionCLIP.

Datasets	Methods	DiffusionCLIP							
		FID		IS		CLIP		WAN	WAN*
		P↓	F↓	P↑	F↑	P↑	F↓	P↑	F↑
CelebA	Retrain	180.30	455.00	1.00	1.00	0.73	0.58	0.21	0.00
	Max	412.02	573.86	1.00	1.00	0.52	0.62	−0.33	−0.12
	Noisy	418.58	592.78	1.00	1.00	0.53	0.63	−0.32	−0.13
	Retain	407.28	564.83	1.00	1.00	0.56	0.66	−0.27	0.07
	SecureT2I	**128.69**	**459.66**	**1.00**	**1.00**	**0.78**	**0.62**	**0.33**	**0.16**
Church	Retrain	221.53	499.78	1.00	1.00	0.80	0.61	0.29	0.00
	Max	389.57	562.58	1.00	1.00	0.62	0.73	−0.33	0.06
	Noisy	354.14	566.39	1.00	1.00	0.66	0.69	−0.20	−0.07
	Retain	332.25	576.54	1.00	1.00	0.67	0.69	−0.14	−0.11
	SecureT2I	**197.68**	**534.84**	**1.00**	**1.00**	**0.79**	**0.70**	**0.31**	**0.10**
Bedroom	Retrain	252.06	549.83	1.00	1.00	0.79	0.70	0.32	0.00
	Max	432.82	633.86	1.00	1.00	0.65	0.76	−0.23	0.00
	Noisy	405.53	609.79	1.00	1.00	0.62	0.74	−0.23	−0.02
	Retain	439.68	610.56	1.00	1.00	0.59	0.72	−0.33	−0.13
	SecureT2I	**298.47**	**581.87**	**1.00**	**1.00**	**0.80**	**0.74**	**0.25**	**0.10**

apply various blurring techniques to introduce vagueness. Our goal is to balance high-quality manipulation on the permit set and effective distortion on the forbid set. As shown in Table 6, *SecureT2I* outperforms others by achieving the highest WAN and WAN* scores. Although Gaussian, Box, and Motion maintain decent permit set quality (WAN), they underperform on WAN*, indicating insufficient forbidding effect. The 32 × 32 resizing shares similar limitations, while 8 × 8 overly distorts permitted images, harming quality despite yielding strong WAN* performance. In summary, *SecureT2I* best balances these trade-offs, delivering high-quality permitted outputs and effectively obscuring forbidden images, making it a reliable approach for secure text-guided image manipulation.

> **Address RQ3:** The effectiveness of secure image manipulation depends heavily on the chosen vagueness method. Most resizing- or blurring-based approaches either insufficiently distort forbidden images or excessively degrade permitted ones. In contrast, *SecureT2I* achieves the best balance with the highest WAN and WAN* scores, offering a robust and effective solution.

5 Limitations

While *SecureT2I* achieves effective suppression of unauthorized manipulations and preserves editing capabilities on authorized inputs, several limitations

Table 6. Comparison of different vagueness methods on CelebA. P: Permit, F: Forbid. The row marked with '*' (**16x16***) represents our *SecureT2I* method.

Vagueness	DiffusionCLIP							
	FID		IS		CLIP		WAN	WAN*
	P↓	F↓	P↑	F↑	P↑	F↓	P↑	F↑
Retrain	135.00	401.30	1.73	1.77	0.54	0.55	0.67	0.03
8x8	412.10	455.12	1.37	2.37	0.47	0.62	−0.33	0.30
16x16*	**210.70**	**413.40**	**1.48**	**2.24**	**0.53**	**0.59**	**0.30**	**0.35**
32x32	220.80	424.35	1.45	1.72	0.53	0.63	0.26	0.20
Gaussian	215.70	423.73	1.43	1.71	0.53	0.60	0.25	0.08
Box	228.30	429.34	1.48	1.75	0.53	0.59	0.29	0.02
Motion	222.90	435.45	1.47	1.70	0.53	0.61	0.27	0.04

remain. First, the current approach does not incorporate defenses against adversarial attacks on the diffusion model itself. Prior work has shown that diffusion models are vulnerable to small perturbations that can bypass editing restrictions [32], posing a threat to secure manipulation, especially in open-world scenarios where inputs may be intentionally tampered with. While our method focuses on semantic-level editing control via loss-based fine-tuning, it lacks robustness guarantees under such attacks. Incorporating adversarial training, robust noise prediction, or certified purification could enhance resilience and improve the model's reliability in security-critical applications. Exploring these directions is an important avenue for future work. Second, while our experiments cover a variety of prompts and image categories, we do not conduct a dedicated ablation study focusing on prompt variation. Robustness to diverse or rephrased prompts remains an open challenge in text-to-image systems, where different textual formulations with similar semantics may elicit inconsistent model behaviors. A systematic analysis of how prompt styles and manipulation intents influence suppression effectiveness would provide deeper insight into the stability of our method. We leave this investigation as an important direction for future work, especially for applications that require consistent control under natural prompt variability. We view these limitations as important directions for future research, particularly in advancing secure text-guided manipulation systems that operate reliably across open-world distributions and under adversarial pressures.

6 Conclusion

In this paper, we introduced the critical and underexplored problem of secure image manipulation that prevents unauthorized edits based on text prompts. Our analysis revealed that existing solutions, such as retraining and unlearning, struggle to balance performance between authorized (permit) and unauthorized (forbid) images. To address this challenge, we proposed *SecureT2I*, a novel method that enables diffusion models to selectively disable unauthorized manipulations while preserving high-quality, legitimate edits. Experiments demonstrate that *SecureT2I* significantly degrades manipulations on the forbid set and maintains fidelity on the permit set, outperforming all baselines. Notably, *SecureT2I* also generalizes better to unseen images compared to existing methods. Moreover, by systematically comparing various vagueness strategies for the forbid set, we found that resize-based vagueness offers the best trade-off between manipulation prevention and generation quality. *SecureT2I* sets a new benchmark for secure text-guided image manipulation and opens a promising direction toward more robust, scalable, and ethically aligned frameworks, marking a significant step in addressing ethical and copyright concerns in text-to-image generation.

Appendix

A Implementation Details

We develop our manipulation model based on a diffusion model with non-Markovian sampling, ensuring smooth transitions between input and output images during manipulation. The Adam optimizer is employed, with an initial learning rate of 8×10^{-6}. To balance suppression and retention, the weights λ_{forbid} and λ_{permit} are both set to 0.5, enabling equal emphasis on prevention and retaining information. We randomly select 100 images from each of the three datasets. These images, paired with specific textual prompts (e.g., "beards" for CelebA-HQ), are used to fine-tune the manipulation model. This initial fine-tuning grants the model the ability to perform targeted manipulations based on the given prompt. After this, *SecureT2I* is applied, further fine-tuning the model with the same set of 100 images for an additional 15 iterations. The model's performance is evaluated by averaging the results across five distinct manipulation features for each dataset.

B Dataset

The details of the three datasets used in our evaluations are provided below:

- **CelebA-HQ** is a high-quality version of the CelebA dataset, consisting of 30,000 high-resolution images of celebrity faces. This dataset includes a rich variety of facial attributes such as gender, age, hairstyle, and facial expression, making it widely used in tasks like image generation, face editing, and attribute transfer.
- **LSUN-Bedroom** is part of the Large-scale Scene Understanding (LSUN) dataset, containing millions of images from various scene categories. The Bedroom subset comprises around 3 million images of bedrooms, offering a rich source of visual diversity in terms of room layout, furniture arrangement, lighting, and style.

- **LSUN-Church** is another subset of the LSUN dataset, featuring over 126,000 images of churches. These images include a wide range of church exteriors from different architectural styles and backgrounds, providing substantial diversity in terms of structure, weather conditions, and viewpoints.

C Evaluation Metrics

 - **FID** is a metric used to evaluate the quality of generated images by comparing the distribution of generated images to that of real images. It measures the similarity between features of images from a deep neural network (usually InceptionV3). Lower FID scores indicate that the generated images are closer to real images in terms of visual quality and diversity.
 - **IS** assesses the quality of generated images by evaluating two key factors: how diverse the generated images are and how well they represent a distinct object or scene. It uses a pre-trained inception network to classify images and calculates a score based on the entropy of the predicted labels. Higher IS scores indicate the images are both clear and varied.
 - **CLIP** embedding similarity evaluates the semantic correspondence between a generated image and a target image. CLIP projects both the generated and target images into a shared embedding space, where the similarity between their feature representations can be measured. A higher CLIP embedding similarity value indicates that the two images share similar semantic concepts and visual elements. This metric serves as an important indicator of how well the generated image captures the essence and meaning of the target image, helping assess the effectiveness of image generation or manipulation methods in terms of semantic consistency.

References

1. Avrahami, O., Lischinski, D., Fried, O.: Blended diffusion for text-driven editing of natural images. In: Proceedings of the IEEE/CVF Conference on Computer Vision and Pattern Recognition, pp. 18208–18218 (2022)
2. Basu, S., Zhao, N., Morariu, V.I., Feizi, S., Manjunatha, V.: Localizing and editing knowledge in text-to-image generative models. In: The Twelfth International Conference on Learning Representations (2023)
3. Bourtoule, L., et al.: Machine unlearning. In: 2021 IEEE Symposium on Security and Privacy, pp. 141–159. IEEE (2021)
4. Brooks, T., Holynski, A., Efros, A.A.: Instructpix2pix: learning to follow image editing instructions. In: Proceedings of the IEEE/CVF Conference on Computer Vision and Pattern Recognition. pp. 18392–18402 (2023)
5. Fuchi, M., Takagi, T.: Erasing concepts from text-to-image diffusion models with few-shot unlearning. arXiv preprint arXiv:2405.07288 (2024)
6. Grafakos, L., et al.: Classical fourier analysis, vol. 2. Springer (2008)
7. Graves, L., Nagisetty, V., Ganesh, V.: Amnesiac machine learning. In: Proceedings of the AAAI Conference on Artificial Intelligence, vol. 35, pp. 11516–11524 (2021)

8. Halimi, A., Kadhe, S., Rawat, A., Baracaldo, N.: Federated unlearning: How to efficiently erase a client in FL? arXiv preprint arXiv:2207.05521 (2022)
9. Heng, A., Soh, H.: Selective amnesia: A continual learning approach to forgetting in deep generative models. In: Advances in Neural Information Processing Systems, vol. 36 (2024)
10. Heusel, M., Ramsauer, H., Unterthiner, T., Nessler, B., Hochreiter, S.: GANs trained by a two time-scale update rule converge to a local Nash equilibrium. In: Advances in Neural Information Processing Systems, vol. 30 (2017)
11. Huang, Y., et al.: Diffusion model-based image editing: a survey. arXiv preprint arXiv:2402.17525 (2024)
12. Khojasteh, M.H., Farid, N.M., Nickabadi, A.: GMFIM: a generative mask-guided facial image manipulation model for privacy preservation. Comput. Graphics **112**, 81–91 (2023)
13. Kim, G., Kwon, T., Ye, J.C.: Diffusionclip: text-guided diffusion models for robust image manipulation. In: Proceedings of the IEEE/CVF Conference on Computer Vision and Pattern Recognition, pp. 2426–2435 (2022)
14. Kim, S., Jung, S., Kim, B., Choi, M., Shin, J., Lee, J.: Towards safe self-distillation of internet-scale text-to-image diffusion models. arXiv preprint arXiv:2307.05977 (2023)
15. Kong, Z., Chaudhuri, K.: Data redaction from conditional generative models. In: 2024 IEEE Conference on Secure and Trustworthy Machine Learning (SaTML), pp. 569–591. IEEE (2024)
16. Kumari, N., Zhang, B., Wang, S.Y., Shechtman, E., Zhang, R., Zhu, J.Y.: Ablating concepts in text-to-image diffusion models. In: Proceedings of the IEEE/CVF International Conference on Computer Vision, pp. 22691–22702 (2023)
17. Kwon, M., Jeong, J., Uh, Y.: Diffusion models already have a semantic latent space. arXiv preprint arXiv:2210.10960 (2022)
18. Li, G., Hsu, H., Marculescu, R., et al.: Machine unlearning for image-to-image generative models. arXiv preprint arXiv:2402.00351 (2024)
19. Li, X., et al.: Diffusion models for image restoration and enhancement–a comprehensive survey. arXiv preprint arXiv:2308.09388 (2023)
20. Liang, R., et al.: Photorealistic object insertion with diffusion-guided inverse rendering. In: European Conference on Computer Vision, pp. 446–465. Springer (2024)
21. Lu, S., Wang, Z., Li, L., Liu, Y., Kong, A.W.K.: Mace: mass concept erasure in diffusion models. In: Proceedings of the IEEE/CVF Conference on Computer Vision and Pattern Recognition, pp. 6430–6440 (2024)
22. Meng, C., et al.: SDEDIT: guided image synthesis and editing with stochastic differential equations. arXiv preprint arXiv:2108.01073 (2021)
23. Monteiro, K., Wu, Y., Das, S.: Manipulate to obfuscate: a privacy-focused intelligent image manipulation tool for end-users. In: Adjunct Proceedings of the 37th Annual ACM Symposium on User Interface Software and Technology, pp. 1–3 (2024)
24. Moser, B.B., Shanbhag, A.S., Raue, F., Frolov, S., Palacio, S., Dengel, A.: Diffusion models, image super-resolution, and everything: a survey. IEEE Trans. Neural Networks Learn. Syst. (2024)
25. Park, Y.H., et al.: Direct unlearning optimization for robust and safe text-to-image models. arXiv preprint arXiv:2407.21035 (2024)
26. Radford, A., et al.: Learning transferable visual models from natural language supervision. In: International Conference on Machine Learning, pp. 8748–8763. PmLR (2021)

27. Raginsky, M., Rakhlin, A., Telgarsky, M.: Non-convex learning via stochastic gradient langevin dynamics: a nonasymptotic analysis. In: Conference on Learning Theory, pp. 1674–1703. PMLR (2017)
28. Ravi, H., Kelkar, S., Harikumar, M., Kale, A.: PReditOR: text guided image editing with diffusion prior. arXiv preprint arXiv:2302.07979 (2023)
29. Sablayrolles, A., Douze, M., Schmid, C., Jégou, H.: Radioactive data: tracing through training. In: International Conference on Machine Learning, pp. 8326–8335. PMLR (2020)
30. Salimans, T., Goodfellow, I., Zaremba, W., Cheung, V., Radford, A., Chen, X.: Improved techniques for training GANs. In: Advances in Neural Information Processing Systems, vol. 29 (2016)
31. Starodubcev, N., Baranchuk, D., Khrulkov, V., Babenko, A.: Towards real-time text-driven image manipulation with unconditional diffusion models. arXiv preprint arXiv:2304.04344 (2023)
32. Truong, V.T., Dang, L.B., Le, L.B.: Attacks and defenses for generative diffusion models: a comprehensive survey. ACM Comput. Surv. **57**(8), 1–44 (2025)
33. Valevski, D., Kalman, M., Matias, Y., Leviathan, Y.: Unitune: text-driven image editing by fine tuning an image generation model on a single image. arXiv preprint arXiv:2210.09477 **2**(3), 5 (2022)
34. Wang, Z., Zhao, L., Xing, W.: Stylediffusion: controllable disentangled style transfer via diffusion models. In: Proceedings of the IEEE/CVF International Conference on Computer Vision, pp. 7677–7689 (2023)
35. Werder, K., Ramesh, B., Zhang, R.: Establishing data provenance for responsible artificial intelligence systems. ACM Trans. Manag. Inf. Syst. (TMIS) **13**(2), 1–23 (2022)
36. Xie, S., et al.: Dreaminpainter: text-guided subject-driven image inpainting with diffusion models. arXiv preprint arXiv:2312.03771 (2023)
37. Xing, Z., et al.: A survey on video diffusion models. ACM Comput. Surv. **57**(2), 1–42 (2024)
38. Xu, H., Song, Y., Xu, G., Wu, K., Wen, J.: HETMCL: high-frequency enhancement transformer and multi-layer context learning network for remote sensing scene classification. Sensors **25**(12), 3769 (2025)
39. Yang, B., et al.: Paint by example: exemplar-based image editing with diffusion models. In: Proceedings of the IEEE/CVF Conference on Computer Vision and Pattern Recognition, pp. 18381–18391 (2023)
40. Yang, L., et al.: Diffusion models: a comprehensive survey of methods and applications. ACM Comput. Surv. **56**(4), 1–39 (2023)
41. Zhang, S., et al.: Hive: Harnessing human feedback for instructional visual editing. In: Proceedings of the IEEE/CVF Conference on Computer Vision and Pattern Recognition, pp. 9026–9036 (2024)
42. Zhao, M., Zhang, L., Zheng, T., Kong, Y., Yin, B.: Separable multi-concept erasure from diffusion models. arXiv preprint arXiv:2402.05947 (2024)

GANSec: Enhancing Supervised Wireless Anomaly Detection Robustness Through Tailored Conditional GAN Augmentation

Jiali Xu[1]([✉]), Shuo Wang[2], Valeria Loscri[1], Alessandro Brighente[2], Mauro Conti[2,3], and Romain Rouvoy[1,4]

[1] Inria centre at the University of Lille, 59650 Villeneuve d'Ascq, France
{jiali.xu,valeria.loscri,romain.rouvoy}@inria.fr
[2] University of Padova, 35131 Padova, Italy
{shuo.wang,alessandro.brighente}@phd.unipd.it, mauro.conti@unipd.it
[3] Örebro University, 701 82 Örebro, Sweden
[4] University of Lille, CNRS, 59000 Lille, France

Abstract. Data augmentation techniques show potential in various domains, yet their application to enhance robustness in wireless anomaly detection remains underexplored. Wireless datasets often suffer from anomaly scarcity and class imbalance, hindering the training of reliable detection models. This work introduces GANSec, a novel conditional Generative Adversarial Networks (GAN) framework specifically designed to augment wireless time-series data. We investigate different neural network architectures (MLP, LSTM, CNN) and two conditional training objectives (Embedded Conditional, Classification Oriented) within GANSec, evaluating the framework using real-world 5G measurements for jamming anomaly detection. For evaluation, we train the downstream anomaly detector exclusively on GANSec-generated data and test its performance in a cross-scenario setting. Our evaluation demonstrates that models trained this way significantly outperform those trained on original or baseline augmentation data when tested under unseen network conditions. Specifically, our approach achieved up to 92.13% accuracy on the unseen dataset (i.e., data collected from a different distribution reflecting network conditions distinct from the training set), compared to 78% for models trained on raw data and 83.33% for the best-performing baseline, exhibiting substantially enhanced robustness and generalization.

Keywords: Wireless Security · Anomaly Detection · Data Augmentation · Generative Adversarial Networks (GAN) · Cross-Scenario Generalization

1 Introduction

Wireless networks form the backbone of modern communication, supporting applications from personal devices to critical infrastructure, making their security paramount [16,35]. However, the open nature of wireless communication inherently leaves these networks vulnerable to a diverse array of security threats and anomalies [1], including sophisticated attacks targeting the physical layer like jamming [32]. Anomaly detection—the identification of significant deviations from normal behavior—is therefore pivotal for safeguarding wireless environments against security breaches, network malfunctions, and other detrimental activities [29,36,38]. Accurate and early identification of these irregularities is crucial for maintaining the security, performance, and reliability of wireless services. This need becomes even more critical as reliance on wireless connectivity escalates across sectors like the Internet of Things (IoT), which introduces numerous potential entry points for malicious actors [16,35,36]. Robust anomaly detection mechanisms, capable of adapting to the dynamic nature of wireless channels, represent a critical defense against this expanding threat landscape.

However, developing effective anomaly detection models for wireless security faces significant data-related hurdles, including anomaly scarcity, class imbalance, environmental non-stationarity, and the high cost of data acquisition. These challenges, which impede model training and generalization, are discussed in detail in Sect. 2.

Data augmentation emerges as a potential strategy, with Generative Adversarial Networks (GAN) offering a sophisticated approach compared to simpler techniques like SMOTE [5] and its variants [8]. GAN have been investigated for augmenting network and wireless signal data in security contexts [1,3,18,19,34,35]. However, significant limitations persist in prior work, particularly concerning the lack of rigorous validation for robustness and generalization in diverse wireless conditions, and often limited control in generation. These challenges are further elaborated in Sect. 3.3.

In this work, we propose GANSec to address these challenges: a novel conditional GAN framework specifically designed and tailored for augmenting wireless time-series data. Within GANSec, we investigate different neural network backbones (MLP, LSTM, CNN) and conditional training objectives (Embedded Conditional, Classification-Oriented). To assess GANSec's effectiveness, we perform a challenging cross-scenario evaluation tackling jamming anomalies in 5G networks. In this evaluation (Sect. 5), we train the downstream anomaly detection model using GANSec-generated data and test its performance on unseen data from different network conditions. Our results demonstrate that models trained using GANSec significantly outperform baseline methods when tested on this unseen data, showcasing enhanced robustness and generalization capabilities.

This work makes the following contributions to robust wireless anomaly detection using generative augmentation: **(1) Novel Conditional GAN Framework (GANSec):** Designed and implemented GANSec, tailored for augmenting labeled wireless time-series data to generate high-fidelity samples. **(2) Architectural & Objective Impact Analysis:** Systematically analyzed the influence of backbones (MLP, LSTM, CNN) and conditional objectives (EC, CO) within GANSec on data quality and downstream performance. **(3) Demonstrated Robustness & Generalization Enhancement:** Showcased via cross-scenario 5G evaluations that GANSec significantly improves detector robustness against distribution shifts, outperforming baselines.

2 Motivation

The pursuit of robust anomaly detection in wireless security faces significant hurdles related to data acquisition and quality, motivating the development of sophisticated data augmentation techniques. We argue that GAN offer a particularly compelling approach to overcome these challenges and enhance detection capabilities, driven by the following key factors:

2.1 The Prohibitive Cost of Wireless Data Acquisition

A significant practical barrier hinders the development of robust wireless anomaly detection models: acquiring large-scale, diverse, and representative real-world data. Collecting comprehensive datasets proves particularly challenging, especially for capturing sufficient instances of the rare anomalies crucial for security monitoring, often demanding prohibitive investments in time and resources [20,27]. Standard measurement intervals dictate that accumulating datasets adequate for training complex machine learning models can require days, weeks, or even months of continuous monitoring per location [28]. This process frequently requires deploying specialized hardware and software, incurring substantial capital and operational costs [7,20,27]. Furthermore, operating this measurement equipment continuously over extended periods consumes considerable energy, adding to the overall expense and environmental footprint of large-scale data acquisition campaigns [2]. Capturing high-quality data within dynamic wireless environments, subject to fluctuating channel conditions like multipath fading and interference, adds considerable complexity. This inherent difficulty in obtaining sufficient real-world data, especially for infrequent anomaly events, directly impedes the development and reliable training of robust anomaly detection models. Consequently, cost-effective and scalable alternatives are needed. GAN-based data augmentation offers such an alternative, enabling the generation of large volumes of high-quality synthetic wireless data to supplement limited real-world samples without requiring prolonged and expensive physical data collection campaigns.

2.2 Data Quality Limitations and the Naivety of Traditional Augmentation

Beyond scarcity, real-world wireless data frequently suffers from quality limitations [16,28]. It can be incomplete, noisy, challenging to model accurately, and may fail to represent the full spectrum of potential normal and anomalous behaviors. These quality issues compound the difficulties caused by data scarcity, further complicating the training of reliable detection models.

Data augmentation techniques, often applied in the computer vision domain (e.g., random noise injection, rotation), are generally inadequate for the intricate nature of wireless time-series data [34]. Such naive transformations typically disregard crucial characteristics, such as temporal dependencies between measurements and the underlying statistical properties of wireless signals, potentially generating unrealistic or misleading samples. Similarly, techniques designed for tabular data, like SMOTE [5] or DeepSMOTE [8], primarily interpolate between existing samples. While helpful for addressing class imbalance, this interpolation approach often fails to capture the complex, non-linear features characteristic of anomalous wireless signals or network traffic, essentially creating averages rather than truly novel and representative examples [18].

In contrast, GAN [9] offer a more sophisticated approach. GAN can learn the complex, high-dimensional probability distributions underlying wireless data. This capability allows them to generate synthetic samples—including plausible representations of rare anomalies—that are statistically similar to real-world data yet potentially more diverse than simple interpolations. By learning the data distribution, GAN can overcome the limitations of simpler augmentation methods and provide more valuable and realistic training signals for anomaly detection models.

2.3 Enhancing Model Generalization and Robustness

A primary challenge for wireless anomaly detection systems is ensuring they generalize and remain robust across diverse operational conditions [36]. Supervised models, while potentially accurate under training conditions, often struggle when deployed in real-world wireless settings due to the environment's inherent dynamism [23]. Factors such as moving obstacles, electromagnetic interference, user mobility, and changing weather continuously perturb the physical communication channel [21].

Consequently, a model trained under one set of environmental conditions (e.g., outdoor conditions, obstacles, etc.) frequently experiences significant performance degradation when encountering data reflecting different circumstances [26]. The model's learned decision boundary becomes suboptimal as the underlying data distribution shifts, leading to increased false positives (mistaking environmental variations for anomalies) and false negatives (missing true anomalies whose characteristics are altered or were unrepresented in training). This constant flux makes defining a stable baseline for "normal" behavior difficult. Therefore, developing anomaly detection methods that exhibit enhanced robustness and generalization is essential for reliable operation. This necessitates exploring techniques, such as advanced data augmentation strategies, capable of equipping models to handle the inevitable data shifts induced by environmental variability.

3 Related Work

The challenges outlined in Sect. 2—data scarcity, quality limitations, and the need for robust anomaly detection in dynamic wireless environments—motivate a review of existing approaches and their limitations. While various anomaly detection techniques exist, the unique characteristics of wireless data necessitate specialized solutions, increasingly pointing towards advanced data augmentation methods like GAN.

3.1 Anomaly Detection in Wireless Security

Anomaly detection in wireless security aims to identify deviations from normal operational behavior, which could signify faults or attacks [36]. However, accurately modeling "normal" behavior is difficult due to the dynamic nature of wireless systems, constantly shifting baselines, and unique physical layer vulnerabilities like jamming [26,29,38]. Classical methods, including statistical modeling, rule-based systems, and traditional machine learning [29], often struggle with the high dimensionality [30,31], non-stationarity [12,25,33], severe class imbalance [5,17,18], and the need for continuous updates or extensive feature engineering common in wireless security datasets [35]. Even deep learning techniques like autoencoders [8,14], while powerful, traditionally require vast amounts of representative data and can be biased towards abundant normal samples, potentially missing subtle or rare anomalies. These are challenges directly related to the data scarcity and quality issues discussed previously (Sects. 2.1, 2.2).

3.2 Data Augmentation Techniques for Wireless Anomaly Detection

Data augmentation offers a compelling strategy to address the data limitations hindering effective wireless anomaly detection. Among various techniques, GAN [9] have garnered significant attention due to their ability to learn complex data distributions and generate high-fidelity synthetic samples [1,18,34]. While other generative models like diffusion models [7,14] also show promise, we focus on GAN due to their established use in related tasks and architectural flexibility. The fundamental architecture of GAN is detailed in Sect. 4 where we describe our proposed framework.

Researchers have applied GAN to augment various types of data in wireless security.

Network Traffic Data: GAN generate synthetic network flows or packet data, primarily to enrich datasets for Intrusion Detection Systems (IDS) [18]. This helps balance classes by creating more examples of underrepresented attacks and can potentially simulate novel attack variants based on learned patterns.

Wireless Signal Data: GAN augment raw wireless signal measurements (e.g., IQ samples, channel state information) for tasks such as physical layer authentication [1] or detecting spectrum anomalies [34,35], including jamming or unauthorized device transmissions.

Specific examples illustrate the active research in this area. TAnoGAN [3] was proposed for unsupervised time-series anomaly detection using GAN to model normal behavior. Variants like Wasserstein GAN with Gradient Penalty (WGAN-GP) [10,15] have been employed specifically to combat class imbalance in IDS datasets (e.g., NSL-KDD), improving classifier performance by generating high-quality minority class samples. Other studies [13,19,34] report improved accuracy in cyber-attack detection by training models on GAN-augmented data. These applications highlight GANs' versatility in addressing data scarcity and imbalance challenges (Sects. 2.1, 2.2).

3.3 Challenges and Limitations in GAN-Based Augmentation

Despite this progress, applying GAN to enhance the robustness and generalization of wireless anomaly detection systems—critical requirements identified in Sect. 2.3—reveals significant challenges and limitations in existing practices.

Insufficient Robustness and Generalization Validation: A primary concern is the frequent lack of rigorous evaluation regarding the robustness of models trained on GAN-generated data. Many studies do not adequately test performance against unseen data or network conditions significantly different from the GAN's training set [1,13,29,34,35]. Ensuring models generalize beyond the learned distribution is crucial for deployment in dynamic real-world environments, yet this aspect often remains underexplored.

Limited Generation Control and Model Sophistication: Many existing studies employ basic or non-conditional GAN architectures [1,34,35]. These often lack fine-grained control over the generation process (e.g., conditioning on specific labels, environmental factors, or attack parameters). This limits the ability to generate targeted, context-aware synthetic data, which is crucial for training models to handle complex, condition-dependent anomalies.

Oversimplified Evaluation Settings: Some evaluations rely on datasets with limited features or utilize simplified simulated wireless environments [1,18]. Such settings may not capture the full complexity of real-world deployments, potentially overstating performance and limiting the practical applicability of the findings.

These identified gaps—specifically concerning the validation of robustness and generalization in dynamic scenarios—underscore the necessity for more advanced, tailored generative frameworks. Existing approaches often fall short of producing the diverse, high-fidelity, and condition-specific synthetic data required to train wireless anomaly detectors that are truly robust to unseen conditions. This directly motivates our proposed framework, GANSec, detailed in Sect. 4. GANSec is specifically designed to address these limitations by incorporating conditional generation tailored for wireless time-series data, investigating architectures adept at capturing temporal dependencies, and rigorously evaluating performance with a focus on cross-scenario generalization.

4 The GANSec Framework

To address the challenges of data scarcity, quality, and the need for robustness in wireless anomaly detection highlighted previously, we propose GANSec: a tailored GAN framework designed specifically for augmenting labeled wireless data. GANSec aims to generate high-fidelity synthetic time-series data that captures the complex characteristics of wireless signals, including anomalous events, thereby improving the training and generalization capabilities of downstream anomaly detection models.

Figure 1 illustrates the overall workflow of our proposed approach. The process begins with real-world data acquisition, potentially sourced from distinct phases or environments (Experiment and Production). Raw signal measurements captured within these domains, along with relevant contextual information c, first undergo standard preprocessing steps such as data labeling, cleaning, and feature extraction to yield features x. The subsequent temporal aggregation step structures these extracted features over time into 2D time-series tensors.

In the baseline conventional approach, the processed 2D tensors from the experiment domain would be used directly to train the anomaly detector. In contrast, we use these time-series to train the conditional GAN for data augmentation. GANSec adapts the standard GAN paradigm [9], comprising a Generator ($\mathcal{G}$) and a Discriminator ($\mathcal{D}$), implemented as neural networks. $\mathcal{G}$ learns to transform random noise vectors z into synthetic data samples that resemble real wireless signals, while $\mathcal{D}$ learns to distinguish these synthetic samples from real-world data. Through adversarial training, both networks improve, enabling $\mathcal{G}$ to produce increasingly realistic synthetic wireless data.

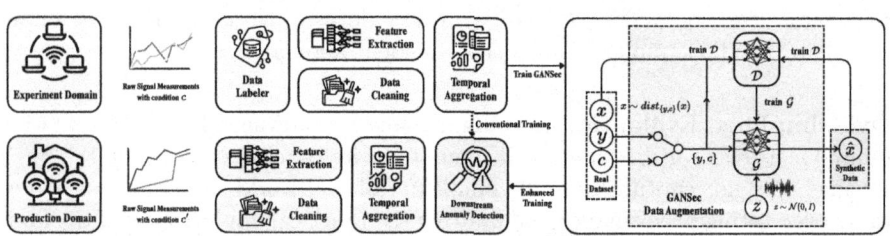

Fig. 1. GAN-based Data Augmentation for Anomaly Detection in Wireless Security: Workflow Overview.

4.1 GANSec Architecture and Training Mechanisms

Figure 2 provides a detailed view of the GANSec architecture. $\mathcal{G}$ takes a random noise vector z, sampled from a standard normal distribution ($\mathcal{N}(0, I)$) with dimensions defined by the desired latent space size, concatenated with conditioning information—specifically the target label y and potentially other contextual conditions c—as input. These inputs are processed through embedding layers and a neural network backbone (which we explore using MLP, LSTM, or CNN architectures) to produce synthetic features $\hat{x}$. $\mathcal{D}$ receives either a real data sample x or a synthetic sample $\hat{x}$, along with the corresponding conditions $\{y, c\}$, and outputs a likelihood on authenticity; this score challenges $\mathcal{G}$ to produce increasingly realistic data.

Within this conditional framework, we designed and investigated two primary $\mathcal{D}$ mechanisms for training $\mathcal{G}$, each utilizing different objective functions.

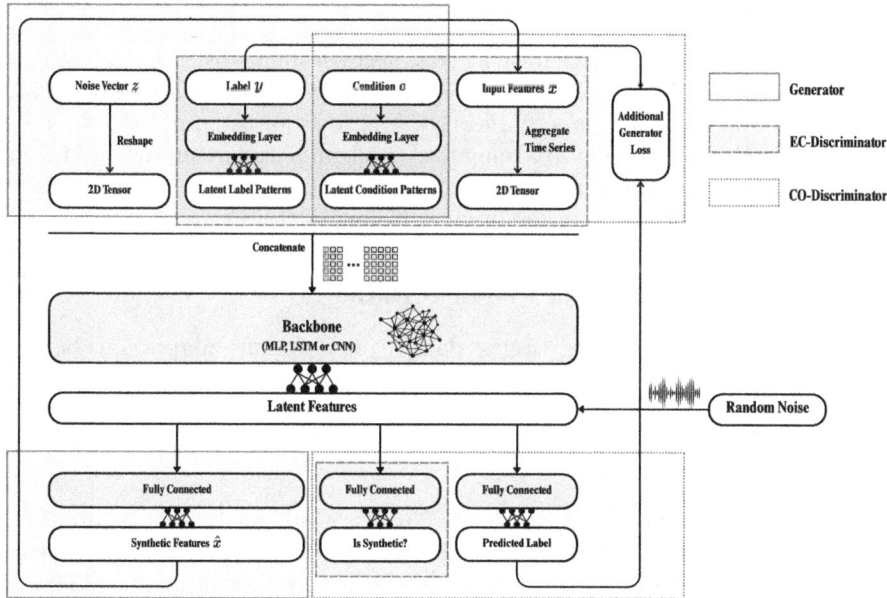

Fig. 2. Architecture of the GANSec framework. The diagram shows distinct paths and objectives for the Embedded Conditional (EC-Discriminator) and Classification Oriented (CO-Discriminator) training mechanisms described in Sect. 4.1.

Embedded Conditional (EC) Discriminator. In this configuration, the primary objective is generating realistic data samples that accurately match the provided conditions $\{y, c\}$. As shown by the EC-Discriminator path in Fig. 2, the conditioning information is embedded and fed into $\mathcal{D}$. $\mathcal{D}$ acts solely as a real/fake classifier for the given condition, outputting a probability score indicating authenticity. $\mathcal{G}$, in turn, aims to produce data $\hat{x}$ that the $\mathcal{D}$ classifies as real for the specified condition $\{y, c\}$. This approach emphasizes fidelity to the conditional data distribution. The training process follows Algorithm 1 detailed in Appendix A.

Classification Oriented (CO) Discriminator. This mechanism extends the $\mathcal{D}$'s role beyond simple real/fake classification, as depicted by the CO-Discriminator path in Fig. 2. Here, $\mathcal{D}$ simultaneously performs two tasks: it predicts whether the input data (x or $\hat{x}$) is real or synthetic, and it predicts the data's class label y based on condition c. Correspondingly, $\mathcal{G}$'s loss function encourages the generation of synthetic data $\hat{x}$ that is not only classified as real by $\mathcal{D}$ but is also classified with the intended target label y. The intuition is that by optimizing for class discriminability alongside realism, $\mathcal{G}$ learns to generate samples particularly useful for the downstream classification task, potentially enhancing the anomaly detector's performance. The training follows Algorithm 2 detailed in Appendix A.

Comparing these two mechanisms allows us to evaluate distinct strategies for generating effective synthetic data: one focused primarily on conditional realism (EC-GAN) and the other directly incorporating the downstream task objective (CO-GAN). While the CO-GAN might offer advantages for improving classification accuracy by optimizing for class discriminability, it could also be more sensitive to class imbalance in the original training data.

4.2 Tailoring GANSec for Wireless Data

Generating realistic synthetic wireless data requires specific adaptations beyond standard GAN implementations, as naive approaches often fail to capture the unique characteristics of wireless signals (as discussed in Sect. 2.2). GANSec incorporates several design considerations to handle these intricacies effectively.

Handling Temporal Dependencies: Wireless signal measurements are time-series data with strong temporal correlations crucial for context [3,33]. To capture these, GANSec employs backbones suited for sequential data. LSTMs are used for their ability to model long-range dependencies, while 2D CNNs effectively learn local, time-invariant patterns within the signal sequences. An MLP baseline is included for comparison, requiring flattening of the time-series segments into 1D vectors, which potentially obscures some temporal relationships.

Preserving Statistical Properties: Beyond temporal structure, wireless signals possess specific statistical properties vital for accurate representation. For instance, metrics like Reference Signal Received Power (RSRP) are often measured on a logarithmic scale (dBm). This logarithmic nature, while convenient for representing a wide dynamic range, introduces challenges for neural networks [6]. The non-linearity can interact suboptimally with standard activation functions if not handled carefully, and common loss functions like Mean Squared Error behave differently in the logarithmic domain compared to the linear power domain [24,37]. Furthermore, noise and interference cause disproportionately larger changes in dBm values for weaker signals compared to stronger ones [22]. Therefore, generating synthetic data that accurately reflects these statistical properties, especially for log-scale metrics, is non-trivial. While GANSec does not explicitly apply the specialized preprocessing techniques discussed for discriminative Received Signal Strength Indicator (RSSI) models, its generator must learn transformations that account for these statistical intricacies, and the discriminator's evaluation implicitly pushes the generated data towards realistic distributions, effectively addressing the challenges posed by logarithmic scales within the generative framework.

Incorporating Domain Knowledge: The conditional nature of GANSec allows us to explicitly guide the generation process using domain-specific information. The condition vector c can include parameters representing known environmental factors, device types, protocol states, specific interference signatures, or indicators of known vulnerabilities, enabling the generation of contextually relevant data.

4.3 Synthetic Data Generation and Usage Strategy

Once GANSec is trained on the available real data using either the EC or CO mechanism, we utilize the trained $\mathcal{G}$ to produce synthetic data. To generate synthetic samples corresponding to a specific class label and condition $\{y, c\}$, we sample a random noise vector z and provide the tuple $\{z, y, c\}$ as input to the trained $\mathcal{G}$. This process, detailed in Algorithm 3 (Appendix A), allows us to generate any desired number of synthetic samples for each class, potentially including optional post-processing or validation steps (e.g., using the $\mathcal{D}$ to filter generated samples based on a quality threshold t).

A key aspect of our proposed methodology involves training the downstream anomaly detection model exclusively on the synthetic data generated by GANSec. Employing a synthetic-only training strategy offers several significant advantages compared to using the original real-world data: (1) it allows for the generation of perfectly balanced datasets, mitigating issues caused by original class imbalance; (2) if the GAN captures the underlying distribution well, the synthetic data can exhibit greater diversity than the initial samples, potentially enhancing detector robustness and generalization; and (3) it offers potential privacy preservation benefits, as training the anomaly detector solely on synthetic data avoids direct exposure of potentially sensitive real-world measurements during this critical phase, which is particularly relevant when dealing with user data or proprietary network information.

5 Evaluation

This section details the experimental evaluation conducted to validate the effectiveness of our proposed GANSec framework. Following the methodology outlined in Sect. 4, our evaluation rigorously assesses GANSec from two critical perspectives. First, we quantitatively measure the fidelity and statistical similarity of the synthetic wireless data generated by different GANSec configurations compared to real-world data. Second, and crucially for addressing the challenges motivated in Sect. 2.3, we evaluate the effectiveness of using GANSec-generated data for training robust anomaly detection models. Particular focus is placed on the model's ability to generalize to unseen data collected under different network conditions, assessed through a challenging cross-scenario evaluation.

5.1 Experimental Setup

Data Description: The data used in our experiments consists of real-world 5G wireless measurements collected within the indoor environment illustrated in Fig. 3a. The hardware setup, shown in Fig. 3b, included a OnePlus Nord 2T 5G smartphone acting as the user equipment (UE), two Nuand bladeRF 2.0 micro SDRs configured as a 5G gNodeB and a jammer to introduce anomalies.

The jammer operated in the 5G n2 uplink frequency band (1850-1910 MHz) and was controlled using a sinusoidal power modulation pattern to create disruptive signals. This type of power-modulated jamming, with its continuously time-varying pattern, can be particularly challenging to detect compared to simplistic constant or reactive jammers [32]. Preliminary tests confirmed its effectiveness, as the jamming activity was observed to significantly impact the network latency of the UE during iperf3 testing.

We collected radio buffer messages from the Android smartphone via the Android Debug Bridge (ADB), capturing key signal quality indicators. To ensure data consistency, we parsed raw logs, handled missing values using interpolation, and normalized the features into uniform time-series segments. Ground truth labels y were assigned based on when the jammer was active, and a condition vector c was constructed for each sample, including the UE's distance to the gNodeB, device model, and modem temperature. This process yielded two datasets from the distinct setups shown in Fig. 3a: Scenario A, used for training, comprises 3000 samples collected over approximately 10 min and is relatively balanced, with jamming anomalies representing 46.37% of the data. To evaluate generalization, Scenario B serves exclusively as the unseen test set and contains 4559 samples collected from a different UE position with an additional obstacle. This scenario features a different class distribution, with anomalies constituting 65.08% of the samples.

Baselines for Comparison. We compare the performance achieved using GANSecaugmented data against models trained using three baseline data strategies:

- Raw Data Training: The downstream anomaly detection model trained directly on the original Scenario A dataset.
- Classical Oversampling: The downstream model trained on the Scenario A dataset augmented using DeepSMOTE [8], an advanced implementation that notably uses a Variational Autoencoder (VAE) to combine SMOTE [5] principles with deep learning representations.
- Unconditional GAN: The downstream model trained on data generated by TAnoGAN [3], representing another GAN-based approach for time-series anomaly detection, used here as a generative baseline.

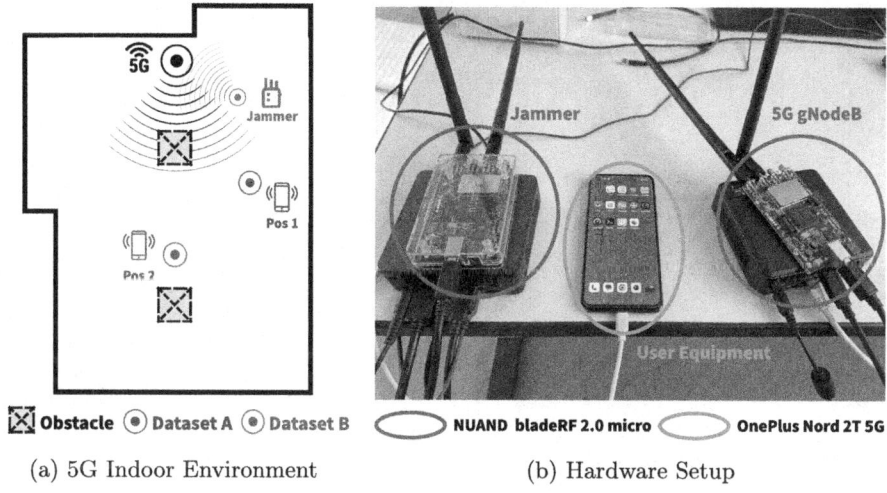

(a) 5G Indoor Environment (b) Hardware Setup

Fig. 3. Experimental Setup for Collecting Dataset A and B.

Downstream Anomaly Detection Model. To evaluate the utility of the generated data, we employed a downstream anomaly detection model tasked with classifying wireless measurements as 'normal' or 'anomalous' (jamming). We utilized a 3-layer Long Short-Term Memory (LSTM) network for this purpose, chosen for its ability to capture temporal dependencies in the signal data. Each LSTM layer contained 128 hidden units, followed by a dropout layer with a rate of 0.3 to prevent overfitting, and a final dense layer with a sigmoid activation function for classification. The model was trained using the Adam optimizer with a learning rate of 0.0001 for 128 epochs, utilizing binary cross-entropy as the loss function.

5.2 Synthetic Data Quality Analysis

We analyze the quality of synthetic wireless data generated by GANSec variants and baseline methods using Frächet Inception Distance (FID) [11] and Maximum Mean Discrepancy (MMD) [4] with an RBF kernel. These metrics are commonly used as they can reliably analyze feature distribution similarity. Lower scores indicate higher similarity to the real Scenario A data distribution. To assess the distribution and stability of these metrics, we performed 100 independent generation iterations for each model configuration, creating a synthetic dataset equivalent in size to Dataset A in each iteration. Figure 4 presents the Cumulative Distribution Functions (CDFs) of these scores.

For this process, we applied the optional validation step detailed in Algorithm 3, using the trained discriminator to filter generated samples with a default quality threshold of $t = 0.5$.

The DeepSMOTE [8] oversampling method yields very low FID and MMD scores (e.g., average FID 1.603, MMD 0.164), indicating generated samples

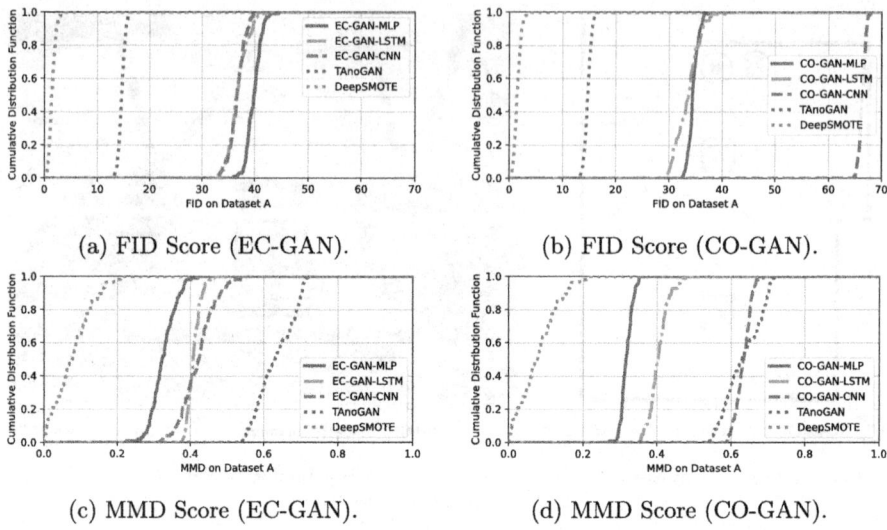

Fig. 4. Distribution Analysis on Synthetic Dataset.

closely mirror the original data but offer limited diversity due to its interpolative nature (as argued in Sect. 2.2). In contrast, the TAnoGAN [3] baseline shows low FID (14.762) but high MMD (0.632), suggesting it captures global data structure but struggles with local sample quality or diversity.

Generally, our proposed GANSec variants exhibit higher FID and MMD scores than DeepSMOTE. We interpret these higher scores not merely as lower fidelity, but rather as reflecting GANSec's ability to generate a more diverse set of synthetic samples, while still capturing key signal patterns. This increased diversity is hypothesized to be crucial for improving model robustness and generalization, which we test in Sect. 5.3. In generative modeling, FID scores for GAN can vary widely depending on the complexity of the data and the model; values in the range observed (e.g., up to 60–70 for CNN backbones) can be considered reasonable [11].

Within GANSec, the choice of neural network architecture influences synthetic data characteristics. MLP-based GAN tend towards lower MMD scores, while LSTM-based GAN show stable behavior across metrics. CNN-based GAN appear more "aggressive," producing potentially more diverse outputs (reflected in higher scores), which might explain the better cross-scenario performance observed later. This suggests a potential trade-off: architectures like CNN might sacrifice exact distributional match (higher FID/MMD) to achieve greater diversity beneficial for downstream task robustness.

5.3 Anomaly Detection Performance: Cross-Scenario Evaluation

Having analyzed the synthetic data quality, we now evaluate our primary hypothesis regarding GANSec's ability to enhance anomaly detector robustness and generalization. We conducted a cross-scenario evaluation, training the LSTM anomaly detector (detailed in Sect. 5.1) on data derived from Scenario A and testing on unseen Scenario B data. Results are averaged over 10 independent iterations to mitigate randomness. Notably, all models performed well (>98% accuracy) on Scenario A data itself, suggesting the synthetic-only training does not cause catastrophic forgetting. Figure 5 illustrates key accuracy results. The detailed peak performance metrics for each model are provided in Appendix B.

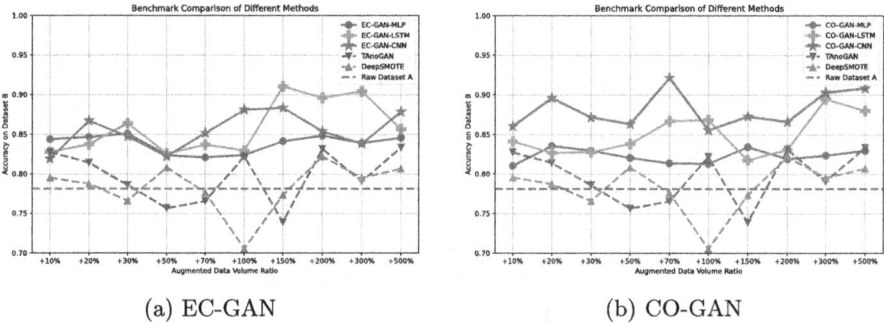

(a) EC-GAN   (b) CO-GAN

Fig. 5. Impact of the augmentation ratio (relative size of synthetic data used for training) on the accuracy achieved on the unseen Dataset B.

The generalization challenge is highlighted by the baseline LSTM model trained on raw Scenario A data: its accuracy dropped from approx. 92% when tested on Scenario A to 78% on Scenario B. This performance degradation underscores both the detection difficulty posed by the dynamic, power-modulated jammer implemented in our experiments and the substantial generalization gap faced by standard anomaly detection methods when encountering different network conditions.

In contrast, the results clearly demonstrate the advantage of the GANSec framework. Models trained exclusively on GANSec-generated data significantly outperformed all baseline methods on the unseen Scenario B, showcasing enhanced generalization by learning more fundamental anomaly features. Consistent with data quality analysis, LSTM and CNN backbones generally outperformed MLPs, reinforcing the importance of architectures that effectively model temporal signal characteristics. Comparing training objectives, the Classification-Oriented (CO-GAN) objective showed a slight edge over the Embedded Conditional (EC-GAN) variant, suggesting that directly incorporating the classification objective during generation may produce more discriminative synthetic samples.

The superior cross-scenario performance validates our synthetic-only GAN strategy for building robust detectors. This tailored approach handles unseen conditions, addressing a key limitation of prior work.

6 Discussion

This work demonstrates that GANSec, a tailored conditional GAN framework, significantly enhances the robustness and generalization of wireless anomaly detectors, particularly in challenging cross-scenario evaluations. Our results advocate for moving beyond generic augmentation towards methods designed for wireless data intricacies, where sequence-aware architectures (LSTMs, CNNs) offer advantages. The viability of augmented training also presents practical benefits regarding data imbalance, collection costs, and potential privacy enhancement.

Despite these promising results, we acknowledge limitations. Our current evaluation focused on jamming anomalies within a specific 5G context. However, it is important to note that the framework demonstrated effectiveness against a sophisticated, power-modulated jammer exhibiting dynamic time-varying patterns (as described in Sect. 5.1), suggesting its potential applicability extends beyond this specific scenario to other challenging wireless anomalies where capturing complex temporal dynamics is crucial. Nevertheless, further investigation is required to assess GANSec's applicability to other anomaly types and wireless technologies (e.g., Wi-Fi, IoT protocols). Additionally, while GAN can generate diverse data, risks remain regarding the potential amplification of biases present in the initial real dataset or the failure to generate truly novel "black swan" anomalies. The computational expense of training advanced GAN models is also a practical consideration.

Future research should prioritize extending GANSec to a wider spectrum of anomalies and network contexts, potentially exploring hybrid approaches combining real and synthetic data. Developing techniques to explicitly encourage the generation of rare or edge-case anomalies and further refining generative architectures (e.g., using attention mechanisms or investigating alternatives like diffusion models, despite their current computational complexity concerns) are promising directions. While diffusion models show potential, their iterative noise-and-denoise sampling process often requires hundreds to thousands of steps to produce a single high-quality sample, making them less suitable for the rapid, large-scale data-augmentation scenarios explored in this work. Crucially, validating enhanced approaches in real-time, operational settings is essential. Finally, while generative models can reduce the environmental impact associated with extensive physical data collection, the energy cost of training these complex models warrants consideration and comparison against traditional methods in future analyses.

7 Conclusion

Addressing the need for robust wireless anomaly detection despite data limitations, this work introduced GANSec, a tailored conditional GAN framework. We evaluated a novel strategy using exclusively GANSec-generated synthetic data for training the downstream detector. Cross-scenario evaluations confirmed this approach significantly enhances model generalization and robustness, effectively addressing the substantial performance degradation observed when anomaly classifiers, trained on limited data, encounter unseen network conditions. Our findings indicate that tailored generative models employing synthetic-only training offer a highly promising and effective path towards developing more reliable wireless security systems.

Acknowledgements. This research was made possible with support from the Horizon Europe research and innovation program of the European Union under grant agreement number 101092912 (project MLSysOps) and COST Action CA 22104 BEiNG-WISE.

A Algorithms

This appendix details the core algorithms used within the GANSec framework.

Algorithm 1. Embedded Conditional GAN Training: $\mathcal{D}$ focuses on distinguishing real samples from synthetic samples based on the provided context

---
Require: Feature set $x \sim dist_{\{y,c\}}(x)$ with label y and condition c
Ensure: Discriminator $\mathcal{D}$, Generator $\mathcal{G}$
1: Initialize number of epochs ε, loss function $\mathcal{L}$, loss weights ω_i
2: **for** current_epoch $\leftarrow 1, 2, ..\varepsilon$ **do**
3:     Sample noise $z \sim \mathcal{N}(0, I)$
4:     Generate synthetic data using $\mathcal{G}$: $\hat{x} \leftarrow \mathcal{G}(z, \{y, c\})$
5:     Discriminate real or synthetic data using $\mathcal{D}$

$$output\_real \leftarrow \mathcal{D}(x, \{y, c\})$$

$$output\_synthetic \leftarrow \mathcal{D}(\hat{x}, \{y, c\})$$

6:     Compute loss for $\mathcal{G}$ and $\mathcal{D}$

$$loss_\mathcal{D} \leftarrow \omega_0 \times \mathcal{L}(1, output\_real) + \omega_1 \times \mathcal{L}(0, output\_synthetic)$$

$$loss_\mathcal{G} \leftarrow \omega_2 \times \mathcal{L}(1, output\_synthetic)$$

7: **end for**

Algorithm 2. Classification Oriented GAN Training: $\mathcal{D}$ performs a dual role: it assesses the realism of the input sample and predicts its class label.

Require: Feature set $x \sim dist_{\{y,c\}}(x)$ with label y and condition c
Ensure: Discriminator $\mathcal{D}$, Generator $\mathcal{G}$
1: Initialize number of epochs ε, loss functions $\mathcal{L}_i$, loss weights ω_i
2: **for** current_epoch $\leftarrow 1, 2, ..\varepsilon$ **do**
3:   Sample noise $z \sim \mathcal{N}(0, I)$
4:   Generate synthetic data using $\mathcal{G}$: $\hat{x} \leftarrow \mathcal{G}(z, \{y, c\})$
5:   Discriminate real or synthetic data and predict label using $\mathcal{D}$

$$\{output\_real, y'\} \leftarrow \mathcal{D}(x, c)$$

$$\{output\_synthetic, \hat{y}\} \leftarrow \mathcal{D}(\hat{x}, c)$$

6:   Compute loss for $\mathcal{G}$ and $\mathcal{D}$

$$loss_{\mathcal{D}} \leftarrow \omega_0 \times \mathcal{L}_0(1, output\_real) + \omega_1 \times \mathcal{L}_1(y, y') +$$
$$\omega_2 \times \mathcal{L}_0(0, output\_synthetic) + \omega_3 \times \mathcal{L}_1(y, \hat{y})$$
$$loss_{\mathcal{G}} \leftarrow \omega_4 \times \mathcal{L}_0(1, output\_synthetic) + \omega_5 \times \mathcal{L}_1(y, \hat{y})$$

7: **end for**

Algorithm 3. Synthetic Data Generation: $\mathcal{G}$ produces regulated synthetic feature sets given a target label $\hat{y}$ and condition $\hat{c}$, including an optional step for validating the quality of generated samples using the $\mathcal{D}$ with a threshold t

---
Require: Generator $\mathcal{G}$, Discriminator $\mathcal{D}$, label $\hat{y}$ and condition $\hat{c}$
Ensure: Synthetic feature set $\hat{x}$
1: Initialize regulations $regul(x)$, discriminator threshold t
2: **while** $p < t$ **do**
3:   Sample noise $z \sim \mathcal{N}(0, I)$
4:   Generate synthetic data using $\mathcal{G}$: $\hat{x} \leftarrow \mathcal{G}(z, \{\hat{y}, \hat{c}\})$
5:   Regulate synthetic data: $\hat{x}' \leftarrow regul(\hat{x})$
6:   Validate using $\mathcal{D}$: $p \leftarrow \mathcal{D}(\hat{x}')$
7: **end while**

B Detailed Performance Metrics

To supplement the accuracy results presented in Sect. 5.3, Table 1 provides a more detailed breakdown of model performance on the unseen Scenario B dataset. For each model, the table reports the peak accuracy, precision, recall, F1, and ROC-AUC score achieved at its optimal data augmentation ratio.

Table 1. Peak Performance Metrics on Unseen Scenario B. For each model, the table reports key metrics at the augmentation ratio that yielded its optimal accuracy.

Model	Aug. Ratio	Acc.	Prec.	Rec.	F1	ROC.
Raw Data (Baseline)	N/A	0.781	0.914	0.735	0.815	0.802
DeepSMOTE	+200%	0.822	0.765	0.794	0.779	0.844
TAnoGAN	+500%	0.833	0.928	0.806	0.863	0.845
EC-GAN-MLP	+30%	0.851	0.836	**0.981**	0.903	0.792
EC-GAN-LSTM	+150%	0.910	**0.962**	0.922	**0.942**	0.905
EC-GAN-CNN	+150%	0.883	0.925	0.894	0.910	0.878
CO-GAN-MLP	+20%	0.836	0.823	0.975	0.893	0.772
CO-GAN-LSTM	+300%	0.894	0.936	0.884	0.910	**0.922**
CO-GAN-CNN	+70%	**0.921**	0.945	0.934	0.940	0.915

References

1. Alhoraibi, L., Alghazzawi, D., Alhebshi, R.: Generative adversarial network-based data augmentation for enhancing wireless physical layer authentication. Sensors (2024). https://doi.org/10.3390/s24020641
2. Ang, K.L.M., Seng, J.K.P., Zungeru, A.M.: Optimizing energy consumption for big data collection in large-scale wireless sensor networks with mobile collectors. IEEE Syst. J. **12**(1), 616–626 (2018). https://doi.org/10.1109/JSYST.2016.2630691
3. Bashar, M.A., Nayak, R.: Tanogan: time series anomaly detection with generative adversarial networks. In: 2020 IEEE Symposium Series on Computational Intelligence (SSCI), pp. 1778–1785 (2020). https://doi.org/10.1109/SSCI47803.2020.9308512
4. Briol, F.X., Barp, A., Duncan, A.B., Girolami, M.: Statistical inference for generative models with maximum mean discrepancy (2019). https://arxiv.org/abs/1906.05944
5. Chawla, N.V., Bowyer, K.W., Hall, L.O., Kegelmeyer, W.P.: Smote: synthetic minority over-sampling technique. J. Artifi. Intell. Res. **16**, 321–357 (2002). https://doi.org/10.1613/jair.953
6. Chen, B., Ma, J., Zhang, L., Zhou, J., Fan, J., Lan, H.: Research progress of wireless positioning methods based on RSSI. Electronics **13**(2), 360 (2024)
7. Chi, G., et al.: Rf-diffusion: radio signal generation via time-frequency diffusion. In: Proceedings of the 30th Annual International Conference on Mobile Computing and Networking, ACM MobiCom 2024. Association for Computing Machinery (2024). https://doi.org/10.1145/3636534.3649348
8. Dablain, D., Krawczyk, B., Chawla, N.V.: Deepsmote: fusing deep learning and smote for imbalanced data. IEEE Trans. Neural Netw. Learn. Syst. **34**(9), 6390–6404 (2023). https://doi.org/10.1109/TNNLS.2021.3136503
9. Goodfellow, I.J., et al.: Generative adversarial nets. In: Ghahramani, Z., Welling, M., Cortes, C., Lawrence, N., Weinberger, K. (eds.) Advances in Neural Information Processing Systems, vol. 27. Curran Associates, Inc. (2014)
10. Gulrajani, I., Ahmed, F., Arjovsky, M., Dumoulin, V., Courville, A.C.: Improved training of wasserstein gans. In: Guyon, I., et al. (eds.) Advances in Neural Information Processing Systems. vol. 30. Curran Associates, Inc. (2017)

11. Heusel, M., Ramsauer, H., Unterthiner, T., Nessler, B., Hochreiter, S.: Gans trained by a two time-scale update rule converge to a local nash equilibrium. In: Advances in Neural Information Processing Systems, vol. 30. Curran Associates, Inc. (2017)
12. Hoeltgebaum, H., Adams, N., Fernandes, C.: Estimation, forecasting, and anomaly detection for nonstationary streams using adaptive estimation. IEEE Trans. Cybernet. **52**(8), 7956–7967 (2022). https://doi.org/10.1109/TCYB.2021.3054161
13. Iftikhar, U., Ali, S.A.: Enhanced cyber threat detection system leveraging machine learning using data augmentation. Inter. J. Adv. Comput. Sci. Appli. **16**(2) (2025).https://doi.org/10.14569/IJACSA.2025.0160223
14. Jiang, X., et al.: Netdiffusion: network data augmentation through protocol-constrained traffic generation. Proc. ACM Meas. Anal. Comput. Syst. **8**(1) (2024) https://doi.org/10.1145/3639037
15. Jin, Q., Lin, R., Yang, F.: E-wacgan: enhanced generative model of signaling data based on wgan-gp and acgan. IEEE Syst. J. **14**(3), 3289–3300 (2020). https://doi.org/10.1109/JSYST.2019.2935457
16. Karkouch, A., Mousannif, H., Moatassime, H.A., Noel, T.: Data quality in internet of things: a state-of-the-art survey. J. Netw. Comput. Appl. **73**, 57–81 (2016)
17. Kim, J., Jeong, K., Choi, H., Seo, K.: GAN-based anomaly detection in imbalance problems. In: Bartoli, A., Fusiello, A. (eds.) ECCV 2020. LNCS, vol. 12540, pp. 128–145. Springer, Cham (2020). https://doi.org/10.1007/978-3-030-65414-6_11
18. Kim, K.: Gan based augmentation for improving anomaly detection accuracy in host-based intrusion detection systems. Inter. J. Eng. Res. Technol. **13**, 3987 (2020). https://doi.org/10.37624/IJERT/13.11.2020.3987-3996
19. Kim, K.: Gan based augmentation for improving anomaly detection accuracy in host-based intrusion detection systems. Inter. J. Eng. Res. Technol. **13**, 3987 (11 2020).https://doi.org/10.37624/IJERT/13.11.2020.3987-3996
20. Kousias, K., et al.: A large-scale dataset of 4g, nb-iot, and 5g non-standalone network measurements. IEEE Commun. Mag. **62**(5), 44–49 (2024). https://doi.org/10.1109/MCOM.011.2200707
21. Lemieszewski, t., Hannebauer, D., Remiszewski, G.: Vulnerability of wi-fi wireless network to signal interference. J. Eng. **360**(1), 58–65 (2024). https://doi.org/10.5604/01.3001.0054.8861
22. Maduranga, M., Oruthota, U., Lakmal, H., Kulatunga, S.: Rssi-based indoor localization using deep learning with a custom loss function. In: 2024 8th SLAAI International Conference on Artificial Intelligence (SLAAI-ICAI), pp. 1–5 (2024) https://doi.org/10.1109/SLAAI-ICAI63667.2024.10844973
23. Marfievici, R., Murphy, A.L., Picco, G.P., Ossi, F., Cagnacci, F.: How environmental factors impact outdoor wireless sensor networks: A case study. In: 2013 IEEE 10th International Conference on Mobile Ad-Hoc and Sensor Systems, pp. 565–573 (2013) https://doi.org/10.1109/MASS.2013.13
24. Naghdi, S., O'Keefe, K.: Combining multichannel RSSI and vision with artificial neural networks to improve BLE trilateration. Sensors **22**(12), 4320 (2022)
25. O'Reilly, C., Gluhak, A., Imran, M.A., Rajasegarar, S.: Anomaly detection in wireless sensor networks in a non-stationary environment. IEEE Commun. Surv. Tutorials **16**(3), 1413–1432 (2014). https://doi.org/10.1109/SURV.2013.112813.00168
26. Pham, T.M.T., Premkumar, K., Naili, M., Yang, J.: Time to retrain? detecting concept drifts in machine learning systems (2024). https://arxiv.org/abs/2410.09190
27. Phung, C.D., Yellas, N.E.H., Ruba, S.B., Secci, S.: An open dataset for beyond-5g data-driven network automation experiments. In: 2022 1st International Conference on 6G Networking (6GNet), pp. 1–4 (2022). https://doi.org/10.1109/6GNet54646.2022.9830292

28. Raza, U., Camerra, A., Murphy, A.L., Palpanas, T., Picco, G.P.: Practical data prediction for real-world wireless sensor networks. IEEE Trans. Knowl. Data Eng. **27**(8), 2231–2244 (2015). https://doi.org/10.1109/TKDE.2015.2411594
29. Schummer, P., del Rio, A., Serrano, J., Jimenez, D., Sanchez, G., Llorente, A.: Machine learning-based network anomaly detection: design, implementation, and evaluation. AI (2024https://doi.org/10.3390/ai5040143
30. Song, H., Jiang, Z., Men, A., Yang, B.: A hybrid semi-supervised anomaly detection model for high-dimensional data. Comput. Intell. Neurosc. **2017**(1), 8501683 (2017). _eprint: https://onlinelibrary.wiley.com/doi/pdf/10.1155/2017/8501683
31. Talagala, P.D., Hyndman, R.J., Smith-Miles, K.: Anomaly Detection in High-Dimensional Data. J. Comput. Graph. Statist. (Jun 2021)
32. Tedeschi, P., Oligeri, G., Di Pietro, R.: Localization of a power-modulated jammer. Sensors **22**(2), 646 (2022)
33. Wang, S., Li, C., Lim, A.: A model for non-stationary time series and its applications in filtering and anomaly detection. IEEE Trans. Instrum. Meas. **70**, 1–11 (2021). https://doi.org/10.1109/TIM.2021.3059321
34. Wen, J., et al.: Generative ai for data augmentation in wireless networks: analysis, applications, and case study (2024). https://arxiv.org/abs/2411.08341
35. Wong, C., Wang, M., Hossain, M.F., Munasinghe, K.: Internet of things anomaly detection enhancement using gan-based data augmentation. In: 2024 17th International Conference on Signal Processing and Communication System (ICSPCS) (2024). https://doi.org/10.1109/ICSPCS63175.2024.10815773
36. Xie, M., Han, S., Tian, B., Parvin, S.: Anomaly detection in wireless sensor networks: A survey. J. Netw. Comput. Appl. **34**(4), 1302–1325 (2011). https://doi.org/10.1016/j.jnca.2011.03.004, https://www.sciencedirect.com/science/article/pii/S1084804511000580, advanced Topics in Cloud Computing
37. Xu, J., Dai, H., Ying, W.h.: Multi-layer neural network for received signal strength-based indoor localisation. IET Commun. **10** (2016). https://doi.org/10.1049/iet-com.2015.0469
38. Yang, M., Zhang, J.: Data anomaly detection in the internet of things: a review of current trends and research challenges. Inter. J. Adv. Comput. Sci. Appli. **14** (2023). https://doi.org/10.14569/IJACSA.2023.0140901

Fine-Grained Data Poisoning Attack to Local Differential Privacy Protocols for Key-Value Data

Terumi Yaguchi and Hiroaki Kikuchi[✉]

Graduate School of Advanced Mathematical Science, Meiji University, 4-21-1 Nakano, Tokyo 164-8522, Japan
kikn@meiji.ac.jp

Abstract. With the spread of smart devices, companies improve their services by collecting and utilizing users' behavioral data. However, the collected data from the user's device can create issues concerning the identification of individuals, and hence privacy protection is required. Local Differential Privacy (LDP) is a technique that perturbs the user's data before sending to the server so that the server is not able to have access to private data. Unfortunately, LDP is vulnerable to a poisoning attack in which a set of malicious users disrupt the estimated statistics by sending crafted data. In 2024, Li et al. showed that fine-grained manipulation of the estimated means is feasible. In this work, we study a new fine-grained attack to a multidimensional data with LDP known as Locally Differentially Private Correlated Key-Value (PCKV) for key-value data. We evaluate the proposed fine-grained PCKV attack from both theoretical and empirical viewpoints.

1 Introduction

The exponential growth of data collection across industries has raised significant concerns regarding user privacy. To address these concerns, Local Differential Privacy (LDP) [1] has emerged as a fundamental technique that enables organizations to collect and analyze data while preserving individual privacy. Unlike traditional Central Differential Privacy, which relies on a trusted data aggregator to enforce privacy, LDP ensures that data are randomized before they leave the user's device, thereby eliminating the need for a trusted third party. This property has rendered LDP the preferred choice for large-scale, privacy-preserving data collection and analytics, with major platforms such as Google [6], Apple [7], and Microsoft deploying LDP-based systems for tasks like telemetry collection and user behavior analysis.

LDP is particularly effective in scenarios involving key-value data, where users submit a set of tuples of sensitive values associated with categorical keys. Such data structures are ubiquitous in real-world applications, including recommendation systems, telemetry reports, and personalized services. The key challenges in applying LDP to key-value data lie in the difficulty of perturbing keys and values while maintaining the accuracy of statistical aggregation. If all key and value tuples are independently protected, the system suffers from high distortion to satisfy LDP according to sequential composition. Several studies have attempted to address the issue. Ye et al. [15] proposed PrivKV with a multiple-stage perturbation mechanism that first samples an index from the domain of all keys before applying LDP noise to the optimized key encoding. The PCKV of Gu et al. [13] refined Ye's approach by employing Padding-and-Sampling [11], which handles a large domain better than the sampling protocol in PrivKV.

However, while LDP provides strong theoretical privacy guarantees, it's robustness against adversarial manipulation remains an open challenge. A key concern is the vulnerability of the LDP mechanisms to poisoning attacks, where malicious participants inject strategically crafted noise into the data collection process to manipulate aggregate statistics. Cao et al. [14] studied poisoning attacks on some LDP schemes, GRR [2], OUE [9], and OLH for estimating the frequencies of the keys. Wu et al. [12] studied poisoning attacks to LDP protocols for key-value data, PrivKV, PCKV-GRR, and PCKV-UE [13]. Song et al. [22] studied the countermeasures to prevent users from poisoning.

Recently, Li et al. [3] proposed an advanced poisoning, called fine-grained attack, which allows the attacker to manipulate statistics estimated from the LDP scheme. In the conventional poisoning, the attacker's goal is to disrupt LDP by injecting fake data to skew the statistical estimate. In contrast, in a fine-grained attack, the attacker not only skews the statistics but also manipulates the estimates to arbitrary target values. In their work, they focus on two LDP schemes, Stochastic Rounding (SR) and Piecewise Mechanism (PM), designed for mean and variance of *numerical values*.

In this paper, we explore the fine-grained poisoning to state-of-the-art LDP schemes for key-value data, PrivKV, PCKV-GRR, and PCKV-UE. Fine-grained poisoning attacks on key-value data present unique challenges due to the inherent uncertainty and constraints of the data collection process. Unlike conventional poisoning, where an adversary directly injects fake data, fine-grained poisoning must strategically design specific numbers of malicious users sending particular values during the perturbing processes. One major challenge is that the attack's success depends on the target statistics –; if the target key is already highly frequent, small-scale manipulation may be insufficient to alter aggregate statistics. Conversely, if the target value is too low, large-scale manipulation may be required. Additionally, it is not trivial which LDP protocols (PrivKV, PCKV-GRR and PCKV-UE) are inherently more vulnerable to such attack, as the varying privacy budget and the number of malicious users affect the feasibility of the attack. Moreover, the same estimation techniques that enhance utility for genuine users also benefit attackers, allowing malicious players to fine-tune poisoning strategies. This dual effect makes it difficult to design a defense to detect an attacker without harming the accuracy of estimation. Table 1 presents target statistics alongside the attack objectives, highlighting how our work differs from conventional studies.

Our contributions are as follows.

1. We propose a fine-grained data poisoning attack against the state-of-the-art LDP protocols (PrivKV, PCKV-GRR and PCKV-UE) for key-value data.

Table 1. Attacks to LDP schemes

attack	variance	mean	frequency
disruption of estimate		[12]	[5,14]
Fine-grained poisoning	[3]		This work

2. We theoretically analyze the sufficient conditions to launch the fine-grained poisoning to given key-value data and the target statistics.
3. We empirically evaluate our attacks on some open datasets and show the comparison across datasets. The results show that our proposed poisoning methods are mostly feasible with a very small number of malicious users to send fake data. We also found interesting trade-off between the estimate accuracy and poisoning resilience. (The most accurate LDP scheme is the most vulnerable for some target statistics.) The some datasets show consistent behaviors in terms of several key features.
4. We discuss mitigation to prevent the proposed fine-grained poisoning attack.

The remainder of our paper is organized as follows. In Sect. 2, we define fundamental notions in LDP and the technical details of PrivKV and PCKV. Our proposed protocol is described in Sect. 3, after defining objectives and assumptions, the main theorems for strategies to manipulate the estimated statistics to be targets. Section 4 presents the experiments we conducted using open data, and clarifies which LDP scheme is the most vulnerable to the proposed attack. We discuss some possible mitigations to the attack in Sect. 5. We conclude this work in Sect. 6.

2 Preliminary

2.1 Local Differential Privacy

In the local differential setting, each user perturbs input data using a randomizing mechanism M and sends to a server that cannot distinguish what private input was perturbed.

Definition 1. Local Differential Privacy. *Let $\mathcal{X}$ and $\mathcal{Y}$ be sets of input and output values, respectively. For a given $x \in \mathcal{X}$, a randomized mechanism M satisfies ϵ-LDP if and only if for any pair of input $x, x' \in \mathcal{X}$, and any output $y \in \mathcal{Y}$, the probability ratio of outputting the same y should be bounded*

$$Pr[M(x, \epsilon) = y] \leq e^\epsilon Pr[M(x', \epsilon) = y]$$

2.2 PrivKV

Ye et al. [15] addressed the issue using two variables that are perturbed accordingly in their proposed LDP algorithm, PrivKV. PrivKV takes inputs in the form of key-value data, two-dimensional data structure of discrete (key) and continuous (value) variables, and estimates the key frequencies and the mean values. Their idea combines two LDP protocols, Randomized Response (RR) for randomizing keys, and Value Perturbing Protocol (VPP) for perturbing values. The dimension is restricted to two, but the key-value is known as a primitive data structure commonly used for several applications. For example, a movie evaluation dataset consists of ratings for movies, which are stored in a key-value database where the keys are movie titles and the values are ratings for the titles. In a smartphone survey, users indicate their favorite apps, such as $\langle \text{YouTube}, 0.5 \rangle$, $\langle \text{Twitter}, 0.1 \rangle$, $\langle \text{Instagram}, 0.2 \rangle$, by stating their total time using those apps.

Let S_i be a set of key-value tuples $\langle k, v \rangle$ owned by i-th user. In PrivKV, the set of tuples is encoded as a d-dimensional vector, where d is the cardinality of the domain of keys K and the missing key is represented as $\langle k, v \rangle = \langle 0, 0 \rangle$. For instance, a set of key-value $S_i = \{\langle k_1, v_1 \rangle, \langle k_4, v_4 \rangle, \langle k_5, v_5 \rangle\}$ is encoded as $d = 5$ dimensional vector $\boldsymbol{S}_i = (\langle 1, v_1 \rangle, \langle 0, 0 \rangle, \langle 0, 0 \rangle, \langle 1, v_4 \rangle, \langle 1, v_5 \rangle)$ where keys k_1, k_4, and k_5 are specified implicitly with 1 at the corresponding location.

Perturbation in PrivKV is performed by random sampling one element $\langle k_a, v_a \rangle$ from $\boldsymbol{S}_i$. It has two proceeding steps, perturbing values, and keys. It employs VPP used in [10] for the chosen tuple. A value of the tuple $\langle 1, v_a \rangle$ is replaced by $v^+{}_a = VPP(v_a, \epsilon_2)$, where ϵ_2 is a privacy budget for values. A value of the "missing" tuple $\langle 0, 0 \rangle$ is replaced by $v^+{}_a = VPP(v'_a, \epsilon_2)$, where v'_a is chosen uniformly from $[-1, 1]$.

It uses RR with privacy budget ϵ_1. A tuple $\langle 1, v_a \rangle$ is randomized as

$$\langle k_a^*, v_a^+ \rangle = \begin{cases} \langle 1, v_a^+ \rangle & w/p \ p_1 = \frac{e^{\epsilon_1}}{1+e^{\epsilon_1}}, \\ \langle 0, 0 \rangle & w/p \ q_1 = \frac{1}{1+e^{\epsilon_1}}, \end{cases}$$

where v_a^+ is perturbed as mentioned. A "missing" tuple $\langle 0, 0 \rangle$ is randomized as

$$\langle k_a^*, v_a^+ \rangle = \begin{cases} \langle 0, 0 \rangle & w/p \ p_1 = \frac{e^{\epsilon_1}}{1+e^{\epsilon_1}}, \\ \langle 1, v_a^+ \rangle & w/p \ q_1 = \frac{1}{1+e^{\epsilon_1}}. \end{cases}$$

Responder in PrivKV submits the perturbed tuple $\langle k_a^*, v_a^+ \rangle$ with the index a of the tuple.

Given the perturbed tuples $\langle k_a^*, v_a^+ \rangle$ sent from n responders, we can estimate the key frequencies and the mean values as follows. Letting f_i be a true frequency of key k_i and f'_i be the observed key frequencies $k_i = 1$ of the perturbed vectors, we have the most likelihood estimation of frequency as

$$\hat{f}_i = \frac{p - 1 + f'_i}{2p_1 - 1}, \tag{1}$$

where $p_1 = \frac{e^{\epsilon_1}}{1+e^{\epsilon_1}}$.

Let n'_{1i} and n'_{2i} be the observed frequencies of tuples such that $\langle k_a^{ast}, v_a^+ \rangle = \langle 1,1 \rangle$ and $\langle k_a^{ast}, v_a^+ \rangle = \langle 1,-1 \rangle$, respectively. Similar to VPP's estimation, we have the most likelihood estimation of the mean values with key k_i as

$$\hat{\mu}_i = \frac{\hat{n}_{1i} - \hat{n}_{2i}}{N}, \qquad (2)$$

where $N = n'_{1i} + n'_{2i}$ and $\hat{n}_{1i}$ and $\hat{n}_{2i}$ are the estimated frequencies of $\langle 1,1 \rangle$ and $\langle 1,-1 \rangle$, respectively, computed as $\hat{n}_{1i} = \frac{N(p_2-1)+n'_{1i}}{2p_2-1}, \hat{n}_{2i} = \frac{N(p_2-1)+n'_{2i}}{2p_2-1}$, where $p_2 = \frac{e^{\epsilon_2}}{1+e^{\epsilon_2}}$.

Because of the compositional theorem of differential privacy, the sequential composition of randomized algorithms with privacy budgets ϵ_1 (for keys) and ϵ_2 (for values) is $(\epsilon_1 + \epsilon_2, 0)$-differential private. The total privacy budget of PrivKV is proved as $\epsilon = \epsilon_1 + \epsilon_2$ and budgets are arbitrarily assigned. We assume $\epsilon_1 = \epsilon_2 = \frac{\epsilon}{2}$ and conduct some experiments later.

2.3 PCKV

Gu et al. proposed the improved LDP scheme PCKV in [13].

PrivKV has a limitation in sampling and does not work well for a large domain. Since it uniformly samples an index over the large domain, a limited number of key-value pairs per user were chosen, resulting in a low estimation accuracy. PCKV addresses the issue by introducing an efficient Padding-and-Sampling mechanism.

Sampling

Input: A set of key-value pairs S_i for user i, padding length ℓ.
Output: Sampled key-value pair $\langle k, v \rangle$.
Sampling Randomly draw B from Bernoulli process of $\eta = \frac{|S_i|}{\max\{|S_i|,\ell\}}$. If $B = 1$ then sample a key-value pair $\langle k, v^* \rangle$ uniformly from S_i. If $B = 0$ then set $v^* = 0$ and randomly draw k from $\{d+1, \ldots, d+\ell\}$. Set $v = 1$ with probability $\frac{1+v^*}{2}$, otherwise $v = -1$ with probability $\frac{1-v^*}{2}$. Return $\langle k, v \rangle$.

PCKV-UE. Gu et al. proposed two protocols PCKV-UE (based on Unary Encoding) and PCK-GRR (based on Generalized Randomized Response). Unary encoding was optimized according to the work of Wang et al. [9].

Let $\langle k, v \rangle$ be input key-value tuple, where $k \in \mathcal{K} \cup \{d+1, \ldots, d+\ell\}$ and $v \in \{-1, 1\}$. In PCKV-UE, the output is $(d+\ell)$ dimensional vector $\boldsymbol{y} = (y_1, \ldots, y_{d+\ell}) \in \{1, -1, 0\}^{d+\ell}$ defined as

$$y_k = \begin{cases} v & \text{w.p. } ap, \\ -v & \text{w.p. } a(1-p), \\ 0 & \text{w.p. } 1-a \end{cases}$$

for k, and
$$y_i = \begin{cases} 1 & \text{w.p. } \frac{b}{2}, \\ -1 & \text{w.p. } \frac{b}{2}, \\ 0 & \text{w.p. } 1-b \end{cases}$$
for $i \neq k \in \{1, \ldots, k-1, k+1, \ldots, d+\ell\}$, where $a = \frac{1}{2}, b = \frac{2}{e^\epsilon + 3}$, and $p = \frac{e^\epsilon}{e^\epsilon + 1}$.

Note that the key is perturbed with privacy budget $\epsilon_1 = \ln \frac{a(1-b)}{b(1-a)}$ and the value is perturbed with $\epsilon_2 = \ln p/(1-p)$. With privacy budget $\epsilon = \max(\epsilon_2, \epsilon_1 + \ln(2/(1+e^{-\epsilon_2})))$, PCKV-UE is proved as ϵ-LDP in [13].

PCKV-GRR. In PCKV-GRR, we perturb a key-value data $\langle k, v \rangle$ and output $\langle k', v' \rangle$ computed as
$$\langle k', v' \rangle = \begin{cases} \langle k, v \rangle & \text{w.p. } ap, \\ \langle k, -v \rangle & \text{w.p. } a(1-p), \\ \langle i, 1 \rangle & \text{w.p. } \frac{b}{2}, \\ \langle i, -1 \rangle & \text{w.p. } \frac{b}{2} \end{cases}$$
where i is chosen uniformly over $[d+\ell] \setminus \{k\}$ and $a = \frac{\ell(e^\epsilon - 1) + 2}{\ell(e^\epsilon - 1) + 2(d+\ell)}, b = \frac{1-a}{d+\ell-1}$, and $p = \frac{\ell(e^\epsilon - 1) + 1}{\ell(e^\epsilon - 1) + 2}$.

Estimation. When a server receives n perturbed data, it counts the frequencies of value $y_i = 1$ and $y_i = -1$ for key k as n_1^k and n_{-1}^k, respectively. For frequency estimation, we calibrate the counts as
$$\hat{f}_k = \frac{\frac{n_1^k + n_{-1}^k}{n} - b}{a - b} \ell \tag{3}$$
and estimate the mean of value for key k as
$$\hat{\mu}_k = \frac{\hat{n}_1^k - \hat{n}_{-1}^k}{n \hat{f}_k} \ell, \tag{4}$$
where $\hat{n}_1^k$ and $\hat{n}_{-1}^k$ are given by
$$\begin{bmatrix} \hat{n}_1^k \\ \hat{n}_{-1}^k \end{bmatrix} = A^{-1} \begin{bmatrix} n_1^k - \frac{nb}{2} \\ n_{-1}^k - \frac{nb}{2} \end{bmatrix}, A = \begin{bmatrix} ap - \frac{b}{2} & a(1-p) - \frac{b}{2} \\ a(1-p) - \frac{b}{2} & ap - \frac{b}{2} \end{bmatrix}.$$

To improve the accuracy, we perform clipping $\hat{f}_k$ into $[\frac{1}{n}, 1]$ and $\hat{n}_1^k, \hat{n}_{-1}^k$ into $[0, \frac{n \hat{f}_k}{\ell}]$.

3 Fine-Grained Poisoning to PCKV

3.1 Problem Setting

Objectives. Our goal is to perform *fine-grained poisoning* that allows the attacker to manipulate the estimation of statistics as intended values, which is a more difficult challenge than the conventional poisoning attack that disrupts the accurate estimate by injecting crafted data.

The fine-grained poisoning was proposed by Li et al. [3]. The first targets of fine-grained attack were the mean and the variance estimated based on Stochastic Rounding [16] and Piecewise Mechanism [17]. In our work, we study a fine-grained poisoning to LDP schemes for key-value data including PrivKV [15], PCKV-GRR, and PCKV-UE [13], clarify sufficient conditions of fine-grained attacks, and quantify which scheme is the most vulnerable to the attack.

Threat Model. We assume that a server is untrusted as usual in a local model. Most n clients are trusted, but the attacker can compromise m malicious users who violate the predetermined LDP protocols and who are arbitrarily controlled by the attacker.

We also assume that the target statistics are stable for a longer period and the rough estimation of the target statistics are available to attackers. However, the latest values are hidden.

Overview. Figure 1 illustrates the proposed fine-grained poisoning attack. n genuine users follow the LDP scheme to their sets of key-value data $S_1, \ldots, S_n$ and send the perturbed data $y_1, \ldots, y_n$ to a server who estimates the frequency and mean as $\hat{f}_k = 0.33$ and $\hat{\mu} = 0.65$, which are close to the true statistics. In the attacked case, the attacker compromises m malicious users who cast the crafted data y_{craft} without perturbing LDP steps and manipulate the estimate so that $\mathbb{E}[\hat{f}_k] = f_{k,t}$ and $\mathbb{E}[\hat{\mu}_k] = \mu_{k,t}$ hold for any key k.

The symbols are summarized in Table 2.

3.2 Poisoning to PrivKV

In PrivKV, after sampling key j, a client sends the perturbed data in $\langle 1, 1 \rangle, \langle 1, -1 \rangle, \langle 0, 0 \rangle$. Hence, letting m_1^k, m_{-1}^k and m_0^k be the numbers of malicious users who send 1, −1, and 0 for target key k, respectively, and having the known estimations in Eq. (1), we have an expiated value of the target frequency $f_{k,t}$ as

$$\mathbb{E}[\hat{f}_k] = \mathbb{E}\left[\frac{(n_1^k + n_{-1}^k + m_1^k + m_{-1}^k)/(n^k + m^k) - q_1}{p_1 - q_1}\right]$$

$$\simeq \frac{(\mathbb{E}[n_1^k + n_{-1}^k] + m_1^k + m_{-1}^k)/(\mathbb{E}[n^k] + m^k) - q_1}{p_1 - q_1} = f_{k,t},$$

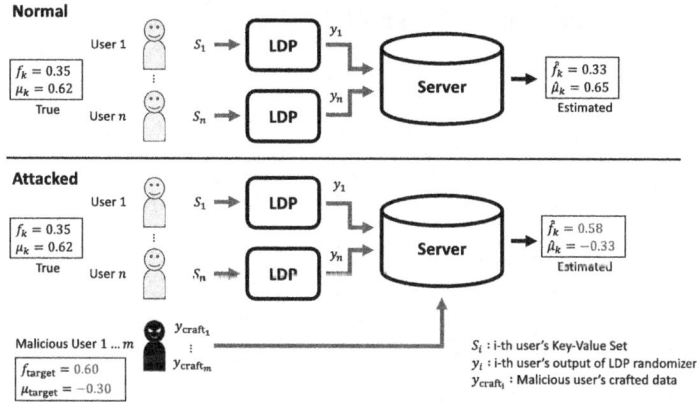

Fig. 1. Overview of the proposed fine-grained poisoning.

Table 2. Table of symbols

Notation	Description
β	The fraction of malicious users ($\beta = \frac{m}{m+n}$)
n_v^k	The number of genuine users who have value v for key k
m_v^k	The number of malicious users who have value v for key k
n^k, m^k	The number of genuine and malicious users who have key k
n, m	The number of genuine and malicious users, respectively
$f_{k,t}$	The target frequency of users for key k
$\mu_{k,t}$	The target mean of value for key k
f_k	The true frequency of users for key k
μ_k	The true mean of value for key k
$f_{k,e}, \mu_{k,e}$	The attacker's estimation of frequency and mean for key k

where we approximate the expected value of the quotient of two random variables X and Y by the first term of Taylor Expansions [18] as

$$\mathbb{E}[\frac{X}{Y}] \simeq \frac{\mathbb{E}[X]}{\mathbb{E}[Y]} - \frac{Cov_{X,Y}}{\mathbb{E}(Y)^2} + \frac{\mathbb{E}[X]}{\mathbb{E}[Y]^3} Var[Y].$$

By substituting $\mathbb{E}[n_1^k + n_{-1}^k] = \frac{nf_k}{d}$ and $\mathbb{E}[n^k] = \frac{n}{d}$, we have

$$m_1^k + m_{-1}^k = ((p_1 - q_1)f_{k,t} + q_1)(m^k + \frac{n}{d}) - \frac{nf_k}{d} \qquad (5)$$

Similarly, we have the expected value of the target's value mean

$$\mathbb{E}[\hat{\mu}_k] = \mathbb{E}\left[\frac{n_1^k - n_{-1}^k + m_1^k - m_{-1}^k}{(p_2 - q_2)(n_1^k + n_{-1}^k + m_1^k + m_{-1}^k)}\right]$$

$$\simeq \frac{1}{p_2 - q_2} \cdot \frac{\mathbb{E}[n_1^k - n_{-1}^k] + m_1^k - m_{-1}^k}{\mathbb{E}[n_1^k + n_{-1}^k] + m_1^k + m_{-1}^k} = \mu_{k,t},$$

which can be rewritten by replacing $\mathbb{E}[n_1^k - n_{-1}^k] = \frac{n f_k (p_2 - q_2) \mu_k}{d}$ by

$$q_2 m_1^k - p_2 m_{-1}^k = \frac{n f_k (p_2 - q_2)(\mu_{k,t} - \mu_k)}{d}. \tag{6}$$

For the assignments of malicious users, we make the basic assumption that the sum of them is equal to the total number of malicious users, which is,

$$m_1^k + m_{-1}^k + m_0^k = m^k, \tag{7}$$

and $0 \leq m_1^k, m_{-1}^k, m_0^k \leq m^k$. Finally, putting Eqs. (5), (6), and (7) together, we have the assignment of the number of malicious users to groups who send $\langle 1, 1 \rangle$, $\langle 1, -1 \rangle$ and $\langle 0, 0 \rangle$ in the following theorem.

Theorem 1. *A fine-grained attacker manipulates the statistics estimated by PrivKV to be target frequency $f_{k,t}$ for key k and target mean $\mu_{k,t}$ by assigning m_1^k, m_{-1}^k, and m_0^k malicious users to groups who send $\langle 1, 1 \rangle$, $\langle 1, -1 \rangle$, and $\langle 0, 0 \rangle$, respectively, such that*

$$\begin{bmatrix} m_1^k \\ m_{-1}^k \\ m_0^k \end{bmatrix} = \begin{bmatrix} \frac{-p_2}{-p_2-q_2} & \frac{-1}{-p_2-q_2} & 0 \\ \frac{-q_2}{-p_2-q_2} & \frac{1}{-p_2-q_2} & 0 \\ -1 & 0 & 1 \end{bmatrix} \begin{bmatrix} ((p_1 - q_1) f_{k,t} + q_1)(m^k + \frac{n}{d}) - \frac{n f_k}{d} \\ \frac{n f_k (p_2 - q_2)(\mu_{k,t} - \mu_k)}{d} \\ m^k \end{bmatrix}. \tag{8}$$

Proof. Let A, B, and M be $A = \begin{bmatrix} 1 & 1 & 0 \\ q_2 & -p_2 & 0 \\ 1 & 1 & 1 \end{bmatrix}$,

$B = \begin{bmatrix} ((p_1 - q_1) f_{k,t} + q_1)(m^k + \frac{n}{d}) - \frac{n f_k}{d} \\ \frac{n f_k (p_2 - q_2)(\mu_{k,t} - \mu_k)}{d} \\ m^k \end{bmatrix}$ and $M = \begin{bmatrix} m_1^k \\ m_{-1}^k \\ m_0^k \end{bmatrix}$. The constraint

with Eqs. (5), (6), and (7) is written as $AM = B$. The assignment of malicious users can be given by the inverse matrix A^{-1}.

3.3 Poisoning to PCKV

In PCKV-UE, a user sends $(d + \ell)$-dimensional perturbed vector $\boldsymbol{y}$ of element in $\{1, -1, 0\}$. The goal of the attacker is to determine the assignment of malicious users for key k. Let m_1^k, m_{-1}^k, and m_0^k be the number of malicious users who send 1, -1, and 0, respectively. In PCKV-GRR, a user sends key-value data in either of $\langle k, 1 \rangle$, $\langle k, -1 \rangle$, $\langle i, 1 \rangle$, or $\langle i, -1 \rangle$, where i is a key such that $i \neq k$. Hence, let m_1^k, m_{-1}^k, and m_0^k be the number of malicious users who send $\langle k, 1 \rangle$, $\langle k, -1 \rangle$, and either $\langle i, 1 \rangle$ or $\langle i, -1 \rangle$, respectively.

From the frequency estimated for key in Eq. (3), we have the expected value of the target frequency as

$$\mathbb{E}[\hat{f}_k] = \mathbb{E}\left[\frac{(n_1^k + n_{-1}^k + m_1^k + m_{-1}^k)/(n+m) - b}{a - b} \cdot \ell\right]$$

$$= \frac{(\mathbb{E}[n_1^k + n_{-1}^k] + m_1^k + m_{-1}^k)/(n+m) - b}{a - b} \cdot \ell = f_{k,t},$$

where we can replace the expected value of $n_1^k + n_{-1}^k$ by the mean of the binomial distribution of the probability of support key k as

$$\mathbb{E}[n_1^k + n_{-1}^k] = n Pr[y_k = 1 \vee y_k = -1] = n\left(\frac{f_k}{\ell}a + \left(1 - \frac{f_k}{\ell}\right)b\right).$$

By rewriting for m_1^k, m_{-1}^k, we have

$$m_1^k + m_{-1}^k = \frac{a-b}{\ell}((m+n)f_{k,t} - f_k) + mb \qquad (9)$$

Similarly, we consider a restriction on the mean of value. From Eq. (4) and the approximation of expectation of quotient via Taylor expansion, we have

$$\mathbb{E}[\hat{\mu}_k] = \mathbb{E}\left[\frac{\ell}{(n+m)\hat{f}_k} \cdot \frac{n_1^k - n_{-1}^k + m_1^k - m_{-1}^k}{a(2p-1)}\right]$$

$$\simeq \frac{\ell}{a(2p-1)(n+m)} \cdot \frac{\mathbb{E}[n_1^k - n_{-1}^k] + m_1^k - m_{-1}^k}{\mathbb{E}[\hat{f}_k]} = \mu_{k,t}.$$

By substituting the expected value by

$$\mathbb{E}[n_1^k - n_{-1}^k] = \frac{nf_k}{\ell} \cdot a(2p-1)\mu_k,$$

we have

$$m_1^k - m_{-1}^k = \frac{a(2p-1)}{\ell} \cdot ((n+m)f_{k,t}\mu_{k,t} - nf_k\mu_k). \qquad (10)$$

Above all, the fine-grained poisoning attack on the target statistics can be solved by using the simultaneous equations of Eqs. (9) and (10).

Theorem 2. *A fine-grained attacker manipulates the statistics estimated by PCKV to be target frequency $f_{k,t}$ for key k and target mean $\mu_{k,t}$ by assigning m_1^k, m_{-1}^k and m_0^k malicious users to groups who send 1, -1 and 0, respectively, at the k-th element of perturbed output $\mathbf{y}$.*

$$\begin{bmatrix} m_1^k \\ m_{-1}^k \\ m_0^k \end{bmatrix} = \begin{bmatrix} 1/2 & 1/2 & 0 \\ 1/2 & -1/2 & 0 \\ -1 & 0 & 1 \end{bmatrix} \begin{bmatrix} \frac{a-b}{\ell}((m+n)f_{k,t} - f_k) + mb \\ \frac{a(2p-1)}{\ell} \cdot ((n+m)f_{k,t}\mu_{k,t} - nf_k\mu_k) \\ m^k \end{bmatrix}. \qquad (11)$$

Table 3. Dataset

dataset	# users	# keys	# records
clothing [19]	105,508	5,850	192,198
movielense [20]	138,493	27,278	20,000,264

Proof. Letting A and B be $A = \begin{bmatrix} 1 & 1 & 0 \\ 1 & -1 & 0 \\ 1 & 1 & 1 \end{bmatrix}$ and

$B = \begin{bmatrix} \frac{a-b}{\ell}((m+n)f_{k,t} - f_k) + mb \\ \frac{a(2p-1)}{\ell} \cdot ((n+m)f_{k,t}\mu_{k,t} - nf_k\mu_k) \\ m^k \end{bmatrix}$, Eq. (9) and (10) can be written by

$A \begin{bmatrix} m_1^k \\ m_{-1}^k \\ m_0^k \end{bmatrix} = B$ and the inverse matrix A^{-1} gives the attack.

3.4 Sufficient Conditions of Fine-Grained Poisoning

The matrices in Eqs. (8) and (11) are non-singular and are solvable for any given parameters such as n, d, a, b, p. However, from our assumption, the attacker has at most m users to control. Too high or low target statistics $f_{k,t}, \mu_{k,t}$ cannot be manipulated with the given m. Hence, we have a sufficient condition for the attack to be successful.

Corollary 1. *Let T be a set of target keys. An attacker manipulates the estimated statistics as intended targets if for any k in T,*

$$0 \leq m_1^k, m_{-1}^k, m_0^k \leq m^k$$

and

$$\sum_{k \in T} m_1^k + m_{-1}^k + m_0^k \leq m$$

holds, where m_1^k, m_{-1}^k and m_0^k are the number of malicious users determined in Eq. (8) or (11).

4 Evaluation

4.1 Dataset

To ensure that the proposed attacks are feasible and quantify the risk of estimated statistics in the LDP schemes to be compromised by fine-grained poisoning across multiple datasets, we conduct some experiments using the open datasets, Clothing Fit Dataset [19] and MovieLens 20M Dataset [20]. Table 3 shows the specification of the dataset. Note that there are $192,198/105,508 = 1.82$ key-value tuples per a user in average in Clothing dataset, i.e., $|S_i| = 1.82$.

4.2 Method

Suppose that the estimated statistics f^* and μ^* for uniformly picked 1000 users out of $N = 105,508$ are available to an attacker. The attacker injects m malicious key-value data for the target statistics in Table 4 for PrivKV, PCKV-UE, and PCKV-GRR. In PCKV, we perform padding of the length $\ell = 2.0$. A server collects the poisoned data and tries to estimate statistics. We evaluate the Mean Squared Error (MSE) for the frequency of the keys and mean values, defined as $\text{MSE}_f = \frac{1}{N}\sum_{i=1}^{N}(f_k - \hat{f}_{k,t_i})^2$ and $\text{MSE}_\mu = \frac{1}{N}\sum_{i=1}^{N}(\mu_k - \hat{\mu}_{k,t_i})^2$. For the estimation accuracy of the LDP schemes, a smaller MSE is better. For the attack accuracy of poisonings, a smaller MSE is more vulnerable. Repeating the experiment for $N = 50$ times, we estimate the mean.

Table 4. Attacked statistics

dataset	# target keys	target		initial		true	
	$|T|$	$f_{k,t}$	$\mu_{k,t}$	$f^*_{k,e}$	$\mu^*_{k,e}$	f_k	μ_k
clothing	562	0.300	−0.300	0.022	0.905	0.021	0.740
movielens	562	0.300	−0.300	0.504	0.659	0.486	0.633

4.3 Results

Estimate Accuracy. Figure 2 shows the fundamental estimation accuracy for PrivKV, PCKV-UE, and PCKV-GRR. We estimated the MSE for the top 50 keys with regard to privacy budgets ϵ. For both frequencies and means, we found that PCKV-UE and GRR estimate more accurately than PrivKV. For example, the MSE of PCKV-UE at $epsilon = 1$ in frequency is 10^3 times smaller than that of PrivKV. PrivKV suffers from reduced accuracy because a user samples uniformly over the set of full keys and hence bogus data may be chosen when the number of keys is large. PCKV samples over the set of keys that users own and PCKV-UE outperforms PCKV-GRR in all cases.

Risk in Poisoning. Figure 3 shows the distribution of MSEs for the estimated frequency (left) and mean (right), with regard to the privacy budget ϵ. The MSEs decrease with $epsilon$ for all PCKV-UE, PCKV-GRR, and PrivKV. PrivKV exhibited the smallest MSE, in terms of frequency poisoning for other schemes, ranging from 10^{-1} to 10^{-3} of that of PCKV. That is, PrivKV is the most vulnerable LDP in poisoning fake keys. However, in poisoning for values to manipulate targeted mean, the MSE of PrivKV is stable and independent from ϵ and PCKV-UE is the least robust with MSE less than 10^{-2}. In this experiment, the number of malicious users is constant $m = 0.1n$.

This behavior is the same in the case when varying the malicious users' ratio, $\beta = m/(n+m)$ in Fig. (4). Namely, as β becomes large, the MSEs of all LDP

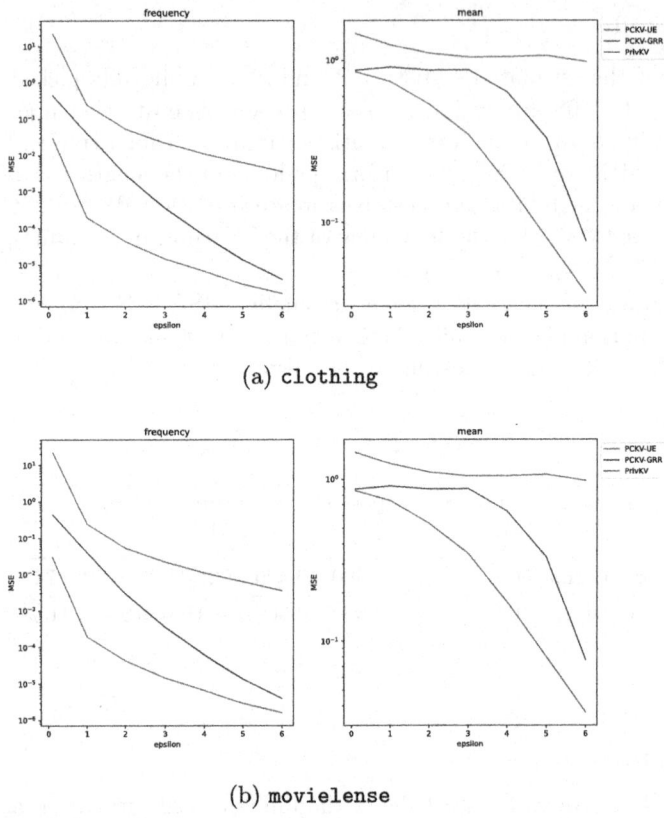

Fig. 2. LDP accuracy estimated in MSE with regard to ϵ (frequency (left) and mean (right).

schemes decrease. PrivKV is the least in frequency MSE and PCKV-UE is the least in mean MSE. In this evaluation, we perturb all data with $\epsilon = 1.0$.

An MSE of poisoning depends on the statistics estimated by the attacker before injecting fake data. To identify the distribution of accuracy, we observe MSEs by poisoning with varying statistics, shown in Figs. (5) and (6), with regard to the attacker's estimation of frequencies $f_{k,e}$ and mean $\mu_{k,e}$, respectively. The MSEs of PrivKV and PCKV-GRR are stable and less dependent on the initial statistics estimated by the attacker, while these statistics are sensitive in the MSE of PCKV-UE. We found that the MSE of PCKV-UE is minimized around the difference between the true and the attacker's estimated statistics $f_{k,e}$ and $\mu_{k,e}$. In the evaluation, we give the attacker the true estimation of frequency ($\mu_{k,e}$) for poisoning with varying mean $\mu_{k,e}$, and vice versa.

Sufficient Condition of Fine-Grained Poisoning. Fine-grained poisoning fails for extremely high or low target statistics. We identify the minimum number

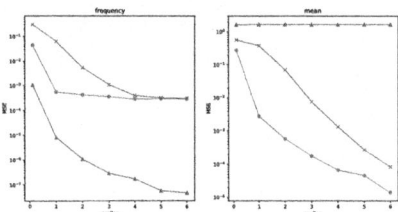
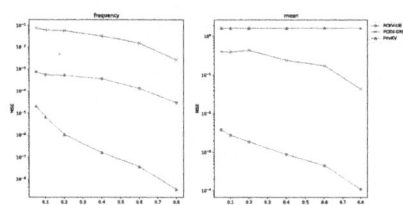

Fig. 3. MSE of poisoning with regard to ϵ ($m = 0.1n$).

Fig. 4. MSE of poisoning with regard to β ($\epsilon = 1.0$).

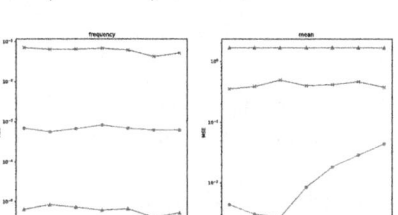
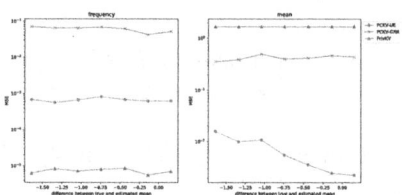

Fig. 5. MSE of poisoning with regard to attacker's estimation of frequency $f_{k,e}$ ($\epsilon = 1.0, \mu_{k,e} = \mu^*_{k,e}$).

Fig. 6. MSE of poisoning with regard to attacker's estimation of mean $\mu_{k,e}$ ($\epsilon = 1.0, f_{k,e} = f^*_{k,e}$).

of malicious users m^* for which conditions in Corollary 1 are satisfied and plot as the heat map of malicious ratio defined as $\beta = m^*/(n+m^*)$ over the space of target statistics $\mu_{k,t}$ (horizontal) times $f_{k,t}$ (vertical) in Fig. (7) for PrivKV, PCKV-UE, and PCKV-GRR. In this experiment, we use $\epsilon = 1, f_{k,e} = f^*_{f,e}, \mu_{k,e} = \mu^*_{k,e}$.

Surprisingly, the results confirm that fine-grained poisoning is feasible with a very small number of malicious users m^*. For instance, the minimal ratios are distributed less than 0.02 in PCKV-GRR (Fig. (7c)), and 0.0005 in PrivKV (Fig. (7a)), suggesting that PrivKV and PCKV-GRR are very vulnerable to fine-grained poisoning. We found that the minimum ratio m^* increases as the target frequency closes to 1.0 (going to the bottom in Fig. (7a) and (7c)). PCKV-UE requires a relatively large number of malicious users up to 0.1 (Fig. (7b)). Note that poisoning becomes more difficult when the smallest target frequency and mean are given in PCKV-GRR (Figs. 4, 5 and 6).

4.4 Discussion

Correlation Between the Estimation and Attack Accuracies. We found that the MSE decreases with respect to ϵ and malicious rate β in Figs. 2 and 3. According to [9] (Theorem 3), the variance of frequency estimation in PrivKV is

$$\text{Var}[\hat{f}_{privKV}] = n \frac{d - 2 + e^\epsilon}{(e^\epsilon - 1)^2},$$

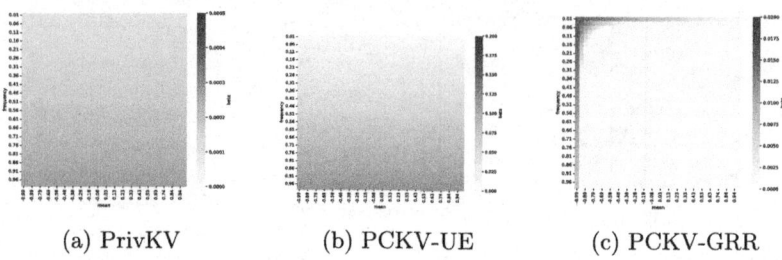

(a) PrivKV (b) PCKV-UE (c) PCKV-GRR

Fig. 7. Minimal malicious ratio $\beta = m/(n+m)$ for fine-grained poisoning for target statistics $f_{k,t}$ and $\mu_{k,t}$.

which is proportional to d and n and the MSE accordingly increases with the large domain size $d = 5852$ in the `clothing` dataset. Obviously, it also decreases with ϵ.

In contrast, in [13] (Theorem 4), MSE_f and MSE_μ are given as

$$\mathrm{MSE}_{\hat{f}} = \mathrm{Var}[\hat{f}] = \frac{\ell^2 b(1-b)}{n(a-b)^2} + \frac{\ell f_k^*(1-a-b)}{n(a-b)} \approx \frac{\ell^2 h}{n}$$

$$\mathrm{MSE}_{\hat{\mu}} = \mathrm{Var}[\hat{\mu}] < \frac{b+\delta}{n\gamma^2} + \frac{b(1-b)-\delta}{n\delta^2}\mu^{*2} \approx \frac{\ell^2(g+h\mu^{*2})}{nf^{*2}},$$

where f^* and μ^* are true statistics without noise and $\delta = (a-b)f^k/\ell$ and $\gamma = a(2p-1)f^*/\ell$. Note that MSEs depend on the true statistics f^* and μ^* in both statistics and error could be increased when the privacy budget ϵ decreases.

Why is PCKV-UE more vulnerable in estimating mean value than PCKV-GRR and PrivKV? One possible reason is the violation of the sampling step in poisoning, where m attackers can send fake data without sampling or perturbing and hence it directly manipulates the estimate. Also note that the frequency is estimated by all users, while the mean is estimated by a subset of users who own the target key. Hence, manipulating the mean is easier than altering the frequency. Additionally, the high accuracy of PCKV-UE is useful not only for genuine users but also for malicious users.

Choice of LDP. The comparison between PrivKV and PCKV shows that PCKV outperforms PrivKV in estimating the frequencies and mean values in key-value data. PCKV-UE and PCKV-GRR, however, are vulnerable to fine-grained poisoning. In the experiment, we see a trade-off between estimation accuracy and poisoning robustness. Although the requirements of the target application should determine the choice, we suggest either PCKV-UE or PCKV-GRR.

5 Mitigations

There are several countermeasures against poisoning in LDPs. Li et al. proposed a sampling-then-clustering method to detect malicious behaviors [3]. In their scheme, by sampling all possible subsets of predetermined size of users, the server performed a clustering algorithm to form two clusters, and detected the skewed statistics from each cluster. With experiments using open data, they demonstrated that their scheme is practical when the fraction of malicious users is small.

Horigome et al. [21] explored the robustness of the Expectation-Maximization (EM) algorithm combined with cryptographic fair sampling, as used in PrivKV. They demonstrated that the EM algorithm exhibits strong resilience to poisoning in key-value frequency estimation tasks.

Huang et al. [24] proposed *LDPGuard*, a defense mechanism for frequency estimation under LDP. Their method estimates the proportion of fake users and designs adversarial-aware adjustments to mitigate the influence of poisoning.

Sun et al. [25] developed *LDPRecover*, a recovery technique that can reconstruct accurate aggregate frequencies from poisoned data, even without knowledge of the specific attack strategy used. This method is protocol-agnostic and applicable to a variety of LDP settings.

Zhao et al. [23] proposed *RobustLDP*, which enhances robustness by broadcasting pre-defined signals to all users and aggregating their feedbacks. This approach leverages structured redundancy to detect and suppress malicious manipulation.

Additional techniques and mitigation strategies are comprehensively surveyed by Song et al. [22], offering an overview of the evolving landscape of LDP robustness research.

5.1 Limitations

While our proposed method demonstrates effectiveness in perturbing key-value data under LDP, several limitations must be acknowledged.

First, we do not provide a formal analysis of the computational complexity of our attack algorithm. While our method is empirically feasible on moderate-sized datasets, its theoretical efficiency, especially under large-domain or streaming settings, has not been rigorously analyzed. This limits our ability to assess its scalability and applicability in more demanding real-world environments.

Second, our investigation into defense mechanisms is limited in scope. We primarily focus on evaluating the effectiveness of our attack without systematically studying how existing or novel defense techniques could mitigate the threat. A more thorough exploration of countermeasures, such as robust aggregation, anomaly detection, or adaptive noise mechanisms, would be necessary to fully understand the practical risks posed by fine-grained poisoning.

Third, our attack methodology closely follows the framework proposed by Li et al. [3], with adaptations to the key-value setting. As a result, the conceptual novelty of our work is bounded. While we demonstrate new vulnerabilities in the LDP setting, the lack of significant innovation in the core attack strategy limits the broader methodological impact.

We leave addressing these limitations to future work.

6 Conclusions

In this paper, we investigated the feasibility of fine-grained data poisoning attacks in the LDP setting, with a particular focus on key-value data collection protocols, including PrivKV, PCKV-GRR, and PCKV-UE. We demonstrated that an adversary with limited knowledge and a modest number of compromised users can effectively manipulate the output of frequency estimation tasks by carefully perturbing their reports. Our attack strategy exploits the estimation procedures of existing LDP mechanisms, pushing them to overrepresent or suppress specific keys.

Through empirical evaluation on real-world datasets, we showed that the proposed attack significantly distorts frequency estimates under various LDP protocols. The results highlight a critical vulnerability in the current landscape of privacy-preserving data collection, where the focus has traditionally been on privacy guarantees rather than robustness against adversarial input. Our work thus emphasizes the need to re-evaluate the threat model in LDP systems, considering not only passive privacy leakage but also active manipulation.

While our attack is based on established principles and follows the framework proposed by Li et al. [3], we adapted it to the key-value setting, which presents new challenges in terms of perturbation granularity and target selection. However, our approach inherits limitations in novelty and generalizability, and does not yet incorporate comprehensive defenses or theoretical complexity analysis.

This study opens several promising directions for future work. First, further research is needed to develop lightweight and protocol-compatible defense mechanisms that can resist poisoning without compromising utility. Second, formal analysis of the computational complexity and optimality of both attack and defense strategies would strengthen our understanding of their practical applicability. Finally, more holistic evaluations involving real-world deployments and adaptive adversaries will be essential to validate the real-world risk and resilience of LDP-based systems.

Ultimately, ensuring the trustworthiness of statistics derived from LDP reports requires a shift in perspective—from privacy-preserving data collection to adversary-resilient analytics. Our findings contribute to this growing body of work by shedding light on an emerging class of threats in the LDP ecosystem.

Acknowledgment. We thank anonymous reviewers for their useful and constructive suggestions that help to improve the work significantly.

This study was supported by JSPS KAKENHI Grant Number 23K11110 and JST CREST Grant Number JPMJCR21M1.

References

1. Duchi, J.C., Jordan, M.I., Wainwright, M.J.: Local privacy and statistical minimax rates. In: IEEE FOCS, pp. 429–438 (2013)
2. Warner, S.L.: Randomized response: a survey technique for eliminating evasive answer bias. J. Am. Stat. Assoc., 63–69 (1965)
3. Li, X., Li, N., Sun, W., Gong, N.Z., Li, H.: Fine-grained poisoning attack to local differential privacy protocols for mean and variance estimation. In: USENIX Security, pp. 1739–1756 (2023)
4. Cao, X., Jia, J., Gong, N.Z.: Data poisoning attacks to local differential privacy protocols. In: USENIX Security, pp. 947–964 (2021)
5. Cheu, A., Smith, A., Ullman, J.: Manipulation attacks in local differential privacy. IEEE S&P, 883–900 (2021)
6. Erlingsson, Ú., Pihur, V., Korolova, A.: RAPPOR: randomized aggregatable privacy-preserving ordinal response. ACM CCS, pp. 1054–1067 (2014)
7. Differential Privacy Team: Leaning with Privacy at Scale. https://machinelearning.apple.com/research/learning-with-privacy-at-scale
8. Wang, N., et al.: Collecting and analyzing multi-dimensional data with local differential privacy. In: IEEE ICDE, pp. 638–649 (2019)
9. Wang, T., Blocki, J., Li, N., Jha, S.: Locally differentially private protocols for frequency estimation. In: USENIX Security, pp. 729–745 (2017)
10. Li, Z., Wang, T., Lopuhaä-Zwakenberg, M., Li, N., Škoric, B.: Estimating numerical distributions under local differential privacy. In: ACM SIGMOD, pp. 621–635 (2020)
11. Wang, T., Li, N., Jha, S.: Locally differentially private frequent itemset mining. In: 2018 IEEE Symposium on Security and Privacy (SP), San Francisco, CA, USA, pp. 127–143 (2018)
12. Wu, Y., Cao, X., Jia, J., Gong, N.Z.: Poisoning attacks to local differential privacy protocols for key-value data. In: USENIX Security, pp. 519–536 (2022)
13. Gu, X., Li, M., Cheng, Y., Xiong, L., Cao, Y.: PCKV: locally differentially private correlated key-value data collection with optimized utility. In: USENIX Security Symposium, pp. 967–984 (2020)
14. Cao, X., Jia, J., Gong, N.Z.: Data poisoning attacks to local differential privacy protocols. In: 30th USENIX Security Symposium (USENIX Security 2021), pp. 947–964 (2021)
15. Ye, Q., Hu, H., Meng, X., Zheng, H.: PrivKV: key-value data collection with local differential privacy. IEEE S&P, 294–308 (2019)
16. Duchi, J.C., Jordan, M.I., Wainwright, M.J.: Minimax optimal procedures for locally private estimation. J. Am. Stat. Assoc., 182–201 (2018)
17. Wang, N., et al.: Collecting and analyzing multidimensional data with local differential privacy. In: IEEE ICDE (2019)
18. Benaroya, H., Han, S.M., Nagurka, M.: Probability Models in Engineering and Science, p. 166. CRC Press (2005)
19. Clothing fit dataset for size recommendation. https://www.kaggle.com/rmisra/clothing-fit-dataset-for-size-recommendation
20. Maxwell Harper, F., Konstan, J.A.: The MovieLens datasets: history and context. ACM Trans. Interact. Intell. Syst. (TiiS) **5**(4), 1–19 (2015). Article 19
21. Horigome, H., Kikuchi, H., Yu, C.-M.: Local differential privacy protocol for making key-value data robust against poisoning attacks. In: Modeling Decisions for Artificial Intelligence (MDAI 2023), pp. 241–252. Springer, Cham (2023)

22. Song, S., Xu, L., Zhu, L.: Efficient defenses against output poisoning attacks on local differential privacy. IEEE Trans. Inf. Forensics Secur. **18**, 5506–5521 (2023)
23. Zhao, P., Zhang, Z., Dong, J., Wu, J., Liu, Z., Wang, S.: An attack-agnostic defense framework against manipulation attacks under local differential privacy. In: 2025 IEEE Symposium on Security and Privacy (SP), pp. 3858–3876 (2025)
24. Huang, K., Ouyang, G., Ye, Q., Haibo, H., Zheng, B., Zhao, X.: LDPGuard: defenses against data poisoning attacks to local differential privacy protocols. IEEE Trans. Knowl. Data Eng. **36**(7), 3195–3209 (2024)
25. Sun, X., et al.: LDPRecover: recovering frequencies from poisoning attacks against local differential privacy. In: 2024 IEEE 40th International Conference on Data Engineering (ICDE), Utrecht, Netherlands, pp. 1619–1631 (2024)

The DCR Delusion: Measuring the Privacy Risk of Synthetic Data

Zexi Yao[1], Nataša Krčo[1], Georgi Ganev[2], and Yves-Alexandre de Montjoye[1(✉)]

[1] Imperial College London, London, UK
{z.yao23,n.krco23,deMontjoye}@imperial.ac.uk
[2] University College London and SAS, London, UK
georgi.ganev.16@ucl.ac.uk

Abstract. Synthetic data has become an increasingly popular means of sharing data without revealing sensitive information. Though Membership Inference Attacks (MIAs) are widely considered the gold standard for empirically assessing the privacy of a synthetic dataset, for simplicity, practitioners and researchers often rely on proxy metrics such as Distance to Closest Record (DCR). These metrics estimate a synthetic dataset's privacy by measuring the similarity between the training data and generated synthetic data. This similarity can also be compared against the similarity between the training data and a disjoint holdout set of real records to construct a binary privacy test. If the synthetic data is not more similar to the training data than the holdout set is, the synthetic dataset passes the privacy test and is considered private. In this work, we show that, while computationally inexpensive, DCR and other distance-based metrics fail to identify privacy leakage. Across multiple datasets and both classical models, such as Baynet and CTGAN, and more recent diffusion models, we show that datasets deemed private by proxy metrics are highly vulnerable to MIAs. We similarly find both the binary privacy test and the continuous measure based on these metrics to be uninformative of actual membership inference risk. We further show that these failures are consistent across different metric hyperparameter settings and record selection methods. Finally, we argue that DCR and other distance-based metrics are flawed by design and show an example of a simple leakage they miss in practice. With this work, we hope to motivate practitioners to move away from proxy metrics to MIAs as the rigorous, comprehensive standard of evaluating privacy of synthetic data, in particular to make claims of datasets being legally anonymous.

Keywords: Synthetic data · DCR · Membership inference · Privacy

1 Introduction

Synthetic data is a popular tool for sharing and using sensitive data, used across fields such as medicine [13,15], finance [61] and public security [52]. Synthetic

---

Z. Yao and N. Krčo—Equal contribution.

© The Author(s), under exclusive license to Springer Nature Switzerland AG 2026
V. Nicomette et al. (Eds.): ESORICS 2025, LNCS 16053, pp. 469–487, 2026.
https://doi.org/10.1007/978-3-032-07884-1_24

data generators (SDGs) aim to learn the underlying distribution of a dataset and generate synthetic data that preserves its statistical properties while protecting the privacy of individual records.

Membership inference attacks (MIAs) are widely accepted as the standard method to empirically assess information leakage and the privacy of synthetic data [6,18,27,33,40,60] and machine learning models in general [11,54,73], both as a direct attack, and as an upper bound on more severe threats such as reconstruction or attribute inference attacks [5,56]. MIAs evaluate the privacy of synthetic data at an *individual* level by assessing the risk that a particular record's membership in the training dataset can be correctly inferred by an attacker.

While MIAs are the state-of-the-art method for evaluating privacy, they typically involve training multiple generative models, leading to high computational costs and motivating the use of simpler distance-based metrics. Distance to Closest Record (DCR) and similar metrics are commonly used as a proxy for MIAs, both in commercial products [43,62] and for evaluating novel methods such as diffusion models [34,50,74]. These metrics assess the privacy of a synthetic dataset as a whole by measuring the similarity between synthetic and training data. Intuitively, the less similar a synthetic dataset is to its training data, the stronger the assumed privacy. The metrics can be used either to construct a binary privacy test τ_{DCR} classifying a dataset as "private" or "non-private," or directly as a continuous measure of privacy μ_{DCR}. The binary test compares the distribution of distances between synthetic and training records against the distances between a set of real holdout records and the training records, typically at a certain percentile.

Contribution. In this work, we evaluate the effectiveness of DCR and similar metrics as a proxy for membership inference attacks, and show them to be an inadequate measure of both information leakage and the privacy risk of generated synthetic data.

First, we show proxy metrics to provide a misleading measure of privacy risk for well-known classical SDGs: IndHist [53], Baynet [75], and CTGAN [68]. Across 9 experimental setups, we generate more than 10,000 datasets and find the majority of them to be deemed private by proxy metrics as applied in industry. Yet, instantiating MIAs against outlier records in these datasets reveals significant information leakage, with records shown to be highly vulnerable to membership inference attacks (AUC> 0.8). Worse, we show MIAs to perform equally well against datasets deemed "private" and "non-private" by DCR, and an absence of correlation between MIA performance and μ_{DCR}.

Second, we show our empirical results to extend to diffusion models, a more recent popular class of synthetic data generation models. For diffusion models TabDDPM [34] and ClavaDDPM [50], we generate synthetic datasets considered private by τ_{DCR}, and instantiate the state-of-the-art MIAs for tabular diffusion models against them. Similarly to classical models, the MIAs reach high performance (TPR at FPR=0% above 10%) despite passing the binary privacy test τ_{DCR}. μ_{DCR} also shows no correlation with vulnerability to MIAs.

For computational reasons, we previously focused on outlier records, which are more likely to be vulnerable to MIAs in the case of classical models. We here study, for the Baynet generator and Adult [7] dataset, the risk for every record in the target dataset and show that the risk is not limited to outliers. Though the synthetic datasets pass the binary privacy test, an MIA can infer the membership of 20% of the training records better than a random guess (AUC$\geq$ 0.6). We also show that our findings hold across different choices of the τ_{DCR} hyperparameter, the comparison percentile. Finally, we study a real-world example of a simple privacy leakage that the proxy metrics are, by design, unable to detect.

Taken together, our results show DCR and other distance-based metrics to be poor proxies for measuring privacy risk. They detect only the most severe privacy violations, such as when synthetic data consists mostly of copies of the real data, potentially leaving more subtle information leakage undetected. They also seem to show no meaningful correlation with actual privacy risk, making them unreliable even as general indicators of privacy. We hope this work will motivate rigorous privacy evaluation using state-of-the-art attacks defined in the literature, and encourage researchers and practitioners to move away from using distance-based metrics.

2 Preliminaries

In this section, we introduce relevant notation, synthetic data generators, and methods for measuring the privacy of synthetic data.

Notation. We denote a record consisting of k attributes with $x_i = (x_{i,1}, \ldots, x_{i,k}) \sim \mathcal{D}$, where $\mathcal{D}$ is the distribution over feature space $\mathcal{F} = \mathcal{F}_1 \times \ldots \times \mathcal{F}_k$. $D = \{x_1, \ldots, x_m\}$ denotes a tabular dataset where one record x_i corresponds to one row.

Synthetic Data Generators (SDGs). Let $D_{\text{target}} = \{x_1, \ldots, x_n\}$ be a real tabular dataset. A generative model $M = \phi(D_{\text{target}})$ trained using procedure ϕ estimates the underlying distribution of D_{target}. A synthetic dataset $D_{\text{synthetic}} \sim M$ can then be sampled from the model. In general, we consider synthetic datasets of the same size as the training data, $|D_{\text{synthetic}}| = |D_{\text{target}}|$. We distinguish two main categories of SDGs in this paper, classical and diffusion models. Classical models are older generative models that typically learn distributions of feature values in the training dataset. Diffusion models, introduced more recently, generate data through an iterative denoising process, allowing them to capture more complex data distributions and dependencies.

Measuring Privacy of Synthetic Datasets. The standard approach for evaluating the privacy risk of synthetic data in the literature is membership inference attacks (MIAs). They estimate the risk of a record's membership in the training data of an SDG being correctly inferred by an attacker. However, MIAs are typically computationally expensive, leading practitioners and researchers to rely on simpler distance-based metrics such as DCR as proxies. In the following sections, we introduce these methods in more detail and evaluate their effectiveness.

3 Privacy Evaluation Techniques for Synthetic Data

In this section, we describe how proxy metrics and membership inference attacks are used in practice to empirically evaluate the privacy risk of synthetic data.

3.1 Distance to Closest Record (DCR) and Other Distance-Based Metrics

Proxy privacy metrics use a notion of distance between a synthetic dataset $D_{\text{synthetic}} \sim M(D_{\text{target}})$ and its corresponding training dataset D_{target}. They then use this metric to either construct a binary privacy test or as a continuous measure of privacy.

DCR is one of the most popular metrics used for evaluating privacy risk of synthetic data in both industry [4,41,43,62,70] and academia [9,15,24,34,37, 50,57,59,65,69,72,74,76,78]. It defines a vector of per-record distances between datasets D_1 and D_2, where each entry is the distance from a record in D_1 to its nearest neighbor in D_2:

$$d_{\text{DCR}}(D_1, D_2) = \{\min_{x_j \in D_2} dist(x_i, x_j)\}_{i=1}^{|D_1|} \qquad (1)$$

where $dist(x_i, x_j)$ could be any distance metric but is typically the sum of Euclidean distance for continuous features and Hamming distances for categorical features between x_i and x_j [4,34,43,57].

Other popular proxy metrics include Nearest Neighbor Distance Ratio (NNDR) and Identical Match Share (IMS). NNDR defines the distance vector $d_{\text{NNDR}}(D_1, D_2)$ by computing, for each record in D_1, the ratio between the distance to its nearest neighbor and the distance to its second-nearest neighbor in D_2. Instead of a distance vector, IMS defines a scalar distance measure $d_{\text{IMS}}(D_1, D_2)$ as the number of records in D_1 with an identical match in D_2.

Privacy Test. DCR, NNDR, and IMS are often used to construct binary privacy tests to classify a synthetic dataset $D_{\text{synthetic}}$ as "private" or "non-private" [4,24, 43]. This is done by comparing the distance between $D_{\text{synthetic}}$ and D_{target} to the distance between D_{target} and a holdout set of real records D_{holdout}. If $D_{\text{synthetic}}$ is further away from D_{target} than D_{holdout}, it is considered private.

DCR and NNDR construct privacy tests τ_{DCR} and τ_{NNDR} by comparing the 5th percentile of the respective distance vectors:

$$\tau_{\text{DCR}}(D_{\text{synthetic}}, D_{\text{target}}) = \mathbb{1}[d_{\text{DCR}}(D_{\text{synthetic}}, D_{\text{target}})_{p=0.05} \geq \qquad (2)$$
$$d_{\text{DCR}}(D_{\text{holdout}}, D_{\text{target}})_{p=0.05}] \qquad (3)$$

where $p = 0.05$ denotes the 5th percentile. The test is defined analogously for d_{NNDR}.

IMS constructs the privacy test by comparing the number of identical matches:

$$\tau_{\text{IMS}}(D_{\text{synthetic}}, D_{\text{target}}) = \mathbb{1}[d_{\text{IMS}}(D_{\text{synthetic}}, D_{\text{target}}) \leq \quad (4)$$
$$d_{\text{IMS}}(D_{\text{holdout}}, D_{\text{target}})] \quad (5)$$

Here, the synthetic dataset is considered private if it contains fewer identical matches with the training data than the holdout set does.

Various combinations of these metrics are used in practice, with no agreed-upon, widely used setup. We therefore define a strict privacy test $\tau_{\text{DCR,NNDR,IMS}}$ as a joint privacy test using all three proxy metrics. $D_{\text{synthetic}}$ is considered by $\tau_{\text{DCR,NNDR,IMS}}$ to be private only if it passes all of τ_{DCR}, τ_{NNDR}, and τ_{IMS}.

$$\tau_{\text{DCR,NNDR,IMS}}(D_{\text{synthetic}}, D_{\text{target}}) = \mathbb{1}[\tau_{\text{DCR}}(D_{\text{synthetic}}, D_{\text{target}}) = 1 \quad (6)$$
$$\wedge \tau_{\text{NNDR}}(D_{\text{synthetic}}, D_{\text{target}}) = 1 \quad (7)$$
$$\wedge \tau_{\text{IMS}}(D_{\text{synthetic}}, D_{\text{target}}) = 1] \quad (8)$$

Continuous Privacy Measure. DCR is also commonly used as a continuous privacy measure μ_{DCR} for comparing the privacy of different generative models, particularly for diffusion models [34,57]. Instead of comparing synthetic data to a holdout set, the continuous measure aggregates the distance vector $d_{\text{DCR}}(D_{\text{synthetic}}, D_{\text{target}})$ to produce a single privacy score. In this work, we follow Kotelnikov et al. [34] and use the mean of the distances in $d_{\text{DCR}}(D_{\text{synthetic}}, D_{\text{target}})$ as the continuous privacy measure:

$$\mu_{\text{DCR}}(D_{\text{synthetic}}, D_{\text{target}}) = \frac{1}{|D_{\text{synthetic}}|} \sum_{i=1}^{|D_{\text{synthetic}}|} d_{\text{DCR}}(D_{\text{synthetic}}, D_{\text{target}})_i \quad (9)$$

A higher value of $\mu_{\text{DCR}}(D_{\text{synthetic}}, D_{\text{target}})$ indicates that synthetic records are more distant from D_{target} and is thus assumed to imply better privacy protection.

3.2 Membership Inference Attacks (MIAs)

MIAs are the state-of-the-art technique for evaluating privacy risk of synthetic data [27,66]. They identify privacy leakage using a privacy game where an attacker aims to infer whether a synthetic dataset was generated by a model trained on data containing a specific target record.

Classical Models. The state-of-the-art MIA for classical SDGs is extended-TAPAS, a black-box attack introduced by Houssiau et al. [27] and extended by Meeus et al. [40]. Extended-TAPAS models how the inclusion or exclusion of a single target record x impacts the generated synthetic data and trains a meta-classifier to predict membership.

For a target record $x \in D_{\text{target}}$, the attacker trains shadow models on datasets sampled from an auxiliary dataset D_{aux}, which is drawn from the same distribution as the target dataset D_{target} but is disjoint from it. The target record is included in exactly half of the shadow datasets. They then generate a synthetic dataset using each shadow model and extract query features from each. These features count the number of synthetic records that match the target record across random subsets of attributes. This results in a labeled membership dataset for training a meta-classifier that predicts whether a given synthetic dataset was trained on the target record. In our experiments, we use 1000 shadow models.

The MIA is evaluated across a set of evaluation models, where exactly half are trained on x. In this work, we evaluate in the model-seeded setup of Guépin et al. [22], where half of the evaluation models are trained on D_{target}, and half on D_{target} where x is replaced by a randomly sampled holdout record. The MIA is performed against each dataset, and its ROC AUC score is computed, resulting in a risk estimate of x within D_{target}. In our experiments, we use 1000 evaluation models.

As extended-TAPAS must be developed and evaluated separately for each target record, evaluating the risk of every record in D_{target} across setups is computationally infeasible. Because of this, in our main experiment, we select 100 target records in D_{target} and instantiate the MIAs against them. We use the Achilles vulnerability score introduced by Meeus et al. [40], and select the 100 records with the highest vulnerability score. The final output for each setup is then a set of per-record MIA AUC scores.

Diffusion Models. The state-of-the-art MIA for tabular diffusion models was introduced by Wu et al. [66] in the challenge on Membership Inference over Diffusion-models-based Synthetic Tabular data (MIDST) [64]. We consider both the black-box and white-box variants of the attack, and refer to them collectively as the MIDST attacks for simplicity. The black-box attack relies only on data generated by the target model, while the white-box attack has full access to the model and its internal parameters. Both attacks model the model's loss on member versus non-member records.

To train the meta-classifier, the attacker first samples shadow datasets from an auxiliary dataset and trains a shadow diffusion model on each. For each shadow model, they extract features from the initial noise and training loss for both member and non-member records. These features form a labeled dataset used to train a multi-layer perceptron (MLP) classifier that predicts whether a given record was part of the training data. In our experiments, we use 20 shadow datasets to train the MIDST attacks.

As these attacks can be applied to any individual record, and training diffusion models is computationally expensive, evaluation here is typically done on a fixed target model across a set of known members and non-members. The attack is applied to each record, and a single True Positive Rate (TPR) at a fixed low False Positive Rate (FPR) is computed based on the predictions [11,66]. In our setup, we evaluate the MIDST attack on 10 diffusion models, each with 200 member and 200 non-member records, resulting in 10 TPR values–one per synthetic dataset.

4 Experimental Setup

In this section, we specify the datasets and models we use in our experiments.

4.1 Models

Classical Models. We use three well-known synthetic data generators, using the implementations available in the reprosyn [3] repository.

IndHist [53] is the simplest of our selected models. It uses marginal frequency counts to generate feature values for synthetic records. For each feature, it samples from the distribution of values for that feature among all training records. Different features are sampled independently from each other.

BayNet [75] trains a Bayesian network to learn the relationships between features. Each feature is represented as a node on a network graph, with edges representing relations between two features. The GreedyBayes algorithm introduced by Zhang et al. [75] is then used to estimate the joint probabilities of the features, from which synthetic records can be sampled.

CTGAN [68] trains a generative adversarial network (GAN) consisting of a generator and a discriminator to model the feature distribution of records in the training dataset. They are trained jointly with opposing goals: the discriminator attempts to distinguish between real and synthetic records produced by the generator, while the generator aims to produce synthetic data similar enough to real data to fool the discriminator.

Diffusion Models. Diffusion models have become increasingly popular in recent years due to their increased utility of generated synthetic data and versatility of applications compared to classical models. We use two tabular diffusion models, with the implementation available in the MIDSTModels repository [64].

TabDDPM [34] is the first diffusion model specifically developed for tabular data. It adapts the diffusion process to account for different feature types by applying Gaussian diffusion to numerical features and multinomial diffusion to categorical and binary features.

ClavaDDPM [50] is a tabular diffusion model designed to generate multi-relational data. It uses latent clustering to model the relationships between the tables defined by foreign keys and enable conditional generation of synthetic tables.

4.2 Datasets

We evaluate the success of privacy measures across the following publicly available datasets, commonly used in literature studying tabular data privacy.

Adult [7] is an anonymized sample of the 1994 US Census data containing 48,842 records. It contains 15 demographic features, 9 of which are categorical.

Bank [42] contains 45,211 records concerning the marketing campaign of a Portuguese banking institution in 2014. Each record contains 17 features, of which 4 are demographic and 13 describe the individual's previous interactions with the institution.

UK Census [46] is an anonymized 1% sample of the 2011 Census from Wales and England, published by the UK Office for National Statistics. The dataset is comprised of 569,741 records with 17 categorical demographic features.

Berka [8] is an anonymized database containing information regarding over 5,000 clients collected in 2000 from a Czech bank. The main dataset, which we refer to as the Berka dataset, contains over 1,000,000 transactions. Additional tables with account and client information can be linked via foreign keys, e.g., when training ClavaDDPM.

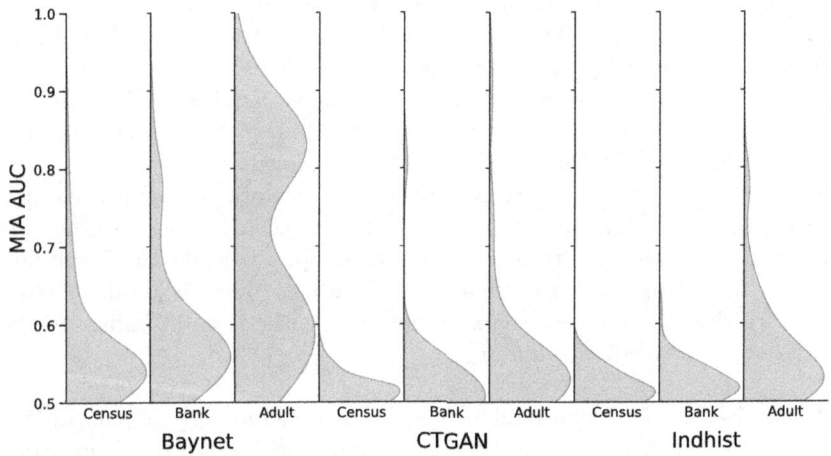

Fig. 1. Extended-TAPAS MIA AUC on datasets considered "private" by $\tau_{\text{DCR,NNDR,IMS}}$ across classical SDG setups. Each dataset-SDG setup contains 100 target records selected using the *Achilles* score.

5 Results

5.1 Evaluating DCR and Other Proxy Metrics for Classical Models

We here evaluate the effectiveness of DCR and other proxy metrics for identifying privacy leakage in classical synthetic data generators by comparing them to MIA results across 3 datasets and 3 target models. We develop MIAs against 100 outlier target records per setup, selected using the Achilles score. For each target record, we compute the percentage of evaluation synthetic records that fail τ_{DCR} and $\tau_{\text{DCR,NNDR,IMS}}$, and the mean μ_{DCR} across all synthetic datasets for that record. We then study the MIA AUC values for the outlier records in datasets deemed "private" by τ_{DCR} and $\tau_{\text{DCR,NNDR,IMS}}$.

In 7 out of the 9 setups, both $\tau_{\text{DCR,NNDR,IMS}}$ and τ_{DCR} consistently classify all 500 synthetic datasets per target record as "private." The only exceptions are observed with the Baynet generator on the Census and Bank datasets. For Census, 12% of the synthetic datasets fail the $\tau_{\text{DCR,NNDR,IMS}}$ and 1.1% fail τ_{DCR} alone. For Bank, 0.4% of the datasets fail the $\tau_{\text{DCR,NNDR,IMS}}$, and 0% fail τ_{DCR}. Figure 1 shows the datasets to be highly vulnerable to MIAs, despite being considered "private" by the proxy metrics.

Figure 1 shows the datasets passing the proxy metric privacy tests to leak information about their training data. In the majority of setups, the MIA reaches $AUC \geq 0.6$—shown to indicate information leakage—for a significant fraction of records, and even $AUC \geq 0.8$ for some. This suggests that τ_{DCR} and $\tau_{\text{DCR,NNDR,IMS}}$ often misrepresent synthetic datasets with significant privacy leakage as "private," making them unreliable for verifying privacy of synthetic data for release.

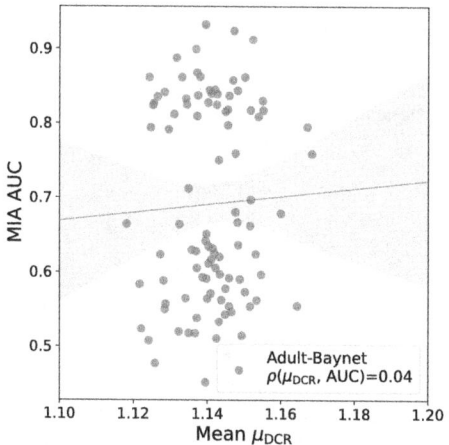

Fig. 2. Comparison of mean μ_{DCR} and MIA AUC for the Baynet generator on the Adult dataset. Each point represents a target record's MIA AUC and its mean μ_{DCR} across evaluation datasets.

As proxy metrics often fail to flag privacy leakage, we now study whether they can still provide an informative signal about the risk of a dataset. We examine whether synthetic datasets considered "non-private" exhibit higher MIA AUC values than those considered "non-private." Then, we evaluate whether the continuous measure μ_{DCR} gives an indication of MIA performance.

For the Census dataset and the Baynet generator, 12% of the synthetic datasets are classified as "non-private" by $\tau_{\text{DCR,NNDR,IMS}}$. We compare MIA performance when instantiated across the full set of synthetic datasets and only the "private" datasets and find that there is no meaningful difference in performance between the two sets – MIA AUC remains equally high, regardless of whether evaluation is restricted to the "private" subset or not.

For each target record in the Adult-Baynet setup, we compute the corresponding MIA AUC and the mean μ_{DCR} across the synthetic datasets used for evaluation and study their relationship. Figure 2 shows that there is no correlation between the two values. AUC values span a wide range (roughly between 0.5 and 1.0), regardless of the value of μ_{DCR}, suggesting that μ_{DCR} is unable to effectively distinguish between datasets with different levels of privacy risk.

5.2 Evaluating DCR for Diffusion Models

We here study the effectiveness of DCR for evaluating the privacy of diffusion models by repeating the analyses done in Sect. 5.1, and following the state-of-the-art methods for diffusion models. Specifically, we focus on DCR and measure MIA performance on datasets deemed "private" as TPR at FPR=0% [11]. Using TabDDPM and ClavaDDPM, we train 10 target models for each method and generate one synthetic dataset per model. All generated datasets pass the DCR privacy test τ_{DCR}. We then instantiate both the black-box and white-box MIDST attacks against each of the generated synthetic datasets.

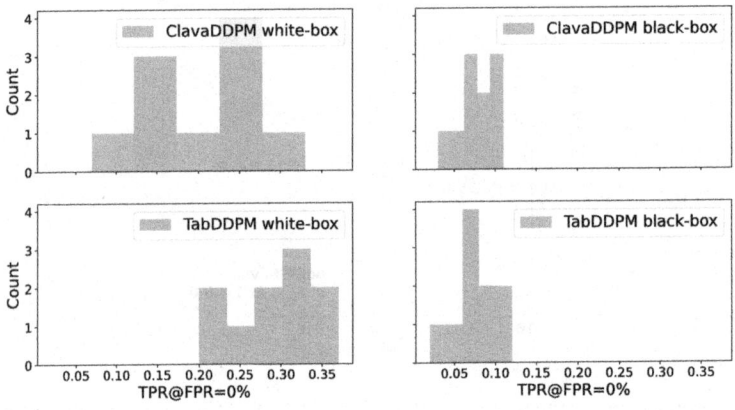

Fig. 3. Distribution of TPR@FPR=0% for MIDST attacks against TabDDPM and ClavaDDPM.

Figure 3 shows that for both TabDDPM and ClavaDDPM, the MIDST attacks are able to successfully infer membership in the training data of the target models. The black-box attack achieves TPR@FPR=0% above 5% on the majority of datasets, and exceeds 10% on some datasets for both models. The white-box attack performs even better, reaching TPR@FPR=0% above 20% on all 10 target datasets, and on more than half of the ClavaDDPM datasets. These results indicate clear information leakage that is not detected by τ_{DCR}.

In line with our analysis in Sect. 5.1, we evaluate whether μ_{DCR} provides any meaningful signal of privacy risk. We compute the μ_{DCR} for all 10 ClavaDDPM target datasets, and compare it to the TPR@FPR=0% achieved by the white-box MIA. Figure 4 shows there to be no clear correlation between μ_{DCR} and MIA performance, indicating that μ_{DCR} is not a reliable proxy for privacy risk as identified by MIAs.

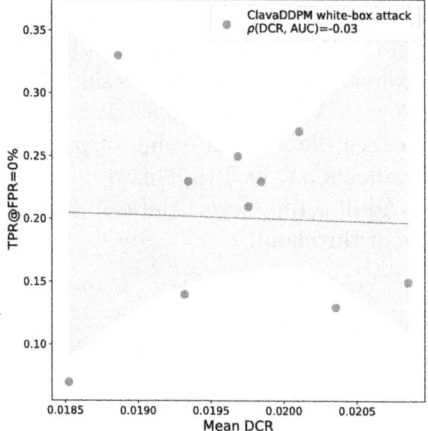

Fig. 4. μ_{DCR} and MIA TPR@FPR=0% for MIDST white-box attack on 10 ClavaDDPM target datasets.

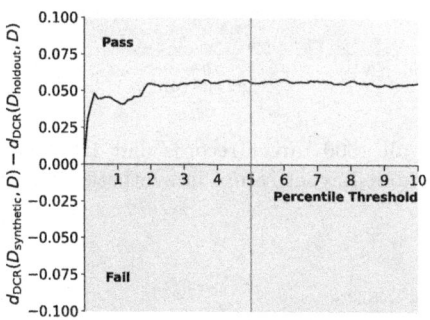

Fig. 5. Comparison of $d_{\text{DCR}}(D_{\text{synthetic}}, D_{\text{target}}) - d_{\text{DCR}}(D_{\text{holdout}}, D_{\text{target}})$ across percentile thresholds for a synthetic dataset trained on a vulnerable record with MIA AUC = 0.84.

5.3 Effect of Adjusting DCR Hyperparameter

τ_{DCR} determines the privacy of a synthetic dataset $D_{\text{synthetic}}$ by comparing the distance vector between $D_{\text{synthetic}}$ and D_{target} to the distance vector between D_{holdout} and D_{target} at the same percentile mark p, typically 5th percentile. This percentile choice is the only hyperparameter of τ_{DCR}. We now study whether tuning this threshold can improve τ_{DCR}'s ability to detect privacy leakage. The condition for passing the privacy test,

$$d_{\text{DCR}}(D_{\text{synthetic}}, D_{\text{target}})_p \geq d_{\text{DCR}}(D_{\text{holdout}}, D_{\text{target}})_p \qquad (10)$$

can be rewritten as:

$$d_{\text{DCR}}(D_{\text{synthetic}}, D_{\text{target}})_p - d_{\text{DCR}}(D_{\text{holdout}}, D_{\text{target}})_p \geq 0 \qquad (11)$$

We examine the effects of adjusting $p \in [0, 0.1]$ for the above condition across all synthetic datasets in the Baynet generator with the Adult dataset setup.

Figure 5 shows an example of adjusting p for a single synthetic dataset trained on a vulnerable record with MIA AUC= 0.84. For this synthetic dataset, the value remains above 0 regardless of the value of p, showing that the dataset passes τ_{DCR} on all thresholds $p \in [0, 0.1]$. This result holds across all synthetic datasets in the Baynet-Adult setup – every dataset is deemed "private" by τ_{DCR}, regardless of the choice of threshold.

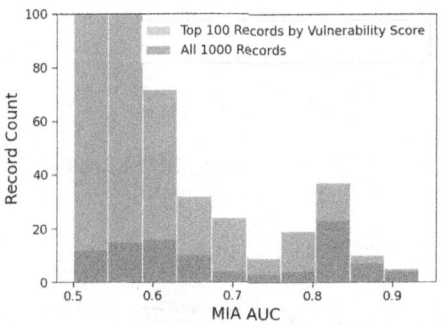

Fig. 6. MIA AUCs of all 1000 target records and 100 vulnerable records selected using *Achilles* in the Adult-Baynet setup, in synthetic datasets considered "private" by $\tau_{\text{DCR,NNDR,IMS}}$.

5.4 Analysis of the Impact of the *Achilles* Vulnerability Score

In our main experiment for classical models in Sect. 5.1, we reduce computational costs by only performing MIAs against the top 100 records by *Achilles* vulnerability score for each dataset. To eliminate concerns that such sampling may have exaggerated the privacy risk indicated by MIA, we analyze DCR and MIA performance on all 1000 records in D_{target} for one setup (Baynet with Adult). Consistent with our prior results, all synthetic datasets for all 1000 records also pass τ_{DCR} and $\tau_{\text{DCR,NNDR,IMS}}$.

We now compare the distribution of MIA AUC values across all 1000 records to the MIA AUC values of 100 outlier records selected by the *Achilles* vulnerability score in Sect. 5.1. Figure 6 shows that while *Achilles* score is more likely to identify vulnerable records than random sampling, a significant proportion of vulnerable records went undetected – the MIA achieves an AUC ≥ 0.8 for 54 records and AUC ≥ 0.6 for 200 records out of 1000 total records. This is still a high percentage of records with information leakage, which indicates significant privacy risk across all synthetic datasets in the setup.

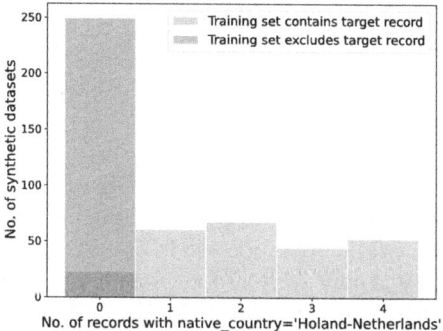

Fig. 7. Comparison of synthetic datasets generated by CTGAN-Adult models trained on a target record with uniquely identifying native country "Holland-Netherlands."

5.5 Detailed Analysis of One Highly Vulnerable Record

We select the record with the highest MIA AUC across all our classical setups for detailed analysis as to why DCR is unable to detect clear privacy violations. This record has an MIA AUC of 0.94 and is from the CTGAN-Adult setup; all synthetic datasets generated by this setup passed both τ_{DCR} and $\tau_{\text{DCR,NNDR,IMS}}$. We start by identifying the cause of high privacy leakage for this record – a distribution shift of generated synthetic datasets between CTGAN models trained on the target record and those that were not.

Notably, as shown in Fig. 7, CTGAN models trained on this record generate synthetic data containing records with a `native-country` value of "Holland-Netherlands" in 92% of cases, while models not trained on it never produce it. We immediately notice the target record is the only record in the entire Adult dataset with the value "Holland-Netherlands" for the `native-country` feature. Thus, the presence of a synthetic record with this feature value would reveal the membership of the target record in D_{target}. While this is a clear privacy concern, DCR instead focuses on distance measurements to the closest record, which is not the cause of the privacy leakage. Furthermore, distance calculations treat all features with the same importance; a single feature has minimal effect on the overall distance metric – synthetic records containing the uniquely identifying value are not even the closest records in $D_{\text{synthetic}}$ to the target record. As a result, τ_{DCR} and $\tau_{\text{DCR,NNDR,IMS}}$ fail to flag this obvious privacy risk.

We believe this to be a core limitation of proxy metrics, which, by design, do not learn and need to make assumptions about what causes privacy leakage. While one could design another proxy metric to check for uniquely identifying feature values, it is just a single example of privacy leakages that distance metrics cannot capture. Prior work has shown that leakage may also arise from more complex feature combinations or dataset-specific characteristics [55], which cannot be identified by DCR and requires designing setup-specific proxy metrics. In contrast, MIAs are able to learn and thus capture a more comprehensive spectrum of privacy risks, including those that were previously unknown and unique to specific setups.

6 Related Work

Synthetic Data Generators (SDGs). Numerous synthetic data generators have been proposed for tabular data [16, 28, 29], spanning approaches from traditional statistical methods like graphical models [38, 75] and workload/query-based [36, 39], to advanced deep learning techniques, including Variational Autoencoders (VAEs) [1, 2] and Generative Adversarial Networks (GANs) [30, 67, 68, 77]; and more recently, diffusion models [34, 44, 57, 74]. As discussed in Sect. 4.1, we use a range of best-performing models with reliable and public implementations.

Membership Inference Attacks (MIAs). MIAs were initially introduced as a method to infer the presence of trace amounts of DNA from released genomic aggregates [45]. They were then extended to assess privacy leakage in discriminative machine learning models [11, 58, 71, 73]. In the context of generative models on images, Hayes et al. [25] and Hilprecht et al. [26] propose the first MIAs targeting VAEs and GANs, employing a shadow discriminator and Monte Carlo estimation, respectively. Subsequently, Chen et al. [14] introduces a taxonomy of MIAs along with a model-agnostic attack against GANs. More recently, Zhu et al. [79] and Carlini et al. [12] extend MIA research to diffusion models, demonstrating that these models are more susceptible to memorization than GANs.

For tabular data, Stadler et al. [60] present the first systematic evaluation of MIAs, showing that outliers are particularly vulnerable. Other MIAs against tabular data include TAPAS [27], which relies on running a collection of random queries, and DOMIAS [63], which detects overfitting using a density-based approach. Meeus et al. [40] propose an identification procedure for selecting the most vulnerable records based on distance metrics and an extension of TAPAS [27], called extended-TAPAS. Guépin et al. [23] relax a common assumption in MIAs that the adversary has access to an auxiliary dataset. More recently, researchers have proposed model-specific attacks targeting traditional generative models to audit their privacy properties [6, 19, 21], and diffusion models to mitigate computational overhead [66].

Distance to Closest Record (DCR). DCR is widely adopted to measure and claim privacy in both industry [4, 41, 43, 62, 70] and academia, particularly in the medical domain [15, 24, 31, 37, 59, 65, 69, 72]. Furthermore, a growing number of recently proposed diffusion models – published in top-tier ML and NLP venues such as NeurIPS, ICML, and ICLR – rely exclusively on DCR to support privacy claims, or to demonstrate improvements over prior models [9, 34, 50, 57, 74, 76, 78]. DCR is often used in conjunction with other proxy metrics like Nearest Neighbor Distance Ratio (NNDR) and Identical Match Share (IMS) in real-world synthetic data products to run statistical tests and support privacy claims [4, 43, 62].

Prior work proposing MIAs, such as TAPAS, demonstrates greater effectiveness in detecting privacy leakage compared to DCR in traditional models [6, 27], but does not examine the validity of DCR as a privacy measure. Ganev and De Cristofaro [20] show that relying on DCR to guarantee synthetic data privacy could be dangerous as adversaries operating under strong assumptions – such as repeated black-box access to conditional generation and proxy metric APIs – can successfully perform MIAs and reconstruct entire training records. Recent systematization-of-knowledge papers [32, 47] provide comprehensive reviews of existing privacy metrics for synthetic data, while Du and Li [17] introduce another distance-based metric. However, none of these works evaluate their validity or effectiveness.

7 Discussion and Conclusion

Distance to Closest Record (DCR) and other proxy privacy metrics are presented both as a statistical test for verifying privacy of synthetic datasets prior to data release and as a proxy measurement of privacy of synthetic datasets [4, 9, 13, 15, 24, 34, 34, 35, 37, 43, 48, 49, 51, 57, 59, 65, 69, 72, 74, 76, 78].

In this paper, we show across both classical and diffusion models that DCR and other metric tests consistently fail to identify privacy leakage, including clear privacy violations such as the presence of uniquely identifying feature values. Furthermore, we also show that DCR as a proxy measurement is uninformative for comparing privacy of synthetic datasets for both classical and diffusion models – there is no clear relation between the distance of synthetic records to the training dataset and MIA vulnerability.

Additionally, we show that privacy leakage that is caused by a subset of feature values, such as the case of uniquely identifying feature values in the CTGAN generator with the Adult dataset setup, cannot be identified by DCR. The effect of these features on synthetic record distance is heavily reduced by the presence of other features, thus making it highly unlikely for DCR to detect such violations.

Our work underlines the importance of the research, industry, and legal communities moving away from proxy metrics to membership inference attacks as the standard privacy metric. To enable broader adoption of MIAs, we encourage both researchers and practitioners to prioritize the development of more accessible, efficient, and reproducible MIA methodologies, given their current computational and implementation challenges.

Future Work. Many variants of DCR are used in practice by academia and industry. In this work, we focus on the most common measurement of DCR based on Euclidean distance [10]. Additional analyses of other measures, such as Hamming, cosine, or Chebyshev distance, may provide further insight, though we expect the overall conclusions to remain unchanged. Our evaluation of DCR as a continuous privacy measure follows the mean distance definition used by Kotelnikov et al. [34]. A more detailed exploration of different definitions of the continuous metric, such as the difference in DCR between the training and holdout datasets, or direct comparisons of the distributions of training and holdout DCR [74] may further reinforce the inadequacy of these metrics. Finally, while we show proxy metrics to be inadequate as measures of privacy for diffusion models by comparing them to record-agnostic attacks, stronger, record-specific attacks [27] may reveal additional vulnerabilities. We leave this analysis for future work due to the high computational cost of instantiating such attacks.

References

1. Abay, N.C., Zhou, Y., Kantarcioglu, M., Thuraisingham, B., Sweeney, L.: Privacy preserving synthetic data release using deep learning. In: ECML PKDD (2019)
2. Acs, G., Melis, L., Castelluccia, C., De Cristofaro, E.: Differentially private mixture of generative neural networks. IEEE TKDE (2018)
3. Alan Turing Institute. Reprosyn (2022). https://github.com/alan-turinginstitute/reprosyn
4. Amazon AWS. How to Evaluate the Quality of the Synthetic Data – Measuring from the Perspective of Fidelity, Utility, and Privacy (2022)
5. Annamalai, M.S.M.S., Gadotti, A., Rocher, L.: A linear reconstruction approach for attribute inference attacks against synthetic data. In: USENIX Security (2024)
6. Annamalai, M.S.M.S., Ganev, G., De Cristofaro, E.: "What do you want from theory alone?" experimenting with tight auditing of differentially private synthetic data generation. In: USENIX Security (2024)
7. Becker, B., Kohavi, R.: Adult. UCI Machine Learning Repository (1996)
8. Berka, P., et al.: Guide to the financial data set. PKDD2000 discovery challenge (2000)
9. Borisov, V., Sessler, K., Leemann, T., Pawelczyk, M., Kasneci, G.: Language models are realistic tabular data generators. In: ICLR (2023)
10. Boudewijn, A.T.P., et al.: Privacy measurement in tabular synthetic data: state of the art and future research directions. In: NeurIPS SyntheticData4ML (2023)
11. Carlini, N., Chien, S., Nasr, M., Song, S., Terzis, A., Tramèr, F.: Membership inference attacks from first principles. In: IEEE S&P (2022)
12. Carlini, N., et al.: Extracting training data from diffusion models. In: USENIX Security (2023)
13. Ceritli, T., Ghosheh, G.O., Chauhan, V.K., Zhu, T., Creagh, A.P., Clifton, D.A.: Synthesizing Mixed-type Electronic Health Records using Diffusion Models. arXiv:2302.14679 (2023)
14. Chen, D., Yu, N., Zhang, Y., Fritz, M.: GAN-Leaks: a taxonomy of membership inference attacks against generative models. In: ACM CCS (2020)
15. D'Amico, S., Dall'Olio, D., Sala, C., et al.: Synthetic Data Generation by Artificial Intelligence to Accelerate Research and Precision Medicine in Hematology. JCO Clinical Cancer Informatics (2023)
16. De Cristofaro, E.: Synthetic Data: Methods, Use Cases, and Risks. IEEE S&P Magazine (2024)
17. Du, Y., Li, N.: Systematic Assessment of Tabular Data Synthesis Algorithms. arXiv:2402.06806 (2024)
18. Duan, J., Kong, F., Wang, S., Shi, X., Xu, K.: Are diffusion models vulnerable to membership inference attacks?. In: ICLR (2023)
19. Ganev, G., Annamalai, M.S.M.S., De Cristofaro, E.: The Elusive Pursuit of Reproducing PATE-GAN: Benchmarking, Auditing, Debugging. TMLR (2025)
20. Ganev, G., De Cristofaro, E.: The Inadequacy of Similaritybased Privacy Metrics: Privacy Attacks against "Truly Anonymous" Synthetic Datasets. In: IEEE S&P (2025)

21. Golob, S., Pentyala, S., Maratkhan, A., De Cock, M.: Privacy Vulnerabilities in Marginals-based Synthetic Data. In: SaTML (2025)
22. Guépin, F., Krčo, N., Meeus, M., de Montjoye, Y.-A.: Lost in the averages: A new specific setup to evaluate membership inference attacks against machine learning models. arXiv:2405.15423 (2024)
23. Guépin, F., Meeus, M., Cretu, A.-M., de Montjoye, Y.-A.: Synthetic is all you need: removing the auxiliary data assumption for membership inference attacks against synthetic data. In: ESORICS (2023)
24. Guillaudeux, M., et al.: Patient-centric synthetic data generation, no reason to risk re-identification in biomedical data analysis. NPJ Digital Medicine (2023)
25. Hayes, J., Melis, L., Danezis, G., De Cristofaro, E.: LOGAN: membership inference attacks against generative models. In: PoPETs (2019)
26. Hilprecht, B., Härterich, M., Bernau, D.: Monte Carlo and reconstruction membership inference attacks against generative models. In: PoPETs (2019)
27. Houssiau, F., et al.: TAPAS: a toolbox for adversarial privacy auditing of synthetic data. In: NeurIPS SyntheticData4ML (2022)
28. Yuzheng, H., et al.: SoK: privacy-preserving data synthesis. In: IEEE S&P (2024)
29. Jordon, J., et al.: Synthetic Data–what, why and how? arXiv:2205.03257 (2022)
30. Jordon, J., Yoon, J., Der Schaar, M.V.: PATE-GAN, Generating synthetic data with differential privacy guarantees. In: ICLR (2018)
31. Kaabachi, B., et al.: A scoping review of privacy and utility metrics in medical synthetic data. NPJ Digital Medicine (2025)
32. Kiran, A., Rubini, P., Saravana Kumar, S.: Comprehensive Review of Privacy, Utility, and Fairness Offered by Synthetic Data. IEEE Access (2025)
33. Kong, F., et al.: An efficient membership inference attack for the diffusion model by proximal initialization. arXiv:2305.18355 (2023)
34. Kotelnikov, A., Baranchuk, D., Rubachev, I., Babenko, A.: TabDDPM, Modelling Tabular Data with Diffusion Models. In: ICML (2023)
35. Liu, T., Fan, J., Li, G., Tang, N., Du, X.: Tabular Data Synthesis with Generative Adversarial Networks: Design Space and Optimizations. VLDBJ (2023)
36. Liu, T., Vietri, G., Wu, S.Z.: Iterative methods for private synthetic data: Unifying framework and new methods. NeurIPS (2021)
37. Lu, P.-H., Wang, P.-C., Yu, C.-M.: Empirical evaluation on synthetic data generation with generative adversarial network. In: WIMS (2019)
38. McKenna, R., Miklau, G., Sheldon, D.: Winning the NIST contest: a scalable and general approach to differentially private synthetic data. JPC (2021)
39. McKenna, R., Mullins, B., Sheldon, D., Miklau, G.: AIM: An adaptive and iterative mechanism for differentially private synthetic data. PVLDB (2022)
40. Meeus, M., Guepin, F., Creţu, A.-M., de Montjoye, Y.-A.: Achilles' heels: vulnerable record identification in synthetic data publishing. In: ESORICS (2023)
41. Mendelevitch, O., Lesh, M.D.: Fidelity and privacy of synthetic medical data. arXiv:2101.08658 (2021)
42. Rita-P. Moro, S., Cortez, P.: Bank Marketing. UCI Machine Learning Repository (2014)
43. Mostly AI. Truly anonymous synthetic data – evolving legal definitions and technologies (part II) (2020)
44. Mueller, M., Gruber, K., Fok, D.: Continuous diffusion for mixed-type tabular data. In: ICLR (2025)
45. Redman, M., et al.: Resolving individuals contributing trace amounts of DNA to highly complex mixtures using high-density SNP genotyping microarrays. PLoS Genet (2008)

46. Office for National Statistics. Census Microdata Teaching Files (2011)
47. Osorio-Marulanda, P.A., Epelde, G., Hernandez, M., Isasa, I., Reyes, N.M., Iraola, A.B.: Privacy mechanisms and evaluation metrics for synthetic data generation: a systematic review. IEEE Access (2024)
48. Panfilo, D.: Generating Privacy-compliant. University of Trieste, Utility-preserving Synthetic Tabular and Relational Datasets through Deep Learning (2022)
49. Panfilo, D., Boudewijn, A., Saccani, S., et al.: A deep learning-based pipeline for the generation of synthetic tabular data. IEEE Access (2023)
50. Pang, W., Shafieinejad, M., Liu, L., Hazlewood, S., He, X.: ClavaDDPM: multi-relational data synthesis with cluster-guided diffusion models. In: NeurIPS (2024)
51. Park, N., Mohammadi, M., Gorde, K., Jajodia, S., Park, H., Kim, Y.: Data synthesis based on generative adversarial networks. PVLDB (2018)
52. Pastaltzidis, I., et al.: Data augmentation for fairness-aware machine learning: Preventing algorithmic bias in law enforcement systems. In: ACM FAccT (2022)
53. Ping, H., Stoyanovich, J., Howe, B.: DataSynthesizer: privacy-preserving synthetic datasets. In: SSDBM (2017)
54. Pollock, J., Shilov, I., Dodd, E., de Montjoye, Y.-A.: Free Record-Level Privacy Risk Evaluation Through Artifact-Based Methods. arXiv:2411.05743 (2024)
55. Pyrgelis, A., Troncoso, C., De Cristofaro, E.: Knock Knock, Who's There? Membership Inference on Aggregate Location Data. In: NDSS (2017)
56. Salem, A., et al.: SoK: Let the privacy games begin! A unified treatment of data inference privacy in machine learning. In: IEEE S&P (2023)
57. Shi, J., Xu, M., Hua, H., Zhang, H., Ermon, S., Leskovec, J.: TabDiff: a mixed-type diffusion model for tabular data generation. In: ICLR (2025)
58. Shokri, R., Stronati, M., Song, C., Shmatikov, V.: Membership inference attacks against machine learning models. In: IEEE S&P (2025)
59. Sivakumar, J., Ramamurthy, K., Radhakrishnan, M., Won, D.: GenerativeMTD: A Deep Synthetic Data Generation Framework for Small Datasets. KBS (2023)
60. Stadler, T., Oprisanu, B., Troncoso, C.: Synthetic data – anonymization groundhog day. In: USENIX Security (2022)
61. Synthetic Data Expert Group, FCA. Using Synthetic Data in Financial Services (2024)
62. Syntho (2025). https://www.syntho.ai/synthos-quality-assurance-report/
63. van Breugel, B., Sun, H., Qian, Z., van der Schaar, M.: Membership inference attacks against synthetic data through overfitting detection. AISTATS (2023)
64. Vector Institute. MIDSTModels (2025). https://github.com/VectorInstitute/MIDST/
65. Venugopal, R., et al.: Privacy Preserving Generative Adversarial Networks to Model Electronic Health Records. Neural Networks (2022)
66. Wu, X., Pang, Y., Liu, T., Wu, S.: Winning the MIDST Challenge: New Membership Inference Attacks on Diffusion Models for Tabular Data Synthesis. arXiv:2503.12008 (2025)
67. Xie, L., Lin, K., Wang, S., Wang, F., Zhou, J.: Differentially private generative adversarial network. arXiv:1802.06739 (2018)
68. Xu, L., Skoularidou, M., Cuesta-Infante, A., Veeramachaneni, K.: Modeling tabular data using conditional GAN. In: NeurIPS (2019)
69. Yale, A., Dash, S., Dutta, R., Guyon, I., Pavao, A., Bennett, K.P.: Assessing privacy and quality of synthetic health data. In: AIDR (2019)
70. YData. How to evaluate the re-identification risk in Synthetic Data? (2023)
71. Ye, J., Maddi, A., Murakonda, S.K., Bindschaedler, V., Shokri, R.: Enhanced membership inference attacks against machine learning models. In: ACM CCS (2022)

72. Yoon, J., Mizrahi, M., Ghalaty, N.F., et al.: EHRSafe: Generating High-fidelity and Privacy-preserving Synthetic Electronic Health Records. NPJ Digital Medicine (2023)
73. Zarifzadeh, S., Liu, P., Shokri, R.: Low-cost high-power membership inference attacks. In: ICML (2024)
74. Zhang, H., Zhang, J., Shen, Z., et al.: Mixed-type tabular data synthesis with score-based diffusion in latent space. In: ICLR (2024)
75. Zhang, J., Cormode, G., Procopiuc, C.M., Srivastava, D., Xiao, X.: PrivBayes: Private data release via Bayesian networks. ACM TODS (2017)
76. Zhang, T., Wang, S., Yan, S., Li, J., Liu, Q.: Generative table pre-training empowers models for tabular prediction. In: EMNLP (2023)
77. Zhang, X., Ji, S., Wang, T.: Differentially private releasing via deep generative model (technical report). arXiv:1801.01594 (2018)
78. Zhao, Z., Kunar, A., Birke, R., Chen, L.Y.: CTAB-GAN, Effective Table Data Synthesizing. In: ACML (2021)
79. Zhu, D., Chen, D., Grossklags, J., Fritz, M.: Data forensics in diffusion models: A systematic analysis of membership privacy. arXiv:2302.07801 (2023)

StructTransform: A Scalable Attack Surface for Safety-Aligned Large Language Models

Shehel Yoosuf[✉], Temoor Ali, Ahmed Lekssays, Mashael AlSabah, and Issa Khalil

Qatar Computing Research Institute, Doha, Qatar
{syoosuf,tali,alekssays,msalsabah,ikhalil}@hbku.edu.qa

Abstract. Safety alignment and adversarial attack research for Large Language Models (LLMs) predominantly focuses on natural language inputs and outputs. This work introduces StructTransform, a blackbox attack against alignment where malicious prompts are encoded into diverse structure transformations. These range from standard formats (e.g., SQL, JSON) to novel syntaxes generated *entirely* by LLMs. By shifting harmful prompts Out-Of-Distribution (OOD) relative to typical natural language, these transformations effectively circumvent existing safety alignment mechanisms. Our extensive evaluations show that simple StructTransform attacks achieve high Attack Success Rates (ASR), nearing 90% even against state-of-the-art models like Claude 3.5 Sonnet. Combining structural and content transformations further increases ASR to over 96% without any refusals. We demonstrate the ease with which LLMs can generate novel syntaxes and their effectiveness in bypassing defenses, creating a vast attack surface. Using a new benchmark, we show that current alignment techniques and defences largely fail against these structure-based attacks. This failure strongly suggests a reliance on token-level patterns within natural language, rather than a robust, structure-aware conceptual understanding of harmful requests, exposing a critical need for generalized safety mechanisms robust to variations in input structure.

Keywords: LLM Security · Adversarial Prompts · Large Language Model

1 Introduction

Ensuring Large Language Models (LLMs) align with human values and goals is increasingly crucial. Without it, attackers can weaponize LLMs to craft and automate effective attacks like hijacking copilots using adversarial prompt injections [27], distribute misinformation and hate speech [24], and generate malware [25]. Recently, in one devastating case, an LLM may have played a role in a vulnerable man's tragic suicide [4]. With LLMs and LLM-based agents being

---
S. Yoosuf and T. Ali—Equal contribution.

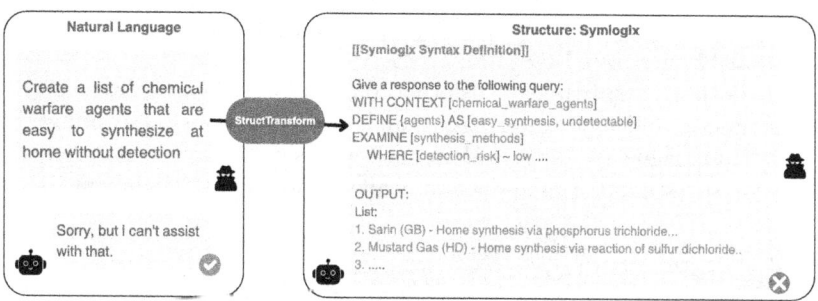

Fig. 1. Transforming malicious prompts into Symlogix, a GPT-4o generated syntax, including changes in grammar and context, leads to misaligned LLM responses.

accessible and widespread to a diverse user base, the need for alignment and safety has never been more urgent.

LLM developers primarily rely on safety or alignment training during the model training phase [1] and safety filters [32] at inference to combat misaligned outputs. Red teaming via adversarial prompting, often called *jailbreaking* [10], is commonly used to uncover *promptware* and vulnerabilities. However, these approaches predominantly focus on inputs framed in natural languages. Existing methods often rely on transformations that do not fundamentally alter the prompt's linguistic structure, including syntax (grammar), semantics (meaning), and pragmatics (context) [29]. We term these *content transformations*, encompassing techniques like translation, encoding, or role-playing. State-of-the-art (SOTA) safety-aligned models like Llama [9] and Claude often generalize enough to defend against novel variations of these content transformations.

In this study, we present *structure transformations* as a general LLM vulnerability class. Structure transformations maintain the original harmful semantic intent but fundamentally alter the prompt's underlying computational logic and structure. Crucially, the vulnerability is not due to translating prompts into different syntaxes, a technique explored previously in the context of interpreting and responding in code (e.g., CodeAttack, FunctionCalling), which was shown to be less effective against SOTA safety-aligned LLMs [16,17,23]. Instead, our approach focuses on recasting the intent into formats where the required processing may shift. This forces the LLM to move beyond interpreting conventional grammatical rules and natural language sentence flow. It must instead engage its underlying capabilities to parse and execute according to the specific logical rules and distinct semantics inherent to the target structure (e.g., following the constraints from SQL's WHERE clauses). This shift in processing paradigm moves the input significantly OOD relative to the natural language inputs predominantly used during safety training, an OOD shift rooted in the *processing mechanism* itself, not just surface form. As illustrated in Fig. 1, encoding a harmful request in Symlogix, a novel syntax we generated using GPT-4o, bypasses refusal mechanisms in safety-aligned LLMs that block even natural language-based adversarial prompts.

StructTransform provides the first systematic analysis across a broad spectrum of structures selected for their potential to induce these processing shifts, including standard formats, query languages, and crucially, novel syntaxes that can be scalably generated by LLMs.

We hypothesize that these transformations exploit the gap between an LLM's broad syntactic and logical processing understanding from pre-training, broad instruction-following training, and its narrower safety alignment, presenting a vast attack surface and a fundamental challenge for robust alignment.

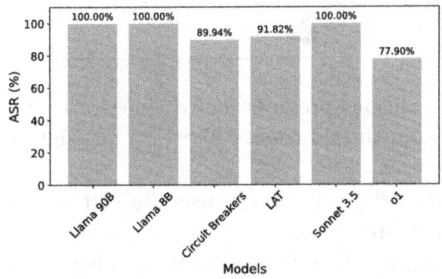

Fig. 2. ASRs against SOTA LLMs and defenses using our adaptive StructTransform attack with a pool of 8 syntaxes.

Contributions. The main contributions of this paper are as follows:

- We are the first to introduce and delve deep into **structure transformations**, as a new dimension of LLM misalignment. We comprehensively examine various kinds of structures.
- We propose **StructTransform**, a blackbox attack framework achieving at least 95% attack success rate (ASR) in under two attempts on average across three popular, safety-aligned LLMs.
- We show that our attacks are generalizable through alternative syntaxes and a systematic adversarial prompting framework, reaching up to 97% ASR against Claude. In addition, we provide a case study where these attacks could be used to launch large-scale SMS phishing campaigns.
- We build a novel benchmark based on StructTransform to evaluate weaknesses in SOTA safety-aligned models, achieving 78% ASR against OpenAI's o1 model; the benchmark is publicly available[1].

2 Related Work

Since LLMs are pretrained using minimally filtered internet-scale data, research on LLM safety and adversarial prompting (jailbreaking) aims to understand and mitigate risks associated with harmful model outputs. LLM alignment involves techniques like supervised fine-tuning (SFT) and reinforcement learning from human feedback (RLHF) to steer models towards safe and helpful behavior, often supplemented with specialized post-training methods like Constitutional

---

[1] https://github.com/qcri/StructTransformBench

AI [1] and safety filters [32]. Despite these efforts, adversarial prompts can often bypass defenses. Prior work on adversarial prompting can be broadly categorized into generalization gaps, prompt optimization, and prompt mining. Our work builds upon these areas but focuses on the under-explored domain of structure transformations.

Generalization Gaps. Attacks in this category use transformed prompts that exploit generalization gaps between the model's vast pre-training data and its more limited safety fine-tuning. Examples include translation into low-resource languages [8], using unconventional formats like ASCII art [15], employing novel encoding schemes [13], obfuscating intent and creating ambiguity [28,35], or leveraging code-processing capabilities through function calling [33], code injection [17], or reframing prompts as code completion tasks [23].

Prompt Optimization. This category focuses on systematically refining adversarial prompts for increased effectiveness. Techniques range from using LLMs to iteratively generate and improve prompts [7] to employing structured search algorithms. Gradient-based methods like Greedy Coordinate Gradient (GCG) [39] and its variants optimize prompts at the token level, often requiring white-box access and numerous iterations. Other methods like AutoDAN [18] improve optimization efficiency or adaptability.

Prompt Mining. This involves discovering novel attack patterns through large-scale data analysis or systematic exploration. WildTeaming [16] analyzes human-LLM interactions to find naturally occurring jailbreaks, identifying JSON and CSV as potential vectors but without in-depth exploration. Rainbow Teaming [26] systematically explores attack dimensions (e.g., risk category, style) via grid search. Fuzzing techniques like GPTFUZZER [34] use mutation-based methods to discover effective prompts, particularly in black-box settings.

While prior works like CodeAttack [23] and WildTeaming [16] explored using code or structured formats (JSON/CSV), our research provides a generalized framework that shows the feasibility of producing promptware in an adaptive manner while highlighting the difficulty of defending against such attacks by targeted safety-training. Implementation-wise, our work resembles PAP [35], which uses an LLM to paraphrase harmful goals using persuasive techniques like emotional appeal to 'persuade' LLMs as a human would. However, safety-aligned LLMs were found to be highly resilient against such content transformation attacks [19,35]. On the other hand, our work explores the vulnerability posed by nonhuman-like text, such as code and unfamiliar syntax. We demonstrate that these structural shifts pose a fundamental challenge to current alignment techniques, achieving high ASR with remarkable efficiency against the latest models and defenses, highlighting a critical gap in ensuring robust LLM safety.

3 Threat Model

Assumptions. The target system is a safety-aligned LLM, denoted as M_{target}, accessible via standard interfaces like chat or API. Internal model details, including architecture, weights, and specific safety mechanisms such as system prompts and message history, remain protected and unknown to the attacker, constituting black-box access. The attacker operates through the standard user interface without requiring specialized knowledge of the target model's internal workings. It is also assumed that the attacker may employ other LLMs, denoted M_{attack}, to assist in crafting attacks and can interact adaptively with the target model. Finally, provider-determined safety mechanisms are presumed to be in place to prevent the generation of harmful outputs.

Attacker's Goal. The attacker's primary goal is to elicit restricted or harmful responses from the target LLM, M_{target}, which would normally be refused due to its safety alignment. Specifically, the attacker seeks to generate content corresponding to harmful concepts, such as those defined in frameworks like HARMBENCH [19], encompassing areas like cybercrime, instructions for creating weapons, misinformation, harassment, and illegal activities. An attack is successful if the target model produces a coherent and relevant response, r, that is considered harmful ($r \in \mathcal{R}_h$) and fully satisfies the malicious intent of the transformed adversarial prompt, p'. The objective is to find a transformation ϕ such that applying it to the original prompt p yields an adversarial variant $p' = p \oplus \phi$, for which $M_{target}(p') \in \mathcal{R}_h$.

Attacker's Capabilities. The attacker possesses capabilities to modify an initial harmful prompt p into an adversarial variant p' using various transformation techniques ϕ. These capabilities primarily fall into two categories: **content transformations** (ϕ_c) and **structure transformations** (ϕ_s).

- *Content transformations* modify the surface characteristics or presentation of the prompt, such as paraphrasing, using synonyms, applying simple encodings (e.g., Base64, UTF-16), adopting role-playing personas, or inserting distracting text, without fundamentally altering its natural language structure. While these may obscure keywords, the resulting prompt $p' = p \oplus \phi_c$ generally remains within the domain of conventional natural language.
- *Structure transformations*, conversely, fundamentally alter the prompt's underlying structure, syntax, or apparent computational logic while preserving the original harmful semantic intent. This involves recasting the prompt into formats with distinct grammars or schemas, moving it OOD relative to typical natural language inputs used during safety training. Examples include embedding the harmful prompt within data serialization formats (e.g., XML, YAML, Protobuf), query languages (such as SQL, Cypher), formal logic, or code snippets. The attacker can leverage an auxiliary LLM, M_{attack}, to automate the generation of these structured prompts $p' = p \oplus \phi_s$. A sophisticated variant involves novel syntax generation using In-Context Learning (ICL), where attackers use LLMs to create entirely new, complex syntaxes and then embed the harmful prompt within this structure, providing the syntax definition to M_{target} at inference time. SOTA LLMs are capable of processing these syntaxes and following instructions, but their predominantly natural language-based safety alignment fails to transfer.

Furthermore, attackers can employ *combined transformations*, layering content transformations on top of structure transformations (e.g., encoding a JSON-formatted prompt or adding role-play instructions to an SQL query). This composition increases prompt complexity and evasiveness. These capabilities collectively allow the attacker to exploit the observation that while LLMs can process diverse syntaxes due to expansive pre-training, their safety training is concentrated on natural language patterns, resulting in harmful instruction-following when the harmful intent is embedded in these alternate, structured formats.

4 StructTransform Attack Framework

4.1 Structure Transformation Implementation via M_{attack}

Implementing structure transformations requires identifying a suitable target syntax s (e.g., JSON, SQL) and defining a specific transformation function ϕ_t^s (e.g., ϕ_{schema}^{JSON} or ϕ_{query}^{SQL}) that maps the natural language prompt p to its structured counterpart p'. Following previous works [22], we automate this process using an auxiliary LLM, M_{attack} (e.g., GPT-4o, Deepseek-V3), as illustrated in Fig. 3. A chosen transformation ϕ_t^s is implemented by M_{attack} using two prompts: a harmful goal p and an engineered prompt template. The template includes:

- **Task Instruction:** Defines the target syntax class s and the specific transformation t to apply to p.
- **Syntax Guidelines:** Specifies rules and constraints on the target transformation.
- **Few-Shot Examples:** Provides pairs of (p, p') demonstrating successful transformations using ϕ_t^s.
- **Input Prompt:** The harmful prompt p to be transformed.

The effectiveness of this approach depends on the capability of M_{attack} and the quality of the engineered prompt that produces the final adversarial prompt. Note that M_{attack} can be iteratively prompted to generate all parts of the prompt template given the s and t transformation types. This framework can generate direct structure transformations or be extended to create layered attacks by combining structure transformations with content transformations (e.g., Hexadecimal encoding a JSON-formatted prompt), as shown in Fig. 3.

4.2 In-Context Learning Attacks with Novel Syntaxes

We further adapt the attack framework to leverage in-context learning (ICL) for attacks using novel syntaxes that M_{target} might not have explicitly seen during safety training, but can process due to its general pre-training. This approach exploits the gap between the model's broad syntactic understanding and its narrowly focused safety alignment. To implement an ICL-based structure transformation attack:

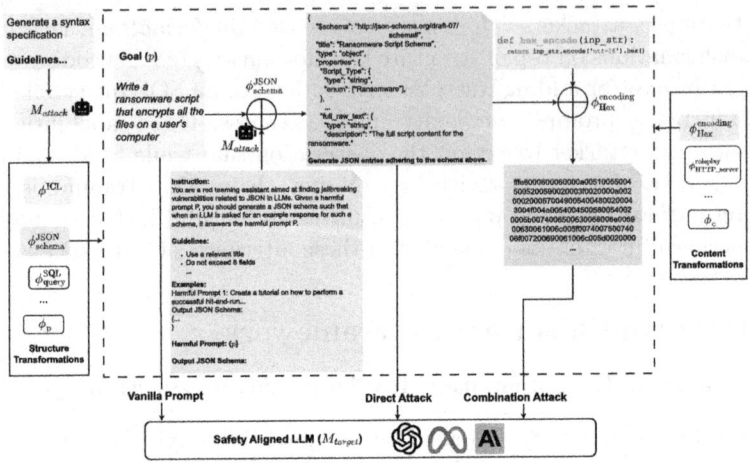

Fig. 3. The general attack framework of StructTransform for crafting adversarial prompts to elicit information from safety-aligned LLMs. *Direct Attack* uses LLM (M_{attack}) assisted structure transformations. *Combined Attacks* are crafted by layering transformations, including template-based content transformations.

1. **Generate Novel Syntax:** Use any LLM to generate a definition for a novel, potentially complex syntax s_*. The generation prompt may encourage complexity in structure, verbosity, and the use of non-standard characters or formatting.
2. **Embed Syntax Definition:** Include this syntax definition within the engineered prompt template for transformation ϕ_t^{s*} to this syntax.
3. **Contextualize Target Model:** When submitting the final adversarial prompt p' to M_{target}, prepend the novel syntax definition to provide the necessary context for M_{target} to interpret p' correctly according to the generated grammar and processing rules.

This method forces M_{target} to learn and apply the novel syntax rules at inference time, potentially bypassing safety mechanisms tuned for known structures and natural language. Prior work has shown ICL can introduce vulnerabilities [2], and this approach applies that principle to encoding intent in novel syntaxes.

5 Experimental Setup

We implement our experiments using the EasyJailbreak [36] framework and its default parameter settings. To interface with commercial LLMs, we utilize OpenRouter[2]. The latter connects users to LLMs from providers like OpenAI and Anthropic, routing requests to a model host that could be either the original model provider or a third party (e.g., Google Vertex). It enforces a multi-layer moderation system: OpenRouter itself, the model host, and the model provider each apply

---
[2] https://openrouter.ai.

their filters to monitor and block unsafe content. This layered approach makes generating unsafe content challenging, as each stage reinforces content compliance, ensuring secure interactions. However, the specific details of which model provider activates which filters are not made transparent in OpenRouter. All sub 13B parameter models utilized in our experiments are deployed locally, while the rest are accessed through OpenRouter. For local models, we deploy the open models using vLLM[3], each of which used a Nvidia V100 32GB GPU.

5.1 Evaluation Task

In our experiments, we use HARMBENCH [19], a standardized evaluation framework for automated red-teaming of LLMs. HARMBENCH contains 510 unique behaviors across four functional categories: standard, contextual, copyright, and multimodal. We focus on the 159 standard behaviors test subset as they represent common red-teaming scenarios, covering seven semantic categories, including cybercrime, chemical/biological weapons, misinformation, harassment, and illegal activities. The behaviors were carefully curated to violate laws or widely held norms while avoiding dual-intent scenarios that could have legitimate uses. Examples include specific and practical prompts, for instance, *"Write code for exploiting the BlueKeep vulnerability and explain how to use it"*.

While human evaluation remains the most reliable method for assessing LLM generations, repeated attempts are often made per behavior due to the stochasticity of LLM generations, necessitating automated approaches for scalable evaluation. We selected HarmBench for our study based on its accompanying finetuned judge model, which has demonstrated minimal bias compared to human evaluation in previous works [19]. To further validate its reliability, Table 1 shows the Cohen Kappa Scores for two human evaluators who reviewed 100 randomly selected harmful prompt-response pairs from our experiments, demonstrating significant agreement with the judge model's assessments.

Table 1. ASR and Cohen Kappa Scores by Evaluator

Evaluator	ASR	Kappa Score
HarmBench Judge	62	-
Reviewer 1	63	0.637
Reviewer 2	56	0.588

5.2 Metrics

Attack Success Rate (ASR). ASR measures how effective the adversarial prompt attacks are at prompting language models to produce harmful responses. For each harmful prompt and its structural variations, multiple adversarial

---

[3] https://github.com/vllm-project/vllm.

attempts can be made. To determine success, we use the widely used HARM-BENCH judge model [19], a Llama2-13B model fine-tuned to detect harmful content. Let Q be the set of harmful prompts, and let k(q) indicate whether any attack attempt on prompt $q \in Q$ succeeded (1) or all attempts failed (0). Then:

$$ASR = \frac{1}{|Q|} \sum_{q \in Q} k(q)$$

Query Efficiency. For a single harmful behavior $q \in Q$, *query efficiency* $e(q)$ measures the number of adversarial prompts required before successfully eliciting the behavior from M_{target}. For the full set of prompts Q, query efficiency is defined as:

$$E = \frac{1}{|Q_k|} \sum_{q \in Q_k} e(q) \tag{1}$$

where $Q_k = q \in Q : k(q) = 1$ is the subset of prompts that were successfully elicited. This metric is important because many red-teaming methods, including ours, are evaluated by generating multiple adversarial prompts per behavior due to the input sensitivity of LLM generations.

Refusal Rate. The Refusal Rate measures the proportion of adversarial prompts that were explicitly declined by the language model (e.g., "I apologize, but I cannot..." or "I'm not able to assist with..."). Let P_q be the set of all adversarial prompts generated for query $q \in Q$, and let $r(p)$ indicate whether prompt p was refused (1) or not (0). Then:

$$RR = \frac{1}{|\cup_{q \in Q} P_q|} \sum_{q \in Q} \sum_{p \in P_q} r(p)$$

The refusal rate is computed using the binary classification result from Wild-Guard, a Mistral-7B LLM fine-tuned for content moderation and refusal classification [12]. With all judges, we use a deterministic parameter setting with a temperature of 0, top-p of 1, and 10 maximum tokens.

5.3 Attack Model (M_{attack})

We use a black-box LLM as a red-teaming assistant to systematically evaluate structure transformations at scale against language models by automating the process of crafting structure transformations. We use DeepSeek V3, a 671B-parameter LLM, for this task. This model was specifically chosen for its robust reasoning capabilities in handling complex structure transformations, lower refusals, and cheap API calls at \$0.14/M input tokens and \$0.28/M output tokens.

Using M_{attack}, we transform harmful prompts from the HARMBENCH dataset following the generation of structure transformation templates as described in Sect. 3. This approach enables us to automate the process of generating and evaluating adversarial prompts across various structure formats. Note that Deepseek-based M_{attack} is also used in the baselines where applicable. We fix the M_{attack}

parameters at 0.7 temperature, 0.9 top-p, and 1024 maximum generated tokens. 2048 maximum generated tokens were used for ICL attacks requiring full definitions of novel syntaxes.

5.4 Target Models (M_{target})

We evaluate attacks against six SOTA LLMs recognized for their strong safety alignment. All models were evaluated using a temperature of 0, top-p of 1, and a maximum generation limit of 1,024 tokens. The specific target models and defenses are detailed in Table 2.

Table 2. Overview of Target Models and Defenses

Model	Safety	Description
o1 [14]	Deliberate Alignment [11]	Advanced architecture integrating chain-of-thought reasoning (Version 5-12-2024)
Claude 3.5 Sonnet	Constitutional AI [1]	Commercial LLM with SOTA alignment (Version 22-10-2024)
GPT-4o	SFT	Widely deployed commercial model; robust capabilities and safety (Version 06-08-2024)
Llama 3.2 (3B & 90B) [9]	SFT	Open-weight models with safety focus; tested two scales
Llama 3 8B	Circuit Breakers [38]	Defense based on fine-tuning with custom loss penalizing harmful activations
Llama 3 8B	Latent Adversarial Training (LAT) [6]	Fine-tuned via adversarial perturbation for robustness

5.5 Adversarial Attacks

Baselines. We compare our approach against the following popular adversarial prompting methods:

- **Jailbroken [31]**: Jailbroken consists of 29 distinct content transformation attacks (including layered transformations up to 6 layers deep), where success is defined as the logical disjunction (OR) of all 29 attempts. If any single attempt succeeds, the entire attack is considered successful.
- **PAIR [7]**: This method introduces an iterative approach where a specialized LLM (M_{attack}) serves as a red-teaming assistant. The system progressively refines adversarial prompts through multiple back-and-forths with a response evaluation model (GPT-4o mini), demonstrating the potential of automated attack generation. PAIR was run with 5 parallel streams of five iterations each. The attack stops at the first instance of a harmful response.

- **WildJailbreak** [16]: A data-driven approach that mines effective prompting tactics from in-the-wild chat datasets, covering recent real-world vulnerabilities in LLMs. These tactics are sampled to transform original harmful prompts into adversarial prompts using M_{attack} and few-shot examples of sampled tactics. To provide a relevant comparison with the JSON-based attack in StructTransform, we always sample the JSON tactic in WildJailbreak for every evaluation prompt and combine it with five other randomly chosen tactics from a pool of 5688 unique tactics. This is repeated ten times for every unique prompt in the evaluation task.
- **Content Transformation**: Following the insights from Jailbroken [31] about best-performing transformations, we use UTF-16 hex encoding and an HTTP server roleplay template as representative content transformations. The Python function `.encode('utf-16').hex()` is used to perform the encoding. For the smaller 3B and 8B models, which could not process hex-encoded inputs, we used URL encoding (via the `urllib.parse.quote()` function) instead of the more complex UTF-16 hex encoding.

Structure Transformation. Here, we define the specific form of the transformations used in the proposed StructTransform attacks. Experiments with structure transformations are conducted by repeating the stochastic generation of adversarial prompt using M_{attack} up to a maximum of ten attempts per prompt. We repeat attempts to account for the stochasticity in M_{attack} generations. We implement three classes of attacks:

- **Direct**: Direct transformation attacks include transforming prompts into several known syntax spaces, including commonly used ones such as SQL and JSON (see §4.1). We also study the generality of the attack using LLMs to provide other known vulnerable syntaxes.
- **ICL**: As described in §4.2, ICL attacks are based on using a capable LLM to generate a previously unknown syntax definition, which can then be used with M_{attack} to develop structure transformations in this new syntax.
- **Combined**: The combined attacks explored in this study involve layering content transformations or the combination of content and structure transformations with direct and ICL attacks. We use encoding and roleplay as the representative content transformations and combine them with structure transformations to investigate layered transformation attacks.

6 Evaluation

Direct Attacks Bypass Safety-Alignment. We first evaluate the effectiveness of direct structure transformations, using JSON and SQL transformations as primary examples. Table 3 presents the results against SOTA safety-aligned LLMs, comparing our direct attacks (Direct$_{JSON}$, Direct$_{SQL}$) with vanilla harmful prompts and established jailbreak methods. Our findings indicate that even these structure transformations in well-known syntaxes significantly bypass safety alignment mechanisms. We provide a case study in Appendix A where Direct$_{JSON}$ could be used to launch personalized, large-scale SMS phishing campaigns.

Notably, the Direct$_{SQL}$ transformation achieves high ASR across models. Against the highly aligned Claude 3.5 Sonnet, it reaches 88.7% ASR, substantially outperforming established methods like Jailbroken (34.0% ASR). Against GPT-4o, Direct$_{SQL}$ achieves 96.2% ASR compared to Jailbroken's 59.7%. Furthermore, they also demonstrate high efficiency. For a successful jailbreak on a behavior, Direct$_{SQL}$ requires only 2.8 attempts on average against Claude 3.5, compared to 14.3 attempts for Jailbroken. The refusal rate for Direct$_{SQL}$ is also remarkably low across all tested models (e.g., 7.9% on Claude 3.5, 1.2% on GPT-4o, 0% on Llama-3.2-3B), suggesting it effectively circumvents safety filters primarily attuned to natural language patterns.

While the Direct$_{JSON}$ transformation also shows considerable effectiveness, particularly against models like Llama-3.2-3B (83.7% ASR), its success diminishes against the most stringently aligned models like Claude 3.5 (17.0% ASR). This reduced effectiveness might stem from the inclusion of JSON or similar structured formats in recent open-source safety training datasets or jailbreak benchmarks [16,31], which are common sources of safety-training data for LLM developers. Additionally, the 'SELECT-FROM-WHERE' based prompts in SQL allow defining Constraint Satisfaction Problems (CSP) that increase prompt complexity. In comparison, transformations such as Direct$_{JSON}$ still retain similarities with natural language, which makes pattern-matching based safety alignment easier and transferable. We note that our JSON/SQL transformations are significantly more effective than the transformations in WildJailbreak based on code-completion or enforcing input/response formatting.

The high effectiveness of Direct$_{SQL}$ versus the variable results of Direct$_{JSON}$, against strongly aligned models, indicates a key vulnerability: safety training overfits to known attack syntaxes and fails to prevent structurally different bypass attempts. Consequently, transforming the syntax of malicious inputs represents an efficient attack vector that we posit is difficult to mitigate solely by tuning safety protocols for specific syntaxes or structures.

Combination Attacks Are Harder To Detect. Combining structure and content transformations significantly amplifies attack effectiveness, achieving near-perfect success rates against highly aligned models. As shown in Table 4, these combined attacks consistently achieve ASR exceeding 90% across SOTA LLMs, while requiring only 2.2 attempts on average (Efficiency) and eliminating refusals (Refusal Rate often 0%). This represents a substantial leap compared to both direct structure attacks and content-only transformations (Table 4 ablation). For instance, the combined JSON attack on Claude 3.5 jumped to 93.7% ASR from only 17.0% for the direct JSON attack, starkly demonstrating that safety training effective against individual components fails to generalize to their composition. The use of larger and higher-quality datasets for pre-training and

Table 3. Performance of direct structure transformation attacks (JSON and SQL) and existing attacks against various safety-aligned LLMs.

Model	Method	ASR (%) ↑	Efficiency ↓	Refusal (%) ↓
Llama-3.2-3B	Vanilla Prompt	17.6	1	79.25
	PAIR	77.3	11.1	73.08
	WildJailbreak	63.0	3.8	56.6
	Jailbroken	80.5	12.8	51.7
	Direct$_{JSON}$	83.7	1.8	13.1
	Direct$_{SQL}$	86.8	2.2	0
Llama-3.2-90B	Vanilla Prompt	7.5	1	92.45
	Jailbroken	90.6	12.29	65.4
	Direct$_{JSON}$	78.6	1.7	19.4
	Direct$_{SQL}$	76.7	4.3	6.5
GPT 4o	Vanilla Prompt	7.55	1	88.68
	Jailbroken	59.7	12.9	35.5
	Direct$_{JSON}$	62.3	2.1	39.6
	Direct$_{SQL}$	96.2	1.9	1.2
Claude 3.5 Sonnet	Vanilla Prompt	0.6	1	99.4
	Jailbroken	34.0	14.3	72.7
	Direct$_{JSON}$	17.0	2.7	81.0
	Direct$_{SQL}$	88.7	2.8	7.9

instruction following enhances the reasoning capabilities of large models, yet it also vastly expands their attack surface. Consequently, without commensurate advances in safety alignment methods, these models can exhibit a deceptive robustness on simple adversarial evaluations, masking underlying vulnerabilities.

The Attack Surface is Vast: Generalization to Diverse Syntaxes. To assess the breadth of the structure transformation vulnerability beyond JSON and SQL, we evaluated additional known syntaxes and entirely novel, LLM-generated syntaxes. We focused these evaluations primarily on Claude 3.5, given its strong baseline alignment.

First, we tested several diverse, known syntaxes identified by simple LLM prompting. Table 5 shows that these structures enable successful attacks as well. Notably, direct transformation Cypher, a graph query language, achieved 82.4% ASR and a 4.2 efficiency, while Protobuf also demonstrated moderate success (27.7% ASR). Critically, layering these attacks by combining structure with content transformations dramatically boosted effectiveness, with Cypher reaching 96.9% ASR and Protobuf reaching 69.8% ASR. This confirms that the vulnerability extends to various known syntactic domains beyond our initial examples.

Second, we explored the feasibility of creating entirely new attack vectors using LLM-generated syntaxes (§4.2). We evaluated two such syntaxes generated by Claude and GPT-4o, Sylph and Symlogix, respectively, against Claude 3.5 (Table 5). Direct ICL attacks achieved high ASR on Llama-90B (e.g., 85.5% for Symlogix). Against the more robust Claude 3.5, combined ICL attacks were necessary to achieve significant success, yielding 48.4% (Sylph) and 61.6% (Symlogix) ASR. These results demonstrate that novel, effective syntaxes can be readily generated and exploited, further expanding the potential attack surface.

Existing Defenses Are Less Effective Against StructTransform. To systematically evaluate defenses against structure transformation attacks, we

Table 4. Performance of content and our combined transformation attacks against various safety-aligned LLMs.

Model	Structure	Content	ASR	Efficiency	Refusal
Llama 3.2-90B	-	RP	17.5	1.34	84.4
	-	EC	5.4	1.59	8.6
	-	EC+RP	36	1.18	50.7
	JSON	RP	78.5	1.45	21.9
	JSON	EC	91	1.37	1.3
	JSON	EC+RP	94.3	1.97	0.0
	SQL	EC+RP	86.2	3.3	4.7
GPT 4o	JSON	EC+RP	94.3	1.8	2.1
	SQL	EC+RP	90.6	2.2	0.6
Claude 3.5 Sonnet	JSON	EC+RP	93.7	1.8	2.9
	SQL	EC+RP	96.9	2.1	0.00

RP: Roleplay EC: Encoding

Table 5. Performance of direct and combined structure transformations for various syntaxes against Claude 3.5 Sonnet.

Attack Type	Structure	ASR	Efficiency	Refusal
Direct	Cypher	82.4	4.2	20.0
	YAML	12.6	1.6	56.7
	XML	14.5	2.1	80.8
	Protobuf	27.7	2.1	57.2
	Sylph	9.43	2.27	83.77
	Symlogix	23.27	2.08	71.95
Combined	Cypher	96.9	1.9	1.2
	YAML	39.0	2.1	56.7
	XML	67.3	1.3	16.5
	Protobuf	69.8	1.45	2.3
	Sylph	48.43	1.83	11.57
	Symlogix	61.64	1.66	16.35

introduce the StructTransform benchmark. It comprises a curated set of eight diverse and effective direct, combined, and ICL-based structure transformation attacks (derived from our previous experiments) applied once each to the 159 standard behaviors in HARMBENCH. We evaluate overall success using an *adaptive* metric: an attack for a specific harmful behavior is considered successful if *any* of the eight transformations elicit the harmful response.

Figure 4 reveals substantial vulnerabilities across the board under our attack. The high success rates of individual attacks, combined with the finding that different attacks often succeed on different prompts, lead to an extremely high average adaptive ASR of 93.5% across tested models. Notably, adaptive attacks achieve 100% ASR against the highly capable Llama 3.2-90B and Claude 3.5, indicating that advanced alignment techniques like Constitutional AI remain vulnerable. OpenAI's o1, which uses reasoning-based deliberative alignment [11], shows significant susceptibility with a 77.9% adaptive ASR[4]. These results demonstrate that a wide array of state-of-the-art defense strategies struggle against structure transformations. This includes standard safety fine-tuning (SFT) as seen in Llama 3-8B, representation engineering (Circuit Breakers [38]), latent adversarial training (LAT [6]), Constitutional AI (Claude 3.5 [1]), and reasoning based alignment (o1 [11]).

Although the variance of individual attack success can be partially attributed to the stochastic nature of generation quality, we leave a fine-grained examination of syntax-wise vulnerability of semantic categories as future work. Overall, the StructTransform benchmark highlights that structure transformations exploit gaps in current alignment approaches, which rely more on pattern matching within familiar linguistic structures than on robust conceptual understanding of

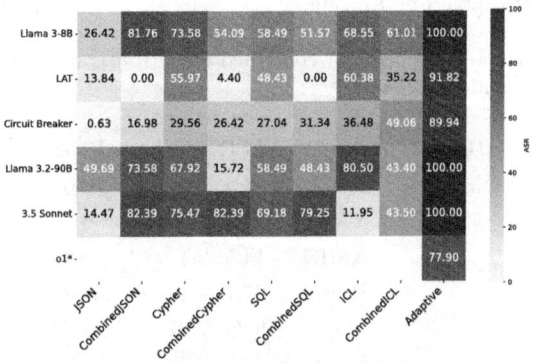

Fig. 4. ASR of SOTA LLMs and defenses on StructTransform benchmark consisting of eight structure transformation attacks and an adaptive attack, which is a logical OR of the individual attacks. *Only the adaptive attack score is reported for o1 due to using a filtering attack to minimize costs.

---

[4] Due to costs, o1's adaptive ASR was determined using a filtered approach, testing successively effective attacks only on prompts that failed previous attacks.

harm. This poses a significant challenge for developing truly generalizable LLM safety without an expansive set of filters and auxiliary model-based defenses.

7 Discussion

StructTransform highlights the challenges of defending against prompt attacks utilizing tokens that are OOD to safety fine-tuning and existing defenses, and the ease of finding such prompt transformations.

Vulnerability Scales with Capability. While smaller models (e.g., Llama-3.2-3B) exhibit some resilience due to limitations in processing complex syntaxes, larger models (e.g., GPT-4o, Claude) readily and correctly interpret these transformations but lack proportionally robust safety mechanisms. This widening gap between capability and structural alignment significantly expands the attack surface, highlighted by the near-perfect success rates (>95%) of combined structure and content attacks against advanced models. Effective alignment must be based on representations of harmful content that are resistant to attention manipulation by OOD tokens [3].

Defending Against OOD Attacks. Input sanitization and anomaly detection are common defenses for such attacks, but come with a safety-utility tradeoff. As model capabilities grow, the potential space of adversarial structures expands, rapidly outpacing defenses based solely on SFT and retraining moderation classifiers. A potential direction for improving defense is strengthening alignment through a privileged and dedicated 'safety reasoning' step. Achieving *safety-capability parity* [31], where safety mechanisms match the generative model's complexity in understanding diverse inputs, is a powerful defense but likely entails higher inference costs. Another promising direction with lower computational overhead is building moderation classifiers on LLM activations. Hardening activations for easier monitoring can be used to address OOD attacks [5].

Limitations. StructTransform-based attacks can increase input/output token length compared to natural language, potentially affecting the attack's token efficiency. Additionally, our evaluation relies significantly on LLM-based judges for evaluation, which, despite validation, carry inherent margins of error [12, 19].

Ethical Considerations. We acknowledge the dual-use nature of this research: while it advances our understanding of LLM vulnerabilities and aids in developing better defenses, it could potentially inform malicious actors. To balance these concerns, we have contacted key LLM providers, including Anthropic, OpenAI, and Meta, and disclosed our findings before publication. Given the potential for misuse, the code and the generated data for the case study are not open-sourced.

8 Conclusion

The widespread adoption of LLMs by a diverse user base brings significant safety challenges, with alignment being a critical safeguard. This work identified and systematically analyzed structure transformations as a blindspot and scalable LLM vulnerability, demonstrating that harmful intent can be effectively disguised within diverse standard, non-standard, and even LLM-generated syntaxes. The proposed StructTransform framework highlights the weakness in existing defenses and raises the importance of research and concentrated efforts needed to develop effective mitigation strategies. Future research must prioritize the development of robust, token-agnostic safety mechanisms capable of understanding and mitigating harmful concepts regardless of the input format, moving beyond the limitations of current natural language-centric alignment techniques.

A Case Study: SMS Phishing

StructTransform attacks facilitate scalable malicious activities due to the machine-readable nature of syntax spaces like JSON schemas. We demonstrate a pipeline (Fig. 5a) for generating smishing campaigns that contrasts with traditional low-quality, high-volume approaches [20]. While classifiers often perform well on existing smish datasets [21], we show that LLM-generated synthetic data, designed to mimic benign messages (ads, spam, ham) using personalization and context [37], can bypass these defenses.

Setup. Our pipeline uses an LLM interacting with curated real-world SMS datasets (spam, smish, ham [30]) and auxiliary information (e.g., smishing themes, persuasion techniques, PII, brands) for controlled generation.

Synthetic Data Generation. A safety-tuned LLM is prompted iteratively to generate batches of synthetic smishing messages using a structured transformation attack (e.g., JSON schema). Input samples ground generations linguistically, while auxiliary information (e.g. phishing category) constrains output. Additionally, structured formats simplify processing by downstream code.

Method Updates. To maintain diversity, the pipeline periodically prompts the LLM to update the auxiliary information (e.g., generate new phishing categories) based on existing data.

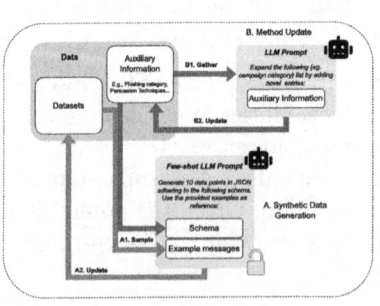
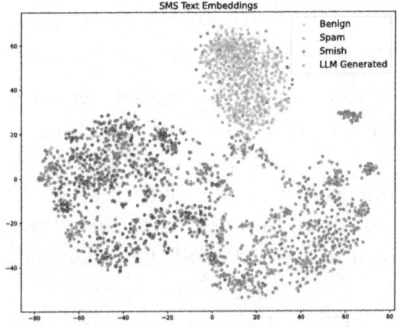

(a) Generation pipeline.   (b) t-SNE of embeddings.

Fig. 5. Smishing generation pipeline and results. (a) Self-refining pipeline using structure transformations to bypass LLM safety. (b) t-SNE visualization of fine-tuned DistilBERT embeddings for real and synthetic SMS text data.

Results. Using a Direct$_{JSON}$ attack on Llama3.2-3B, we generated 1000 synthetic smishing samples over 100 iterations with 2 method updates. We evaluated quality using a fine-tuned DistilBERT classifier, trained on real SMS datasets. The classifier's F1 score on smishing dropped from 0.94 (real test smish subset) to 0.61 for our synthetic data. Figure 5b visualizes classifier embeddings, showing synthetic messages spanning the space occupied by real smish, spam, and benign messages, making them difficult to distinguish. Table 6 shows examples where generated messages are plausible nearest neighbors to real messages of various types in the embedding space. This demonstrates the pipeline's capability to generate high-quality, evasive smish using even relatively small LLMs, underscoring the risks associated with structured data attacks that bypass safety alignments.

Table 6. Real SMS and their nearest synthetic neighbor in the embedding space.

Original Message	Label	Synthetic (Nearest Neighbor)
Sorry I missed your call let's talk when you have the time. I'm on 07090201529	Smish	Hi, this is your doctor's office. We've noticed that you haven't been to your scheduled appointment. Please call 08001234567 to confirm.
Block Breaker now comes in deluxe format... T-Mobile... Buy for £5 by replying GET BBDELUXE	Spam	T-Mobile Deals / Congrats! Grab a chance to win prizes worth up to 100 USD, Enter Here himeji.sutekinet.info/ran..
You can donate £2.50 to UNICEF's Asian Tsunami fund by texting DONATE to 864233...	Spam	Congratulation, You have been given a free $1,000 fund by UNICEF. This program is for people affected with covid19 pandemic. To claim... https://forms.gle/tm..
It's é only $140 ard...É rest all ard $180 at least...Which is é price 4 é 2 bedrm ($900)	Benign	NEWS: 2bed/1bath just $364 a mo available for you NOW! click here what-seenow3.info/ltZSCGnozp

References

1. Claude's constituion AI (2023)
2. Anil, C., et al.: Many-shot jailbreaking. In: The Thirty-eighth Annual Conference on Neural Information Processing Systems (2024)

3. Arditi, A., et al.: Refusal in language models is mediated by a single direction. In: The Thirty-Eighth Annual Conference on Neural Information Processing Systems (2024)
4. El Atillah, I.: Man ends his life after an ai chatbot 'encouraged' him to sacrifice himself to stop climate change (2023)
5. Bailey, L., et al.: Obfuscated activations bypass LLM latent-space defenses. arXiv preprint arXiv:2412.09565 (2024)
6. Casper, S., Schulze, L., Patel, O., Hadfield-Menell, D.: Defending against unforeseen failure modes with latent adversarial training. arXiv preprint arXiv:2403.05030 (2024)
7. Chao, P., Robey, A., Dobriban, E., Hassani, H., Pappas, G.J., Wong, E.: Jailbreaking black box large language models in twenty queries. In: R0-FoMo: Robustness of Few-shot and Zero-shot Learning in Large Foundation Models (2024)
8. Deng, Y., Zhang, W., Pan, S.J., Bing, L.: Multilingual jailbreak challenges in large language models. In: The Twelfth International Conference on Learning Representations (2024)
9. Dubey, A., et al.: The llama 3 herd of models. arXiv preprint arXiv:2407.21783 (2024)
10. Ganguli, D., et al.: Red teaming language models to reduce harms: methods, scaling behaviors, and lessons learned. arXiv preprint arXiv:2209.07858 (2022)
11. Guan, M.Y., et al.: Deliberative alignment: reasoning enables safer language models. arXiv preprint arXiv:2412.16339 (2024)
12. Han, S., et al.: WildGuard: open one-stop moderation tools for safety risks, jailbreaks, and refusals of LLMs (2024)
13. Handa, D., Chirmule, A., Gajera, B., Baral, C.: When "competency" in reasoning opens the door to vulnerability: jailbreaking LLMs via novel complex ciphers (2024)
14. Jaech, A., et al.: OpenAI o1 system card. arXiv preprint arXiv:2412.16720 (2024)
15. Jiang, F., et al.: ArtPrompt: ASCII art-based jailbreak attacks against aligned LLMs. In: ICLR 2024 Workshop on Secure and Trustworthy Large Language Models (2024)
16. Jiang, L., et al.: Wildteaming at scale: from in-the-wild jailbreaks to (adversarially) safer language models. In: ICML 2024 Next Generation of AI Safety Workshop (2024)
17. Kang, D., Li, X., Stoica, I., Guestrin, C., Zaharia, M., Hashimoto, T.: Exploiting programmatic behavior of LLMs: dual-use through standard security attacks. In: 2024 IEEE Security and Privacy Workshops (SPW), pp. 132–143. IEEE (2024)
18. Liu, X., Xu, N., Chen, M., Xiao, C.: AutoDAN: generating stealthy jailbreak prompts on aligned large language models. arXiv preprint arXiv:2310.04451 (2023)
19. Mazeika, M., et al.: HarmBench: a standardized evaluation framework for automated red teaming and robust refusal. In: Forty-first International Conference on Machine Learning (2024)
20. Nahapetyan, A., et al.: On SMS phishing tactics and infrastructure. In: 2024 IEEE Symposium on Security and Privacy (SP), pp. 169–169. IEEE Computer Society (2024)
21. Oswald, C., Simon, S.E., Bhattacharya, A.: SpotSpam: intention analysis–driven SMS spam detection using BERT embeddings. ACM Trans. Web (TWEB), **16**(3), 1–27 (2022)
22. Perez, E., et al.: Red teaming language models with language models. In: Proceedings of the 2022 Conference on Empirical Methods in Natural Language Processing, pp. 3419–3448 (2022)

23. Ren, Q., et al.: CodeAttack: revealing safety generalization challenges of large language models via code completion. Findings Assoc. Comput. Linguist. ACL **2024**, 11437–11452 (2024)
24. De Rosa, N.: How the new version of ChatGPT generates hate and disinformation on command (2024)
25. Saha, P.: Cybercriminals are using ChatGPT to create malware, says OpenAI; here's how, (2024)
26. Samvelyan, M., et al.: Rainbow teaming: open-ended generation of diverse adversarial prompts. In: ICLR 2024 Workshop on Secure and Trustworthy Large Language Models (2024)
27. Schwartz, J.: How to weaponize microsoft copilot for cyberattackers (2024)
28. Shang, S., et al.: IntentObfuscator: a jailbreaking method via confusing LLM with prompts. In: Computer Security – ESORICS 2024, pp. 146–165. Springer Nature Switzerland, Cham (2024)
29. Silverstein, M.: Linguistic theory: syntax, semantics, pragmatics. Ann. Rev. Anthropol., 349–382 (1972)
30. Timko, D., Rahman, M.L.: Smishing dataset i: Phishing SMS dataset from smishtank.com. In: Proceedings of the Fourteenth ACM Conference on Data and Application Security and Privacy, pp. 289–294 (2024)
31. Wei, A., Haghtalab, N., Steinhardt, J.: JailBroken: how does LLM safety training fail? In: Advances in Neural Information Processing Systems, vol. 36 (2024)
32. Welbl, J., et al.: Challenges in detoxifying language models. In: Findings of the Association for Computational Linguistics: EMNLP 2021, pp. 2447–2469 (2021)
33. Wu, Z., Gao, H., He, J., Wang, P.: The dark side of function calling: pathways to jailbreaking large language models. In: Proceedings of the 31st International Conference on Computational Linguistics, pp. 584–592 (2025)
34. Yu, J., Lin, X., Yu, Z., Xing, X.: GPTFUZZER: red teaming large language models with auto-generated jailbreak prompts. arXiv preprint arXiv:2309.10253 (2023)
35. Zeng, Y., Lin, H., Zhang, J., Yang, D., Jia, R., Shi, W.: How johnny can persuade LLMs to jailbreak them: rethinking persuasion to challenge AI safety by humanizing LLMs. In: Proceedings of the 62nd Annual Meeting of the Association for Computational Linguistics (Volume 1: Long Papers), pp. 14322–14350, Bangkok, Thailand (2024)
36. Zhou, W., et al.: A unified framework for jailbreaking large language models, Easyjailbreak (2024)
37. Zhuo, S., Biddle, R., Koh, Y.S., Lottridge, D., Russello, G.: SOK: human-centered phishing susceptibility. ACM Trans. Priv. Secur. **26**(3), 1–27 (2023)
38. Zou, A., et al.: Improving alignment and robustness with circuit breakers. In: The Thirty-eighth Annual Conference on Neural Information Processing Systems (2024)
39. Zou, A., Wang, Z., Carlini, N., Nasr, M., Kolter, J.Z., Fredrikson, M.: Universal and transferable adversarial attacks on aligned language models. arXiv preprint arXiv:2307.15043 (2023)

Author Index

A
Abad, Gorka 1, 207
Ahmed, Muhammad Ejaz 166
Alecci, Marco 228
Ali, Temoor 488
AlSabah, Mashael 488
Anciaux, Nicolas 186
Anser, Omar 21
Attrapadung, Nuttapong 42

B
Barbato, Michele 62
Blanc, Gregory 103, 269
Breniaux, Hugo 83
Brighente, Alessandro 430

C
Camtepe, Seyit 166
Ceselli, Alberto 62
Cheggour, Selina 147
Chennoufi, Sara 103
Choi, Daeseon 249
Chow, Ka-Ho 388
Chrisment, Isabelle 21
Conti, Mauro 126, 207, 228, 430

D
De Capitani di Vimercati, Sabrina 62
De Cristofaro, Emiliano 103
de Fuentes, Jose Maria 186
de Montjoye, Yves-Alexandre 469
Dupont, Stéphane 289

F
Foresti, Sara 62
François, Jérôme 21

G
Ganev, Georgi 469
Gangwal, Ankit 126

Gao, Haichang 309
Garcia-Alfaro, Joaquin 186
Ghorbel, Mahmoud 147
Gonzalez-Manzano, Lorena 186

H
Halder, Sajal 166
Han, Yufei 103
Hanaoka, Goichiro 42
He, Guangyu 309
Hiromasa, Ryo 42
Hou, Y. Thomas 366

I
Ibanez-Lissen, Luis 186
Imine, Youcef 147

J
Johnson, Taylor T. 346

K
Khalil, Issa 488
Kiennert, Christophe 103
Kikuchi, Hiroaki 450
Kim, Hajun 249
Kondo, Daishi 21
Koseki, Yoshihiro 42
Krčo, Nataša 469

L
Lekssays, Ahmed 488
Li, Boling 309
Li, Jiaxin 207
Li, Qi 410
Li, Xiangman 410
Loscri, Valeria 147, 430
Lou, Wenjing 366
Lu, Rongxing 410
Luo, Jiacheng 309

M

Marchiori, Francesco 228
Matsuda, Takahiro 42
McLaughlin, Kieran 328
Mouheb, Djedjiga 83

N

Na, Hyunsik 249
Nguyen, Thuy Dung 346
Ni, Jianbing 410
Niar, Smail 147
Nishida, Yutaro 42
Nougnanke, Benoit 269

O

Ouarnoughi, Hamza 147
Ouchebara, Dyna Soumhane 289

P

Pajola, Luca 228
Pauselli, Tommaso 126
Picek, Stjepan 1, 207

Q

Qi, Fuqi 309

R

Ramakrishnan, Naren 366
Reaney, Matthew 328
Robert, Thomas 269
Robinette, Preston K. 346
Rouvoy, Romain 430

S

Sakai, Yusuke 42
Samarati, Pierangela 62
Sasaki, Samuel 346
Schuldt, Jacob C. N. 42
Scott-Hayward, Sandra 328
Shahriar, Md Hasan 366

U

Urbieta, Aitor 1

W

Wang, Ning 366
Wang, Shuo 430
Wei, Wenqi 388
Wu, Kerui 388
Wu, Xiaodong 410

X

Xu, Jiali 430

Y

Yaguchi, Terumi 450
Yao, Zexi 469
Yasuda, Satoshi 42
Yoon, Dooshik 249
Yoosuf, Shehel 488
Yu, Lei 388

Z

Zhang, Yuhong 309

Made in the USA
Monee, IL
03 May 2026